Weiss Ratings'
Guide to
Life and Annuity Insurers

Weiss Ratings' Guide to Life and Annuity Insurers

A Quarterly Compilation of Insurance Company Ratings and Analyses

Summer 2022

GREY HOUSE PUBLISHING

Weiss Ratings
11780 US Highway 1, Suite 201
Palm Beach Gardens, FL 33408
561-627-3300

Published by Grey House Publishing, Inc., located at 4919 Route 22, Amenia, NY 12501; telephone 518-789-8700. Grey House Publishing neither guarantees the accuracy of the data contained herein nor assumes any responsibility for errors, omissions or discrepancies. Grey House Publishing accepts no payment for listing; inclusion in the publication of any organization, agency, institution, publication, service or individual does not imply endorsement of the publisher.

Grey House
Publishing
4919 Route 22
PO Box 56
Amenia, NY 12501-0056

Edition No. 128, Summer 2022

ISBN: 978-1-63700-186-8
ISSN: 2158-527X

Contents

Introduction

Appendix

Terms and Conditions

This document is prepared strictly for the confidential use of our customer(s). It has been provided to you at your specific request. It is not directed to, or intended for distribution to or use by, any person or entity who is a citizen or resident of or located in any locality, state, country or other jurisdiction where such distribution, publication, availability or use would be contrary to law or regulation or which would subject Weiss Ratings or its affiliates to any registration or licensing requirement within such jurisdiction.

No part of the analysts' compensation was, is, or will be, directly or indirectly, related to the specific recommendations or views expressed in this research report.

This document is not intended for the direct or indirect solicitation of business. Weiss Ratings, LLC., and its affiliates disclaims any and all liability to any person or entity for any loss or damage caused, in whole or in part, by any error (negligent or otherwise) or other circumstances involved in, resulting from or relating to the procurement, compilation, analysis, interpretation, editing, transcribing, publishing and/or dissemination or transmittal of any information contained herein.

Weiss Ratings has not taken any steps to ensure that the securities or investment vehicle referred to in this report are suitable for any particular investor. The investment or services contained or referred to in this report may not be suitable for you and it is recommended that you consult an independent investment advisor if you are in doubt about such investments or investment services. Nothing in this report constitutes investment, legal, accounting or tax advice or a representation that any investment or strategy is suitable or appropriate to your individual circumstances or otherwise constitutes a personal recommendation to you.

The ratings and other opinions contained in this document must be construed solely as statements of opinion from Weiss Ratings, LLC., and not statements of fact. Each rating or opinion must be weighed solely as a factor in your choice of an institution and should not be construed as a recommendation to buy, sell or otherwise act with respect to the particular product or company involved.

Past performance should not be taken as an indication or guarantee of future performance, and no representation or warranty, expressed or implied, is made regarding future performance. Information, opinions and estimates contained in this report reflect a judgment at its original date of publication and are subject to change without notice. Weiss Ratings offers a notification service for rating changes on companies you specify. For more information visit WeissRatings.com or call 1-877-934-7778. The price, value and income from any of the securities or financial instruments mentioned in this report can fall as well as rise.

This document and the information contained herein is copyrighted by Weiss Ratings, LLC. Any copying, displaying, selling, distributing or otherwise reproducing or delivering this information or any part of this document to any other person or entity is prohibited without the express written consent of Weiss Ratings, LLC, with the exception of a reviewer or editor who may quote brief passages in connection with a review or a news story.

Message To Insurers

All survey data received on or before October 24, 2022 has been considered or incorporated into this edition of the Directory. If there are particular circumstances which you believe could affect your rating, please use the online survey (**http://weissratings.com/survey/**) or e-mail Weiss Ratings, LLC (**insurancesurvey@weissinc.com**) with documentation to support your request. If warranted, we will make every effort to incorporate the changes in our next edition.

Welcome to Weiss Ratings'
Guide to Life and Annuity Insurers

Most people automatically assume their insurance company will survive, year after year. However, prudent consumers and professionals realize that in this world of shifting risks, the solvency of insurance companies can't be taken for granted.

If you are looking for accurate, unbiased ratings and data to help you choose life and annuity insurance for yourself, your family, your company or your clients, *Weiss Ratings' Guide to Life and Annuity Insurers* gives you precisely what you need.

In fact, it's the only source that currently provides ratings and analyses on over 650 life and annuity insurers.

Weiss Ratings' Mission Statement

Weiss Ratings' mission is to empower consumers, professionals, and institutions with high quality advisory information for selecting or monitoring a financial services company or financial investment.

In doing so, Weiss Ratings will adhere to the highest ethical standards by maintaining our independent, unbiased outlook and approach to advising our customers.

Why rely on Weiss Ratings?

Weiss Ratings provides fair, objective ratings to help professionals and consumers alike make educated purchasing decisions.

At Weiss Ratings, integrity is number one. Weiss Ratings never takes a penny from insurance companies for its ratings. And, we publish Weiss Safety Ratings without regard for insurers' preferences. However, other rating agencies like A.M. Best, Fitch, Moody's and Standard & Poor's are paid by insurance companies for their ratings and may even suppress unfavorable ratings at an insurer's request.

Our ratings are more frequently reviewed and updated than any other ratings. You can be sure that the information you receive is accurate and current – providing you with advance warning of financial vulnerability early enough to do something about it.

Other rating agencies focus primarily on a company's current claims paying ability and consider only mild economic adversity. Weiss Ratings also considers these issues, but in addition, our analysis covers a company's ability to deal with severe economic adversity and a sharp increase in claims.

Our use of more rigorous standards stems from the viewpoint that an insurance company's obligations to its policyholders should not depend on favorable business conditions. An insurer must be able to honor its policy commitments in bad times as well as good.

Our rating scale, from A to F, is easy to understand. Only a few outstanding companies receive an A (Excellent) rating, although there are many to choose from within the B (Good) category. An even larger group falls into the broad average range which receives C (Fair) ratings. Companies that demonstrate marked vulnerabilities receive either D (Weak) or E (Very Weak) ratings.

How to Use This Guide

The purpose of the *Guide to Life and Annuity Insurers* is to provide policyholders and prospective policy purchasers with a reliable source of insurance company ratings and analyses on a timely basis. We realize that the financial strength of an insurer is an important factor to consider when making the decision to purchase a policy or change companies. The ratings and analyses in this Guide can make that evaluation easier when you are considering:

- Life insurance

- Annuities

- Health insurance

- Guaranteed Investment Contracts (GICs) and other pension products

This Guide also includes ratings for some Blue Cross Blue Shield plans.

The rating for a particular company indicates our opinion regarding that company's ability to meet its commitments to the policyholder – not only under current economic conditions, but also during a declining economy or in an environment of increased liquidity demands.

To use this Guide most effectively, we recommend you follow the steps outlined below:

Step 1 To ensure you evaluate the correct company, verify the company's exact name and state of domicile as it was given to you or appears on your policy. Many companies have similar names but are not related to one another, so you want to make sure the company you look up is really the one you are interested in evaluating.

Step 2 Turn to Section I, the Index of Companies, and locate the company you are evaluating. This section contains all companies analyzed by Weiss Ratings including those that did not receive a Safety Rating. It is sorted alphabetically by the name of the company and shows the state of domicile following the name for additional verification. Once you have located your specific company, the first column after the state of domicile shows its Weiss Safety Rating. Turn to *About Weiss Safety Ratings* for information about what this rating means. If the rating has changed since the last issue of this Guide, a downgrade will be indicated with a down triangle ▼ to the left of the company name; an upgrade will be indicated with an up triangle ▲.

Step 3 Following Weiss Safety Rating are some of the various indexes that our analysts used in rating the company. Refer to the Critical Ranges in our Indexes table for an interpretation of which index values are considered strong, good, fair or weak. You can also turn to the introduction of Section I to see what each of these factors measures. In most cases, lower rated companies will have a low index value in one or more of the factors shown. Bear in mind, however, that a Weiss Safety Rating is the result of a complex proprietary quantitative and qualitative analysis which cannot be reproduced using only the data provided here.

Step 4 The quality of a company's investment portfolio – bonds, mortgages and other investments – is an integral part of our analysis. So, the right hand page of Section I shows you where the company has invested its premiums. Again, refer to the introduction of Section I for a description of each investment category.

Step 5   Some insurers have a bullet ● preceding the company name on the right hand page of Section I. If the company you are evaluating is identified with a bullet, turn to Section II, the Analysis of Largest Companies, and locate it there (otherwise skip to step 8). Section II contains the largest insurers rated by Weiss Ratings, regardless of rating. It too is sorted alphabetically by the name of the company.

Step 6   Once you have identified your company in Section II, you will find its Safety Rating and a description of the rating immediately to the right of the company name. Then, below the company name is a description of the various rating factors that were considered in assigning the company's rating. These factors and the information below them are designed to give you a better feel for the company and its strengths and weaknesses. See the Section II introduction, to get a better understanding of what each of these factors means.

Step 7   To the right, you will find a five-year summary of the company's Safety Rating, capitalization and income. Look for positive or negative trends in this data. Below the five-year summary, we have included a graphic illustration of the most critical factor or factors impacting the company's rating. Again, the Section II introduction provides an overview of the content of each graph or table.

Step 8   If the company you are evaluating is not highly rated and you want to find an insurer with a higher rating, turn to the page in Section IV that has your state's name at the top. This section contains those Recommended Companies (rating of A+, A, A- or B+) that are licensed to underwrite insurance in your state, sorted by rating. From here you can select a company and then refer back to Sections I and II to analyze it.

Step 9   If you decide that you would like to contact one of Weiss Recommended Companies about obtaining a policy or for additional information, refer to Section III. Following each company's name is its address and phone number to assist you in making contact.

Step 10   In order to use Weiss Safety Ratings most effectively, we strongly recommend you consult the Important Warnings and Cautions listed. These are more than just "standard disclaimers"; they are very important factors you should be aware of before using this Guide. If you have any questions regarding the precise meaning of specific terms used in the Guide, refer to the Glossary.

Step 11   The Appendix contains information about State Guaranty Associations and the types of coverage they provide to policyholders when an insurance company fails. Keep in mind that while guaranty funds have now been established in all states, many do not cover all types of insurance. Furthermore, all of these funds have limits on their amount of coverage. Use the table to determine whether the level of coverage is applicable to your policy and the limits are adequate for your needs. You should pay particular attention to the notes regarding whether the coverage is for residents of the state or companies domiciled in the state.

Step 12   If you want more information on your state's guaranty fund, call the State Commissioner's Office directly.

Step 13   Keep in mind that good coverage from a state guaranty association is no substitute for dealing with a financially strong company. Weiss Ratings only recommends those companies which we feel are most able to stand on their own, even in a recession or downturn in the economy.

Step 14 Make sure you stay up to date with the latest information available since the publication of this Guide. For information on how to set up a rating change notification service, acquire follow-up reports or receive a more in-depth analysis of an individual company, call 1-877-934-7778 or visit www.weissratings.com.

Data Sources: Annual and quarterly statutory statements filed with state insurance commissioners and data provided by the insurance companies being rated. The National Association of Insurance Commissioners has provided some of the raw data. Any analyses or conclusions are not provided or endorsed by the NAIC.

Date of data analyzed: December 31 , 2021 unless otherwise noted.

About Weiss Safety Ratings

The Weiss Ratings of insurers are based upon the annual and quarterly financial statements filed with state insurance commissioners. This data may be supplemented by information that we request from the insurance companies themselves. However, if a company chooses not to provide supplemental data, we reserve the right to rate the company based exclusively on publicly available data.

The Weiss Ratings are based on a complex analysis of hundreds of factors that are synthesized into a series of indexes: capitalization, investment safety (life, health and annuity companies only), reserve adequacy (property and casualty companies only), profitability, liquidity, and stability. These indexes are then used to arrive at a letter grade rating. A weak score on any one index can result in a low rating, as financial problems can be caused by any one of a number of factors, such as inadequate capital, unpredictable claims experience, poor liquidity, speculative investments, inadequate reserving, or consistent operating losses.

Our **Capital Index** gauges capital adequacy in terms of each insurer's ability to handle a variety of business and economic scenarios as they may impact investment performance, claims experience, persistency, and market position. The index combines two Risk-Adjusted Capital ratios as well as a leverage test that examines pricing risk.

Our **Investment Safety Index** measures the exposure of the company's investment portfolio to loss of principal and/or income due to default and market risks. Each investment area is rated by a factor that takes into consideration both quality and liquidity. (This factor is measured as a separate index only for life, health, and annuity insurers.)

Our **Profitability Index** measures the soundness of the company's operations and the contribution of profits to the company's financial strength. The profitability index is a composite of five sub-factors: 1) gain or loss on operations; 2) consistency of operating results; 3) impact of operating results on surplus; 4) adequacy of investment income as compared to the needs of policy reserves (life, health and annuity companies only); and 5) expenses in relation to industry norms for the types of policies that the company offers.

Our **Liquidity Index** evaluates a company's ability to raise the necessary cash to settle claims and honor cash withdrawal obligations. We model various cash flow scenarios, applying liquidity tests to determine how the company might fare in the event of an unexpected spike in claims and/or a run on policy surrenders.

Our **Stability Index** integrates a number of sub-factors that affect consistency (or lack thereof) in maintaining financial strength over time. These sub-factors will vary depending on the type of insurance company being evaluated but may include such things as 1) risk diversification in terms of company size, group size, number of policies in force, types of policies written, and use of reinsurance; 2) deterioration of operations as reported in critical asset, liability, income and expense items, such as surrender rates and premium volume; 3) years in operation; 4) former problem areas where, despite recent improvement, the company has yet to establish a record of stable performance over a suitable period of time; 5) a substantial shift in the company's operations; 6) potential instabilities such as reinsurance quality, asset/liability matching, and sources of capital; and 7) relationships with holding companies and affiliates.

In order to help guarantee our objectivity, we reserve the right to publish ratings expressing our opinion of a company's financial stability based exclusively on publicly available data and our own proprietary standards for safety.

Each of these indexes is measured according to the following range of values.

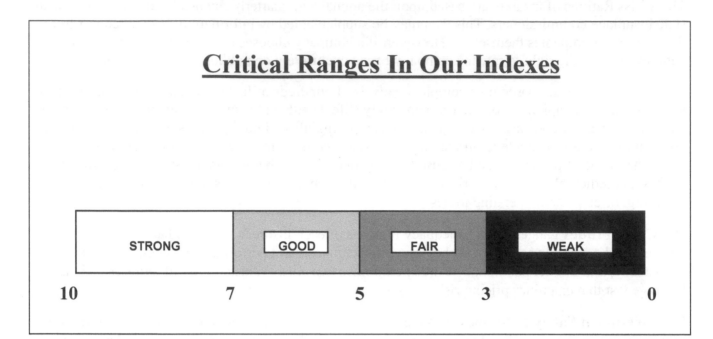

What Our Ratings Mean

A   **Excellent.** The company offers excellent financial security. It has maintained a conservative stance in its investment strategies, business operations and underwriting commitments. While the financial position of any company is subject to change, we believe that this company has the resources necessary to deal with severe economic conditions.

B   **Good.** The company offers good financial security and has the resources to deal with a variety of adverse economic conditions. It comfortably exceeds the minimum levels for all of our rating criteria, and is likely to remain healthy for the near future. However, in the event of a severe recession or major financial crisis, we feel that this assessment should be reviewed to make sure that the firm is still maintaining adequate financial strength.

C   **Fair.** The company offers fair financial security and is currently stable. But during an economic downturn or other financial pressures, we feel it may encounter difficulties in maintaining its financial stability.

D   **Weak.** The company currently demonstrates what, in our opinion, we consider to be significant weaknesses which could negatively impact policyholders. In an unfavorable economic environment, these weaknesses could be magnified.

E   **Very Weak.** The company currently demonstrates what we consider to be significant weaknesses and has also failed some of the basic tests that we use to identify fiscal stability. Therefore, even in a favorable economic environment, it is our opinion that policyholders could incur significant risks.

F   **Failed.** The company is deemed failed if it is either 1) under supervision of an insurance regulatory authority; 2) in the process of rehabilitation; 3) in the process of liquidation; or 4) voluntarily dissolved after disciplinary or other regulatory action by an insurance regulatory authority.

+   The **plus sign** is an indication that the company is in the upper third of the letter grade.

-   The **minus sign** is an indication that the company is in the lower third of the letter grade.

U   **Unrated.** The company is unrated for one or more of the following reasons: (1) total assets are less than $1 million; (2) premium income for the current year was less than $100,000; (3) the company functions almost exclusively as a holding company rather than as an underwriter; (4) in our opinion, we do not have enough information to reliably issue a rating.

How Our Ratings Differ From Those of Other Services

Weiss Safety Ratings are conservative and consumer-oriented. We use tougher standards than other rating agencies because our system is specifically designed to inform risk-averse consumers about the financial strength of life and annuity insurers.

Our rating scale (A to F) is easy to understand by the general public. Users can intuitively understand that an A+ rating is at the top of the scale rather than in the middle like some of the other rating agencies.

Other rating agencies give top ratings more generously so that most companies receive excellent ratings.

More importantly, other rating agencies focus primarily on a company's *current* claims paying ability or consider only relatively mild economic adversity. We also consider these scenarios but extend our analysis to cover a company's ability to deal with severe economic adversity and potential liquidity problems. This stems from the viewpoint that an insurance company's obligations to its policyholders should not be contingent upon a healthy economy. The company must be capable of honoring its policy commitments in bad times as well.

Looking at the insurance industry as a whole, we note that several major rating firms have poor historical track records in identifying troubled companies. The 1980s saw a persistent decline in capital ratios, increased holdings of risky investments in the life and health industry as well as recurring long-term claims liabilities in the property and casualty industry. The insurance industry experienced similar issues before and during the Great Recession of 2007-2009. Despite these clear signs that insolvency risk was rising, other rating firms failed to downgrade at-risk insurance companies. Instead, they often rated companies by shades of excellence, understating the gravity of potential problems.

Other ratings agencies have not issued clear warnings that the ordinary consumer can understand. Few, if any, companies receive "weak" or "poor" ratings. Surely, weak companies do exist. However, the other rating agencies apparently do not view themselves as consumer advocates with the responsibility of warning the public about the risks involved in doing business with such companies.

Additionally, these firms will at times agree *not* to issue a rating if a company denies them permission to do so. In short, too often insurance rating agencies work hand-in-glove with the companies they rate.

At Weiss Ratings, although we seek to maintain good relationships with the firms, we owe our primary obligation to the consumer, not the industry. We reserve the right to rate companies based on publicly available data and make the necessary conservative assumptions when companies choose not to provide additional data we might request.

Comparison of Insurance Company Rating Agency Scales

Weiss Ratings [a]	Best [a]	S&P	Moody's	Fitch
A+, A, A-	A++, A+	AAA	Aaa	AAA
B+, B, B-	A, A-	AA+, AA AA-	Aa1, Aa2, Aa3	AA+, AA, AA-
C+, C, C-	B++, B+,	A+, A, A-, BBB+, BBB, BBB-	A1, A2, A3, Baa1, Baa2, Baa3	A+, A, A-, BBB+, BBB, BBB-
D+, D, D-	B, B- C++, C+, C, C-	BB+, BB, BB-, B+, B, B-	Ba1, Ba2, Ba3, B1, B2, B3	BB+, BB, BB-, B+, B, B-
E+, E, E- F	D E, F	CCC R	Caa, Ca, C	CCC+, CCC, CCC- DD

[a] Weiss Ratings and Best use additional symbols to designate that they recognize an insurer's existence but do not provide a rating. These symbols are not included in this table.

Rate of Insurance Company Failures

Weiss Ratings provides quarterly Safety Ratings for thousands of insurance companies each year. Weiss Ratings strives for fairness and objectivity in its ratings and analyses, ensuring that each company receives the rating that most accurately depicts its current financial status, and more importantly, its ability to deal with severe economic adversity and a sharp increase in claims. Weiss Ratings has every confidence that its Safety Ratings provide an accurate representation of a company's stability.

In order for these ratings to be of any true value, it is important that they prove accurate over time. One way to determine the accuracy of a rating is to examine those insurance companies that have failed, and their respective Weiss Safety Ratings. A high percentage of failed companies with "A" ratings would indicate that Weiss Ratings is not being conservative enough with its "secure" ratings, while conversely, a low percentage of failures with "vulnerable" ratings would show that Weiss Ratings is overly conservative.

Over the past 33 years (1989–2021) Weiss Ratings has rated 690 insurance companies, for all industries, that subsequently failed. The chart below shows the number of failed companies in each rating category, the average number of companies rated in each category per year, and the percentage of annual failures for each letter grade.

	Safety Rating	Number of Failed Companies	Average Number of Companies Rated per year	Percentage of Failed Companies per year (by ratings category)*
Secure	A	1	148	0.02%
	B	7	1,118	0.02%
	C	85	1,617	0.16%
Vulnerable	D	294	721	1.24%
	E	303	212	4.34%

A=Excellent, B=Good, C=Fair, D=Weak, E=Very Weak

On average, only 0.10% of the companies Weiss Ratings rates as "secure" fail each year. On the other hand, an average of 1.94% of the companies Weiss Ratings rates as "vulnerable" fail annually. That means that a company rated by Weiss Ratings as "Vulnerable" is 19.8 times more likely to fail than a company rated as "Secure".

When considering a Weiss Safety Rating, one can be sure that they are getting the most fair, objective, and accurate financial rating available anywhere.

*Percentage of Failed Companies per year = (Number of Failed Companies) / [(Average Number of Companies Rated per year) x (years in study)]

Data as of December 2021 for Life & Annuity Insurers

Data as of December 2020 for Property & Casualty Insurers, and Health Insurers.

What Does Average Mean?

At Weiss Ratings, we consider the words average and fair to mean just that – average and fair. So when we assign our ratings to insurers, a large percentage of companies receive an average C rating. That way, you can be sure that a company receiving Weiss B or A rating is truly above average. Likewise, you can feel confident that companies with D or E ratings are truly below average. In recent years, life and health insurers have experienced consistent, solid performance resulting in a shift in the rating distribution so that more insurers than ever are rated B or better.

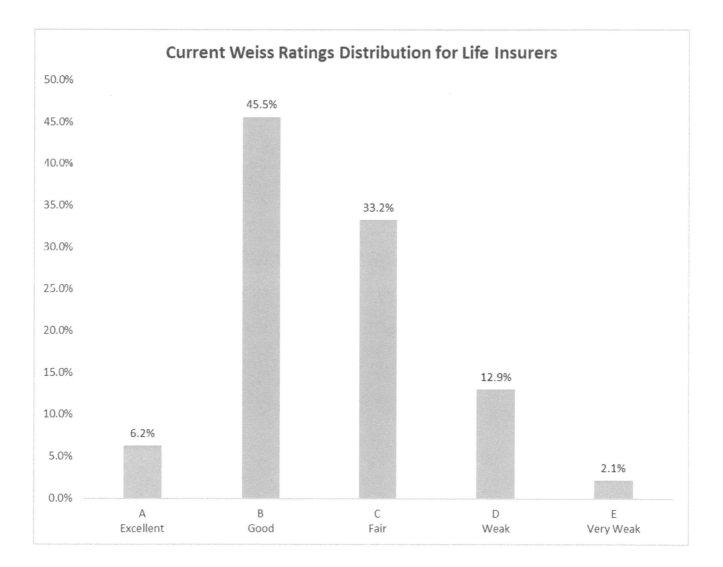

Current Weiss Ratings Distribution for Life Insurers

Rating	Percentage
A Excellent	6.2%
B Good	45.5%
C Fair	33.2%
D Weak	12.9%
E Very Weak	2.1%

Important Warnings and Cautions

1. A rating alone cannot tell the whole story. Please read the explanatory information contained in this publication. It is provided in order to give you an understanding of our rating philosophy, as well as paint a more complete picture of how we arrive at our opinion of a company's strengths and weaknesses.

2. Weiss Safety Ratings represent our opinion of a company's insolvency risk. As such, a high rating means we feel that the company has less chance of running into financial difficulties. A high rating is not a guarantee of solvency nor is a low rating a prediction of insolvency. Weiss Safety Ratings are not deemed to be a recommendation concerning the purchase or sale of the securities of any insurance company that is publicly owned.

3. Company performance is only one factor in determining a rating. Conditions in the marketplace and overall economic conditions are additional factors that may affect the company's financial strength. Therefore, a rating upgrade or downgrade does not necessarily reflect changes in the company's profits, capital or other financial measures, but may be due to external factors. Likewise, changes in Weiss indexes may reflect changes in our risk assessment of business or economic conditions as well as changes in company performance.

4. All firms that have the same Safety Rating should be considered to be essentially equal in strength. This is true regardless of any differences in the underlying numbers which might appear to indicate greater strengths. Weiss Safety Rating already takes into account a number of lesser factors which, due to space limitations, cannot be included in this publication.

5. A good rating requires consistency. If a company is excellent on four indicators and fair on one, the company may receive a fair rating. This requirement is necessary due to the fact that fiscal problems can arise from any *one* of several causes including speculative investments, inadequate capital resources or operating losses.

6. We are an independent rating agency and do not depend on the cooperation of the companies we rate. Our data are derived from annual and quarterly financial statements that we obtain from federal regulators and filings with state insurance commissioners. The latter may be supplemented by information insurance companies voluntarily provide upon request. Although we seek to maintain an open line of communication with the companies, we do not grant them the right to stop or influence publication of the ratings. This policy stems from the fact that this publication is designed for the protection of the consumer.

7. Affiliated companies do not automatically receive the same rating. We recognize that a troubled company may expect financial support from its parent or affiliates. Weiss Safety Ratings reflect our opinion of the measure of support that may become available to a subsidiary, if the subsidiary were to experience serious financial difficulties. In the case of a strong parent and a weaker subsidiary, the affiliate relationship will generally result in a higher rating for the subsidiary than it would have on a stand-alone basis. Seldom, however, would the rating be brought up to the level of the parent. This treatment is appropriate because we do not assume the parent would have either the resources or the will to "bail out" a troubled subsidiary during a severe economic crisis. Even when there is a binding legal obligation for a parent corporation to honor the policy obligations of its subsidiaries, the possibility exists that the subsidiary could be sold and lose its parental support. Therefore, it is quite common for one affiliate to have a higher rating than another. This is another reason why it is especially important that you have the precise name of the company you are evaluating.

Section I

Index of Companies

An analysis of all rated and unrated
U.S. Life and Annuity Insurers.

Companies are listed in alphabetical order.

Section I Contents

This section contains the key rating factors and investment portfolio analysis for all rated and unrated insurers analyzed by Weiss Ratings. An explanation of each of the footnotes and stability factors appears at the end of this section.

Left Pages

1. Insurance Company Name

The legally registered name, which can sometimes differ from the name that the company uses for advertising. If you cannot find the company you are interested in, or if you have any doubts regarding the precise name, verify the information with the company before looking the name up in this Guide. Also, determine the domicile state for confirmation. (See column 2.)

2. Domicile State

The state which has primary regulatory responsibility for the company. It may differ from the location of the company's corporate headquarters. You do not have to be living in the domicile state to purchase insurance from this firm, provided it is licensed to do business in your state.

Also use this column to confirm that you have located the correct company. It is possible for two unrelated companies to have the same name if they are domiciled in different states.

3. Safety Rating

Our rating is measured on a scale from A to F and considers a wide range of factors. Please see What Our Ratings Mean for specific descriptions of each letter grade. Also, refer to how our ratings differ from those of other rating agencies. Most important, when using this rating, please be sure to consider the warnings regarding the ratings' limitations and the underlying assumptions. Notes in this column refer to the date of the data included in the rating evaluation and are explained.

4. Total Assets

All assets admitted by state insurance regulators in millions of dollars. This includes investments, current business assets, and separate accounts. The year-end figure is used to correspond with the figures on the right-hand pages, some of which are only available on an annual basis.

The overall size is an important factor which affects the ability of a company to manage risk. Mortality, morbidity (sickness) and investment risks can be more effectively diversified by large companies. Because the insurance business is based on probability, the number of policies must be large enough so that actuarial statistics are valid. Life insurance policies, for example, are based on mortality tables containing the expected number of deaths per thousand at various ages.

The larger the number of policyholders, the more reliable the actuarial projections will be. A large company with a correspondingly large policy base can spread its risk and minimize the effects of claims experience that exceeds actuarial expectations.

5. **Capital and Surplus**

The company's statutory net worth in millions of dollars. Consumers may wish to limit the size of any policy so that the policyholder's maximum benefits do not exceed approximately 1% of the company's capital and surplus. For example, when buying a policy from a company with capital and surplus of $10,000,000, the 1% limit would be $100,000. (When performing this calculation, do not forget that figures in this column are expressed in millions of dollars.)

Critical Ranges In Our Indexes and Ratios

Indicators	*Strong*	*Good*	*Fair*	*Weak*
Risk-Adjusted Capital Ratio #1	—	1.0 or more	0.75 - 0.99	0.74 or less
Risk-Adjusted Capital Ratio #2	1.0 or more	0.75 - 0.99	0.5 - 0.74	0.49 or less
Capitalization Index	6.9 – 10	4.9 - 6.8	2.9 - 4.8	Less than 2.9
5 Year Profitability Index	6.9 – 10	4.9 - 6.8	2.9 - 4.8	Less than 2.9
Liquidity Index	6.9 – 10	4.9 - 6.8	2.9 - 4.8	Less than 2.9
Investment Safety Index	6.9 – 10	4.9 - 6.8	2.9 - 4.8	Less than 2.9
Stability Index	6.9 – 10	4.9 - 6.8	2.9 - 4.8	Less than 2.9

6. **Risk-Adjusted Capital Ratio #1**

This ratio examines the adequacy of the company's capital base and whether the company has sufficient capital resources to cover potential losses which might occur in an average recession or other moderate loss scenario. Specifically, the figure cited in the table answers the question: For every dollar of capital that we feel would be needed, how many dollars in capital resources does the company actually have? (See the table above for the levels which we believe are critical.) You may find that some companies have unusually high levels of capital. This often reflects special circumstances related to the small size or unusual operations of the company.

7. **Risk-Adjusted Capital Ratio #2**

This is similar to item 6. But in this case, the question relates to whether the company has enough capital cushion to withstand a *severe* recession or other severe loss scenario.

8. **Capitalization Index**

An index that measures the adequacy of the company's capital resources to deal with a variety of business and economic scenarios. It combines Risk-Adjusted Capital Ratios #1 and #2 as well as a leverage test that examines pricing risk. (See the table above for the levels which we believe are critical.)

9. Investment Safety Index	An index that measures the exposure of the company's investment portfolio to a loss of principal and/or income due to default and market risks. It is the composite of a series of elements, some of which are shown on the right pages. Each investment area is rated by a factor that takes into consideration both quality and liquidity. (See the table on the next page for the levels which we believe are critical.)
10. 5-Year Profitability Index	An index that measures the soundness of the company's operations and the contribution of profits to the company's fiscal strength. The Profitability Index is a composite of five factors: (1) gain or loss on operations; (2) consistency of operating results; (3) impact of operating results on surplus; (4) adequacy of investment income as compared to the needs of policy reserves; and (5) expenses in relation to industry averages for the types of policies that the company offers. This factor is especially important among health insurers including Blue Cross Blue Shield companies that rely more heavily on current earnings than do life and annuity writers. After factoring out the normal cycle, companies with stable earnings and capital growth are viewed more favorably than those whose results are erratic from year to year. (See the table for the levels which we believe are critical.)
11. Liquidity Index	An index which measures the company's ability to raise the necessary cash to meet policyholder obligations. This index includes a stress test which considers the consequences of a spike in claims or a run on policy surrenders. Sometimes a company may appear to have the necessary resources, but may be unable to sell its investments at the prices at which they are valued in the company's financial statements. (See the table for the levels which we believe are critical.)
12. Stability Index	An index which integrates a number of factors such as: (1) risk diversification in terms of company size, number of policies in force, use of reinsurance and other items related to spread of risk; (2) deterioration of operations as reported in critical asset, liability, income or expense items such as surrender rates and premium volume; (3) former problem areas where, despite recent improvement, the company has yet to establish a record of stable performance over a suitable period of time; (4) a substantial shift in the company's operations; (5) potential instabilities such as reinsurance quality, asset/liability matching and sources of capital; plus (6) relationships to holding companies and affiliates. (See the table for the levels which we believe are critical.)
13. Stability Factors	Indicates those specific areas that have negatively impacted the company's Stability Index.

Right Pages

1. Net Premiums   The amount of insurance premiums received from policyholders less any premiums that have been transferred to other companies through reinsurance agreements. This figure is updated through the most recent quarterly report available. Generally speaking, companies with large net premium volume generally have more predictable claims experience.

2. Invested Assets   The value of the firm's total investment portfolio, measured in millions of dollars. The year-end figure is used to correspond with the following figures, some of which are only available on an annual basis. Use the figure in this column to determine the actual dollar amounts invested in each asset category shown in columns 3 through 11 on the right-side pages. For example, if the firm has $500 million in invested assets and column 3 shows that 10% of its portfolio is in cash, the company has $50 million in cash.

Looking at the right-side pages, columns 3 through 11 will, unless otherwise noted, add up to approximately 100%. Column 12 (investments in affiliates) is already included in other columns (usually 4, 5 or 6) depending upon the specific investment vehicle.

3. Cash   Cash on hand and demand deposits at year-end. A negative cash position implies checks outstanding exceed cash balances, a situation not unusual for insurance companies.

4. CMOs (Collateralized Mortgage Obligations) and Other Structured Securities   Mortgage-backed bonds at year-end that split the payments from mortgage pools into different classes, called tranches. The split may be based on maturity dates or a variety of other factors. For example, the owner of one type of CMO, called a PAC, receives principal and interest payments made by the mortgage holders between specific dates. The large majority of CMOs held by insurance companies are those issued by government agencies and carry very little risk of default. Virtually all of the CMOs included here are investment grade. However, they all carry some measure of risk based on the payment speed of the underlying mortgages.

5. Other Investment Grade Bonds

All year-end investment grade bonds other than the CMOs included in column 4. Specifically, this includes: (1) issues guaranteed by U.S. and foreign governments which are rated as "highest quality" (Class 1) by state insurance commissioners; (2) nonguaranteed obligations of governments, such as Fannie Maes, which do not carry full faith and credit guarantees; (3) obligations of governments rated as "high quality" (Class 2) by state insurance commissioners; (4) state and municipal bonds; plus (5) investment-grade corporate bonds as defined by the state insurance commissioners. The data shown in this column are based exclusively on the definition used by state insurance commissioners. However, on the companies for which a more detailed breakdown of bond ratings is available, the actual bond ratings - and not the data shown in this column - are used in our rating process to calculate the Investment Safety Index.

6. Noninvestment Grade Bonds

Low-rated issues at year-end– commonly known as "junk bonds" – which carry a high risk as defined by the state insurance commissioners. In an unfavorable economic environment, we generally assume that these will be far more subject to default than other categories of corporate bonds.

7. Common and Preferred Stock

Year-end common and preferred equities. Although a certain amount is acceptable for the sake of diversification, excessive investment in this area is viewed as a factor that can increase the company's overall vulnerability to market declines.

8. Mortgages In Good Standing

Year-end mortgages which are current in their payments. Mortgage-backed securities are excluded.

9. Non-performing Mortgages

Mortgages which are (a) 90 days or more past due; or (b) in process of foreclosure. These are year-end figures. If the mortgages have already been foreclosed, the asset is transferred to the next category - real estate. Clearly, a high level of nonperforming mortgages is a negative, reflecting on the quality of the entire mortgage portfolio.

10. Real Estate

Year-end direct real estate investments including (a) property occupied by the company; and (b) properties acquired through foreclosure. A certain amount of real estate investment is considered acceptable for portfolio diversification. However, excessive amounts may subject the company to losses during a recessionary period.

11. Other Investments

Items such as premium notes, collateral loans, short-term investments, policy loans and a long list of miscellaneous items at year-end.

12. Investments in Affiliates

Year-end bonds, preferred and common stocks, as well as other vehicles which many insurance companies use to invest in - and establish a corporate link with - affiliated companies. Since these can often be non-income-producing paper assets, they are considered less desirable than the equivalent securities of publicly traded companies. Investments in affiliates are also included in other columns (usually 4, 5 or 6). Therefore, the percentage shown here represents a duplication of some of the amounts shown in the other columns.

Footnotes:

(1)   Data items shown are from the company's 2020 annual statutory statement except for Risk-Adjusted Capital Indexes 1 and 2, Profitability Index, Investment Safety Index, Liquidity Index and Stability Index which have been updated using the company's September 2021 quarterly statutory statement. Other more recent data may have been factored into the rating when available.

(2)   Data items shown are from the company's 2020 annual statutory statement except for Risk-Adjusted Capital Indexes 1 and 2, Profitability Index, Investment Safety Index, Liquidity Index and Stability Index which have been updated using the company's June 2021 quarterly statutory statement. Other more recent data may have been factored into the rating when available.

(3)   Data items shown are from the company's 2020 annual statutory statement except for Risk-Adjusted Capital Indexes 1 and 2, Profitability Index, Investment Safety Index, Liquidity Index and Stability Index which have been updated using the company's March 2021 quarterly statutory statement. Other more recent data may have been factored into the rating when available.

(4)   Data items shown are from the company's 2020 annual statutory statement. Other more recent data may have been factored into the rating when available.

(5)   These companies have data items that are older than September 30, 2020. They will be unrated (U) if they are not failed companies (F).

(*)   Breakdown of the company's investment portfolio, shown in percentages in columns 3-11 on the right hand page, does not total to 100% due to the inclusion of non–admitted assets in the bond or mortgage figures, or due to other accounting adjustments.

Stability Factors

(A)   Stability Index was negatively impacted by the financial problems or weaknesses of a parent or **affiliate** company.

(C)   Stability Index was negatively impacted by past results on our Risk-Adjusted **Capital** tests. In general, the Stability Index of any company can be affected by past results even if current results show improvement. While such improvement is a plus, the improved results must be maintained for a period of time to assure that the improvement is not a temporary fluctuation. During a five-year period, the impact of poor past results on the Stability Index gradually diminishes.

(D)   Stability Index was negatively impacted by limited **diversification** of general business, policy, and/or investment risk. This factor especially affects smaller companies that do not issue as many policies as larger firms. It can also affect firms that specialize in only one line of business.

(E)   Stability Index was negatively impacted due to a lack of operating **experience**. The company has been in operation for less than five years. Consequently, it has not been able to establish the kind of stable track record that we believe is needed to demonstrate financial permanence and strength.

(F)   Stability Index was negatively impacted by negative cash **flow**. In other words, the company paid out more in claims and expenses than it received in premiums and investment income.

(G)   Stability Index was negatively impacted by fast asset or premium **growth**. Fast growth can pose a serious problem for insurers. It is generally achieved by offering policies with premiums that are too low, benefits that are too costly, or agents commissions that are too high. Due to the highly competitive nature of the insurance marketplace, rapid growth has been a factor in many insurance insolvencies.

(I)   Stability Index was negatively impacted by past results on our **Investment** Safety Index. This can pose a problem for insurers even after risky investments have been sold off. To illustrate, consider those companies that have sold off their junk bonds and now carry much smaller junk bond risk. For a period of time the company that had the junk bonds incorporated the expectation of higher yields into its policy design and marketing strategy. Only time will tell how the company's investment income margins and future sales will be affected by the junk bond sell off. So, while the Investment Safety Index would improve right away, the Stability Index would improve only gradually over a period of three years, if the transition to lower yielding investments is handled smoothly.

(L)   Stability Index was negatively impacted by past results on our **liquidity** tests. In general, the Stability Index of any company can be affected by past results even if current results show improvement. While such improvement is a plus, the improved results must be maintained for a period of time to assure that the improvement is not a temporary fluctuation. During a five-year period, the impact of poor past results on the Stability Index gradually diminishes.

(O)   Stability Index was negatively impacted by significant changes in the company's business **operations**. These changes can include shifts in the kinds of insurance offered by the company, a temporary or permanent freeze on the sale of new policies, or recent release from conservatorship. In these circumstances, past performance cannot be a reliable indicator of future financial strength.

(R)   Stability Index was negatively impacted by concerns about the financial strength of its **reinsurers**.

(T)   Stability Index was negatively impacted by significant **trends** in critical asset, liability, income or expense items. Examples include increasing surrender rates, increasing mortgage defaults, and shrinking premium volume.

(Z)   This company is unrated due to data, as received by Weiss Ratings, that are either incomplete in substantial ways or contain items that, in the opinion of Weiss Ratings analysts, may not be reliable.

INSURANCE COMPANY NAME	DOM. STATE	RATING	TOTAL ASSETS ($MIL)	CAPITAL & SURPLUS ($MIL)	RISK ADJUSTED CAPITAL RATIO 1	RISK ADJUSTED CAPITAL RATIO 2	CAPITAL-IZATION INDEX (PTS)	INVEST. SAFETY INDEX (PTS)	PROFIT-ABILITY INDEX (PTS)	LIQUIDITY INDEX (PTS)	STAB INDEX (PTS)	STABILITY FACTOR
4 EVER LIFE INS CO	IL	B	193.1	80.0	8.78	6.44	10.0	6.5	3.9	6.7	5.2	A
AAA LIFE INS CO	MI	B	764.0	202.0	3.73	2.04	8.6	6.1	5.3	6.4	6.1	I
AAA LIFE INS CO OF NY	NY	B	13.0	4.4	1.61	1.45	7.7	8.7	1.1	0.6	4.7	ADFG
▲ ABILITY INS CO	NE	D-	915.1	21.2	1.23	0.46	4.0	0.0	1.8	9.2	1.0	CFIT
ACADEME INC	WA	U	--	--	--	--	--	--	--	--	--	Z
ACCORDIA LIFE & ANNUITY CO	IA	C+	12709.0	952.6	1.15	0.79	5.3	4.8	2.5	5.8	4.7	IT
ACE LIFE INS CO	CT	C+	37.0	8.1	1.51	1.36	7.5	8.8	1.6	6.8	4.4	AFT
ADVANCE INS CO OF KANSAS	KS	B+	78.4	63.5	4.08	2.66	9.5	3.9	8.2	7.3	6.3	AFI
▲ AETNA HEALTH & LIFE INS CO	CT	C	656.5	318.9	0.95	0.75	4.1	6.5	2.8	1.5	3.5	CDLT
AETNA LIFE INS CO	CT	B	25501.2	6134.9	1.34	1.06	5.8	6.2	9.5	5.3	5.4	AIL
AGC LIFE INS CO	MO	U	--	--	--	--	--	--	--	--	--	Z
ALABAMA LIFE REINS CO INC	AL	D	19.0	5.2	1.73	1.56	7.8	5.9	1.4	9.3	1.5	DFT
ALFA LIFE INS CORP	AL	C	1642.9	227.4	2.04	1.10	7.2	4.0	1.9	5.7	4.2	I
ALL SAVERS LIFE INS CO OF CA	CA	U (5)	--	--	--	--	--	--	--	--	--	Z
ALLIANZ LIFE INS CO OF NORTH AMERICA	MN	B-	174000.0	10704.7	4.20	2.23	8.8	6.7	2.8	5.3	5.2	F
▼ ALLIANZ LIFE INS CO OF NY	NY	B-	5071.6	163.0	3.27	2.48	9.2	7.6	3.0	9.2	5.3	AG
ALLIED FINANCIAL INS CO	TX	U (5)	--	--	--	--	--	--	--	--	--	Z
AMALGAMATED LIFE & HEALTH INS CO	IL	C (5)	--	--	--	--	--	--	--	--	--	Z
▼ AMALGAMATED LIFE INS CO	NY	B	144.3	72.6	3.49	2.67	9.5	8.2	4.3	5.9	5.7	F
▼ AMER MONUMENTAL LIFE INS CO	LA	B-	37.1	3.2	0.63	0.57	3.6	2.7	1.4	7.3	3.7	ACGIT
AMERICAN BANKERS LIFE ASR CO OF FL	FL	B	267.8	53.0	5.10	2.91	9.9	6.1	7.9	7.3	4.9	AFIT
AMERICAN BENEFIT LIFE INS CO	OK	B	238.9	32.7	2.46	1.55	7.8	5.0	9.1	6.2	5.7	ADI
AMERICAN CENTURY LIFE INS CO	OK	D+	92.5	6.8	0.87	0.78	5.2	1.8	3.7	5.3	2.6	DI
AMERICAN CENTURY LIFE INS CO TX	TX	D+	69.9	4.7	0.65	0.44	2.3	2.4	9.1	7.1	2.3	CDGI
AMERICAN COMMUNITY MUT INS CO	MI	F (5)	--	--	--	--	--	--	--	--	--	Z
AMERICAN CONTINENTAL INS CO	TN	B+	439.4	235.4	4.11	2.98	10.0	7.7	7.2	6.7	6.8	AD
AMERICAN CREDITORS LIFE INS CO	DE	U	--	--	--	--	--	--	--	--	--	Z
▼ AMERICAN EQUITY INVEST LIFE INS CO	IA	C+	60422.4	4078.5	2.28	1.26	7.4	5.6	2.4	4.8	4.4	FLT
AMERICAN EQUITY INVESTMENT LIFE NY	NY	B	170.4	43.6	4.65	3.60	10.0	6.7	6.2	6.5	4.5	ADFT
AMERICAN FAMILY LIFE ASR CO OF NY	NY	A	1108.3	359.8	6.28	4.15	10.0	7.9	9.3	7.6	7.7	
AMERICAN FAMILY LIFE INS CO	WI	A+	5473.4	445.4	2.64	1.43	7.6	5.9	4.7	5.0	7.0	AIL
AMERICAN FARM LIFE INS CO	TX	B	5.1	2.0	1.30	1.17	7.3	8.6	3.5	7.0	4.1	AD
AMERICAN FARMERS & RANCHERS LIFE INS	OK	C	33.3	1.9	0.41	0.37	1.4	5.4	1.9	2.6	2.4	ACDL
AMERICAN FEDERATED LIFE INS CO	MS	C+	26.2	8.3	1.99	1.73	8.1	8.6	4.2	7.5	4.5	AF
AMERICAN FIDELITY ASR CO	OK	B+	7628.5	616.8	2.12	1.22	7.3	6.2	8.3	6.6	6.8	I
AMERICAN FIDELITY LIFE INS CO	FL	B	385.7	67.7	2.07	1.27	7.4	4.6	5.5	8.0	5.8	DI
AMERICAN FINANCIAL SECURITY L I C	MO	D	23.0	12.1	2.84	2.14	8.7	8.5	3.7	7.8	2.3	DFT
AMERICAN GENERAL LIFE INS CO	TX	B	217000.0	8532.5	2.90	1.37	7.6	4.6	6.7	5.3	5.4	AGILT
▲ AMERICAN HEALTH & LIFE INS CO	TX	B+	1264.4	292.2	4.49	2.72	9.6	6.3	8.9	7.7	6.8	IT
AMERICAN HERITAGE LIFE INS CO	FL	B	2325.5	350.7	1.23	0.91	6.3	4.7	3.8	6.4	5.6	CI
AMERICAN HOME LIFE INS CO	KS	C-	283.7	22.2	2.01	1.00	7.0	3.4	2.4	4.7	3.0	DIL
AMERICAN INCOME LIFE INS CO	IN	B-	4889.9	408.1	1.69	0.98	6.8	4.8	5.2	2.0	4.0	AIL
AMERICAN INDEPENDENT NETWORK INS CO	NY	E-	14.8	-41.7	-6.84	-4.67	0.0	4.6	0.9	7.0	0.0	CDFT
AMERICAN LABOR LIFE INS CO	AZ	D	12.4	10.5	3.90	3.51	10.0	9.3	8.6	10.0	1.9	D
AMERICAN LIFE & ACC INS CO OF KY	KY	C	300.0	172.2	2.72	1.63	7.9	1.8	8.5	6.9	3.9	DI
AMERICAN LIFE & ANNUITY CO	AR	D+	53.9	3.4	0.57	0.52	3.2	3.6	3.4	3.6	2.4	CDIL
AMERICAN LIFE & SECURITY CORP	NE	D+	1121.1	74.0	1.39	0.64	5.6	3.2	1.9	8.6	2.5	GIT
AMERICAN LIFE INS CO	DE	C	13159.6	5583.9	1.00	0.97	6.8	3.0	7.1	8.5	4.1	I
AMERICAN MATURITY LIFE INS CO	CT	B	68.1	50.7	6.75	6.07	10.0	9.6	7.2	10.0	6.1	A
▲ AMERICAN MEMORIAL LIFE INS CO	SD	B	4034.0	221.0	1.91	1.00	7.0	4.7	7.0	5.7	5.6	ACI
AMERICAN NATIONAL INS CO	TX	B	23828.7	3989.5	4.67	2.37	9.1	5.3	7.0	6.7	5.4	GI
AMERICAN NATIONAL LIFE INS CO OF NY	NY	B-	2874.9	240.4	2.57	1.29	7.4	5.0	3.8	5.8	4.9	IT

See Page 27 for explanation of footnotes and Page 28 for explanation of stability factors.
Arrows denote recent upgrades ▲ or downgrades▼ (see Section VI for explanations)

30

www.weissratings.com

NET PREMIUM ($MIL)	IN-VESTED ASSETS ($MIL)	CASH	CMO & STRUCT. SECS.	OTH.INV. GRADE BONDS	NON-INV. GRADE BONDS	CMMON & PREF. STOCK	MORT IN GOOD STAND.	NON-PERF. MORT.	REAL ESTATE	OTHER INVEST-MENTS	INVEST. IN AFFIL	INSURANCE COMPANY NAME
59.0	162.5 (*)	11.6	24.4	45.1	5.6	6.2	0.0	0.0	0.0	4.9	0.0	● 4 EVER LIFE INS CO
131.8	639.2	0.0	20.3	66.4	9.4	1.2	0.0	0.0	0.0	2.7	0.7	● AAA LIFE INS CO
10.0	9.6 (*)	9.0	0.0	77.4	0.0	0.0	0.0	0.0	0.0	0.5	0.0	AAA LIFE INS CO OF NY
-12.2	897.9	3.1	41.0	30.5	8.2	0.5	12.4	0.0	0.0	4.2	0.0	ABILITY INS CO
--	--	--	--	--	--	--	--	--	--	--	--	ACADEME INC
519.4	11,118.4 (*)	0.6	25.0	50.3	1.9	5.2	9.2	0.0	0.0	5.8	6.8	● ACCORDIA LIFE & ANNUITY CO
3.9	30.8 (*)	0.1	0.0	78.3	0.0	0.0	0.0	0.0	0.0	0.0	0.0	ACE LIFE INS CO
11.6	77.8 (*)	0.1	30.5	26.4	0.2	39.4	0.0	0.0	0.0	0.0	2.9	● ADVANCE INS CO OF KANSAS
2,041.6	544.1 (*)	0.0	31.6	57.7	8.4	0.0	0.0	0.0	0.0	4.4	4.4	● AETNA HEALTH & LIFE INS CO
26,542.8	15,025.9	0.0	15.3	50.1	7.3	5.9	5.3	0.0	1.2	14.8	5.8	● AETNA LIFE INS CO
--	--	--	--	--	--	--	--	--	--	--	--	AGC LIFE INS CO
0.3	18.9	82.4	0.0	0.6	0.0	17.0	0.0	0.0	0.0	0.0	0.0	ALABAMA LIFE REINS CO INC
170.4	1,614.0 (*)	0.5	14.9	46.0	9.5	12.5	0.0	0.0	0.0	12.6	0.0	● ALFA LIFE INS CORP
--	--	--	--	--	--	--	--	--	--	--	--	ALL SAVERS LIFE INS CO OF CA
14,125.2	123,000.0 (*)	0.0	14.8	60.2	2.0	1.3	14.0	0.0	0.1	1.4	1.5	● ALLIANZ LIFE INS CO OF NORTH AMERICA
688.6	610.7	0.0	20.4	73.3	1.3	0.0	0.0	0.0	0.0	4.9	0.0	● ALLIANZ LIFE INS CO OF NY
--	--	--	--	--	--	--	--	--	--	--	--	ALLIED FINANCIAL INS CO
--	--	--	--	--	--	--	--	--	--	--	--	AMALGAMATED LIFE & HEALTH INS CO
137.1	125.1	0.0	22.8	74.5	0.1	0.0	0.0	0.0	0.0	2.6	0.0	● AMALGAMATED LIFE INS CO
13.2	35.7	6.2	21.8	67.6	0.0	0.0	2.2	0.0	0.4	1.8	0.0	AMER MONUMENTAL LIFE INS CO
93.3	231.5 (*)	3.2	7.3	58.7	0.5	2.2	2.7	0.0	19.1	1.0	0.0	● AMERICAN BANKERS LIFE ASR CO OF FL
34.8	226.1	0.4	13.2	54.0	2.2	3.1	24.0	0.0	0.6	2.5	2.8	● AMERICAN BENEFIT LIFE INS CO
9.0	91.4	4.7	10.1	77.0	7.8	0.0	0.0	0.0	0.4	0.1	0.0	AMERICAN CENTURY LIFE INS CO
31.5	69.0	0.8	18.5	0.1	0.0	0.0	76.4	0.0	4.2	0.1	0.0	AMERICAN CENTURY LIFE INS CO TX
--	--	--	--	--	--	--	--	--	--	--	--	AMERICAN COMMUNITY MUT INS CO
423.3	407.3 (*)	0.0	26.8	71.1	1.5	0.0	1.4	0.0	0.0	1.6	0.0	● AMERICAN CONTINENTAL INS CO
--	--	--	--	--	--	--	--	--	--	--	--	AMERICAN CREDITORS LIFE INS CO
-4,146.6	59,421.3 (*)	-0.1	18.9	59.8	2.1	0.9	10.3	0.1	0.0	2.3	0.8	● AMERICAN EQUITY INVEST LIFE INS CO
0.0	100.0 (*)	0.1	17.9	73.0	2.7	0.0	0.0	0.0	0.0	1.9	0.0	● AMERICAN EQUITY INVESTMENT LIFE NY
327.4	1,047.6 (*)	2.3	0.0	91.8	1.5	0.0	0.0	0.0	0.0	0.4	0.0	● AMERICAN FAMILY LIFE ASR CO OF NY
429.2	4,920.4	0.0	23.0	60.1	0.2	0.1	12.0	0.0	0.0	4.5	0.5	● AMERICAN FAMILY LIFE INS CO
0.4	4.8 (*)	8.7	2.3	80.8	2.1	0.0	0.0	0.0	0.0	5.0	0.0	AMERICAN FARM LIFE INS CO
2.9	32.7 (*)	0.7	0.6	96.4	0.8	0.0	0.0	0.0	0.0	0.4	0.0	AMERICAN FARMERS & RANCHERS LIFE INS
16.9	23.6	5.3	1.4	93.3	0.0	0.0	0.0	0.0	0.0	0.0	0.0	AMERICAN FEDERATED LIFE INS CO
1,300.9	5,888.5	4.3	16.9	60.5	1.5	0.6	11.3	0.0	0.4	4.7	0.0	● AMERICAN FIDELITY ASR CO
9.6	380.0	2.7	0.0	63.8	9.3	8.6	6.6	0.0	6.9	2.1	11.3	● AMERICAN FIDELITY LIFE INS CO
20.7	16.9	22.5	0.0	74.6	0.0	2.9	0.0	0.0	0.0	0.0	0.0	AMERICAN FINANCIAL SECURITY L I C
15,308.5	143,000.0 (*)	-0.1	18.4	52.0	5.4	0.9	15.6	0.0	0.0	5.7	1.9	● AMERICAN GENERAL LIFE INS CO
289.3	1,179.0	1.1	20.0	73.2	3.4	1.6	0.1	0.0	0.0	0.4	0.0	● AMERICAN HEALTH & LIFE INS CO
1,159.4	2,086.8	0.0	0.7	64.4	11.6	9.3	4.5	0.0	1.0	8.5	6.5	● AMERICAN HERITAGE LIFE INS CO
27.6	271.7 (*)	0.4	20.3	54.3	8.9	1.3	7.4	0.0	0.4	5.5	0.0	AMERICAN HOME LIFE INS CO
842.1	4,506.6	0.2	0.4	80.5	4.3	1.9	0.6	0.0	0.1	11.7	2.4	● AMERICAN INCOME LIFE INS CO
1.6	14.7 (*)	1.6	11.2	48.3	3.3	27.2	0.0	0.0	0.0	4.9	0.0	AMERICAN INDEPENDENT NETWORK INS CO
2.4	12.2	85.3	0.0	12.7	0.0	1.4	0.0	0.0	0.0	0.5	0.0	AMERICAN LABOR LIFE INS CO
51.8	299.3 (*)	1.6	0.7	8.3	0.0	80.5	0.0	0.0	5.5	0.1	0.0	● AMERICAN LIFE & ACC INS CO OF KY
4.7	52.7	0.5	30.8	62.4	2.4	2.8	0.0	0.0	0.2	0.2	0.0	AMERICAN LIFE & ANNUITY CO
107.8	1,104.3 (*)	11.0	31.9	24.9	5.0	2.5	11.3	0.0	0.0	11.5	0.0	● AMERICAN LIFE & SECURITY CORP
1,408.4	10,299.9	8.3	1.5	12.0	16.5	60.0	0.3	0.0	0.1	1.4	60.9	● AMERICAN LIFE INS CO
0.0	51.2	7.8	0.0	92.3	0.0	0.0	0.0	0.0	0.0	0.0	0.0	● AMERICAN MATURITY LIFE INS CO
672.5	3,907.2	0.0	13.7	68.6	2.6	0.1	12.3	0.0	0.0	2.8	0.0	● AMERICAN MEMORIAL LIFE INS CO
2,583.1	21,999.5 (*)	0.3	1.4	45.0	1.7	0.3	21.8	0.0	1.6	22.2	20.7	● AMERICAN NATIONAL INS CO
94.1	2,830.5 (*)	0.4	1.1	71.6	2.7	0.1	16.5	0.0	0.2	4.0	0.0	● AMERICAN NATIONAL LIFE INS CO OF NY

● Bullets denote a more detailed analysis is available in Section II.
(*) Asset category percentages do not add up to 100%

INSURANCE COMPANY NAME	DOM. STATE	RATING	TOTAL ASSETS ($MIL)	CAPITAL & SURPLUS ($MIL)	RISK ADJUSTED CAPITAL RATIO 1	RISK ADJUSTED CAPITAL RATIO 2	CAPITAL-IZATION INDEX (PTS)	INVEST. SAFETY INDEX (PTS)	PROFIT-ABILITY INDEX (PTS)	LIQUIDITY INDEX (PTS)	STAB. INDEX (PTS)	STABILITY FACTORS
AMERICAN NATIONAL LIFE INS CO OF TX	TX	C+	137.2	37.0	3.44	2.40	9.1	7.1	4.0	6.9	4.7	
AMERICAN PROGRESSIVE L&H I C OF NY	NY	C	350.4	137.2	0.91	0.74	4.9	7.4	5.1	0.7	2.8	CDFGL
AMERICAN PUBLIC LIFE INS CO	OK	B	100.9	35.5	2.67	1.99	8.5	7.9	7.0	6.8	4.8	FT
AMERICAN REPUBLIC CORP INS CO	IA	C	19.4	8.2	2.40	2.16	8.0	8.4	5.8	8.7	3.9	AG
AMERICAN REPUBLIC INS CO	IA	B-	1561.0	585.9	3.44	2.53	9.3	5.8	9.1	6.8	4.9	T
AMERICAN RETIREMENT LIFE INS CO	OH	C+	147.8	76.9	1.49	1.14	5.7	7.6	1.9	5.6	4.7	D
AMERICAN SAVINGS LIFE INS CO	AZ	C	73.3	15.5	1.56	1.00	7.0	3.1	6.7	7.7	3.7	DI
AMERICAN SERVICE LIFE INS CO	AR	U	--	--	--	--	--	--	--	--	--	Z
AMERICAN UNITED LIFE INS CO	IN	B-	39048.1	1371.0	2.54	1.25	7.4	5.4	2.7	5.8	5.0	I
AMERICAN-AMICABLE LIFE INS CO OF TX	TX	C	465.9	137.2	1.41	1.24	7.4	6.4	2.8	5.8	4.1	AD
AMERICO FINANCIAL LIFE & ANNUITY INS	TX	B-	6268.1	814.2	2.50	1.41	7.6	4.6	3.4	5.9	5.3	AI
AMERITAS LIFE INS CORP	NE	B	27493.5	1977.3	2.50	1.44	7.7	4.9	6.5	6.1	5.8	I
AMERITAS LIFE INS CORP OF NY	NY	B-	1818.3	119.4	2.13	1.13	7.2	4.4	2.7	4.3	4.9	IL
AMICA LIFE INS CO	RI	A-	1465.4	357.0	4.37	2.52	9.3	6.2	6.7	6.6	7.0	AI
ANNUITY INVESTORS LIFE INS CO	OH	A-	3225.7	370.5	3.89	1.94	8.4	6.4	8.2	6.7	6.1	AFI
ANTHEM LIFE & DISABILITY INS CO	NY	B	48.6	22.2	1.64	1.27	7.4	4.8	1.7	5.1	5.7	FGIL
▼ ANTHEM LIFE INS CO	IN	B	869.7	163.2	1.71	1.22	7.3	7.2	1.9	6.1	6.3	F
ARKANSAS BANKERS LIFE INS CO	AR	C	2.5	1.7	1.94	1.75	8.1	9.4	4.2	9.8	3.0	DG
ASPIDA LIFE INSURANCE CO	CA	U	--	--	--	--	--	--	--	--	--	Z
ASSURITY LIFE INS CO	NE	B+	2660.6	394.6	2.93	1.67	8.0	5.5	6.6	5.9	6.6	IL
ASSURITY LIFE INS CO OF NY	NY	B	8.2	6.7	3.20	2.88	9.8	8.5	2.5	7.0	5.1	DF
ATHENE ANNUITY & LIFE ASR CO	DE	C	37921.8	1604.5	0.79	0.51	3.3	3.6	2.6	4.8	3.3	CGIL
ATHENE ANNUITY & LIFE ASR CO OF NY	NY	B-	4008.7	304.2	1.77	1.04	7.1	4.3	5.0	9.6	4.9	AFGI
ATHENE ANNUITY & LIFE CO	IA	C	106000.0	1278.9	0.80	0.45	3.4	2.4	4.6	3.7	3.4	CGIL
ATHENE LIFE INS CO OF NEW YORK	NY	C	971.0	85.7	2.97	1.46	7.7	6.5	4.3	7.0	2.9	T
▲ ATLANTA LIFE INS CO	GA	E	36.3	20.7	2.05	1.56	7.8	9.2	1.4	0.0	0.1	CFGIL
ATLANTIC COAST LIFE INS CO	SC	C-	1076.9	61.4	1.20	0.61	5.3	4.0	2.6	8.1	2.4	ACGIT
AURORA NATIONAL LIFE ASR CO	CA	C	2954.8	159.4	1.97	0.96	6.7	4.9	6.1	1.6	3.6	FIL
AUTO CLUB LIFE INS CO	MI	C	973.1	82.5	0.86	0.62	4.0	4.7	1.3	4.0	4.0	CL
▼ AUTO-OWNERS LIFE INS CO	MI	C+	4655.6	618.7	2.46	1.44	4.0	4.6	2.5	6.6	3.9	IT
AUTOMOBILE CLUB OF SOUTHERN CA INS	CA	C+	1676.3	84.5	1.09	0.60	5.1	3.1	1.2	2.4	4.4	CIL
BALTIMORE LIFE INS CO	MD	B	1299.4	87.5	1.81	0.93	6.4	4.8	5.0	2.0	4.1	CIL
BANKERS CONSECO LIFE INS CO	NY	D	559.3	70.9	4.27	2.17	8.8	5.7	7.6	6.3	1.8	T
BANKERS FIDELITY ASR CO	GA	C	10.1	8.0	3.29	2.15	8.0	8.3	1.9	10.0	3.8	AF
BANKERS FIDELITY LIFE INS CO	GA	C-	162.5	38.6	1.30	0.96	6.7	4.8	1.9	5.2	3.3	CDFI
BANKERS LIFE & CAS CO	IL	D+	18541.7	1241.2	1.83	0.99	6.9	4.7	5.8	4.8	2.7	AIL
BANKERS LIFE INS CO	FL	F (5)	--	--	--	--	--	--	--	--	--	Z
▼ BANKERS LIFE INS CO OF AMERICA	TX	D	6.1	1.0	0.65	0.58	3.6	3.7	1.9	6.6	2.1	CDFI
BANKERS LIFE OF LOUISIANA	LA	C	20.8	8.8	2.45	2.21	8.8	8.5	2.9	7.7	3.8	AD
BANNER LIFE INS CO	MD	C-	7266.8	766.4	1.87	1.34	7.5	5.6	1.9	3.4	2.7	LT
BENEFICIAL LIFE INS CO	UT	B	1944.1	198.2	3.46	1.87	8.3	6.9	4.2	5.3	6.0	FL
BENEVOLENT LIFE INS CO INC	LA	D	2.0	0.4	0.62	0.56	3.5	8.3	1.9	9.9	2.1	CFT
BERKLEY LIFE & HEALTH INS CO	IA	A	478.2	293.7	8.37	5.76	10.0	7.6	8.6	8.8	7.8	AD
BERKSHIRE HATHAWAY LIFE INS CO OF NE	NE	C+	23719.2	9283.7	1.58	1.31	4.0	3.8	4.6	6.9	3.7	AFIT
BERKSHIRE LIFE INS CO OF AMERICA	MA	B	4680.8	220.9	2.65	1.28	7.4	4.4	6.7	8.2	6.2	I
BEST LIFE & HEALTH INS CO	TX	B+	31.3	21.5	1.80	1.46	7.7	8.0	8.7	7.1	6.0	T
BEST MERIDIAN INS CO	FL	C-	399.4	40.9	1.02	0.67	5.0	3.4	1.7	6.5	3.1	I
BESTOW LIFE INS CO	IA	U	--	--	--	--	--	--	--	--	--	Z
BESTOW NATL LIFE INS CO	TX	U (5)	--	--	--	--	--	--	--	--	--	Z
BLUE CROSS BLUE SHIELD OF KANSAS INC	KS	B	2277.0	1085.8	2.10	1.62	7.9	4.6	7.8	5.7	6.0	FI
BLUE SHIELD OF CALIFORNIA L&H INS CO	CA	B	256.1	146.9	4.30	3.24	10.0	8.1	5.0	6.6	5.5	
BLUE SPIRIT INS CO	VT	U	--	--	--	--	--	--	--	--	--	Z

See Page 27 for explanation of footnotes and Page 28 for explanation of stability factors.
Arrows denote recent upgrades ▲ or downgrades▼ (see Section VI for explanations)

32

www.weissratings.com

NET PREMIUM ($MIL)	IN-VESTED ASSETS ($MIL)	CASH	CMO & STRUCT. SECS.	OTH.INV. GRADE BONDS	NON-INV. GRADE BONDS	CMMON & PREF. STOCK	MORT IN GOOD STAND.	NON-PERF. MORT.	REAL ESTATE	OTHER INVEST-MENTS	INVEST. IN AFFIL	INSURANCE COMPANY NAME
47.1	124.7 (*)	1.6	0.0	91.3	0.0	0.0	0.0	0.0	0.0	2.1	0.0 •	AMERICAN NATIONAL LIFE INS CO OF TX
828.0	253.4 (*)	-0.4	6.8	82.4	1.4	0.8	0.0	0.0	0.0	0.0	0.0 •	AMERICAN PROGRESSIVE L&H I C OF NY
84.2	96.0	2.1	22.4	61.8	0.0	1.5	10.6	0.0	0.8	0.8	0.0 •	AMERICAN PUBLIC LIFE INS CO
0.0	11.4 (*)	25.0	13.0	58.9	0.0	0.0	0.0	0.0	0.0	0.1	0.0	AMERICAN REPUBLIC CORP INS CO
663.3	1,398.2 (*)	0.5	18.1	55.4	4.0	7.4	9.4	0.0	2.1	1.9	6.0 •	AMERICAN REPUBLIC INS CO
385.5	135.0	0.0	0.0	99.5	0.7	0.0	0.0	0.0	0.0	0.0	0.0 •	AMERICAN RETIREMENT LIFE INS CO
2.6	72.4 (*)	22.7	1.7	4.4	0.0	2.5	54.9	5.3	4.3	0.1	0.8	AMERICAN SAVINGS LIFE INS CO
--	--	--	--	--	--	--	--	--	--	--	--	AMERICAN SERVICE LIFE INS CO
5,007.0	17,069.2 (*)	0.4	17.2	54.3	3.5	0.5	14.5	0.0	0.5	5.0	0.0 •	AMERICAN UNITED LIFE INS CO
87.1	450.4	0.0	0.3	73.2	0.0	18.2	2.2	0.0	1.1	5.1	18.2 •	AMERICAN-AMICABLE LIFE INS CO OF TX
872.2	5,743.5 (*)	0.2	14.0	47.0	3.2	18.4	7.6	0.0	0.0	6.7	1.4 •	AMERICO FINANCIAL LIFE & ANNUITY INS
3,652.2	14,985.0 (*)	-0.1	15.4	50.5	3.2	4.0	14.9	0.0	0.3	9.2	1.6 •	AMERITAS LIFE INS CORP
168.1	1,284.0	0.0	13.7	60.1	2.4	0.1	18.3	0.0	0.0	4.6	0.0 •	AMERITAS LIFE INS CORP OF NY
75.2	1,372.6 (*)	0.5	25.5	50.4	0.0	7.9	5.2	0.0	0.0	7.5	0.0 •	AMICA LIFE INS CO
97.4	2,507.8 (*)	0.4	23.9	67.6	1.6	0.3	0.0	0.0	0.0	2.6	0.0 •	ANNUITY INVESTORS LIFE INS CO
41.7	44.3 (*)	14.9	5.3	45.0	0.8	0.0	0.0	0.0	0.0	0.0	0.0	ANTHEM LIFE & DISABILITY INS CO
513.4	792.2 (*)	0.0	25.9	56.3	1.2	1.0	0.0	0.0	0.0	3.7	0.0 •	ANTHEM LIFE INS CO
0.7	2.5 (*)	64.8	0.0	18.8	0.0	0.0	0.0	0.0	0.0	0.0	0.0	ARKANSAS BANKERS LIFE INS CO
--	--	--	--	--	--	--	--	--	--	--	--	ASPIDA LIFE INSURANCE CO
198.0	2,576.1	0.0	9.4	57.5	1.3	6.0	16.6	0.0	1.9	7.4	1.0 •	ASSURITY LIFE INS CO
0.7	7.9	0.0	0.0	99.9	0.0	0.0	0.0	0.0	0.0	0.0	0.0	ASSURITY LIFE INS CO OF NY
839.6	32,231.1	2.2	33.1	32.8	5.1	4.9	14.7	0.1	0.0	6.4	19.9 •	ATHENE ANNUITY & LIFE ASR CO
563.7	3,021.5	1.9	17.8	66.0	6.6	3.3	2.1	0.0	0.0	2.3	3.2 •	ATHENE ANNUITY & LIFE ASR CO OF NY
3,651.0	73,228.0 (*)	3.5	29.9	34.8	3.3	1.2	18.4	0.7	0.0	6.6	14.1 •	ATHENE ANNUITY & LIFE CO
0.6	950.8	4.6	4.0	85.8	2.5	0.5	2.1	0.0	0.0	0.7	0.0 •	ATHENE LIFE INS CO OF NEW YORK
12.4	4.0 (*)	6.6	13.2	74.7	0.0	0.0	0.0	0.0	0.2	1.6	0.0	ATLANTA LIFE INS CO
132.7	1,036.5 (*)	20.3	22.1	32.6	2.5	0.9	12.0	0.0	0.0	1.9	3.5 •	ATLANTIC COAST LIFE INS CO
0.4	2,927.4	1.4	7.7	58.8	4.4	0.7	20.4	0.0	0.0	5.6	0.0 •	AURORA NATIONAL LIFE ASR CO
211.8	902.1 (*)	0.0	20.4	61.7	8.5	6.4	0.0	0.0	0.0	1.6	6.0 •	AUTO CLUB LIFE INS CO
220.1	3,593.7	1.4	14.8	49.5	2.9	5.1	14.0	1.9	5.2	4.2	0.0 •	AUTO-OWNERS LIFE INS CO
350.1	1,557.5 (*)	0.0	23.0	64.5	9.9	0.2	0.0	0.0	0.0	1.0	0.0 •	AUTOMOBILE CLUB OF SOUTHERN CA INS
83.2	1,256.1	0.2	3.2	80.3	2.4	0.1	0.6	0.0	0.7	11.9	0.2 •	BALTIMORE LIFE INS CO
70.1	536.8	0.0	11.7	79.7	3.1	0.2	0.0	0.0	0.0	5.4	0.0 •	BANKERS CONSECO LIFE INS CO
0.0	9.1 (*)	7.3	0.0	80.8	0.0	0.0	0.0	0.0	0.0	0.0	0.0	BANKERS FIDELITY ASR CO
116.7	153.2 (*)	1.4	10.2	67.6	1.2	16.1	0.0	0.0	0.0	1.3	5.3 •	BANKERS FIDELITY LIFE INS CO
2,727.2	17,968.5 (*)	0.7	28.6	51.9	5.3	1.7	4.9	0.0	0.0	5.3	0.9 •	BANKERS LIFE & CAS CO
--	--	--	--	--	--	--	--	--	--	--	--	BANKERS LIFE INS CO
1.0	5.8	6.4	0.0	53.9	3.5	0.8	0.0	0.0	26.2	9.4	0.0	BANKERS LIFE INS CO OF AMERICA
12.4	18.6 (*)	1.7	35.9	57.5	0.0	0.0	0.0	0.0	0.0	0.0	0.0	BANKERS LIFE OF LOUISIANA
477.9	4,655.0 (*)	0.1	8.0	54.6	2.1	6.2	16.0	0.0	0.0	1.4	6.0 •	BANNER LIFE INS CO
22.7	1,883.0 (*)	0.5	7.0	81.8	1.0	0.6	0.4	0.0	0.0	5.5	0.0 •	BENEFICIAL LIFE INS CO
0.1	1.9 (*)	57.0	0.0	16.0	0.0	2.0	0.0	0.0	2.9	0.0	0.0	BENEVOLENT LIFE INS CO INC
239.9	453.9	6.2	47.7	46.1	0.0	0.0	0.0	0.0	0.0	0.0	0.0 •	BERKLEY LIFE & HEALTH INS CO
1,075.4	22,242.5 (*)	0.1	0.8	19.6	0.0	51.1	0.0	0.0	0.0	26.6	39.2 •	BERKSHIRE HATHAWAY LIFE INS CO OF NE
143.7	4,578.0	0.1	0.1	92.7	1.9	0.0	1.2	0.0	0.3	3.9	0.4 •	BERKSHIRE LIFE INS CO OF AMERICA
47.1	30.3 (*)	48.5	0.1	16.9	0.4	16.6	0.0	0.0	0.0	0.0	0.0	BEST LIFE & HEALTH INS CO
158.6	321.9	22.0	12.0	44.0	1.6	0.2	4.8	2.9	9.6	2.6	0.2 •	BEST MERIDIAN INS CO
--	--	--	--	--	--	--	--	--	--	--	--	BESTOW LIFE INS CO
--	--	--	--	--	--	--	--	--	--	--	--	BESTOW NATL LIFE INS CO
2,323.0	2,041.6	0.0	17.6	31.2	2.4	26.2	0.0	0.0	1.6	21.0	8.5 •	BLUE CROSS BLUE SHIELD OF KANSAS INC
227.1	251.8 (*)	0.7	47.0	44.7	0.1	0.0	0.0	0.0	0.0	0.0	0.0 •	BLUE SHIELD OF CALIFORNIA L&H INS CO
--	--	--	--	--	--	--	--	--	--	--	--	BLUE SPIRIT INS CO

• Bullets denote a more detailed analysis is available in Section II.
(*) Asset category percentages do not add up to 100%

INSURANCE COMPANY NAME	DOM. STATE	RATING	TOTAL ASSETS ($MIL)	CAPITAL & SURPLUS ($MIL)	RISK ADJUSTED CAPITAL RATIO 1	RISK ADJUSTED CAPITAL RATIO 2	CAPITAL-IZATION INDEX (PTS)	INVEST. SAFETY INDEX (PTS)	PROFIT-ABILITY INDEX (PTS)	LIQUIDITY INDEX (PTS)	STAB INDEX (PTS)	STABILI FACTOR
BLUEBONNET LIFE INS CO	MS	A-	71.5	66.7	8.69	7.82	10.0	8.1	8.4	10.0	6.4	D
BOSTON MUTUAL LIFE INS CO	MA	B+	1634.0	284.2	2.36	1.54	7.8	5.8	7.3	5.4	6.4	IL
BRIGHTHOUSE LIFE INS CO OF NY	NY	C	11631.9	356.8	3.07	1.52	7.8	6.5	1.2	8.8	4.2	FGT
BRIGHTHOUSE LIFE INSURANCE CO	DE	B-	201000.0	7762.7	3.83	1.98	8.5	6.6	5.3	6.8	5.3	
BROOKE LIFE INS CO	MI	C	6432.0	6095.7	0.99	0.88	6.0	1.2	6.4	7.0	3.5	FI
CALPERS LONG-TERM CARE PROGRAM		U	--	--	--	--	--	--	--	--	--	Z
CANADA LIFE ASSURANCE CO-US BRANCH	MI	C	3928.3	188.2	1.69	0.89	6.1	5.9	2.1	3.8	2.6	LT
CANADA LIFE REINSURANCE COMPANY	PA	C+	54.1	33.6	4.87	4.38	10.0	8.4	4.1	9.5	3.0	DT
CANOPY INSURANCE CORP	AL	U	--	--	--	--	--	--	--	--	--	Z
CANYON STATE LIFE INS CO	AZ	U	--	--	--	--	--	--	--	--	--	Z
CAPITOL LIFE INS CO	TX	B-	540.9	53.2	2.82	1.36	7.5	4.3	4.7	6.6	5.0	DGIT
CAPITOL SECURITY LIFE INS CO	TX	D-	3.9	1.6	1.27	1.15	7.2	9.4	2.1	8.4	1.0	ADF
CAREAMERICA LIFE INS CO	CA	U	--	--	--	--	--	--	--	--	--	Z
CARIBBEAN AMERICAN LIFE ASR CO	PR	B	41.5	12.7	1.70	1.49	7.7	7.7	3.5	8.8	4.1	FGT
CATERPILLAR LIFE INS CO	MO	U	--	--	--	--	--	--	--	--	--	Z
CENTRAL SECURITY LIFE INS CO	TX	C	81.2	6.9	0.87	0.78	5.2	6.4	2.8	4.6	3.4	CDFL
▲ CENTRAL STATES H & L CO OF OMAHA	NE	A-	386.9	182.5	4.04	3.06	10.0	5.8	7.8	7.0	6.9	DFI
CENTRE LIFE INS CO	MA	C	1450.2	83.2	4.16	2.30	9.0	6.4	2.1	9.2	4.3	A
CHESAPEAKE LIFE INS CO	OK	A+	251.1	113.3	2.16	1.68	8.0	8.3	2.9	7.6	6.3	ADT
CHESTERFIELD REINS CO	MO	D+	342.2	91.0	2.05	1.43	7.6	4.5	2.3	0.0	2.0	DFIL
▼ CHRISTIAN FIDELITY LIFE INS CO	TX	B+	44.0	17.1	2.85	2.23	8.8	7.8	6.8	7.2	5.3	ADT
CHURCH LIFE INS CORP	NY	B-	309.4	77.9	5.05	2.73	9.6	6.2	4.5	6.5	5.2	DF
CICA LIFE INS CO OF AMERICA	CO	C	151.5	43.1	2.07	1.74	8.1	5.7	5.4	6.4	3.6	ADT
CIGNA ARBOR LIFE INS CO	CT	U	--	--	--	--	--	--	--	--	--	Z
▼ CIGNA HEALTH & LIFE INS CO	CT	C+	13549.9	5700.3	2.00	1.49	7.7	3.7	9.3	1.3	3.4	IL
CIGNA INSURANCE CO	OH	U	--	--	--	--	--	--	--	--	--	Z
CIGNA NATIONAL HEALTH INS CO	OH	B	15.1	9.0	0.75	0.67	4.4	4.9	1.7	4.6	4.4	ACDF
CIGNA WORLDWIDE INS CO	DE	B	59.4	19.1	2.88	2.59	9.4	8.1	8.4	10.0	4.5	AFGT
CINCINNATI EQUITABLE LIFE INS CO	OH	B	192.3	7.1	0.91	0.58	4.3	2.2	1.8	0.7	4.9	ACDIL
CINCINNATI LIFE INS CO	OH	B-	4966.1	270.1	1.52	0.81	5.8	3.6	6.7	5.1	5.2	CI
CITIZENS FIDELITY INS CO	AR	C+	79.8	15.7	2.23	1.46	7.7	3.8	8.2	6.7	4.5	DFI
▼ CITIZENS NATIONAL LIFE INS CO	TX	C-	11.9	1.8	3.02	2.71	9.6	7.6	1.6	6.8	3.0	ADF
CITIZENS SECURITY LIFE INS CO	KY	C	36.3	23.6	0.86	0.77	5.2	3.6	8.5	7.1	4.1	CDI
CL LIFE AND ANNUITY INS CO	TX	U	--	--	--	--	--	--	--	--	--	Z
CLEAR SPRING LIFE & ANNTY CO	DE	B-	14709.5	1163.3	2.79	1.48	7.7	4.5	8.1	6.1	5.1	AI
CM LIFE INS CO	CT	B+	9072.1	1634.3	3.19	2.03	8.5	5.3	6.9	6.5	6.7	AI
▲ CMFG LIFE INS CO	IA	B	26335.6	2824.1	1.23	1.04	7.1	5.3	7.7	6.7	5.5	I
COLONIAL LIFE & ACCIDENT INS CO	SC	C+	3861.4	705.2	2.82	1.79	8.2	5.7	8.7	6.8	4.8	A
COLONIAL PENN LIFE INS CO	PA	D+	884.8	84.5	1.14	0.68	5.2	4.6	1.6	0.0	2.0	ACFIL
COLONIAL SECURITY LIFE INS CO	TX	D+	2.8	2.0	2.30	2.07	8.6	3.7	6.5	7.0	2.7	DI
COLORADO BANKERS LIFE INS CO	NC	F (5)	--	--	--	--	--	--	--	--	--	Z
COLUMBIAN LIFE INS CO	IL	C-	387.9	40.6	2.67	1.45	7.7	7.4	1.8	3.8	3.3	FLRT
COLUMBIAN MUTUAL LIFE INS CO	NY	C+	1478.1	77.1	1.05	0.71	5.1	6.0	3.4	0.6	3.0	CL
COLUMBUS LIFE INS CO	OH	C+	4628.7	372.4	2.10	1.08	7.1	4.1	1.9	5.3	4.5	I
COMBINED INS CO OF AMERICA	IL	C	2672.9	412.3	1.66	1.26	7.4	6.6	2.9	7.2	4.1	C
COMBINED LIFE INS CO OF NEW YORK	NY	C+	586.3	111.2	2.94	2.03	8.5	7.9	2.9	7.8	4.5	A
COMM TRAVELERS LIFE INS CO	NY	B	12.2	8.1	3.04	2.73	9.6	8.5	1.0	6.5	4.2	DFGT
COMMONWEALTH ANNUITY & LIFE INS CO	MA	C	60138.2	3888.2	0.87	0.64	4.1	4.8	5.5	8.8	3.9	CGIT
COMMONWEALTH DEALERS LIFE INS CO	VA	U (5)	--	--	--	--	--	--	--	--	--	Z
COMPANION LIFE INS CO	NY	B-	1193.1	75.9	2.15	1.16	7.2	6.2	4.4	3.7	4.9	ILT
COMPANION LIFE INS CO	SC	B+	689.7	391.4	3.74	2.82	9.7	5.4	8.3	7.4	6.6	DI
COMPANION LIFE INS CO OF CA	CA	B+	34.1	13.3	2.79	2.51	9.3	8.9	3.6	7.7	6.3	D

See Page 27 for explanation of footnotes and Page 28 for explanation of stability factors.
Arrows denote recent upgrades ▲ or downgrades▼ (see Section VI for explanations)

34   www.weissratings.com

NET PREMIUM ($MIL)	IN-VESTED ASSETS ($MIL)	CASH	CMO & STRUCT. SECS.	OTH.INV. GRADE BONDS	NON-INV. GRADE BONDS	CMMON & PREF. STOCK	MORT IN GOOD STAND.	NON-PERF. MORT.	REAL ESTATE	OTHER INVEST-MENTS	INVEST. IN AFFIL	INSURANCE COMPANY NAME
3.4	70.7	0.4	27.9	59.7	0.9	0.9	0.0	0.0	0.0	10.2	0.0 ●	BLUEBONNET LIFE INS CO
189.2	1,492.6	0.4	4.1	57.1	1.2	10.1	13.3	0.0	1.1	11.9	2.6 ●	BOSTON MUTUAL LIFE INS CO
964.9	3,061.4 (*)	13.3	10.4	48.4	2.3	0.1	8.9	0.0	0.0	2.6	0.0 ●	BRIGHTHOUSE LIFE INS CO OF NY
9,077.0	74,955.5 (*)	2.6	18.7	46.7	3.5	0.7	16.3	0.1	0.0	7.3	0.6 ●	BRIGHTHOUSE LIFE INSURANCE CO
30.5	6,422.5	0.0	0.6	4.3	0.1	95.0	0.0	0.0	0.0	0.0	95.0 ●	BROOKE LIFE INS CO
--	--	--	--	--	--	--	--	--	--	--	--	CALPERS LONG-TERM CARE PROGRAM
99.5	2,533.5	1.8	14.2	58.9	1.1	0.0	15.0	0.0	0.0	8.3	0.0 ●	CANADA LIFE ASSURANCE CO-US BRANCH
0.1	46.4 (*)	6.9	12.5	77.7	0.3	0.0	0.0	0.0	0.0	0.0	0.0 ●	CANADA LIFE REINSURANCE COMPANY
--	--	--	--	--	--	--	--	--	--	--	--	CANOPY INSURANCE CORP
--	--	--	--	--	--	--	--	--	--	--	--	CANYON STATE LIFE INS CO
122.6	529.2	6.4	19.3	49.6	3.9	0.2	18.9	0.0	0.0	1.7	0.0 ●	CAPITOL LIFE INS CO
0.4	3.7	5.6	0.0	94.4	0.0	0.0	0.0	0.0	0.0	0.0	0.0	CAPITOL SECURITY LIFE INS CO
--	--	--	--	--	--	--	--	--	--	--	--	CAREAMERICA LIFE INS CO
12.5	40.4 (*)	14.1	3.2	62.1	0.0	16.7	0.0	0.0	0.0	0.0	16.7	CARIBBEAN AMERICAN LIFE ASR CO
--	--	--	--	--	--	--	--	--	--	--	--	CATERPILLAR LIFE INS CO
1.4	79.7 (*)	0.1	45.3	37.0	1.0	3.3	0.0	0.0	0.0	5.8	3.3	CENTRAL SECURITY LIFE INS CO
114.7	378.4 (*)	0.3	22.0	36.7	1.1	12.9	5.2	0.0	0.7	17.7	8.2 ●	CENTRAL STATES H & L CO OF OMAHA
0.9	1,434.5	0.0	22.4	76.9	0.0	0.0	0.0	0.0	0.0	0.0	0.0 ●	CENTRE LIFE INS CO
274.7	241.2 (*)	2.8	29.7	35.3	0.0	0.0	0.0	0.0	0.0	0.8	0.0 ●	CHESAPEAKE LIFE INS CO
223.8	78.4 (*)	0.4	15.9	58.0	2.6	0.0	0.0	0.0	0.0	0.0	0.0 ●	CHESTERFIELD REINS CO
17.6	42.1	7.7	7.7	82.9	0.2	0.1	0.4	0.0	0.0	1.1	0.0	CHRISTIAN FIDELITY LIFE INS CO
36.4	306.4	0.0	27.6	61.1	4.3	6.4	0.0	0.0	0.0	0.6	0.0 ●	CHURCH LIFE INS CORP
4.0	142.7 (*)	0.3	13.4	69.4	1.4	12.0	0.1	0.0	0.0	1.6	12.0 ●	CICA LIFE INS CO OF AMERICA
--	--	--	--	--	--	--	--	--	--	--	--	CIGNA ARBOR LIFE INS CO
21,984.8	8,931.6	0.0	3.3	26.8	14.0	4.5	10.5	0.0	0.2	40.5	29.7 ●	CIGNA HEALTH & LIFE INS CO
--	--	--	--	--	--	--	--	--	--	--	--	CIGNA INSURANCE CO
14.1	14.4 (*)	0.0	0.0	31.0	0.0	70.9	0.0	0.0	0.0	0.0	70.9	CIGNA NATIONAL HEALTH INS CO
0.0	42.8 (*)	33.4	0.0	57.5	0.0	0.0	0.0	0.0	0.0	0.0	15.7	CIGNA WORLDWIDE INS CO
37.6	186.1	0.0	6.3	83.2	2.6	2.4	4.2	0.0	0.0	1.4	1.0	CINCINNATI EQUITABLE LIFE INS CO
341.5	3,864.2	0.8	5.5	84.3	6.8	0.3	0.0	0.0	0.0	2.3	0.1 ●	CINCINNATI LIFE INS CO
3.1	78.7 (*)	2.3	0.4	72.5	4.0	13.7	0.0	0.0	4.1	0.7	0.0	CITIZENS FIDELITY INS CO
0.7	11.6 (*)	6.5	14.8	67.4	0.0	4.8	0.0	0.0	0.0	1.5	0.0	CITIZENS NATIONAL LIFE INS CO
99.2	26.7	45.2	0.0	9.5	1.7	25.6	0.0	0.0	18.0	0.4	0.0	CITIZENS SECURITY LIFE INS CO
--	--	--	--	--	--	--	--	--	--	--	--	CL LIFE AND ANNUITY INS CO
954.1	10,012.9 (*)	0.5	21.2	58.2	1.9	2.9	2.8	0.0	0.0	10.0	7.2 ●	CLEAR SPRING LIFE & ANNTY CO
276.4	6,731.2 (*)	1.1	9.3	44.6	6.5	4.5	15.5	0.1	0.0	9.1	7.9 ●	CM LIFE INS CO
4,488.6	15,779.6 (*)	0.0	14.9	40.5	3.1	12.7	12.4	0.0	0.7	12.6	26.6 ●	CMFG LIFE INS CO
1,623.2	3,537.6	0.0	1.5	81.3	2.6	0.1	11.5	0.0	1.5	1.9	0.0 ●	COLONIAL LIFE & ACCIDENT INS CO
433.3	800.9 (*)	3.3	12.1	74.7	2.4	0.4	0.1	0.0	0.7	5.0	0.0 ●	COLONIAL PENN LIFE INS CO
0.5	2.8	4.8	0.0	50.9	15.4	15.2	0.0	0.0	0.0	13.6	0.0	COLONIAL SECURITY LIFE INS CO
--	--	--	--	--	--	--	--	--	--	--	--	COLORADO BANKERS LIFE INS CO
51.1	358.0 (*)	3.8	6.1	74.4	0.0	0.0	5.0	0.0	0.0	8.6	0.0 ●	COLUMBIAN LIFE INS CO
166.0	1,397.7	0.0	3.9	72.2	0.0	3.4	14.2	0.0	0.2	6.2	3.0 ●	COLUMBIAN MUTUAL LIFE INS CO
273.6	4,470.0 (*)	0.0	13.0	54.5	5.3	3.7	11.4	0.0	0.0	9.1	2.7 ●	COLUMBUS LIFE INS CO
923.0	2,529.6	2.2	16.7	68.0	7.0	4.4	0.0	0.0	0.0	1.1	4.4 ●	COMBINED INS CO OF AMERICA
164.2	563.9	0.0	29.9	63.6	0.0	0.1	0.0	0.0	0.0	6.5	0.0 ●	COMBINED LIFE INS CO OF NEW YORK
3.7	11.7	7.9	3.1	88.2	0.0	0.0	0.0	0.0	0.0	0.0	0.0	COMM TRAVELERS LIFE INS CO
-710.1	53,553.3 (*)	0.2	33.5	36.2	2.9	6.6	16.1	0.0	0.0	2.2	7.4 ●	COMMONWEALTH ANNUITY & LIFE INS CO
--	--	--	--	--	--	--	--	--	--	--	--	COMMONWEALTH DEALERS LIFE INS CO
93.1	1,095.3	1.3	14.8	74.6	0.8	0.1	4.7	0.0	0.0	3.7	0.0 ●	COMPANION LIFE INS CO
295.4	593.1 (*)	14.1	15.4	36.9	0.0	26.7	0.0	0.0	0.0	0.0	5.9 ●	COMPANION LIFE INS CO
12.4	27.7 (*)	28.1	16.8	46.6	0.0	0.0	0.0	0.0	0.0	0.0	0.0	COMPANION LIFE INS CO OF CA

● Bullets denote a more detailed analysis is available in Section II.
(*) Asset category percentages do not add up to 100%

INSURANCE COMPANY NAME	DOM. STATE	RATING	TOTAL ASSETS ($MIL)	CAPITAL & SURPLUS ($MIL)	RISK ADJUSTED CAPITAL RATIO 1	RISK ADJUSTED CAPITAL RATIO 2	CAPITAL-IZATION INDEX (PTS)	INVEST. SAFETY INDEX (PTS)	PROFIT-ABILITY INDEX (PTS)	LIQUIDITY INDEX (PTS)	STAB. INDEX (PTS)	STABILITY FACTORS
CONCERT HEALTH PLAN INS CO	IL	F (5)	--	--	--	--	--	--	--	--	--	Z
CONNECTICUT GENERAL LIFE INS CO	CT	B-	21459.7	6385.3	1.22	1.15	7.2	4.4	8.4	8.5	3.9	AIT
CONSECO LIFE INS CO OF TX	TX	U	--	--	--	--	--	--	--	--	--	Z
CONTINENTAL AMERICAN INS CO	SC	B	933.7	243.5	3.15	2.35	9.0	7.5	1.9	6.8	5.8	DFT
CONTINENTAL GENERAL INS CO	OH	C	4340.3	346.9	2.77	1.39	7.6	4.1	6.2	7.4	4.1	IT
CONTINENTAL LIFE INS CO OF BRENTWOOD	TN	C+	629.5	399.1	1.23	1.13	7.2	5.4	4.7	6.7	4.5	D
COOPERATIVA DE SEGUROS DE VIDA DE PR	PR	D	610.0	22.3	0.71	0.39	2.7	3.3	2.8	5.1	1.4	CI
CORPORATE SOLUTIONS LIFE REINS CO	DE	C	20868.3	1903.1	3.41	1.65	8.0	4.6	4.0	1.7	2.8	AFGILT
COTTON STATES LIFE INS CO	GA	B	316.4	67.5	4.15	2.25	8.9	6.0	6.1	6.4	6.3	DFI
COUNTRY INVESTORS LIFE ASR CO	IL	A-	323.0	216.2	14.89	7.19	8.0	8.0	7.7	9.0	7.1	A
COUNTRY LIFE INS CO	IL	A+	9442.8	1534.9	2.62	1.65	4.0	5.8	8.2	6.4	6.5	IT
CROWN GLOBAL INS CO OF AMERICA	DE	E	846.8	2.4	0.13	0.12	0.0	6.4	5.2	10.0	0.0	CGT
CSI LIFE INS CO	NE	B-	23.6	18.4	4.73	4.26	10.0	9.4	4.1	7.5	5.2	AF
CYRUS LIFE INSURANCE CO	AR	E	25.8	1.0	0.26	0.23	0.0	0.3	1.8	0.3	0.0	CIL
DAKOTA CAPITAL LIFE INS CO	ND	D-	24.7	3.9	1.06	0.95	6.6	3.1	4.3	6.4	1.3	ACGIT
DAYFORWARD LIFE INSURANCE CO	TX	U	--	--	--	--	--	--	--	--	--	Z
▼ DEARBORN LIFE INS CO	IL	B	1647.0	409.1	3.05	1.87	8.3	5.8	2.5	6.3	5.5	FI
DEARBORN NATIONAL LIFE INS CO OF NY	NY	U	--	--	--	--	--	--	--	--	--	Z
DELAWARE AMERICAN LIFE INS CO	DE	A-	106.3	53.0	3.73	2.77	9.7	7.8	5.7	6.9	6.6	A
DELAWARE LIFE INS CO	DE	C	44380.7	2076.3	1.70	1.03	7.0	4.7	7.8	6.8	4.2	I
DELAWARE LIFE INS CO OF NEW YORK	NY	B	2151.9	444.0	12.05	5.58	10.0	6.4	8.1	6.9	5.5	AFI
▼ DELTA LIFE INS CO	GA	E-	70.9	1.2	0.25	0.17	0.0	0.8	0.7	0.6	0.0	CDFILT
DESERET MUTUAL INS CO	UT	U	--	--	--	--	--	--	--	--	--	Z
DESTINY HEALTH INS CO	IL	U (5)	--	--	--	--	--	--	--	--	--	Z
DIRECT GENERAL LIFE INS CO	SC	A	33.5	26.8	5.41	4.87	10.0	9.2	8.9	6.8	6.2	AD
DIRECTORS LIFE ASR CO	OK	E+	39.9	2.4	0.45	0.34	1.1	0.4	4.0	0.6	0.7	CDIL
DL REINSURANCE CO	DE	U	--	--	--	--	--	--	--	--	--	Z
EAGLE LIFE INS CO	IA	B	3050.9	343.4	3.17	1.56	7.8	5.8	8.6	3.7	4.7	AILT
EDUCATORS LIFE INS CO OF AMERICA	IL	U	--	--	--	--	--	--	--	--	--	Z
ELCO MUTUAL LIFE & ANNUITY	IL	B	993.1	76.1	2.08	1.02	7.0	4.7	7.7	7.0	4.4	DIT
ELIPS LIFE INS CO	MO	C	81.0	58.5	7.20	6.48	10.0	8.6	1.8	9.4	2.7	FGT
EMC NATIONAL LIFE CO	IA	B	844.9	106.5	2.78	1.58	7.9	6.5	4.7	5.5	6.3	F
EMPIRE FIDELITY INVESTMENTS L I C	NY	A	4201.6	110.4	2.45	2.06	8.6	8.1	8.4	9.2	7.6	G
EMPLOYERS PROTECTIVE INS CO	HI	B	5.2	3.9	2.46	2.21	8.8	9.6	1.3	9.3	4.0	ADEFC
EMPLOYERS REASSURANCE CORP	KS	C-	22443.7	1731.7	1.48	0.96	6.7	4.7	0.9	6.9	2.9	IT
EMPOWER ANNTY INS CO AM	CO	C	75889.8	2915.6	1.79	0.98	6.8	4.8	1.9	4.5	2.4	FILT
▲ EMPOWER LIFE & ANNTY INS CO NY	NY	C	4138.8	193.3	2.84	1.43	7.6	5.7	1.8	5.8	2.1	FT
▲ ENCOVA LIFE INSURANCE CO	OH	B	607.8	79.1	3.36	1.73	8.1	6.5	6.6	5.6	5.5	T
ENTERPRISE LIFE INS CO	TX	B+	159.9	97.5	1.04	0.95	6.6	6.4	8.9	7.5	6.4	CDI
EQUITABLE FINL LIFE & ANNUITY CO	CO	C+	587.0	54.6	2.47	1.29	7.4	7.4	1.0	0.0	3.0	CFLT
EQUITABLE FINL LIFE INS CO	NY	B	248000.0	5393.9	2.47	1.25	7.4	6.3	3.4	5.4	4.1	FIT
EQUITABLE FINL LIFE INS CO OF AMER	AZ	C+	6242.0	322.8	2.08	1.24	7.4	5.6	1.6	3.5	4.4	GLT
EQUITRUST LIFE INS CO	IL	B-	25685.5	1631.8	1.78	0.87	6.2	3.7	8.4	3.9	5.0	IL
ERIE FAMILY LIFE INS CO	PA	C+	3055.6	439.2	3.66	2.00	8.5	5.9	2.1	5.8	4.4	
EVERENCE INS CO	IN	U	--	--	--	--	--	--	--	--	--	Z
EVERGREEN LIFE INS CO	TX	U	--	--	--	--	--	--	--	--	--	Z
EVERLAKE ASSURANCE COMPANY	IL	C+	172.7	34.7	3.63	3.26	4.0	6.3	2.9	10.0	3.3	T
EVERLAKE LIFE INS CO	IL	B	28147.6	2601.2	3.29	1.67	8.0	5.1	3.9	6.8	4.4	FIT
FAMILY BENEFIT LIFE INS CO	MO	D	252.3	11.8	1.27	0.66	5.4	3.5	4.5	4.5	2.1	ACDIL
FAMILY HERITAGE LIFE INS CO OF AMER	OH	B-	1588.1	155.6	1.92	1.12	7.2	5.6	5.5	8.5	5.1	A
FAMILY LIBERTY LIFE INS CO	TX	D	34.7	7.2	1.82	1.12	7.2	4.2	2.4	6.7	2.2	D
FAMILY LIFE INS CO	TX	C	140.0	28.6	3.12	2.10	8.7	7.9	7.6	6.3	4.2	DF

See Page 27 for explanation of footnotes and Page 28 for explanation of stability factors.
Arrows denote recent upgrades ▲ or downgrades ▼ (see Section VI for explanations)

36

www.weissratings.com

NET PREMIUM ($MIL)	IN-VESTED ASSETS ($MIL)	CASH	CMO & STRUCT. SECS.	OTH.INV. GRADE BONDS	NON-INV. GRADE BONDS	CMMON & PREF. STOCK	MORT IN GOOD STAND.	NON-PERF. MORT.	REAL ESTATE	OTHER INVEST-MENTS	INVEST. IN AFFIL	INSURANCE COMPANY NAME
--	--	--	--	--	--	--	--	--	--	--	--	CONCERT HEALTH PLAN INS CO
142.1	11,059.9 (*)	0.1	1.3	25.9	1.2	51.6	2.8	0.0	2.1	13.9	52.4 ●	CONNECTICUT GENERAL LIFE INS CO
--	--	--	--	--	--	--	--	--	--	--	--	CONSECO LIFE INS CO OF TX
516.2	746.5 (*)	8.8	0.0	79.3	1.4	0.0	0.0	0.0	0.0	0.7	0.0 ●	CONTINENTAL AMERICAN INS CO
106.3	4,287.7 (*)	2.0	11.1	72.0	4.1	6.0	0.1	0.2	0.0	0.7	1.6 ●	CONTINENTAL GENERAL INS CO
737.2	576.4 (*)	0.0	24.2	34.4	1.8	40.8	0.9	0.0	0.0	0.2	40.8 ●	CONTINENTAL LIFE INS CO OF BRENTWOOD
84.4	463.6 (*)	2.6	0.0	73.6	1.1	8.3	0.3	0.4	6.7	5.4	0.0	COOPERATIVA DE SEGUROS DE VIDA DE PR
14,868.0	20,389.6 (*)	0.1	18.7	61.6	2.5	0.7	4.2	0.0	0.0	2.4	0.1 ●	CORPORATE SOLUTIONS LIFE REINS CO
16.0	308.6	0.0	28.6	46.6	3.1	6.9	0.0	0.0	0.0	14.8	0.0 ●	COTTON STATES LIFE INS CO
0.0	244.7	0.0	35.5	52.0	1.2	0.0	0.0	0.0	0.0	11.4	0.0 ●	COUNTRY INVESTORS LIFE ASR CO
562.7	9,166.5 (*)	0.0	20.1	52.9	4.0	7.5	3.9	0.0	0.4	10.0	2.8 ●	COUNTRY LIFE INS CO
44.8	3.1	20.4	0.3	71.5	7.8	0.0	0.0	0.0	0.0	0.0	0.0	CROWN GLOBAL INS CO OF AMERICA
1.4	19.6 (*)	9.0	0.0	61.3	0.0	0.0	0.0	0.0	0.0	0.1	43.4	CSI LIFE INS CO
2.8	25.4 (*)	4.1	0.7	71.7	3.9	9.0	2.4	0.0	0.0	0.8	0.0	CYRUS LIFE INSURANCE CO
3.7	24.1 (*)	9.6	7.2	45.7	6.7	8.9	1.4	0.0	5.9	0.4	0.0	DAKOTA CAPITAL LIFE INS CO
--	--	--	--	--	--	--	--	--	--	--	--	DAYFORWARD LIFE INSURANCE CO
568.0	1,555.2	0.0	21.9	49.7	9.3	0.4	13.3	0.0	0.0	5.4	0.3 ●	DEARBORN LIFE INS CO
--	--	--	--	--	--	--	--	--	--	--	--	DEARBORN NATIONAL LIFE INS CO OF NY
77.0	87.7	5.5	46.7	47.6	0.2	0.0	0.0	0.0	0.0	0.0	0.0 ●	DELAWARE AMERICAN LIFE INS CO
2,292.7	21,238.9 (*)	2.0	17.7	41.7	2.8	8.4	4.5	0.0	0.0	19.1	10.0 ●	DELAWARE LIFE INS CO
12.1	1,088.1	4.1	16.0	69.5	3.1	0.8	3.2	0.0	0.0	3.4	0.0 ●	DELAWARE LIFE INS CO OF NEW YORK
15.5	69.6	0.9	6.3	33.1	2.0	32.2	0.0	0.0	18.7	6.1	25.5	DELTA LIFE INS CO
--	--	--	--	--	--	--	--	--	--	--	--	DESERET MUTUAL INS CO
--	--	--	--	--	--	--	--	--	--	--	--	DESTINY HEALTH INS CO
10.4	24.2	1.0	8.4	90.0	0.0	0.0	0.0	0.0	0.0	0.0	0.0 ●	DIRECT GENERAL LIFE INS CO
5.7	38.5	0.1	0.3	76.5	13.1	8.2	0.0	0.0	0.0	1.0	0.0	DIRECTORS LIFE ASR CO
--	--	--	--	--	--	--	--	--	--	--	--	DL REINSURANCE CO
-25.2	3,025.6 (*)	0.1	22.2	34.6	1.3	0.0	12.5	0.0	0.0	0.1	0.0 ●	EAGLE LIFE INS CO
--	--	--	--	--	--	--	--	--	--	--	--	EDUCATORS LIFE INS CO OF AMERICA
219.2	969.3 (*)	2.9	22.7	68.6	0.2	0.2	0.0	0.0	0.3	2.6	0.0 ●	ELCO MUTUAL LIFE & ANNUITY
-6.6	79.2	1.2	0.0	98.8	0.0	0.0	0.0	0.0	0.0	0.0	0.0 ●	ELIPS LIFE INS CO
47.6	792.2	0.0	7.6	72.7	0.5	4.8	8.1	0.0	0.1	6.1	0.3 ●	EMC NATIONAL LIFE CO
157.7	232.9	0.0	0.3	92.4	0.4	0.0	0.0	0.0	0.0	7.0	0.0 ●	EMPIRE FIDELITY INVESTMENTS L I C
1.0	4.9	7.0	0.0	92.3	0.0	0.0	0.0	0.0	0.0	0.0	0.0	EMPLOYERS PROTECTIVE INS CO
504.1	20,114.0	0.1	16.2	54.5	9.6	4.5	4.5	0.0	0.0	10.1	4.9 ●	EMPLOYERS REASSURANCE CORP
6,298.4	38,855.2 (*)	0.9	17.7	53.8	1.6	0.9	11.1	0.0	0.1	11.9	2.8 ●	EMPOWER ANNTY INS CO AM
524.1	3,144.6 (*)	1.4	12.3	75.1	0.3	0.0	6.8	0.0	0.0	1.0	0.0 ●	EMPOWER LIFE & ANNTY INS CO NY
42.5	574.9 (*)	1.1	15.9	63.8	8.1	0.0	0.0	0.0	0.0	8.6	0.0 ●	ENCOVA LIFE INSURANCE CO
292.2	151.8 (*)	23.5	9.0	29.3	0.0	36.6	0.0	0.0	0.0	0.0	36.6 ●	ENTERPRISE LIFE INS CO
-0.8	534.4	0.0	0.5	45.6	0.0	0.0	0.0	0.0	0.0	53.9	0.0 ●	EQUITABLE FINL LIFE & ANNUITY CO
4,891.8	65,360.8 (*)	0.2	4.8	61.9	3.8	1.1	17.6	0.0	0.0	9.2	3.6 ●	EQUITABLE FINL LIFE INS CO
1,071.4	2,288.7 (*)	0.6	4.9	82.1	0.2	1.0	0.7	0.0	0.0	5.5	0.0 ●	EQUITABLE FINL LIFE INS CO OF AMER
1,578.7	24,074.1 (*)	0.2	25.4	40.9	6.9	2.5	13.1	0.1	0.0	7.7	1.5 ●	EQUITRUST LIFE INS CO
228.3	2,921.6 (*)	0.9	1.0	83.0	2.8	1.6	0.0	0.0	0.0	2.5	0.0 ●	ERIE FAMILY LIFE INS CO
--	--	--	--	--	--	--	--	--	--	--	--	EVERENCE INS CO
--	--	--	--	--	--	--	--	--	--	--	--	EVERGREEN LIFE INS CO
0.0	129.0	21.8	0.0	78.2	0.0	0.0	0.0	0.0	0.0	0.0	0.0 ●	EVERLAKE ASSURANCE COMPANY
-5,889.4	24,455.6	0.5	12.0	59.5	6.4	0.2	12.1	0.0	0.0	8.3	1.1 ●	EVERLAKE LIFE INS CO
21.9	243.0	11.8	2.5	47.2	0.4	0.4	36.7	0.2	0.1	0.8	0.0	FAMILY BENEFIT LIFE INS CO
350.0	1,541.3	0.0	0.8	86.3	3.9	0.0	1.1	0.0	0.0	7.9	0.0 ●	FAMILY HERITAGE LIFE INS CO OF AMER
2.3	34.3 (*)	2.0	0.3	55.8	2.2	16.2	0.9	0.0	0.1	15.0	0.0	FAMILY LIBERTY LIFE INS CO
27.0	128.0 (*)	5.3	1.1	79.4	0.2	1.6	0.0	0.0	0.0	7.5	0.0 ●	FAMILY LIFE INS CO

● Bullets denote a more detailed analysis is available in Section II.
(*) Asset category percentages do not add up to 100%

INSURANCE COMPANY NAME	DOM. STATE	RATING	TOTAL ASSETS ($MIL)	CAPITAL & SURPLUS ($MIL)	RISK ADJUSTED CAPITAL RATIO 1	RISK ADJUSTED CAPITAL RATIO 2	CAPITAL-IZATION INDEX (PTS)	INVEST. SAFETY INDEX (PTS)	PROFIT-ABILITY INDEX (PTS)	LIQUIDITY INDEX (PTS)	STAB. INDEX (PTS)	STABILI FACTOR
FAMILY SECURITY LIFE INS CO INC	MS	C-	6.7	1.6	0.90	0.81	5.5	6.1	2.3	8.4	3.1	DF
FAMILY SERVICE LIFE INS CO	TX	U	--	--	--	--	--	--	--	--	--	Z
FARM BUREAU LIFE INS CO	IA	B+	9888.5	670.8	2.20	1.16	7.2	5.6	7.6	5.0	6.4	IL
FARM BUREAU LIFE INS CO OF MICHIGAN	MI	A-	2709.6	520.9	3.91	2.15	8.7	6.1	7.0	6.0	6.9	I
▼ FARM BUREAU LIFE INS CO OF MISSOURI	MO	B	698.8	98.3	1.72	1.14	7.2	4.8	3.0	6.0	6.1	I
FARMERS LIFE INS CO	TN	U	--	--	--	--	--	--	--	--	--	Z
FARMERS NEW WORLD LIFE INS CO	WA	B-	5670.8	342.0	1.69	0.89	6.1	5.5	2.9	5.1	4.8	A
▼ FEDERAL LIFE INS CO	IL	D+	270.5	18.5	2.27	1.26	7.4	4.5	1.8	4.9	2.6	DFILT
FEDERATED LIFE INS CO	MN	A	2427.1	550.0	4.89	2.54	9.3	6.4	8.9	6.6	7.4	AI
FIDELITY & GUARANTY LIFE INS CO	IA	C-	38358.1	1472.7	0.75	0.51	3.1	3.5	5.3	7.1	2.9	CGIT
FIDELITY & GUARANTY LIFE INS CO NY	NY	C	556.8	99.2	3.97	1.91	8.4	3.8	6.0	6.6	3.9	AGIT
FIDELITY INVESTMENTS LIFE INS CO	UT	A	44295.4	1086.8	2.70	1.84	8.3	6.6	9.2	10.0	7.7	GI
FIDELITY LIFE ASSN A LEGAL RESERVE	IL	C+	418.7	98.2	5.67	2.98	10.0	6.3	3.2	6.7	4.8	FT
FIDELITY MUTUAL LIFE INS CO	PA	F (5)	--	--	--	--	--	--	--	--	--	Z
FIDELITY SECURITY LIFE INS CO	MO	A-	982.0	309.9	4.67	2.90	9.9	6.7	7.6	6.8	6.9	I
FIDELITY SECURITY LIFE INS CO OF NY	NY	A-	39.3	14.5	3.00	1.57	7.9	6.6	7.7	6.8	6.9	AFI
FIDELITY STANDARD LIFE INSURANCE COM	TX	C-	9.9	2.8	1.31	0.93	6.4	2.3	4.1	6.9	3.3	DFIT
FINANCIAL AMERICAN LIFE INS CO	KS	U	--	--	--	--	--	--	--	--	--	Z
FIRST ALLMERICA FINANCIAL LIFE INS	MA	C+	3262.6	121.5	4.14	1.92	4.0	6.5	3.2	6.7	4.0	FT
FIRST ASR LIFE OF AMERICA	LA	B	42.6	38.6	3.48	3.31	10.0	8.4	6.3	9.2	5.9	ADF
FIRST BERKSHIRE HATHAWAY LIFE INS CO	NY	C+	250.6	129.1	8.27	4.79	10.0	5.3	2.6	9.9	4.4	
FIRST COMMAND LIFE INS CO	TX	B-	48.1	11.2	1.76	1.58	7.9	7.5	5.6	6.5	4.3	D
FIRST CONTINENTAL LIFE & ACC INS CO	TX	D- (5)	--	--	--	--	--	--	--	--	--	Z
FIRST DIMENSION LIFE INS CO INC	OK	U	--	--	--	--	--	--	--	--	--	Z
FIRST GUARANTY INS CO	LA	D	52.1	7.7	1.22	1.10	7.2	3.7	8.4	6.0	1.4	ADGI
FIRST HEALTH LIFE & HEALTH INS CO	TX	C+	150.0	32.9	0.99	0.79	5.3	8.3	6.2	7.2	4.6	DFT
FIRST LANDMARK LIFE INS CO	NE	U	--	--	--	--	--	--	--	--	--	Z
FIRST NATIONAL LIFE INS CO	NE	D	6.1	2.4	1.32	0.84	5.7	3.7	1.9	4.6	2.2	FILT
FIRST PENN-PACIFIC LIFE INS CO	IN	B-	1157.8	126.0	3.05	1.58	4.0	6.4	3.8	4.4	3.8	AFLT
FIRST RELIANCE STANDARD LIFE INS CO	NY	A-	259.1	100.9	6.20	4.29	10.0	7.8	7.0	7.1	5.8	AD
FIRST SECURITY BENEFIT LIFE & ANN	NY	B	556.7	31.3	2.35	1.04	7.1	3.5	3.4	9.1	5.4	DFI
FIRST SYMETRA NATL LIFE INS CO OF NY	NY	C+	3477.6	179.2	1.44	0.72	5.7	4.1	3.0	4.9	4.7	CIL
FIRST UNUM LIFE INS CO	NY	C+	4405.9	392.4	2.80	1.48	7.7	4.8	6.5	7.3	4.8	AI
FIVE STAR LIFE INS CO	NE	C	324.2	30.3	2.07	1.29	7.4	7.2	3.6	1.4	3.4	FL
FLORIDA COMBINED LIFE INS CO INC	FL	D+	39.0	23.3	4.27	3.84	8.0	8.7	2.8	6.9	2.4	
FORETHOUGHT LIFE INS CO	IN	B	47725.7	2372.4	1.78	0.86	6.2	4.4	7.8	6.4	5.8	ACI
▼ FORTITUDE LIFE INS & ANNTY CO	AZ	B-	48354.5	1013.9	2.60	2.02	8.5	4.9	4.8	9.9	3.8	IT
FORTITUDE US REINSURANCE COMPA	AZ	C+	9.8	9.7	4.31	3.88	8.0	7.5	5.6	9.3	4.3	AFT
▼ FOUNDATION LIFE INS CO OF AR	AR	D	4.7	0.5	0.68	0.56	3.5	2.2	1.0	7.1	1.6	CFIT
FOXO LIFE INS CO	AR	D	5.0	5.0	3.27	2.94	9.9	9.8	3.6	10.0	2.3	GT
FRANDISCO LIFE INS CO	GA	A	121.9	96.2	10.49	9.44	10.0	8.9	9.3	8.4	7.1	AD
FREEDOM LIFE INS CO OF AMERICA	TX	B+	462.4	280.1	1.40	1.23	7.3	7.3	8.3	7.4	6.5	T
FUNERAL DIRECTORS LIFE INS CO	TX	B	1718.8	155.2	1.94	0.99	6.9	4.7	7.7	6.1	5.8	I
GAINBRIDGE LIFE INSURANCE CO	TX	U	--	--	--	--	--	--	--	--	--	Z
GARDEN STATE LIFE INS CO	TX	A	143.5	92.2	9.97	8.97	10.0	6.9	9.0	7.2	7.8	AI
GENERAL RE LIFE CORP	CT	C	5020.2	878.1	2.41	1.62	7.9	6.9	2.0	9.0	4.1	I
GENWORTH INSURANCE CO	NC	U	--	--	--	--	--	--	--	--	--	Z
GENWORTH LIFE & ANNUITY INS CO	VA	C	19843.6	864.6	1.56	0.87	6.0	5.0	1.8	5.0	3.6	AFT
GENWORTH LIFE INS CO	DE	B-	41321.0	2937.1	1.70	1.09	7.1	5.1	5.4	6.9	5.0	ACI
GENWORTH LIFE INS CO OF NEW YORK	NY	C	7569.5	224.2	1.35	0.68	5.5	3.4	2.3	5.9	3.8	ACFI
GERBER LIFE INS CO	NY	B+	5146.7	540.1	2.45	1.36	7.5	5.8	6.0	5.2	6.4	AIL
GERMANIA LIFE INS CO	TX	B-	107.9	11.7	1.40	1.26	7.4	6.0	2.9	5.3	5.0	D

See Page 27 for explanation of footnotes and Page 28 for   38   www.weissratings.com
explanation of stability factors.
Arrows denote recent upgrades ▲ or downgrades▼ (see Section VI for explanations)

NET PREMIUM ($MIL)	IN-VESTED ASSETS ($MIL)	CASH	CMO & STRUCT. SECS.	OTH.INV. GRADE BONDS	NON-INV. GRADE BONDS	CMMON & PREF. STOCK	MORT IN GOOD STAND.	NON-PERF. MORT.	REAL ESTATE	OTHER INVEST-MENTS	INVEST. IN AFFIL	INSURANCE COMPANY NAME
0.8	6.6	36.8	4.3	51.9	3.0	1.2	0.0	0.0	2.9	0.0	0.0	FAMILY SECURITY LIFE INS CO INC
--	--	--	--	--	--	--	--	--	--	--	--	FAMILY SERVICE LIFE INS CO
624.0	8,902.6	0.4	25.1	53.6	2.8	1.4	11.1	0.0	0.0	4.8	0.1 ●	FARM BUREAU LIFE INS CO
116.1	2,531.3	0.0	0.7	66.5	2.6	7.4	18.0	0.0	0.6	4.3	0.0 ●	FARM BUREAU LIFE INS CO OF MICHIGAN
43.5	682.7	0.2	11.3	66.1	0.8	16.9	0.0	0.0	0.0	4.2	3.7 ●	FARM BUREAU LIFE INS CO OF MISSOURI
--	--	--	--	--	--	--	--	--	--	--	--	FARMERS LIFE INS CO
542.1	4,119.7	0.0	22.6	49.3	2.1	0.0	13.0	0.0	2.9	10.2	2.4 ●	FARMERS NEW WORLD LIFE INS CO
22.7	220.2 (*)	0.3	29.2	55.8	4.3	0.3	0.8	0.0	0.8	4.1	0.3	FEDERAL LIFE INS CO
251.7	2,370.4 (*)	0.0	16.9	67.1	6.2	3.9	0.0	0.0	0.0	2.8	0.0 ●	FEDERATED LIFE INS CO
903.8	34,588.8	3.4	33.6	33.0	7.2	8.6	2.8	0.0	0.0	10.4	5.0 ●	FIDELITY & GUARANTY LIFE INS CO
40.9	550.4	5.6	15.3	57.8	9.8	5.5	0.0	0.0	0.0	5.6	0.0 ●	FIDELITY & GUARANTY LIFE INS CO NY
2,253.7	1,320.5	0.0	0.3	74.5	5.8	8.4	0.0	0.0	0.0	11.0	8.4 ●	FIDELITY INVESTMENTS LIFE INS CO
61.0	394.3	4.6	23.8	53.1	3.4	0.7	12.0	0.0	0.0	2.4	0.0 ●	FIDELITY LIFE ASSN A LEGAL RESERVE
--	--	--	--	--	--	--	--	--	--	--	--	FIDELITY MUTUAL LIFE INS CO
145.7	918.1 (*)	3.2	42.5	37.4	1.7	4.0	0.4	0.0	0.0	6.1	2.5 ●	FIDELITY SECURITY LIFE INS CO
6.1	37.0 (*)	3.2	28.7	59.3	5.2	0.6	0.0	0.0	0.0	1.4	0.0	FIDELITY SECURITY LIFE INS CO OF NY
0.6	9.8	5.8	0.0	36.5	10.9	41.1	0.0	0.0	5.1	0.5	0.0	FIDELITY STANDARD LIFE INSURANCE COM
--	--	--	--	--	--	--	--	--	--	--	--	FINANCIAL AMERICAN LIFE INS CO
177.4	2,407.8 (*)	1.9	13.6	79.7	0.5	0.0	0.2	0.0	0.0	1.8	0.6 ●	FIRST ALLMERICA FINANCIAL LIFE INS
3.2	39.5 (*)	1.2	0.0	68.1	0.0	26.2	0.0	0.0	0.0	0.0	26.2 ●	FIRST ASR LIFE OF AMERICA
1.9	245.0 (*)	1.4	4.3	66.5	2.1	10.8	0.0	0.0	0.0	0.0	14.0 ●	FIRST BERKSHIRE HATHAWAY LIFE INS CO
2.2	47.3 (*)	0.1	16.7	78.9	1.0	0.0	0.0	0.0	0.0	1.0	0.0	FIRST COMMAND LIFE INS CO
--	--	--	--	--	--	--	--	--	--	--	--	FIRST CONTINENTAL LIFE & ACC INS CO
--	--	--	--	--	--	--	--	--	--	--	--	FIRST DIMENSION LIFE INS CO INC
5.8	50.8 (*)	0.4	6.5	70.4	3.1	3.1	6.1	0.0	0.0	0.4	0.0	FIRST GUARANTY INS CO
182.1	138.0 (*)	51.4	11.0	31.1	2.6	1.6	0.0	0.0	0.0	0.1	0.0 ●	FIRST HEALTH LIFE & HEALTH INS CO
--	--	--	--	--	--	--	--	--	--	--	--	FIRST LANDMARK LIFE INS CO
1.8	5.7	1.3	0.0	15.0	10.3	9.4	0.0	0.0	0.0	63.9	0.0	FIRST NATIONAL LIFE INS CO
29.6	1,068.5	0.0	7.1	77.4	3.1	0.7	9.0	0.0	0.0	3.1	0.0 ●	FIRST PENN-PACIFIC LIFE INS CO
98.6	244.2	0.0	8.4	86.8	1.7	0.0	0.0	0.0	0.0	3.1	0.0 ●	FIRST RELIANCE STANDARD LIFE INS CO
8.8	369.4 (*)	3.9	50.4	38.5	4.1	1.1	0.0	0.0	0.0	0.6	0.0 ●	FIRST SECURITY BENEFIT LIFE & ANN
601.6	3,438.5	1.5	18.2	61.3	1.6	0.1	17.3	0.0	0.0	0.0	0.0 ●	FIRST SYMETRA NATL LIFE INS CO OF NY
530.0	4,278.6	0.0	2.3	81.4	5.7	0.1	9.1	0.0	0.0	1.2	0.0 ●	FIRST UNUM LIFE INS CO
165.2	248.2	1.2	9.6	83.8	1.0	0.3	0.0	0.0	0.0	3.7	0.1 ●	FIVE STAR LIFE INS CO
0.0	22.8	26.6	11.0	61.8	0.0	0.0	0.0	0.0	0.0	0.0	0.0	FLORIDA COMBINED LIFE INS CO INC
4,546.3	43,640.8 (*)	0.1	42.6	23.9	3.1	0.9	24.5	0.4	0.0	2.7	2.7 ●	FORETHOUGHT LIFE INS CO
-4,050.5	5,573.7 (*)	2.9	18.9	64.0	0.4	0.1	0.0	0.0	0.0	1.0	0.0 ●	FORTITUDE LIFE INS & ANNTY CO
0.0	9.8 (*)	8.7	3.2	27.1	0.8	0.0	0.0	0.0	0.0	0.1	0.0	FORTITUDE US REINSURANCE COMPA
1.3	4.3	22.6	0.0	26.4	1.4	35.0	1.1	0.0	12.7	1.0	0.0	FOUNDATION LIFE INS CO OF AR
0.0	5.0 (*)	97.2	0.0	0.0	0.0	0.0	0.0	0.0	0.0	0.0	0.0	FOXO LIFE INS CO
24.3	119.1 (*)	0.1	0.0	92.0	0.0	0.0	0.0	0.0	0.0	0.0	0.0 ●	FRANDISCO LIFE INS CO
834.7	440.2	21.7	15.9	39.6	0.0	22.2	0.0	0.0	0.0	0.0	22.2 ●	FREEDOM LIFE INS CO OF AMERICA
338.7	1,690.4	0.1	16.2	62.8	6.0	1.0	12.2	0.0	1.3	0.3	0.9 ●	FUNERAL DIRECTORS LIFE INS CO
--	--	--	--	--	--	--	--	--	--	--	--	GAINBRIDGE LIFE INSURANCE CO
25.6	132.2 (*)	1.1	0.8	93.8	0.4	0.0	0.0	0.0	0.0	1.9	0.0 ●	GARDEN STATE LIFE INS CO
1,485.6	4,350.3 (*)	1.1	0.0	74.4	0.1	5.9	0.0	0.0	0.0	17.2	17.6 ●	GENERAL RE LIFE CORP
--	--	--	--	--	--	--	--	--	--	--	--	GENWORTH INSURANCE CO
-1,249.1	13,102.2	0.0	11.7	63.6	3.6	1.4	13.4	0.0	0.1	5.8	1.0 ●	GENWORTH LIFE & ANNUITY INS CO
2,350.0	40,360.8	0.0	6.7	63.9	5.5	2.8	11.1	0.0	0.0	10.0	2.6 ●	GENWORTH LIFE INS CO
240.9	7,021.8	0.0	17.2	66.5	3.3	0.1	8.0	0.0	0.0	5.0	0.0 ●	GENWORTH LIFE INS CO OF NEW YORK
863.6	4,791.1	0.0	13.5	69.6	6.6	1.7	2.6	0.0	0.0	5.1	0.0 ●	GERBER LIFE INS CO
6.3	102.4 (*)	0.1	19.5	70.4	2.8	4.8	0.0	0.0	0.0	1.0	0.0	GERMANIA LIFE INS CO

● Bullets denote a more detailed analysis is available in Section II.
(*) Asset category percentages do not add up to 100%

INSURANCE COMPANY NAME	DOM. STATE	RATING	TOTAL ASSETS ($MIL)	CAPITAL & SURPLUS ($MIL)	RISK ADJUSTED CAPITAL RATIO 1	RISK ADJUSTED CAPITAL RATIO 2	CAPITAL-IZATION INDEX (PTS)	INVEST. SAFETY INDEX (PTS)	PROFIT-ABILITY INDEX (PTS)	LIQUIDITY INDEX (PTS)	STAB. INDEX (PTS)	STABILITY FACTORS
GERTRUDE GEDDES WILLIS LIFE INS CO	LA	F (5)	--	--	--	--	--	--	--	--	--	Z
GLOBE LIFE & ACCIDENT INS CO	NE	C	5236.5	343.8	0.96	0.63	4.7	4.0	7.9	1.1	3.1	CIL
GLOBE LIFE INSURANCE CO OF NY	NY	B	266.6	36.6	2.02	1.24	7.4	5.1	7.2	4.7	5.9	AIL
GMHP HEALTH INS LMTD	GU	U (5)	--	--	--	--	--	--	--	--	--	Z
GOLDEN RULE INS CO	IN	B (3)	632.3	318.3	1.44	1.14	5.2	8.0	9.2	6.7	5.2	A
GOVERNMENT PERSONNEL MUTUAL L I C	TX	B-	799.8	96.5	1.95	1.27	7.4	5.7	1.9	5.4	4.9	DF
GPM HEALTH & LIFE INS CO	WA	B	140.7	22.1	2.46	2.14	8.7	5.6	6.0	6.3	5.7	AFI
GRANGE LIFE INS CO	OH	C+	470.1	29.9	1.52	0.87	6.0	5.2	1.6	4.2	4.4	DLT
▼ GRANULAR INSURANCE CO	SC	D	69.3	43.6	5.60	4.20	10.0	8.5	1.0	7.2	1.7	DGT
GREAT AMERICAN LIFE,INS CO	OH	B-	38448.9	2878.1	1.85	1.01	4.0	5.1	7.1	6.2	4.0	IT
GREAT REPUBLIC LIFE INS CO	WA	F (5)	--	--	--	--	--	--	--	--	--	Z
▼ GREAT SOUTHERN LIFE INS CO	TX	C	191.1	36.2	2.82	1.73	8.1	7.5	1.7	6.7	3.7	DFT
GREAT WESTERN INS CO	UT	C-	1191.0	47.5	1.43	0.70	4.0	2.1	1.8	7.4	2.9	CFIT
GREATER GEORGIA LIFE INS CO	GA	B	106.1	30.9	2.25	1.57	7.9	6.7	1.7	6.5	6.3	FG
GREENFIELDS LIFE INS CO	CO	B	10.0	9.0	3.71	3.34	8.0	8.7	4.0	10.0	6.3	A
GRIFFIN LEGGETT BURIAL INS CO	AR	U	--	--	--	--	--	--	--	--	--	Z
GUARANTEE TRUST LIFE INS CO	IL	B	791.2	153.5	2.77	1.75	8.1	6.5	7.7	7.2	5.8	T
GUARANTY INCOME LIFE INS CO	IA	B	3458.1	631.7	1.18	0.96	6.7	4.5	8.2	7.1	5.4	GI
GUARDIAN INS & ANNUITY CO INC	DE	B	14206.8	548.9	2.66	1.39	7.6	5.7	7.5	6.1	4.8	IT
GUARDIAN LIFE INS CO OF AMERICA	NY	A	72127.3	8589.0	3.06	1.92	8.4	6.7	7.6	5.7	7.5	I
▼ GULF GUARANTY LIFE INS CO	MS	D+	34.9	10.1	0.74	0.56	3.5	3.7	1.8	5.9	2.4	CDGI
GULF STATES LIFE INS CO INC	LA	U (5)	--	--	--	--	--	--	--	--	--	Z
HANNOVER LIFE REASSURANCE CO OF AMER	FL	B	17746.6	625.2	1.43	0.94	6.5	7.4	8.0	6.7	4.0	GT
HARLEYSVILLE LIFE INS CO	OH	B (4)	409.2	57.6	3.65	1.89	8.3	6.2	4.7	5.9	5.4	ADI
HARTFORD LIFE & ACCIDENT INS CO	CT	B-	13021.6	2410.1	3.49	2.16	8.7	6.5	3.7	6.8	5.3	A
HAWKEYE LIFE INS GROUP INC	IA	C	11.4	9.7	3.77	3.40	10.0	8.7	6.8	9.3	3.3	D
HAWTHORN LIFE INS CO	TX	D	11.2	3.3	0.26	0.26	0.1	3.0	8.0	6.2	0.7	ACDFI
HAYMARKET INS CO	NE	D-	2707.8	54.2	0.57	0.27	1.6	0.8	2.7	9.1	0.9	CIT
HCC LIFE INS CO	IN	B	1491.3	750.0	3.96	2.96	9.9	7.8	9.2	6.8	5.8	A
HEALTH NET LIFE INS CO	CA	B	616.8	353.3	3.91	3.07	10.0	8.1	4.8	7.0	4.0	T
HEARTLAND NATIONAL LIFE INS CO	IN	B	13.9	6.9	1.88	1.34	7.5	5.1	6.1	7.2	4.6	DI
HERITAGE LIFE INS CO	AZ	C+	7707.6	960.7	1.64	1.00	7.0	3.6	6.9	6.5	4.5	IT
HIGGINBOTHAM BURIAL INS CO	AR	F (5)	--	--	--	--	--	--	--	--	--	Z
HM LIFE INS CO	PA	B+	881.3	498.1	4.84	3.20	10.0	5.0	6.8	6.9	6.5	DI
HM LIFE INS CO OF NEW YORK	NY	B	81.4	55.6	6.83	5.76	10.0	8.6	5.2	7.7	5.9	AD
HOMESTEADERS LIFE CO	IA	B	3451.6	194.7	1.79	0.93	6.4	4.7	4.6	7.0	5.5	CI
HORACE MANN LIFE INS CO	IL	B	9032.1	472.6	1.90	0.97	6.8	5.0	7.4	5.0	5.3	AIT
▼ HUMANA INS CO OF KENTUCKY	KY	C	234.1	131.6	1.34	1.07	7.1	7.3	4.2	0.8	2.9	DGL
▼ HUMANA INS CO OF PUERTO RICO INC	PR	C	79.6	45.0	2.08	1.57	7.9	6.7	2.6	6.6	4.2	D
IA AMERICAN LIFE INS CO	TX	C	267.4	143.4	1.00	0.97	6.8	4.5	2.8	6.7	4.1	ADI
IBC LIFE INS CO	TX	U (5)	--	--	--	--	--	--	--	--	--	Z
IBEXIS LIFE & ANNUITY INS CO	MO	C	49.0	47.1	7.47	6.73	4.0	5.9	4.3	10.0	3.5	GT
IDEALIFE INS CO	CT	C+	20.3	18.8	5.33	4.80	10.0	9.4	2.5	10.0	4.4	FT
ILLINOIS MUTUAL LIFE INS CO	IL	B+	1595.0	277.6	3.70	2.01	8.5	5.9	7.0	6.5	6.7	FI
INDEPENDENCE INS INC	DE	U	--	--	--	--	--	--	--	--	--	Z
INDEPENDENCE LIFE & ANNUITY CO	DE	D+	3445.7	189.5	4.88	3.73	4.0	7.5	7.4	6.8	2.6	AT
INDEPENDENT LIFE INSURANCE CO	TX	D	468.3	80.9	4.61	2.16	4.0	4.4	1.8	7.7	2.2	DEGI
INDIVIDUAL ASR CO LIFE HEALTH & ACC	OK	C	18.7	8.7	1.69	1.43	7.6	7.0	4.6	7.1	4.0	AT
INDUSTRIAL ALLIANCE INS & FIN SERV	TX	C	295.2	38.4	2.65	1.59	7.9	7.4	1.4	3.5	3.6	DL
INDY HEALTH INSURANCE COMPANY	AR	F (4)	8.4	6.5	2.86	2.57	9.4	8.2	2.0	9.5	2.2	DFG
INTEGRITY LIFE INS CO	OH	C+	9956.3	1481.4	1.89	1.28	7.4	5.0	2.8	6.6	4.7	T
INTERNATIONAL AMERICAN LIFE INS CO	TX	D-	3.3	0.4	0.35	0.31	0.7	9.8	0.9	9.2	0.7	CDGT

See Page 27 for explanation of footnotes and Page 28 for explanation of stability factors.
Arrows denote recent upgrades ▲ or downgrades▼ (see Section VI for explanations)

40

www.weissratings.com

NET PREMIUM ($MIL)	IN-VESTED ASSETS ($MIL)	% OF INVESTED ASSETS IN:									INVEST. IN AFFIL		INSURANCE COMPANY NAME
		CASH	CMO & STRUCT. SECS.	OTH.INV. GRADE BONDS	NON-INV. GRADE BONDS	CMMON & PREF. STOCK	MORT IN GOOD STAND.	NON-PERF. MORT.	REAL ESTATE	OTHER INVEST-MENTS			
--	--	--	--	--	--	--	--	--	--	--	--		GERTRUDE GEDDES WILLIS LIFE INS CO
799.5	4,878.1	0.0	0.6	82.7	4.8	3.2	1.1	0.0	0.1	7.9	5.3	●	GLOBE LIFE & ACCIDENT INS CO
73.7	250.7	0.0	2.5	86.8	4.8	0.0	0.0	0.0	0.0	6.0	0.0	●	GLOBE LIFE INSURANCE CO OF NY
--	--	--	--	--	--	--	--	--	--	--	--		GMHP HEALTH INS LMTD
428.8	573.7 (*)	-1.1	20.8	60.3	0.0	0.0	0.0	0.0	0.4	1.4	0.0	●	GOLDEN RULE INS CO
59.0	762.8 (*)	5.9	3.3	52.6	2.1	3.6	19.4	0.0	2.3	7.5	3.1	●	GOVERNMENT PERSONNEL MUTUAL L I C
8.3	131.7 (*)	6.2	5.3	66.9	4.1	0.7	0.0	0.0	0.0	7.7	0.0	●	GPM HEALTH & LIFE INS CO
46.8	409.2 (*)	0.3	21.2	73.4	0.2	0.0	0.0	0.0	0.0	3.3	0.0	●	GRANGE LIFE INS CO
43.9	66.7 (*)	30.0	0.0	63.5	0.0	0.0	0.0	0.0	0.0	0.0	0.0	●	GRANULAR INSURANCE CO
5,027.0	37,304.9 (*)	0.7	29.8	51.6	3.9	2.9	5.8	0.0	0.0	3.3	1.0	●	GREAT AMERICAN LIFE INS CO
--	--	--	--	--	--	--	--	--	--	--	--		GREAT REPUBLIC LIFE INS CO
36.7	179.0	0.0	3.5	80.1	2.2	12.3	0.0	0.0	0.0	2.0	0.0	●	GREAT SOUTHERN LIFE INS CO
-2.3	1,149.0	0.1	9.7	76.5	4.7	0.4	5.6	0.0	0.0	2.5	0.0	●	GREAT WESTERN INS CO
46.8	98.8 (*)	0.0	7.7	57.3	5.8	0.0	0.0	0.0	0.0	15.2	0.0	●	GREATER GEORGIA LIFE INS CO
0.0	9.9	21.2	71.3	7.5	0.0	0.0	0.0	0.0	0.0	0.0	0.0		GREENFIELDS LIFE INS CO
--	--	--	--	--	--	--	--	--	--	--	--		GRIFFIN LEGGETT BURIAL INS CO
255.5	766.2 (*)	0.7	29.1	49.2	5.6	0.9	10.2	0.0	0.3	2.8	2.0	●	GUARANTEE TRUST LIFE INS CO
552.4	3,332.3 (*)	2.0	22.8	41.9	6.3	16.9	4.9	0.0	0.1	3.5	13.1	●	GUARANTY INCOME LIFE INS CO
151.5	4,363.2	0.0	2.0	75.3	1.9	0.0	13.6	0.0	0.0	7.6	0.0	●	GUARDIAN INS & ANNUITY CO INC
9,452.9	66,043.7	-0.1	4.9	67.6	4.6	2.0	8.1	0.0	0.4	12.4	1.8	●	GUARDIAN LIFE INS CO OF AMERICA
50.9	33.3 (*)	19.0	0.0	9.7	0.9	33.0	0.4	0.0	5.0	1.3	10.3		GULF GUARANTY LIFE INS CO
--	--	--	--	--	--	--	--	--	--	--	--		GULF STATES LIFE INS CO INC
477.3	3,289.6	1.4	4.9	85.8	1.6	4.6	0.0	0.0	0.0	1.7	4.3	●	HANNOVER LIFE REASSURANCE CO OF AMER
13.8	394.9	0.0	5.5	83.5	2.6	0.0	0.0	0.0	0.0	8.4	0.0	●	HARLEYSVILLE LIFE INS CO
3,658.2	12,028.4 (*)	0.2	17.4	53.4	4.1	2.5	12.3	0.0	0.0	7.1	0.0	●	HARTFORD LIFE & ACCIDENT INS CO
1.4	11.2 (*)	0.8	23.0	70.8	0.0	0.0	0.0	0.0	0.0	0.0	5.6		HAWKEYE LIFE INS GROUP INC
0.3	11.0	4.0	12.8	6.4	0.0	76.9	0.0	0.0	0.0	0.0	76.4		HAWTHORN LIFE INS CO
55.6	2,607.1	6.9	18.1	37.9	4.9	0.6	9.5	0.0	0.0	22.2	8.8	●	HAYMARKET INS CO
1,501.8	1,408.3	0.0	49.6	49.2	0.3	0.1	0.0	0.0	0.0	0.9	0.1	●	HCC LIFE INS CO
524.2	480.1 (*)	23.9	18.5	49.4	0.8	0.0	0.0	0.0	0.0	4.1	0.0	●	HEALTH NET LIFE INS CO
10.7	9.7	0.0	0.1	72.4	0.0	0.0	0.0	0.0	10.8	16.8	0.0		HEARTLAND NATIONAL LIFE INS CO
212.0	6,778.1 (*)	0.2	16.3	55.2	7.0	5.8	0.0	0.0	0.0	12.4	4.6	●	HERITAGE LIFE INS CO
--	--	--	--	--	--	--	--	--	--	--	--		HIGGINBOTHAM BURIAL INS CO
450.2	829.7 (*)	0.0	16.1	43.1	6.6	19.3	0.0	0.0	0.0	0.2	0.0	●	HM LIFE INS CO
35.7	78.2	15.7	23.0	59.3	1.0	0.0	0.0	0.0	0.0	0.0	0.0	●	HM LIFE INS CO OF NEW YORK
561.7	3,354.7	0.6	22.1	66.2	2.5	0.2	6.1	0.0	0.3	1.4	0.1	●	HOMESTEADERS LIFE CO
571.3	5,434.8 (*)	0.0	23.7	53.9	4.1	3.3	0.7	0.0	0.0	12.7	0.6	●	HORACE MANN LIFE INS CO
518.3	193.5 (*)	1.4	32.6	47.0	4.0	0.0	0.0	0.0	0.0	0.0	0.0	●	HUMANA INS CO OF KENTUCKY
119.6	69.5	7.3	32.1	37.8	4.4	0.0	0.0	0.0	0.0	18.4	0.0	●	HUMANA INS CO OF PUERTO RICO INC
48.0	259.9	2.1	0.2	39.0	0.0	55.4	0.1	0.0	0.0	2.5	55.4	●	IA AMERICAN LIFE INS CO
--	--	--	--	--	--	--	--	--	--	--	--		IBC LIFE INS CO
0.0	48.8 (*)	5.3	3.5	35.1	0.0	0.1	0.0	0.0	0.0	0.0	0.0	●	IBEXIS LIFE & ANNUITY INS CO
-0.3	19.6	4.7	0.0	87.3	0.0	0.0	0.0	0.0	0.0	8.0	0.0		IDEALIFE INS CO
98.0	1,455.9	0.6	14.4	62.8	5.3	6.5	6.0	0.0	0.3	3.5	0.1	●	ILLINOIS MUTUAL LIFE INS CO
--	--	--	--	--	--	--	--	--	--	--	--		INDEPENDENCE INS INC
2.4	214.2	0.5	33.5	60.6	0.0	0.0	0.0	0.0	0.0	5.4	0.0	●	INDEPENDENCE LIFE & ANNUITY CO
18.6	460.4 (*)	1.7	4.2	68.0	6.1	4.6	0.0	0.0	0.0	13.5	0.0	●	INDEPENDENT LIFE INSURANCE CO
3.2	14.5 (*)	11.8	18.2	21.4	0.0	38.8	0.0	0.0	0.0	8.2	24.1		INDIVIDUAL ASR CO LIFE HEALTH & ACC
119.0	289.3	1.3	0.3	94.3	0.7	0.0	0.0	0.0	0.0	2.8	0.0	●	INDUSTRIAL ALLIANCE INS & FIN SERV
0.3	7.9	41.6	0.2	55.2	0.0	2.7	0.0	0.0	0.0	0.0	0.0		INDY HEALTH INSURANCE COMPANY
373.2	7,819.6 (*)	0.0	22.1	40.2	5.2	14.9	9.6	0.0	0.0	5.5	8.3	●	INTEGRITY LIFE INS CO
1.9	3.0	97.7	0.0	2.3	0.0	0.0	0.0	0.0	0.0	0.0	0.0		INTERNATIONAL AMERICAN LIFE INS CO

● Bullets denote a more detailed analysis is available in Section II.
(*) Asset category percentages do not add up to 100%

INSURANCE COMPANY NAME	DOM. STATE	RATING	TOTAL ASSETS ($MIL)	CAPITAL & SURPLUS ($MIL)	RISK ADJUSTED CAPITAL RATIO 1	RISK ADJUSTED CAPITAL RATIO 2	CAPITAL-IZATION INDEX (PTS)	INVEST. SAFETY INDEX (PTS)	PROFIT-ABILITY INDEX (PTS)	LIQUIDITY INDEX (PTS)	STAB. INDEX (PTS)	STABILITY FACTOR
INTRAMERICA LIFE INS CO	NY	B (5)	--	--	--	--	--	--	--	--	--	Z
INVESTORS HERITAGE LIFE INS CO	KY	C	1398.4	170.8	2.84	1.40	7.6	3.9	3.3	6.9	3.3	GIRT
▼ INVESTORS LIFE INS CO NORTH AMERICA	TX	B-	512.5	25.7	1.87	0.99	4.0	3.5	6.2	5.2	3.5	FIT
INVESTORS PREFERRED LIFE INS CO	SD	E	1011.5	3.5	0.18	0.12	0.0	9.8	4.6	9.5	0.0	CGT
JACKSON GRIFFIN INS CO	AR	D+ (1)	14.3	1.7	0.66	0.59	3.7	3.1	6.1	9.4	1.7	CDFI
JACKSON NATIONAL LIFE INS CO	MI	C+	303000.0	6098.2	2.07	1.15	4.0	5.8	8.0	7.3	4.0	T
▲ JACKSON NATIONAL LIFE INS CO OF NY	NY	B	19048.2	661.9	3.74	2.58	9.4	5.4	8.2	7.0	5.5	AFI
▲ JAMESTOWN LIFE INS CO	VA	C+	5.2	2.3	1.50	1.35	7.5	9.7	5.3	9.2	3.4	ADFT
JEFFERSON NATIONAL LIFE INS CO	TX	C+	10807.0	102.6	1.13	0.84	5.7	6.3	8.9	10.0	4.8	CG
JEFFERSON NATIONAL LIFE INS CO OF NY	NY	B-	282.3	6.7	0.63	0.57	3.6	9.3	3.7	10.0	3.6	ACDG
JOHN ALDEN LIFE INS CO	WI	C+	181.7	20.8	4.81	4.33	10.0	7.7	2.8	6.5	4.0	FT
JOHN HANCOCK LIFE & HEALTH INS CO	MA	B	19441.1	1448.4	5.38	2.87	9.8	6.2	9.4	9.0	6.2	AIT
JOHN HANCOCK LIFE INS CO (USA)	MI	B-	273000.0	10411.6	1.88	1.20	7.3	5.1	5.0	6.8	5.2	IT
JOHN HANCOCK LIFE INS CO OF NY	NY	C+	19494.3	1320.4	3.87	2.00	8.5	6.0	3.0	5.9	4.5	T
JORDAN FUNERAL & INS CO INC	AL	F (5)	--	--	--	--	--	--	--	--	--	Z
JRD LIFE INS CO	AZ	U	--	--	--	--	--	--	--	--	--	Z
KANSAS CITY LIFE INS CO	MO	B	3770.7	245.3	1.57	0.91	6.3	4.9	3.4	5.0	5.5	CFILT
KENTUCKY FUNERAL DIRECTORS LIFE INS	KY	B-	25.9	6.6	1.61	1.45	7.7	7.6	7.9	6.2	4.8	DG
KENTUCKY HOME LIFE INS CO	KY	C-	5.3	3.2	2.89	2.61	9.4	6.3	2.1	7.8	3.0	AFT
▲ KILPATRICK LIFE INS CO	LA	C-	206.7	15.6	1.83	1.29	7.4	6.3	5.6	8.6	3.0	D
LADDER LIFE INSURANCE CO	CA	F	10.3	9.6	3.89	3.50	10.0	8.4	1.9	6.8	0.0	FT
LAFAYETTE LIFE INS CO	OH	B	6345.5	404.3	1.98	1.00	7.0	4.2	4.2	5.5	5.6	AI
LANDCAR LIFE INS CO	UT	U (5)	--	--	--	--	--	--	--	--	--	Z
▼ LANDMARK LIFE INS CO	TX	C	49.1	5.3	0.87	0.78	5.2	6.4	3.5	4.5	3.7	CDIL
LANGHORNE REINSURANCE AZ LTD	AZ	D	9.7	8.9	3.77	3.39	10.0	9.5	1.9	9.0	1.6	DFGT
LEADERS LIFE INS CO	OK	B	8.7	3.5	1.58	1.42	7.6	7.4	1.9	5.7	6.3	AD
LEGACY LIFE INS CO OF MO	MO	B	6.4	6.2	3.47	3.12	10.0	8.3	4.0	9.5	6.0	AD
LEWER LIFE INS CO	MO	C	34.9	14.0	2.81	1.73	8.1	4.9	5.8	6.7	3.6	D
LIBERTY BANKERS LIFE INS CO	OK	B-	2323.6	278.4	1.16	0.83	5.6	4.2	8.7	6.7	5.1	GI
LIBERTY NATIONAL LIFE INS CO	NE	B-	8756.8	579.7	1.78	0.95	6.6	4.7	5.8	3.0	5.0	AIL
LIFE ASR CO OF AMERICA	IL	U	--	--	--	--	--	--	--	--	--	Z
LIFE ASSURANCE CO INC	OK	C	3.7	3.1	2.66	2.40	4.0	8.9	7.6	10.0	3.4	T
LIFE INS CO OF ALABAMA	AL	C+	130.7	33.2	2.58	1.65	8.0	5.6	4.6	6.7	4.6	
▼ LIFE INS CO OF BOSTON & NEW YORK	NY	B+	193.4	38.3	3.67	2.13	8.7	6.4	5.3	6.6	6.4	DI
LIFE INS CO OF LOUISIANA	LA	D	12.0	5.5	2.37	1.40	7.6	3.0	2.9	7.6	2.1	DI
▼ LIFE INS CO OF NORTH AMERICA	PA	B	9002.2	1670.2	4.43	2.59	9.4	5.4	4.2	6.9	5.3	IT
LIFE INS CO OF THE SOUTHWEST	TX	B	27512.1	1973.9	2.50	1.25	7.4	4.7	5.9	5.5	5.5	AI
▲ LIFE OF AMERICA INS CO	TX	B-	8.8	3.3	1.06	0.79	5.3	6.1	8.0	3.4	4.7	ACDIL
LIFE OF THE SOUTH INS CO	GA	C-	143.9	31.3	0.85	0.72	4.8	5.8	2.9	7.8	3.2	CF
LIFECARE ASSURANCE CO	AZ	C	2933.0	100.0	1.48	0.75	5.7	3.2	3.9	8.7	4.2	CI
LIFEMAP ASR CO	OR	B-	107.2	61.7	2.83	2.02	8.5	4.9	4.0	6.7	5.3	FI
▲ LIFESECURE INS CO	MI	B-	582.7	55.4	2.25	1.28	7.4	4.3	5.0	9.1	5.1	ADI
LIFESHIELD NATIONAL INS CO	OK	C+	78.6	23.1	0.97	0.87	6.0	4.0	4.9	6.6	4.4	CFIT
LINCOLN BENEFIT LIFE CO	NE	C+	12067.4	436.8	0.99	0.56	4.9	3.6	8.4	5.6	4.8	CFIT
LINCOLN HERITAGE LIFE INS CO	IL	B-	1118.1	89.9	2.07	1.13	7.2	6.6	2.7	5.3	5.1	
LINCOLN LIFE & ANNUITY CO OF NY	NY	B	17305.7	991.3	3.54	1.83	8.2	6.1	5.3	5.3	5.5	AIL
LINCOLN LIFE ASSR CO OF BOSTON	NH	C+ (5)	--	--	--	--	--	--	--	--	--	Z
▼ LINCOLN NATIONAL LIFE INS CO	IN	C+	317000.0	8447.1	1.33	0.92	6.4	6.3	2.3	5.6	4.6	AF
LIVE OAK INSURANCE CO	LA	D	9.9	1.7	0.75	0.68	4.4	3.3	2.7	6.4	2.1	CDI
LOCOMOTIVE ENGRS&COND MUT PROT ASSN	MI	B	100.1	85.7	6.78	4.05	10.0	3.4	6.7	7.4	5.7	DI
LOMBARD INTL LIFE ASR CO	PA	E	7923.8	17.6	0.20	0.12	0.0	8.1	1.7	10.0	0.0	CT
LOMBARD INTL LIFE ASR CO OF NY	NY	U	--	--	--	--	--	--	--	--	--	Z

See Page 27 for explanation of footnotes and Page 28 for explanation of stability factors.

Arrows denote recent upgrades ▲ or downgrades▼ (see Section VI for explanations)

42   www.weissratings.com

NET PREMIUM ($MIL)	IN- VESTED ASSETS ($MIL)	CASH	CMO & STRUCT. SECS.	OTH.INV. GRADE BONDS	NON-INV. GRADE BONDS	CMMON & PREF. STOCK	MORT IN GOOD STAND.	NON- PERF. MORT.	REAL ESTATE	OTHER INVEST- MENTS	INVEST. IN AFFIL	INSURANCE COMPANY NAME
--	--	--	--	--	--	--	--	--	--	--	--	INTRAMERICA LIFE INS CO
455.9	1,283.8 (*)	0.6	20.3	40.6	6.6	5.3	5.7	0.2	0.0	16.4	0.5 ●	INVESTORS HERITAGE LIFE INS CO
3.2	326.2	0.0	12.6	64.0	4.9	12.6	0.0	0.0	0.0	5.9	1.5 ●	INVESTORS LIFE INS CO NORTH AMERICA
190.6	110.8	4.3	0.0	0.0	0.0	0.0	0.0	0.0	0.0	95.7	0.0	INVESTORS PREFERRED LIFE INS CO
0.6	14.0 (*)	6.1	0.0	71.3	4.7	19.7	0.0	0.0	0.0	0.0	0.0	JACKSON GRIFFIN INS CO
19,845.3	69,805.0 (*)	0.4	17.7	48.0	2.5	1.5	16.3	0.3	0.4	9.8	2.2 ●	JACKSON NATIONAL LIFE INS CO
148.7	1,328.4	0.0	22.2	71.6	2.6	0.0	0.0	0.0	0.0	3.5	0.0 ●	JACKSON NATIONAL LIFE INS CO OF NY
0.6	5.1	41.6	0.0	58.4	0.0	0.0	0.0	0.0	0.0	0.0	0.0	JAMESTOWN LIFE INS CO
1,387.5	527.4 (*)	16.7	16.6	54.4	3.4	4.0	1.1	0.0	0.0	1.0	1.3 ●	JEFFERSON NATIONAL LIFE INS CO
65.6	6.8	0.0	8.4	40.8	0.0	0.0	0.0	0.0	0.0	50.8	0.0	JEFFERSON NATIONAL LIFE INS CO OF NY
-1.4	173.6 (*)	1.8	9.5	73.9	0.1	1.8	0.0	0.0	0.0	5.9	0.0	JOHN ALDEN LIFE INS CO
677.5	5,991.4 (*)	0.1	4.0	64.3	1.7	1.2	8.0	0.0	2.7	9.3	0.4 ●	JOHN HANCOCK LIFE & HEALTH INS CO
15,930.9	104,000.0 (*)	-0.1	5.8	46.8	2.7	4.3	11.0	0.0	4.1	13.2	6.4 ●	JOHN HANCOCK LIFE INS CO (USA)
1,005.6	8,869.9 (*)	0.2	3.4	61.4	0.8	1.0	7.4	0.0	2.7	10.8	0.0 ●	JOHN HANCOCK LIFE INS CO OF NY
--	--	--	--	--	--	--	--	--	--	--	--	JORDAN FUNERAL & INS CO INC
--	--	--	--	--	--	--	--	--	--	--	--	JRD LIFE INS CO
265.2	3,143.5	0.0	7.0	64.5	1.1	1.9	17.7	0.0	4.2	3.8	1.6 ●	KANSAS CITY LIFE INS CO
3.6	25.5	1.9	0.0	96.4	1.5	0.0	0.0	0.0	0.0	0.0	0.0	KENTUCKY FUNERAL DIRECTORS LIFE INS
1.7	5.0	3.3	0.4	78.9	0.0	17.4	0.0	0.0	0.0	0.1	0.0	KENTUCKY HOME LIFE INS CO
12.2	201.5 (*)	12.2	11.2	16.1	0.3	1.5	17.5	0.3	1.2	37.9	0.0	KILPATRICK LIFE INS CO
0.0	10.0 (*)	4.0	0.0	0.0	0.0	0.0	0.0	0.0	0.0	0.0	0.0	LADDER LIFE INSURANCE CO
643.5	6,188.7 (*)	0.1	16.3	44.3	5.4	3.1	10.4	0.0	0.0	17.9	1.8 ●	LAFAYETTE LIFE INS CO
--	--	--	--	--	--	--	--	--	--	--	--	LANDCAR LIFE INS CO
9.0	43.8	5.2	17.2	65.8	1.6	0.1	1.2	0.0	5.8	3.1	0.0	LANDMARK LIFE INS CO
0.3	9.6	0.8	0.0	97.4	0.0	0.0	0.0	0.0	0.0	1.0	0.0	LANCHORNE REINSURANCE AZ LTD
6.7	6.5	18.0	0.0	74.2	0.8	6.4	0.0	0.0	0.0	0.0	0.0	LEADERS LIFE INS CO
0.1	6.4 (*)	1.9	0.0	72.7	0.0	0.0	0.0	0.0	0.0	0.0	0.0	LEGACY LIFE INS CO OF MO
10.1	32.4 (*)	0.8	22.0	50.8	5.8	17.8	0.0	0.0	0.0	0.7	0.0	LEWER LIFE INS CO
548.1	2,256.4	6.3	9.1	41.5	2.6	9.5	23.8	0.1	3.1	3.9	8.1 ●	LIBERTY BANKERS LIFE INS CO
1,148.5	8,290.9	-0.1	0.7	76.1	5.3	3.8	0.6	0.0	0.0	13.5	7.2 ●	LIBERTY NATIONAL LIFE INS CO
--	--	--	--	--	--	--	--	--	--	--	--	LIFE ASR CO OF AMERICA
0.0	3.4	68.3	12.2	0.0	0.0	16.5	0.0	0.0	0.0	2.9	0.0	LIFE ASSURANCE CO INC
36.5	120.3	1.3	16.6	62.5	0.0	9.5	0.0	0.0	3.9	6.1	0.0 ●	LIFE INS CO OF ALABAMA
22.5	181.1	4.0	5.9	62.0	1.5	6.6	0.0	0.0	0.0	19.1	0.0 ●	LIFE INS CO OF BOSTON & NEW YORK
0.1	11.1	8.0	0.0	29.1	0.0	50.6	1.8	0.0	0.0	10.5	11.1	LIFE INS CO OF LOUISIANA
2,661.9	8,098.4	0.0	8.4	77.4	6.4	0.0	8.7	0.0	0.0	0.0	0.0 ●	LIFE INS CO OF NORTH AMERICA
3,275.6	26,916.9 (*)	0.1	14.1	52.1	3.1	0.4	16.6	0.0	0.0	6.5	0.0 ●	LIFE INS CO OF THE SOUTHWEST
9.6	3.7 (*)	16.7	0.0	56.8	9.4	0.0	9.7	0.0	0.0	0.0	0.0	LIFE OF AMERICA INS CO
79.6	104.4 (*)	4.2	25.4	34.5	0.0	27.9	0.0	0.0	0.0	3.3	20.0 ●	LIFE OF THE SOUTH INS CO
198.5	2,859.9	0.0	23.6	67.7	3.2	0.0	1.6	0.0	0.0	3.2	0.0 ●	LIFECARE ASSURANCE CO
68.9	102.6 (*)	1.5	31.8	39.5	0.0	25.9	0.0	0.0	0.0	0.0	1.9 ●	LIFEMAP ASR CO
93.3	569.2	1.8	6.6	86.7	5.1	0.0	0.0	0.0	0.0	0.0	0.0 ●	LIFESECURE INS CO
26.1	71.2 (*)	9.0	32.0	18.2	1.4	31.8	0.0	0.0	0.0	2.2	28.0	LIFESHIELD NATIONAL INS CO
-156.4	9,967.9 (*)	1.5	20.7	57.8	3.2	3.7	8.4	0.0	0.0	3.2	1.8 ●	LINCOLN BENEFIT LIFE CO
374.2	987.0 (*)	8.1	31.1	41.4	0.1	0.6	5.6	0.0	1.2	7.4	0.0 ●	LINCOLN HERITAGE LIFE INS CO
824.6	8,600.1	0.0	6.6	77.5	1.6	0.1	11.2	0.0	0.0	2.9	0.0 ●	LINCOLN LIFE & ANNUITY CO OF NY
--	--	--	--	--	--	--	--	--	--	--	--	LINCOLN LIFE ASSR CO OF BOSTON
17,319.5	121,000.0 (*)	0.0	7.6	64.0	1.9	3.6	12.2	0.0	0.1	4.8	6.6 ●	LINCOLN NATIONAL LIFE INS CO
1.9	9.7	11.6	0.0	72.3	0.0	5.3	1.2	0.0	8.6	0.1	0.0	LIVE OAK INSURANCE CO
17.9	99.7 (*)	1.1	0.1	46.3	0.0	46.0	0.0	0.0	0.0	0.0	0.0 ●	LOCOMOTIVE ENGRS&COND MUT PROT ASSN
839.0	130.5 (*)	1.3	0.0	11.5	0.0	3.5	0.0	0.0	0.0	81.4	3.5	LOMBARD INTL LIFE ASR CO
--	--	--	--	--	--	--	--	--	--	--	--	LOMBARD INTL LIFE ASR CO OF NY

● Bullets denote a more detailed analysis is available in Section II.
(*) Asset category percentages do not add up to 100%

INSURANCE COMPANY NAME	DOM. STATE	RATING	TOTAL ASSETS ($MIL)	CAPITAL & SURPLUS ($MIL)	RISK ADJUSTED CAPITAL RATIO 1	RISK ADJUSTED CAPITAL RATIO 2	CAPITAL-IZATION INDEX (PTS)	INVEST. SAFETY INDEX (PTS)	PROFIT-ABILITY INDEX (PTS)	LIQUIDITY INDEX (PTS)	STAB. INDEX (PTS)	STABILITY FACTOR
LONE STAR LIFE INS CO	TX	F (5)	--	--	--	--	--	--	--	--	--	Z
LOYAL AMERICAN LIFE INS CO	OH	B	403.0	133.6	1.07	0.93	6.4	6.1	6.4	6.8	5.6	ACDI
LUMICO LIFE INSURANCE CO	MO	C	201.9	85.3	8.75	6.35	10.0	7.5	1.9	7.4	2.7	FGT
LUMICO LIFE INSURANCE CO OF NY	NY	U	--	--	--	--	--	--	--	--	--	Z
M LIFE INS CO	CO	B+	479.6	168.1	7.64	5.06	10.0	8.5	4.4	9.0	6.8	DG
MADISON NATIONAL LIFE INS CO INC	WI	B	236.9	92.9	4.40	3.28	10.0	8.6	5.3	9.0	4.1	AT
MAGNOLIA GUARANTY LIFE INS CO	MS	D+	11.2	1.5	0.64	0.58	3.6	5.3	1.4	7.3	2.4	CDFG
MAJESTIC LIFE INS CO	LA	D	16.2	5.5	1.19	0.71	5.3	1.5	2.5	6.5	2.3	CDFI
MANHATTAN LIFE INS CO	NY	B	632.6	77.6	1.74	1.21	7.3	6.1	5.4	6.2	4.0	AFIT
MANHATTAN NATIONAL LIFE INS CO	OH	B	141.2	13.1	1.52	1.37	7.6	3.9	1.8	6.2	5.4	DFI
MANHATTANLIFE INS & ANNUITY CO	AR	C+	792.0	219.4	0.91	0.81	5.5	5.2	6.7	6.5	4.8	T
MAPFRE LIFE INS CO OF PR	PR	B	59.3	29.9	2.63	2.04	8.6	8.3	5.7	6.6	5.1	ADF
MARQUETTE INDEMNITY & LIFE INS CO	AZ	D+	4.8	2.4	1.66	1.50	7.8	3.7	4.5	9.1	2.4	FIT
MASSACHUSETTS MUTUAL LIFE INS CO	MA	B	315000.0	26979.3	1.41	1.09	7.1	6.0	7.3	6.4	4.2	GIT
MCS LIFE INS CO	PR	D-	90.5	36.1	0.65	0.53	3.2	9.5	5.6	1.4	1.0	DFLT
MEDAMERICA INS CO	PA	C	1146.3	40.5	1.18	0.63	4.0	2.6	0.9	6.9	3.8	CFI
MEDAMERICA INS CO OF FL	FL	C	74.9	9.4	1.24	1.12	7.2	4.6	0.9	9.2	3.8	ADI
MEDAMERICA INS CO OF NEW YORK	NY	D+	1128.1	28.1	0.77	0.45	3.2	2.7	0.9	8.1	2.2	CI
MEDICAL BENEFITS MUTUAL LIFE INS CO	OH	D+	17.3	12.8	2.22	1.78	8.2	3.0	3.3	6.9	2.6	DI
MEDICO CORP LIFE INS CO	NE	B-	72.9	27.8	3.60	3.24	8.0	7.6	8.1	7.5	4.9	AG
MEDICO INS CO	NE	B-	75.0	32.4	4.14	3.73	4.0	7.7	4.8	7.1	4.0	AG
MEDICO LIFE & HEALTH INS CO	IA	C	14.0	11.5	4.04	3.64	8.0	7.8	4.7	7.7	4.2	A
▼ MEDMUTUAL LIFE INS CO	OH	B-	60.0	33.2	1.81	1.39	7.6	9.3	1.8	6.0	5.3	FG
MELLON LIFE INS CO	DE	U (5)	--	--	--	--	--	--	--	--	--	Z
MEMBERS LIFE INS CO	IA	B	386.6	35.6	3.08	2.77	8.0	9.0	5.7	6.8	6.2	A
MEMORIAL LIFE INS CO	LA	D	3.8	1.5	1.39	1.10	7.2	2.7	2.4	8.3	2.1	DI
MERIT LIFE INS CO	TX	C	56.9	25.0	3.67	3.31	8.0	3.8	2.4	6.6	4.1	AFI
METLIFE INSURANCE LTD	GU	U (5)	--	--	--	--	--	--	--	--	--	Z
METROPOLITAN LIFE INS CO	NY	B	404000.0	11803.8	2.48	1.26	7.4	5.3	8.4	6.8	5.9	I
METROPOLITAN TOWER LIFE INS CO	NE	C+	43883.0	1638.2	2.29	1.11	7.2	5.4	3.9	6.4	4.8	T
MID-WEST NATIONAL LIFE INS CO OF TN	TX	C	42.9	19.7	3.34	3.00	10.0	8.0	1.3	10.0	3.4	FT
▼ MIDLAND NATIONAL LIFE INS CO	IA	B	74313.6	5248.4	2.32	1.18	7.3	4.5	9.2	5.6	4.5	IT
MIDWESTERN UNITED LIFE INS CO	IN	B	248.1	145.3	14.40	12.96	10.0	7.7	5.5	7.0	6.0	AD
MILILANI LIFE INS CO	HI	U	--	--	--	--	--	--	--	--	--	Z
MINNESOTA LIFE INS CO	MN	C+	66996.4	3402.9	2.15	1.32	7.5	5.8	1.9	6.0	4.4	
MML BAY STATE LIFE INS CO	CT	B-	5462.8	265.4	4.74	3.46	4.0	6.7	5.8	7.2	4.0	T
MOLINA HEALTHCARE OF TEXAS INS CO	TX	D	10.1	9.6	3.95	3.55	8.0	9.8	8.5	10.0	1.9	A
MONARCH LIFE INS CO	MA	F	627.8	5.9	0.52	0.32	1.2	0.4	2.9	0.0	0.0	CFILT
MONITOR LIFE INS CO OF NEW YORK	NY	C	20.4	17.1	4.80	4.32	10.0	9.0	6.1	10.0	3.7	AFT
MONY LIFE INS CO	NY	B-	6597.6	334.5	1.88	0.99	6.9	5.3	2.9	4.2	5.0	AFIL
MOUNTAIN LIFE INS CO	TN	C-	4.8	3.0	2.09	1.88	8.3	7.3	1.9	7.6	3.0	AFT
MULHEARN PROTECTIVE INS CO	LA	D+	12.2	3.0	1.13	0.68	5.2	1.8	2.6	7.7	2.5	DFI
MULTINATIONAL LIFE INS CO	PR	C-	132.4	25.8	2.26	1.30	7.5	5.5	2.9	7.2	3.3	A
MUNICH AMERICAN REASSURANCE CO	GA	C	9176.0	607.7	2.67	1.64	8.0	7.1	1.5	6.1	3.0	FT
MUNICH RE US LIFE CORP	GA	U	--	--	--	--	--	--	--	--	--	Z
MUTUAL OF AMERICA LIFE INS CO	NY	B	28283.4	762.1	1.46	0.90	6.2	5.7	2.4	6.7	4.6	CFGIT
MUTUAL OF OMAHA INS CO	NE	B	10341.8	3996.6	1.25	1.13	7.2	4.9	5.7	7.0	5.5	I
MUTUAL SAVINGS LIFE INS CO	AL	B-	110.1	22.0	2.96	2.34	4.0	6.4	6.1	6.8	4.0	AFT
MUTUAL TRUST LIFE INS CO	IL	B	2259.5	165.1	2.07	1.04	7.1	4.3	5.4	5.2	5.9	IL
NASSAU LIFE & ANNUITY CO	CT	D	1935.6	116.5	1.69	0.85	6.0	4.0	1.6	8.9	1.8	AGIT
NASSAU LIFE INS CO OF KS	KS	D-	77.9	14.3	1.93	1.74	8.1	4.8	2.5	7.2	1.2	ADFIT
NASSAU LIFE INSURANCE CO	NY	D-	14014.5	376.4	1.33	0.67	5.5	4.8	5.0	3.6	1.3	CFIL

See Page 27 for explanation of footnotes and Page 28 for explanation of stability factors.
Arrows denote recent upgrades ▲ or downgrades▼ (see Section VI for explanations)

44

www.weissratings.com

NET PREMIUM ($MIL)	IN-VESTED ASSETS ($MIL)	% OF INVESTED ASSETS IN:									INVEST. IN AFFIL	INSURANCE COMPANY NAME
		CASH	CMO & STRUCT. SECS.	OTH.INV. GRADE BONDS	NON-INV. GRADE BONDS	CMMON & PREF. STOCK	MORT IN GOOD STAND.	NON-PERF. MORT.	REAL ESTATE	OTHER INVEST-MENTS		
--	--	--	--	--	--	--	--	--	--	--	--	LONE STAR LIFE INS CO
363.3	370.8	0.0	0.0	77.2	0.5	20.7	0.0	0.0	0.0	1.5	20.7 ●	LOYAL AMERICAN LIFE INS CO
21.3	192.0	-0.2	17.7	76.6	0.0	4.8	0.0	0.0	0.0	0.8	0.0 ●	LUMICO LIFE INSURANCE CO
--	--	--	--	--	--	--	--	--	--	--	--	LUMICO LIFE INSURANCE CO OF NY
539.9	260.4 (*)	1.9	14.9	80.0	0.0	0.0	0.0	0.0	0.0	1.0	0.0 ●	M LIFE INS CO
112.5	213.9 (*)	3.3	0.0	87.0	0.0	0.0	0.0	0.0	0.0	0.3	0.0 ●	MADISON NATIONAL LIFE INS CO INC
2.1	10.8 (*)	2.3	24.8	61.2	1.5	5.4	0.0	0.0	0.0	0.0	0.0	MAGNOLIA GUARANTY LIFE INS CO
0.6	16.1 (*)	0.4	0.0	9.0	0.0	78.0	0.9	0.0	0.1	2.9	0.0	MAJESTIC LIFE INS CO
68.5	620.2 (*)	1.7	11.0	67.1	2.0	7.1	6.3	0.0	0.0	2.2	4.6 ●	MANHATTAN LIFE INS CO
5.5	134.1 (*)	1.1	5.1	70.0	4.2	0.0	0.0	0.0	0.0	3.5	0.0	MANHATTAN NATIONAL LIFE INS CO
280.7	700.6 (*)	0.8	2.9	54.7	0.2	27.4	4.9	0.0	2.7	1.4	26.7 ●	MANHATTANLIFE INS & ANNUITY CO
51.7	55.9	8.1	0.1	88.4	0.0	3.0	0.0	0.0	0.0	0.3	0.0 ●	MAPFRE LIFE INS CO OF PR
0.3	4.7 (*)	11.2	4.2	58.9	18.3	0.9	0.0	0.0	0.0	3.0	0.0	MARQUETTE INDEMNITY & LIFE INS CO
19,868.0	230,000.0 (*)	0.6	9.1	41.4	5.4	11.5	11.5	0.0	0.2	13.0	16.2 ●	MASSACHUSETTS MUTUAL LIFE INS CO
290.0	47.9	51.2	0.2	48.6	0.0	0.0	0.0	0.0	0.0	0.0	0.0 ●	MCS LIFE INS CO
-41.2	1,132.4 (*)	0.5	3.8	69.4	4.5	6.3	4.1	0.0	0.0	8.2	0.8 ●	MEDAMERICA INS CO
4.1	73.6 (*)	3.8	0.1	92.5	0.3	0.0	0.0	0.0	0.0	0.7	0.0	MEDAMERICA INS CO OF FL
44.2	1,112.7 (*)	1.7	1.0	71.7	1.5	15.8	2.7	0.0	0.0	4.2	0.0 ●	MEDAMERICA INS CO OF NEW YORK
0.4	13.6 (*)	0.5	2.5	17.4	0.0	66.4	0.0	0.0	4.0	0.0	31.0	MEDICAL BENEFITS MUTUAL LIFE INS CO
0.0	31.6 (*)	13.4	13.9	68.3	1.7	0.7	0.0	0.0	0.0	0.0	0.0 ●	MEDICO CORP LIFE INS CO
0.0	42.1 (*)	5.8	18.5	73.3	0.0	0.7	0.0	0.0	0.0	0.3	0.0 ●	MEDICO INS CO
0.0	10.8 (*)	4.1	15.5	70.3	2.4	0.0	0.0	0.0	0.0	2.6	0.0	MEDICO LIFE & HEALTH INS CO
39.9	50.3 (*)	10.6	0.0	57.4	0.0	0.0	0.0	0.0	0.0	0.0	0.0 ●	MEDMUTUAL LIFE INS CO
--	--	--	--	--	--	--	--	--	--	--	--	MELLON LIFE INS CO
0.0	66.2 (*)	1.2	5.7	35.8	0.0	0.0	0.0	0.0	0.0	0.0	0.0 ●	MEMBERS LIFE INS CO
0.3	3.8 (*)	19.6	0.0	4.3	0.0	39.3	24.8	2.6	0.0	0.0	0.0	MEMORIAL LIFE INS CO
0.0	55.5	3.3	16.5	62.1	13.4	2.4	0.0	0.0	0.0	1.5	0.0 ●	MERIT LIFE INS CO
--	--	--	--	--	--	--	--	--	--	--	--	METLIFE INSURANCE LTD
22,761.2	252,000.0 (*)	1.9	17.4	40.8	3.8	0.6	21.1	0.1	0.7	11.3	4.3 ●	METROPOLITAN LIFE INS CO
2,528.2	27,223.8	0.4	20.7	46.8	3.1	0.3	16.8	0.0	0.2	11.2	1.5 ●	METROPOLITAN TOWER LIFE INS CO
4.6	41.3 (*)	15.7	3.1	54.3	0.0	0.0	0.0	0.0	0.0	4.0	0.0	MID-WEST NATIONAL LIFE INS CO OF TN
4,077.7	65,386.0	1.9	26.4	49.0	6.5	4.2	5.6	0.0	0.2	5.4	2.7 ●	MIDLAND NATIONAL LIFE INS CO
2.3	245.9	3.0	19.3	69.6	1.7	0.0	4.5	0.0	0.0	1.9	0.0 ●	MIDWESTERN UNITED LIFE INS CO
--	--	--	--	--	--	--	--	--	--	--	--	MILILANI LIFE INS CO
7,746.6	32,075.4 (*)	0.0	15.2	53.1	2.5	3.5	15.0	0.0	0.2	6.6	2.0 ●	MINNESOTA LIFE INS CO
11.4	432.3	1.7	18.3	56.6	2.1	0.0	0.4	0.0	0.0	21.0	0.2 ●	MML BAY STATE LIFE INS CO
0.0	9.6	78.9	0.0	21.1	0.0	0.0	0.0	0.0	0.0	0.0	0.0	MOLINA HEALTHCARE OF TEXAS INS CO
1.5	381.6 (*)	0.7	5.3	77.4	2.0	0.0	0.0	0.0	0.0	13.4	0.0	MONARCH LIFE INS CO
0.0	20.3 (*)	8.3	0.0	88.5	0.0	0.0	0.0	0.0	0.0	0.0	0.0	MONITOR LIFE INS CO OF NEW YORK
190.1	6,275.2 (*)	0.3	11.3	66.7	2.3	0.3	5.9	0.0	0.0	11.8	0.0 ●	MONY LIFE INS CO
1.1	4.0	9.5	0.3	77.6	0.0	12.6	0.0	0.0	0.0	0.0	0.0	MOUNTAIN LIFE INS CO
0.9	12.1	18.1	0.4	25.4	0.0	56.1	0.0	0.0	0.0	0.1	0.0	MULHEARN PROTECTIVE INS CO
31.2	119.6	15.2	10.4	58.5	2.7	2.6	2.0	0.0	7.7	1.0	0.0 ●	MULTINATIONAL LIFE INS CO
35.7	7,833.9 (*)	0.0	1.4	94.2	0.6	0.1	0.0	0.0	0.0	2.2	0.0 ●	MUNICH AMERICAN REASSURANCE CO
--	--	--	--	--	--	--	--	--	--	--	--	MUNICH RE US LIFE CORP
2,372.9	8,950.1 (*)	-0.1	27.1	61.3	2.7	3.1	0.0	0.0	0.1	3.9	2.7 ●	MUTUAL OF AMERICA LIFE INS CO
3,779.1	9,006.1 (*)	-0.2	9.2	44.4	1.6	29.3	5.0	0.0	0.3	7.0	31.4 ●	MUTUAL OF OMAHA INS CO
0.0	92.9 (*)	0.9	1.0	85.6	3.3	4.4	0.0	0.0	0.0	0.0	4.4	MUTUAL SAVINGS LIFE INS CO
212.1	2,190.8	0.4	17.7	60.7	4.1	1.4	0.4	0.0	0.2	14.4	0.0 ●	MUTUAL TRUST LIFE INS CO
196.0	1,844.4 (*)	2.7	28.9	45.1	5.0	1.2	9.5	0.0	0.0	5.4	1.4 ●	NASSAU LIFE & ANNUITY CO
8.1	68.0 (*)	8.7	12.2	64.2	3.3	3.6	0.0	0.0	0.0	0.2	3.2	NASSAU LIFE INS CO OF KS
285.8	10,945.2	0.7	13.9	49.1	2.5	0.8	5.2	0.0	0.3	27.6	0.3 ●	NASSAU LIFE INSURANCE CO

● Bullets denote a more detailed analysis is available in Section II.
(*) Asset category percentages do not add up to 100%

INSURANCE COMPANY NAME	DOM. STATE	RATING	TOTAL ASSETS ($MIL)	CAPITAL & SURPLUS ($MIL)	RISK ADJUSTED CAPITAL RATIO 1	RISK ADJUSTED CAPITAL RATIO 2	CAPITAL-IZATION INDEX (PTS)	INVEST. SAFETY INDEX (PTS)	PROFIT-ABILITY INDEX (PTS)	LIQUIDITY INDEX (PTS)	STAB. INDEX (PTS)	STABILIT FACTOR
NATIONAL BENEFIT LIFE INS CO	NY	A-	675.0	133.6	4.69	2.52	9.3	6.6	6.2	6.8	7.1	ADI
▼ NATIONAL FAMILY CARE LIFE INS CO	TX	C-	15.6	9.3	3.05	2.74	9.6	9.5	2.6	7.4	3.0	DF
NATIONAL FARM LIFE INS CO	TX	B	443.8	51.7	2.72	1.63	7.9	6.5	5.1	6.1	5.5	D
NATIONAL FARMERS UNION LIFE INS CO	TX	B+	158.8	29.5	3.38	1.90	8.4	5.4	5.6	6.2	6.2	ADI
NATIONAL FOUNDATION LIFE INS CO	TX	A	94.2	55.6	2.31	1.81	8.2	8.8	9.1	7.5	7.1	A
▼ NATIONAL GUARDIAN LIFE INS CO	WI	B-	4698.1	495.1	2.52	1.41	7.6	5.3	7.3	6.6	3.5	IT
▲ NATIONAL HEALTH INS CO	TX	B+	181.1	79.9	4.79	1.98	8.5	8.5	7.2	7.3	6.5	AFGT
NATIONAL INCOME LIFE INS CO	NY	B	390.6	41.7	2.14	1.25	7.4	6.3	4.3	4.5	5.9	ADIL
NATIONAL INTEGRITY LIFE INS CO	NY	C+	4580.3	426.3	4.18	1.96	8.4	5.7	2.6	6.3	4.8	G
NATIONAL LIFE INS CO	VT	B	11011.8	2878.8	1.22	1.09	7.1	6.0	7.9	6.9	5.8	AI
NATIONAL SECURITY INS CO	AL	B-	55.2	11.0	1.72	1.27	7.4	4.5	5.9	6.6	5.1	AI
NATIONAL SECURITY LIFE & ANNUITY CO	NY	B-	482.6	36.6	2.98	2.68	4.0	7.4	7.7	7.3	4.0	A
NATIONAL TEACHERS ASSOCIATES L I C	TX	B-	657.1	49.5	1.64	0.92	6.4	4.8	5.4	7.7	4.9	DI
NATIONAL WESTERN LIFE INS CO	CO	B	10771.7	1580.2	2.64	1.71	4.0	6.4	7.2	6.7	4.2	IT
NATIONWIDE LIFE & ANNUITY INS CO	OH	C	42615.4	2553.4	2.79	1.34	7.5	4.7	1.9	5.1	4.2	AIT
NATIONWIDE LIFE INS CO	OH	B-	179000.0	9091.4	2.16	1.53	7.8	6.3	8.3	6.6	5.1	A
NETCARE LIFE & HEALTH INS CO	GU	D-	34.6	3.4	0.69	0.62	4.0	7.6	2.0	6.5	1.1	C
NEW ENGLAND LIFE INS CO	MA	B-	9856.9	138.7	1.40	0.72	5.6	6.4	2.9	5.0	5.0	C
NEW ERA LIFE INS CO	TX	B-	641.7	150.6	1.07	0.88	6.0	3.8	8.6	6.6	4.9	I
NEW ERA LIFE INS CO OF THE MIDWEST	TX	C+	188.9	24.8	1.95	1.12	7.2	3.8	9.0	7.2	4.8	DI
NEW YORK LIFE INS CO	NY	A-	214000.0	24566.4	1.36	1.09	7.1	6.8	7.8	5.8	7.0	I
NIAGARA LIFE & HEALTH INS CO	NY	B+	20.4	11.4	3.21	2.89	9.8	9.1	5.2	9.1	6.5	T
NORTH AMERICAN CO FOR LIFE & H INS	IA	B	35313.3	1930.9	1.86	0.88	6.3	3.6	8.6	4.5	4.4	CILT
▼ NORTH AMERICAN INS CO	WI	B	19.8	8.0	2.34	2.11	8.7	7.9	6.5	7.3	5.6	AD
NORTH AMERICAN NATIONAL RE INS CO	AZ	C-	39.7	14.6	2.01	1.08	7.1	2.0	6.6	6.6	3.0	GI
NORTH CAROLINA MUTUAL LIFE INS CO	NC	F (5)	--	--	--	--	--	--	--	--	--	Z
NORTHWESTERN LONG TERM CARE INS CO	WI	B+	320.0	218.3	11.75	4.74	8.0	8.2	7.7	7.3	6.8	A
NORTHWESTERN MUTUAL LIFE INS CO	WI	B+	335000.0	29283.2	3.73	1.89	8.3	6.0	5.1	5.8	6.7	IL
NTA LIFE INS CO OF NEW YORK	NY	B	10.1	7.7	3.16	2.84	9.8	8.9	8.4	10.0	5.5	AD
NY LIFE GROUP INS CO OF NY	NY	B	503.4	111.9	2.31	1.56	7.8	5.6	6.3	6.5	6.3	I
NY LIFE INS & ANNUITY CORP	DE	B+	183000.0	9734.4	3.41	1.72	8.1	6.0	7.2	5.6	6.8	IL
NYLIFE INS CO OF ARIZONA	AZ	B+	159.0	109.1	11.51	10.36	10.0	8.5	5.4	7.5	5.5	DT
OCCIDENTAL LIFE INS CO OF NC	TX	C	295.3	36.6	3.17	1.83	8.2	7.4	4.0	3.5	4.2	ADL
▼ OCEANVIEW LIFE AND ANNUITY CO	TX	C	3661.7	308.5	0.83	0.57	3.6	1.9	1.9	7.9	3.6	CGIT
OHIO NATIONAL LIFE ASR CORP	OH	B	3181.4	246.8	2.00	1.05	7.1	5.6	5.2	5.4	5.6	AIL
OHIO NATIONAL LIFE INS CO	OH	C+	28854.3	1455.5	1.63	1.13	7.2	5.7	6.1	6.2	4.2	AT
OHIO STATE LIFE INS CO	TX	D	148.7	18.7	4.52	2.73	9.6	6.1	1.8	6.9	1.5	DG
OLD AMERICAN INS CO	MO	B-	303.1	18.3	1.84	1.00	7.0	3.8	1.8	0.7	3.5	IL
OLD REPUBLIC LIFE INS CO	IL	B+	106.8	48.0	5.94	3.84	10.0	5.5	5.8	7.6	6.6	AI
OLD SPARTAN LIFE INS CO INC	SC	C	28.3	20.6	2.75	1.71	8.1	2.9	8.5	9.2	3.8	I
OLD SURETY INSURANCE CO	OK	U	--	--	--	--	--	--	--	--	--	Z
OLD SURETY LIFE INS CO	OK	C	40.7	21.0	0.94	0.74	4.9	7.3	9.1	6.4	4.3	CD
OLD UNITED LIFE INS CO	AZ	B	129.8	89.4	5.69	3.50	10.0	3.9	7.4	10.0	5.6	ADGI
OMAHA INS CO	NE	B-	114.7	52.7	1.71	0.89	6.1	7.1	1.9	6.2	4.9	
OMAHA SUPPLEMENTAL INS CO	NE	B	25.1	18.3	3.45	1.84	8.3	8.7	1.8	7.3	5.5	FGIT
OPTIMUM RE INS CO	TX	C+	282.9	48.7	2.48	1.52	7.8	7.1	2.4	7.0	4.6	F
OPTUM INS OF OH INC	OH	B-	251.7	39.5	3.87	3.48	8.0	9.8	5.2	9.1	4.5	AFT
OXFORD LIFE INS CO	AZ	B+	2955.5	230.2	2.20	1.21	7.3	5.7	8.1	5.5	5.9	I
OZARK NATIONAL LIFE INS CO	MO	C+	849.9	105.8	3.71	2.07	8.6	7.2	2.9	6.1	4.5	D
PACIFIC CENTURY LIFE INS CORP	AZ	U	--	--	--	--	--	--	--	--	--	Z
PACIFIC GUARDIAN LIFE INS CO LTD	HI	B	594.9	86.3	3.32	1.88	8.3	6.6	3.0	5.6	5.9	
PACIFIC LIFE & ANNUITY CO	AZ	B+	8615.1	536.9	4.09	1.94	8.4	6.4	6.6	6.0	6.5	AI

See Page 27 for explanation of footnotes and Page 28 for explanation of stability factors.

Arrows denote recent upgrades ▲ or downgrades▼ (see Section VI for explanations)

46   www.weissratings.com

NET PREMIUM ($MIL)	IN-VESTED ASSETS ($MIL)	% OF INVESTED ASSETS IN:										INSURANCE COMPANY NAME
		CASH	CMO & STRUCT. SECS.	OTH.INV. GRADE BONDS	NON-INV. GRADE BONDS	CMMON & PREF. STOCK	MORT IN GOOD STAND.	NON-PERF. MORT.	REAL ESTATE	OTHER INVEST-MENTS	INVEST. IN AFFIL	
116.0	645.4 (*)	0.0	23.8	64.5	3.6	1.5	0.0	0.0	0.0	3.2	0.0	● NATIONAL BENEFIT LIFE INS CO
5.7	14.7	8.5	0.0	91.5	0.0	0.0	0.0	0.0	0.0	0.0	0.0	NATIONAL FAMILY CARE LIFE INS CO
26.6	430.0 (*)	0.6	2.8	81.2	1.1	5.0	2.3	0.0	0.1	4.9	0.5	● NATIONAL FARM LIFE INS CO
4.7	144.7	0.0	13.0	60.0	5.1	10.6	1.3	0.0	0.0	9.9	3.5	● NATIONAL FARMERS UNION LIFE INS CO
149.7	92.7 (*)	22.3	16.3	60.0	0.0	0.0	0.0	0.0	0.0	0.0	0.0	● NATIONAL FOUNDATION LIFE INS CO
60.2	4,437.9 (*)	0.7	8.9	74.9	4.6	1.8	3.1	0.0	0.2	4.7	1.1	● NATIONAL GUARDIAN LIFE INS CO
12.0	119.8 (*)	15.7	0.0	82.1	0.0	0.0	0.0	0.0	0.0	0.0	0.0	● NATIONAL HEALTH INS CO
106.5	354.8 (*)	1.3	0.5	86.3	2.4	0.0	0.0	0.0	0.0	7.9	0.0	● NATIONAL INCOME LIFE INS CO
359.3	3,200.3	0.0	24.5	56.0	6.0	0.7	7.2	0.0	0.0	5.8	2.5	● NATIONAL INTEGRITY LIFE INS CO
418.0	9,456.0 (*)	0.5	11.7	49.0	2.8	21.3	5.1	0.0	0.6	6.9	20.9	● NATIONAL LIFE INS CO
5.6	53.6	0.4	10.0	71.2	4.7	7.4	0.3	0.0	2.7	3.4	0.0	NATIONAL SECURITY INS CO
-2.8	65.6	8.5	10.7	78.2	2.6	0.0	0.0	0.0	0.0	0.0	0.0	● NATIONAL SECURITY LIFE & ANNUITY CO
94.4	636.8 (*)	0.4	34.9	48.0	3.1	2.5	0.0	0.0	0.0	8.7	0.0	● NATIONAL TEACHERS ASSOCIATES L I C
725.4	10,618.3 (*)	0.8	14.0	66.7	1.8	4.7	4.4	0.0	0.4	1.3	4.6	● NATIONAL WESTERN LIFE INS CO
5,254.6	39,219.4 (*)	0.0	6.3	61.0	4.2	0.1	18.6	0.0	0.0	3.6	1.8	● NATIONWIDE LIFE & ANNUITY INS CO
12,663.4	52,140.4 (*)	0.0	11.5	57.1	4.1	5.8	15.7	0.0	0.0	4.3	6.1	● NATIONWIDE LIFE INS CO
17.3	32.1	3.2	5.9	81.5	0.0	0.0	0.0	0.0	0.0	9.0	0.0	NETCARE LIFE & HEALTH INS CO
90.6	1,519.5	5.3	10.5	47.1	5.3	0.0	4.1	0.0	0.0	27.1	0.0	● NEW ENGLAND LIFE INS CO
199.1	631.3	4.7	3.6	41.3	13.1	18.1	18.3	0.0	0.0	0.1	17.7	● NEW ERA LIFE INS CO
83.9	183.2	16.9	4.7	51.7	13.8	0.5	11.4	0.0	0.0	0.1	0.0	NEW ERA LIFE INS CO OF THE MIDWEST
17,733.8	189,000.0	-0.1	16.2	46.2	3.8	7.9	10.6	0.0	1.1	13.3	12.8	● NEW YORK LIFE INS CO
6.6	15.7 (*)	52.3	11.1	29.6	0.0	0.0	0.0	0.0	0.0	0.0	0.0	NIAGARA LIFE & HEALTH INS CO
2,637.4	34,629.3	1.8	28.0	47.7	6.3	3.9	6.0	0.0	0.0	5.4	2.2	● NORTH AMERICAN CO FOR LIFE & H INS
6.9	18.9	10.4	5.2	82.4	1.9	0.1	0.0	0.0	0.0	0.0	0.0	NORTH AMERICAN INS CO
0.4	36.8 (*)	3.1	0.0	12.7	4.3	49.8	2.2	0.0	18.2	4.6	3.3	NORTH AMERICAN NATIONAL RE INS CO
--	--	--	--	--	--	--	--	--	--	--	--	NORTH CAROLINA MUTUAL LIFE INS CO
0.0	219.6	-1.0	0.0	101.0	0.0	0.0	0.0	0.0	0.0	0.0	0.0	● NORTHWESTERN LONG TERM CARE INS CO
22,551.3	284,000.0	0.1	12.6	46.1	5.4	1.5	16.9	0.0	1.1	16.1	6.9	● NORTHWESTERN MUTUAL LIFE INS CO
1.7	9.9 (*)	19.5	32.5	26.3	0.0	0.0	0.0	0.0	0.0	0.0	0.0	NTA LIFE INS CO OF NEW YORK
257.3	459.3	0.1	9.1	80.0	6.1	0.0	4.5	0.0	0.0	0.0	0.0	● NY LIFE GROUP INS CO OF NY
13,964.3	113,000.0	-0.2	25.3	52.5	4.2	1.4	12.7	0.0	0.1	3.5	4.3	● NY LIFE INS & ANNUITY CORP
3.7	142.7	0.4	19.1	80.4	0.1	0.0	0.0	0.0	0.0	0.0	0.0	● NYLIFE INS CO OF ARIZONA
68.7	287.1 (*)	0.5	0.6	87.8	0.0	0.0	1.6	0.0	0.0	4.2	0.0	● OCCIDENTAL LIFE INS CO OF NC
1,620.8	2,887.8 (*)	9.0	27.0	6.5	2.3	0.4	40.6	12.6	0.0	0.3	0.0	● OCEANVIEW LIFE AND ANNUITY CO
153.8	2,647.6 (*)	1.8	9.8	58.3	3.4	1.4	15.9	0.0	0.0	6.0	0.0	● OHIO NATIONAL LIFE ASR CORP
-17,687.3	9,485.5 (*)	2.0	9.3	51.0	2.5	5.4	11.2	0.0	0.3	13.1	6.6	● OHIO NATIONAL LIFE INS CO
51.3	145.2	2.5	12.7	61.0	9.5	13.3	0.0	0.0	0.0	0.0	3.6	OHIO STATE LIFE INS CO
98.3	286.4 (*)	0.1	3.0	74.9	0.8	0.5	15.0	0.0	0.0	3.5	0.0	OLD AMERICAN INS CO
10.8	101.8 (*)	1.6	0.0	66.4	0.2	18.3	0.0	0.0	0.0	0.4	0.0	● OLD REPUBLIC LIFE INS CO
4.8	27.8 (*)	10.0	0.0	23.0	0.0	57.4	0.0	0.0	0.0	0.0	0.0	OLD SPARTAN LIFE INS CO INC
--	--	--	--	--	--	--	--	--	--	--	--	OLD SURETY INSURANCE CO
66.0	39.0	17.8	0.1	58.2	0.8	10.7	1.2	0.0	9.9	0.6	10.7	OLD SURETY LIFE INS CO
12.0	129.1	0.9	1.4	56.8	0.2	40.7	0.0	0.0	0.0	0.0	0.0	● OLD UNITED LIFE INS CO
79.7	96.6	0.0	59.7	41.0	0.0	0.0	0.0	0.0	0.0	0.3	0.0	● OMAHA INS CO
8.9	21.4	60.6	28.7	10.7	0.0	0.0	0.0	0.0	0.0	0.0	0.0	OMAHA SUPPLEMENTAL INS CO
71.5	201.5	18.8	0.0	73.3	0.3	4.5	0.0	0.0	1.6	1.6	1.6	● OPTIMUM RE INS CO
0.0	91.3	96.8	0.0	2.5	0.0	0.0	0.0	0.0	0.0	0.0	0.0	● OPTUM INS OF OH INC
417.9	2,902.1	1.5	14.4	66.8	1.4	1.9	12.1	0.0	1.2	0.4	1.4	● OXFORD LIFE INS CO
77.0	809.0 (*)	0.7	10.8	84.1	0.9	0.0	0.0	0.0	0.0	2.4	0.0	● OZARK NATIONAL LIFE INS CO
--	--	--	--	--	--	--	--	--	--	--	--	PACIFIC CENTURY LIFE INS CORP
72.3	568.5	2.4	8.5	43.4	2.5	0.0	37.2	0.0	0.0	5.4	0.0	● PACIFIC GUARDIAN LIFE INS CO LTD
583.0	5,048.6	0.0	4.3	83.3	2.2	0.1	7.5	0.0	0.0	2.3	0.0	● PACIFIC LIFE & ANNUITY CO

● Bullets denote a more detailed analysis is available in Section II.
(*) Asset category percentages do not add up to 100%

INSURANCE COMPANY NAME	DOM. STATE	RATING	TOTAL ASSETS ($MIL)	CAPITAL & SURPLUS ($MIL)	RISK ADJUSTED CAPITAL RATIO 1	RISK ADJUSTED CAPITAL RATIO 2	CAPITAL-IZATION INDEX (PTS)	INVEST. SAFETY INDEX (PTS)	PROFIT-ABILITY INDEX (PTS)	LIQUIDITY INDEX (PTS)	STAB. INDEX (PTS)	STABILITY FACTORS
PACIFIC LIFE INS CO	NE	A-	178000.0	11353.2	3.63	1.99	8.5	5.6	2.8	6.0	6.9	AI
PACIFICARE LIFE & HEALTH INS CO	IN	B- (5)	--	--	--	--	--	--	--	--	--	Z
PAN AMERICAN ASR CO	LA	B+	26.7	19.9	4.73	2.78	9.7	7.5	7.6	10.0	6.0	A
PAN AMERICAN ASR CO INTL INC	FL	U	--	--	--	--	--	--	--	--	--	Z
PAN AMERICAN LIFE INS CO OF PR	PR	B	8.4	5.0	2.37	2.13	8.7	6.7	1.5	6.6	4.5	ADFT
PAN-AMERICAN LIFE INS CO	LA	B	1236.0	267.9	2.81	1.76	8.1	5.4	7.1	6.4	5.6	AFI
PARK AVENUE LIFE INS CO	DE	B	199.4	46.7	1.11	0.99	6.9	6.2	8.1	6.5	5.2	DFI
PARKER CENTENNIAL ASR CO	WI	A-	99.1	47.9	5.37	4.84	10.0	8.4	7.6	6.8	7.1	ADG
PARTNERRE LIFE RE CO OF AM	AR	C	417.3	48.8	2.79	1.87	8.3	8.5	1.7	6.6	3.8	G
PATRIOT LIFE INS CO	MI	C+	30.7	21.6	4.82	3.11	10.0	5.4	1.9	7.0	4.6	DF
PAUL REVERE LIFE INS CO	MA	C+	745.4	270.0	18.78	16.90	4.0	4.9	7.4	6.6	4.0	AFIT
PAVONIA LIFE INS CO OF MICHIGAN	MI	C	1005.1	54.8	1.46	0.79	5.7	4.7	2.4	2.3	3.5	CFIL
PAVONIA LIFE INS CO OF NEW YORK	NY	C	27.2	7.1	1.74	1.56	7.8	8.1	1.1	6.7	4.0	ADFT
PEKIN LIFE INS CO	IL	B	1626.3	122.0	1.72	0.97	6.8	5.5	3.7	5.1	5.7	IL
PELLERIN LIFE INS CO	LA	C	1.7	1.6	2.60	2.06	8.6	9.8	2.5	7.1	2.8	CFT
PENN INS & ANNTY CO OF NY	NY	B	385.7	37.9	2.48	1.29	3.0	4.8	2.6	5.5	4.0	IT
PENN INS & ANNUITY CO	DE	C+	9532.6	669.0	1.99	1.16	7.2	5.5	2.8	5.7	4.8	
PENN MUTUAL LIFE INS CO	PA	B	27994.9	2571.6	1.88	1.28	4.0	5.8	3.8	6.6	4.2	I
PERFORMANCE LIFE OF AMERICA	LA	B-	26.5	15.5	3.70	3.33	10.0	8.3	6.6	9.1	5.2	ADF
PHILADELPHIA AMERICAN LIFE INS CO	TX	B	390.4	84.6	1.70	1.05	7.1	3.7	9.1	5.8	5.8	ADI
▲ PHL VARIABLE INS CO	CT	E+	5173.0	53.0	0.55	0.25	1.4	0.8	1.2	10.0	0.7	CIT
▼ PHYSICIANS LIFE INS CO	NE	B+	1783.0	172.5	2.86	1.42	7.6	5.6	5.9	5.5	6.4	FIL
PHYSICIANS MUTUAL INS CO	NE	A+	2785.1	1161.7	3.42	2.47	9.2	5.6	9.0	7.3	7.9	I
PILLAR LIFE INSURANCE CO	PA	U	--	--	--	--	--	--	--	--	--	Z
PINE BELT LIFE INS CO	MS	U (5)	--	--	--	--	--	--	--	--	--	Z
PIONEER AMERICAN INS CO	TX	C-	122.3	45.3	4.96	4.47	10.0	8.4	1.8	6.3	3.2	DT
PIONEER MILITARY INS CO	NV	U (5)	--	--	--	--	--	--	--	--	--	Z
PIONEER MUTUAL LIFE INS CO	ND	C	63.9	52.4	8.31	6.71	10.0	6.9	3.8	7.8	3.7	DFIT
PIONEER SECURITY LIFE INS CO	TX	C-	192.0	144.0	1.03	1.01	7.0	2.9	2.7	6.8	3.3	DGI
PLATEAU INS CO	TN	B	28.9	19.2	3.76	2.76	9.6	8.3	8.1	7.7	5.4	AR
POPULAR LIFE RE	PR	B+	70.2	43.7	5.71	5.14	10.0	8.9	8.0	9.2	5.0	T
PRCPL RE CO OF VERMONT II	IA	U	--	--	--	--	--	--	--	--	--	Z
PREFERRED SECURITY LIFE INS CO	TX	C	8.0	3.2	0.91	0.77	5.2	2.6	3.9	6.8	2.8	ACDFI
PRENEED REINS CO OF AMERICA	AZ	B-	22.7	18.4	4.86	4.37	10.0	8.9	4.2	1.3	3.7	LT
PRESIDENTIAL LIFE INS CO	NC	C-	9.8	4.6	2.03	1.83	8.2	8.2	5.3	7.4	2.7	DFGIT
PRIMERICA LIFE INS CO	TN	B	2064.3	779.6	1.88	1.55	7.8	4.3	8.5	7.4	5.8	I
PRINCIPAL LIFE INS CO	IA	B+	239000.0	5375.2	2.01	1.13	7.2	5.7	6.5	5.4	5.5	IL
PRINCIPAL NATIONAL LIFE INS CO	IA	B	832.4	269.5	5.63	2.78	9.7	7.3	2.9	10.0	5.7	G
PROFESSIONAL INS CO	TX	D+	84.5	27.2	3.36	3.03	10.0	6.7	6.3	6.9	2.6	ADT
PROFESSIONAL LIFE & CAS CO	AZ	C+	11.6	10.6	4.26	3.83	8.0	5.4	3.0	10.0	4.5	FIT
PROGRESSIVE LIFE INSURANCE CO	OH	U	--	--	--	--	--	--	--	--	--	Z
PROTECTIVE LIFE & ANNUITY INS CO	AL	C+	6210.6	505.4	2.63	1.37	7.6	6.0	3.0	5.3	3.3	FT
PROTECTIVE LIFE INS CO	TN	B	80820.8	5318.6	1.52	1.05	7.1	6.4	5.1	5.4	5.8	AILT
PROVIDENT AMER LIFE & HEALTH INS CO	OH	B	11.0	10.2	2.40	2.22	8.8	7.3	9.2	7.3	5.5	AD
PROVIDENT AMERICAN INS CO	TX	C-	36.9	14.4	0.79	0.61	3.9	3.7	9.4	1.4	3.2	CDILT
PROVIDENT LIFE & ACCIDENT INS CO	TN	C+	6214.2	971.3	3.97	2.11	4.0	5.2	6.5	6.7	4.0	AT
▲ PROVIDENT LIFE & CAS INS CO	TN	B	861.9	173.5	5.13	2.98	10.0	5.3	8.1	7.1	5.4	AI
PRUCO LIFE INS CO	AZ	C	167000.0	5954.6	2.74	1.57	7.9	5.7	3.0	6.7	2.8	ACFG
PRUCO LIFE INS CO OF NEW JERSEY	NJ	B-	20574.7	591.6	2.96	1.50	7.8	5.7	2.8	6.6	5.0	
PRUDENTIAL INS CO OF AMERICA	NJ	B	324000.0	19122.9	1.49	1.17	7.3	6.3	6.9	6.7	5.8	AI
PRUDENTIAL LEGACY INS CO OF NJ	NJ	C	55451.9	400.0	0.69	0.60	3.8	9.1	5.4	0.0	2.8	CL
PRUDENTIAL RETIREMENT INS & ANNUITY	CT	B-	100000.0	1495.2	1.90	1.08	7.1	4.7	5.1	10.0	5.1	I

See Page 27 for explanation of footnotes and Page 28 for explanation of stability factors.
Arrows denote recent upgrades ▲ or downgrades ▼ (see Section VI for explanations)

48

www.weissratings.com

NET PREMIUM ($MIL)	IN-VESTED ASSETS ($MIL)	CASH	CMO & STRUCT. SECS.	OTH.INV. GRADE BONDS	NON-INV. GRADE BONDS	CMMON & PREF. STOCK	MORT IN GOOD STAND.	NON-PERF. MORT.	REAL ESTATE	OTHER INVEST-MENTS	INVEST. IN AFFIL	INSURANCE COMPANY NAME
					% OF INVESTED ASSETS IN:							
13,984.3	104,000.0 (*)	0.6	9.5	51.1	4.3	0.7	15.3	0.0	0.1	12.7	5.0 ●	PACIFIC LIFE INS CO
--	--	--	--	--	--	--	--	--	--	--	--	PACIFICARE LIFE & HEALTH INS CO
0.0	26.2 (*)	50.5	1.4	39.2	3.8	3.2	0.0	0.0	0.0	0.0	0.0	PAN AMERICAN ASR CO
--	--	--	--	--	--	--	--	--	--	--	--	PAN AMERICAN ASR CO INTL INC
4.7	7.1 (*)	22.1	9.4	53.8	6.5	0.0	0.0	0.0	0.0	0.0	0.0	PAN AMERICAN LIFE INS CO OF PR
262.3	1,107.5 (*)	3.8	22.8	51.7	6.5	4.4	0.0	0.0	0.0	8.9	1.8 ●	PAN-AMERICAN LIFE INS CO
1.1	195.8	0.4	0.0	76.7	2.4	19.4	0.0	0.0	0.0	0.9	19.4 ●	PARK AVENUE LIFE INS CO
4.9	97.5	0.0	0.0	96.8	1.6	0.0	0.0	0.0	0.0	1.6	0.0	PARKER CENTENNIAL ASR CO
19.5	113.8 (*)	5.4	32.6	56.3	0.0	0.0	0.0	0.0	0.0	0.0	0.0 ●	PARTNERRE LIFE RE CO OF AM
2.1	29.4	2.5	5.0	72.0	0.0	20.3	0.0	0.0	0.0	0.0	0.0	PATRIOT LIFE INS CO
-318.8	687.9	0.0	2.5	91.7	0.8	0.0	3.2	0.0	0.0	2.0	0.0 ●	PAUL REVERE LIFE INS CO
33.2	986.5	1.6	17.8	76.8	1.0	0.0	0.0	0.0	0.0	2.3	0.0 ●	PAVONIA LIFE INS CO OF MICHIGAN
2.3	26.0 (*)	2.9	0.0	93.2	0.0	0.0	0.0	0.0	0.0	0.0	0.0	PAVONIA LIFE INS CO OF NEW YORK
197.3	1,578.2	0.2	21.5	63.5	4.0	2.4	6.6	0.0	0.1	0.9	0.0 ●	PEKIN LIFE INS CO
-9.8	0.2 (*)	95.2	0.0	0.0	0.0	0.0	0.0	0.0	0.0	0.0	0.0	PELLERIN LIFE INS CO
29.8	370.9 (*)	1.1	36.4	55.2	1.6	1.3	0.0	0.0	0.0	0.1	0.0 ●	PENN INS & ANNTY CO OF NY
845.4	8,216.3 (*)	0.1	27.6	45.1	2.8	2.5	0.0	0.0	0.0	13.0	1.4 ●	PENN INS & ANNUITY CO
1,245.9	16,984.1 (*)	0.2	25.8	42.5	3.2	5.3	0.0	0.0	0.2	15.9	5.9 ●	PENN MUTUAL LIFE INS CO
6.2	21.6 (*)	0.1	0.0	94.3	0.0	0.0	0.0	0.0	0.0	0.0	0.0	PERFORMANCE LIFE OF AMERICA
336.8	364.7 (*)	0.0	7.6	52.7	24.6	0.4	14.5	0.0	0.0	2.0	0.0 ●	PHILADELPHIA AMERICAN LIFE INS CO
0.0	1,421.5	1.7	26.5	53.7	4.1	0.9	3.5	0.0	0.0	9.1	0.0 ●	PHL VARIABLE INS CO
242.1	1,754.3	0.0	26.0	61.3	7.1	2.9	0.0	0.0	0.0	2.3	0.0 ●	PHYSICIANS LIFE INS CO
519.8	2,752.0 (*)	0.3	23.2	47.9	7.2	18.3	0.0	0.0	0.7	0.7	6.3 ●	PHYSICIANS MUTUAL INS CO
--	--	--	--	--	--	--	--	--	--	--	--	PILLAR LIFE INSURANCE CO
--	--	--	--	--	--	--	--	--	--	--	--	PINE BELT LIFE INS CO
52.2	117.4 (*)	0.8	0.2	89.6	0.0	0.0	1.5	0.0	0.0	4.6	0.0 ●	PIONEER AMERICAN INS CO
--	--	--	--	--	--	--	--	--	--	--	--	PIONEER MILITARY INS CO
5.0	38.0	0.6	1.6	77.0	4.0	0.0	10.6	0.0	0.0	6.2	0.0 ●	PIONEER MUTUAL LIFE INS CO
24.9	189.1 (*)	0.2	0.0	23.5	0.0	72.6	0.2	0.0	0.0	2.4	72.6 ●	PIONEER SECURITY LIFE INS CO
18.3	26.3 (*)	15.4	0.0	76.9	1.4	3.6	0.0	0.0	0.6	0.3	0.0	PLATEAU INS CO
16.5	68.1	4.6	57.3	38.1	0.0	0.0	0.0	0.0	0.0	0.0	0.0 ●	POPULAR LIFE RE
--	--	--	--	--	--	--	--	--	--	--	--	PRCPL RE CO OF VERMONT II
0.1	8.0	2.8	0.0	29.0	6.4	59.3	0.5	0.0	0.0	2.0	35.4	PREFERRED SECURITY LIFE INS CO
3.1	20.7 (*)	0.6	0.0	91.2	0.0	0.0	0.0	0.0	0.0	0.0	0.0	PRENEED REINS CO OF AMERICA
2.8	4.1	91.9	0.0	0.0	0.0	6.4	0.0	0.0	0.0	1.5	0.0	PRESIDENTIAL LIFE INS CO
721.6	2,093.3 (*)	0.0	22.7	50.4	3.6	18.4	0.0	0.0	0.0	1.4	16.7 ●	PRIMERICA LIFE INS CO
5,946.4	84,858.6 (*)	0.1	19.9	46.4	4.8	1.3	18.8	0.0	0.6	5.5	4.8 ●	PRINCIPAL LIFE INS CO
0.0	258.7	8.8	12.0	77.3	1.1	0.0	0.0	0.0	0.0	0.8	0.0 ●	PRINCIPAL NATIONAL LIFE INS CO
12.9	80.3	1.7	18.5	70.5	5.5	0.0	0.0	0.0	0.0	3.9	0.0 ●	PROFESSIONAL INS CO
0.0	11.5 (*)	26.5	0.0	25.6	0.0	0.0	0.0	0.0	0.0	0.0	0.0	PROFESSIONAL LIFE & CAS CO
--	--	--	--	--	--	--	--	--	--	--	--	PROGRESSIVE LIFE INSURANCE CO
181.9	5,933.8 (*)	0.4	20.9	66.5	2.9	0.4	5.8	0.0	0.0	1.5	0.0 ●	PROTECTIVE LIFE & ANNUITY INS CO
5,094.2	62,827.5 (*)	0.1	13.9	58.3	2.8	3.6	15.2	0.0	0.2	3.0	3.2 ●	PROTECTIVE LIFE INS CO
4.1	10.2 (*)	7.8	0.0	33.8	0.0	30.2	0.0	0.0	0.0	0.0	30.2	PROVIDENT AMER LIFE & HEALTH INS CO
66.0	19.8 (*)	4.1	0.9	29.1	21.8	0.0	14.4	0.0	0.0	1.6	0.0	PROVIDENT AMERICAN INS CO
644.8	5,717.2	0.0	1.7	76.7	5.0	0.3	9.8	0.0	1.8	4.5	0.0 ●	PROVIDENT LIFE & ACCIDENT INS CO
112.6	839.5	0.0	1.9	89.5	3.6	0.0	2.1	0.0	0.0	2.9	0.0 ●	PROVIDENT LIFE & CAS INS CO
12,934.2	32,242.6 (*)	0.2	5.8	34.2	3.9	2.2	7.6	0.0	0.0	26.0	3.6 ●	PRUCO LIFE INS CO
321.9	2,391.5 (*)	0.0	16.9	56.4	2.9	0.0	4.9	0.0	0.0	17.1	1.9 ●	PRUCO LIFE INS CO OF NEW JERSEY
33,229.1	155,000.0 (*)	0.6	14.7	47.1	4.4	8.7	13.6	0.0	0.3	7.9	12.2 ●	PRUDENTIAL INS CO OF AMERICA
1,781.9	407.2	0.0	0.0	79.2	0.0	0.0	0.0	0.0	0.0	20.8	24.6 ●	PRUDENTIAL LEGACY INS CO OF NJ
1,744.2	28,875.7 (*)	0.3	18.2	58.4	2.7	0.0	17.6	0.0	0.0	0.2	0.0 ●	PRUDENTIAL RETIREMENT INS & ANNUITY

● Bullets denote a more detailed analysis is available in Section II.
(*) Asset category percentages do not add up to 100%

INSURANCE COMPANY NAME	DOM. STATE	RATING	TOTAL ASSETS ($MIL)	CAPITAL & SURPLUS ($MIL)	RISK ADJUSTED CAPITAL RATIO 1	RISK ADJUSTED CAPITAL RATIO 2	CAPITAL-IZATION INDEX (PTS)	INVEST. SAFETY INDEX (PTS)	PROFIT-ABILITY INDEX (PTS)	LIQUIDITY INDEX (PTS)	STAB. INDEX (PTS)	STABILI FACTOI
PURITAN LIFE INS CO	TX	C-	31.1	29.1	0.74	0.67	4.0	2.8	2.3	6.8	2.9	CDFG
PURITAN LIFE INS CO OF AMERICA	TX	C	271.6	27.5	2.64	1.34	7.5	4.6	1.9	6.0	3.5	DIT
REGAL LIFE OF AMERICA INS CO	TX	D-	6.9	5.2	1.29	1.27	7.4	4.9	2.2	7.2	1.0	ADFT
REGAL REINSURANCE COMPANY	MA	U	--	--	--	--	--	--	--	--	--	Z
REINSURANCE CO OF MO INC	MO	C	2697.7	2361.7	1.01	0.91	6.3	1.4	3.5	7.0	4.2	FI
RELIABLE LIFE INS CO	MO	B-	38.2	15.5	2.43	1.20	7.3	8.4	8.6	8.7	4.4	AGT
RELIABLE LIFE INS CO	LA	D-	7.0	1.7	1.10	0.66	5.2	1.4	1.8	6.2	1.3	CFIT
RELIABLE SERVICE INS CO	LA	U	--	--	--	--	--	--	--	--	--	Z
RELIANCE STANDARD LIFE INS CO	IL	C+	18943.6	1843.1	1.56	0.89	6.1	2.6	7.6	6.1	4.5	CI
RELIANCE STANDARD LIFE INS CO OF TX	TX	U	--	--	--	--	--	--	--	--	--	Z
RELIASTAR LIFE INS CO	MN	B-	15173.4	1781.7	1.96	1.34	7.5	5.9	1.8	6.0	3.9	T
RELIASTAR LIFE INS CO OF NEW YORK	NY	B-	2258.6	433.0	6.25	3.33	10.0	6.5	5.6	6.5	4.0	FT
RENAISSANCE L&H INS CO OF AMERICA	DE	B	97.9	48.9	1.33	0.99	6.9	4.8	3.8	5.2	5.4	FIL
RENAISSANCE L&H INS CO OF NY	NY	B-	15.6	9.6	1.86	1.43	7.6	7.1	8.1	7.0	5.2	T
▼ RESERVE NATIONAL INS CO	OK	C+	50.8	24.7	3.77	3.39	10.0	7.8	1.8	10.0	3.1	T
RESOLUTION LIFE COLORADO INC	CO	C	1510.0	1339.8	0.98	0.90	3.0	1.0	2.9	7.0	3.0	EFIT
RESOURCE LIFE INS CO	IL	U	--	--	--	--	--	--	--	--	--	Z
RGA REINSURANCE CO	MO	B-	49440.5	2367.9	1.54	0.83	5.8	4.1	6.2	4.4	5.3	AGIL
RIVERSOURCE LIFE INS CO	MN	B	116000.0	3412.5	2.09	1.35	7.5	5.9	5.2	8.1	4.8	IT
RIVERSOURCE LIFE INS CO OF NY	NY	C	8277.9	309.1	2.93	1.46	7.7	5.7	2.8	7.8	4.3	
ROYAL STATE NATIONAL INS CO LTD	HI	U	--	--	--	--	--	--	--	--	--	Z
ROYALTY CAPITAL LIFE INS CO	MO	D (3)	3.5	3.2	2.81	2.53	9.3	8.4	2.0	9.2	1.6	ADFT
RUSH LIFE INS CO	LA	C-	30.1	12.2	1.70	1.13	7.2	3.7	2.9	7.3	3.3	DI
S USA LIFE INS CO INC	AZ	B-	1514.6	139.1	2.66	1.19	7.3	3.8	1.7	8.1	3.5	AGIT
SAGICOR LIFE INS CO	TX	D-	2997.6	169.7	0.89	0.45	4.1	2.5	1.6	4.5	1.3	CIL
SB MUTL LIFE INS CO OF MA	MA	B	3563.5	206.6	1.99	1.03	7.0	5.5	5.9	5.7	4.7	IT
SBLI USA MUT LIFE INS CO INC	NY	B-	2554.3	134.7	1.37	0.68	5.6	3.8	6.7	5.2	5.2	CI
SCOR GLOBAL LIFE AMERICAS REIN CO	DE	C-	738.5	142.6	0.95	0.68	4.6	7.9	1.2	5.8	3.3	CFT
▼ SCOR GLOBAL LIFE REINS CO OF DE	DE	C-	347.8	63.3	3.74	2.41	9.1	8.5	0.9	5.7	3.3	FT
SCOR GLOBAL LIFE USA RE CO	DE	C+	787.5	184.1	2.29	1.40	7.6	6.8	1.9	0.3	2.9	AFL
SCOTTISH RE US INC	DE	F (5)	--	--	--	--	--	--	--	--	--	Z
▼ SECU LIFE INS CO	NC	B-	75.7	32.2	4.11	3.23	10.0	7.9	8.6	7.0	3.8	T
▼ SECURIAN LIFE INS CO	MN	B-	2066.0	476.1	4.26	2.65	9.5	7.4	2.9	6.4	4.9	AT
SECURICO LIFE INS CO	TX	D	29.3	26.8	5.42	4.87	10.0	6.1	1.9	7.0	2.0	DFGT
SECURITY BENEFIT LIFE INS CO	KS	B	46517.4	4436.3	3.10	1.46	7.7	4.3	8.3	7.2	5.5	IT
SECURITY LIFE OF DENVER INS CO	CO	B-	34605.0	1213.6	1.33	0.71	5.5	3.7	1.8	0.6	3.6	CFGIL
SECURITY MUTUAL LIFE INS CO OF NY	NY	C	2996.8	188.4	1.76	0.94	6.5	6.1	5.9	0.6	2.9	L
SECURITY NATIONAL LIFE INS CO	UT	D	702.8	57.4	1.01	0.61	5.0	2.7	8.2	8.1	1.4	CDI
SECURITY PLAN LIFE INS CO	LA	D	317.9	12.4	0.70	0.46	2.6	2.8	1.3	1.8	2.0	CDIL
▼ SELECTED FUNERAL AND LIFE INS CO	AR	C+	194.3	29.2	2.88	1.45	7.7	4.5	4.2	5.2	4.4	DI
SENIOR HEALTH INS CO OF PENNSYLVANIA	PA	F (5)	--	--	--	--	--	--	--	--	--	Z
SENIOR LIFE INS CO	GA	D+	89.0	13.1	1.73	0.92	6.4	5.1	1.9	5.5	2.5	CDI
SENIOR LIFE INS CO OF TEXAS	TX	D	2.1	0.7	0.96	0.87	6.0	5.9	1.9	8.6	2.0	CD
SENTINEL AMERICAN LIFE INS CO	TX	U	--	--	--	--	--	--	--	--	--	Z
SENTINEL SECURITY LIFE INS CO	UT	D	858.0	63.0	0.90	0.48	4.2	3.4	2.4	7.8	1.5	ACGI
SENTRY LIFE INS CO	WI	A	9857.5	335.1	3.40	1.90	8.4	7.2	7.9	6.1	7.4	AF
SENTRY LIFE INS CO OF NEW YORK	NY	B	168.1	10.0	1.07	0.96	6.7	8.0	5.8	6.9	6.3	D
SERVICE LIFE & CAS INS CO	TX	U (5)	--	--	--	--	--	--	--	--	--	Z
SETTLERS LIFE INS CO	WI	B-	413.8	25.9	2.15	1.19	7.3	4.4	3.5	2.7	4.5	DILT
SHELTER LIFE INS CO	MO	B	1404.6	266.0	3.87	2.25	8.9	6.8	4.7	6.2	5.4	
SHELTERPOINT INS CO	FL	B	13.2	9.4	3.73	3.36	8.0	8.8	5.0	7.0	6.3	
SHELTERPOINT LIFE INS CO	NY	A	392.4	162.9	2.36	1.97	8.5	7.5	8.1	7.5	7.3	DG

See Page 27 for explanation of footnotes and Page 28 for explanation of stability factors.
Arrows denote recent upgrades ▲ or downgrades▼ (see Section VI for explanations)

50

www.weissratings.com

NET PREMIUM ($MIL)	IN-VESTED ASSETS ($MIL)	CASH	CMO & STRUCT. SECS.	OTH.INV. GRADE BONDS	NON-INV. GRADE BONDS	CMMON & PREF. STOCK	MORT IN GOOD STAND.	NON-PERF. MORT.	REAL ESTATE	OTHER INVEST-MENTS	INVEST. IN AFFIL	INSURANCE COMPANY NAME
-0.1	30.1 (*)	0.0	0.0	1.8	0.0	91.3	0.0	0.0	0.0	0.0	91.3	● PURITAN LIFE INS CO
48.4	261.2 (*)	3.9	19.4	52.3	3.3	2.3	4.4	0.0	0.0	7.5	0.0	● PURITAN LIFE INS CO OF AMERICA
0.3	6.9	11.7	0.0	31.2	0.0	56.1	0.0	0.0	0.0	1.0	56.1	REGAL LIFE OF AMERICA INS CO
--	--	--	--	--	--	--	--	--	--	--	--	REGAL REINSURANCE COMPANY
31.5	2,693.7	0.0	1.3	6.8	0.0	87.9	0.0	0.0	0.0	3.6	87.9	● REINSURANCE CO OF MO INC
0.0	41.4 (*)	0.0	0.0	100.9	0.0	0.0	0.0	0.0	0.0	2.7	0.0	RELIABLE LIFE INS CO
0.4	6.9 (*)	0.4	0.0	15.6	0.0	58.6	0.5	0.0	3.6	0.0	1.5	RELIABLE LIFE INS CO
--	--	--	--	--	--	--	--	--	--	--	--	RELIABLE SERVICE INS CO
2,057.3	18,370.2 (*)	0.5	24.5	19.3	11.2	2.4	33.9	1.9	0.1	4.5	1.6	● RELIANCE STANDARD LIFE INS CO
--	--	--	--	--	--	--	--	--	--	--	--	RELIANCE STANDARD LIFE INS CO OF TX
-4,852.1	11,532.1 (*)	0.9	21.2	46.1	3.6	6.0	10.9	0.1	0.4	8.3	5.6	● RELIASTAR LIFE INS CO
-928.8	1,520.9 (*)	2.6	22.0	55.7	3.8	0.5	8.2	0.0	0.0	4.7	0.4	● RELIASTAR LIFE INS CO OF NEW YORK
181.9	82.4 (*)	0.2	28.2	42.6	2.1	23.0	0.0	0.0	0.0	0.0	0.0	● RENAISSANCE L&H INS CO OF AMERICA
19.0	11.8	32.3	0.0	54.7	0.0	12.3	0.0	0.0	0.0	0.0	0.0	RENAISSANCE L&H INS CO OF NY
0.0	50.6 (*)	11.1	5.0	76.4	0.0	0.0	0.0	0.0	0.0	1.6	2.0	RESERVE NATIONAL INS CO
153.4	1,383.9	0.2	2.1	2.3	0.0	94.2	0.0	0.0	0.0	1.2	94.5	RESOLUTION LIFE COLORADO INC
--	--	--	--	--	--	--	--	--	--	--	--	RESOURCE LIFE INS CO
6,598.5	33,541.3 (*)	1.2	12.5	51.3	7.4	0.8	15.6	0.0	0.0	9.6	2.3	● RGA REINSURANCE CO
-1,346.3	22,207.0 (*)	0.7	15.0	27.2	3.6	3.4	6.8	0.0	0.4	5.6	4.7	● RIVERSOURCE LIFE INS CO
300.7	2,726.1 (*)	3.5	25.8	42.9	3.9	0.0	5.7	0.0	0.0	2.2	0.0	● RIVERSOURCE LIFE INS CO OF NY
--	--	--	--	--	--	--	--	--	--	--	--	ROYAL STATE NATIONAL INS CO LTD
0.1	3.6 (*)	2.3	0.0	87.9	0.8	0.0	0.0	0.0	0.0	0.0	0.0	ROYALTY CAPITAL LIFE INS CO
1.8	30.0 (*)	9.8	0.1	23.9	0.0	38.2	17.1	0.0	9.2	0.0	10.2	RUSH LIFE INS CO
454.2	1,460.1 (*)	0.8	53.8	24.4	0.4	0.5	15.7	0.0	0.0	0.3	0.0	● S USA LIFE INS CO INC
471.6	2,914.7 (*)	2.0	24.4	48.4	3.8	9.7	3.4	0.0	0.0	1.8	0.0	● SAGICOR LIFE INS CO
130.6	3,349.6	0.0	12.9	71.9	2.8	1.9	0.0	0.0	0.3	10.2	0.1	● SB MUTL LIFE INS CO OF MA
506.1	2,514.0 (*)	0.4	44.3	46.5	0.6	0.5	0.5	0.0	0.0	4.8	0.2	● SBLI USA MUT LIFE INS CO INC
225.9	535.0	2.9	6.0	67.8	0.1	11.9	0.0	0.0	0.0	10.5	20.3	● SCOR GLOBAL LIFE AMERICAS REIN CO
70.6	243.8 (*)	2.1	22.5	44.4	0.0	0.1	0.0	0.0	0.0	4.6	0.0	● SCOR GLOBAL LIFE REINS CO OF DE
302.4	398.9	3.9	13.2	57.1	0.0	0.1	0.0	0.0	0.0	25.5	22.6	● SCOR GLOBAL LIFE USA RE CO
--	--	--	--	--	--	--	--	--	--	--	--	SCOTTISH RE US INC
14.2	73.3	6.8	0.0	55.1	0.0	0.0	38.0	0.0	0.0	0.0	0.0	● SECU LIFE INS CO
532.3	1,062.2 (*)	0.0	10.6	62.0	1.2	0.6	14.9	0.0	0.0	0.9	0.0	● SECURIAN LIFE INS CO
1.3	28.9 (*)	0.1	0.0	17.2	0.0	8.5	0.0	0.0	0.0	0.0	0.0	● SECURICO LIFE INS CO
-855.0	39,060.0	1.6	33.1	16.5	7.3	1.9	2.6	0.0	0.1	36.1	35.3	● SECURITY BENEFIT LIFE INS CO
16,469.5	31,728.5 (*)	1.1	16.4	62.3	2.3	0.7	7.7	0.0	0.0	7.8	0.5	● SECURITY LIFE OF DENVER INS CO
241.5	2,802.6 (*)	1.3	1.4	65.2	0.2	0.1	8.1	0.1	0.4	20.3	0.0	● SECURITY MUTUAL LIFE INS CO OF NY
92.9	676.4 (*)	5.3	1.2	18.1	1.0	5.6	12.4	0.3	16.7	37.3	4.6	● SECURITY NATIONAL LIFE INS CO
45.6	303.0	0.3	8.8	79.8	1.2	4.7	0.0	0.0	0.7	3.5	2.4	SECURITY PLAN LIFE INS CO
18.3	191.0	2.3	6.0	75.0	9.7	5.7	0.0	0.2	0.9	0.4	0.0	● SELECTED FUNERAL AND LIFE INS CO
--	--	--	--	--	--	--	--	--	--	--	--	SENIOR HEALTH INS CO OF PENNSYLVANIA
34.9	68.6	18.7	0.1	48.0	0.0	5.3	0.0	0.0	18.2	9.8	1.0	SENIOR LIFE INS CO
0.7	1.9 (*)	42.5	0.0	37.6	0.0	16.5	0.0	0.0	0.0	0.0	0.0	SENIOR LIFE INS CO OF TEXAS
--	--	--	--	--	--	--	--	--	--	--	--	SENTINEL AMERICAN LIFE INS CO
205.4	821.7 (*)	12.2	24.9	35.8	5.6	0.8	10.5	0.0	0.9	2.7	1.8	● SENTINEL SECURITY LIFE INS CO
862.0	2,683.0	0.0	5.0	91.6	1.7	0.4	0.0	0.0	0.0	0.3	0.4	● SENTRY LIFE INS CO
16.4	42.7 (*)	2.0	11.3	84.1	0.5	0.0	0.0	0.0	0.0	0.7	0.0	SENTRY LIFE INS CO OF NEW YORK
--	--	--	--	--	--	--	--	--	--	--	--	SERVICE LIFE & CAS INS CO
39.3	401.2 (*)	0.3	0.0	94.0	0.0	0.0	0.0	0.0	0.0	2.4	0.0	● SETTLERS LIFE INS CO
152.0	1,331.3	0.2	34.6	47.5	1.0	0.5	4.5	0.0	0.0	11.1	1.1	● SHELTER LIFE INS CO
0.0	9.8 (*)	18.6	8.9	57.4	0.0	0.0	0.0	0.0	0.0	0.0	0.0	SHELTERPOINT INS CO
478.5	313.1 (*)	4.5	8.9	25.4	0.2	3.1	0.0	0.0	0.0	0.0	3.1	● SHELTERPOINT LIFE INS CO

● Bullets denote a more detailed analysis is available in Section II.
(*) Asset category percentages do not add up to 100%

INSURANCE COMPANY NAME	DOM. STATE	RATING	TOTAL ASSETS ($MIL)	CAPITAL & SURPLUS ($MIL)	RISK ADJUSTED CAPITAL RATIO 1	RISK ADJUSTED CAPITAL RATIO 2	CAPITAL-IZATION INDEX (PTS)	INVEST. SAFETY INDEX (PTS)	PROFIT-ABILITY INDEX (PTS)	LIQUIDITY INDEX (PTS)	STAB. INDEX (PTS)	STABILIT FACTOR
SHENANDOAH LIFE INS CO	VA	C	1850.5	101.0	1.61	0.87	6.0	4.8	2.8	0.3	2.5	FGILT
SHERIDAN LIFE INS CO	OK	U	--	--	--	--	--	--	--	--	--	Z
▼ SILAC INSURANCE CO	UT	C-	6778.9	271.4	0.79	0.42	3.3	1.3	6.2	8.4	3.3	CGI
SMITH BURIAL & LIFE INS CO	AR	E	4.5	0.4	0.33	0.29	0.5	8.1	2.9	2.5	0.1	CDFL
SOUTHERN FARM BUREAU LIFE INS CO	MS	A	15730.7	3074.3	4.38	2.36	9.0	5.7	7.7	6.4	7.4	I
SOUTHERN FIDELITY LIFE INS CO	AR	U	--	--	--	--	--	--	--	--	--	Z
SOUTHERN FINANCIAL LIFE INS CO	KY	C	16.0	5.0	1.63	1.47	7.7	8.3	6.6	8.4	3.8	AF
SOUTHERN FINANCIAL LIFE INS CO	LA	D+	169.4	60.9	2.71	1.58	7.9	2.7	8.6	6.7	2.8	DI
SOUTHERN LIFE & HEALTH INS CO	WI	C	34.3	5.5	1.13	1.02	7.0	6.1	6.0	5.1	2.6	CDFGT
SOUTHERN NATL LIFE INS CO INC	LA	B	23.1	18.8	3.67	2.44	9.2	4.1	7.9	7.7	4.8	DI
SOUTHERN SECURITY LIFE INS CO INC	MS	D	1.6	1.6	2.59	2.33	8.0	7.2	3.9	10.0	1.4	A
SOUTHLAND NATIONAL INS CORP	NC	F (5)	--	--	--	--	--	--	--	--	--	Z
SOUTHWEST CREDIT LIFE INC	NM	U (5)	--	--	--	--	--	--	--	--	--	Z
SOUTHWEST SERVICE LIFE INS CO	TX	D-	9.6	3.8	0.85	0.74	4.9	8.8	1.7	6.7	0.9	DFT
SQUIRE REASSURANCE CO LLC	MI	U (5)	--	--	--	--	--	--	--	--	--	Z
STANDARD INS CO	OR	B+	32461.1	1433.2	2.09	1.07	7.1	5.1	7.3	6.4	6.5	AI
STANDARD LIFE & ACCIDENT INS CO	TX	B	488.4	307.0	16.35	9.94	10.0	4.9	4.1	8.7	.5.4	AFIT
STANDARD LIFE & CAS INS CO	UT	B-	45.3	8.6	1.38	1.25	7.4	5.0	3.0	5.9	5.0	ADI
STANDARD LIFE INS CO OF NY	NY	A	325.0	142.5	6.14	4.21	10.0	7.4	8.3	7.4	7.7	AD
STANDARD SECURITY LIFE INS CO OF NY	NY	A-	152.8	73.6	4.41	3.60	10.0	8.2	8.0	8.5	6.3	DG
STARMOUNT LIFE INS CO	ME	C	132.1	66.9	1.93	1.50	7.8	7.4	1.8	1.3	3.3	DFL
STATE FARM HEALTH INS CO	IL	U	--	--	--	--	--	--	--	--	--	Z
STATE FARM LIFE & ACCIDENT ASR CO	IL	A+	3528.9	611.4	3.82	2.21	8.8	6.3	3.0	6.4	7.9	AI
STATE FARM LIFE INS CO	IL	A+	86273.0	14931.3	4.96	2.78	9.7	6.2	7.4	6.5	7.9	AI
STATE LIFE INS CO	IN	B	10441.4	581.6	1.76	0.89	6.1	4.4	5.5	3.6	5.4	ACGIL
STATE LIFE INS FUND	WI	B	112.9	10.5	1.31	1.18	7.3	7.6	5.6	5.7	4.2	DF
STATE MUTUAL INS CO	GA	D	217.6	26.7	0.90	0.70	4.6	3.8	1.9	7.4	1.8	CDGIT
▲ STERLING INVESTORS LIFE INS CO	IN	C+	96.8	13.5	1.65	1.42	7.6	3.6	6.6	6.2	4.6	AFIT
▼ STERLING LIFE INS CO	IL	B	33.7	16.8	1.20	0.93	6.4	8.0	9.0	7.2	5.9	ACD
STERLING NATL LIFE INS CO	CT	U	--	--	--	--	--	--	--	--	--	Z
STRUCTURED ANNUITY RE CO	IA	U	--	--	--	--	--	--	--	--	--	Z
SUN LIFE & HEALTH INS CO	MI	D+	1078.5	133.9	2.39	1.43	7.6	6.8	2.4	6.0	2.6	A
SUN LIFE ASR CO OF CANADA	MI	D	19675.7	798.3	0.53	0.31	1.2	1.1	5.2	3.7	1.2	CFIL
SURENCY LIFE & HEALTH INS CO	KS	B	21.2	17.5	4.21	2.98	10.0	6.0	6.5	7.5	5.4	DGI
SURETY LIFE & CASUALTY INS CO	ND	C-	14.8	5.4	2.18	1.89	8.3	4.4	7.7	7.6	2.8	DI
SURETY LIFE INS CO	NE	D	29.5	27.4	3.55	1.90	8.4	5.6	2.8	9.7	2.0	T
SWBC LIFE INS CO	TX	A-	42.4	25.4	3.95	2.67	9.5	6.2	7.8	9.0	6.2	I
SWISS RE LIFE & HEALTH AMER INC	MO	C+	13957.8	1556.0	1.91	1.25	7.4	6.6	5.0	5.0	4.7	AFGT
SYMETRA LIFE INS CO	IA	B-	46627.5	2331.6	1.89	1.01	7.0	4.7	1.9	5.6	4.8	I
SYMETRA NATIONAL LIFE INS CO	IA	B+	24.4	12.2	3.06	2.76	9.6	8.9	6.9	6.9	5.9	AD
T J M LIFE INS CO	TX	D+	18.2	1.4	0.53	0.48	2.8	0.8	2.9	5.4	2.7	CDI
TALCOTT RESOLUTION INTL LIFE	CT	U	--	--	--	--	--	--	--	--	--	Z
TALCOTT RESOLUTION LIFE	CT	B-	36351.0	772.4	2.07	1.04	7.1	5.6	5.4	6.5	5.0	T
TALCOTT RESOLUTION LIFE INS CO	CT	B-	101000.0	2153.5	1.39	0.90	4.0	5.5	2.9	6.1	4.0	FT
TEACHERS INS & ANNUITY ASN OF AM	NY	A+	343000.0	42972.7	3.88	2.26	8.9	6.4	8.9	6.1	7.0	I
TENNESSEE FARMERS LIFE INS CO	TN	B+	2599.1	590.9	2.65	1.72	8.1	5.1	7.0	6.5	6.6	AI
TEXAS DIRECTORS LIFE INS CO	TX	B-	4.8	1.1	0.76	0.69	4.5	5.6	6.0	6.4	4.5	ACDF
TEXAS LIFE INS CO	TX	C+	1632.4	114.5	1.59	0.83	5.9	3.5	6.5	5.4	4.4	AI
▲ TEXAS REPUB LIFE INS CO	TX	E	31.4	1.8	0.41	0.37	1.4	5.4	1.1	7.6	0.1	CDIT
TEXAS SERVICE LIFE INS CO	TX	C-	120.9	17.7	2.03	1.73	8.1	6.8	2.6	6.1	3.1	D
THE EPIC LIFE INSURANCE CO	WI	C-	31.6	17.2	3.43	2.26	8.9	5.5	2.1	6.8	3.2	F
THE UNION LABOR LIFE INS CO	MD	B	4752.2	154.7	2.18	1.46	7.7	7.1	8.2	6.6	5.5	T

See Page 27 for explanation of footnotes and Page 28 for explanation of stability factors.

Arrows denote recent upgrades ▲ or downgrades▼ (see Section VI for explanations)

52   www.weissratings.com

NET PREMIUM ($MIL)	IN-VESTED ASSETS ($MIL)	CASH	CMO & STRUCT. SECS.	OTH.INV. GRADE BONDS	NON-INV. GRADE BONDS	CMMON & PREF. STOCK	MORT IN GOOD STAND.	NON-PERF. MORT.	REAL ESTATE	OTHER INVEST-MENTS	INVEST. IN AFFIL	INSURANCE COMPANY NAME
493.0	1,012.2 (*)	0.3	39.8	46.4	0.9	0.8	4.3	0.0	0.0	6.2	1.5 ●	SHENANDOAH LIFE INS CO
--	--	--	--	--	--	--	--	--	--	--	--	SHERIDAN LIFE INS CO
1,299.7	6,590.7 (*)	7.7	20.0	46.6	9.5	1.3	9.4	0.0	1.2	2.9	0.2 ●	SILAC INSURANCE CO
0.3	4.4	5.2	0.0	94.8	0.0	0.0	0.0	0.0	0.0	0.0	0.0	SMITH BURIAL & LIFE INS CO
945.6	15,120.6	0.2	13.1	52.4	3.3	7.1	12.9	0.0	0.1	10.7	6.9 ●	SOUTHERN FARM BUREAU LIFE INS CO
--	--	--	--	--	--	--	--	--	--	--	--	SOUTHERN FIDELITY LIFE INS CO
3.7	12.0 (*)	11.3	26.8	49.7	0.0	0.0	0.0	0.0	0.0	0.0	0.0	SOUTHERN FINANCIAL LIFE INS CO
19.8	164.3 (*)	1.0	0.0	44.2	7.5	41.5	0.0	0.0	0.0	4.5	0.0 ●	SOUTHERN FINANCIAL LIFE INS CO
2.4	33.1	1.5	0.0	1.6	0.0	96.3	0.0	0.0	0.0	0.1	0.0	SOUTHERN LIFE & HEALTH INS CO
3.4	21.5	5.8	19.7	34.3	0.0	39.0	0.0	0.0	0.0	0.3	3.9	SOUTHERN NATL LIFE INS CO INC
0.0	1.5 (*)	36.9	25.8	20.4	2.7	6.7	0.0	0.0	0.0	0.0	0.0	SOUTHERN SECURITY LIFE INS CO INC
--	--	--	--	--	--	--	--	--	--	--	--	SOUTHLAND NATIONAL INS CORP
--	--	--	--	--	--	--	--	--	--	--	--	SOUTHWEST CREDIT LIFE INC
8.0	9.2	7.9	0.0	68.1	0.0	24.0	0.0	0.0	0.0	0.0	24.0	SOUTHWEST SERVICE LIFE INS CO
--	--	--	--	--	--	--	--	--	--	--	--	SQUIRE REASSURANCE CO LLC
6,353.4	20,393.8 (*)	0.9	8.9	44.3	4.0	0.3	39.3	0.0	0.4	3.6	0.0 ●	STANDARD INS CO
66.0	466.8 (*)	0.3	0.0	86.4	2.3	0.0	5.2	0.0	0.0	0.7	0.1 ●	STANDARD LIFE & ACCIDENT INS CO
10.6	37.3 (*)	3.4	1.6	82.2	2.7	0.7	0.0	0.0	0.0	6.5	0.0	STANDARD LIFE & CAS INS CO
118.3	308.7	10.4	0.0	50.0	0.0	0.0	39.6	0.0	0.0	0.0	0.0 ●	STANDARD LIFE INS CO OF NY
173.7	122.0 (*)	0.7	0.0	96.1	0.0	0.0	0.0	0.0	0.0	0.3	0.0 ●	STANDARD SECURITY LIFE INS CO OF NY
272.9	111.3	0.0	0.0	81.4	0.0	0.0	0.0	0.0	4.8	13.9	0.0 ●	STARMOUNT LIFE INS CO
--	--	--	--	--	--	--	--	--	--	--	--	STATE FARM HEALTH INS CO
266.7	3,414.2	0.0	19.9	65.6	0.7	7.4	0.0	0.0	0.0	6.4	1.3 ●	STATE FARM LIFE & ACCIDENT ASR CO
5,479.3	83,922.6	0.0	15.0	49.4	0.5	8.7	14.1	0.0	0.0	12.3	2.7 ●	STATE FARM LIFE INS CO
691.0	10,308.8 (*)	0.8	13.8	62.8	3.0	0.4	14.7	0.0	0.0	1.7	0.0 ●	STATE LIFE INS CO
1.0	111.6 (*)	0.3	0.0	91.4	0.9	0.0	0.0	0.0	0.0	4.2	0.0	STATE LIFE INS FUND
101.9	194.3 (*)	6.9	11.3	38.9	2.4	14.0	1.9	0.0	8.2	9.1	12.5 ●	STATE MUTUAL INS CO
3.1	89.3 (*)	5.8	10.1	72.7	7.0	0.0	1.1	0.0	0.0	1.6	0.0	STERLING INVESTORS LIFE INS CO
45.0	30.5	2.9	0.0	96.3	0.0	0.0	0.0	0.0	0.0	0.8	0.6	STERLING LIFE INS CO
--	--	--	--	--	--	--	--	--	--	--	--	STERLING NATL LIFE INS CO
--	--	--	--	--	--	--	--	--	--	--	--	STRUCTURED ANNUITY RE CO
152.2	838.5	0.8	16.9	73.5	1.5	0.5	5.5	0.0	0.0	1.3	0.0 ●	SUN LIFE & HEALTH INS CO
2,339.4	18,083.2	-0.1	15.4	56.8	2.2	1.9	15.2	0.0	4.4	3.9	1.2 ●	SUN LIFE ASR CO OF CANADA
13.9	20.7	30.5	5.7	45.0	0.0	17.9	0.0	0.0	0.0	0.0	0.0	SURENCY LIFE & HEALTH INS CO
1.5	14.4	2.6	0.0	72.6	2.2	19.8	0.0	0.0	0.3	2.4	0.0	SURETY LIFE & CASUALTY INS CO
0.4	27.1 (*)	0.0	6.8	73.7	0.0	24.0	0.0	0.0	0.0	0.0	0.0 ●	SURETY LIFE INS CO
17.6	40.9 (*)	28.2	0.0	47.0	1.1	14.4	0.0	0.0	0.0	0.0	0.0 ●	SWBC LIFE INS CO
3,509.7	10,818.1 (*)	-0.1	8.0	70.3	2.3	1.1	11.3	0.0	0.0	4.5	7.7 ●	SWISS RE LIFE & HEALTH AMER INC
4,609.0	38,859.0	2.7	21.7	51.6	2.8	1.5	17.5	0.0	0.0	1.6	0.6 ●	SYMETRA LIFE INS CO
2.3	23.7	2.1	24.2	73.1	0.0	0.0	0.0	0.0	0.0	0.7	0.0	SYMETRA NATIONAL LIFE INS CO
1.4	18.0 (*)	3.3	5.6	58.5	14.0	0.0	0.0	0.0	10.1	0.5	0.0	T J M LIFE INS CO
--	--	--	--	--	--	--	--	--	--	--	--	TALCOTT RESOLUTION INTL LIFE
-13,324.6	6,661.1 (*)	0.2	17.9	50.8	1.6	0.6	12.2	0.0	0.0	10.7	0.2 ●	TALCOTT RESOLUTION LIFE
1,161.0	18,893.5 (*)	0.2	16.3	56.5	1.7	4.7	6.2	0.0	0.1	11.1	4.4 ●	TALCOTT RESOLUTION LIFE INS CO
13,772.5	288,000.0 (*)	0.0	18.5	44.0	6.2	3.5	12.8	0.0	1.3	12.4	10.0 ●	TEACHERS INS & ANNUITY ASN OF AM
205.9	2,501.7 (*)	0.0	0.0	76.8	5.2	14.7	0.2	0.0	0.5	1.4	3.5 ●	TENNESSEE FARMERS LIFE INS CO
0.1	4.7 (*)	7.8	0.1	82.9	4.1	0.6	0.0	0.0	0.0	0.3	0.0	TEXAS DIRECTORS LIFE INS CO
314.9	1,602.9 (*)	0.9	29.8	22.5	14.1	5.3	4.8	0.0	0.0	20.7	0.0 ●	TEXAS LIFE INS CO
3.8	30.2 (*)	9.5	1.2	28.5	0.0	0.2	18.6	0.6	0.0	24.2	0.2	TEXAS REPUB LIFE INS CO
21.7	111.5 (*)	3.3	4.9	53.9	0.5	4.3	0.0	0.0	3.1	0.9	0.0	TEXAS SERVICE LIFE INS CO
12.4	27.8 (*)	2.0	19.4	57.2	1.2	18.4	0.0	0.0	0.0	0.0	0.0	THE EPIC LIFE INSURANCE CO
190.4	409.4	0.0	23.3	49.6	0.3	9.0	8.1	0.0	0.0	9.9	5.5 ●	THE UNION LABOR LIFE INS CO

● Bullets denote a more detailed analysis is available in Section II.
(*) Asset category percentages do not add up to 100%

INSURANCE COMPANY NAME	DOM. STATE	RATING	TOTAL ASSETS ($MIL)	CAPITAL & SURPLUS ($MIL)	RISK ADJUSTED CAPITAL RATIO 1	RISK ADJUSTED CAPITAL RATIO 2	CAPITAL-IZATION INDEX (PTS)	INVEST. SAFETY INDEX (PTS)	PROFIT-ABILITY INDEX (PTS)	LIQUIDITY INDEX (PTS)	STAB. INDEX (PTS)	STABIL FACTOR
TIAA-CREF LIFE INS CO	NY	B	17626.1	841.7	2.39	1.27	7.4	6.3	5.8	3.0	5.0	IL
TIER ONE INSURANCE CO	NE	B	73.6	57.0	7.30	6.57	8.0	9.3	1.6	7.0	4.4	DFT
TIME INS CO	PR	F (5)	--	--	--	--	--	--	--	--	--	Z
TOWN & COUNTRY LIFE INS CO	UT	C-	10.6	7.9	2.95	2.49	9.2	5.4	8.2	7.4	2.7	D
TRANS CITY LIFE INS CO	AZ	C-	20.5	10.4	3.54	3.19	10.0	7.5	2.3	9.5	2.9	DG
TRANS OCEANIC LIFE INS CO	PR	B+	407.4	39.3	2.17	1.42	7.6	4.9	8.8	7.7	6.4	GI
TRANS WORLD ASR CO	CA	B+	341.0	85.3	3.33	2.16	8.7	5.6	6.1	8.0	6.7	ADI
TRANS-WESTERN LIFE INS CO	TX	U	--	--	--	--	--	--	--	--	--	Z
TRANSAMERICA FINANCIAL LIFE INS CO	NY	B	35545.8	1088.6	3.04	1.49	7.7	5.3	6.5	7.7	5.6	AI
TRANSAMERICA LIFE INS CO	IA	B	203000.0	7276.9	1.48	1.05	7.1	6.3	4.8	6.3	5.4	I
TRANSAMERICA PACIFIC RE INC	VT	C (4)	2280.3	271.2	5.44	3.14	3.0	4.9	0.9	7.0	3.0	ET
▲ TRINITY LIFE INS CO	OK	D	349.6	14.3	0.64	0.41	2.1	1.9	2.3	5.1	1.5	CDI
TRIPLE S VIDA INC	PR	C+	810.1	58.3	0.98	0.62	4.8	3.3	5.0	6.0	4.6	CI
TRIPLE-S BLUE II	PR	D+	18.2	2.8	0.77	0.60	3.8	8.3	1.7	6.4	1.3	DT
TRUSTMARK INS CO	IL	B	1807.8	320.4	2.83	1.59	7.9	4.8	3.2	7.0	5.4	I
TRUSTMARK LIFE INS CO	IL	A-	249.3	152.4	7.01	4.80	10.0	7.1	6.2	6.8	5.5	ADT
TRUSTMARK LIFE INS CO OF NEW YORK	NY	B	11.7	6.4	2.47	2.22	8.8	8.7	2.5	6.9	5.3	AD
UNICARE LIFE & HEALTH INS CO	IN	B	957.9	289.4	5.03	3.54	10.0	3.7	6.7	0.0	4.9	DILT
▼ UNIFIED LIFE INS CO	TX	C+	206.8	20.2	1.47	0.88	6.0	3.3	3.6	1.8	3.8	FILT
UNIMERICA INS CO	WI	B-	427.6	260.2	6.25	4.81	10.0	8.5	9.0	7.1	5.0	AD
UNIMERICA LIFE INS CO OF NY	NY	B-	35.6	24.8	4.80	4.32	10.0	8.5	7.2	7.5	5.1	A
UNION FIDELITY LIFE INS CO	KS	C	19882.4	862.7	1.83	0.92	6.4	3.7	1.8	4.4	3.6	AFIL
UNION NATIONAL LIFE INS CO	LA	B-	21.4	11.6	3.25	1.62	7.9	8.8	6.2	10.0	4.4	AT
UNION SECURITY INS CO	KS	B	3149.8	205.6	4.92	2.50	9.3	5.4	8.3	6.3	4.8	AFIT
▲ UNION SECURITY LIFE INS CO OF NY	NY	B	55.8	42.7	6.12	5.50	10.0	8.1	5.2	10.0	6.2	AT
UNITED AMERICAN INS CO	NE	B	714.5	191.6	1.63	1.24	7.4	6.2	8.0	5.7	5.9	AI
UNITED ASR LIFE INS CO	TX	D-	2.3	0.6	0.80	0.72	4.8	9.2	1.6	7.7	1.0	ADF
UNITED FARM FAMILY LIFE INS CO	IN	B+	2457.7	363.7	3.30	2.02	8.5	7.0	4.2	5.9	6.5	L
UNITED FIDELITY LIFE INS CO	TX	C	1121.1	879.8	0.86	0.85	5.8	2.8	7.2	6.9	4.1	CI
UNITED FUNERAL BENEFIT LIFE INS CO	OK	D	54.4	7.9	0.84	0.68	4.4	4.5	6.3	7.0	2.1	ACDI
UNITED FUNERAL DIR BENEFIT LIC	TX	D	154.8	7.7	0.65	0.59	3.7	0.8	5.6	5.4	2.1	CDI
UNITED HEALTHCARE INS CO	CT	C	22699.4	7379.6	0.88	0.76	4.8	6.4	7.5	1.3	3.3	CL
UNITED HERITAGE LIFE INS CO	ID	B	682.2	76.1	2.21	1.14	7.2	3.9	7.8	4.7	5.7	IL
UNITED HOME LIFE INS CO	IN	B	193.7	30.1	3.16	2.77	9.7	7.8	5.8	6.1	5.4	DG
UNITED INS CO OF AMERICA	IL	B-	5067.0	445.0	1.58	0.94	6.5	4.4	6.5	4.7	5.3	AILT
▼ UNITED LIFE INS CO	IA	B-	2915.1	256.8	2.23	1.04	7.1	3.8	4.1	8.2	3.9	GIT
▲ UNITED NATIONAL LIFE INS CO OF AM	IL	B+	52.1	19.9	2.24	1.60	7.9	7.8	8.1	7.9	5.9	AD
UNITED OF OMAHA LIFE INS CO	NE	B	31183.6	1924.8	1.96	1.12	7.2	5.1	7.1	5.4	6.0	IL
UNITED SECURITY ASR CO OF PA	PA	C	55.4	12.1	1.75	1.57	7.9	8.2	5.3	8.0	3.3	D
UNITED STATES LIFE INS CO IN NYC	NY	C+	32282.1	2020.0	2.51	1.21	7.3	4.9	5.5	5.2	4.8	AFGIT
UNITED WORLD LIFE INS CO	NE	B+	160.3	59.5	3.36	1.38	7.6	7.4	7.3	6.6	6.7	A
UNITY FINANCIAL LIFE INS CO	OH	C-	345.1	17.0	1.52	0.79	5.8	3.4	4.5	7.0	3.2	DI
UNIVANTAGE INS CO	UT	U	--	--	--	--	--	--	--	--	--	Z
UNIVERSAL FIDELITY LIFE INS CO	OK	B-	18.8	7.9	1.04	0.95	6.6	5.9	2.7	6.3	4.7	AF
UNIVERSAL GUARANTY LIFE INS CO	OH	C+	360.0	64.7	1.79	1.04	7.1	2.4	2.9	6.4	4.4	DFI
▼ UNIVERSAL LIFE INS CO	PR	B	2445.4	165.9	2.01	0.97	6.8	3.8	8.2	7.5	5.8	I
UNUM INS CO	ME	C	117.9	74.2	3.54	2.61	9.4	7.1	2.2	7.8	3.8	ADG
UNUM LIFE INS CO OF AMERICA	ME	C+	22629.7	1296.7	2.08	1.06	7.1	3.4	4.6	6.9	3.4	AGIT
▲ UPSTREAM LIFE INS CO	TX	E+	218.9	11.1	1.08	0.54	5.1	1.4	1.1	6.5	0.7	CDFIT
US ALLIANCE LIFE & SEC CO (MT)	MT	U	--	--	--	--	--	--	--	--	--	Z
US ALLIANCE LIFE & SECURITY CO	KS	D-	85.6	7.4	0.79	0.53	3.3	4.5	1.8	0.0	1.3	CILT
US FINANCIAL LIFE INS CO	OH	B	373.7	124.5	11.12	5.24	10.0	7.0	8.3	9.0	4.2	AFT

See Page 27 for explanation of footnotes and Page 28 for explanation of stability factors.
Arrows denote recent upgrades ▲ or downgrades▼ (see Section VI for explanations)

54

www.weissratings.com

NET PREMIUM ($MIL)	IN-VESTED ASSETS ($MIL)	CASH	CMO & STRUCT. SECS.	OTH.INV. GRADE BONDS	NON-INV. GRADE BONDS	CMMON & PREF. STOCK	MORT IN GOOD STAND.	NON-PERF. MORT.	REAL ESTATE	OTHER INVEST-MENTS	INVEST. IN AFFIL	INSURANCE COMPANY NAME
433.6	12,669.2	0.0	12.5	87.0	0.0	0.1	0.0	0.0	0.0	0.4	0.0	● TIAA-CREF LIFE INS CO
3.4	73.2 (*)	31.0	0.0	54.6	0.0	0.0	0.0	0.0	0.0	0.0	0.0	● TIER ONE INSURANCE CO
--	--	--	--	--	--	--	--	--	--	--	--	TIME INS CO
4.6	10.4	13.9	0.0	23.3	0.0	10.5	19.7	0.0	0.0	32.7	0.0	TOWN & COUNTRY LIFE INS CO
2.6	19.6 (*)	31.9	0.0	32.5	0.0	23.1	0.0	0.0	2.3	0.0	24.7	TRANS CITY LIFE INS CO
32.3	87.7 (*)	12.8	6.8	42.4	0.0	17.6	0.3	0.0	11.4	1.6	4.5	● TRANS OCEANIC LIFE INS CO
12.4	336.0	3.5	0.0	74.4	7.2	5.1	5.7	0.0	3.0	1.2	10.1	● TRANS WORLD ASR CO
--	--	--	--	--	--	--	--	--	--	--	--	TRANS-WESTERN LIFE INS CO
5,206.8	8,704.1 (*)	1.7	11.8	51.4	3.4	0.2	18.8	0.0	0.0	4.5	2.0	● TRANSAMERICA FINANCIAL LIFE INS CO
14,263.3	73,792.7 (*)	0.3	8.4	56.1	3.4	5.0	12.4	0.0	0.1	6.8	6.3	● TRANSAMERICA LIFE INS CO
29.8	981.3 (*)	0.0	12.8	76.8	0.2	0.0	0.0	0.0	0.0	1.3	0.0	● TRANSAMERICA PACIFIC RE INC
38.7	335.4 (*)	3.0	4.1	44.1	5.1	3.8	36.2	0.3	0.1	1.8	3.5	TRINITY LIFE INS CO
227.7	752.5	1.2	19.9	53.1	0.0	20.8	0.0	0.0	0.0	5.1	0.4	● TRIPLE S VIDA INC
12.3	11.8	24.7	30.7	42.0	0.0	0.0	0.0	0.0	2.5	0.1	0.0	TRIPLE-S BLUE II
389.7	1,765.4	0.0	21.3	43.1	4.6	6.7	7.9	0.0	1.1	15.3	0.0	● TRUSTMARK INS CO
119.6	233.5	0.0	18.6	64.0	0.3	4.0	4.1	0.0	0.0	9.1	0.0	● TRUSTMARK LIFE INS CO
2.5	11.1	6.2	8.0	85.0	0.0	0.0	0.0	0.0	0.0	0.2	0.0	TRUSTMARK LIFE INS CO OF NEW YORK
404.3	388.2 (*)	1.8	0.0	69.0	16.3	0.1	0.0	0.0	0.0	9.5	0.0	● UNICARE LIFE & HEALTH INS CO
55.1	190.7 (*)	1.9	7.3	68.0	8.1	6.7	0.0	0.0	0.0	4.7	0.0	UNIFIED LIFE INS CO
312.0	412.7	0.0	15.9	70.6	0.0	0.0	0.0	0.0	0.0	13.5	0.0	● UNIMERICA INS CO
7.6	34.5 (*)	0.5	27.8	70.5	0.0	0.0	0.0	0.0	0.0	0.0	0.0	UNIMERICA LIFE INS CO OF NY
225.3	19,538.0	0.3	6.4	82.6	3.2	0.2	4.6	0.0	0.0	2.1	0.9	● UNION FIDELITY LIFE INS CO
0.0	21.3	0.0	0.0	99.8	0.0	0.0	0.0	0.0	0.0	0.2	0.0	UNION NATIONAL LIFE INS CO
4.1	916.4	0.0	17.7	68.6	2.8	3.3	4.8	0.0	0.0	2.8	0.0	● UNION SECURITY INS CO
0.5	42.8 (*)	0.5	15.7	54.0	0.0	0.0	0.0	0.0	0.0	0.7	0.0	● UNION SECURITY LIFE INS CO OF NY
547.4	617.2	0.0	1.8	82.5	2.8	5.9	0.0	0.0	0.0	7.6	10.1	● UNITED AMERICAN INS CO
0.4	2.1	18.5	0.0	81.5	0.0	0.0	0.0	0.0	0.0	0.0	0.0	UNITED ASR LIFE INS CO
118.8	2,382.7	0.1	5.5	67.9	1.2	3.1	16.3	0.0	0.2	5.2	1.8	● UNITED FARM FAMILY LIFE INS CO
4.8	1,116.3	0.0	4.6	11.5	0.5	80.8	1.2	0.0	0.2	1.2	79.1	● UNITED FIDELITY LIFE INS CO
1.8	54.0	7.0	53.1	14.5	8.4	16.4	0.0	0.0	0.0	0.6	14.3	UNITED FUNERAL BENEFIT LIFE INS CO
11.2	151.4	3.9	50.7	32.9	5.2	1.9	2.8	0.0	0.0	2.7	0.0	UNITED FUNERAL DIR BENEFIT LIC
52,670.9	14,516.5	0.0	19.6	38.9	7.4	25.4	0.0	0.0	1.7	7.1	23.9	● UNITED HEALTHCARE INS CO
100.1	660.5	0.3	7.0	71.5	6.1	8.4	0.6	0.0	1.5	4.5	0.0	● UNITED HERITAGE LIFE INS CO
32.5	168.5 (*)	3.3	3.4	87.0	0.5	1.4	0.0	0.0	0.0	3.3	0.0	● UNITED HOME LIFE INS CO
599.7	4,577.3	0.0	16.0	56.8	5.4	8.8	0.1	0.0	2.1	9.8	1.6	● UNITED INS CO OF AMERICA
279.1	2,822.1 (*)	2.6	31.7	42.8	7.3	3.9	3.9	0.0	0.0	5.6	0.2	● UNITED LIFE INS CO
26.5	49.6	1.6	24.3	62.1	3.1	0.4	7.2	0.0	0.0	0.3	0.0	UNITED NATIONAL LIFE INS CO OF AM
4,840.6	25,220.3 (*)	-0.1	16.4	57.8	2.8	1.6	13.8	0.0	0.2	4.1	3.7	● UNITED OF OMAHA LIFE INS CO
7.2	53.8 (*)	1.7	16.8	76.2	0.0	0.0	0.0	0.0	0.0	0.1	0.0	UNITED SECURITY ASR CO OF PA
2,436.8	25,635.9 (*)	-0.1	17.7	54.1	5.9	0.1	12.4	0.0	0.0	7.8	1.0	● UNITED STATES LIFE INS CO IN NYC
0.9	141.9 (*)	0.0	53.8	39.4	0.4	0.4	0.0	0.0	0.0	0.4	0.0	● UNITED WORLD LIFE INS CO
41.9	338.1	1.5	22.1	73.8	0.4	0.8	0.0	0.0	0.0	0.8	0.0	UNITY FINANCIAL LIFE INS CO
--	--	--	--	--	--	--	--	--	--	--	--	UNIVANTAGE INS CO
8.3	12.4 (*)	11.7	0.2	9.3	0.0	63.3	0.0	0.0	7.1	1.6	48.3	UNIVERSAL FIDELITY LIFE INS CO
4.6	356.3	3.4	0.0	35.9	0.0	28.9	7.6	0.6	4.0	18.7	4.0	● UNIVERSAL GUARANTY LIFE INS CO
112.5	1,864.4 (*)	3.5	27.9	29.7	13.9	17.6	0.0	0.0	0.0	5.0	0.0	● UNIVERSAL LIFE INS CO
140.7	91.0	0.0	4.0	73.6	0.0	0.0	0.0	0.0	0.0	22.4	0.0	● UNUM INS CO
3,162.7	21,414.7	0.0	2.3	76.7	10.1	0.1	5.5	0.0	0.4	5.0	0.0	● UNUM LIFE INS CO OF AMERICA
10.7	215.4	15.2	20.8	43.8	3.3	8.3	2.1	0.0	0.0	6.6	0.0	UPSTREAM LIFE INS CO
--	--	--	--	--	--	--	--	--	--	--	--	US ALLIANCE LIFE & SEC CO (MT)
13.8	33.8 (*)	3.1	11.5	40.9	1.6	30.8	9.8	0.0	0.0	0.7	16.7	US ALLIANCE LIFE & SECURITY CO
0.0	302.2	0.0	25.8	63.4	4.9	2.7	0.0	0.0	0.0	3.7	0.0	● US FINANCIAL LIFE INS CO

● Bullets denote a more detailed analysis is available in Section II.
(*) Asset category percentages do not add up to 100%

INSURANCE COMPANY NAME	DOM. STATE	RATING	TOTAL ASSETS ($MIL)	CAPITAL & SURPLUS ($MIL)	RISK ADJUSTED CAPITAL RATIO 1	RISK ADJUSTED CAPITAL RATIO 2	CAPITAL-IZATION INDEX (PTS)	INVEST. SAFETY INDEX (PTS)	PROFIT-ABILITY INDEX (PTS)	LIQUIDITY INDEX (PTS)	STAB. INDEX (PTS)	STABILIT FACTOR
USA INS CO	MS	C-	5.2	4.3	2.80	2.52	9.3	3.0	2.8	6.9	2.2	DIT
USA LIFE ONE INS CO OF INDIANA	IN	C-	31.0	13.3	2.87	2.59	9.4	7.3	2.8	8.4	3.3	DF
▼ USAA LIFE INS CO	TX	B+	26197.9	2583.2	3.83	2.09	8.6	6.7	5.9	5.7	5.2	AFIT
USAA LIFE INS CO OF NEW YORK	NY	B	665.9	85.5	3.03	1.65	8.0	6.2	3.9	5.4	4.1	FIT
USABLE LIFE	AR	B+	505.6	229.2	2.53	1.84	8.3	6.3	4.7	6.3	6.4	FI
USIC LIFE INS CO	PR	U	--	--	--	--	--	--	--	--	--	Z
UTIC INS CO	AL	B	165.0	46.7	3.51	2.07	8.6	3.8	4.5	7.8	5.9	DI
VANTIS LIFE INS CO	CT	C+	542.5	60.5	2.83	1.41	7.6	4.6	1.9	5.5	3.1	FGIT
VARIABLE ANNUITY LIFE INS CO	TX	B	95249.3	3280.6	2.63	1.30	7.5	5.5	7.9	5.3	5.8	AIL
VENERABLE INS AND ANNTY CO	IA	C	38977.6	2087.2	0.88	0.68	4.4	4.8	1.9	5.7	2.6	ACT
VERSANT LIFE INS CO	MS	B-	5.2	4.6	2.95	2.65	9.5	8.6	5.8	9.6	4.5	ADFT
VOYA RETIREMENT INS & ANNUITY CO	CT	B+	129000.0	2232.0	2.13	1.08	7.1	5.6	7.4	6.1	5.1	IT
WASHINGTON NATIONAL INS CO	IN	D+	5828.8	361.0	1.66	0.96	6.7	5.3	7.0	6.4	2.7	A
WEA INS CORP	WI	C	786.8	163.2	1.22	0.88	6.0	3.7	1.8	5.8	3.7	FI
WEST COAST LIFE INS CO	NE	B	4377.3	403.8	2.91	1.42	7.6	4.4	7.5	5.8	4.3	AFIT
WESTERN & SOUTHERN LIFE INS CO	OH	B	12681.6	6756.1	1.36	1.24	7.4	3.4	7.7	7.0	5.7	AI
WESTERN AMERICAN LIFE INS CO	TX	C	25.1	2.6	0.67	0.61	3.9	6.9	3.0	4.7	3.4	ACDFL
WESTERN UNITED LIFE ASR CO	WA	B-	1473.0	102.0	1.55	0.81	5.8	4.0	4.8	6.0	5.0	GI
WESTERN-SOUTHERN LIFE ASR CO	OH	B	19537.6	1539.3	1.90	1.03	7.0	4.3	7.4	6.4	5.9	AI
▼ WICHITA NATIONAL LIFE INS CO	OK	D	13.4	6.1	2.18	1.93	8.4	8.8	1.9	9.2	2.3	DF
▲ WILCAC LIFE INS CO	IL	C	5581.8	238.6	2.14	1.05	7.1	4.2	5.1	5.6	4.0	AFIT
WILLIAM PENN LIFE INS CO OF NEW YORK	NY	C	1356.2	123.8	2.77	1.35	4.0	5.9	4.7	6.7	3.6	AT
WILLIAMS PROGRESSIVE LIFE & ACC I C	LA	E	11.9	1.0	0.45	0.27	0.4	1.1	5.0	5.3	0.1	CDI
WILTON REASSURANCE CO	MN	C	22558.5	1372.7	1.01	0.71	4.0	4.8	5.7	5.9	3.4	CFIT
▼ WILTON REASSURANCE LIFE CO OF NY	NY	C-	7515.8	327.6	2.09	1.00	7.0	4.2	0.9	4.9	2.9	FGILT
WINDSOR LIFE INS CO	TX	B-	3.3	3.1	2.91	2.62	9.4	8.7	6.2	9.2	3.5	ADT
WYSH L&H INSURANCE CO	AZ	B	9.5	8.7	3.75	3.37	8.0	9.5	1.6	4.8	6.3	FLT
ZALICONY HNW PPVA SERIES ACT	NY	C	149.5	20.3	2.15	1.93	8.4	9.6	2.8	10.0	4.3	ADGT
ZURICH AMERICAN LIFE INS CO	IL	C-	16900.4	163.6	1.66	0.99	6.9	7.9	1.7	7.1	3.1	FGT

See Page 27 for explanation of footnotes and Page 28 for explanation of stability factors.
Arrows denote recent upgrades ▲ or downgrades▼ (see Section VI for explanations)

56

www.weissratings.com

NET PREMIUM ($MIL)	IN-VESTED ASSETS ($MIL)	CASH	CMO & STRUCT. SECS.	OTH.INV. GRADE BONDS	NON-INV. GRADE BONDS	CMMON & PREF. STOCK	MORT IN GOOD STAND.	NON-PERF. MORT.	REAL ESTATE	OTHER INVEST-MENTS	INVEST. IN AFFIL	INSURANCE COMPANY NAME
						% OF INVESTED ASSETS IN:						
0.2	2.1	0.0	0.0	0.0	0.0	0.1	63.9	0.0	32.6	3.7	0.0	USA INS CO
0.4	30.8	3.3	0.2	92.4	2.7	0.1	0.0	0.0	0.0	1.3	0.0	USA LIFE ONE INS CO OF INDIANA
-3,771.0	25,684.5	0.0	10.9	72.5	2.5	0.7	9.0	0.0	0.0	3.7	0.4 ●	USAA LIFE INS CO
-159.2	643.5	1.9	12.8	78.7	2.1	0.0	2.8	0.0	0.0	1.0	0.0 ●	USAA LIFE INS CO OF NEW YORK
498.8	424.2	0.0	9.1	78.5	0.0	11.0	0.0	0.0	0.0	2.0	0.0 ●	USABLE LIFE
--	--	--	--	--	--	--	--	--	--	--	--	USIC LIFE INS CO
15.2	152.2 (*)	4.4	1.6	61.2	0.5	23.0	0.0	0.0	0.0	5.5	0.0 ●	UTIC INS CO
26.7	473.1 (*)	0.8	14.4	69.8	8.1	1.4	0.0	0.0	1.1	2.5	0.0 ●	VANTIS LIFE INS CO
3,931.3	48,810.5 (*)	0.0	21.1	52.5	5.3	0.3	13.7	0.0	0.0	5.5	1.2 ●	VARIABLE ANNUITY LIFE INS CO
-4,618.6	13,307.4	0.1	18.7	42.8	2.7	13.3	16.5	0.0	0.0	5.1	16.1 ●	VENERABLE INS AND ANNTY CO
0.4	4.7 (*)	1.7	0.0	88.3	0.0	0.0	0.0	0.0	0.0	0.0	0.0	VERSANT LIFE INS CO
7,984.3	31,032.5 (*)	0.2	20.5	51.3	3.4	1.3	13.6	0.0	0.2	5.4	1.7 ●	VOYA RETIREMENT INS & ANNUITY CO
731.3	5,684.4	0.7	15.0	72.3	2.5	1.6	2.1	0.0	0.8	4.5	1.1 ●	WASHINGTON NATIONAL INS CO
651.3	776.9 (*)	1.6	16.4	48.0	0.2	27.4	0.0	0.0	0.0	1.0	2.5 ●	WEA INS CORP
2.2	4,212.7	1.6	4.0	70.0	6.7	2.9	11.5	0.0	0.0	2.6	0.0 ●	WEST COAST LIFE INS CO
220.3	11,236.9	-0.2	2.6	24.5	0.9	49.5	0.5	0.0	0.2	21.3	58.5 ●	WESTERN & SOUTHERN LIFE INS CO
1.9	24.4	0.0	49.6	40.0	0.5	0.1	0.0	0.0	0.0	9.8	0.0	WESTERN AMERICAN LIFE INS CO
352.9	1,438.0 (*)	2.1	12.6	63.6	1.7	2.0	12.8	0.0	1.6	0.0	0.6 ●	WESTERN UNITED LIFE ASR CO
2,988.2	18,624.4 (*)	0.0	32.2	35.5	8.5	5.1	14.9	0.0	0.0	2.5	2.7 ●	WESTERN-SOUTHERN LIFE ASR CO
2.4	12.9	75.2	0.5	0.0	0.0	16.5	0.0	0.0	1.3	6.5	16.5	WICHITA NATIONAL LIFE INS CO
108.6	5,058.0 (*)	0.8	20.2	46.6	6.6	5.2	5.1	0.0	0.0	13.6	0.0 ●	WILCAC LIFE INS CO
71.9	1,305.0	0.0	6.2	56.1	8.4	0.0	14.3	0.0	0.0	15.0	0.0 ●	WILLIAM PENN LIFE INS CO OF NEW YORK
1.4	11.9 (*)	4.8	0.1	22.8	5.2	31.0	24.6	2.4	1.9	4.6	0.8	WILLIAMS PROGRESSIVE LIFE & ACC I C
4,356.0	17,832.7	1.3	15.9	57.6	5.8	6.6	4.6	0.0	0.0	7.8	4.9 ●	WILTON REASSURANCE CO
-4,000.0	7,005.3 (*)	0.5	5.8	71.9	5.6	1.5	6.6	0.0	0.0	5.9	0.0 ●	WILTON REASSURANCE LIFE CO OF NY
0.1	3.2	7.3	0.0	92.7	0.0	0.0	0.0	0.0	0.0	0.0	0.0	WINDSOR LIFE INS CO
0.0	9.4 (*)	12.4	0.0	71.0	0.0	0.0	0.0	0.0	0.0	0.0	0.0	WYSH L&H INSURANCE CO
29.7	24.4	0.0	0.0	92.1	0.0	0.0	0.0	0.0	0.0	7.9	0.0	ZALICONY HNW PPVA SERIES ACT
862.8	1,240.7 (*)	0.3	13.4	65.0	0.4	1.6	0.0	0.0	0.0	14.2	1.6 ●	ZURICH AMERICAN LIFE INS CO

● Bullets denote a more detailed analysis is available in Section II.
(*) Asset category percentages do not add up to 100%

Section II

Analysis of Largest Companies

A summary analysis of those

U.S. Life and Annuity Insurers

with capital in excess of $25 million.

Companies are listed in alphabetical order

Section II Contents

This section contains rating factors, historical data and general information on each of the largest life and health insurers. Companies with capital and surplus of less than $25 million, Blue Cross Blue Shield plans and companies lacking year-end data do not appear in this section. You can find information on these firms in Section I.

1. Safety Rating

The current rating appears to the right of the company name. Our ratings are designed to distinguish levels of insolvency risk and are measured on a scale from A (Excellent) to F (Failed). Highly rated companies are, in our opinion, less likely to experience financial difficulties than lower rated firms. See *About Weiss Safety Ratings* for more information.

2. Major Rating Factors

A synopsis of the key indexes and sub-factors that have most influenced the rating of a particular insurer. Items are presented in the approximate order of their importance to the rating. There may be additional factors which have influenced the rating but do not appear due to space limitations or confidentiality agreements with insurers.

3. Other Rating Factors

A summary of those Weiss Ratings indexes that were not included as Major Rating Factors, but nevertheless, may have had some impact on the final grade.

4. Principal Business

The major types of policies written by an insurer along with the percentages for each line in relation to the entire book of business, including direct premium and deposit funds (from Exhibit 1 Part 1 of the annual statutory statement). Lines of business written by life, health and annuity insurers are individual life, individual health, individual annuities, group life, group health, group retirement contracts, credit life, credit health and reinsurance. The data used to calculate these amounts are the latest available from the National Association of Insurance Commissioners.

Note: Percentages contained in this column may not agree with similar figures displayed in Section III which are based on net premium after reinsurance.

5. Principal Investments

The major investments in an insurer's portfolio. These include non CMO Bonds (debt obligations which are rated Class 1 through Class 6 based on risk of default), CMOs and other structured securities, which consist primarily of mortgage-backed bonds, real estate, mortgages in good standing, nonperforming mortgages, common and preferred stocks, policy loans (which are loans given to policyholders), miscellaneous investments and cash.

6.	**Investments in Affiliates**	The percentage of bonds, common and preferred stocks and other financial instruments an insurer has invested with affiliated companies. This is not a subcategory of "Principal Investments."
7.	**Group Affiliation**	The name of the group of companies to which a particular insurer belongs.
8.	**Licensed in**	List of the states in which an insurer is licensed to conduct business.
9.	**Commenced Business**	The date when the company first opened for business.
10.	**Address**	The address of an insurer's corporate headquarters. This location may differ from the company's state of domicile.
11.	**Phone**	The telephone number of an insurer's corporate headquarters.
12.	**Domicile State**	The state that has primary regulatory responsibility for this company. You do not have to live in the domicile state to do business with this firm, provided it is registered to do business in your state.
13.	**NAIC Code**	The identification number assigned to an insurer by the National Association of Insurance Commissioners (NAIC).
14.	**Historical Data**	Five years of background data for Weiss Safety Rating, risk-adjusted capital ratios (moderate and severe loss scenarios), total assets, capital (including capital stock and retained earnings), net premium and net income. See the following page for more details on how to read the historical data table.
15.	**Customized Graph (or Table)**	A graph or table depicting one of the company's major strengths or weaknesses. See the following page for more details.

How to Read the Historical Data Table

Data Date: The quarterly or annual date of the financial statements that provide the source of the data.	**RACR#1:** Ratio of the capital resources an insurer currently has to the resources that would be needed to deal with a modest loss scenario.	**Total Assets:** Total admitted assets in millions of dollars, including investments and other business assets.	**Net Premiums:** The total volume of premium dollars, in millions, retained by an insurer. This figure is equal to direct premiums written plus deposit funds, and reinsurance assumed, less reinsurance ceded.

Data Date	Safety Rating	RACR #1	RACR #2	Total Assets ($mil)	Capital ($mil)	Net Premium ($mil)	Net Income ($mil)
2021	B	8.78	6.44	193.1	80.0	59.0	7.5
2020	B	4.43	2.74	173.5	50.1	53.2	6.1
2019	B	6.33	4.12	176.9	78.6	64.3	4.0
2018	B	6.41	4.26	182.0	81.4	69.8	5.5
2017	B	5.81	3.81	212.5	85.0	76.8	5.1

Safety Rating: Our opinion of the financial risk of an insurer based on data from that time period.	**RACR #2:** Ratio of the capital resources an insurer currently has to the resources that would be needed to deal with a severe loss scenario.	**Capital:** The equity or net worth of an insurer in millions of dollars.	**Net Income:** Profit gained on operations and investments, after expenses and taxes.

Row Descriptions:

Row 1 contains the most recent quarterly data as filed with state regulators and is presented on a year-to-date basis. For example, the figure for third quarter premiums includes premiums received through the third quarter. Row 2 consists of data from the same quarter of the prior year. Compare current quarterly results to those of a year ago.

Row 3 contains data from the most recent annual statutory filing. **Rows 4-7** include data from year-end statements going back four years from the most recent annual filing. Compare current year-end results to those of the previous four years. With the exception of Total Assets and Capital, quarterly data are not comparable with annual data.

Customized Graphs

In the lower right-hand corner of each company section, a customized graph or text block highlights a key factor affecting that company's financial strength. One of thirteen types of information is found, identified by one of the following headings:

Adverse Trends in Operations lists changes in key balance sheet and income statement items which may be leading indicators of deteriorating business performance.

Exposure to Withdrawals Without Penalty answers the question: For each dollar of capital and surplus, how much does the company have in annuity and deposit funds that can be withdrawn by policyholders with minimal or no penalty? The figures do not include the effects of reinsurance or funds subject to withdrawals from cash value life insurance policies.

Group Ratings shows the group name, a composite Weiss Safety Rating for the group, and a list of the largest members with their ratings. The composite Safety Rating is made up of the weighted average, by assets, of the individual ratings of each company in the group (including life/health companies, property/casualty companies or HMOs) plus a factor for the financial strength of the holding company, where applicable.

High Risk Assets as a % of Capital answers the question: For each dollar of capital and surplus, how much does the company have in junk bonds, nonperforming mortgages and repossessed real estate? Accumulations in the Asset Valuation Reserve or AVR, which provide some protection against investment losses, have not been included in the figure for capital. These figures are based on year-end data.

Investment Income Compared to Needs of Reserves answers the question: Is the company earning enough investment income to meet the expectations of actuaries when they priced their policies and set reserve levels? According to state insurance regulators, it would be "unusual" if an insurer were to have less than $1.25 in actual investment income for each dollar of investment income that it projected in its actuarial forecasts. This provides an excess margin of at least 25 cents on the dollar to cover any unexpected decline in income or increase in claims. This graph shows whether or not the company is maintaining the appropriate 25% margin and is based on year-end data.

Junk Bonds as a % of Capital answers the question: For each dollar of capital and surplus, how much does the company have in junk bonds? In addition, it shows a breakdown of the junk bond portfolio by bond rating – BB, B, CCC or in default. Accumulations in the Asset Valuation Reserve or AVR, which provide some protection against investment losses, have not been included in the figure for capital. These figures are based on year-end data.

Net Income History plots operating gains and losses over the most recent five-year period.

Policy Leverage answers the question: To what degree is this insurer capable of handling an unexpected spike in claims? Low leverage indicates low exposure; high leverage is high exposure.

Premium Growth History depicts the change in the insurer's net premiums written. Such changes may be the result of issuing more policies or changes in reinsurance arrangements. In either case, growth rates above 20% per year are considered excessive. "Standard" growth is under 20%; "shrinkage" refers to net declines.

Rating Indexes illustrate the score and range – strong, good, fair or weak – on each of the five Weiss Ratings indexes. The indexes are **capitalization**, **stability**, **investment safety**, **profitability** and **liquidity**.

Risk-Adjusted Capital Ratio #1 answers the question: In each of the past five years, does the insurer have sufficient capital to cover potential losses in its investments and business operations in a *moderate* loss scenario?

Risk-Adjusted Capital Ratio #2 answers the question: In each of the past five years, does the insurer have sufficient capital to cover potential losses in its investments and business operations in a *severe* loss scenario?

Risk-Adjusted Capital Ratios answers these questions for both a moderate loss scenario (RACR #1 shown by the dark bar) and a severe loss scenario (RACR #2, light bar).

4 EVER LIFE INS CO
B **Good**

Major Rating Factors: Good overall results on stability tests (5.2 on a scale of 0 to 10). Stability strengths include good operational trends and good risk diversification. Good quality investment portfolio (6.5) despite mixed results such as: no exposure to mortgages and substantial holdings of BBB bonds but small junk bond holdings. Good liquidity (6.7) with sufficient resources to handle a spike in claims.

Other Rating Factors: Fair profitability (3.9). Strong capitalization (10.0) based on excellent risk adjusted capital (severe loss scenario).

Principal Business: Group health insurance (61%), reinsurance (36%), and group life insurance (2%).

Principal Investments: NonCMO investment grade bonds (45%), CMOs and structured securities (24%), cash (12%), common & preferred stock (6%), and noninv. grade bonds (6%).

Investments in Affiliates: None

Group Affiliation: BCS Financial Corp

Licensed in: All states, the District of Columbia and Puerto Rico

Commenced Business: November 1949

Address: 2 Mid America Plaza Suite 200, Oakbrook Terrace, IL 60181

Phone: (630) 472-7700 **Domicile State:** IL **NAIC Code:** 80985

Data Date	Rating	RACR #1	RACR #2	Total Assets ($mil)	Capital ($mil)	Net Premium ($mil)	Net Income ($mil)
2021	B	8.78	6.44	193.1	80.0	59.0	7.5
2020	B	4.43	2.74	173.1	50.1	53.2	6.1
2019	B	6.33	4.12	176.9	78.6	64.3	4.0
2018	B	6.41	4.26	182.0	81.4	69.8	5.5
2017	B	5.81	3.83	212.5	85.0	76.8	5.1

Adverse Trends in Operations

Decrease in asset base during 2020 (2%)
Decrease in premium volume from 2019 to 2020 (17%)
Decrease in capital during 2020 (36%)
Decrease in premium volume from 2017 to 2018 (9%)
Decrease in asset base during 2018 (14%)

AAA LIFE INS CO
B **Good**

Major Rating Factors: Good quality investment portfolio (6.1 on a scale of 0 to 10) despite mixed results such as: large holdings of BBB rated bonds but moderate junk bond exposure. Good overall profitability (5.3) although investment income, in comparison to reserve requirements, is below regulatory standards. Good liquidity (6.4).

Other Rating Factors: Good overall results on stability tests (6.1) excellent operational trends and excellent risk diversification. Strong capitalization (8.6) based on excellent risk adjusted capital (severe loss scenario).

Principal Business: Individual life insurance (59%), group life insurance (31%), group health insurance (6%), and individual annuities (3%).

Principal Investments: NonCMO investment grade bonds (67%), CMOs and structured securities (20%), noninv. grade bonds (9%), common & preferred stock (1%), and policy loans (1%).

Investments in Affiliates: 1%

Group Affiliation: ACLI Acquisition Co

Licensed in: All states except NY, PR

Commenced Business: July 1969

Address: 17900 N Laurel Park Drive, Livonia, MI 48152

Phone: (734) 779-2600 **Domicile State:** MI **NAIC Code:** 71854

Data Date	Rating	RACR #1	RACR #2	Total Assets ($mil)	Capital ($mil)	Net Premium ($mil)	Net Income ($mil)
2021	B	3.73	2.04	764.0	202.0	131.8	6.4
2020	B	3.56	2.01	755.6	199.4	129.5	17.5
2019	B	3.53	1.96	709.9	184.4	125.3	17.8
2018	B	3.34	1.89	678.2	172.5	120.3	18.2
2017	B	3.08	1.77	652.0	155.4	116.1	12.7

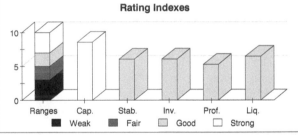

Rating Indexes

ACCORDIA LIFE & ANNUITY CO
C+ **Fair**

Major Rating Factors: Fair quality investment portfolio (4.8 on a scale of 0 to 10). Fair overall results on stability tests (4.7). Good capitalization (5.3) based on good risk adjusted capital (severe loss scenario). Capital levels have been relatively consistent over the last five years.

Other Rating Factors: Good liquidity (5.8). Weak profitability (2.5).

Principal Business: Individual life insurance (93%) and reinsurance (7%).

Principal Investments: NonCMO investment grade bonds (50%), CMOs and structured securities (25%), mortgages in good standing (9%), common & preferred stock (5%), and misc. investments (9%).

Investments in Affiliates: 7%

Group Affiliation: Global Atlantic Financial Group

Licensed in: All states except NY, PR

Commenced Business: September 1967

Address: 215 10TH STREET SUITE 1100, DES MOINES, IA 50309

Phone: (855) 887-4487 **Domicile State:** IA **NAIC Code:** 62200

Data Date	Rating	RACR #1	RACR #2	Total Assets ($mil)	Capital ($mil)	Net Premium ($mil)	Net Income ($mil)
2021	C+	1.15	0.79	12,709.0	952.6	519.4	6.4
2020	C+	1.22	0.84	11,882.1	849.6	1,421.0	-47.3
2019	C	1.17	0.81	10,071.7	736.3	547.7	48.9
2018	C	1.20	0.83	9,098.7	765.6	329.8	23.3
2017	C	1.18	0.81	8,916.2	684.9	380.8	-114.3

Rating Indexes

ADVANCE INS CO OF KANSAS *   B+   Good

Major Rating Factors: Good overall results on stability tests (6.3 on a scale of 0 to 10) despite negative cash flow from operations for 2021. Other stability subfactors include excellent operational trends and excellent risk diversification. Fair quality investment portfolio (3.9). Strong capitalization (9.5) based on excellent risk adjusted capital (severe loss scenario).

Other Rating Factors: Excellent profitability (8.2) with operating gains in each of the last five years. Excellent liquidity (7.3).

Principal Business: Group life insurance (54%), group health insurance (35%), and individual life insurance (11%).

Principal Investments: Common & preferred stock (39%), CMOs and structured securities (30%), and nonCMO investment grade bonds (27%).

Investments in Affiliates: 3%

Group Affiliation: Blue Cross Blue Shield Kansas

Licensed in: KS

Commenced Business: July 2004

Address: 1133 SW Topeka Blvd, Topeka, KS 66629-0001

Phone: (785) 273-9804 **Domicile State:** KS **NAIC Code:** 12143

Data Date	Rating	RACR #1	RACR #2	Total Assets ($mil)	Capital ($mil)	Net Premium ($mil)	Net Income ($mil)
2021	B+	4.08	2.66	78.4	63.5	11.6	5.4
2020	B+	4.13	2.69	71.9	58.6	11.3	1.4
2019	B+	4.11	2.70	65.7	55.3	11.1	2.9
2018	B+	4.09	2.69	58.3	49.9	10.9	1.8
2017	B+	3.95	2.59	59.7	49.7	10.9	2.7

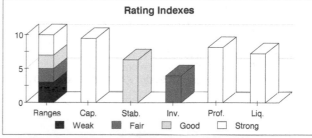

Rating Indexes

AETNA HEALTH & LIFE INS CO   C   Fair

Major Rating Factors: Fair current capitalization (4.1 on a scale of 0 to 10) based on mixed results -- excessive policy leverage mitigated by good risk adjusted capital (severe loss scenario) reflecting some improvement over results in 2020. Fair overall results on stability tests (3.5) including fair risk adjusted capital in prior years. Good quality investment portfolio (6.5).

Other Rating Factors: Weak profitability (2.8). Weak liquidity (1.5).

Principal Business: Individual health insurance (98%) and group health insurance (2%).

Principal Investments: NonCMO investment grade bonds (57%), CMOs and structured securities (32%), and noninv. grade bonds (8%).

Investments in Affiliates: 4%

Group Affiliation: Aetna Inc

Licensed in: All states except PR

Commenced Business: October 1971

Address: 151 FARMINGTON AVENUE, HARTFORD, CT 6156

Phone: (800) 872-3862 **Domicile State:** CT **NAIC Code:** 78700

Data Date	Rating	RACR #1	RACR #2	Total Assets ($mil)	Capital ($mil)	Net Premium ($mil)	Net Income ($mil)
2021	C	0.95	0.75	656.5	318.9	2,041.6	94.8
2020	C-	0.68	0.55	516.7	206.3	1,852.9	58.6
2019	C-	0.95	0.73	134.5	53.0	442.8	-62.4
2018	C	2.11	1.59	185.2	106.5	374.0	-13.0
2017	C+	5.60	3.55	388.4	307.3	-1,183.1	418.9

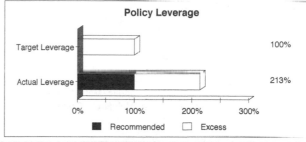

Policy Leverage

AETNA LIFE INS CO   B   Good

Major Rating Factors: Good current capitalization (5.8 on a scale of 0 to 10) based on mixed results -- excessive policy leverage mitigated by excellent risk adjusted capital (severe loss scenario) reflecting improvement over results in 2017. Good quality investment portfolio (6.2) despite mixed results such as: minimal exposure to mortgages and large holdings of BBB rated bonds but small junk bond holdings. Good liquidity (5.3).

Other Rating Factors: Good overall results on stability tests (5.4) excellent operational trends and excellent risk diversification. Excellent profitability (9.5) with operating gains in each of the last five years.

Principal Business: Individual health insurance (57%), group health insurance (42%), and reinsurance (1%).

Principal Investments: NonCMO investment grade bonds (50%), CMOs and structured securities (15%), noninv. grade bonds (7%), common & preferred stock (6%), and misc. investments (15%).

Investments in Affiliates: 6%

Group Affiliation: Aetna Inc

Licensed in: All states, the District of Columbia and Puerto Rico

Commenced Business: December 1850

Address: 151 FARMINGTON AVENUE, HARTFORD, CT 6156

Phone: (800) 872-3862 **Domicile State:** CT **NAIC Code:** 60054

Data Date	Rating	RACR #1	RACR #2	Total Assets ($mil)	Capital ($mil)	Net Premium ($mil)	Net Income ($mil)
2021	B	1.34	1.06	25,501.2	6,134.9	26,542.8	2,034.3
2020	B	1.21	0.96	24,057.3	5,163.6	23,885.1	2,247.5
2019	B	1.13	0.87	22,016.5	3,852.5	23,423.9	1,805.9
2018	B	1.28	0.97	20,230.7	3,697.1	19,837.6	1,933.0
2017	B	1.12	0.84	19,894.8	2,904.0	17,984.7	1,339.4

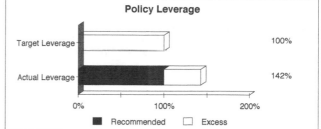

Policy Leverage

ALFA LIFE INS CORP   C   Fair

Major Rating Factors: Fair quality investment portfolio (4.0 on a scale of 0 to 10) with large holdings of BBB rated bonds in addition to junk bond exposure equal to 51% of capital. Fair overall results on stability tests (4.2). Good liquidity (5.7) with sufficient resources to handle a spike in claims as well as a significant increase in policy surrenders.

Other Rating Factors: Weak profitability (1.9) with operating losses during 2021. Strong capitalization (7.2) based on excellent risk adjusted capital (severe loss scenario).

Principal Business: Individual life insurance (95%), individual annuities (4%), and group life insurance (1%).

Principal Investments: NonCMO investment grade bonds (46%), CMOs and structured securities (15%), common & preferred stock (12%), noninv. grade bonds (9%), and policy loans (5%).

Investments in Affiliates: None
Group Affiliation: Alfa Ins Group
Licensed in: AL, AR, FL, GA, LA, MS, MO, NC, SC, TN, VA
Commenced Business: March 1955
Address: 2108 East South Boulevard, Montgomery, AL 36116
Phone: (334) 288-3900 **Domicile State:** AL **NAIC Code:** 79049

Data Date	Rating	RACR #1	RACR #2	Total Assets ($mil)	Capital ($mil)	Net Premium ($mil)	Net Income ($mil)
2021	C	2.04	1.10	1,642.9	227.4	170.4	-30.3
2020	B-	2.13	1.16	1,581.1	235.4	163.0	7.4
2019	B-	2.70	1.50	1,543.9	269.8	159.3	8.3
2018	B-	N/A	N/A	1,462.1	257.3	155.5	10.9
2017	B-	3.02	1.69	1,430.2	269.0	151.8	16.5

Rating Indexes

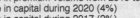

Ranges: Weak/Fair/Good/Strong ranges; Cap., Stab., Inv., Prof., Liq.

■ Weak ■ Fair ▨ Good □ Strong

ALLIANZ LIFE INS CO OF NORTH AMERICA   B-   Good

Major Rating Factors: Good quality investment portfolio (6.7 on a scale of 0 to 10) despite large holdings of BBB rated bonds in addition to moderate junk bond exposure. Exposure to mortgages is significant, but the mortgage default rate has been low. Good liquidity (5.3) with sufficient resources to handle a spike in claims as well as a significant increase in policy surrenders. Good overall results on stability tests (5.2) despite negative cash flow from operations for 2021 and excessive premium growth excellent operational trends and excellent risk diversification.

Other Rating Factors: Weak profitability (2.8). Strong capitalization (8.8) based on excellent risk adjusted capital (severe loss scenario).

Principal Business: Individual annuities (89%), individual life insurance (10%), and individual health insurance (1%).

Principal Investments: NonCMO investment grade bonds (60%), CMOs and structured securities (15%), mortgages in good standing (14%), noninv. grade bonds (2%), and common & preferred stock (1%).

Investments in Affiliates: 1%
Group Affiliation: Allianz Ins Group
Licensed in: All states except NY
Commenced Business: December 1979
Address: 5701 Golden Hills Drive, Minneapolis, MN 55416-1297
Phone: (800) 328-5601 **Domicile State:** MN **NAIC Code:** 90611

Data Date	Rating	RACR #1	RACR #2	Total Assets ($mil)	Capital ($mil)	Net Premium ($mil)	Net Income ($mil)
2021	B-	4.20	2.23	174,000	10,704.7	14,125.2	1,290.6
2020	B-	3.13	1.66	173,000	7,660.4	10,346.2	739.1
2019	B-	3.41	1.85	158,000	7,953.6	12,805.0	542.8
2018	C	2.87	1.58	142,000	6,575.5	11,925.2	769.6
2017	C	2.06	1.16	138,000	6,011.2	9,982.6	805.2

Adverse Trends in Operations

Decrease in premium volume from 2019 to 2020 (19%)
Decrease in capital during 2020 (4%)
Decrease in capital during 2017 (2%)
Decrease in premium volume from 2016 to 2017 (21%)

ALLIANZ LIFE INS CO OF NY   B-   Good

Major Rating Factors: Good overall results on stability tests (5.3 on a scale of 0 to 10) despite excessive premium growth. Other stability subfactors include excellent operational trends and excellent risk diversification. Fair profitability (3.0) with investment income below regulatory standards in relation to interest assumptions of reserves. Strong capitalization (9.2) based on excellent risk adjusted capital (severe loss scenario).

Other Rating Factors: High quality investment portfolio (7.6). Excellent liquidity (9.2).

Principal Business: Individual annuities (99%).

Principal Investments: NonCMO investment grade bonds (74%), CMOs and structured securities (20%), and noninv. grade bonds (1%).

Investments in Affiliates: None
Group Affiliation: Allianz Ins Group
Licensed in: CT, DC, IL, MN, MO, NY, ND
Commenced Business: April 1984
Address: 28 Liberty Street 38th Floor, New York, NY 10019-7585
Phone: (800) 328-5600 **Domicile State:** NY **NAIC Code:** 64190

Data Date	Rating	RACR #1	RACR #2	Total Assets ($mil)	Capital ($mil)	Net Premium ($mil)	Net Income ($mil)
2021	B-	3.27	2.48	5,071.6	163.0	688.6	5.6
2020	B+	3.49	2.59	4,377.6	156.0	428.5	-15.5
2019	B+	4.20	3.11	3,846.4	171.3	375.0	-42.8
2018	B+	6.04	4.29	3,340.5	223.7	301.7	47.9
2017	A	4.63	2.69	3,396.4	173.1	268.0	-5.3

Adverse Trends in Operations

Decrease in capital during 2020 (9%)
Decrease in capital during 2019 (23%)
Decrease in asset base during 2018 (2%)
Decrease in capital during 2017 (14%)
Increase in policy surrenders from 2016 to 2017 (45%)

ALLSTATE LIFE INS CO   B   Good

Major Rating Factors: Good quality investment portfolio (5.1 on a scale of 0 to 10) despite large holdings of BBB rated bonds in addition to significant exposure to junk bonds. Exposure to mortgages is significant, but the mortgage default rate has been low. Good liquidity (6.8) with sufficient resources to handle a spike in claims as well as a significant increase in policy surrenders. Fair profitability (3.9).

Other Rating Factors: Fair overall results on stability tests (4.4) including negative cash flow from operations for 2021. Strong overall capitalization (8.0) based on mixed results -- excessive policy leverage mitigated by excellent risk adjusted capital (severe loss scenario).

Principal Business: Reinsurance (71%), individual life insurance (26%), group life insurance (1%), individual annuities (1%), and group health insurance (1%).

Principal Investments: NonCMO investment grade bonds (60%), mortgages in good standing (12%), CMOs and structured securities (12%), noninv. grade bonds (6%), and policy loans (2%).

Investments in Affiliates: 1%

Group Affiliation: Allstate Group

Licensed in: All states except NY

Commenced Business: September 1957

Address: 3075 SANDERS ROAD SUITE I2W, NORTHBROOK, IL 60062

Phone: (847) 402-5000 **Domicile State:** IL **NAIC Code:** 60186

Data Date	Rating	RACR #1	RACR #2	Total Assets ($mil)	Capital ($mil)	Net Premium ($mil)	Net Income ($mil)
2021	B	3.29	1.67	28,147.6	2,601.2	-5,889.4	1,246.9
2020	B	2.43	1.43	30,842.9	3,926.8	1,483.8	57.0
2019	B	2.31	1.38	30,166.4	3,816.9	924.9	486.5
2018	B	2.03	1.22	30,130.1	3,471.2	958.4	342.7
2017	B	2.05	1.21	31,567.3	3,408.1	751.1	846.7

Junk Bonds as a % of Capital

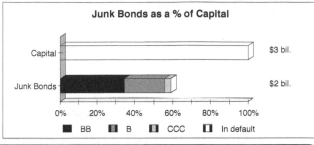

AMALGAMATED LIFE INS CO   B   Good

Major Rating Factors: Good liquidity (5.9 on a scale of 0 to 10) with sufficient resources to handle a spike in claims. Good overall results on stability tests (5.7) despite negative cash flow from operations for 2021. Other stability subfactors include good operational trends and excellent risk diversification. Fair profitability (4.3) with operating losses during 2021. Return on equity has been low, averaging 4.4%.

Other Rating Factors: Strong capitalization (9.5) based on excellent risk adjusted capital (severe loss scenario). High quality investment portfolio (8.2).

Principal Business: Group life insurance (37%), group health insurance (31%), reinsurance (25%), and individual health insurance (7%).

Principal Investments: NonCMO investment grade bonds (74%) and CMOs and structured securities (23%).

Investments in Affiliates: None

Group Affiliation: National Retirement Fund

Licensed in: All states except PR

Commenced Business: February 1944

Address: 333 WESTCHESTER AVENUE, WHITE PLAINS, NY 10604

Phone: (914) 367-5275 **Domicile State:** NY **NAIC Code:** 60216

Data Date	Rating	RACR #1	RACR #2	Total Assets ($mil)	Capital ($mil)	Net Premium ($mil)	Net Income ($mil)
2021	B	3.49	2.67	144.3	72.6	137.1	-9.1
2020	A	3.98	3.02	155.6	80.3	116.3	4.9
2019	A	4.19	3.18	143.0	75.6	99.7	9.2
2018	A	3.96	3.00	146.5	66.8	96.5	4.9
2017	A	4.24	3.24	127.5	61.7	82.7	5.5

Adverse Trends in Operations

Decrease in asset base during 2019 (2%)
Increase in policy surrenders from 2018 to 2019 (35%)

AMERICAN BANKERS LIFE ASR CO OF FL   B   Good

Major Rating Factors: Good quality investment portfolio (6.1 on a scale of 0 to 10) despite mixed results such as: minimal exposure to mortgages and substantial holdings of BBB bonds but minimal holdings in junk bonds. Fair overall results on stability tests (4.9) including negative cash flow from operations for 2021. Strong capitalization (9.9) based on excellent risk adjusted capital (severe loss scenario).

Other Rating Factors: Excellent profitability (7.9) with operating gains in each of the last five years. Excellent liquidity (7.3).

Principal Business: Credit health insurance (48%), credit life insurance (46%), reinsurance (2%), group health insurance (2%), and individual life insurance (2%).

Principal Investments: NonCMO investment grade bonds (59%), real estate (19%), CMOs and structured securities (7%), cash (3%), and misc. investments (7%).

Investments in Affiliates: None

Group Affiliation: Assurant Inc

Licensed in: All states except NY

Commenced Business: April 1952

Address: 11222 QUAIL ROOST DRIVE, MIAMI, FL 33157-6596

Phone: (305) 253-2244 **Domicile State:** FL **NAIC Code:** 60275

Data Date	Rating	RACR #1	RACR #2	Total Assets ($mil)	Capital ($mil)	Net Premium ($mil)	Net Income ($mil)
2021	B	5.10	2.91	267.8	53.0	93.3	19.0
2020	B	5.10	2.87	341.9	54.9	96.6	21.9
2019	B	4.68	2.71	353.4	52.8	103.2	20.6
2018	C+	4.75	2.72	338.4	47.9	95.1	23.0
2017	C+	5.57	3.05	364.0	53.0	79.1	23.8

Rating Indexes

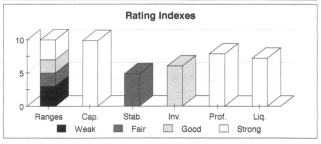

AMERICAN BENEFIT LIFE INS CO

B Good

Major Rating Factors: Good overall results on stability tests (5.7 on a scale of 0 to 10). Stability strengths include excellent operational trends and good risk diversification. Good quality investment portfolio (5.0) despite significant exposure to mortgages . Mortgage default rate has been low. large holdings of BBB rated bonds in addition to small junk bond holdings. Good liquidity (6.2).

Other Rating Factors: Strong capitalization (7.8) based on excellent risk adjusted capital (severe loss scenario). Excellent profitability (9.1) with operating gains in each of the last five years.

Principal Business: Reinsurance (60%), individual life insurance (35%), and individual annuities (4%).

Principal Investments: NonCMO investment grade bonds (54%), mortgages in good standing (24%), CMOs and structured securities (13%), common & preferred stock (3%), and misc. investments (6%).

Investments in Affiliates: 3%

Group Affiliation: Liberty Life Group Trust

Licensed in: AL, AZ, AR, CO, DC, DE, FL, GA, IL, IN, IA, KS, KY, LA, MD, MI, MN, MS, MO, MT, NE, NH, NJ, NM, NC, ND, OH, OK, OR, PA, SC, SD, TN, TX, UT, VT, VA, WV, WI

Commenced Business: May 1909

Address: 1605 LBJ Freeway Suite 710, Dallas, TX 75234

Phone: (469) 522-4400 **Domicile State:** OK **NAIC Code:** 66001

Data Date	Rating	RACR #1	RACR #2	Total Assets ($mil)	Capital ($mil)	Net Premium ($mil)	Net Income ($mil)
2021	B	2.46	1.55	238.9	32.7	34.8	7.7
2020	B-	2.42	1.52	222.7	29.3	32.7	9.3
2019	C	3.12	1.74	202.9	25.7	33.4	3.1
2018	C	3.04	1.79	187.0	24.7	27.9	1.9
2017	C	2.62	1.68	141.1	21.8	26.5	2.3

Adverse Trends in Operations

Decrease in premium volume from 2019 to 2020 (2%)
Increase in policy surrenders from 2018 to 2019 (109%)

AMERICAN CONTINENTAL INS CO *

B+ Good

Major Rating Factors: Good overall results on stability tests (6.8 on a scale of 0 to 10). Stability strengths include excellent operational trends and excellent risk diversification. Good liquidity (6.7) with sufficient resources to handle a spike in claims as well as a significant increase in policy surrenders. Strong capitalization (10.0) based on excellent risk adjusted capital (severe loss scenario).

Other Rating Factors: High quality investment portfolio (7.7). Excellent profitability (7.2) despite modest operating losses during 2017 and 2018.

Principal Business: Individual health insurance (91%) and individual life insurance (9%).

Principal Investments: NonCMO investment grade bonds (71%), CMOs and structured securities (27%), policy loans (1%), noninv. grade bonds (1%), and mortgages in good standing (1%).

Investments in Affiliates: None

Group Affiliation: Aetna Inc

Licensed in: AL, AZ, AR, CO, FL, GA, IL, IN, IA, KS, KY, LA, MI, MN, MS, MO, MT, NE, NV, NM, NC, ND, OH, OK, PA, SC, SD, TN, TX, UT, VA, WV, WI, WY

Commenced Business: September 2005

Address: 800 CRESENT CENTRE DR STE 200, FRANKLIN, TN 37064

Phone: (800) 264-4000 **Domicile State:** TN **NAIC Code:** 12321

Data Date	Rating	RACR #1	RACR #2	Total Assets ($mil)	Capital ($mil)	Net Premium ($mil)	Net Income ($mil)
2021	B+	4.11	2.98	439.4	235.4	423.3	59.3
2020	B	3.04	2.24	386.3	182.5	458.8	35.1
2019	C	2.02	1.51	299.3	124.8	485.4	0.0
2018	C	1.86	1.39	285.8	118.3	499.4	-5.1
2017	B-	1.82	1.37	276.9	115.2	506.3	-15.0

Rating Indexes

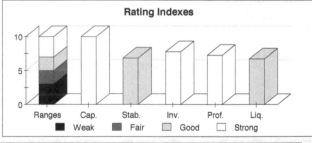

Ranges | Cap. | Stab. | Inv. | Prof. | Liq.
■ Weak ■ Fair ☐ Good ☐ Strong

AMERICAN EQUITY INVEST LIFE INS CO

C+ Fair

Major Rating Factors: Fair liquidity (4.8 on a scale of 0 to 10) as cash from operations and sale of marketable assets may not be adequate to cover a spike in claims or a run on policy withdrawals. Fair overall results on stability tests (4.4) including negative cash flow from operations for 2021. Good quality investment portfolio (5.6).

Other Rating Factors: Weak profitability (2.4) with operating losses during 2021. Strong overall capitalization (7.4) based on mixed results -- excessive policy leverage mitigated by excellent risk adjusted capital (severe loss scenario).

Principal Business: Individual annuities (61%) and reinsurance (39%).

Principal Investments: NonCMO investment grade bonds (60%), CMOs and structured securities (19%), mortgages in good standing (10%), noninv. grade bonds (2%), and common & preferred stock (1%).

Investments in Affiliates: 1%

Group Affiliation: American Equity Investment Group

Licensed in: All states except NY, PR

Commenced Business: January 1981

Address: 6000 WESTOWN PARKWAY, WEST DES MOINES, IA 50266-5921

Phone: (888) 222-1234 **Domicile State:** IA **NAIC Code:** 92738

Data Date	Rating	RACR #1	RACR #2	Total Assets ($mil)	Capital ($mil)	Net Premium ($mil)	Net Income ($mil)
2021	C+	2.28	1.26	60,422.4	4,078.5	-4,146.6	-863.8
2020	B-	2.34	1.25	57,643.5	3,728.7	2,221.4	-34.5
2019	B-	2.29	1.21	57,673.2	3,490.2	4,015.8	143.3
2018	B-	2.23	1.16	53,705.2	3,251.9	3,520.8	210.0
2017	B-	2.32	1.23	51,891.7	3,005.7	3,393.5	375.9

Rating Indexes

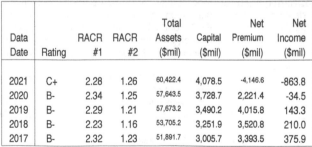

Ranges | Cap. | Stab. | Inv. | Prof. | Liq.
■ Weak ■ Fair ☐ Good ☐ Strong

AMERICAN EQUITY INVESTMENT LIFE NY   B   Good

Major Rating Factors: Good quality investment portfolio (6.7 on a scale of 0 to 10) despite mixed results such as: no exposure to mortgages and large holdings of BBB rated bonds but minimal holdings in junk bonds. Good overall profitability (6.2). Excellent expense controls. Return on equity has been fair, averaging 5.8%. Good liquidity (6.5).

Other Rating Factors: Fair overall results on stability tests (4.5) including fair financial strength of affiliated American Equity Investment Group and negative cash flow from operations for 2021. Strong capitalization (10.0) based on excellent risk adjusted capital (severe loss scenario).

Principal Business: Individual annuities (100%).

Principal Investments: NonCMO investment grade bonds (74%), CMOs and structured securities (18%), and noninv. grade bonds (3%).

Investments in Affiliates: None

Group Affiliation: American Equity Investment Group

Licensed in: NY

Commenced Business: July 2001

Address: 1979 MARCUS AVENUE STE 210, LAKE SUCCESS, NY 11042

Phone: (866) 233-6660 **Domicile State:** NY **NAIC Code:** 11135

Data Date	Rating	RACR #1	RACR #2	Total Assets ($mil)	Capital ($mil)	Net Premium ($mil)	Net Income ($mil)
2021	B	4.65	3.60	170.4	43.6	0.0	1.5
2020	B	4.46	3.16	181.3	42.2	0.3	1.9
2019	B	4.24	2.85	188.6	40.3	1.6	2.8
2018	B	3.93	2.44	196.2	37.4	0.2	2.4
2017	B-	3.61	2.20	208.5	34.6	0.2	3.2

Rating Indexes

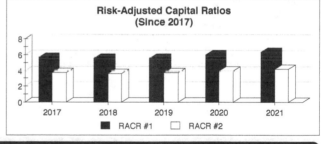

AMERICAN FAMILY LIFE ASR CO OF NY *   A   Excellent

Major Rating Factors: Strong capitalization (10.0 on a scale of 0 to 10) based on excellent risk adjusted capital (severe loss scenario). Furthermore, this high level of risk adjusted capital has been consistently maintained over the last five years. High quality investment portfolio (7.9) despite no exposure to mortgages and large holdings of BBB rated bonds but minimal holdings in junk bonds. Excellent profitability (9.3) with operating gains in each of the last five years.

Other Rating Factors: Excellent liquidity (7.6). Excellent overall results on stability tests (7.7) excellent operational trends and excellent risk diversification.

Principal Business: Individual health insurance (91%), individual life insurance (4%), group health insurance (3%), and reinsurance (2%).

Principal Investments: NonCMO investment grade bonds (92%), noninv. grade bonds (2%), and cash (2%).

Investments in Affiliates: None

Group Affiliation: AFLAC Inc

Licensed in: CT, MA, NJ, NY, ND, VT

Commenced Business: December 1964

Address: 22 Corporate Woods Blvd Ste 2, Albany, NY 12211

Phone: (706) 243 8708 **Domicile State:** NY **NAIC Code:** 60526

Data Date	Rating	RACR #1	RACR #2	Total Assets ($mil)	Capital ($mil)	Net Premium ($mil)	Net Income ($mil)
2021	A	6.28	4.15	1,108.3	359.8	327.4	82.5
2020	A	5.97	3.97	1,077.1	351.6	341.5	75.5
2019	A-	5.57	3.76	982.9	319.5	342.5	75.1
2018	A-	5.55	3.65	965.2	310.1	335.4	66.6
2017	A-	5.60	3.74	915.6	300.6	326.8	58.9

Risk-Adjusted Capital Ratios (Since 2017)

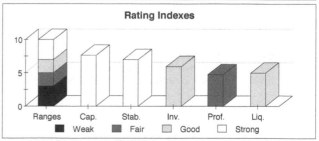

AMERICAN FAMILY LIFE INS CO *   A+   Excellent

Major Rating Factors: Good quality investment portfolio (5.9 on a scale of 0 to 10) despite significant exposure to mortgages . Mortgage default rate has been low. large holdings of BBB rated bonds in addition to minimal holdings in junk bonds. Good liquidity (5.0) with sufficient resources to handle a spike in claims as well as a significant increase in policy surrenders. Fair profitability (4.7) with investment income below regulatory standards in relation to interest assumptions of reserves.

Other Rating Factors: Excellent overall results on stability tests (7.0) excellent operational trends and excellent risk diversification. Strong capitalization (7.6) based on excellent risk adjusted capital (severe loss scenario).

Principal Business: Individual life insurance (94%), individual annuities (3%), group life insurance (2%), and reinsurance (1%).

Principal Investments: NonCMO investment grade bonds (60%), CMOs and structured securities (23%), mortgages in good standing (12%), and policy loans (3%).

Investments in Affiliates: 1%

Group Affiliation: American Family Ins Group

Licensed in: All states except NY, PR

Commenced Business: December 1957

Address: 6000 AMERICAN PARKWAY, MADISON, WI 53783-0001

Phone: (608) 249-2111 **Domicile State:** WI **NAIC Code:** 60399

Data Date	Rating	RACR #1	RACR #2	Total Assets ($mil)	Capital ($mil)	Net Premium ($mil)	Net Income ($mil)
2021	A+	2.64	1.43	5,473.4	445.4	429.2	39.6
2020	A+	2.52	1.35	5,346.9	404.9	393.9	51.2
2019	A+	3.77	2.03	5,454.3	685.1	380.3	72.0
2018	A+	3.71	2.00	5,274.1	646.9	369.3	102.9
2017	A+	5.04	2.70	5,676.1	1,059.7	359.0	69.4

Rating Indexes

AMERICAN FIDELITY ASR CO *   B+   Good

Major Rating Factors: Good quality investment portfolio (6.2 on a scale of 0 to 10) despite significant exposure to mortgages . Mortgage default rate has been low. large holdings of BBB rated bonds in addition to small junk bond holdings. Good liquidity (6.6) with sufficient resources to handle a spike in claims as well as a significant increase in policy surrenders. Good overall results on stability tests (6.8) excellent operational trends and excellent risk diversification.

Other Rating Factors: Strong capitalization (7.3) based on excellent risk adjusted capital (severe loss scenario). Excellent profitability (8.3) with operating gains in each of the last five years.

Principal Business: Group health insurance (42%), individual health insurance (24%), individual annuities (15%), individual life insurance (14%), and reinsurance (3%).

Principal Investments: NonCMO investment grade bonds (60%), CMOs and structured securities (17%), mortgages in good standing (11%), cash (4%), and misc. investments (7%).

Investments in Affiliates: None
Group Affiliation: Cameron Associates Inc
Licensed in: All states except NY
Commenced Business: December 1960
Address: 9000 Cameron Parkway, Oklahoma City, OK 73114-3701
Phone: (405) 523-2000 **Domicile State:** OK **NAIC Code:** 60410

Data Date	Rating	RACR #1	RACR #2	Total Assets ($mil)	Capital ($mil)	Net Premium ($mil)	Net Income ($mil)
2021	B+	2.12	1.22	7,628.5	616.8	1,300.9	166.9
2020	B+	2.15	1.24	7,092.7	590.7	1,213.6	130.1
2019	B+	2.14	1.26	6,656.8	544.3	1,176.2	90.3
2018	B+	2.05	1.17	6,101.2	505.2	1,091.7	98.9
2017	B+	1.78	1.04	5,896.7	430.6	957.4	66.2

Adverse Trends in Operations

Increase in policy surrenders from 2018 to 2019 (40%)

AMERICAN FIDELITY LIFE INS CO   B   Good

Major Rating Factors: Good overall profitability (5.5 on a scale of 0 to 10) although investment income, in comparison to reserve requirements, is below regulatory standards. Good overall results on stability tests (5.8). Stability strengths include good operational trends and good risk diversification. Fair quality investment portfolio (4.6).

Other Rating Factors: Strong capitalization (7.4) based on excellent risk adjusted capital (severe loss scenario). Excellent liquidity (8.0).

Principal Business: Individual life insurance (54%), individual annuities (23%), and reinsurance (22%).

Principal Investments: NonCMO investment grade bonds (64%), common & preferred stock (9%), noninv. grade bonds (9%), mortgages in good standing (7%), and misc. investments (12%).

Investments in Affiliates: 11%
Group Affiliation: AMFI Corp
Licensed in: All states except NY, VT, PR
Commenced Business: September 1956
Address: 500 So Palafox St Ste 200, Pensacola, FL 32502
Phone: (850) 456-7401 **Domicile State:** FL **NAIC Code:** 60429

Data Date	Rating	RACR #1	RACR #2	Total Assets ($mil)	Capital ($mil)	Net Premium ($mil)	Net Income ($mil)
2021	B	2.07	1.27	385.7	67.7	9.6	1.3
2020	B	1.95	1.28	396.7	69.0	10.5	1.7
2019	B	2.02	1.39	401.1	68.9	9.4	2.6
2018	B	2.07	1.41	401.3	68.6	10.2	3.6
2017	B	1.78	1.29	410.2	67.3	9.6	1.3

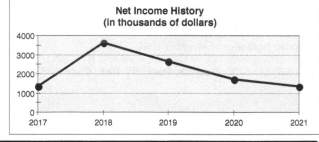

Net Income History
(in thousands of dollars)

AMERICAN GENERAL LIFE INS CO   B   Good

Major Rating Factors: Good overall profitability (6.7 on a scale of 0 to 10). Return on equity has been fair, averaging 9.6%. Good liquidity (5.3) with sufficient resources to handle a spike in claims as well as a significant increase in policy surrenders. Good overall results on stability tests (5.4) despite excessive premium growth good operational trends and excellent risk diversification.

Other Rating Factors: Fair quality investment portfolio (4.6). Strong capitalization (7.6) based on excellent risk adjusted capital (severe loss scenario).

Principal Business: Individual annuities (65%), individual life insurance (18%), reinsurance (12%), and group retirement contracts (4%).

Principal Investments: NonCMO investment grade bonds (52%), CMOs and structured securities (18%), mortgages in good standing (16%), noninv. grade bonds (5%), and misc. investments (7%).

Investments in Affiliates: 2%
Group Affiliation: American International Group
Licensed in: All states except NY
Commenced Business: August 1960
Address: 2727-A Allen Parkway 3-D1, Houston, TX 77019
Phone: (713) 522-1111 **Domicile State:** TX **NAIC Code:** 60488

Data Date	Rating	RACR #1	RACR #2	Total Assets ($mil)	Capital ($mil)	Net Premium ($mil)	Net Income ($mil)
2021	B	2.90	1.37	217,000	8,532.5	15,308.5	2,244.5
2020	B	2.74	1.29	205,000	7,511.1	10,863.8	-31.0
2019	B	2.49	1.17	192,000	6,288.7	14,264.7	91.6
2018	B	2.54	1.19	177,000	6,350.3	-10,118.3	564.9
2017	B	2.98	1.40	179,000	7,983.6	10,972.7	612.3

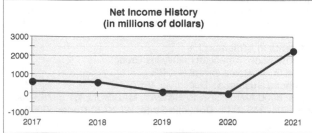

Net Income History
(in millions of dollars)

AMERICAN HEALTH & LIFE INS CO *   B+   Good

Major Rating Factors: Good quality investment portfolio (6.3 on a scale of 0 to 10) despite mixed results such as: minimal exposure to mortgages and large holdings of BBB rated bonds but small junk bond holdings. Good overall results on stability tests (6.8). Stability strengths include excellent operational trends and excellent risk diversification. Strong capitalization (9.6) based on excellent risk adjusted capital (severe loss scenario).

Other Rating Factors: Excellent profitability (8.9) with operating gains in each of the last five years. Excellent liquidity (7.7).

Principal Business: Credit health insurance (42%), credit life insurance (38%), individual life insurance (7%), reinsurance (7%), and other lines (6%).

Principal Investments: NonCMO investment grade bonds (73%), CMOs and structured securities (20%), noninv. grade bonds (3%), common & preferred stock (2%), and cash (1%).

Investments in Affiliates: None

Group Affiliation: Citigroup Inc

Licensed in: All states except NY, PR

Commenced Business: June 1954

Address: 3001 Meacham Blvd Ste 100, Fort Worth, TX 76137-4615

Phone: (800) 307-0048   **Domicile State:** TX   **NAIC Code:** 60518

Data Date	Rating	RACR #1	RACR #2	Total Assets ($mil)	Capital ($mil)	Net Premium ($mil)	Net Income ($mil)
2021	B+	4.49	2.72	1,264.4	292.2	289.3	79.5
2020	B-	4.53	2.71	1,251.0	261.3	236.1	114.0
2019	B-	2.58	1.67	1,281.6	192.4	479.7	55.9
2018	A-	2.00	1.28	1,038.1	128.5	377.6	32.1
2017	A-	2.70	1.70	883.2	130.3	251.1	34.5

Adverse Trends in Operations

Decrease in premium volume from 2019 to 2020 (51%)
Increase in policy surrenders from 2018 to 2019 (118%)
Decrease in capital during 2018 (1%)
Increase in policy surrenders from 2017 to 2018 (1066%)
Decrease in capital during 2017 (39%)

AMERICAN HERITAGE LIFE INS CO   B   Good

Major Rating Factors: Good current capitalization (6.3 on a scale of 0 to 10) based on good risk adjusted capital (severe loss scenario), although results have slipped from the excellent range over the last year. Good liquidity (6.4) with sufficient resources to handle a spike in claims as well as a significant increase in policy surrenders. Good overall results on stability tests (5.6) despite excessive premium growth excellent operational trends and excellent risk diversification.

Other Rating Factors: Fair quality investment portfolio (4.7). Fair profitability (3.8) with investment income below regulatory standards in relation to interest assumptions of reserves.

Principal Business: Group health insurance (63%), individual health insurance (16%), group life insurance (10%), individual life insurance (6%), and reinsurance (5%).

Principal Investments: NonCMO investment grade bonds (64%), noninv. grade bonds (12%), common & preferred stock (9%), policy loans (7%), and misc. investments (6%).

Investments in Affiliates: 6%

Group Affiliation: Allstate Group

Licensed in: All states except NY

Commenced Business: December 1956

Address: 1776 AMERICAN HERITAGE LIFE DR, JACKSONVILLE, FL 32224-6688

Phone: (904) 992-1776   **Domicile State:** FL   **NAIC Code:** 60534

Data Date	Rating	RACR #1	RACR #2	Total Assets ($mil)	Capital ($mil)	Net Premium ($mil)	Net Income ($mil)
2021	B	1.23	0.91	2,325.5	350.7	1,159.4	92.6
2020	B	1.36	1.02	2,071.7	364.5	926.8	94.6
2019	B	1.27	0.96	2,075.3	344.9	958.8	91.9
2018	B	1.18	0.91	2,003.1	323.9	952.5	101.8
2017	B	1.08	0.82	1,922.0	306.0	905.3	55.3

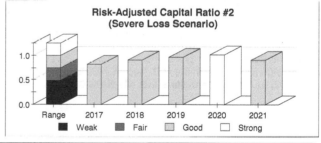

Risk-Adjusted Capital Ratio #2 (Severe Loss Scenario)

Range	2017	2018	2019	2020	2021
■ Weak	▨ Fair	▥ Good	☐ Strong		

AMERICAN INCOME LIFE INS CO   B-   Good

Major Rating Factors: Good capitalization (6.8 on a scale of 0 to 10) based on good risk adjusted capital (severe loss scenario). Capital levels have been relatively consistent over the last five years. Good overall profitability (5.2) although investment income, in comparison to reserve requirements, is below regulatory standards. Fair overall results on stability tests (4.0) including fair financial strength of affiliated Torchmark Corp.

Other Rating Factors: Fair quality investment portfolio (4.8). Weak liquidity (2.0).

Principal Business: Individual life insurance (92%) and individual health insurance (7%).

Principal Investments: NonCMO investment grade bonds (81%), policy loans (5%), noninv. grade bonds (4%), common & preferred stock (2%), and mortgages in good standing (1%).

Investments in Affiliates: 2%

Group Affiliation: Torchmark Corp

Licensed in: All states except NY, PR

Commenced Business: August 1954

Address: 8604 ALLISONVILLE RD SUITE 151, INDIANAPOLIS, IN 46250

Phone: (254) 761-6400   **Domicile State:** IN   **NAIC Code:** 60577

Data Date	Rating	RACR #1	RACR #2	Total Assets ($mil)	Capital ($mil)	Net Premium ($mil)	Net Income ($mil)
2021	B-	1.69	0.98	4,889.9	408.1	842.1	178.5
2020	B-	1.43	0.83	4,674.9	338.9	896.7	184.0
2019	B-	1.58	0.93	4,391.1	347.3	847.5	198.5
2018	B-	1.60	0.95	4,156.8	343.0	800.7	190.7
2017	B-	1.34	0.79	3,919.7	270.3	811.7	141.5

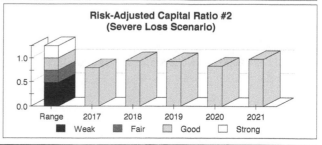

Risk-Adjusted Capital Ratio #2 (Severe Loss Scenario)

Range	2017	2018	2019	2020	2021
■ Weak	▨ Fair	▥ Good	☐ Strong		

AMERICAN LIFE & ACC INS CO OF KY

C Fair

Major Rating Factors: Fair overall results on stability tests (3.9 on a scale of 0 to 10). Good liquidity (6.9) with sufficient resources to handle a spike in claims. Low quality investment portfolio (1.8).

Other Rating Factors: Strong capitalization (7.9) based on excellent risk adjusted capital (severe loss scenario). Excellent profitability (8.5) with operating gains in each of the last five years.

Principal Business: Reinsurance (100%).

Principal Investments: Common & preferred stock (80%), nonCMO investment grade bonds (8%), real estate (6%), cash (2%), and CMOs and structured securities (1%).

Investments in Affiliates: None

Group Affiliation: Hardscuffle Inc

Licensed in: AR, GA, IN, KY, MD, OH, PA, TN

Commenced Business: July 1906

Address: 3 Riverfront Plz 471 W Main St, Louisville, KY 40202

Phone: (502) 585-5347 **Domicile State:** KY **NAIC Code:** 60666

Data Date	Rating	RACR #1	RACR #2	Total Assets ($mil)	Capital ($mil)	Net Premium ($mil)	Net Income ($mil)
2021	C	2.72	1.63	300.0	172.2	51.8	18.2
2020	C	2.56	1.54	261.0	138.8	66.0	4.2
2019	C	2.62	1.58	263.4	142.2	62.6	4.1
2018	C	2.67	1.61	226.5	121.7	63.9	20.9
2017	C	2.67	1.63	252.4	144.9	90.2	3.4

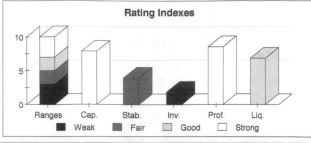

Rating Indexes

AMERICAN LIFE & SECURITY CORP

D+ Weak

Major Rating Factors: Weak profitability (1.9 on a scale of 0 to 10) with operating losses during 2021. Return on equity has been low, averaging -18.3%. Weak overall results on stability tests (2.5). Fair quality investment portfolio (3.2) with large holdings of BBB rated bonds in addition to junk bond exposure equal to 52% of capital. Exposure to mortgages is significant, but the mortgage default rate has been low.

Other Rating Factors: Good capitalization (5.6) based on good risk adjusted capital (moderate loss scenario). Excellent liquidity (8.6).

Principal Business: Individual annuities (100%).

Principal Investments: CMOs and structured securities (32%), nonCMO investment grade bonds (25%), cash (11%), mortgages in good standing (11%), and misc. investments (13%).

Investments in Affiliates: None

Group Affiliation: Midwest Holding Inc

Licensed in: AZ, CO, DC, HI, ID, IL, IN, IA, KS, LA, MI, MO, MT, NE, NV, NM, ND, OH, OK, SD, TX, UT

Commenced Business: October 1961

Address: 2900 South 70th St Ste 400, Lincoln, NE 68506

Phone: (402) 817-5701 **Domicile State:** NE **NAIC Code:** 67253

Data Date	Rating	RACR #1	RACR #2	Total Assets ($mil)	Capital ($mil)	Net Premium ($mil)	Net Income ($mil)
2021	D+	1.39	0.64	1,121.1	74.0	107.8	-6.4
2020	D	2.68	1.20	654.6	77.4	39.9	3.9
2019	E+	2.05	1.24	186.1	19.5	0.9	1.3
2018	E	5.62	5.06	22.3	21.0	1.5	-4.3
2017	E+	0.72	0.65	23.9	3.0	5.2	-2.1

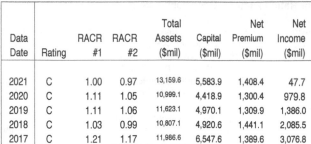

Net Income History
(in thousands of dollars)

AMERICAN LIFE INS CO

C Fair

Major Rating Factors: Fair quality investment portfolio (3.0 on a scale of 0 to 10). Fair overall results on stability tests (4.1). Good current capitalization (6.8) based on good risk adjusted capital (severe loss scenario), although results have slipped from the excellent range over the last year.

Other Rating Factors: Excellent profitability (7.1) with operating gains in each of the last five years. Excellent liquidity (8.5).

Principal Business: Individual life insurance (60%), group health insurance (20%), reinsurance (9%), individual health insurance (7%), and other lines (4%).

Principal Investments: Common & preferred stock (60%), noninv. grade bonds (16%), nonCMO investment grade bonds (12%), cash (8%), and misc. investments (2%).

Investments in Affiliates: 61%

Group Affiliation: MetLife Inc

Licensed in: DE

Commenced Business: August 1921

Address: 1209 Orange Street, Wilmington, DE 19801

Phone: (302) 594-2000 **Domicile State:** DE **NAIC Code:** 60690

Data Date	Rating	RACR #1	RACR #2	Total Assets ($mil)	Capital ($mil)	Net Premium ($mil)	Net Income ($mil)
2021	C	1.00	0.97	13,159.6	5,583.9	1,408.4	47.7
2020	C	1.11	1.05	10,999.1	4,418.9	1,300.4	979.8
2019	C	1.11	1.06	11,623.1	4,970.1	1,309.9	1,386.0
2018	C	1.03	0.99	10,807.1	4,920.6	1,441.1	2,085.5
2017	C	1.21	1.17	11,986.6	6,547.6	1,389.6	3,076.8

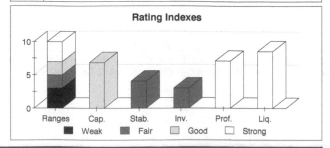

Rating Indexes

AMERICAN MATURITY LIFE INS CO
B   **Good**

Major Rating Factors: Good overall results on stability tests (6.1 on a scale of 0 to 10). Stability strengths include excellent operational trends and excellent risk diversification. Strong capitalization (10.0) based on excellent risk adjusted capital (severe loss scenario). High quality investment portfolio (9.6).
Other Rating Factors: Excellent profitability (7.2) with operating gains in each of the last five years. Excellent liquidity (10.0).
Principal Business: Group retirement contracts (75%) and individual annuities (25%).
Principal Investments: NonCMO investment grade bonds (92%) and cash (8%).
Investments in Affiliates: None
Group Affiliation: Hartford Financial Services Inc
Licensed in: All states except PR
Commenced Business: March 1973
Address: One Hartford Plaza, Windsor, CT 06095-1512
Phone: (800) 862-6668 **Domicile State:** CT **NAIC Code:** 81213

Data Date	Rating	RACR #1	RACR #2	Total Assets ($mil)	Capital ($mil)	Net Premium ($mil)	Net Income ($mil)
2021	B	6.75	6.07	68.1	50.7	0.0	0.4
2020	B	6.78	6.10	65.8	50.3	0.0	0.6
2019	B-	6.77	6.09	63.8	49.6	0.0	0.7
2018	B-	6.76	6.09	61.6	48.9	0.1	0.7
2017	B	6.65	5.99	62.5	48.3	0.0	0.3

Adverse Trends in Operations

Decrease in premium volume from 2018 to 2019 (95%)
Increase in policy surrenders from 2017 to 2018 (125%)
Decrease in asset base during 2018 (1%)

AMERICAN MEMORIAL LIFE INS CO
B   **Good**

Major Rating Factors: Good overall results on stability tests (5.6 on a scale of 0 to 10) despite fair risk adjusted capital in prior years. Other stability subfactors include excellent operational trends and excellent risk diversification. Good liquidity (5.7) with sufficient resources to handle a spike in claims as well as a significant increase in policy surrenders. Fair quality investment portfolio (4.7).
Other Rating Factors: Strong capitalization (7.0) based on excellent risk adjusted capital (severe loss scenario). Excellent profitability (7.0) with operating gains in each of the last five years.
Principal Business: Group life insurance (64%) and individual life insurance (36%).
Principal Investments: NonCMO investment grade bonds (68%), CMOs and structured securities (14%), mortgages in good standing (12%), and noninv. grade bonds (3%).
Investments in Affiliates: None
Group Affiliation: Assurant Inc
Licensed in: All states except NY, PR
Commenced Business: October 1959
Address: 440 MOUNT RUSHMORE ROAD, RAPID CITY, SD 57701
Phone: (608) 238-5851 **Domicile State:** SD **NAIC Code:** 67989

Data Date	Rating	RACR #1	RACR #2	Total Assets ($mil)	Capital ($mil)	Net Premium ($mil)	Net Income ($mil)
2021	B	1.91	1.00	4,034.0	221.0	672.5	17.5
2020	B-	1.61	0.82	3,749.1	193.8	569.7	39.8
2019	B-	1.43	0.74	3,558.6	158.7	592.3	33.9
2018	B-	1.40	0.72	3,339.1	147.4	562.1	39.1
2017	B-	1.35	0.69	3,166.4	128.5	544.3	32.0

Adverse Trends in Operations

Decrease in premium volume from 2019 to 2020 (4%)

AMERICAN NATIONAL INS CO
B   **Good**

Major Rating Factors: Good quality investment portfolio (5.3 on a scale of 0 to 10) despite significant exposure to mortgages . Mortgage default rate has been low. large holdings of BBB rated bonds in addition to small junk bond holdings. Good liquidity (6.7) with sufficient resources to handle a spike in claims as well as a significant increase in policy surrenders. Good overall results on stability tests (5.4) despite excessive premium growth good operational trends, good risk adjusted capital for prior years and excellent risk diversification.
Other Rating Factors: Strong capitalization (9.1) based on excellent risk adjusted capital (severe loss scenario). Excellent profitability (7.0) despite modest operating losses during 2019 and 2020.
Principal Business: Individual annuities (63%), individual life insurance (29%), reinsurance (3%), group retirement contracts (2%), and other lines (3%).
Principal Investments: NonCMO investment grade bonds (45%), mortgages in good standing (22%), noninv. grade bonds (2%), real estate (2%), and misc. investments (23%).
Investments in Affiliates: 21%
Group Affiliation: American National Group Inc
Licensed in: All states except NY
Commenced Business: March 1905
Address: ONE MOODY PLAZA, GALVESTON, TX 77550
Phone: (409) 763-4661 **Domicile State:** TX **NAIC Code:** 60739

Data Date	Rating	RACR #1	RACR #2	Total Assets ($mil)	Capital ($mil)	Net Premium ($mil)	Net Income ($mil)
2021	B	4.67	2.37	23,828.7	3,989.5	2,583.1	878.3
2020	B	1.04	0.89	22,203.3	3,644.4	1,565.6	-47.5
2019	B	1.08	0.93	21,443.4	3,477.7	1,735.0	-21.9
2018	B	1.13	0.94	20,467.5	3,162.8	1,949.9	42.4
2017	B	1.16	0.97	20,146.6	3,293.5	2,131.3	20.1

Adverse Trends in Operations

Decrease in premium volume from 2019 to 2020 (10%)
Decrease in premium volume from 2018 to 2019 (11%)
Decrease in premium volume from 2017 to 2018 (9%)
Decrease in capital during 2018 (4%)

AMERICAN NATIONAL LIFE INS CO OF TX | C+ | Fair

Major Rating Factors: Fair profitability (4.0 on a scale of 0 to 10). Return on equity has been low, averaging -0.3%. Fair overall results on stability tests (4.7). Good liquidity (6.9) with sufficient resources to handle a spike in claims as well as a significant increase in policy surrenders.

Other Rating Factors: Strong capitalization (9.1) based on excellent risk adjusted capital (severe loss scenario). High quality investment portfolio (7.1).

Principal Business: Reinsurance (56%), group health insurance (27%), individual health insurance (14%), and individual life insurance (2%).

Principal Investments: NonCMO investment grade bonds (91%), policy loans (2%), and cash (2%).

Investments in Affiliates: None

Group Affiliation: American National Group Inc

Licensed in: All states except ME, NJ, NY, VT, PR

Commenced Business: December 1954

Address: ONE MOODY PLAZA, GALVESTON, TX 77550

Phone: (409) 763-4461 **Domicile State:** TX **NAIC Code:** 71773

Data Date	Rating	RACR #1	RACR #2	Total Assets ($mil)	Capital ($mil)	Net Premium ($mil)	Net Income ($mil)
2021	C+	3.44	2.40	137.2	37.0	47.1	1.4
2020	B-	2.60	1.83	132.8	35.1	60.3	-1.6
2019	B-	3.00	2.06	131.6	35.4	52.0	1.8
2018	B-	3.59	2.39	127.7	33.0	39.2	-1.5
2017	B-	3.85	2.99	123.7	34.2	28.8	-0.5

Net Income History
(in thousands of dollars)

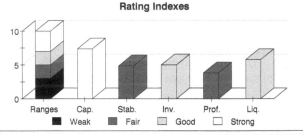

AMERICAN NATIONAL LIFE INSURANCE COMPANY OF NEW YO | B- | Good

Major Rating Factors: Good quality investment portfolio (5.0 on a scale of 0 to 10) despite large holdings of BBB rated bonds in addition to moderate junk bond exposure. Exposure to mortgages is significant, but the mortgage default rate has been low. Good liquidity (5.8) with sufficient resources to handle a spike in claims as well as a significant increase in policy surrenders. Fair profitability (3.8).

Other Rating Factors: Fair overall results on stability tests (4.9). Strong capitalization (7.4) based on excellent risk adjusted capital (severe loss scenario).

Principal Business: Individual life insurance (57%), individual annuities (38%), individual health insurance (4%), credit health insurance (1%), and credit life insurance (1%).

Principal Investments: NonCMO investment grade bonds (72%), mortgages in good standing (17%), noninv. grade bonds (3%), policy loans (1%), and CMOs and structured securities (1%).

Investments in Affiliates: None

Group Affiliation: American National Group Inc

Licensed in: CT, DE, ME, MD, MA, NH, NJ, NY, PA, RI, VT, VA, WV

Commenced Business: January 1954

Address: 344 ROUTE 9W, GLENMONT, NY 12077

Phone: (800) 392-0644 **Domicile State:** NY **NAIC Code:** 63126

Data Date	Rating	RACR #1	RACR #2	Total Assets ($mil)	Capital ($mil)	Net Premium ($mil)	Net Income ($mil)
2021	B-	2.57	1.29	2,874.9	240.4	94.1	12.4
2020	B-	2.50	1.26	2,788.8	234.3	89.1	10.6
2019	B-	2.53	1.29	2,779.2	228.9	437.8	44.7
2018	B-	2.29	1.22	2,367.3	237.0	262.3	-1.1
2017	B	2.67	1.51	1,369.9	207.7	57.3	15.0

Rating Indexes

Ranges · Cap. · Stab. · Inv. · Prof. · Liq.
■ Weak   ▨ Fair   ▧ Good   □ Strong

AMERICAN PROGRESSIVE L&H I C OF NY | C | Fair

Major Rating Factors: Fair current capitalization (4.9 on a scale of 0 to 10) based on mixed results -- excessive policy leverage mitigated by fair risk adjusted capital (severe loss scenario), although results have slipped from the excellent range over the last year. Good overall profitability (5.1) despite operating losses during 2021. Return on equity has been fair, averaging 5.5%. Weak liquidity (0.7).

Other Rating Factors: Weak overall results on stability tests (2.8) including excessive premium growth and negative cash flow from operations for 2021. High quality investment portfolio (7.4).

Principal Business: Individual health insurance (98%), group health insurance (1%), and individual life insurance (1%).

Principal Investments: NonCMO investment grade bonds (82%), CMOs and structured securities (7%), noninv. grade bonds (1%), and common & preferred stock (1%).

Investments in Affiliates: None

Group Affiliation: WellCare Health Plans Inc

Licensed in: AL, AR, CO, CT, DC, DE, GA, HI, IL, IN, LA, ME, MD, MA, MN, MO, NH, NJ, NY, NC, OH, OK, OR, PA, RI, SC, TX, VT, VA, WV

Commenced Business: March 1946

Address: 44 South Broadway Suite 1200, New York, NY 10004

Phone: (314) 725-4477 **Domicile State:** NY **NAIC Code:** 80624

Data Date	Rating	RACR #1	RACR #2	Total Assets ($mil)	Capital ($mil)	Net Premium ($mil)	Net Income ($mil)
2021	C	0.91	0.74	350.4	137.2	828.0	-26.5
2020	C+	1.32	1.05	314.4	138.5	565.1	31.8
2019	C	1.04	0.84	301.2	126.1	656.9	26.3
2018	C	1.05	0.86	250.8	116.5	602.8	12.0
2017	C	1.04	0.84	222.9	102.1	535.7	-6.6

Policy Leverage

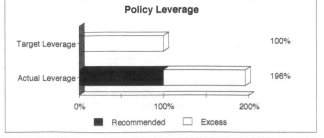

Target Leverage — 100%
Actual Leverage — 196%

■ Recommended   □ Excess

AMERICAN PUBLIC LIFE INS CO   B   Good

Major Rating Factors: Good liquidity (6.8 on a scale of 0 to 10) with sufficient resources to handle a spike in claims. Fair overall results on stability tests (4.8) including negative cash flow from operations for 2021. Strong overall capitalization (8.5) based on excellent risk adjusted capital (severe loss scenario). However, capital levels have fluctuated somewhat during past years.

Other Rating Factors: High quality investment portfolio (7.9). Excellent profitability (7.0) with operating gains in each of the last five years.

Principal Business: Group health insurance (84%), individual health insurance (11%), reinsurance (2%), group life insurance (2%), and individual life insurance (1%).

Principal Investments: NonCMO investment grade bonds (62%), CMOs and structured securities (22%), mortgages in good standing (11%), cash (2%), and misc. investments (4%).

Investments in Affiliates: None

Group Affiliation: Cameron Associates Inc

Licensed in: All states except NY, PR

Commenced Business: March 1946

Address: 9000 Cameron Parkway, Oklahoma City, OK 73114

Phone: (601) 936-6600 **Domicile State:** OK **NAIC Code:** 60801

Data Date	Rating	RACR #1	RACR #2	Total Assets ($mil)	Capital ($mil)	Net Premium ($mil)	Net Income ($mil)
2021	B	2.67	1.99	100.9	35.5	84.2	4.9
2020	B	2.60	1.96	111.9	36.6	93.3	9.4
2019	B	2.18	1.65	99.2	33.8	96.5	7.1
2018	B	2.34	1.77	100.8	35.2	96.6	5.2
2017	B	2.11	1.59	99.5	30.8	90.9	5.5

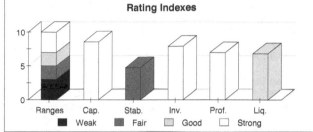

AMERICAN REPUBLIC INS CO   B-   Good

Major Rating Factors: Good quality investment portfolio (5.8 on a scale of 0 to 10) despite mixed results such as: minimal exposure to mortgages and large holdings of BBB rated bonds but minimal holdings in junk bonds. Good liquidity (6.8) with sufficient resources to handle a spike in claims as well as a significant increase in policy surrenders. Fair overall results on stability tests (4.9).

Other Rating Factors: Strong capitalization (9.3) based on excellent risk adjusted capital (severe loss scenario). Excellent profitability (9.1) with operating gains in each of the last five years.

Principal Business: Reinsurance (88%), individual health insurance (7%), group health insurance (4%), and individual life insurance (1%).

Principal Investments: NonCMO investment grade bonds (56%), CMOs and structured securities (18%), mortgages in good standing (9%), common & preferred stock (7%), and misc. investments (7%).

Investments in Affiliates: 6%

Group Affiliation: American Enterprise Mutual Holding

Licensed in: All states except NY, PR

Commenced Business: May 1929

Address: 601 Sixth Avenue, Des Moines, IA 50309

Phone: (800) 247-2190 **Domicile State:** IA **NAIC Code:** 60836

Data Date	Rating	RACR #1	RACR #2	Total Assets ($mil)	Capital ($mil)	Net Premium ($mil)	Net Income ($mil)
2021	B-	3.44	2.53	1,561.0	585.9	663.3	19.6
2020	B-	3.51	2.63	1,267.1	569.5	575.8	42.5
2019	B-	3.57	2.69	1,135.3	519.7	626.9	31.3
2018	B-	5.87	3.64	1,057.0	481.8	675.9	26.3
2017	A-	4.18	2.99	937.4	445.0	442.0	23.3

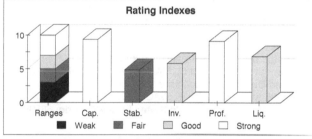

AMERICAN RETIREMENT LIFE INS CO   C+   Fair

Major Rating Factors: Fair overall results on stability tests (4.7 on a scale of 0 to 10). Good current capitalization (5.7) based on mixed results -- excessive policy leverage mitigated by excellent risk adjusted capital (severe loss scenario) reflecting improvement over results in 2018. Good liquidity (5.6) with sufficient resources to handle a spike in claims.

Other Rating Factors: Weak profitability (1.9). High quality investment portfolio (7.6).

Principal Business: Individual health insurance (100%).

Principal Investments: NonCMO investment grade bonds (99%) and noninv. grade bonds (1%).

Investments in Affiliates: None

Group Affiliation: CIGNA Corp

Licensed in: AL, AZ, AR, CA, CO, DE, FL, GA, IL, IN, IA, KS, KY, LA, MD, MN, MS, MO, MT, NE, NV, NH, NM, NC, ND, OH, OK, OR, PA, RI, SC, SD, TN, TX, UT, VA, WV, WI, WY

Commenced Business: November 1978

Address: 1300 East Ninth Street, Cleveland, OH 44114

Phone: (512) 451-2224 **Domicile State:** OH **NAIC Code:** 88366

Data Date	Rating	RACR #1	RACR #2	Total Assets ($mil)	Capital ($mil)	Net Premium ($mil)	Net Income ($mil)
2021	C+	1.49	1.14	147.8	76.9	385.5	12.0
2020	C+	1.55	1.19	151.2	84.5	409.9	20.2
2019	C+	1.23	0.95	131.7	68.7	420.5	-27.4
2018	C+	1.17	0.91	123.9	63.1	401.2	-42.6
2017	C+	1.27	0.99	121.0	59.7	345.2	-38.1

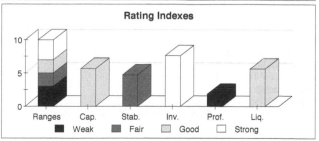

AMERICAN UNITED LIFE INS CO

B- **Good**

Major Rating Factors: Good quality investment portfolio (5.4 on a scale of 0 to 10) despite large holdings of BBB rated bonds in addition to moderate junk bond exposure. Exposure to mortgages is significant, but the mortgage default rate has been low. Good liquidity (5.8) with sufficient resources to handle a spike in claims as well as a significant increase in policy surrenders. Good overall results on stability tests (5.0) excellent operational trends and excellent risk diversification.

Other Rating Factors: Weak profitability (2.7) with investment income below regulatory standards in relation to interest assumptions of reserves. Strong capitalization (7.4) based on excellent risk adjusted capital (severe loss scenario).

Principal Business: Group retirement contracts (82%), individual life insurance (7%), reinsurance (3%), group health insurance (3%), and other lines (5%).

Principal Investments: NonCMO investment grade bonds (55%), CMOs and structured securities (17%), mortgages in good standing (15%), noninv. grade bonds (4%), and misc. investments (6%).

Investments in Affiliates: None

Group Affiliation: American United Life Group

Licensed in: All states except PR

Commenced Business: November 1877

Address: ONE AMERICAN SQUARE, INDIANAPOLIS, IN 46282-0001

Phone: (317) 285-1877 **Domicile State:** IN **NAIC Code:** 60895

Data Date	Rating	RACR #1	RACR #2	Total Assets ($mil)	Capital ($mil)	Net Premium ($mil)	Net Income ($mil)
2021	B-	2.54	1.25	39,048.1	1,371.0	5,007.0	38.8
2020	B-	2.57	1.27	35,827.4	1,323.1	4,638.5	6.1
2019	B+	2.29	1.15	31,388.9	1,024.7	4,303.7	0.1
2018	B+	2.51	1.26	27,997.6	1,052.6	3,902.4	54.1
2017	B+	2.35	1.18	28,805.0	1,025.6	4,271.4	61.4

Adverse Trends In Operations

Decrease in capital during 2019 (3%)
Decrease in premium volume from 2017 to 2018 (9%)
Decrease in asset base during 2018 (3%)

AMERICAN-AMICABLE LIFE INS CO OF TX

C **Fair**

Major Rating Factors: Fair overall results on stability tests (4.1 on a scale of 0 to 10) including fair financial strength of affiliated Industrial Alliance Ins & Financial and fair risk adjusted capital in prior years. Good quality investment portfolio (6.4) despite mixed results such as: minimal exposure to mortgages and large holdings of BBB rated bonds but minimal holdings in junk bonds. Good liquidity (5.8).

Other Rating Factors: Weak profitability (2.8) with investment income below regulatory standards in relation to interest assumptions of reserves. Strong capitalization (7.4) based on excellent risk adjusted capital (severe loss scenario).

Principal Business: Individual life insurance (94%), individual annuities (5%), and group life insurance (1%).

Principal Investments: NonCMO investment grade bonds (74%), common & preferred stock (18%), policy loans (4%), mortgages in good standing (2%), and real estate (1%).

Investments in Affiliates: 18%

Group Affiliation: Industrial Alliance Ins & Financial

Licensed in: All states except IA, MA, MI, NH, NJ, NY, RI, VT, PR

Commenced Business: December 1981

Address: 425 AUSTIN AVENUE, WACO, TX 76701

Phone: (254) 297-2777 **Domicile State:** TX **NAIC Code:** 68594

Data Date	Rating	RACR #1	RACR #2	Total Assets ($mil)	Capital ($mil)	Net Premium ($mil)	Net Income ($mil)
2021	C	1.41	1.24	465.9	137.2	87.1	5.9
2020	C	1.10	0.98	406.7	103.2	82.0	0.1
2019	C	0.92	0.81	336.0	66.8	81.4	9.5
2018	C	0.84	0.75	313.1	63.1	51.6	2.5
2017	C	0.80	0.69	297.7	46.5	72.2	-1.7

Industrial Alliance Ins Financial
Composite Group Rating: C
Largest Group Members

	Assets ($mil)	Rating
AMERICAN-AMICABLE LIFE INS CO OF TX	407	C
INDUSTRIAL ALLIANCE INS FIN SERV	281	C
OCCIDENTAL LIFE INS CO OF NC	277	C
IA AMERICAN LIFE INS CO	211	C
DEALERS ASR CO	199	B-

AMERICO FINANCIAL LIFE & ANNUITY INSURANCE

B- **Good**

Major Rating Factors: Good liquidity (5.9 on a scale of 0 to 10) with sufficient resources to handle a spike in claims as well as a significant increase in policy surrenders. Good overall results on stability tests (5.3). Stability strengths include excellent operational trends and excellent risk diversification. Fair quality investment portfolio (4.6).

Other Rating Factors: Fair profitability (3.4) with investment income below regulatory standards in relation to interest assumptions of reserves. Strong capitalization (7.6) based on excellent risk adjusted capital (severe loss scenario).

Principal Business: Individual annuities (50%), individual life insurance (40%), reinsurance (6%), individual health insurance (3%), and group life insurance (1%).

Principal Investments: NonCMO investment grade bonds (47%), common & preferred stock (18%), CMOs and structured securities (14%), mortgages in good standing (8%), and misc. investments (10%).

Investments in Affiliates: 1%

Group Affiliation: Americo Life Inc

Licensed in: All states except NY

Commenced Business: July 1946

Address: PO Box 139061, Dallas, TX 75313-9061

Phone: (816) 391-2000 **Domicile State:** TX **NAIC Code:** 61999

Data Date	Rating	RACR #1	RACR #2	Total Assets ($mil)	Capital ($mil)	Net Premium ($mil)	Net Income ($mil)
2021	B-	2.50	1.41	6,268.1	814.2	872.2	113.4
2020	B-	2.14	1.20	5,508.1	598.4	811.7	1.3
2019	B-	2.28	1.26	4,935.9	569.4	688.4	112.1
2018	B-	1.86	1.08	4,570.3	467.0	551.8	86.6
2017	B-	1.86	1.08	4,484.6	505.2	514.4	72.4

Adverse Trends In Operations

Decrease in capital during 2018 (8%)

AMERITAS LIFE INS CORP   B   Good

Major Rating Factors: Good overall profitability (6.5 on a scale of 0 to 10). Return on equity has been low, averaging 3.7%. Good liquidity (6.1) with sufficient resources to handle a spike in claims as well as a significant increase in policy surrenders. Good overall results on stability tests (5.8). Stability strengths include excellent operational trends and excellent risk diversification.

Other Rating Factors: Fair quality investment portfolio (4.9). Strong capitalization (7.7) based on excellent risk adjusted capital (severe loss scenario).

Principal Business: Group retirement contracts (31%), group health insurance (21%), individual life insurance (18%), individual annuities (18%), and other lines (13%).

Principal Investments: NonCMO investment grade bonds (51%), mortgages in good standing (15%), CMOs and structured securities (15%), policy loans (4%), and misc. investments (13%).

Investments in Affiliates: 2%
Group Affiliation: Ameritas Mutual Holding Co
Licensed in: All states except NY, PR
Commenced Business: May 1887
Address: 5900 O Street, Lincoln, NE 68510-2234
Phone: (402) 467-1122 **Domicile State:** NE **NAIC Code:** 61301

Data Date	Rating	RACR #1	RACR #2	Total Assets ($mil)	Capital ($mil)	Net Premium ($mil)	Net Income ($mil)
2021	B	2.50	1.44	27,493.5	1,977.3	3,652.2	96.2
2020	B	2.50	1.41	25,697.2	1,750.7	3,143.9	64.4
2019	B	2.44	1.43	24,057.1	1,693.3	3,113.1	91.2
2018	B	2.27	1.33	21,734.8	1,510.6	2,781.7	71.3
2017	B	2.25	1.34	20,076.5	1,555.6	2,724.5	106.3

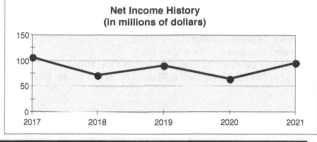

Net Income History
(in millions of dollars)

AMERITAS LIFE INS CORP OF NY   B-   Good

Major Rating Factors: Fair quality investment portfolio (4.4 on a scale of 0 to 10) with large holdings of BBB rated bonds in addition to moderate junk bond exposure. Exposure to mortgages is significant, but the mortgage default rate has been low. Fair liquidity (4.3) as cash from operations and sale of marketable assets may not be adequate to cover a spike in claims or a run on policy withdrawals. Fair overall results on stability tests (4.9).

Other Rating Factors: Weak profitability (2.7). Strong capitalization (7.2) based on excellent risk adjusted capital (severe loss scenario).

Principal Business: Individual life insurance (38%), group retirement contracts (31%), group health insurance (18%), individual health insurance (6%), and reinsurance (6%).

Principal Investments: NonCMO investment grade bonds (60%), mortgages in good standing (18%), CMOs and structured securities (14%), policy loans (2%), and noninv. grade bonds (2%).

Investments in Affiliates: None
Group Affiliation: Ameritas Mutual Holding Co
Licensed in: NY
Commenced Business: May 1994
Address: 1350 Broadway Suite 2201, New York, NY 10018-7722
Phone: (402) 467-1122 **Domicile State:** NY **NAIC Code:** 60033

Data Date	Rating	RACR #1	RACR #2	Total Assets ($mil)	Capital ($mil)	Net Premium ($mil)	Net Income ($mil)
2021	B-	2.13	1.13	1,818.3	119.4	168.1	33.0
2020	B-	1.61	0.85	1,792.2	87.8	191.9	-22.6
2019	B-	2.06	1.10	1,746.7	108.2	185.6	-15.8
2018	B-	1.82	0.97	1,648.4	92.5	129.2	-11.8
2017	B-	2.29	1.22	1,275.7	106.4	154.8	0.0

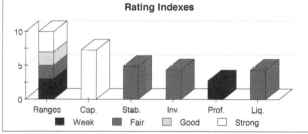

Rating Indexes

Ranges | Cap. | Stab. | Inv. | Prof. | Liq.
■ Weak ▨ Fair ▥ Good □ Strong

AMICA LIFE INS CO *   A-   Excellent

Major Rating Factors: Good quality investment portfolio (6.2 on a scale of 0 to 10) despite mixed results such as: minimal exposure to mortgages and substantial holdings of BBB bonds but minimal holdings in junk bonds. Good overall profitability (6.7). Return on equity has been low, averaging 1.6%. Good liquidity (6.6).

Other Rating Factors: Excellent overall results on stability tests (7.0) excellent operational trends and excellent risk diversification. Strong capitalization (9.3) based on excellent risk adjusted capital (severe loss scenario).

Principal Business: Individual life insurance (89%), group life insurance (6%), and individual annuities (5%).

Principal Investments: NonCMO investment grade bonds (51%), CMOs and structured securities (25%), common & preferred stock (8%), mortgages in good standing (5%), and misc. investments (9%).

Investments in Affiliates: None
Group Affiliation: Amica Mutual Group
Licensed in: All states except PR
Commenced Business: May 1970
Address: 100 AMICA WAY, LINCOLN, RI 02865-1156
Phone: (800) 652-6422 **Domicile State:** RI **NAIC Code:** 72222

Data Date	Rating	RACR #1	RACR #2	Total Assets ($mil)	Capital ($mil)	Net Premium ($mil)	Net Income ($mil)
2021	A-	4.37	2.52	1,465.4	357.0	75.2	7.4
2020	A-	5.07	2.91	1,460.2	354.7	72.7	5.7
2019	A-	5.22	3.01	1,361.2	338.1	73.7	12.8
2018	B+	5.22	3.00	1,322.4	328.3	69.8	11.5
2017	B+	5.03	2.90	1,283.4	310.2	69.6	12.7

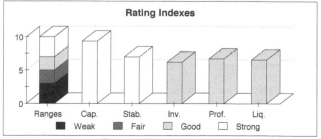

Rating Indexes

Ranges | Cap. | Stab. | Inv. | Prof. | Liq.
■ Weak ▨ Fair ▥ Good □ Strong

ANNUITY INVESTORS LIFE INS CO ^

A-   Excellent

Major Rating Factors: Good overall results on stability tests (6.1 on a scale of 0 to 10) despite negative cash flow from operations for 2021. Strengths that enhance stability include good operational trends and excellent risk diversification. Good quality investment portfolio (6.4) despite mixed results such as: no exposure to mortgages and large holdings of BBB rated bonds but small junk bond holdings. Good liquidity (6.7).

Other Rating Factors: Strong capitalization (8.4) based on excellent risk adjusted capital (severe loss scenario). Excellent profitability (8.2) with operating gains in each of the last five years.

Principal Business: Individual annuities (79%) and group retirement contracts (21%).

Principal Investments: NonCMO investment grade bonds (68%), CMOs and structured securities (24%), policy loans (2%), and noninv. grade bonds (2%).

Investments in Affiliates: None

Group Affiliation: American Financial Group Inc

Licensed in: All states except NY, VT, PR

Commenced Business: December 1981

Address: 301 East Fourth Street, Cincinnati, OH 45202

Phone: (513) 357-3300 **Domicile State:** OH **NAIC Code:** 93661

Data Date	Rating	RACR #1	RACR #2	Total Assets ($mil)	Capital ($mil)	Net Premium ($mil)	Net Income ($mil)
2021	A-	3.89	1.94	3,225.7	370.5	97.4	28.1
2020	A-	3.47	1.73	3,232.3	343.3	121.1	29.0
2019	A-	3.52	1.77	3,213.6	349.3	160.8	20.2
2018	A-	3.15	1.59	3,133.0	312.7	195.4	35.8
2017	A-	3.03	1.53	3,191.3	294.7	211.4	23.8

Adverse Trends in Operations

Decrease in premium volume from 2019 to 2020 (25%)
Decrease in capital during 2020 (2%)
Decrease in premium volume from 2018 to 2019 (18%)
Decrease in premium volume from 2017 to 2018 (8%)
Decrease in asset base during 2018 (2%)

ANTHEM LIFE INS CO

B   Good

Major Rating Factors: Good liquidity (6.1 on a scale of 0 to 10) with sufficient resources to handle a spike in claims. Good overall results on stability tests (6.3) despite negative cash flow from operations for 2021. Strengths include potential support from affiliation with Anthem Inc, excellent operational trends and excellent risk diversification. Weak profitability (1.9) with operating losses during 2021.

Other Rating Factors: Strong capitalization (7.3) based on excellent risk adjusted capital (severe loss scenario). High quality investment portfolio (7.2).

Principal Business: Group health insurance (59%), group life insurance (25%), and reinsurance (15%).

Principal Investments: NonCMO investment grade bonds (56%), CMOs and structured securities (26%), noninv. grade bonds (1%), and common & preferred stock (1%).

Investments in Affiliates: None

Group Affiliation: Anthem Inc

Licensed in: All states except NY, RI, VT, PR

Commenced Business: June 1956

Address: 120 MONUMENT CIRCLE, INDIANAPOLIS, IN 46204

Phone: (614) 433-8800 **Domicile State:** IN **NAIC Code:** 61069

Data Date	Rating	RACR #1	RACR #2	Total Assets ($mil)	Capital ($mil)	Net Premium ($mil)	Net Income ($mil)
2021	B	1.71	1.22	869.7	163.2	513.4	-57.8
2020	B+	1.76	1.25	801.1	166.0	612.8	-21.9
2019	B+	2.30	1.62	761.7	180.6	508.0	23.2
2018	B	2.11	1.46	732.3	148.9	430.8	21.9
2017	B-	1.98	1.37	674.7	125.1	412.0	12.3

Anthem Inc
Composite Group Rating: A

Largest Group Members	Assets ($mil)	Rating
BLUE CROSS OF CALIFORNIA	6274	A+
UNICARE LIFE HEALTH INS CO	1033	B
ANTHEM LIFE INS CO	801	B+
CAREMORE HEALTH PLAN	299	B
GREATER GEORGIA LIFE INS CO	78	B

ASSURITY LIFE INS CO *

B+   Good

Major Rating Factors: Good quality investment portfolio (5.5 on a scale of 0 to 10) despite significant exposure to mortgages . Mortgage default rate has been low. large holdings of BBB rated bonds in addition to small junk bond holdings. Good overall profitability (6.6). Return on equity has been low, averaging 3.4%. Good liquidity (5.9).

Other Rating Factors: Good overall results on stability tests (6.6) excellent operational trends and excellent risk diversification. Strong capitalization (8.0) based on excellent risk adjusted capital (severe loss scenario).

Principal Business: Individual life insurance (44%), group health insurance (25%), individual health insurance (24%), group life insurance (4%), and reinsurance (1%).

Principal Investments: NonCMO investment grade bonds (58%), mortgages in good standing (17%), CMOs and structured securities (9%), common & preferred stock (6%), and misc. investments (11%).

Investments in Affiliates: 1%

Group Affiliation: Assurity Security Group Inc

Licensed in: All states except NY, PR

Commenced Business: March 1964

Address: 2000 Q STREET, LINCOLN, NE 68503

Phone: (402) 476-6500 **Domicile State:** NE **NAIC Code:** 71439

Data Date	Rating	RACR #1	RACR #2	Total Assets ($mil)	Capital ($mil)	Net Premium ($mil)	Net Income ($mil)
2021	B+	2.93	1.67	2,660.6	394.6	198.0	21.9
2020	B+	2.64	1.51	2,642.8	368.2	196.5	12.6
2019	B+	2.67	1.55	2,571.2	345.3	199.2	11.9
2018	B+	2.50	1.46	2,626.8	337.5	198.7	11.1
2017	B+	2.54	1.47	2,632.3	334.7	189.2	16.8

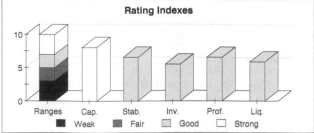

Rating Indexes

ATHENE ANNUITY & LIFE ASR CO

C   **Fair**

Major Rating Factors: Fair capitalization (3.3 on a scale of 0 to 10) based on fair risk adjusted capital (moderate loss scenario). Fair quality investment portfolio (3.6) with large holdings of BBB rated bonds in addition to significant exposure to junk bonds. Exposure to mortgages is significant, but the mortgage default rate has been low. Fair liquidity (4.8).

Other Rating Factors: Fair overall results on stability tests (3.3) including excessive premium growth and fair risk adjusted capital in prior years. Weak profitability (2.6) with operating losses during 2021.

Principal Business: Reinsurance (98%) and individual life insurance (2%).

Principal Investments: CMOs and structured securities (33%), nonCMO investment grade bonds (33%), mortgages in good standing (15%), noninv. grade bonds (5%), and misc. investments (13%).

Investments in Affiliates: 20%

Group Affiliation: BRH Holdings GP Ltd

Licensed In: All states except NY

Commenced Business: July 1909

Address: 1209 ORANGE STREET, WILMINGTON, DE 19808

Phone: (888) 266-8489   **Domicile State:** DE   **NAIC Code:** 61492

Data Date	Rating	RACR #1	RACR #2	Total Assets ($mil)	Capital ($mil)	Net Premium ($mil)	Net Income ($mil)
2021	C	0.79	0.51	37,921.8	1,604.5	839.6	-70.2
2020	C	0.88	0.57	34,397.6	1,699.9	450.9	53.9
2019	C	0.84	0.56	28,470.7	1,525.7	1,213.9	-85.8
2018	C	0.86	0.61	21,930.1	1,544.1	4,544.5	18.2
2017	C	0.92	0.71	13,205.1	1,347.7	51.2	24.3

Junk Bonds as a % of Capital

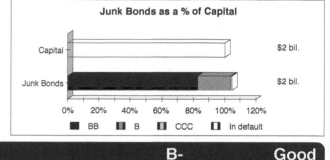

ATHENE ANNUITY & LIFE ASR CO OF NY

B-   **Good**

Major Rating Factors: Good profitability (5.0 on a scale of 0 to 10) despite operating losses during 2021. Return on equity has been low, averaging 3.6%. Fair overall results on stability tests (4.9) including fair financial strength of affiliated BRH Holdings GP Ltd and negative cash flow from operations for 2021. Fair quality investment portfolio (4.3).

Other Rating Factors: Strong capitalization (7.1) based on excellent risk adjusted capital (severe loss scenario). Excellent liquidity (9.6).

Principal Business: Group retirement contracts (85%), individual annuities (14%), and individual life insurance (1%).

Principal Investments: NonCMO investment grade bonds (66%), CMOs and structured securities (18%), noninv. grade bonds (7%), common & preferred stock (3%), and misc. investments (6%).

Investments in Affiliates: 3%

Group Affiliation: BRH Holdings GP Ltd

Licensed In: All states except PR

Commenced Business: October 1966

Address: 69 LYDECKER STREET, PEARL RIVER, NY 10965

Phone: (800) 926-7599   **Domicile State:** NY   **NAIC Code:** 68039

Data Date	Rating	RACR #1	RACR #2	Total Assets ($mil)	Capital ($mil)	Net Premium ($mil)	Net Income ($mil)
2021	B-	1.77	1.04	4,008.7	304.2	563.7	-8.3
2020	C+	1.79	1.06	3,532.4	319.8	241.9	-24.5
2019	C+	2.09	1.17	3,243.4	318.2	183.7	33.0
2018	C+	2.05	1.17	3,148.1	282.1	20.7	6.3
2017	C	1.92	1.06	3,165.0	267.5	10.7	28.7

BRH Holdings GP Ltd Composite Group Rating: C Largest Group Members	Assets ($mil)	Rating
ATHENE ANNUITY LIFE CO	76556	C
VENERABLE INS AND ANNTY CO	40468	C
ATHENE ANNUITY LIFE ASR CO	34398	C
ATHENE ANNUITY LIFE ASR CO OF NY	3532	B-
ASPEN AMERICAN INS CO	1248	C+

ATHENE ANNUITY & LIFE CO

C   **Fair**

Major Rating Factors: Fair capitalization (3.4 on a scale of 0 to 10) based on fair risk adjusted capital (moderate loss scenario). Fair profitability (4.6) with operating losses during 2021. Return on equity has been fair, averaging 6.3%. Fair liquidity (3.7) as cash from operations and sale of marketable assets may not be adequate to cover a spike in claims or a run on policy withdrawals.

Other Rating Factors: Fair overall results on stability tests (3.4) including excessive premium growth and weak risk adjusted capital in prior years. Low quality investment portfolio (2.4).

Principal Business: Group retirement contracts (60%) and individual annuities (39%).

Principal Investments: NonCMO investment grade bonds (35%), CMOs and structured securities (30%), mortgages in good standing (18%), noninv. grade bonds (3%), and misc. investments (11%).

Investments in Affiliates: 14%

Group Affiliation: BRH Holdings GP Ltd

Licensed In: All states except NY

Commenced Business: February 1896

Address: 7700 MILLS CIVIC PARKWAY, WEST DES MOINES, IA 50266-3862

Phone: (888) 266-8489   **Domicile State:** IA   **NAIC Code:** 61689

Data Date	Rating	RACR #1	RACR #2	Total Assets ($mil)	Capital ($mil)	Net Premium ($mil)	Net Income ($mil)
2021	C	0.80	0.45	106,000	1,278.9	3,651.0	-181.5
2020	C	0.97	0.52	76,555.5	1,312.2	1,856.5	-8.0
2019	C	0.97	0.51	65,504.9	1,208.6	1,696.4	241.0
2018	C	0.98	0.52	57,997.0	1,234.2	1,272.5	80.6
2017	C	0.97	0.51	54,933.3	1,164.2	1,533.9	239.3

Junk Bonds as a % of Capital

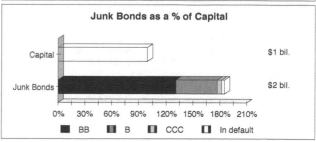

ATHENE LIFE INS CO OF NEW YORK — C — Fair

Major Rating Factors: Fair profitability (4.3 on a scale of 0 to 10) with operating losses during 2021. Return on equity has been low, averaging -0.4%. Good quality investment portfolio (6.5) despite mixed results such as: large holdings of BBB rated bonds but moderate junk bond exposure. Weak overall results on stability tests (2.9) including weak results on operational trends.

Other Rating Factors: Strong capitalization (7.7) based on excellent risk adjusted capital (severe loss scenario). Excellent liquidity (7.0).

Principal Business: Individual life insurance (94%), reinsurance (2%), group life insurance (2%), individual health insurance (1%), and individual annuities (1%).

Principal Investments: NonCMO investment grade bonds (86%), cash (5%), CMOs and structured securities (4%), noninv. grade bonds (2%), and mortgages in good standing (2%).

Investments in Affiliates: None

Group Affiliation: BRH Holdings GP Ltd

Licensed in: CT, FL, IL, IN, IA, KS, KY, MA, MI, MS, NV, NJ, NY, NC, PA, RI, VT

Commenced Business: November 1958

Address: 69 LYDECKER STREET, PEARL RIVER, NY 10965

Phone: (516) 364-5900 **Domicile State:** NY **NAIC Code:** 63932

Data Date	Rating	RACR #1	RACR #2	Total Assets ($mil)	Capital ($mil)	Net Premium ($mil)	Net Income ($mil)
2021	C	2.97	1.46	971.0	85.7	0.6	-1.5
2020	C	3.00	1.46	950.1	87.6	18.6	15.3
2019	C	2.34	1.13	957.6	68.9	-23.8	-1.2
2018	C	2.29	1.11	971.3	69.8	2.0	-21.5
2017	C	2.41	1.17	967.9	75.5	19.1	6.3

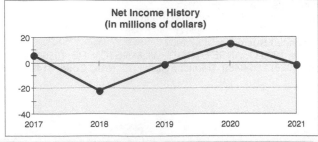

Net Income History
(in millions of dollars)

ATLANTIC COAST LIFE INS CO — C- — Fair

Major Rating Factors: Fair quality investment portfolio (4.0 on a scale of 0 to 10) with significant exposure to mortgages . Mortgage default rate has been low. Weak overall results on stability tests (2.4) including potential financial drain due to affiliation with Advantage Capital Partners LLC. Weak profitability (2.6) with investment income below regulatory standards in relation to interest assumptions of reserves.

Other Rating Factors: Good capitalization (5.3) based on good risk adjusted capital (moderate loss scenario). Excellent liquidity (8.1).

Principal Business: Individual annuities (92%), group life insurance (3%), individual health insurance (2%), and individual life insurance (2%).

Principal Investments: NonCMO investment grade bonds (33%), CMOs and structured securities (22%), cash (20%), mortgages in good standing (12%), and misc. investments (6%).

Investments in Affiliates: 4%

Group Affiliation: Advantage Capital Partners LLC

Licensed in: AL, AK, AZ, AR, CO, DE, FL, GA, HI, IL, IN, IA, KS, KY, LA, MD, MA, MS, MO, MT, NE, NV, NM, NC, ND, OH, OK, OR, PA, RI, SC, SD, TN, TX, UT, VT, VA, WA, WV, WY

Commenced Business: March 1925

Address: 1565 SAM RITTENBERG BOULEVARD, CHARLESTON, SC 29407

Phone: (844) 442-3847 **Domicile State:** SC **NAIC Code:** 61115

Data Date	Rating	RACR #1	RACR #2	Total Assets ($mil)	Capital ($mil)	Net Premium ($mil)	Net Income ($mil)
2021	C-	1.20	0.61	1,076.9	61.4	132.7	4.7
2020	C-	1.45	0.73	758.0	56.7	135.4	7.3
2019	C-	1.52	0.75	466.4	41.0	53.4	8.7
2018	C	1.60	0.79	531.9	28.7	-28.3	5.2
2017	B-	1.66	0.80	445.1	23.7	77.1	3.9

Advantage Capital Partners LLC Composite Group Rating: D Largest Group Members	Assets ($mil)	Rating
HAYMARKET INS CO	2515	D-
ATLANTIC COAST LIFE INS CO	758	C-
SENTINEL SECURITY LIFE INS CO	694	D

AURORA NATIONAL LIFE ASR CO — C — Fair

Major Rating Factors: Fair quality investment portfolio (4.9 on a scale of 0 to 10) with large holdings of BBB rated bonds in addition to junk bond exposure equal to 80% of capital. Exposure to mortgages is significant, but the mortgage default rate has been low. Fair overall results on stability tests (3.6) including negative cash flow from operations for 2021. Good capitalization (6.7) based on good risk adjusted capital (severe loss scenario).

Other Rating Factors: Good overall profitability (6.1) although investment income, in comparison to reserve requirements, is below regulatory standards. Weak liquidity (1.6).

Principal Business: Individual life insurance (97%) and group life insurance (3%).

Principal Investments: NonCMO investment grade bonds (58%), mortgages in good standing (20%), CMOs and structured securities (8%), noninv. grade bonds (4%), and misc. investments (7%).

Investments in Affiliates: None

Group Affiliation: Reinsurance Group of America Inc

Licensed in: All states except CT, ME, NH, NY, PR

Commenced Business: December 1961

Address: 818 WEST 7TH STREET, LOS ANGELES, CA 90017

Phone: (800) 265-2652 **Domicile State:** CA **NAIC Code:** 61182

Data Date	Rating	RACR #1	RACR #2	Total Assets ($mil)	Capital ($mil)	Net Premium ($mil)	Net Income ($mil)
2021	C	1.97	0.96	2,954.8	159.4	0.4	0.9
2020	C	1.74	0.87	2,939.4	145.7	0.4	2.9
2019	C	1.70	0.87	2,936.6	137.7	0.5	8.1
2018	C	1.72	0.89	3,067.2	147.2	0.5	10.4
2017	B	1.64	0.85	3,063.2	140.2	0.7	9.1

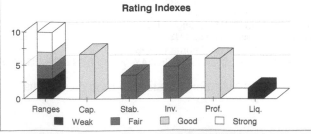

Rating Indexes

Ranges | Cap. | Stab. | Inv. | Prof. | Liq.
■ Weak ■ Fair ☐ Good ☐ Strong

AUTO CLUB LIFE INS CO | C | Fair

Major Rating Factors: Fair capitalization (4.0 on a scale of 0 to 10) based on fair risk adjusted capital (moderate loss scenario). Fair quality investment portfolio (4.7) with large holdings of BBB rated bonds in addition to junk bond exposure equal to 94% of capital. Fair liquidity (4.0) as cash from operations and sale of marketable assets may not be adequate to cover a spike in claims or a run on policy withdrawals.

Other Rating Factors: Fair overall results on stability tests (4.0) including fair risk adjusted capital in prior years. Weak profitability (1.3) with operating losses during 2021.

Principal Business: Reinsurance (97%) and individual life insurance (2%).

Principal Investments: NonCMO investment grade bonds (62%), CMOs and structured securities (20%), noninv. grade bonds (9%), common & preferred stock (6%), and policy loans (1%).

Investments in Affiliates: 6%

Group Affiliation: Automobile Club of Michigan Group

Licensed in: AZ, AR, CA, CO, FL, IL, IN, IA, KS, KY, MD, MI, MN, MO, NE, NM, NC, ND, OH, OK, PA, SC, SD, TX, VA, WA, WI

Commenced Business: August 1974

Address: 1 Auto Club Drive, Dearborn, MI 48126

Phone: (313) 336-1234 **Domicile State:** MI **NAIC Code:** 84522

Data Date	Rating	RACR #1	RACR #2	Total Assets ($mil)	Capital ($mil)	Net Premium ($mil)	Net Income ($mil)
2021	C	0.86	0.62	973.1	82.5	211.8	-29.0
2020	C	0.96	0.69	933.9	91.3	193.6	-22.0
2019	C	1.02	0.73	886.9	91.0	189.3	-4.8
2018	C	1.07	0.77	836.5	90.9	181.6	-2.7
2017	C+	0.98	0.70	760.8	76.4	162.2	-7.0

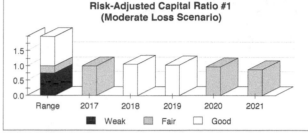

Risk-Adjusted Capital Ratio #1
(Moderate Loss Scenario)

AUTO-OWNERS LIFE INS CO | C+ | Fair

Major Rating Factors: Strong capitalization (4.0 on a scale of 0 to 10) based on excellent risk adjusted capital (severe loss scenario). Moreover, capital levels have been consistently high over the last five years. Fair quality investment portfolio (4.6) with significant exposure to mortgages . Mortgage default rate has been low. Fair overall results on stability tests (3.9).

Other Rating Factors: Good liquidity (6.6). Weak profitability (2.5) with investment income below regulatory standards in relation to interest assumptions of reserves.

Principal Business: Individual life insurance (55%), individual annuities (34%), individual health insurance (6%), group retirement contracts (3%), and group life insurance (1%).

Principal Investments: NonCMO investment grade bonds (49%), CMOs and structured securities (15%), mortgages in good standing (14%), real estate (5%), and misc. investments (15%).

Investments in Affiliates: None

Group Affiliation: Auto-Owners Group

Licensed in: AL, AZ, AR, CO, FL, GA, ID, IL, IN, IA, KS, KY, ME, MA, MI, MN, MS, MO, NE, NV, NH, NM, NC, ND, OH, OR, PA, SC, SD, TN, UT, VT, VA, WA, WI

Commenced Business: January 1966

Address: 6101 ANACAPRI BOULEVARD, LANSING, MI 48917-3968

Phone: (517) 323-1200 **Domicile State:** MI **NAIC Code:** 61190

Data Date	Rating	RACR #1	RACR #2	Total Assets ($mil)	Capital ($mil)	Net Premium ($mil)	Net Income ($mil)
2021	C+	2.46	1.44	4,655.6	618.7	220.1	31.0
2020	B-	3.88	1.96	4,516.8	595.5	-734.4	17.5
2019	B-	3.17	1.71	4,201.1	537.3	243.2	42.8
2018	B	3.21	1.70	3,997.1	489.4	-32.5	29.2
2017	B+	2.82	1.49	4,211.4	451.0	433.6	19.3

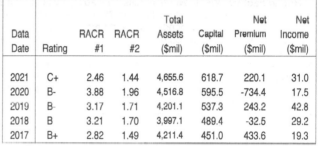

Risk-Adjusted Capital Ratio #2
(Severe Loss Scenario)

AUTOMOBILE CLUB OF SOUTHERN CA INS | C+ | Fair

Major Rating Factors: Fair quality investment portfolio (3.1 on a scale of 0 to 10) with large holdings of BBB rated bonds in addition to significant exposure to junk bonds. Fair overall results on stability tests (4.4) including fair risk adjusted capital in prior years. Good capitalization (5.1) based on good risk adjusted capital (moderate loss scenario).

Other Rating Factors: Weak profitability (1.2) with operating losses during 2021. Weak liquidity (2.4).

Principal Business: Reinsurance (100%).

Principal Investments: NonCMO investment grade bonds (65%), CMOs and structured securities (23%), noninv. grade bonds (10%), and policy loans (1%).

Investments in Affiliates: None

Group Affiliation: Interins Exch Automobile Club

Licensed in: CA, MI

Commenced Business: December 1999

Address: 3333 Fairview Road, Costa Mesa, CA 92626-1698

Phone: (714) 850-5111 **Domicile State:** CA **NAIC Code:** 60256

Data Date	Rating	RACR #1	RACR #2	Total Assets ($mil)	Capital ($mil)	Net Premium ($mil)	Net Income ($mil)
2021	C+	1.09	0.60	1,676.3	84.5	350.1	-47.7
2020	C+	1.30	0.71	1,575.3	100.9	331.6	-43.0
2019	B-	1.43	0.80	1,460.0	101.4	317.5	-17.4
2018	B-	1.40	0.79	1,336.3	93.6	305.2	-15.6
2017	B-	1.19	0.67	1,199.0	72.9	282.2	-17.3

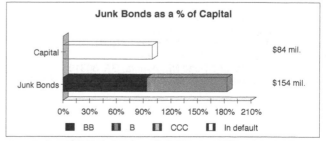

Junk Bonds as a % of Capital

BALTIMORE LIFE INS CO   B   Good

Major Rating Factors: Good capitalization (6.4 on a scale of 0 to 10) based on good risk adjusted capital (severe loss scenario). Good profitability (5.0) despite operating losses during 2021. Return on equity has been low, averaging 1.8%. Fair quality investment portfolio (4.8) with large holdings of BBB rated bonds in addition to junk bond exposure equal to 56% of capital.

Other Rating Factors: Fair overall results on stability tests (4.1). Weak liquidity (2.0).

Principal Business: Individual life insurance (89%) and individual annuities (10%).

Principal Investments: NonCMO investment grade bonds (81%), CMOs and structured securities (3%), noninv. grade bonds (2%), policy loans (1%), and misc. investments (12%).

Investments in Affiliates: None

Group Affiliation: Baltimore Life Holdings Inc

Licensed in: All states except NY, PR

Commenced Business: March 1882

Address: 10075 Red Run Boulevard, Owings Mills, MD 21117

Phone: (410) 581-6600 **Domicile State:** MD **NAIC Code:** 61212

Data Date	Rating	RACR #1	RACR #2	Total Assets ($mil)	Capital ($mil)	Net Premium ($mil)	Net Income ($mil)
2021	B	1.81	0.93	1,299.4	87.5	83.2	-0.9
2020	B	1.81	0.92	1,299.2	92.0	83.5	3.4
2019	B	1.85	0.96	1,306.4	90.7	111.9	3.3
2018	B	1.73	0.90	1,296.5	84.2	119.6	0.1
2017	B	1.68	0.88	1,268.8	81.8	124.6	2.4

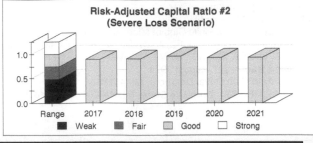

Risk-Adjusted Capital Ratio #2
(Severe Loss Scenario)

BANKERS CONSECO LIFE INS CO   D   Weak

Major Rating Factors: Weak overall results on stability tests (1.8 on a scale of 0 to 10). Good quality investment portfolio (5.7) despite mixed results such as: large holdings of BBB rated bonds but moderate junk bond exposure. Good liquidity (6.3) with sufficient resources to handle a spike in claims as well as a significant increase in policy surrenders.

Other Rating Factors: Strong capitalization (8.8) based on excellent risk adjusted capital (severe loss scenario). Excellent profitability (7.6).

Principal Business: Individual life insurance (70%), individual health insurance (16%), and individual annuities (14%).

Principal Investments: NonCMO investment grade bonds (79%), CMOs and structured securities (12%), noninv. grade bonds (3%), and policy loans (1%).

Investments in Affiliates: None

Group Affiliation: CNO Financial Group Inc

Licensed in: NY

Commenced Business: July 1987

Address: 350 JERICHO TURNPIKE SUITE 304, JERICHO, NY 11753

Phone: (317) 817-6100 **Domicile State:** NY **NAIC Code:** 68560

Data Date	Rating	RACR #1	RACR #2	Total Assets ($mil)	Capital ($mil)	Net Premium ($mil)	Net Income ($mil)
2021	D	4.27	2.17	559.3	70.9	70.1	7.4
2020	D	3.84	1.92	536.6	64.8	63.4	3.1
2019	D	3.64	1.89	523.5	61.5	65.9	0.3
2018	D	3.37	1.69	496.1	59.4	61.2	0.6
2017	D	3.31	1.67	478.1	58.2	58.3	-1.4

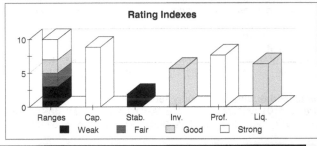

Rating Indexes

BANKERS FIDELITY LIFE INS CO   C-   Fair

Major Rating Factors: Fair quality investment portfolio (4.8 on a scale of 0 to 10). Fair overall results on stability tests (3.3) including negative cash flow from operations for 2021, fair risk adjusted capital in prior years. Weak profitability (1.9). Excellent expense controls. Return on equity has been low, averaging -7.9%.

Other Rating Factors: Good capitalization (6.7) based on good risk adjusted capital (severe loss scenario). Good liquidity (5.2).

Principal Business: Individual health insurance (66%), reinsurance (26%), individual life insurance (4%), group health insurance (2%), and group life insurance (2%).

Principal Investments: NonCMO investment grade bonds (68%), common & preferred stock (16%), CMOs and structured securities (10%), policy loans (1%), and misc. investments (2%).

Investments in Affiliates: 5%

Group Affiliation: Atlantic American Corp

Licensed in: All states except CA, CT, NY, VT, PR

Commenced Business: November 1955

Address: 4370 Peachtree Road NE, Atlanta, GA 30319

Phone: (800) 241-1439 **Domicile State:** GA **NAIC Code:** 61239

Data Date	Rating	RACR #1	RACR #2	Total Assets ($mil)	Capital ($mil)	Net Premium ($mil)	Net Income ($mil)
2021	C-	1.30	0.96	162.5	38.6	116.7	0.2
2020	C-	1.33	1.00	164.7	42.3	121.0	8.2
2019	C	0.85	0.72	159.1	35.5	123.3	-8.9
2018	C	1.09	0.87	152.5	34.2	119.0	-3.4
2017	B-	1.21	0.93	150.0	34.1	109.6	-2.9

Rating Indexes

BANKERS LIFE & CAS CO | D+ | Weak

Major Rating Factors: Weak overall results on stability tests (2.7 on a scale of 0 to 10). Fair quality investment portfolio (4.7) with large holdings of BBB rated bonds in addition to junk bond exposure equal to 76% of capital. Fair liquidity (4.8) as cash from operations and sale of marketable assets may not be adequate to cover a spike in claims or a run on policy withdrawals.

Other Rating Factors: Good capitalization (6.9) based on good risk adjusted capital (severe loss scenario). Good overall profitability (5.8).

Principal Business: Individual annuities (47%), individual health insurance (21%), individual life insurance (17%), reinsurance (13%), and group health insurance (1%).

Principal Investments: NonCMO investment grade bonds (52%), CMOs and structured securities (29%), noninv. grade bonds (5%), mortgages in good standing (5%), and misc. investments (8%).

Investments in Affiliates: 1%

Group Affiliation: CNO Financial Group Inc

Licensed in: All states except NY, PR

Commenced Business: January 1879

Address: 111 EAST WACKER DRIVE STE 2100, CHICAGO, IL 60601-4508

Phone: (312) 396-6000 **Domicile State:** IL **NAIC Code:** 61263

Data Date	Rating	RACR #1	RACR #2	Total Assets ($mil)	Capital ($mil)	Net Premium ($mil)	Net Income ($mil)
2021	D+	1.83	0.99	18,541.7	1,241.2	2,727.2	194.8
2020	D+	1.90	1.03	17,025.1	1,234.7	2,505.5	339.5
2019	D+	1.78	1.00	16,369.5	1,176.7	2,646.3	225.9
2018	D+	1.64	0.92	15,514.6	1,110.2	2,556.4	-299.9
2017	D+	2.10	1.11	18,273.9	1,336.8	2,581.5	249.3

Rating Indexes

Ranges | Cap. | Stab. | Inv. | Prof. | Liq.
■ Weak ■ Fair □ Good □ Strong

BANNER LIFE INS CO | C- | Fair

Major Rating Factors: Fair liquidity (3.4 on a scale of 0 to 10) as cash from operations and sale of marketable assets may not be adequate to cover a spike in claims or a run on policy withdrawals. Weak profitability (1.9). Excellent expense controls. Return on equity has been low, averaging -10.0%. Weak overall results on stability tests (2.7) including weak results on operational trends.

Other Rating Factors: Good quality investment portfolio (5.6). Strong capitalization (7.5) based on excellent risk adjusted capital (severe loss scenario).

Principal Business: Individual life insurance (53%) and group retirement contracts (46%).

Principal Investments: NonCMO investment grade bonds (55%), mortgages in good standing (16%), CMOs and structured securities (8%), common & preferred stock (6%), and noninv. grade bonds (2%).

Investments in Affiliates: 6%

Group Affiliation: Legal & General America Inc

Licensed in: All states except NY

Commenced Business: October 1981

Address: 3275 BENNETT CREEK AVENUE, FREDERICK, MD 21704

Phone: (301) 279-4800 **Domicile State:** MD **NAIC Code:** 94250

Data Date	Rating	RACR #1	RACR #2	Total Assets ($mil)	Capital ($mil)	Net Premium ($mil)	Net Income ($mil)
2021	C-	1.87	1.34	7,266.8	766.4	477.9	24.4
2020	C-	1.67	1.22	6,462.0	660.3	1,090.3	107.0
2019	C	1.90	1.35	5,048.0	615.3	362.5	-59.0
2018	C	3.28	2.16	4,385.5	735.9	1,298.3	-512.8
2017	B-	3.96	2.72	3,850.8	751.6	967.6	65.5

Adverse Trends in Operations

Change in premium mix from 2019 to 2020 (22.5%)
Decrease in capital during 2019 (16%)
Change in premium mix from 2018 to 2019 (37%)
Decrease in premium volume from 2018 to 2019 (72%)
Decrease in capital during 2018 (2%)

BENEFICIAL LIFE INS CO | B | Good

Major Rating Factors: Good quality investment portfolio (6.9 on a scale of 0 to 10) despite mixed results such as: minimal exposure to mortgages and large holdings of BBB rated bonds but small junk bond holdings. Good liquidity (5.3) with sufficient resources to handle a spike in claims as well as a significant increase in policy surrenders. Good overall results on stability tests (6.0) despite negative cash flow from operations for 2021 good operational trends and excellent risk diversification.

Other Rating Factors: Fair profitability (4.2) with investment income below regulatory standards in relation to interest assumptions of reserves. Strong capitalization (8.3) based on excellent risk adjusted capital (severe loss scenario).

Principal Business: Individual life insurance (93%), individual annuities (4%), and reinsurance (3%).

Principal Investments: NonCMO investment grade bonds (82%), CMOs and structured securities (7%), policy loans (5%), common & preferred stock (1%), and misc. investments (3%).

Investments in Affiliates: None

Group Affiliation: DMC Reserve Trust

Licensed in: All states except NY, PR

Commenced Business: May 1905

Address: 55 North 300 West Suite 375, Salt Lake City, UT 84101

Phone: (801) 933-1100 **Domicile State:** UT **NAIC Code:** 61395

Data Date	Rating	RACR #1	RACR #2	Total Assets ($mil)	Capital ($mil)	Net Premium ($mil)	Net Income ($mil)
2021	B	3.46	1.87	1,944.1	198.2	22.7	4.1
2020	B	3.27	1.75	2,005.5	194.4	23.5	-0.6
2019	B	3.30	1.78	2,068.0	196.7	29.3	9.9
2018	B	2.88	1.52	2,132.4	184.9	28.2	13.1
2017	B	2.36	1.31	2,251.3	205.7	32.2	13.4

Adverse Trends in Operations

Decrease in asset base during 2020 (3%)
Decrease in premium volume from 2019 to 2020 (20%)
Decrease in capital during 2018 (10%)
Decrease in premium volume from 2017 to 2018 (12%)
Decrease in premium volume from 2016 to 2017 (9%)

BERKLEY LIFE & HEALTH INS CO ^   A   Excellent

Major Rating Factors: Excellent overall results on stability tests (7.8 on a scale of 0 to 10). Strengths that enhance stability include excellent operational trends and excellent risk diversification. Strong capitalization (10.0) based on excellent risk adjusted capital (severe loss scenario). Furthermore, this high level of risk adjusted capital has been consistently maintained over the last five years. High quality investment portfolio (7.6).

Other Rating Factors: Excellent profitability (8.6) with operating gains in each of the last five years. Excellent liquidity (8.8).

Principal Business: Group health insurance (99%) and reinsurance (1%).

Principal Investments: CMOs and structured securities (48%), nonCMO investment grade bonds (46%), and cash (6%).

Investments in Affiliates: None

Group Affiliation: W R Berkley Corp

Licensed in: All states except PR

Commenced Business: July 1963

Address: 11201 DOUGLAS AVE, URBANDALE, IA 50322

Phone: (609) 584-6990 **Domicile State:** IA **NAIC Code:** 64890

Data Date	Rating	RACR #1	RACR #2	Total Assets ($mil)	Capital ($mil)	Net Premium ($mil)	Net Income ($mil)
2021	A	8.37	5.76	478.2	293.7	239.9	57.4
2020	A	7.62	5.42	395.7	237.0	221.4	45.2
2019	A	5.18	3.72	363.1	194.5	271.6	28.0
2018	A	4.59	3.35	324.2	166.6	268.0	16.5
2017	A	4.73	3.50	277.3	150.7	238.1	8.2

Adverse Trends in Operations

Decrease in premium volume from 2019 to 2020 (19%)

BERKSHIRE HATHAWAY LIFE INS CO OF NE   C+   Fair

Major Rating Factors: Fair overall results on stability tests (3.7 on a scale of 0 to 10) including fair financial strength of affiliated Berkshire-Hathaway and negative cash flow from operations for 2021. Strong capitalization (4.0) based on excellent risk adjusted capital (severe loss scenario). Capital levels have been relatively consistent over the last five years. Fair quality investment portfolio (3.8).

Other Rating Factors: Fair profitability (4.6). Good liquidity (6.9).

Principal Business: Reinsurance (69%), group retirement contracts (26%), and individual annuities (5%).

Principal Investments: Common & preferred stock (51%), nonCMO investment grade bonds (19%), and CMOs and structured securities (1%).

Investments in Affiliates: 39%

Group Affiliation: Berkshire-Hathaway

Licensed in: All states except PR

Commenced Business: June 1993

Address: 1314 Douglas Street Suite 1400, Omaha, NE 68102-1944

Phone: (402) 916-3000 **Domicile State:** NE **NAIC Code:** 62345

Data Date	Rating	RACR #1	RACR #2	Total Assets ($mil)	Capital ($mil)	Net Premium ($mil)	Net Income ($mil)
2021	C+	1.58	1.31	23,719.2	9,283.7	1,075.4	128.1
2020	C+	1.51	1.25	23,422.1	7,486.9	-1,634.2	-847.2
2019	C+	1.69	1.40	20,830.4	7,524.1	1,283.7	1,489.8
2018	C+	1.24	1.05	18,411.7	5,414.2	2,549.0	118.1
2017	C+	1.52	1.31	19,610.1	4,816.0	225.2	437.6

Berkshire-Hathaway
Composite Group Rating: C+
Largest Group Members

	Assets ($mil)	Rating
NATIONAL INDEMNITY CO	317406	C+
GOVERNMENT EMPLOYEES INS CO	44674	B
COLUMBIA INS CO	32046	C+
BERKSHIRE HATHAWAY LIFE INS CO OF NE	23422	C+
GENERAL REINS CORP	18513	C+

BERKSHIRE LIFE INS CO OF AMERICA   B   Good

Major Rating Factors: Good overall profitability (6.7 on a scale of 0 to 10) despite operating losses during 2021. Return on equity has been fair, averaging 9.3%. Good overall results on stability tests (6.2). Strengths include excellent financial support from affiliation with Guardian Group, excellent operational trends and excellent risk diversification. Fair quality investment portfolio (4.4).

Other Rating Factors: Strong capitalization (7.4) based on excellent risk adjusted capital (severe loss scenario). Excellent liquidity (8.2).

Principal Business: Individual health insurance (82%), reinsurance (16%), and individual life insurance (1%).

Principal Investments: NonCMO investment grade bonds (93%), noninv. grade bonds (2%), and mortgages in good standing (1%).

Investments in Affiliates: None

Group Affiliation: Guardian Group

Licensed in: All states except PR

Commenced Business: July 2001

Address: 700 SOUTH STREET, PITTSFIELD, MA 1201

Phone: (413) 499-4321 **Domicile State:** MA **NAIC Code:** 71714

Data Date	Rating	RACR #1	RACR #2	Total Assets ($mil)	Capital ($mil)	Net Premium ($mil)	Net Income ($mil)
2021	B	2.65	1.28	4,680.8	220.9	143.7	-4.2
2020	B	2.58	1.24	4,410.8	213.0	139.1	15.4
2019	B	2.85	1.40	4,181.5	219.9	135.3	83.6
2018	B	2.44	1.16	3,927.6	192.7	131.4	-13.3
2017	B	2.57	1.20	3,717.7	189.1	126.9	10.2

Rating Indexes

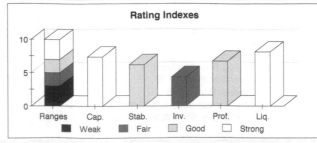

Ranges   Cap.   Stab.   Inv.   Prof.   Liq.

■ Weak   ■ Fair   ☐ Good   ☐ Strong

BEST MERIDIAN INS CO

C- **Fair**

Major Rating Factors: Fair quality investment portfolio (3.4 on a scale of 0 to 10). Fair overall results on stability tests (3.1) including fair risk adjusted capital in prior years. Weak profitability (1.7) with operating losses during 2021.

Other Rating Factors: Good capitalization (5.0) based on good risk adjusted capital (moderate loss scenario). Good liquidity (6.5).

Principal Business: Reinsurance (62%), individual life insurance (30%), individual health insurance (7%), and group health insurance (1%).

Principal Investments: NonCMO investment grade bonds (44%), cash (22%), CMOs and structured securities (12%), real estate (10%), and misc. investments (12%).

Investments in Affiliates: None

Group Affiliation: BMI Financial Group

Licensed in: FL

Commenced Business: August 1987

Address: 8950 SW 74TH COURT, MIAMI, FL 33156

Phone: (305) 443-2898 **Domicile State:** FL **NAIC Code:** 63886

Data Date	Rating	RACR #1	RACR #2	Total Assets ($mil)	Capital ($mil)	Net Premium ($mil)	Net Income ($mil)
2021	C-	1.02	0.67	399.4	40.9	158.6	-16.4
2020	C	1.31	0.89	383.9	58.9	159.2	0.8
2019	B-	1.65	1.09	376.2	61.5	119.8	3.1
2018	B-	1.72	1.13	350.4	59.9	119.8	1.9
2017	B-	1.64	1.06	336.9	54.2	111.5	1.1

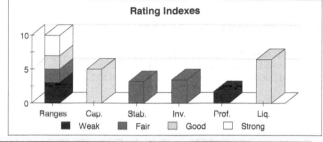

Rating Indexes

BLUE CROSS BLUE SHIELD OF KANSAS INCORPORATED

B **Good**

Major Rating Factors: Good liquidity (5.7 on a scale of 0 to 10) with sufficient resources to handle a spike in claims. Good overall results on stability tests (6.0) despite negative cash flow from operations for 2021. Other stability subfactors include excellent operational trends and excellent risk diversification. Fair quality investment portfolio (4.6).

Other Rating Factors: Strong capitalization (7.9) based on excellent risk adjusted capital (severe loss scenario). Excellent profitability (7.8) with operating gains in each of the last five years.

Principal Business: Group health insurance (72%) and individual health insurance (28%).

Principal Investments: NonCMO investment grade bonds (31%), common & preferred stock (26%), CMOs and structured securities (18%), noninv. grade bonds (2%), and real estate (2%).

Investments in Affiliates: 8%

Group Affiliation: Blue Cross Blue Shield Kansas

Licensed in: KS

Commenced Business: July 1942

Address: 1133 SW Topeka Boulevard, Topeka, KS 66629-0001

Phone: (785) 291-7000 **Domicile State:** KS **NAIC Code:** 70729

Data Date	Rating	RACR #1	RACR #2	Total Assets ($mil)	Capital ($mil)	Net Premium ($mil)	Net Income ($mil)
2021	B	2.10	1.62	2,277.0	1,085.8	2,323.0	77.9
2020	B	1.71	1.32	2,209.7	898.6	2,426.8	32.8
2019	B	2.10	1.60	1,929.4	976.6	2,367.7	65.5
2018	B	1.89	1.45	1,765.8	892.5	2,259.0	105.1
2017	B	2.06	1.54	1,730.4	791.6	1,775.0	3.4

Adverse Trends in Operations

Decrease in capital during 2020 (8%)
Decrease in premium volume from 2016 to 2017 (7%)

BLUE SHIELD OF CALIFORNIA L&H INS CO

B **Good**

Major Rating Factors: Good profitability (5.0 on a scale of 0 to 10) despite operating losses during 2021. Return on equity has been fair, averaging 5.6%. Good liquidity (6.6) with sufficient resources to handle a spike in claims. Good overall results on stability tests (5.5) excellent operational trends and excellent risk diversification.

Other Rating Factors: Strong capitalization (10.0) based on excellent risk adjusted capital (severe loss scenario). High quality investment portfolio (8.1).

Principal Business: Individual health insurance (57%), group health insurance (39%), and group life insurance (4%).

Principal Investments: CMOs and structured securities (47%), nonCMO investment grade bonds (45%), and cash (1%).

Investments in Affiliates: None

Group Affiliation: Blue Shield of California

Licensed in: CA

Commenced Business: July 1954

Address: 50 Beale Street, Oakland, CA 94607

Phone: (800) 642-5599 **Domicile State:** CA **NAIC Code:** 61557

Data Date	Rating	RACR #1	RACR #2	Total Assets ($mil)	Capital ($mil)	Net Premium ($mil)	Net Income ($mil)
2021	B	4.30	3.24	256.1	146.9	227.1	-6.9
2020	B	4.25	3.19	250.6	157.0	245.1	21.9
2019	B	3.73	2.83	253.9	135.2	242.3	9.1
2018	B	5.09	3.75	303.2	191.1	242.3	12.4
2017	B	4.61	3.41	303.5	179.2	253.4	9.7

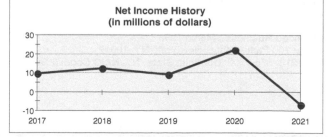

Net Income History
(in millions of dollars)

BLUEBONNET LIFE INS CO ^   A-   Excellent

Major Rating Factors: Good overall results on stability tests (6.4 on a scale of 0 to 10). Strengths that enhance stability include excellent operational trends and good risk diversification. Strong capitalization (10.0) based on excellent risk adjusted capital (severe loss scenario). Furthermore, this high level of risk adjusted capital has been consistently maintained over the last five years. High quality investment portfolio (8.1).

Other Rating Factors: Excellent profitability (8.4) with operating gains in each of the last five years. Excellent liquidity (10.0).

Principal Business: Group life insurance (97%) and individual life insurance (3%).

Principal Investments: NonCMO investment grade bonds (60%), CMOs and structured securities (28%), noninv. grade bonds (1%), and common & preferred stock (1%).

Investments in Affiliates: None

Group Affiliation: Bl Cross & Bl Shield of Mississippi

Licensed in: AL, AR, LA, MS, TN

Commenced Business: June 1984

Address: 3545 Lakeland Dr, Flowood, MS 39232

Phone: (601) 664-4218 **Domicile State:** MS **NAIC Code:** 68535

Data Date	Rating	RACR #1	RACR #2	Total Assets ($mil)	Capital ($mil)	Net Premium ($mil)	Net Income ($mil)
2021	A-	8.69	7.82	71.5	66.7	3.4	2.6
2020	A-	8.70	7.83	70.5	66.5	3.6	2.7
2019	A-	8.46	7.62	67.5	63.6	4.4	2.8
2018	B+	8.28	7.45	64.2	60.9	4.5	3.1
2017	B+	7.91	7.12	61.3	57.2	4.6	2.6

Adverse Trends in Operations

Decrease in premium volume from 2019 to 2020 (17%)
Decrease in premium volume from 2018 to 2019 (2%)
Decrease in premium volume from 2017 to 2018 (2%)
Decrease in premium volume from 2016 to 2017 (2%)

BOSTON MUTUAL LIFE INS CO *   B+   Good

Major Rating Factors: Good quality investment portfolio (5.8 on a scale of 0 to 10) despite significant exposure to mortgages . Mortgage default rate has been low. large holdings of BBB rated bonds in addition to small junk bond holdings. Good liquidity (5.4) with sufficient resources to handle a spike in claims as well as a significant increase in policy surrenders. Good overall results on stability tests (6.4) excellent operational trends and excellent risk diversification.

Other Rating Factors: Strong capitalization (7.8) based on excellent risk adjusted capital (severe loss scenario). Excellent profitability (7.3).

Principal Business: Individual life insurance (61%), group life insurance (18%), group health insurance (18%), and individual health insurance (2%).

Principal Investments: NonCMO investment grade bonds (57%), mortgages in good standing (13%), policy loans (11%), common & preferred stock (10%), and misc. investments (6%).

Investments in Affiliates: 3%

Group Affiliation: Boston Mutual Group

Licensed in: All states, the District of Columbia and Puerto Rico

Commenced Business: February 1892

Address: 120 Royall Street, Canton, MA 02021-1098

Phone: (781) 828-7000 **Domicile State:** MA **NAIC Code:** 61476

Data Date	Rating	RACR #1	RACR #2	Total Assets ($mil)	Capital ($mil)	Net Premium ($mil)	Net Income ($mil)
2021	B+	2.36	1.54	1,634.0	284.2	189.2	37.5
2020	B+	2.19	1.42	1,582.4	256.2	201.5	-0.3
2019	B+	2.24	1.45	1,529.5	245.9	200.9	18.1
2018	B+	2.02	1.34	1,465.1	219.1	202.3	13.9
2017	B+	2.26	1.48	1,430.5	209.4	196.7	13.9

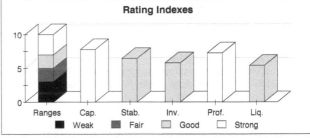

Rating Indexes — Ranges, Cap., Stab., Inv., Prof., Liq. — ■ Weak ■ Fair ☐ Good ☐ Strong

BRIGHTHOUSE LIFE INS CO OF NY   C   Fair

Major Rating Factors: Fair overall results on stability tests (4.2 on a scale of 0 to 10) including excessive premium growth and negative cash flow from operations for 2021. Good quality investment portfolio (6.5) despite mixed results such as: minimal exposure to mortgages and large holdings of BBB rated bonds but small junk bond holdings. Weak profitability (1.2) with operating losses during 2021.

Other Rating Factors: Strong capitalization (7.8) based on excellent risk adjusted capital (severe loss scenario). Excellent liquidity (8.8).

Principal Business: Individual annuities (94%) and individual life insurance (6%).

Principal Investments: NonCMO investment grade bonds (49%), cash (13%), CMOs and structured securities (10%), mortgages in good standing (9%), and noninv. grade bonds (2%).

Investments in Affiliates: None

Group Affiliation: Brighthouse Financial Inc

Licensed in: NY

Commenced Business: March 1993

Address: 200 Park Avenue, New York, NY 10017

Phone: (212) 578-9500 **Domicile State:** NY **NAIC Code:** 60992

Data Date	Rating	RACR #1	RACR #2	Total Assets ($mil)	Capital ($mil)	Net Premium ($mil)	Net Income ($mil)
2021	C	3.07	1.52	11,631.9	356.8	964.9	-52.1
2020	C-	2.90	1.51	9,819.9	372.9	646.3	-390.1
2019	C+	6.01	2.92	8,660.0	578.9	-191.2	-139.1
2018	C+	2.04	1.10	7,484.4	279.2	462.5	18.8
2017	C+	2.50	1.27	7,834.7	294.3	285.4	22.2

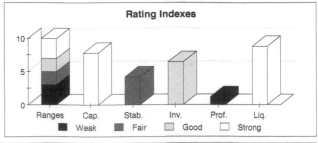

Rating Indexes — Ranges, Cap., Stab., Inv., Prof., Liq. — ■ Weak ■ Fair ☐ Good ☐ Strong

BRIGHTHOUSE LIFE INSURANCE CO

B-   **Good**

Major Rating Factors: Good quality investment portfolio (6.6 on a scale of 0 to 10) despite substantial holdings of BBB bonds in addition to moderate junk bond exposure. Exposure to mortgages is significant, but the mortgage default rate has been low. Good overall profitability (5.3) despite operating losses during 2021. Return on equity has been good over the last five years, averaging 10.6%. Good liquidity (6.8).

Other Rating Factors: Good overall results on stability tests (5.3) excellent operational trends and excellent risk diversification. Strong capitalization (8.5) based on excellent risk adjusted capital (severe loss scenario).

Principal Business: Individual annuities (70%), individual life insurance (19%), reinsurance (9%), and individual health insurance (2%).

Principal Investments: NonCMO investment grade bonds (46%), CMOs and structured securities (19%), mortgages in good standing (16%), noninv. grade bonds (4%), and misc. investments (11%).

Investments in Affiliates: 1%

Group Affiliation: Brighthouse Financial Inc

Licensed in: All states except NY

Commenced Business: April 1864

Address: 1209 Orange Street, Wilmington, DE 19801

Phone: (980) 365-7100 **Domicile State:** DE **NAIC Code:** 87726

Data Date	Rating	RACR #1	RACR #2	Total Assets ($mil)	Capital ($mil)	Net Premium ($mil)	Net Income ($mil)
2021	B-	3.83	1.98	201,000	7,762.7	9,077.0	-155.7
2020	C+	3.60	1.90	188,000	7,409.8	8,037.8	-979.0
2019	B	3.90	2.16	177,000	8,746.3	7,150.1	1,074.4
2018	B	3.13	1.66	164,000	6,730.8	6,127.9	-1,104.0
2017	B	3.06	1.61	176,000	5,594.3	11,351.1	-424.8

Rating Indexes

BROOKE LIFE INS CO

C   **Fair**

Major Rating Factors: Fair overall results on stability tests (3.5 on a scale of 0 to 10) including negative cash flow from operations for 2021. Good capitalization (6.0) based on good risk adjusted capital (severe loss scenario). Capital levels have been relatively consistent over the last five years. Good overall profitability (6.4) despite operating losses during 2021. Return on equity has been fair, averaging 6.4%.

Other Rating Factors: Low quality investment portfolio (1.2). Excellent liquidity (7.0).

Principal Business: Reinsurance (86%) and individual annuities (14%).

Principal Investments: Common & preferred stock (95%), nonCMO investment grade bonds (4%), and CMOs and structured securities (1%).

Investments in Affiliates: 95%

Group Affiliation: Prudential plc

Licensed in: MI

Commenced Business: August 1987

Address: 1 CORPORATE WAY, LANSING, MI 48951

Phone: (517) 381-5500 **Domicile State:** MI **NAIC Code:** 78620

Data Date	Rating	RACR #1	RACR #2	Total Assets ($mil)	Capital ($mil)	Net Premium ($mil)	Net Income ($mil)
2021	C	0.99	0.88	6,432.0	6,095.7	30.5	-94.1
2020	U	0.92	0.82	5,066.1	4,722.5	33.2	-85.1
2019	B-	0.92	0.82	5,087.9	4,760.5	32.5	511.3
2018	B-	1.17	1.04	5,178.3	4,852.5	33.1	461.5
2017	B	1.15	1.02	4,299.7	3,936.5	39.3	604.7

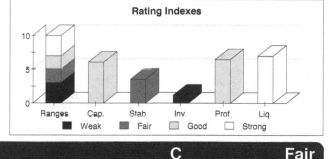

Rating Indexes

CANADA LIFE ASSURANCE CO-US BRANCH

C   **Fair**

Major Rating Factors: Fair liquidity (3.8 on a scale of 0 to 10) as cash from operations and sale of marketable assets may not be adequate to cover a spike in claims or a run on policy withdrawals. Good current capitalization (6.1) based on good risk adjusted capital (severe loss scenario), although results have slipped from the excellent range over the last year. Good quality investment portfolio (5.9).

Other Rating Factors: Weak profitability (2.1) with operating losses during 2021. Weak overall results on stability tests (2.6) including weak results on operational trends.

Principal Business: Reinsurance (100%).

Principal Investments: NonCMO investment grade bonds (59%), mortgages in good standing (15%), CMOs and structured securities (14%), policy loans (8%), and misc. investments (4%).

Investments in Affiliates: None

Group Affiliation: Great West Life Asr

Licensed in: All states except PR

Commenced Business: August 1847

Address: 330 University Avenue, Toronto, ON M5G 1R8

Phone: (303) 737-3000 **Domicile State:** MI **NAIC Code:** 80659

Data Date	Rating	RACR #1	RACR #2	Total Assets ($mil)	Capital ($mil)	Net Premium ($mil)	Net Income ($mil)
2021	C	1.69	0.89	3,928.3	188.2	99.5	-67.4
2020	C	2.31	1.24	4,210.2	259.0	197.4	13.3
2019	C	1.68	0.90	4,120.7	204.0	-58.3	65.3
2018	C	1.41	0.75	4,538.0	187.3	146.1	29.4
2017	C	1.18	0.63	4,581.8	147.1	134.6	-3.9

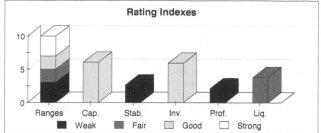

Rating Indexes

CANADA LIFE REINSURANCE COMPANY

C+   Fair

Major Rating Factors: Fair profitability (4.1 on a scale of 0 to 10). Excellent expense controls. Return on equity has been low, averaging 3.7%. Fair overall results on stability tests (3.0) including weak results on operational trends. Strong overall capitalization (10.0) based on excellent risk adjusted capital (severe loss scenario). Nevertheless, capital levels have fluctuated during prior years.

Other Rating Factors: High quality investment portfolio (8.4). Excellent liquidity (9.5).

Principal Business: N/A

Principal Investments: NonCMO investment grade bonds (78%), CMOs and structured securities (12%), and cash (7%).

Investments in Affiliates: None

Group Affiliation: Great West Life Asr

Licensed in: All states, the District of Columbia and Puerto Rico

Commenced Business: December 1969

Address: 1787 Sentry Pkwy W Bldg 16, Blue Bell, PA 19422-2240

Phone: (215) 542-4301   **Domicile State:** PA   **NAIC Code:** 76694

Data Date	Rating	RACR #1	RACR #2	Total Assets ($mil)	Capital ($mil)	Net Premium ($mil)	Net Income ($mil)
2021	C+	4.87	4.38	54.1	33.6	0.1	1.7
2020	C+	3.79	2.99	99.9	33.9	5.9	3.3
2019	C+	6.37	5.62	144.1	59.4	2.3	-2.9
2018	C+	6.75	5.06	154.3	63.2	-55.6	4.7
2017	C+	5.97	3.66	204.0	58.3	1.1	0.9

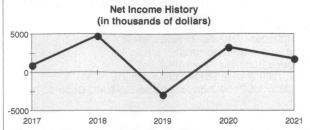

Net Income History (in thousands of dollars)

CAPITOL LIFE INS CO

B-   Good

Major Rating Factors: Good liquidity (6.6 on a scale of 0 to 10) with sufficient resources to handle a spike in claims as well as a significant increase in policy surrenders. Good overall results on stability tests (5.0). Stability strengths include good operational trends and good risk diversification. Fair quality investment portfolio (4.3).

Other Rating Factors: Fair profitability (4.7) with investment income below regulatory standards in relation to interest assumptions of reserves. Strong capitalization (7.5) based on excellent risk adjusted capital (severe loss scenario).

Principal Business: Individual annuities (85%), individual health insurance (12%), and individual life insurance (3%).

Principal Investments: NonCMO investment grade bonds (50%), mortgages in good standing (19%), CMOs and structured securities (19%), cash (6%), and noninv. grade bonds (4%).

Investments in Affiliates: None

Group Affiliation: Liberty Life Group Trust

Licensed in: All states except NY, PR

Commenced Business: August 1905

Address: 1605 LBJ Freeway Suite 710, Dallas, TX 75234

Phone: (469) 522-4400   **Domicile State:** TX   **NAIC Code:** 61581

Data Date	Rating	RACR #1	RACR #2	Total Assets ($mil)	Capital ($mil)	Net Premium ($mil)	Net Income ($mil)
2021	B-	2.82	1.36	540.9	53.2	122.6	1.5
2020	C+	3.64	1.74	385.7	43.9	104.2	0.5
2019	C	3.25	1.55	298.9	31.9	18.8	2.7
2018	C	2.98	1.58	301.6	29.6	23.5	3.2
2017	C	2.62	1.44	301.3	25.6	72.2	1.0

Adverse Trends in Operations

Increase in policy surrenders from 2019 to 2020 (77%)
Decrease in premium volume from 2018 to 2019 (20%)
Increase in policy surrenders from 2017 to 2018 (75%)
Decrease in premium volume from 2017 to 2018 (68%)
Change in premium mix from 2016 to 2017 (16.4%)

CENTRAL STATES H & L CO OF OMAHA *

A-   Excellent

Major Rating Factors: Good quality investment portfolio (5.8 on a scale of 0 to 10) despite mixed results such as: minimal exposure to mortgages and substantial holdings of BBB bonds but minimal holdings in junk bonds. Good overall results on stability tests (6.9) despite negative cash flow from operations for 2021. Strengths that enhance stability include good operational trends and excellent risk diversification. Strong capitalization (10.0) based on excellent risk adjusted capital (severe loss scenario).

Other Rating Factors: Excellent profitability (7.8) despite modest operating losses during 2018. Excellent liquidity (7.0).

Principal Business: Reinsurance (47%), credit life insurance (26%), individual health insurance (13%), credit health insurance (12%), and individual life insurance (1%).

Principal Investments: NonCMO investment grade bonds (37%), CMOs and structured securities (22%), common & preferred stock (13%), mortgages in good standing (5%), and misc. investments (19%).

Investments in Affiliates: 8%

Group Affiliation: Central States Group

Licensed in: All states except NY, PR

Commenced Business: June 1932

Address: 1212 North 96th Street, Omaha, NE 68114

Phone: (402) 397-1111   **Domicile State:** NE   **NAIC Code:** 61751

Data Date	Rating	RACR #1	RACR #2	Total Assets ($mil)	Capital ($mil)	Net Premium ($mil)	Net Income ($mil)
2021	A-	4.04	3.06	386.9	182.5	114.7	12.1
2020	B+	4.07	3.08	391.6	172.4	110.7	12.3
2019	B	3.62	2.70	379.1	149.2	108.4	7.7
2018	B	3.45	2.58	383.8	137.1	111.3	-0.5
2017	A-	4.58	3.30	407.5	151.9	37.8	13.0

Adverse Trends in Operations

Decrease in asset base during 2019 (1%)
Change in premium mix from 2017 to 2018 (16.8%)
Decrease in capital during 2018 (10%)
Decrease in asset base during 2017 (3%)
Decrease in premium volume from 2016 to 2017 (26%)

CENTRE LIFE INS CO   C   Fair

Major Rating Factors: Fair overall results on stability tests (4.3 on a scale of 0 to 10) including fair financial strength of affiliated Zurich Financial Services Group. Good quality investment portfolio (6.4) despite mixed results such as: no exposure to mortgages and substantial holdings of BBB bonds but minimal holdings in junk bonds. Weak profitability (2.1) with operating losses during 2021.
Other Rating Factors: Strong capitalization (9.0) based on excellent risk adjusted capital (severe loss scenario). Excellent liquidity (9.2).
Principal Business: Reinsurance (55%) and individual health insurance (45%).
Principal Investments: NonCMO investment grade bonds (77%) and CMOs and structured securities (22%).
Investments in Affiliates: None
Group Affiliation: Zurich Financial Services Group
Licensed in: All states except PR
Commenced Business: October 1927
Address: 1350 MAIN STREET SUITE 1600, SPRINGFIELD, MA 01103-1641
Phone: (212) 859-2640 **Domicile State:** MA **NAIC Code:** 80896

Data Date	Rating	RACR #1	RACR #2	Total Assets ($mil)	Capital ($mil)	Net Premium ($mil)	Net Income ($mil)
2021	C	4.16	2.30	1,450.2	83.2	0.9	-2.1
2020	C	4.11	2.41	1,521.6	85.0	1.0	-2.0
2019	C	4.09	2.45	1,591.5	87.3	1.0	-6.5
2018	B-	4.22	2.46	1,680.2	93.9	1.3	0.5
2017	B-	4.04	2.40	1,790.7	93.6	1.4	-1.7

Zurich Financial Services Group
Composite Group Rating: C
Largest Group Members

	Assets ($mil)	Rating
ZURICH AMERICAN INS CO	29991	C
ZURICH AMERICAN LIFE INS CO	15907	C-
FARMERS NEW WORLD LIFE INS CO	5427	B-
RURAL COMMUNITY INS CO	2048	B-
CENTRE LIFE INS CO	1522	C

CHESAPEAKE LIFE INS CO *   A+   Excellent

Major Rating Factors: Good overall results on stability tests (6.3 on a scale of 0 to 10) despite fair financial strength of affiliated Blackstone Investor Group. Strengths that enhance stability include excellent risk diversification. Weak profitability (2.9) with investment income below regulatory standards in relation to interest assumptions of reserves. Strong capitalization (8.0) based on excellent risk adjusted capital (severe loss scenario).
Other Rating Factors: High quality investment portfolio (8.3). Excellent liquidity (7.6).
Principal Business: Individual health insurance (88%), individual life insurance (11%), and reinsurance (1%).
Principal Investments: NonCMO investment grade bonds (35%), CMOs and structured securities (30%), and cash (3%).
Investments in Affiliates: None
Group Affiliation: Blackstone Investor Group
Licensed in: All states except NJ, NY, VT, PR
Commenced Business: October 1956
Address: 1833 SOUTH MORGAN ROAD, OKLAHOMA CITY, OK 73128
Phone: (817) 255-3100 **Domicile State:** OK **NAIC Code:** 61832

Data Date	Rating	RACR #1	RACR #2	Total Assets ($mil)	Capital ($mil)	Net Premium ($mil)	Net Income ($mil)
2021	A+	2.16	1.68	251.1	113.3	274.7	30.6
2020	A+	3.36	2.64	267.2	157.6	246.9	30.8
2019	A+	3.40	2.73	242.5	147.9	233.0	22.6
2018	A-	2.90	2.30	197.7	121.3	213.4	28.9
2017	B	2.21	1.76	158.7	86.7	200.8	16.6

Blackstone Investor Group
Composite Group Rating: C
Largest Group Members

	Assets ($mil)	Rating
UNITED HEALTHCARE INS CO	21587	C
UHC OF CALIFORNIA INC	793	C-
GOLDEN RULE INS CO	629	B
UNIMERICA INS CO	450	B-
OPTUM INS OF OH INC	424	B-

CHESTERFIELD REINS CO   D+   Weak

Major Rating Factors: Weak profitability (2.3 on a scale of 0 to 10) with operating losses during 2021. Weak liquidity (0.0) as a spike in claims may stretch capacity. Weak overall results on stability tests (2.0) including negative cash flow from operations for 2021.
Other Rating Factors: Fair quality investment portfolio (4.5). Strong capitalization (7.6) based on excellent risk adjusted capital (severe loss scenario).
Principal Business: Reinsurance (100%).
Principal Investments: NonCMO investment grade bonds (58%), CMOs and structured securities (16%), and noninv. grade bonds (3%).
Investments in Affiliates: None
Group Affiliation: Reinsurance Group of America Inc
Licensed in: MO
Commenced Business: October 2014
Address: 16600 Swingley Ridge Road, Chesterfield, MO 63017-1706
Phone: (636) 736-7000 **Domicile State:** MO **NAIC Code:** 15604

Data Date	Rating	RACR #1	RACR #2	Total Assets ($mil)	Capital ($mil)	Net Premium ($mil)	Net Income ($mil)
2021	D+	2.05	1.43	342.2	91.0	223.8	-14.1
2020	C	2.37	1.63	334.9	101.3	215.2	24.7
2019	C	1.77	1.24	318.0	87.0	216.3	19.2
2018	C	2.16	1.50	335.0	101.0	209.0	41.4
2017	C	1.67	1.17	326.1	95.3	201.1	40.6

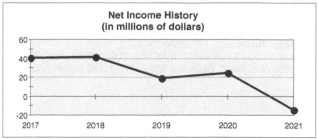

Net Income History
(in millions of dollars)

CHURCH LIFE INS CORP

B-   **Good**

Major Rating Factors: Good quality investment portfolio (6.2 on a scale of 0 to 10) despite mixed results such as: no exposure to mortgages and large holdings of BBB rated bonds but small junk bond holdings. Good liquidity (6.5) with sufficient resources to handle a spike in claims as well as a significant increase in policy surrenders. Good overall results on stability tests (5.2) despite negative cash flow from operations for 2021 good operational trends and good risk diversification.

Other Rating Factors: Fair profitability (4.5). Strong capitalization (9.6) based on excellent risk adjusted capital (severe loss scenario).

Principal Business: Group life insurance (60%), group retirement contracts (36%), individual annuities (3%), and individual life insurance (1%).

Principal Investments: NonCMO investment grade bonds (61%), CMOs and structured securities (28%), common & preferred stock (6%), and noninv. grade bonds (4%).

Investments in Affiliates: None
Group Affiliation: Church Pension Fund
Licensed in: All states except PR
Commenced Business: July 1922
Address: 19 East 34th Street, New York, NY 10016-4303
Phone: (212) 592-1800 **Domicile State:** NY **NAIC Code:** 61875

Data Date	Rating	RACR #1	RACR #2	Total Assets ($mil)	Capital ($mil)	Net Premium ($mil)	Net Income ($mil)
2021	B-	5.05	2.73	309.4	77.9	36.4	7.4
2020	B-	4.43	2.41	317.8	70.5	43.7	7.2
2019	B-	4.19	2.29	305.3	63.5	35.7	7.0
2018	B-	3.68	2.00	301.0	51.6	44.9	-12.4
2017	B	4.72	2.58	294.2	64.7	34.6	8.1

Adverse Trends in Operations

Decrease in premium volume from 2018 to 2019 (20%)
Decrease in capital during 2018 (20%)
Decrease in premium volume from 2016 to 2017 (21%)

CICA LIFE INS CO OF AMERICA

C   **Fair**

Major Rating Factors: Fair overall results on stability tests (3.6 on a scale of 0 to 10) including potential financial drain due to affiliation with Citizens Inc and weak risk adjusted capital in prior years. Good quality investment portfolio (5.7) despite mixed results such as: minimal exposure to mortgages and large holdings of BBB rated bonds but minimal holdings in junk bonds. Good overall profitability (5.4) although investment income, in comparison to reserve requirements, is below regulatory standards.

Other Rating Factors: Good liquidity (6.4). Strong capitalization (8.1) based on excellent risk adjusted capital (severe loss scenario).

Principal Business: Individual life insurance (56%), individual annuities (20%), credit health insurance (12%), credit life insurance (9%), and reinsurance (2%).

Principal Investments: NonCMO investment grade bonds (70%), CMOs and structured securities (13%), common & preferred stock (12%), policy loans (1%), and noninv. grade bonds (1%).

Investments in Affiliates: 12%
Group Affiliation: Citizens Inc
Licensed in: AL, AZ, AR, CO, DC, GA, HI, ID, IN, KS, KY, LA, MN, MS, MO, MT, NE, NV, NM, ND, OK, OR, PA, SC, SD, TN, TX, UT, WA, WV, WY
Commenced Business: June 1968
Address: 1560 Broadway Suite 2090, Denver, CO 80202
Phone: (512) 837-7100 **Domicile State:** CO **NAIC Code:** 71463

Data Date	Rating	RACR #1	RACR #2	Total Assets ($mil)	Capital ($mil)	Net Premium ($mil)	Net Income ($mil)
2021	C	2.07	1.74	151.5	43.1	4.0	9.7
2020	C	1.63	1.40	147.6	39.6	3.9	10.4
2019	C	1.69	1.46	153.6	41.3	4.6	3.6
2018	C-	1.90	1.66	159.4	47.3	-722.5	21.6
2017	D	0.64	0.44	1,000.2	35.1	157.1	5.8

Citizens Inc
Composite Group Rating: D+

Largest Group Members	Assets ($mil)	Rating
SECURITY PLAN LIFE INS CO	318	D
CICA LIFE INS CO OF AMERICA	148	C
CITIZENS NATIONAL LIFE INS CO	13	C
MAGNOLIA GUARANTY LIFE INS CO	11	D+
SECURITY PLAN FIRE INS CO	7	D

CIGNA HEALTH & LIFE INS CO

C+   **Fair**

Major Rating Factors: Fair quality investment portfolio (3.7 on a scale of 0 to 10) with large holdings of BBB rated bonds in addition to moderate junk bond exposure. Exposure to mortgages is significant, but the mortgage default rate has been low. Fair overall results on stability tests (3.4). Weak liquidity (1.3).

Other Rating Factors: Strong capitalization (7.7) based on excellent risk adjusted capital (severe loss scenario). Excellent profitability (9.3) with operating gains in each of the last five years.

Principal Business: Group health insurance (81%), individual health insurance (17%), and reinsurance (2%).

Principal Investments: NonCMO investment grade bonds (27%), noninv. grade bonds (14%), mortgages in good standing (10%), common & preferred stock (5%), and CMOs and structured securities (3%).

Investments in Affiliates: 30%
Group Affiliation: CIGNA Corp
Licensed in: All states, the District of Columbia and Puerto Rico
Commenced Business: February 1964
Address: 900 COTTAGE GROVE ROAD, BLOOMFIELD, CT 6002
Phone: (860) 226-6000 **Domicile State:** CT **NAIC Code:** 67369

Data Date	Rating	RACR #1	RACR #2	Total Assets ($mil)	Capital ($mil)	Net Premium ($mil)	Net Income ($mil)
2021	C+	2.00	1.49	13,549.9	5,700.3	21,984.8	2,066.6
2020	B	2.17	1.61	13,453.7	5,955.4	19,991.6	2,432.5
2019	B	2.06	1.57	11,675.8	5,207.4	18,363.8	2,184.5
2018	B	2.09	1.59	10,489.2	4,801.1	16,629.8	2,197.3
2017	B	1.86	1.42	9,002.2	3,680.6	13,779.7	1,569.1

Rating Indexes

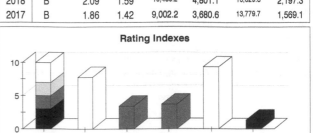

	Weak	Fair	Good	Strong

CINCINNATI LIFE INS CO
B- **Good**

Major Rating Factors: Good current capitalization (5.8 on a scale of 0 to 10) based on good risk adjusted capital (moderate loss scenario) reflecting some improvement over results in 2018. Good overall profitability (6.7). Excellent expense controls. Return on equity has been good over the last five years, averaging 10.4%. Good liquidity (5.1).

Other Rating Factors: Good overall results on stability tests (5.2) despite fair risk adjusted capital in prior years excellent operational trends and excellent risk diversification. Fair quality investment portfolio (3.6).

Principal Business: Individual life insurance (87%), individual annuities (11%), individual health insurance (1%), and group life insurance (1%).

Principal Investments: NonCMO investment grade bonds (84%), noninv. grade bonds (7%), CMOs and structured securities (6%), policy loans (1%), and cash (1%).

Investments in Affiliates: None
Group Affiliation: Cincinnati Financial Corp
Licensed in: All states except NY, PR
Commenced Business: February 1988
Address: 6200 SOUTH GILMORE ROAD, FAIRFIELD, OH 45014-5141
Phone: (513) 870-2000 **Domicile State:** OH **NAIC Code:** 76236

Data Date	Rating	RACR #1	RACR #2	Total Assets ($mil)	Capital ($mil)	Net Premium ($mil)	Net Income ($mil)
2021	B-	1.52	0.81	4,966.1	270.1	341.5	41.1
2020	B-	1.33	0.70	4,809.7	241.5	324.0	26.6
2019	C+	1.28	0.69	4,674.8	203.8	313.2	18.9
2018	B-	1.25	0.67	4,532.9	190.6	293.3	0.0
2017	B	1.31	0.70	4,407.2	195.1	272.8	12.4

Junk Bonds as a % of Capital

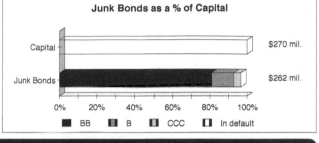

Capital — $270 mil.
Junk Bonds — $262 mil.

0% 20% 40% 60% 80% 100%

■ BB ▨ B ▥ CCC ▢ In default

CM LIFE INS CO *
B+ **Good**

Major Rating Factors: Good overall results on stability tests (6.7 on a scale of 0 to 10). Stability strengths include good operational trends and excellent risk diversification. Good quality investment portfolio (5.0) despite large holdings of BBB rated bonds in addition to moderate junk bond exposure. Exposure to mortgages is significant, but the mortgage default rate has been low. Good overall profitability (6.9).

Other Rating Factors: Good liquidity (6.5). Strong capitalization (8.5) based on excellent risk adjusted capital (severe loss scenario).

Principal Business: Individual annuities (83%) and individual life insurance (17%).

Principal Investments: NonCMO investment grade bonds (45%), mortgages in good standing (16%), CMOs and structured securities (9%), noninv. grade bonds (7%), and misc. investments (15%).

Investments in Affiliates: 8%
Group Affiliation: Massachusetts Mutual Group
Licensed in: All states except NY
Commenced Business: May 1981
Address: 100 BRIGHT MEADOW BOULEVARD, ENFIELD, CT 6082
Phone: (413) 788-8411 **Domicile State:** CT **NAIC Code:** 93432

Data Date	Rating	RACR #1	RACR #2	Total Assets ($mil)	Capital ($mil)	Net Premium ($mil)	Net Income ($mil)
2021	B+	3.19	2.03	9,072.1	1,634.3	276.4	87.8
2020	B+	3.25	2.03	9,411.2	1,738.8	276.2	102.0
2019	B+	3.16	1.99	8,639.0	1,735.0	312.3	115.6
2018	B	2.96	1.90	8,312.7	1,637.3	330.7	87.1
2017	B	2.93	1.86	8,657.3	1,573.2	283.4	67.1

Adverse Trends in Operations

Decrease in premium volume from 2019 to 2020 (12%)
Decrease in premium volume from 2018 to 2019 (6%)
Decrease in asset base during 2018 (4%)
Change in premium mix from 2016 to 2017 (78.3%)

CMFG LIFE INS CO
B **Good**

Major Rating Factors: Good quality investment portfolio (5.3 on a scale of 0 to 10) despite significant exposure to mortgages . Mortgage default rate has been low. large holdings of BBB rated bonds in addition to small junk bond holdings. Good liquidity (6.7) with sufficient resources to handle a spike in claims as well as a significant increase in policy surrenders. Good overall results on stability tests (5.5) excellent operational trends and excellent risk diversification.

Other Rating Factors: Strong capitalization (7.1) based on excellent risk adjusted capital (severe loss scenario). Excellent profitability (7.7) with operating gains in each of the last five years.

Principal Business: Reinsurance (34%), group retirement contracts (27%), individual life insurance (16%), group health insurance (6%), and other lines (17%).

Principal Investments: NonCMO investment grade bonds (40%), CMOs and structured securities (15%), common & preferred stock (13%), mortgages in good standing (12%), and misc. investments (17%).

Investments in Affiliates: 27%
Group Affiliation: CUNA Mutual Ins Group
Licensed in: All states, the District of Columbia and Puerto Rico
Commenced Business: August 1935
Address: 2000 HERITAGE WAY, WAVERLY, IA 50677
Phone: (608) 238-5851 **Domicile State:** IA **NAIC Code:** 62626

Data Date	Rating	RACR #1	RACR #2	Total Assets ($mil)	Capital ($mil)	Net Premium ($mil)	Net Income ($mil)
2021	B	1.23	1.04	26,335.6	2,824.1	4,488.6	156.1
2020	B-	1.53	1.19	24,022.2	2,175.0	4,705.5	162.8
2019	B-	1.57	1.21	21,403.6	2,197.6	3,961.9	204.5
2018	B-	1.56	1.22	18,292.1	2,254.8	3,474.2	127.7
2017	B-	1.59	1.24	18,078.3	2,107.2	3,130.1	227.3

Adverse Trends in Operations

Decrease in capital during 2020 (1%)
Decrease in capital during 2019 (3%)

COLONIAL LIFE & ACCIDENT INS CO   C+   **Fair**

Major Rating Factors: Fair overall results on stability tests (4.8 on a scale of 0 to 10) including fair financial strength of affiliated Unum Group. Good quality investment portfolio (5.7) despite significant exposure to mortgages . Mortgage default rate has been low. large holdings of BBB rated bonds in addition to small junk bond holdings. Good liquidity (6.8).

Other Rating Factors: Strong capitalization (8.2) based on excellent risk adjusted capital (severe loss scenario). Excellent profitability (8.7) with operating gains in each of the last five years.

Principal Business: Individual health insurance (63%), individual life insurance (22%), group health insurance (12%), and group life insurance (3%).

Principal Investments: NonCMO investment grade bonds (82%), mortgages in good standing (11%), noninv. grade bonds (3%), policy loans (2%), and misc. investments (3%).

Investments in Affiliates: None
Group Affiliation: Unum Group
Licensed in: All states except NY
Commenced Business: September 1939
Address: 1200 COLONIAL LIFE BOULEVARD, COLUMBIA, SC 29210
Phone: (803) 798-7000 **Domicile State:** SC **NAIC Code:** 62049

Data Date	Rating	RACR #1	RACR #2	Total Assets ($mil)	Capital ($mil)	Net Premium ($mil)	Net Income ($mil)
2021	C+	2.82	1.79	3,861.4	705.2	1,623.2	254.8
2020	C+	2.86	1.82	3,760.5	719.0	1,638.3	240.3
2019	C+	2.00	1.35	3,525.2	610.9	1,612.7	233.4
2018	C+	2.20	1.40	3,421.9	528.0	1,589.6	200.4
2017	C+	2.14	1.35	3,220.0	490.4	1,503.0	157.9

Unum Group Composite Group Rating: C+ Largest Group Members	Assets ($mil)	Rating
UNUM LIFE INS CO OF AMERICA	21791	C+
PROVIDENT LIFE ACCIDENT INS CO	6172	C+
FIRST UNUM LIFE INS CO	4249	C+
COLONIAL LIFE ACCIDENT INS CO	3760	C+
PAUL REVERE LIFE INS CO	1280	C+

COLONIAL PENN LIFE INS CO   D+   **Weak**

Major Rating Factors: Weak overall results on stability tests (2.0 on a scale of 0 to 10) including weak financial strength of affiliated CNO Financial Group Inc and negative cash flow from operations for 2021. Weak profitability (1.6) with operating losses during 2021. Weak liquidity (0.0) as a spike in claims or a run on policy withdrawals may stretch capacity.

Other Rating Factors: Fair quality investment portfolio (4.6). Good capitalization (5.2) based on good risk adjusted capital (moderate loss scenario).

Principal Business: Individual health insurance (60%), individual life insurance (28%), and group life insurance (12%).

Principal Investments: NonCMO investment grade bonds (75%), CMOs and structured securities (12%), policy loans (3%), cash (3%), and misc. investments (5%).

Investments in Affiliates: None
Group Affiliation: CNO Financial Group Inc
Licensed in: All states except NY
Commenced Business: September 1959
Address: 399 MARKET STREET, PHILADELPHIA, PA 19181
Phone: (215) 928-8000 **Domicile State:** PA **NAIC Code:** 62065

Data Date	Rating	RACR #1	RACR #2	Total Assets ($mil)	Capital ($mil)	Net Premium ($mil)	Net Income ($mil)
2021	D+	1.14	0.68	884.8	84.5	433.3	-41.1
2020	D+	1.35	0.80	893.6	105.5	413.2	-23.6
2019	D+	1.13	0.67	835.7	82.2	390.6	-24.5
2018	D+	1.19	0.69	869.9	92.4	379.0	-21.1
2017	D+	1.28	0.73	868.5	99.7	366.4	-11.7

CNO Financial Group Inc Composite Group Rating: D+ Largest Group Members	Assets ($mil)	Rating
BANKERS LIFE CAS CO	17025	D+
WASHINGTON NATIONAL INS CO	5742	D+
COLONIAL PENN LIFE INS CO	894	D+
BANKERS CONSECO LIFE INS CO	537	D

COLUMBIAN LIFE INS CO   C-   **Fair**

Major Rating Factors: Fair liquidity (3.8 on a scale of 0 to 10) as cash from operations and sale of marketable assets may not be adequate to cover a spike in claims or a run on policy withdrawals. Fair overall results on stability tests (3.3) including negative cash flow from operations for 2021. Weak profitability (1.8) with operating losses during 2021.

Other Rating Factors: Strong capitalization (7.7) based on excellent risk adjusted capital (severe loss scenario). High quality investment portfolio (7.4).

Principal Business: Individual life insurance (77%), group life insurance (20%), and individual annuities (3%).

Principal Investments: NonCMO investment grade bonds (74%), policy loans (9%), CMOs and structured securities (6%), mortgages in good standing (5%), and cash (4%).

Investments in Affiliates: None
Group Affiliation: Columbian Life Group
Licensed in: All states except AK, ME, NY, ND, PR
Commenced Business: June 1988
Address: 111 South Wacker Drive, Chicago, IL 60602
Phone: (607) 724-2472 **Domicile State:** IL **NAIC Code:** 76023

Data Date	Rating	RACR #1	RACR #2	Total Assets ($mil)	Capital ($mil)	Net Premium ($mil)	Net Income ($mil)
2021	C-	2.67	1.45	387.9	40.6	51.1	-8.2
2020	C	2.55	1.39	357.6	37.5	50.2	-5.0
2019	C	1.59	0.89	338.3	22.6	59.4	-4.1
2018	C	2.25	1.24	340.7	32.3	58.8	-5.2
2017	C	1.99	1.11	335.8	26.3	61.2	4.0

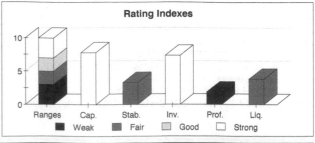

Rating Indexes

COLUMBIAN MUTUAL LIFE INS CO   C+   Fair

Major Rating Factors: Fair profitability (3.4 on a scale of 0 to 10) with investment income below regulatory standards in relation to interest assumptions of reserves. Fair overall results on stability tests (3.0) including fair risk adjusted capital in prior years. Good capitalization (5.1) based on good risk adjusted capital (moderate loss scenario).

Other Rating Factors: Good quality investment portfolio (6.0). Weak liquidity (0.6).

Principal Business: Reinsurance (72%), individual life insurance (26%), individual annuities (1%), group retirement contracts (1%), and individual health insurance (1%).

Principal Investments: NonCMO investment grade bonds (72%), mortgages in good standing (14%), policy loans (4%), CMOs and structured securities (4%), and common & preferred stock (3%).

Investments in Affiliates: 3%
Group Affiliation: Columbian Life Group
Licensed in: All states except PR
Commenced Business: February 1883
Address: 4704 Vestal Pkwy E PO Box 1381, Binghamton, NY 13902-1381
Phone: (607) 724-2472 **Domicile State:** NY **NAIC Code:** 62103

Data Date	Rating	RACR #1	RACR #2	Total Assets ($mil)	Capital ($mil)	Net Premium ($mil)	Net Income ($mil)
2021	C+	1.05	0.71	1,478.1	77.1	166.0	12.9
2020	C+	0.93	0.62	1,482.5	60.6	168.3	-10.8
2019	B	1.50	0.95	1,455.7	87.1	178.2	10.5
2018	B	1.41	0.93	1,454.3	95.9	179.7	3.2
2017	B	1.67	1.08	1,449.4	106.7	180.4	9.0

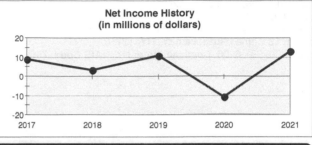

Net Income History
(in millions of dollars)

COLUMBUS LIFE INS CO   C+   Fair

Major Rating Factors: Fair quality investment portfolio (4.1 on a scale of 0 to 10) with large holdings of BBB rated bonds in addition to junk bond exposure equal to 63% of capital. Exposure to mortgages is significant, but the mortgage default rate has been low. Fair overall results on stability tests (4.5). Good liquidity (5.3).

Other Rating Factors: Weak profitability (1.9) with operating losses during 2021. Strong capitalization (7.1) based on excellent risk adjusted capital (severe loss scenario).

Principal Business: Individual life insurance (90%) and individual annuities (10%).

Principal Investments: NonCMO investment grade bonds (55%), CMOs and structured securities (13%), mortgages in good standing (11%), noninv. grade bonds (5%), and misc. investments (13%).

Investments in Affiliates: 3%
Group Affiliation: Western & Southern Group
Licensed in: All states except NY, PR
Commenced Business: July 1988
Address: 400 EAST 4TH STREET, CINCINNATI, OH 45202-3302
Phone: (513) 357-4000 **Domicile State:** OH **NAIC Code:** 99937

Data Date	Rating	RACR #1	RACR #2	Total Assets ($mil)	Capital ($mil)	Net Premium ($mil)	Net Income ($mil)
2021	C+	2.10	1.08	4,628.7	372.4	273.6	-4.9
2020	C+	1.80	0.92	4,305.7	284.7	244.4	-26.0
2019	C+	1.81	0.94	4,286.5	264.2	276.0	-49.3
2018	C+	1.95	1.00	4,091.4	273.5	325.6	-48.0
2017	C+	2.03	1.04	4,104.5	294.4	273.7	-39.5

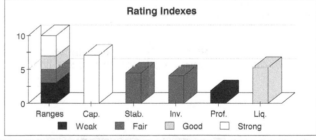

Rating Indexes

Ranges   Cap.   Stab.   Inv.   Prof.   Liq.
■ Weak   ■ Fair   ▨ Good   □ Strong

COMBINED INS CO OF AMERICA   C   Fair

Major Rating Factors: Fair overall results on stability tests (4.1 on a scale of 0 to 10) including fair risk adjusted capital in prior years. Good quality investment portfolio (6.6) despite mixed results such as: substantial holdings of BBB bonds but moderate junk bond exposure. Weak profitability (2.9) with investment income below regulatory standards in relation to interest assumptions of reserves.

Other Rating Factors: Strong capitalization (7.4) based on excellent risk adjusted capital (severe loss scenario). Excellent liquidity (7.2).

Principal Business: Individual health insurance (58%), group health insurance (23%), group life insurance (12%), individual life insurance (6%), and reinsurance (1%).

Principal Investments: NonCMO investment grade bonds (68%), CMOs and structured securities (17%), noninv. grade bonds (7%), common & preferred stock (4%), and misc. investments (3%).

Investments in Affiliates: 4%
Group Affiliation: Chubb Limited
Licensed in: All states except NY
Commenced Business: January 1922
Address: 111 E Wacker Drive, Chicago, IL 60601
Phone: (800) 225-4500 **Domicile State:** IL **NAIC Code:** 62146

Data Date	Rating	RACR #1	RACR #2	Total Assets ($mil)	Capital ($mil)	Net Premium ($mil)	Net Income ($mil)
2021	C	1.66	1.26	2,672.9	412.3	923.0	154.3
2020	C	1.22	0.90	2,568.2	289.6	996.1	78.2
2019	C	0.97	0.72	2,417.9	218.7	1,076.4	16.8
2018	C	1.03	0.72	2,364.2	174.4	646.5	-158.7
2017	C+	1.37	0.97	1,495.7	178.7	480.2	33.4

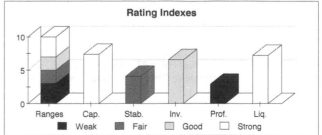

Rating Indexes

Ranges   Cap.   Stab.   Inv.   Prof.   Liq.
■ Weak   ■ Fair   ▨ Good   □ Strong

COMBINED LIFE INS CO OF NEW YORK   C+   Fair

Major Rating Factors: Fair overall results on stability tests (4.5 on a scale of 0 to 10) including fair financial strength of affiliated Chubb Limited. Weak profitability (2.9) with investment income below regulatory standards in relation to interest assumptions of reserves. Strong capitalization (8.5) based on excellent risk adjusted capital (severe loss scenario).

Other Rating Factors: High quality investment portfolio (7.9). Excellent liquidity (7.8).

Principal Business: Individual health insurance (81%), individual life insurance (13%), group health insurance (5%), and group life insurance (2%).

Principal Investments: NonCMO investment grade bonds (64%), CMOs and structured securities (30%), and policy loans (2%).

Investments in Affiliates: None

Group Affiliation: Chubb Limited

Licensed in: IL, NY

Commenced Business: June 1971

Address: 13 Cornell Road, Latham, NY 12110

Phone: (800) 951-6206 **Domicile State:** NY **NAIC Code:** 78697

Data Date	Rating	RACR #1	RACR #2	Total Assets ($mil)	Capital ($mil)	Net Premium ($mil)	Net Income ($mil)
2021	C+	2.94	2.03	586.3	111.2	164.2	26.3
2020	C+	2.21	1.53	540.0	85.3	168.3	15.3
2019	C+	1.78	1.25	502.8	69.1	176.4	13.8
2018	C+	1.42	1.01	472.3	52.7	167.2	7.8
2017	C+	1.21	0.86	441.6	44.3	163.4	10.0

Chubb Limited Composite Group Rating: C+ Largest Group Members	Assets ($mil)	Rating
ACE AMERICAN INS CO	26083	C
FEDERAL INS CO	16527	C+
ACE PC INS CO	12629	C
PACIFIC INDEMNITY CO	12486	B
EXECUTIVE RISK INDEMNITY INC	6115	C+

COMMONWEALTH ANNUITY & LIFE INS CO   C   Fair

Major Rating Factors: Fair overall capitalization (4.1 on a scale of 0 to 10) based on mixed results -- excessive policy leverage mitigated by fair risk adjusted capital (moderate loss scenario). Fair quality investment portfolio (4.8) with significant exposure to mortgages . Mortgage default rate has been low. Fair overall results on stability tests (3.9) including fair risk adjusted capital in prior years.

Other Rating Factors: Good overall profitability (5.5) despite operating losses during 2021. Excellent liquidity (8.8).

Principal Business: Reinsurance (100%).

Principal Investments: NonCMO investment grade bonds (37%), CMOs and structured securities (33%), mortgages in good standing (16%), common & preferred stock (7%), and misc. investments (5%).

Investments in Affiliates: 7%

Group Affiliation: Global Atlantic Financial Group

Licensed in: All states except NY, PR

Commenced Business: January 1967

Address: 132 TURNPIKE ROAD SUITE 210, SOUTHBOROUGH, MA 2135

Phone: (508) 460-2400 **Domicile State:** MA **NAIC Code:** 84824

Data Date	Rating	RACR #1	RACR #2	Total Assets ($mil)	Capital ($mil)	Net Premium ($mil)	Net Income ($mil)
2021	C	0.87	0.64	60,138.2	3,888.2	-710.1	-18.8
2020	C	0.79	0.63	42,763.8	3,366.5	5,829.8	70.7
2019	C+	0.77	0.66	23,126.0	2,845.8	1,591.8	-32.5
2018	B-	0.88	0.75	19,255.4	2,788.0	1,372.6	-22.9
2017	B-	0.93	0.86	11,301.5	2,488.2	40.1	267.8

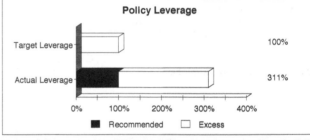

Policy Leverage

Target Leverage — 100%
Actual Leverage — 311%

■ Recommended □ Excess

COMPANION LIFE INS CO   B-   Good

Major Rating Factors: Good quality investment portfolio (6.2 on a scale of 0 to 10) despite mixed results such as: minimal exposure to mortgages and large holdings of BBB rated bonds but small junk bond holdings. Fair profitability (4.4) with investment income below regulatory standards in relation to interest assumptions of reserves. Fair liquidity (3.7).

Other Rating Factors: Fair overall results on stability tests (4.9). Strong capitalization (7.2) based on excellent risk adjusted capital (severe loss scenario).

Principal Business: Individual life insurance (75%), group life insurance (16%), group retirement contracts (9%), and individual annuities (1%).

Principal Investments: NonCMO investment grade bonds (74%), CMOs and structured securities (15%), mortgages in good standing (5%), policy loans (3%), and misc. investments (3%).

Investments in Affiliates: None

Group Affiliation: Mutual Of Omaha Group

Licensed in: CT, NJ, NY

Commenced Business: July 1949

Address: 888 VETERANS MEM HWY STE 515, MELVILLE, NY 11747

Phone: (800) 877-5399 **Domicile State:** NY **NAIC Code:** 62243

Data Date	Rating	RACR #1	RACR #2	Total Assets ($mil)	Capital ($mil)	Net Premium ($mil)	Net Income ($mil)
2021	B-	2.15	1.16	1,193.1	75.9	93.1	24.0
2020	B-	1.50	0.80	1,154.4	50.2	90.8	-4.9
2019	B-	1.62	0.87	1,108.2	52.6	-23.9	-13.3
2018	B-	1.56	0.82	1,171.0	56.3	97.9	1.7
2017	B-	1.64	0.87	1,130.4	57.4	99.7	-13.2

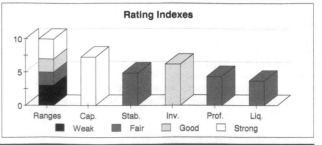

Rating Indexes

Ranges Cap. Stab. Inv. Prof. Liq.

■ Weak ▨ Fair ▨ Good □ Strong

COMPANION LIFE INS CO *　　　　　　　　　　　B+　　　Good

Major Rating Factors: Good quality investment portfolio (5.4 on a scale of 0 to 10) despite mixed results such as: no exposure to mortgages and substantial holdings of BBB bonds but minimal holdings in junk bonds. Good overall results on stability tests (6.6). Stability strengths include excellent operational trends and excellent risk diversification. Strong capitalization (9.7) based on excellent risk adjusted capital (severe loss scenario).

Other Rating Factors: Excellent profitability (8.3) with operating gains in each of the last five years. Excellent liquidity (7.4).

Principal Business: Group health insurance (75%), individual health insurance (13%), reinsurance (7%), and group life insurance (4%).

Principal Investments: NonCMO investment grade bonds (37%), common & preferred stock (27%), CMOs and structured securities (15%), and cash (14%).

Investments in Affiliates: 6%

Group Affiliation: Blue Cross Blue Shield of S Carolina

Licensed in: All states except CA, CT, HI, NJ, NY, PR

Commenced Business: July 1970

Address: 2501 Faraway Drive, Columbia, SC 29219

Phone: (800) 753-0404　**Domicile State:** SC　**NAIC Code:** 77828

Data Date	Rating	RACR #1	RACR #2	Total Assets ($mil)	Capital ($mil)	Net Premium ($mil)	Net Income ($mil)
2021	B+	3.74	2.82	689.7	391.4	295.4	28.8
2020	B+	3.31	2.54	632.3	341.9	323.1	18.6
2019	B+	2.80	2.16	464.3	254.0	324.0	18.8
2018	B+	2.80	2.17	395.7	228.1	279.8	18.8
2017	B+	2.71	2.08	373.6	212.4	253.2	19.4

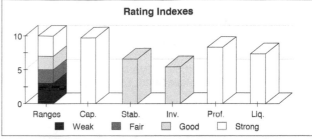

Rating Indexes

CONNECTICUT GENERAL LIFE INS CO　　　　　B-　　　Good

Major Rating Factors: Fair quality investment portfolio (4.4 on a scale of 0 to 10). Fair overall results on stability tests (3.9). Strong capitalization (7.2) based on excellent risk adjusted capital (severe loss scenario). Capital levels have been relatively consistent over the last five years.

Other Rating Factors: Excellent profitability (8.4) with operating gains in each of the last five years. Excellent liquidity (8.5).

Principal Business: Group life insurance (50%), individual life insurance (43%), reinsurance (4%), group health insurance (2%), and individual health insurance (1%).

Principal Investments: Common & preferred stock (52%), nonCMO investment grade bonds (26%), policy loans (11%), mortgages in good standing (3%), and misc. investments (7%).

Investments in Affiliates: 52%

Group Affiliation: CIGNA Corp

Licensed in: All states, the District of Columbia and Puerto Rico

Commenced Business: October 1865

Address: 900 COTTAGE GROVE ROAD, BLOOMFIELD, CT 6002

Phone: (860) 226-6000　**Domicile State:** CT　**NAIC Code:** 62308

Data Date	Rating	RACR #1	RACR #2	Total Assets ($mil)	Capital ($mil)	Net Premium ($mil)	Net Income ($mil)
2021	B-	1.22	1.15	21,459.7	6,385.3	142.1	2,621.9
2020	B-	1.19	1.13	21,488.1	6,583.7	315.0	1,846.7
2019	B-	1.23	1.17	10,753.4	5,934.0	310.7	1,881.7
2018	B-	1.25	1.17	19,056.7	5,494.5	333.7	1,239.4
2017	B-	1.32	1.22	18,137.2	4,412.2	346.3	1,013.8

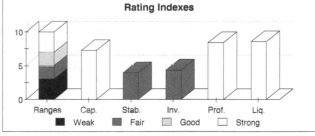

Rating Indexes

CONTINENTAL AMERICAN INS CO　　　　　　　B　　　Good

Major Rating Factors: Good liquidity (6.8 on a scale of 0 to 10) with sufficient resources to handle a spike in claims. Good overall results on stability tests (5.8) despite negative cash flow from operations for 2021. Strengths include good financial support from affiliation with AFLAC Inc, good operational trends and excellent risk diversification. Weak profitability (1.9) with operating losses during 2021.

Other Rating Factors: Strong capitalization (9.0) based on excellent risk adjusted capital (severe loss scenario). High quality investment portfolio (7.5).

Principal Business: Group health insurance (96%) and group life insurance (4%).

Principal Investments: NonCMO investment grade bonds (79%), cash (9%), noninv. grade bonds (1%), and policy loans (1%).

Investments in Affiliates: None

Group Affiliation: AFLAC Inc

Licensed in: All states except NY, PR

Commenced Business: January 1969

Address: 1600 Williams Street, Omaha, NE 68114-3743

Phone: (706) 243-8708　**Domicile State:** SC　**NAIC Code:** 71730

Data Date	Rating	RACR #1	RACR #2	Total Assets ($mil)	Capital ($mil)	Net Premium ($mil)	Net Income ($mil)
2021	B	3.15	2.35	933.7	243.5	516.2	-30.0
2020	B	3.70	2.77	896.9	271.2	495.9	1.0
2019	B	1.74	1.30	674.3	127.8	434.5	-16.3
2018	B	1.70	1.28	665.1	157.3	587.6	5.9
2017	B	1.79	1.33	673.3	153.4	524.7	-21.7

AFLAC Inc Composite Group Rating: B+ Largest Group Members	Assets ($mil)	Rating
AMERICAN FAMILY LIFE ASR CO OF NY	1077	A
CONTINENTAL AMERICAN INS CO	897	B

CONTINENTAL GENERAL INS CO | C | Fair

Major Rating Factors: Fair quality investment portfolio (4.1 on a scale of 0 to 10) with large holdings of BBB rated bonds in addition to junk bond exposure equal to 63% of capital. Fair overall results on stability tests (4.1) including fair risk adjusted capital in prior years. Good overall profitability (6.2). Excellent expense controls. Return on equity has been low, averaging 3.8%.

Other Rating Factors: Strong capitalization (7.6) based on excellent risk adjusted capital (severe loss scenario). Excellent liquidity (7.4).

Principal Business: Individual health insurance (84%), group health insurance (7%), individual life insurance (5%), reinsurance (3%), and group retirement contracts (1%).

Principal Investments: NonCMO investment grade bonds (72%), CMOs and structured securities (11%), common & preferred stock (6%), noninv. grade bonds (4%), and cash (2%).

Investments in Affiliates: 2%

Group Affiliation: HC2 Holdings Inc

Licensed in: All states except NY, PR

Commenced Business: July 1961

Address: 11001 Lakeline Blvd Ste 120, Austin, TX 78717

Phone: (866) 830-0607 **Domicile State:** OH **NAIC Code:** 71404

Data Date	Rating	RACR #1	RACR #2	Total Assets ($mil)	Capital ($mil)	Net Premium ($mil)	Net Income ($mil)
2021	C	2.77	1.39	4,340.3	346.9	106.3	162.7
2020	C	2.40	1.21	4,392.7	297.8	117.7	0.1
2019	C+	2.10	1.14	4,297.3	300.5	119.9	64.6
2018	C+	1.78	0.96	4,206.9	255.5	126.2	-99.8
2017	C+	1.12	0.68	1,385.8	74.7	82.7	-0.1

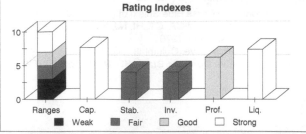

Rating Indexes

Ranges, Cap., Stab., Inv., Prof., Liq. — Weak, Fair, Good, Strong

CONTINENTAL LIFE INS CO OF BRENTWOOD | C+ | Fair

Major Rating Factors: Fair profitability (4.7 on a scale of 0 to 10). Excellent expense controls. Return on equity has been low, averaging -0.6%. Fair overall results on stability tests (4.5). Good quality investment portfolio (5.4) despite mixed results such as: minimal exposure to mortgages and substantial holdings of BBB bonds but minimal holdings in junk bonds.

Other Rating Factors: Good liquidity (6.7). Strong capitalization (7.2) based on excellent risk adjusted capital (severe loss scenario).

Principal Business: Individual health insurance (99%) and individual life insurance (1%).

Principal Investments: Common & preferred stock (41%), nonCMO investment grade bonds (35%), CMOs and structured securities (24%), noninv. grade bonds (2%), and mortgages in good standing (1%).

Investments in Affiliates: 41%

Group Affiliation: Aetna Inc

Licensed in: All states except AK, DC, HI, ME, NY, PR

Commenced Business: December 1983

Address: 800 CRESCENT CENTRE DR STE 200, FRANKLIN, TN 37064

Phone: (800) 264-4000 **Domicile State:** TN **NAIC Code:** 68500

Data Date	Rating	RACR #1	RACR #2	Total Assets ($mil)	Capital ($mil)	Net Premium ($mil)	Net Income ($mil)
2021	C+	1.23	1.13	629.5	399.1	737.2	55.4
2020	C+	0.99	0.90	492.9	265.3	659.1	21.4
2019	C+	0.98	0.88	377.3	195.1	575.9	-26.9
2018	C+	1.10	0.99	366.7	204.0	508.5	-13.5
2017	C+	1.10	0.99	345.6	194.4	468.0	-9.5

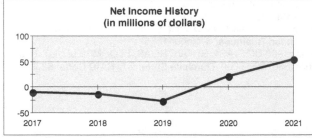

Net Income History
(in millions of dollars)

CORPORATE SOLUTIONS LIFE REINSURANCE COMPANY | C | Fair

Major Rating Factors: Fair quality investment portfolio (4.6 on a scale of 0 to 10). Fair profitability (4.0). Excellent expense controls. Return on equity has been fair, averaging 6.4%. Weak overall results on stability tests (2.8) including fair financial strength of affiliated AXA Financial Inc, weak results on operational trends and negative cash flow from operations for 2021.

Other Rating Factors: Weak liquidity (1.7). Strong capitalization (8.0) based on excellent risk adjusted capital (severe loss scenario).

Principal Business: Reinsurance (100%).

Principal Investments: NonCMO investment grade bonds (61%), CMOs and structured securities (19%), mortgages in good standing (4%), noninv. grade bonds (2%), and common & preferred stock (1%).

Investments in Affiliates: None

Group Affiliation: AXA Financial Inc

Licensed in: All states except FL, PR

Commenced Business: January 1983

Address: 2711 Centerville Rd Ste 400, Wilmington, DE 19801

Phone: (610) 249-9531 **Domicile State:** DE **NAIC Code:** 68365

Data Date	Rating	RACR #1	RACR #2	Total Assets ($mil)	Capital ($mil)	Net Premium ($mil)	Net Income ($mil)
2021	C	3.41	1.65	20,868.3	1,903.1	14,868.0	30.5
2020	B	1.63	1.56	257.0	194.3	1.6	28.2
2019	B	1.33	1.28	284.6	170.3	3.8	-2.0
2018	B	1.38	1.32	264.6	163.4	2.9	12.5
2017	B	1.44	1.37	259.9	160.0	4.6	54.2

AXA Financial Inc
Composite Group Rating: C
Largest Group Members

	Assets ($mil)	Rating
ATHENE ANNUITY LIFE CO	76556	C
VENERABLE INS AND ANNTY CO	49488	C
ATHENE ANNUITY LIFE ASR CO	34398	C
ATHENE ANNUITY LIFE ASR CO OF NY	3532	B-
ASPEN AMERICAN INS CO	1248	C+

COTTON STATES LIFE INS CO　　　　　　　　　B　　Good

Major Rating Factors: Good quality investment portfolio (6.0 on a scale of 0 to 10) despite mixed results such as: no exposure to mortgages and large holdings of BBB rated bonds but small junk bond holdings. Good overall profitability (6.1). Excellent expense controls. Return on equity has been low, averaging 3.6%. Good liquidity (6.4).

Other Rating Factors: Good overall results on stability tests (6.3) despite negative cash flow from operations for 2021 excellent operational trends and excellent risk diversification. Strong capitalization (8.9) based on excellent risk adjusted capital (severe loss scenario).

Principal Business: Individual life insurance (99%) and individual annuities (1%).

Principal Investments: NonCMO investment grade bonds (46%), CMOs and structured securities (29%), common & preferred stock (7%), policy loans (4%), and noninv. grade bonds (3%).

Investments in Affiliates: None

Group Affiliation: COUNTRY Financial

Licensed in: AL, FL, GA, KY, LA, MS, NC, SC, TN, VA

Commenced Business: December 1955

Address: 13560 MORRIS ROAD SUITE 4000, ALPHARETTA, GA 30004

Phone: (309) 821-3000　**Domicile State:** GA　**NAIC Code:** 62537

Data Date	Rating	RACR #1	RACR #2	Total Assets ($mil)	Capital ($mil)	Net Premium ($mil)	Net Income ($mil)
2021	B	4.15	2.25	316.4	67.5	16.0	2.0
2020	B	4.30	2.36	319.4	65.7	17.3	4.1
2019	B	3.84	2.15	319.1	60.3	18.9	4.8
2018	A-	5.02	2.76	336.7	74.1	20.8	3.3
2017	A-	4.64	2.56	335.9	71.0	21.9	2.8

COUNTRY INVESTORS LIFE ASR CO *　　　A-　　Excellent

Major Rating Factors: Excellent overall results on stability tests (7.1 on a scale of 0 to 10). Strengths that enhance stability include excellent operational trends and excellent risk diversification. Strong capitalization (8.0) based on excellent risk adjusted capital (severe loss scenario). Furthermore, this high level of risk adjusted capital has been consistently maintained over the last five years. High quality investment portfolio (8.0).

Other Rating Factors: Excellent profitability (7.7) with operating gains in each of the last five years. Excellent liquidity (9.0).

Principal Business: Individual annuities (64%) and individual life insurance (36%).

Principal Investments: NonCMO investment grade bonds (53%), CMOs and structured securities (35%), and noninv. grade bonds (1%).

Investments in Affiliates: None

Group Affiliation: COUNTRY Financial

Licensed in: All states except CA, DC, HI, NH, NJ, NY, UT, VT, PR

Commenced Business: November 1981

Address: 1701 N TOWANDA AVENUE, BLOOMINGTON, IL 61701-2090

Phone: (309) 821-3000　**Domicile State:** IL　**NAIC Code:** 94218

Data Date	Rating	RACR #1	RACR #2	Total Assets ($mil)	Capital ($mil)	Net Premium ($mil)	Net Income ($mil)
2021	A-	14.89	7.19	323.0	216.2	0.0	5.3
2020	A-	14.69	7.09	316.0	211.0	0.0	5.4
2019	A-	14.96	7.34	305.5	205.1	0.0	5.8
2018	A-	14.54	7.10	303.6	199.2	0.0	5.7
2017	A-	14.39	7.03	299.2	193.1	0.0	4.1

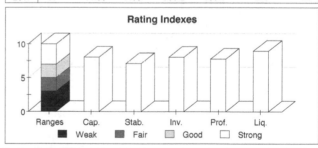

COUNTRY LIFE INS CO *　　　　　　　　　　A+　　Excellent

Major Rating Factors: Good quality investment portfolio (5.8 on a scale of 0 to 10) despite mixed results such as: minimal exposure to mortgages and large holdings of BBB rated bonds but small junk bond holdings. Good liquidity (6.4) with sufficient resources to handle a spike in claims as well as a significant increase in policy surrenders. Good overall results on stability tests (6.5) excellent historical risk adjusted capital and excellent risk diversification.

Other Rating Factors: Strong capitalization (4.0) based on excellent risk adjusted capital (severe loss scenario). Excellent profitability (8.2) with operating gains in each of the last five years.

Principal Business: Individual life insurance (64%), reinsurance (19%), individual health insurance (16%), and group life insurance (1%).

Principal Investments: NonCMO investment grade bonds (53%), CMOs and structured securities (20%), common & preferred stock (7%), policy loans (4%), and misc. investments (12%).

Investments in Affiliates: 3%

Group Affiliation: COUNTRY Financial

Licensed in: All states except CA, DC, HI, NH, NJ, NY, VT, PR

Commenced Business: December 1928

Address: 1701 N TOWANDA AVENUE, BLOOMINGTON, IL 61701-2090

Phone: (309) 821-3000　**Domicile State:** IL　**NAIC Code:** 62553

Data Date	Rating	RACR #1	RACR #2	Total Assets ($mil)	Capital ($mil)	Net Premium ($mil)	Net Income ($mil)
2021	A+	2.62	1.65	9,442.8	1,534.9	562.7	116.3
2020	A+	2.46	1.57	8,962.5	1,357.9	-860.6	117.8
2019	A+	2.29	1.47	10,006.2	1,272.8	638.9	38.1
2018	A+	2.07	1.37	9,656.3	1,207.6	603.7	60.1
2017	A+	2.09	1.37	9,459.6	1,185.3	603.7	63.4

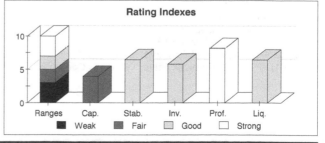

DEARBORN LIFE INS CO
B   **Good**

Major Rating Factors: Good quality investment portfolio (5.8 on a scale of 0 to 10) despite large holdings of BBB rated bonds in addition to moderate junk bond exposure. Exposure to mortgages is significant, but the mortgage default rate has been low. Good liquidity (6.3) with sufficient resources to handle a spike in claims as well as a significant increase in policy surrenders. Good overall results on stability tests (5.5) despite negative cash flow from operations for 2021 excellent operational trends and excellent risk diversification.

Other Rating Factors: Weak profitability (2.5) with operating losses during 2021. Strong capitalization (8.3) based on excellent risk adjusted capital (severe loss scenario).

Principal Business: Group life insurance (58%), group health insurance (40%), and individual life insurance (1%).

Principal Investments: NonCMO investment grade bonds (50%), CMOs and structured securities (22%), mortgages in good standing (13%), and noninv. grade bonds (9%).

Investments in Affiliates: None

Group Affiliation: HCSC Group

Licensed in: All states except NY

Commenced Business: April 1969

Address: 300 East Randolph Street, Chicago, IL 60601-5099

Phone: (800) 633-3696 **Domicile State:** IL **NAIC Code:** 71129

Data Date	Rating	RACR #1	RACR #2	Total Assets ($mil)	Capital ($mil)	Net Premium ($mil)	Net Income ($mil)
2021	B	3.05	1.87	1,647.0	409.1	568.0	-44.2
2020	B+	3.45	2.09	1,647.0	461.1	536.8	0.1
2019	B+	3.59	2.18	1,660.0	461.7	491.4	17.6
2018	B+	3.33	2.06	1,676.5	453.0	462.0	25.7
2017	B+	3.40	2.09	1,785.1	474.3	437.9	34.0

Adverse Trends in Operations

Decrease in capital during 2018 (4%)
Decrease in asset base during 2018 (6%)
Decrease in capital during 2017 (5%)
Decrease in asset base during 2017 (5%)

DELAWARE AMERICAN LIFE INS CO *
A-   **Excellent**

Major Rating Factors: Good overall results on stability tests (6.6 on a scale of 0 to 10). Strengths that enhance stability include good operational trends and excellent risk diversification. Good overall profitability (5.7). Return on equity has been good over the last five years, averaging 12.4%. Good liquidity (6.9) with sufficient resources to handle a spike in claims.

Other Rating Factors: Strong capitalization (9.7) based on excellent risk adjusted capital (severe loss scenario). High quality investment portfolio (7.8).

Principal Business: Group health insurance (69%), reinsurance (15%), group life insurance (14%), and individual life insurance (1%).

Principal Investments: CMOs and structured securities (47%), nonCMO investment grade bonds (47%), and cash (5%).

Investments in Affiliates: None

Group Affiliation: MetLife Inc

Licensed in: All states except PR

Commenced Business: August 1966

Address: 1209 Orange Street, Wilmington, DE 19801

Phone: (302) 594-2000 **Domicile State:** DE **NAIC Code:** 62634

Data Date	Rating	RACR #1	RACR #2	Total Assets ($mil)	Capital ($mil)	Net Premium ($mil)	Net Income ($mil)
2021	A-	3.73	2.77	106.3	53.0	77.0	0.9
2020	B+	4.34	3.26	109.6	59.9	81.6	8.9
2019	B+	4.50	3.39	115.1	61.8	89.0	8.8
2018	B+	4.07	3.02	117.0	65.1	93.0	12.5
2017	B+	3.36	2.53	120.2	61.8	96.4	7.2

Adverse Trends in Operations

Decrease in asset base during 2020 (5%)
Decrease in capital during 2019 (5%)
Decrease in premium volume from 2017 to 2018 (4%)
Decrease in asset base during 2017 (9%)
Decrease in capital during 2017 (15%)

DELAWARE LIFE INS CO
C   **Fair**

Major Rating Factors: Fair quality investment portfolio (4.7 on a scale of 0 to 10). Fair overall results on stability tests (4.2). Good liquidity (6.8) with sufficient resources to handle a spike in claims as well as a significant increase in policy surrenders.

Other Rating Factors: Strong capitalization (7.0) based on excellent risk adjusted capital (severe loss scenario). Excellent profitability (7.8) with operating gains in each of the last five years.

Principal Business: Individual annuities (92%), group retirement contracts (7%), and individual life insurance (1%).

Principal Investments: NonCMO investment grade bonds (41%), CMOs and structured securities (18%), common & preferred stock (8%), mortgages in good standing (5%), and misc. investments (17%).

Investments in Affiliates: 10%

Group Affiliation: Delaware Life Partners LLC

Licensed in: All states except NY

Commenced Business: January 1973

Address: 1209 Orange Street, Wilmington, DE 19801

Phone: (781) 790-8600 **Domicile State:** DE **NAIC Code:** 79065

Data Date	Rating	RACR #1	RACR #2	Total Assets ($mil)	Capital ($mil)	Net Premium ($mil)	Net Income ($mil)
2021	C	1.70	1.03	44,380.7	2,076.3	2,292.7	215.4
2020	C	1.18	0.77	41,746.9	1,598.5	2,668.1	220.6
2019	C	1.25	0.83	37,830.6	1,583.3	2,412.3	270.4
2018	C	1.42	0.90	36,852.6	1,555.3	-10,314.1	198.8
2017	C	1.20	0.75	37,207.3	1,463.4	2,033.4	281.4

Rating Indexes

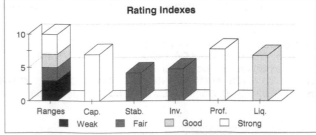

DELAWARE LIFE INS CO OF NEW YORK   B   Good

Major Rating Factors: Good overall results on stability tests (5.5 on a scale of 0 to 10) despite fair financial strength of affiliated Delaware Life Partners LLC and negative cash flow from operations for 2021. Other stability subfactors include good operational trends and excellent risk diversification. Good quality investment portfolio (6.4) despite mixed results such as: minimal exposure to mortgages and large holdings of BBB rated bonds but minimal holdings in junk bonds. Good liquidity (6.9).

Other Rating Factors: Strong capitalization (10.0) based on excellent risk adjusted capital (severe loss scenario). Excellent profitability (8.1) with operating gains in each of the last five years.

Principal Business: Individual life insurance (60%), individual annuities (39%), and group life insurance (1%).

Principal Investments: NonCMO investment grade bonds (70%), CMOs and structured securities (16%), cash (4%), noninv. grade bonds (3%), and misc. investments (8%).

Investments in Affiliates: None

Group Affiliation: Delaware Life Partners LLC

Licensed in: CT, NY, RI

Commenced Business: August 1985

Address: 1115 Broadway 12th Floor, New York, NY 10017

Phone: (781) 790-8600 **Domicile State:** NY **NAIC Code:** 72664

Data Date	Rating	RACR #1	RACR #2	Total Assets ($mil)	Capital ($mil)	Net Premium ($mil)	Net Income ($mil)
2021	B	12.05	5.58	2,151.9	444.0	12.1	54.0
2020	B-	11.77	5.51	2,243.9	450.3	13.3	57.9
2019	B-	10.26	4.95	2,250.9	398.5	12.4	35.1
2018	B-	9.05	4.40	2,264.1	366.4	12.5	15.2
2017	B-	9.44	4.55	2,505.3	369.2	19.0	19.2

Delaware Life Partners LLC
Composite Group Rating: C+

Largest Group Members	Assets ($mil)	Rating
DELAWARE LIFE INS CO	41747	C
CLEAR SPRING LIFE ANNTY CO	13825	B-
DELAWARE LIFE INS CO OF NEW YORK	2244	B
LACKAWANNA CASUALTY CO	515	C
CLEAR SPRING PC CO	328	E-

DIRECT GENERAL LIFE INS CO *   A   Excellent

Major Rating Factors: Good overall results on stability tests (6.2 on a scale of 0 to 10). Strengths that enhance stability include good operational trends and excellent risk diversification. Good liquidity (6.8) with sufficient resources to handle a spike in claims. Strong capitalization (10.0) based on excellent risk adjusted capital (severe loss scenario).

Other Rating Factors: High quality investment portfolio (9.2). Excellent profitability (8.9) with operating gains in each of the last five years.

Principal Business: Individual life insurance (100%).

Principal Investments: NonCMO investment grade bonds (90%), CMOs and structured securities (8%), and cash (1%).

Investments in Affiliates: None

Group Affiliation: National General Holdings Corporatio

Licensed in: All states except HI, IA, MI, NH, NY, VT, WY, PR

Commenced Business: December 1982

Address: 911 Chestnut Street, Orangeburg, SC 29115

Phone: (336) 435-2000 **Domicile State:** SC **NAIC Code:** 97705

Data Date	Rating	RACR #1	RACR #2	Total Assets ($mil)	Capital ($mil)	Net Premium ($mil)	Net Income ($mil)
2021	A	5.41	4.87	33.5	26.8	10.4	1.6
2020	B+	5.43	4.89	35.0	27.8	12.9	5.4
2019	C	4.92	4.43	29.6	22.3	9.6	7.3
2018	C-	4.70	4.23	33.1	23.1	10.1	7.8
2017	B-	4.43	3.98	33.0	21.7	12.0	7.2

Adverse Trends in Operations

Decrease in premium volume from 2018 to 2019 (5%)
Decrease in capital during 2019 (3%)
Decrease in asset base during 2019 (11%)
Decrease in premium volume from 2017 to 2018 (16%)
Decrease in premium volume from 2016 to 2017 (32%)

EAGLE LIFE INS CO   B   Good

Major Rating Factors: Good quality investment portfolio (5.8 on a scale of 0 to 10) despite significant exposure to mortgages . Mortgage default rate has been low. large holdings of BBB rated bonds in addition to small junk bond holdings. Fair overall results on stability tests (4.7) including fair financial strength of affiliated American Equity Investment Group. Fair liquidity (3.7).

Other Rating Factors: Strong overall capitalization (7.8) based on mixed results -- excessive policy leverage mitigated by excellent risk adjusted capital (severe loss scenario). Excellent profitability (8.6) with operating gains in each of the last five years.

Principal Business: Individual annuities (100%).

Principal Investments: NonCMO investment grade bonds (35%), CMOs and structured securities (22%), mortgages in good standing (13%), and noninv. grade bonds (1%).

Investments in Affiliates: None

Group Affiliation: American Equity Investment Group

Licensed in: All states except ID, NY, PR

Commenced Business: August 2008

Address: 6000 WESTOWN PARKWAY, WEST DES MOINES, IA 50266-5921

Phone: (515) 221-0002 **Domicile State:** IA **NAIC Code:** 13183

Data Date	Rating	RACR #1	RACR #2	Total Assets ($mil)	Capital ($mil)	Net Premium ($mil)	Net Income ($mil)
2021	B	3.17	1.56	3,050.9	343.4	-25.2	21.1
2020	B+	2.57	1.27	2,972.1	247.1	1,218.4	0.0
2019	B+	2.89	1.37	1,689.9	207.9	548.2	16.2
2018	B+	3.52	1.67	1,151.4	182.6	342.5	10.3
2017	B	4.37	2.08	810.3	172.4	284.3	7.2

Rating Indexes

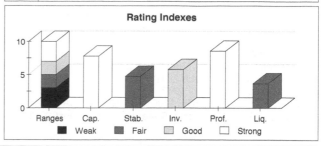

Weak ■   Fair ■   Good □   Strong □

ELCO MUTUAL LIFE & ANNUITY

B   Good

Major Rating Factors: Fair quality investment portfolio (4.7 on a scale of 0 to 10). Fair overall results on stability tests (4.4). Strong current capitalization (7.0) based on excellent risk adjusted capital (severe loss scenario) reflecting improvement over results in 2017.

Other Rating Factors: Excellent profitability (7.7) with operating gains in each of the last five years. Excellent liquidity (7.0).

Principal Business: Individual annuities (93%) and individual life insurance (7%).

Principal Investments: NonCMO investment grade bonds (68%), CMOs and structured securities (23%), and cash (3%).

Investments in Affiliates: None

Group Affiliation: None

Licensed in: All states except CT, MA, NH, NJ, NY, RI, VT, PR

Commenced Business: May 1946

Address: 916 Sherwood Drive, Lake Bluff, IL 60044

Phone: (847) 295-6000   **Domicile State:** IL   **NAIC Code:** 84174

Data Date	Rating	RACR #1	RACR #2	Total Assets ($mil)	Capital ($mil)	Net Premium ($mil)	Net Income ($mil)
2021	B	2.08	1.02	993.1	76.1	219.2	2.8
2020	B	2.20	1.08	934.1	74.2	187.6	2.7
2019	B	2.10	1.02	941.4	71.7	242.4	3.2
2018	C+	2.15	1.03	878.4	68.3	256.2	9.8
2017	C-	1.92	0.92	763.1	58.5	202.1	9.7

Rating Indexes

(Bar chart showing Ranges, Cap., Stab., Inv., Prof., Liq. with legend: Weak, Fair, Good, Strong)

ELIPS LIFE INS CO

C   Fair

Major Rating Factors: Weak profitability (1.8 on a scale of 0 to 10) with operating losses during 2021. Return on equity has been low, averaging -11.1%. Weak overall results on stability tests (2.7) including weak results on operational trends, negative cash flow from operations for 2021. Strong overall capitalization (10.0) based on mixed results -- excessive policy leverage mitigated by excellent risk adjusted capital (severe loss scenario).

Other Rating Factors: High quality investment portfolio (8.6). Excellent liquidity (9.4).

Principal Business: Group health insurance (57%), individual health insurance (28%), group life insurance (13%), and individual life insurance (2%).

Principal Investments: NonCMO investment grade bonds (99%) and cash (1%).

Investments in Affiliates: None

Group Affiliation: MAPFRE Ins Group

Licensed in: All states except NY, PR

Commenced Business: October 1975

Address: 116 WEST WATER STREET, JEFFERSON CITY, MO 65101

Phone: (847) 273-1261   **Domicile State:** MO   **NAIC Code:** 85561

Data Date	Rating	RACR #1	RACR #2	Total Assets ($mil)	Capital ($mil)	Net Premium ($mil)	Net Income ($mil)
2021	C	7.20	6.48	81.0	58.5	-6.6	-7.8
2020	C	5.62	5.06	54.2	38.9	10.2	-6.0
2019	C	6.08	5.47	38.5	33.4	1.6	-0.6
2018	C	5.99	5.39	40.5	34.3	0.1	-6.0
2017	C	5.39	4.85	22.6	20.4	-0.1	-1.7

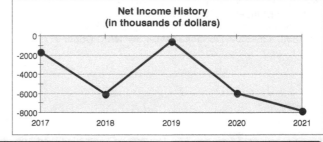

Net Income History
(in thousands of dollars)

EMC NATIONAL LIFE CO

B   Good

Major Rating Factors: Good quality investment portfolio (6.5 on a scale of 0 to 10) despite mixed results such as: minimal exposure to mortgages and large holdings of BBB rated bonds but minimal holdings in junk bonds. Good liquidity (5.5) with sufficient resources to handle a spike in claims as well as a significant increase in policy surrenders. Good overall results on stability tests (6.3) despite negative cash flow from operations for 2021 good operational trends and excellent risk diversification.

Other Rating Factors: Fair profitability (4.7). Strong capitalization (7.9) based on excellent risk adjusted capital (severe loss scenario).

Principal Business: Individual life insurance (79%), individual annuities (9%), reinsurance (6%), group life insurance (5%), and individual health insurance (1%).

Principal Investments: NonCMO investment grade bonds (72%), mortgages in good standing (8%), CMOs and structured securities (8%), common & preferred stock (5%), and misc. investments (4%).

Investments in Affiliates: None

Group Affiliation: Employers Mutual Group

Licensed in: All states except NJ, NY, PR

Commenced Business: April 1963

Address: 699 WALNUT ST STE 1100, DES MOINES, IA 50309-3965

Phone: (515) 280-2511   **Domicile State:** IA   **NAIC Code:** 62928

Data Date	Rating	RACR #1	RACR #2	Total Assets ($mil)	Capital ($mil)	Net Premium ($mil)	Net Income ($mil)
2021	B	2.78	1.58	844.9	106.5	47.6	1.5
2020	B	2.62	1.50	871.6	105.7	47.6	3.2
2019	B	2.68	1.53	886.5	104.6	56.2	5.7
2018	B	2.92	1.64	909.5	115.6	54.4	15.0
2017	B	2.64	1.49	954.8	105.6	56.6	6.3

Adverse Trends in Operations

Decrease in premium volume from 2019 to 2020 (15%)
Decrease in asset base during 2020 (2%)
Decrease in capital during 2019 (10%)
Decrease in premium volume from 2017 to 2018 (4%)
Decrease in premium volume from 2016 to 2017 (6%)

EMPIRE FIDELITY INVESTMENTS L I C *   A   Excellent

Major Rating Factors: Strong capitalization (8.6 on a scale of 0 to 10) based on excellent risk adjusted capital (severe loss scenario). Furthermore, this high level of risk adjusted capital has been consistently maintained over the last five years. High quality investment portfolio (8.1) despite no exposure to mortgages and large holdings of BBB rated bonds but minimal holdings in junk bonds. Excellent profitability (8.4) with operating gains in each of the last five years.

Other Rating Factors: Excellent liquidity (9.2). Excellent overall results on stability tests (7.6) excellent operational trends and excellent risk diversification.

Principal Business: Individual annuities (99%) and individual life insurance (1%).

Principal Investments: NonCMO investment grade bonds (93%).

Investments in Affiliates: None

Group Affiliation: FMR LLC

Licensed in: NY

Commenced Business: June 1992

Address: 640 Fifth Avenue 5th floor, New York, NY 10019

Phone: (401) 292-4717   **Domicile State:** NY   **NAIC Code:** 71228

Data Date	Rating	RACR #1	RACR #2	Total Assets ($mil)	Capital ($mil)	Net Premium ($mil)	Net Income ($mil)
2021	A	2.45	2.06	4,201.6	110.4	157.7	10.7
2020	A	2.74	2.29	3,660.7	110.4	112.6	10.8
2019	B+	2.75	2.29	3,216.7	100.0	132.9	9.2
2018	B+	2.83	2.33	2,714.8	90.2	121.3	7.8
2017	B+	2.46	2.06	2,928.6	83.1	138.8	6.4

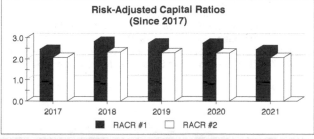

Risk-Adjusted Capital Ratios (Since 2017)

EMPLOYERS REASSURANCE CORP   C-   Fair

Major Rating Factors: Fair quality investment portfolio (4.7 on a scale of 0 to 10) with large holdings of BBB rated bonds in addition to junk bond exposure equal to 90% of capital. Weak profitability (0.9) with operating losses during 2021. Return on equity has been low, averaging -145.6%. Weak overall results on stability tests (2.9).

Other Rating Factors: Good capitalization (6.7) based on good risk adjusted capital (severe loss scenario). Good liquidity (6.9).

Principal Business: Reinsurance (100%).

Principal Investments: NonCMO investment grade bonds (55%), CMOs and structured securities (16%), noninv. grade bonds (10%), common & preferred stock (4%), and mortgages in good standing (4%).

Investments in Affiliates: 5%

Group Affiliation: GE Insurance Solutions

Licensed in: All states except NY

Commenced Business: November 1907

Address: 7101 College Blvd Ste 1400, Overland Park, KS 66211

Phone: (913) 982-3700   **Domicile State:** KS   **NAIC Code:** 68276

Data Date	Rating	RACR #1	RACR #2	Total Assets ($mil)	Capital ($mil)	Net Premium ($mil)	Net Income ($mil)
2021	C-	1.48	0.96	22,443.7	1,731.7	504.1	-1,799.7
2020	D	1.28	0.86	19,963.9	1,433.6	502.2	-1,797.7
2019	D	1.22	0.87	17,871.8	1,233.2	699.7	-1,647.4
2018	D	1.14	0.88	15,739.3	966.6	407.3	-1,511.8
2017	C-	1.16	0.91	14,815.8	816.5	236.7	-2,332.7

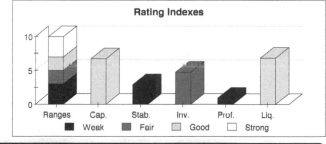

Rating Indexes

ENCOVA LIFE INSURANCE CO   B   Good

Major Rating Factors: Good quality investment portfolio (6.5 on a scale of 0 to 10) despite mixed results such as: substantial holdings of BBB bonds but junk bond exposure equal to 50% of capital. Good overall profitability (6.6). Return on equity has been low, averaging 4.0%. Good liquidity (5.6).

Other Rating Factors: Good overall results on stability tests (5.5) good operational trends and excellent risk diversification. Strong capitalization (8.1) based on excellent risk adjusted capital (severe loss scenario).

Principal Business: Individual life insurance (87%), individual annuities (12%), and group life insurance (1%).

Principal Investments: NonCMO investment grade bonds (64%), CMOs and structured securities (16%), noninv. grade bonds (8%), policy loans (3%), and cash (1%).

Investments in Affiliates: None

Group Affiliation: The Motorists Group

Licensed in: AR, FL, GA, IL, IN, IA, KY, MA, MI, MN, MO, NE, NH, OH, PA, RI, SC, TN, VA, WV, WI

Commenced Business: January 1967

Address: 471 EAST BROAD STREET, Columbus, OH 43215

Phone: (888) 876-6542   **Domicile State:** OH   **NAIC Code:** 66311

Data Date	Rating	RACR #1	RACR #2	Total Assets ($mil)	Capital ($mil)	Net Premium ($mil)	Net Income ($mil)
2021	B	3.36	1.73	607.8	79.1	42.5	2.7
2020	B-	3.34	1.75	624.1	76.5	42.7	2.4
2019	B-	3.65	1.98	595.5	73.3	43.9	7.7
2018	B	2.96	1.64	590.4	68.5	154.3	5.6
2017	B	3.53	1.95	471.7	68.6	36.7	3.2

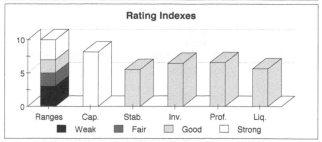

Rating Indexes

ENTERPRISE LIFE INS CO *   B+   Good

Major Rating Factors: Good current capitalization (6.6 on a scale of 0 to 10) based on good risk adjusted capital (severe loss scenario), although results have slipped from the excellent range over the last year. Good quality investment portfolio (6.4) with no exposure to mortgages and no exposure to junk bonds. Good overall results on stability tests (6.4) despite excessive premium growth and fair risk adjusted capital in prior years excellent operational trends and excellent risk diversification.

Other Rating Factors: Excellent profitability (8.9) with operating gains in each of the last five years. Excellent liquidity (7.5).

Principal Business: Reinsurance (97%) and group health insurance (3%).

Principal Investments: Common & preferred stock (37%), nonCMO investment grade bonds (29%), cash (24%), and CMOs and structured securities (9%).

Investments in Affiliates: 37%

Group Affiliation: Credit Suisse Group

Licensed in: AZ, AR, IL, KS, LA, MS, NE, NM, OK, OR, TX, WI

Commenced Business: September 1978

Address: 300 Burnett Street Suite 200, Fort Worth, TX 76102-2734

Phone: (817) 878-3300 **Domicile State:** TX **NAIC Code:** 89087

Data Date	Rating	RACR #1	RACR #2	Total Assets ($mil)	Capital ($mil)	Net Premium ($mil)	Net Income ($mil)
2021	B+	1.04	0.95	159.9	97.5	292.2	40.4
2020	B+	1.19	1.10	150.7	105.2	229.7	32.2
2019	B+	1.07	0.98	110.3	84.0	181.3	21.1
2018	B	0.84	0.74	73.5	49.1	145.8	15.2
2017	C+	0.77	0.69	47.9	29.6	103.3	7.4

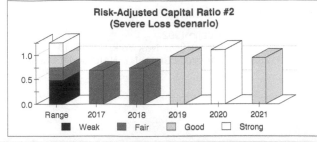

Risk-Adjusted Capital Ratio #2 (Severe Loss Scenario)

EQUITABLE FINANCIAL LIFE INSURANCE COMPANY OF AMERIC   C+   Fair

Major Rating Factors: Fair liquidity (3.5 on a scale of 0 to 10) as cash from operations and sale of marketable assets may not be adequate to cover a spike in claims or a run on policy withdrawals. Fair overall results on stability tests (4.4) including excessive premium growth. Good quality investment portfolio (5.6).

Other Rating Factors: Weak profitability (1.6) with operating losses during 2021. Strong capitalization (7.4) based on excellent risk adjusted capital (severe loss scenario).

Principal Business: N/A

Principal Investments: NonCMO investment grade bonds (82%), CMOs and structured securities (5%), policy loans (5%), common & preferred stock (1%), and misc. investments (2%).

Investments in Affiliates: None

Group Affiliation: AXA Financial Inc

Licensed in: All states except NY

Commenced Business: June 1969

Address: 3030 N Third Street Suite 790, Phoenix, AZ 85012

Phone: (201) 743-5073 **Domicile State:** AZ **NAIC Code:** 78077

Data Date	Rating	RACR #1	RACR #2	Total Assets ($mil)	Capital ($mil)	Net Premium ($mil)	Net Income ($mil)
2021	C+	2.08	1.24	6,242.0	322.8	1,071.4	-44.3
2020	C+	2.30	1.56	5,254.3	432.5	653.3	-20.0
2019	B	1.54	1.04	4,460.5	266.6	633.5	-29.8
2018	B	1.54	1.05	3,704.8	222.4	591.4	-89.4
2017	B	2.38	1.62	3,735.1	302.7	519.4	-12.5

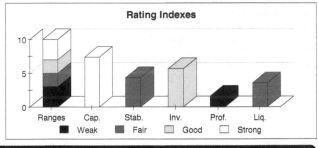

Rating Indexes

EQUITABLE FINL LIFE & ANNUITY CO   C+   Fair

Major Rating Factors: Fair overall results on stability tests (3.0 on a scale of 0 to 10) including weak risk adjusted capital in prior years, negative cash flow from operations for 2021. Weak profitability (1.0) with operating losses during 2021. Return on equity has been low, averaging -80.7%. Weak liquidity (0.0) as a spike in claims or a run on policy withdrawals may stretch capacity.

Other Rating Factors: Strong overall capitalization (7.4) based on mixed results -- excessive policy leverage mitigated by excellent risk adjusted capital (severe loss scenario). High quality investment portfolio (7.4).

Principal Business: Individual life insurance (100%).

Principal Investments: NonCMO investment grade bonds (46%) and policy loans (45%).

Investments in Affiliates: None

Group Affiliation: AXA Financial Inc

Licensed in: All states except NY, PR

Commenced Business: June 1984

Address: 8742 Lucent Boulevard Ste 600, Lakewood, CO 80401

Phone: (704) 341-6308 **Domicile State:** CO **NAIC Code:** 62880

Data Date	Rating	RACR #1	RACR #2	Total Assets ($mil)	Capital ($mil)	Net Premium ($mil)	Net Income ($mil)
2021	C+	2.47	1.29	587.0	54.6	-0.8	-27.0
2020	C+	0.97	0.51	550.5	22.0	0.2	-24.8
2019	B	0.92	0.47	551.3	25.8	-0.9	-51.8
2018	B	0.92	0.48	480.7	19.3	-2.2	-6.3
2017	B	0.55	0.28	486.4	12.0	0.4	-2.5

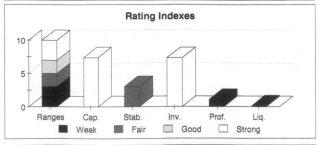

Rating Indexes

EQUITABLE FINL LIFE INS CO
B   Good

Major Rating Factors: Good quality investment portfolio (6.3 on a scale of 0 to 10) despite large holdings of BBB rated bonds in addition to moderate junk bond exposure. Exposure to mortgages is significant, but the mortgage default rate has been low. Good liquidity (5.4) with sufficient resources to handle a spike in claims as well as a significant increase in policy surrenders. Fair profitability (3.4) with operating losses during 2021.

Other Rating Factors: Fair overall results on stability tests (4.1) including negative cash flow from operations for 2021. Strong capitalization (7.4) based on excellent risk adjusted capital (severe loss scenario).

Principal Business: Individual annuities (68%), group retirement contracts (18%), individual life insurance (13%), and reinsurance (1%).

Principal Investments: NonCMO investment grade bonds (62%), mortgages in good standing (18%), policy loans (5%), CMOs and structured securities (5%), and misc. investments (9%).

Investments in Affiliates: 4%

Group Affiliation: AXA Financial Inc

Licensed in: All states, the District of Columbia and Puerto Rico

Commenced Business: July 1859

Address: 1290 Avenue of the Americas, New York, NY 10104

Phone: (212) 554-1234 **Domicile State:** NY **NAIC Code:** 62944

Data Date	Rating	RACR #1	RACR #2	Total Assets ($mil)	Capital ($mil)	Net Premium ($mil)	Net Income ($mil)
2021	B	2.47	1.25	248,000	5,393.9	4,891.8	-808.0
2020	B	2.67	1.37	236,000	6,113.5	13,005.7	412.7
2019	B	3.65	1.91	216,000	8,146.0	14,390.9	3,893.5
2018	B+	3.54	1.85	190,000	7,575.1	12,667.8	3,120.2
2017	B+	3.77	1.95	195,000	7,422.3	12,867.4	893.8

Rating Indexes

EQUITRUST LIFE INS CO
B-   Good

Major Rating Factors: Good current capitalization (6.2 on a scale of 0 to 10) based on good risk adjusted capital (moderate loss scenario) reflecting some improvement over results in 2018. Good overall results on stability tests (5.0) despite fair risk adjusted capital in prior years. Other stability subfactors include excellent operational trends and excellent risk diversification. Fair quality investment portfolio (3.7).

Other Rating Factors: Fair liquidity (3.9). Excellent profitability (8.4) with operating gains in each of the last five years.

Principal Business: Individual annuities (98%), group retirement contracts (1%), and individual life insurance (1%).

Principal Investments: NonCMO investment grade bonds (41%), CMOs and structured securities (25%), mortgages in good standing (13%), noninv. grade bonds (7%), and common & preferred stock (2%).

Investments in Affiliates: 2%

Group Affiliation: Magic Johnson Enterprises Inc

Licensed in: All states except NY, PR

Commenced Business: July 1967

Address: 222 WEST ADAMS ST STE 2150, CHICAGO, IL 60606

Phone: (515) 225-5400 **Domicile State:** IL **NAIC Code:** 62510

Data Date	Rating	RACR #1	RACR #2	Total Assets ($mil)	Capital ($mil)	Net Premium ($mil)	Net Income ($mil)
2021	B-	1.78	0.87	25,685.5	1,631.8	1,578.7	242.6
2020	B-	1.64	0.82	22,988.5	1,362.9	1,923.9	203.2
2019	B-	1.60	0.77	20,735.6	1,186.0	1,787.0	186.1
2018	B-	1.20	0.59	18,595.3	840.0	1,556.6	215.2
2017	B-	1.24	0.62	18,168.7	872.7	1,671.3	210.7

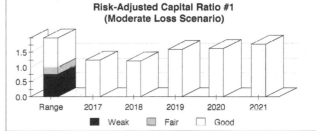

Risk-Adjusted Capital Ratio #1
(Moderate Loss Scenario)

ERIE FAMILY LIFE INS CO
C+   Fair

Major Rating Factors: Fair overall results on stability tests (4.4 on a scale of 0 to 10). Good quality investment portfolio (5.9) despite mixed results such as: no exposure to mortgages and large holdings of BBB rated bonds but small junk bond holdings. Good liquidity (5.8) with sufficient resources to handle a spike in claims as well as a significant increase in policy surrenders.

Other Rating Factors: Weak profitability (2.1) with operating losses during 2021. Strong capitalization (8.5) based on excellent risk adjusted capital (severe loss scenario).

Principal Business: Individual life insurance (88%), individual annuities (9%), and individual health insurance (3%).

Principal Investments: NonCMO investment grade bonds (83%), noninv. grade bonds (3%), common & preferred stock (2%), CMOs and structured securities (1%), and misc. investments (4%).

Investments in Affiliates: None

Group Affiliation: Erie Ins Group

Licensed in: DC, IL, IN, KY, MD, MN, NC, OH, PA, TN, VA, WV, WI

Commenced Business: September 1967

Address: 100 Erie Insurance Place, Erie, PA 16530

Phone: (800) 458-0811 **Domicile State:** PA **NAIC Code:** 70769

Data Date	Rating	RACR #1	RACR #2	Total Assets ($mil)	Capital ($mil)	Net Premium ($mil)	Net Income ($mil)
2021	C+	3.66	2.00	3,055.6	439.2	228.3	-41.9
2020	C+	2.65	1.46	2,824.1	294.9	203.1	-12.5
2019	B	2.98	1.65	2,677.5	310.3	208.7	-3.6
2018	A-	3.10	1.71	2,498.6	313.4	184.9	0.6
2017	A-	2.91	1.59	2,433.1	303.6	170.8	7.5

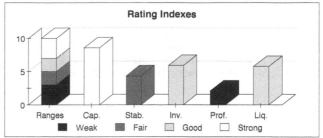

Rating Indexes

EVERLAKE ASSURANCE COMPANY   C | Fair

Major Rating Factors: Fair overall capitalization (4.0 on a scale of 0 to 10) based on excellent risk adjusted capital (severe loss scenario). Nevertheless, capital levels have fluctuated during prior years. Fair overall results on stability tests (3.3). Good quality investment portfolio (6.3).

Other Rating Factors: Weak profitability (2.9) with operating losses during 2021. Excellent liquidity (10.0).

Principal Business: Individual life insurance (100%).

Principal Investments: NonCMO investment grade bonds (78%) and cash (22%).

Investments in Affiliates: None

Group Affiliation: Allstate Group

Licensed in: All states except NY, PR

Commenced Business: July 1967

Address: 3075 SANDERS ROAD SUITE I2W, NORTHBROOK, IL 60062

Phone: (847) 665-9930 **Domicile State:** IL **NAIC Code:** 70866

Data Date	Rating	RACR #1	RACR #2	Total Assets ($mil)	Capital ($mil)	Net Premium ($mil)	Net Income ($mil)
2021	C+	3.63	3.26	172.7	34.7	0.0	-6.5
2020	C+	9.15	8.24	155.4	86.3	-318.2	43.8
2019	C+	2.33	1.36	776.0	164.1	240.7	-33.1
2018	C+	2.53	1.46	693.3	141.0	166.5	-46.0
2017	C+	3.55	1.88	674.1	135.8	57.6	-7.3

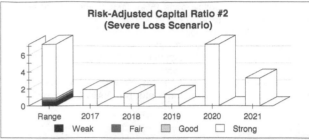

Risk-Adjusted Capital Ratio #2
(Severe Loss Scenario)

FAMILY HERITAGE LIFE INS CO OF AMER   B- Good

Major Rating Factors: Good overall results on stability tests (5.1 on a scale of 0 to 10) despite fair financial strength of affiliated Torchmark Corp. Other stability subfactors include good operational trends and excellent risk diversification. Good quality investment portfolio (5.6) despite mixed results such as: large holdings of BBB rated bonds but moderate junk bond exposure. Good overall profitability (5.5) although investment income, in comparison to reserve requirements, is below regulatory standards.

Other Rating Factors: Strong capitalization (7.2) based on excellent risk adjusted capital (severe loss scenario). Excellent liquidity (8.5).

Principal Business: Individual health insurance (94%), group health insurance (5%), and individual life insurance (1%).

Principal Investments: NonCMO investment grade bonds (86%), noninv. grade bonds (4%), mortgages in good standing (1%), and CMOs and structured securities (1%).

Investments in Affiliates: None

Group Affiliation: Torchmark Corp

Licensed in: All states except NY

Commenced Business: November 1989

Address: 6001 East Royalton Rd Ste 200, Cleveland, OH 44147-3529

Phone: (440) 922-5252 **Domicile State:** OH **NAIC Code:** 77968

Data Date	Rating	RACR #1	RACR #2	Total Assets ($mil)	Capital ($mil)	Net Premium ($mil)	Net Income ($mil)
2021	B-	1.92	1.12	1,588.1	155.6	350.0	41.1
2020	B-	1.87	1.11	1,435.8	135.9	321.8	36.2
2019	B-	1.65	1.00	1,287.3	109.7	298.7	32.0
2018	B-	2.04	1.25	1,196.8	125.4	170.0	31.5
2017	B+	1.65	1.01	1,290.4	100.3	284.3	23.0

Torchmark Corp
Composite Group Rating: C+
Largest Group Members

Largest Group Members	Assets ($mil)	Rating
LIBERTY NATIONAL LIFE INS CO	8308	B-
GLOBE LIFE ACCIDENT INS CO	5074	C
AMERICAN INCOME LIFE INS CO	4675	B-
FAMILY HERITAGE LIFE INS CO OF AMER	1436	B-
UNITED AMERICAN INS CO	729	B

FAMILY LIFE INS CO   C Fair

Major Rating Factors: Fair overall results on stability tests (4.2 on a scale of 0 to 10) including negative cash flow from operations for 2021. Good liquidity (6.3) with sufficient resources to handle a spike in claims as well as a significant increase in policy surrenders. Strong capitalization (8.7) based on excellent risk adjusted capital (severe loss scenario).

Other Rating Factors: High quality investment portfolio (7.9). Excellent profitability (7.6) with operating gains in each of the last five years.

Principal Business: Individual health insurance (68%) and individual life insurance (32%).

Principal Investments: NonCMO investment grade bonds (79%), policy loans (8%), cash (5%), common & preferred stock (2%), and CMOs and structured securities (1%).

Investments in Affiliates: None

Group Affiliation: Manhattan Life Group Inc

Licensed in: All states except NY, PR

Commenced Business: June 1949

Address: 10777 Northwest Freeway, Houston, TX 77092

Phone: (713) 529-0045 **Domicile State:** TX **NAIC Code:** 63053

Data Date	Rating	RACR #1	RACR #2	Total Assets ($mil)	Capital ($mil)	Net Premium ($mil)	Net Income ($mil)
2021	C	3.12	2.10	140.0	28.6	27.0	1.6
2020	C	3.15	2.28	143.3	28.9	27.0	1.0
2019	C	2.89	2.18	141.2	26.6	26.5	1.8
2018	C	3.06	2.40	146.8	28.4	25.6	1.6
2017	C	3.33	2.72	150.8	31.1	25.6	2.7

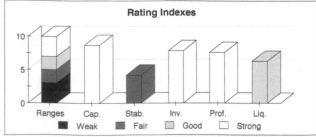

Rating Indexes

FARM BUREAU LIFE INS CO *

B+   Good

Major Rating Factors: Good quality investment portfolio (5.6 on a scale of 0 to 10) despite large holdings of BBB rated bonds in addition to moderate junk bond exposure. Exposure to mortgages is significant, but the mortgage default rate has been low. Good liquidity (5.0) with sufficient resources to handle a spike in claims as well as a significant increase in policy surrenders. Good overall results on stability tests (6.4) excellent operational trends and excellent risk diversification.

Other Rating Factors: Strong capitalization (7.2) based on excellent risk adjusted capital (severe loss scenario). Excellent profitability (7.6) with operating gains in each of the last five years.

Principal Business: Individual life insurance (59%), individual annuities (37%), reinsurance (2%), group retirement contracts (1%), and individual health insurance (1%).

Principal Investments: NonCMO investment grade bonds (54%), CMOs and structured securities (25%), mortgages in good standing (11%), noninv. grade bonds (3%), and misc. investments (6%).

Investments in Affiliates: None

Group Affiliation: Iowa Farm Bureau

Licensed in: AZ, CO, ID, IA, KS, MN, MT, NE, NV, NM, ND, OK, OR, SD, UT, WA, WI, WY

Commenced Business: January 1945

Address: 5400 University Avenue, West Des Moines, IA 50266-5997

Phone: (515) 225-5400 **Domicile State:** IA **NAIC Code:** 63088

Data Date	Rating	RACR #1	RACR #2	Total Assets ($mil)	Capital ($mil)	Net Premium ($mil)	Net Income ($mil)
2021	B+	2.20	1.16	9,888.5	670.8	624.0	110.9
2020	B+	2.05	1.07	9,573.0	628.0	550.6	72.6
2019	B+	2.18	1.15	9,340.7	642.4	603.7	100.1
2018	B+	2.19	1.15	9,120.8	637.2	641.8	103.9
2017	B+	2.04	1.06	9,068.7	616.0	632.8	104.9

Adverse Trends in Operations

Decrease in premium volume from 2019 to 2020 (9%)
Decrease in capital during 2020 (2%)
Decrease in premium volume from 2018 to 2019 (6%)
Decrease in premium volume from 2016 to 2017 (8%)

FARM BUREAU LIFE INS CO OF MICHIGAN *

A-   Excellent

Major Rating Factors: Good quality investment portfolio (6.1 on a scale of 0 to 10) despite significant exposure to mortgages . Mortgage default rate has been low. substantial holdings of BBB bonds in addition to small junk bond holdings. Good liquidity (6.0) with sufficient resources to handle a spike in claims as well as a significant increase in policy surrenders. Good overall results on stability tests (6.9) excellent operational trends and excellent risk diversification.

Other Rating Factors: Strong capitalization (8.7) based on excellent risk adjusted capital (severe loss scenario). Excellent profitability (7.0) with operating gains in each of the last five years.

Principal Business: Individual life insurance (78%), individual annuities (19%), reinsurance (1%), group retirement contracts (1%), and group life insurance (1%).

Principal Investments: NonCMO investment grade bonds (66%), mortgages in good standing (18%), common & preferred stock (7%), noninv. grade bonds (2%), and misc. investments (6%).

Investments in Affiliates: None

Group Affiliation: Michigan Farm Bureau

Licensed in: MI, OH, OK

Commenced Business: September 1951

Address: 7373 WEST SAGINAW HIGHWAY, LANSING, MI 48917

Phone: (517) 323-7000 **Domicile State:** MI **NAIC Code:** 63096

Data Date	Rating	RACR #1	RACR #2	Total Assets ($mil)	Capital ($mil)	Net Premium ($mil)	Net Income ($mil)
2021	A-	3.91	2.15	2,709.6	520.9	116.1	33.1
2020	A-	3.81	2.09	2,643.9	482.4	111.7	36.4
2019	A-	3.51	1.95	2,574.3	444.0	114.0	27.4
2018	A-	3.72	2.07	2,488.2	448.6	115.0	27.2
2017	A-	3.61	2.00	2,487.4	443.3	151.6	24.9

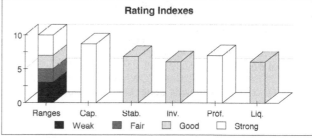

Rating Indexes

FARM BUREAU LIFE INS CO OF MISSOURI

B   Good

Major Rating Factors: Good liquidity (6.0 on a scale of 0 to 10) with sufficient resources to handle a spike in claims as well as a significant increase in policy surrenders. Good overall results on stability tests (6.1). Stability strengths include excellent operational trends and excellent risk diversification. Fair quality investment portfolio (4.8).

Other Rating Factors: Fair profitability (3.0) with investment income below regulatory standards in relation to interest assumptions of reserves. Strong capitalization (7.2) based on excellent risk adjusted capital (severe loss scenario).

Principal Business: Individual life insurance (86%), individual annuities (13%), and group life insurance (1%).

Principal Investments: NonCMO investment grade bonds (66%), common & preferred stock (17%), CMOs and structured securities (11%), policy loans (4%), and noninv. grade bonds (1%).

Investments in Affiliates: 4%

Group Affiliation: Missouri Farm Bureau

Licensed in: MO

Commenced Business: July 1950

Address: 701 South Country Club Drive, Jefferson City, MO 65109-4515

Phone: (573) 893-1400 **Domicile State:** MO **NAIC Code:** 63118

Data Date	Rating	RACR #1	RACR #2	Total Assets ($mil)	Capital ($mil)	Net Premium ($mil)	Net Income ($mil)
2021	B	1.72	1.14	698.8	98.3	43.5	2.7
2020	A-	1.59	1.05	657.9	82.4	42.8	0.9
2019	A-	1.70	1.14	632.7	80.6	40.3	2.4
2018	A-	1.57	1.05	599.8	68.5	39.7	4.8
2017	A-	1.65	1.09	586.5	68.8	37.0	2.6

Adverse Trends in Operations

Decrease in premium volume from 2016 to 2017 (9%)

FARMERS NEW WORLD LIFE INS CO   B-   Good

Major Rating Factors: Good overall capitalization (6.1 on a scale of 0 to 10) based on good risk adjusted capital (severe loss scenario). Nevertheless, capital levels have fluctuated during prior years. Good quality investment portfolio (5.5) despite substantial holdings of BBB bonds in addition to moderate junk bond exposure. Exposure to mortgages is significant, but the mortgage default rate has been low. Good liquidity (5.1).

Other Rating Factors: Fair overall results on stability tests (4.8) including fair financial strength of affiliated Zurich Financial Services Group. Weak profitability (2.9) with investment income below regulatory standards in relation to interest assumptions of reserves.

Principal Business: Individual life insurance (96%), individual annuities (2%), and individual health insurance (2%).

Principal Investments: NonCMO investment grade bonds (49%), CMOs and structured securities (23%), mortgages in good standing (13%), policy loans (7%), and misc. investments (8%).

Investments in Affiliates: 2%

Group Affiliation: Zurich Financial Services Group

Licensed in: All states except NY, PR

Commenced Business: May 1911

Address: 3003 77TH AVENUE SOUTHEAST, BELLEVUE, WA 98005-4491

Phone: (206) 232-8400 **Domicile State:** WA **NAIC Code:** 63177

Data Date	Rating	RACR #1	RACR #2	Total Assets ($mil)	Capital ($mil)	Net Premium ($mil)	Net Income ($mil)
2021	B-	1.69	0.89	5,670.8	342.0	542.1	79.2
2020	B-	1.85	0.97	5,427.5	379.5	537.6	114.2
2019	B-	2.20	1.17	5,260.9	439.8	539.6	162.0
2018	B-	2.29	1.21	5,046.7	448.2	540.1	159.6
2017	B-	2.06	1.13	5,127.3	468.9	-1,738.6	148.9

Risk-Adjusted Capital Ratio #2 (Severe Loss Scenario)

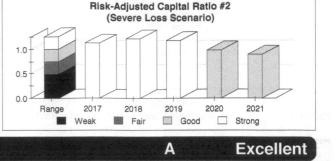

Weak   Fair   Good   Strong

FEDERATED LIFE INS CO *   A   Excellent

Major Rating Factors: Good quality investment portfolio (6.4 on a scale of 0 to 10) despite mixed results such as: large holdings of BBB rated bonds but moderate junk bond exposure. Good liquidity (6.6) with sufficient resources to handle a spike in claims as well as a significant increase in policy surrenders. Excellent overall results on stability tests (7.4) excellent operational trends and excellent risk diversification.

Other Rating Factors: Strong capitalization (9.3) based on excellent risk adjusted capital (severe loss scenario). Excellent profitability (8.9) with operating gains in each of the last five years.

Principal Business: Individual life insurance (75%), individual health insurance (13%), individual annuities (11%), and group life insurance (1%).

Principal Investments: NonCMO investment grade bonds (67%), CMOs and structured securities (17%), noninv. grade bonds (6%), common & preferred stock (4%), and policy loans (1%).

Investments in Affiliates: None

Group Affiliation: Federated Mutual Ins Group

Licensed in: All states except AK, DC, HI, PR

Commenced Business: January 1959

Address: 121 EAST PARK SQUARE, OWATONNA, MN 55060

Phone: (507) 455-5200 **Domicile State:** MN **NAIC Code:** 63258

Data Date	Rating	RACR #1	RACR #2	Total Assets ($mil)	Capital ($mil)	Net Premium ($mil)	Net Income ($mil)
2021	A	4.89	2.54	2,427.1	550.0	251.7	42.9
2020	A	4.72	2.44	2,255.8	506.2	216.3	43.2
2019	A	4.96	2.66	2,139.6	467.7	209.7	37.6
2018	A	4.86	2.62	2,007.4	425.5	199.0	43.8
2017	A	4.39	2.35	1,877.4	382.4	192.7	32.6

Adverse Trends in Operations

Decrease in premium volume from 2016 to 2017 (2%)

FIDELITY & GUARANTY LIFE INS CO   C-   Fair

Major Rating Factors: Fair capitalization for the current period (3.1 on a scale of 0 to 10) based on fair risk adjusted capital (moderate loss scenario) reflecting some improvement over results in 2020. Fair quality investment portfolio (3.5) with large holdings of BBB rated bonds in addition to significant exposure to junk bonds. Weak overall results on stability tests (2.9) including weak risk adjusted capital in prior years.

Other Rating Factors: Good overall profitability (5.3). Excellent liquidity (7.1).

Principal Business: Individual annuities (79%), group retirement contracts (14%), and individual life insurance (6%).

Principal Investments: CMOs and structured securities (34%), nonCMO investment grade bonds (33%), common & preferred stock (9%), noninv. grade bonds (7%), and misc. investments (15%).

Investments in Affiliates: 5%

Group Affiliation: FGL Holdings

Licensed in: All states except NY

Commenced Business: November 1960

Address: 601 Locust Street, Des Moines, IA 50309

Phone: (410) 895-0100 **Domicile State:** IA **NAIC Code:** 63274

Data Date	Rating	RACR #1	RACR #2	Total Assets ($mil)	Capital ($mil)	Net Premium ($mil)	Net Income ($mil)
2021	C-	0.75	0.51	38,358.1	1,472.7	903.8	351.0
2020	C-	0.69	0.44	29,409.8	1,248.7	-594.7	-46.0
2019	C+	0.90	0.56	26,975.9	1,513.3	2,569.8	151.7
2018	C+	1.21	0.69	24,714.5	1,545.2	-1,613.2	-151.1
2017	C+	1.15	0.61	22,380.8	919.0	2,392.4	222.4

Junk Bonds as a % of Capital

Capital — $1 bil.

Junk Bonds — $2 bil.

0% 20% 40% 60% 80% 100%120%140%160%180%

BB   B   CCC   In default

FIDELITY & GUARANTY LIFE INS CO NY | C | Fair

Major Rating Factors: Fair overall results on stability tests (3.9 on a scale of 0 to 10) including potential financial drain due to affiliation with FGL Holdings. Fair quality investment portfolio (3.8) with large holdings of BBB rated bonds in addition to junk bond exposure equal to 74% of capital. Good overall profitability (6.0). Excellent expense controls. Return on equity has been fair, averaging 8.6%.

Other Rating Factors: Good liquidity (6.6). Strong capitalization (8.4) based on excellent risk adjusted capital (severe loss scenario).

Principal Business: Group retirement contracts (61%), individual annuities (34%), and individual life insurance (4%).

Principal Investments: NonCMO investment grade bonds (58%), CMOs and structured securities (15%), noninv. grade bonds (10%), cash (6%), and common & preferred stock (5%).

Investments in Affiliates: None

Group Affiliation: FGL Holdings

Licensed in: NY

Commenced Business: November 1962

Address: 445 Park Avenue 9th Floor, New York, NY 10174

Phone: (800) 495-1123 **Domicile State:** NY **NAIC Code:** 69434

Data Date	Rating	RACR #1	RACR #2	Total Assets ($mil)	Capital ($mil)	Net Premium ($mil)	Net Income ($mil)
2021	C	3.97	1.91	556.8	99.2	40.9	3.7
2020	C+	3.75	1.77	523.2	93.2	14.9	-2.0
2019	B	4.16	1.97	534.6	94.9	15.7	-0.9
2018	B	4.18	2.14	532.1	85.1	11.1	-2.6
2017	B-	4.44	2.23	548.9	88.6	9.6	41.0

FGL Holdings
Composite Group Rating: D+
Largest Group Members

	Assets ($mil)	Rating
FIDELITY GUARANTY LIFE INS CO	29410	C-
FIDELITY GUARANTY LIFE INS CO NY	523	C

FIDELITY INVESTMENTS LIFE INS CO * | A | Excellent

Major Rating Factors: Good quality investment portfolio (6.6 on a scale of 0 to 10) despite mixed results such as: no exposure to mortgages and large holdings of BBB rated bonds but minimal holdings in junk bonds. Strong capitalization (8.3) based on excellent risk adjusted capital (severe loss scenario). Furthermore, this high level of risk adjusted capital has been consistently maintained over the last five years. Excellent profitability (9.2) with operating gains in each of the last five years.

Other Rating Factors: Excellent liquidity (10.0). Excellent overall results on stability tests (7.7) excellent operational trends and excellent risk diversification.

Principal Business: Individual annuities (99%) and individual life insurance (1%).

Principal Investments: NonCMO investment grade bonds (75%), common & preferred stock (8%), and noninv. grade bonds (6%).

Investments in Affiliates: 8%

Group Affiliation: FMR LLC

Licensed in: All states except NY, PR

Commenced Business: December 1981

Address: 49 North 400 West 6th Floor, Salt Lake City, UT 84101

Phone: (401) 292-4717 **Domicile State:** UT **NAIC Code:** 93696

Data Date	Rating	RACR #1	RACR #2	Total Assets ($mil)	Capital ($mil)	Net Premium ($mil)	Net Income ($mil)
2021	A	2.70	1.84	44,295.4	1,086.8	2,253.7	125.3
2020	A	3.08	2.01	37,999.7	1,069.0	1,374.6	103.9
2019	A-	3.51	2.25	32,999.0	1,061.9	1,402.9	102.7
2018	A-	3.72	2.37	27,887.6	957.5	1,400.4	91.3
2017	A-	3.23	2.02	29,539.9	876.1	1,384.4	73.6

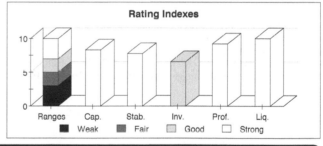

Rating Indexes

Ranges | Cap. | Stab. | Inv. | Prof. | Liq.

■ Weak ■ Fair ▨ Good □ Strong

FIDELITY LIFE ASSN A LEGAL RESERVE | C+ | Fair

Major Rating Factors: Fair profitability (3.2 on a scale of 0 to 10) with operating losses during 2021. Return on equity has been low, averaging 0.3%. Fair overall results on stability tests (4.8) including negative cash flow from operations for 2021. Good quality investment portfolio (6.3) despite significant exposure to mortgages . Mortgage default rate has been low. large holdings of BBB rated bonds in addition to minimal holdings in junk bonds.

Other Rating Factors: Good liquidity (6.7). Strong capitalization (10.0) based on excellent risk adjusted capital (severe loss scenario).

Principal Business: Individual life insurance (73%), reinsurance (20%), and group life insurance (7%).

Principal Investments: NonCMO investment grade bonds (53%), CMOs and structured securities (24%), mortgages in good standing (12%), cash (5%), and misc. investments (7%).

Investments in Affiliates: None

Group Affiliation: Vericity Inc

Licensed in: All states except NY, PR

Commenced Business: February 1896

Address: 8700 W Bryn Mawr Ave Suite 900, Chicago, IL 60631

Phone: (312) 379-2397 **Domicile State:** IL **NAIC Code:** 63290

Data Date	Rating	RACR #1	RACR #2	Total Assets ($mil)	Capital ($mil)	Net Premium ($mil)	Net Income ($mil)
2021	C+	5.67	2.98	418.7	98.2	61.0	-8.7
2020	C+	6.49	3.37	422.4	112.3	69.7	6.2
2019	C+	7.58	3.88	420.5	114.7	-1.2	7.6
2018	C+	5.70	3.08	407.0	121.9	61.5	2.3
2017	C+	6.25	3.29	406.3	127.6	61.1	1.0

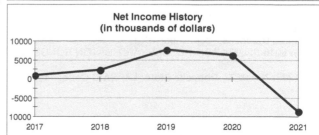

Net Income History
(in thousands of dollars)

FIDELITY SECURITY LIFE INS CO *   A-   Excellent

Major Rating Factors: Good quality investment portfolio (6.7 on a scale of 0 to 10) despite mixed results such as: minimal exposure to mortgages and large holdings of BBB rated bonds but minimal holdings in junk bonds. Good liquidity (6.8) with sufficient resources to handle a spike in claims. Good overall results on stability tests (6.9) excellent operational trends and excellent risk diversification.

Other Rating Factors: Strong capitalization (9.9) based on excellent risk adjusted capital (severe loss scenario). Excellent profitability (7.6) with operating gains in each of the last five years.

Principal Business: Group health insurance (87%), reinsurance (7%), individual health insurance (2%), individual life insurance (2%), and other lines (2%).

Principal Investments: CMOs and structured securities (43%), nonCMO investment grade bonds (37%), common & preferred stock (4%), cash (3%), and misc. investments (8%).

Investments in Affiliates: 2%

Group Affiliation: Fidelity Security Group

Licensed in: All states except PR

Commenced Business: July 1969

Address: 3130 Broadway, Kansas City, MO 64111-2452

Phone: (816) 750-1060 **Domicile State:** MO **NAIC Code:** 71870

Data Date	Rating	RACR #1	RACR #2	Total Assets ($mil)	Capital ($mil)	Net Premium ($mil)	Net Income ($mil)
2021	A-	4.67	2.90	982.0	309.9	145.7	18.7
2020	A-	5.20	3.23	955.5	293.5	128.3	28.9
2019	A-	4.93	3.04	952.3	266.6	126.8	25.5
2018	A-	4.60	2.81	999.4	242.3	119.4	39.2
2017	B	3.87	2.36	949.5	204.4	115.0	22.8

Adverse Trends in Operations

Decrease in asset base during 2019 (5%)
Decrease in premium volume from 2016 to 2017 (5%)

FIRST ALLMERICA FINANCIAL LIFE INS   C+   Fair

Major Rating Factors: Fair overall capitalization (4.0 on a scale of 0 to 10) based on excellent risk adjusted capital (severe loss scenario). Nevertheless, capital levels have fluctuated during prior years. Fair profitability (3.2). Return on equity has been low, averaging 2.2%. Fair overall results on stability tests (4.0) including negative cash flow from operations for 2021.

Other Rating Factors: Good quality investment portfolio (6.5). Good liquidity (6.7).

Principal Business: Reinsurance (83%), individual life insurance (15%), and group life insurance (1%).

Principal Investments: NonCMO investment grade bonds (79%), CMOs and structured securities (14%), policy loans (2%), cash (2%), and noninv. grade bonds (1%).

Investments in Affiliates: 1%

Group Affiliation: Global Atlantic Financial Group

Licensed in: All states except PR

Commenced Business: June 1845

Address: 132 TURNPIKE ROAD SUITE 210, SOUTHBOROUGH, MA 2135

Phone: (508) 460-2400 **Domicile State:** MA **NAIC Code:** 69140

Data Date	Rating	RACR #1	RACR #2	Total Assets ($mil)	Capital ($mil)	Net Premium ($mil)	Net Income ($mil)
2021	C+	4.14	1.92	3,262.6	121.5	177.4	6.5
2020	B-	4.32	1.97	3,062.3	115.6	-921.9	-10.6
2019	B	5.80	2.72	3,233.8	245.6	41.4	-5.8
2018	B	4.88	2.28	3,264.6	224.0	23.5	9.2
2017	B-	5.18	2.44	3,420.3	240.3	28.6	28.7

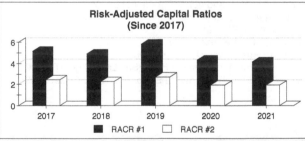

Risk-Adjusted Capital Ratios (Since 2017)

FIRST ASR LIFE OF AMERICA   B   Good

Major Rating Factors: Good overall results on stability tests (5.9 on a scale of 0 to 10) despite fair financial strength of affiliated LDS Group and negative cash flow from operations for 2021. Other stability subfactors include excellent operational trends and good risk diversification. Good overall profitability (6.3). Return on equity has been low, averaging 2.0%. Strong capitalization (10.0) based on excellent risk adjusted capital (severe loss scenario).

Other Rating Factors: High quality investment portfolio (8.4). Excellent liquidity (9.2).

Principal Business: N/A

Principal Investments: NonCMO investment grade bonds (68%), common & preferred stock (26%), and cash (1%).

Investments in Affiliates: 26%

Group Affiliation: LDS Group

Licensed in: LA, MS

Commenced Business: September 1981

Address: 9016 BLUEBONNET BOULEVARD, BATON ROUGE, LA 70810-2810

Phone: (225) 769-9923 **Domicile State:** LA **NAIC Code:** 94579

Data Date	Rating	RACR #1	RACR #2	Total Assets ($mil)	Capital ($mil)	Net Premium ($mil)	Net Income ($mil)
2021	B	3.48	3.31	42.6	38.6	3.2	0.5
2020	B	3.41	3.24	42.4	38.3	3.2	0.6
2019	B	3.34	3.15	42.0	37.6	2.9	0.7
2018	B	3.30	3.09	41.6	36.9	2.0	0.9
2017	B	3.28	3.08	41.0	35.8	1.9	1.2

LDS Group
Composite Group Rating: C+
Largest Group Members

	Assets ($mil)	Rating
VERSANT CASUALTY INS CO	73	C
FIRST ASR LIFE OF AMERICA	42	B
PERFORMANCE LIFE OF AMERICA	28	B-
VERSANT LIFE INS CO	6	B-

FIRST BERKSHIRE HATHAWAY LIFE INS CO — C+ — Fair

Major Rating Factors: Fair overall results on stability tests (4.4 on a scale of 0 to 10). Good quality investment portfolio (5.3) despite mixed results such as: no exposure to mortgages and substantial holdings of BBB bonds but small junk bond holdings. Weak profitability (2.6) with investment income below regulatory standards in relation to interest assumptions of reserves.

Other Rating Factors: Strong capitalization (10.0) based on excellent risk adjusted capital (severe loss scenario). Excellent liquidity (9.9).

Principal Business: Group retirement contracts (100%).

Principal Investments: NonCMO investment grade bonds (67%), common & preferred stock (20%), CMOs and structured securities (4%), noninv. grade bonds (2%), and cash (1%).

Investments in Affiliates: 14%

Group Affiliation: Berkshire-Hathaway

Licensed in: MO, NE, NY

Commenced Business: March 2003

Address: Marine Air Terminal LaGuardia, NEW YORK, NY 10118

Phone: (402) 916-3000 **Domicile State:** NY **NAIC Code:** 11591

Data Date	Rating	RACR #1	RACR #2	Total Assets ($mil)	Capital ($mil)	Net Premium ($mil)	Net Income ($mil)
2021	C+	8.27	4.79	250.6	129.1	1.9	1.2
2020	C+	10.69	5.92	232.9	119.9	2.5	-2.7
2019	C+	12.53	8.89	221.2	122.8	1.2	2.1
2018	C+	12.11	7.65	215.4	119.3	4.2	3.4
2017	C+	11.80	6.75	228.6	116.1	6.8	-3.6

Rating Indexes

Ranges / Cap. / Stab. / Inv. / Prof. / Liq.
Weak / Fair / Good / Strong

FIRST HEALTH LIFE & HEALTH INS CO — C+ — Fair

Major Rating Factors: Fair overall results on stability tests (4.6 on a scale of 0 to 10) including negative cash flow from operations for 2021. Good current capitalization (5.3) based on mixed results -- excessive policy leverage mitigated by good risk adjusted capital (severe loss scenario), although results have slipped from the excellent range over the last year. Good overall profitability (6.2). Excellent expense controls.

Other Rating Factors: High quality investment portfolio (8.3). Excellent liquidity (7.2).

Principal Business: N/A

Principal Investments: Cash (51%), nonCMO investment grade bonds (31%), CMOs and structured securities (11%), noninv. grade bonds (3%), and common & preferred stock (2%).

Investments in Affiliates: None

Group Affiliation: Aetna Inc

Licensed in: All states except PR

Commenced Business: June 1979

Address: DOWNERS GROVE, IL 60515

Phone: (630) 737-7900 **Domicile State:** TX **NAIC Code:** 90328

Data Date	Rating	RACR #1	RACR #2	Total Assets ($mil)	Capital ($mil)	Net Premium ($mil)	Net Income ($mil)
2021	C+	0.99	0.79	150.0	32.9	182.1	12.3
2020	C+	1.25	1.01	144.9	38.4	166.3	18.1
2019	C+	2.26	1.85	391.7	220.5	550.6	55.3
2018	C+	1.86	1.53	371.1	192.8	559.3	53.3
2017	B-	1.70	1.39	400.7	227.8	761.1	16.5

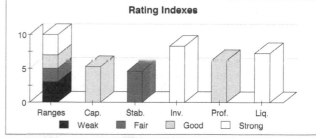

Rating Indexes

Ranges / Cap. / Stab. / Inv. / Prof. / Liq.
Weak / Fair / Good / Strong

FIRST PENN-PACIFIC LIFE INS CO — B- — Good

Major Rating Factors: Fair overall capitalization (4.0 on a scale of 0 to 10) based on excellent risk adjusted capital (severe loss scenario). Nevertheless, capital levels have fluctuated during prior years. Fair profitability (3.8). Excellent expense controls. Return on equity has been fair, averaging 6.8%. Fair liquidity (4.4).

Other Rating Factors: Fair overall results on stability tests (3.8) including negative cash flow from operations for 2021. Good quality investment portfolio (6.4).

Principal Business: Individual life insurance (99%) and reinsurance (1%).

Principal Investments: NonCMO investment grade bonds (77%), mortgages in good standing (9%), CMOs and structured securities (7%), noninv. grade bonds (3%), and misc. investments (4%).

Investments in Affiliates: None

Group Affiliation: Lincoln National Corp

Licensed in: All states except NY, PR

Commenced Business: June 1964

Address: 1300 South Clinton Street, Fort Wayne, IN 46802-3425

Phone: (800) 444-2363 **Domicile State:** IN **NAIC Code:** 67652

Data Date	Rating	RACR #1	RACR #2	Total Assets ($mil)	Capital ($mil)	Net Premium ($mil)	Net Income ($mil)
2021	B-	3.05	1.58	1,157.8	126.0	29.6	22.8
2020	B-	3.61	1.84	1,193.7	155.7	-33.0	-23.8
2019	B	2.38	1.28	1,360.7	138.8	120.3	29.3
2018	B	2.85	1.52	1,442.4	179.9	126.6	6.0
2017	B	2.87	1.54	1,504.1	189.0	130.2	16.0

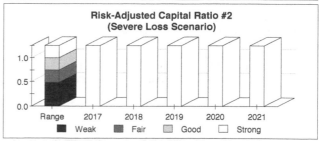

Risk-Adjusted Capital Ratio #2
(Severe Loss Scenario)

Range / 2017 / 2018 / 2019 / 2020 / 2021
Weak / Fair / Good / Strong

FIRST RELIANCE STANDARD LIFE INS CO *   A-   Excellent

Major Rating Factors: Good overall results on stability tests (5.8 on a scale of 0 to 10) despite fair financial strength of affiliated Tokio Marine Holdings Inc. Strengths that enhance stability include excellent operational trends and excellent risk diversification. Strong capitalization (10.0) based on excellent risk adjusted capital (severe loss scenario). Moreover, capital levels have been consistently high over the last five years. High quality investment portfolio (7.8).

Other Rating Factors: Excellent profitability (7.0) despite modest operating losses during 2017 and 2018. Excellent liquidity (7.1).

Principal Business: Group health insurance (77%) and group life insurance (23%).

Principal Investments: NonCMO investment grade bonds (87%), CMOs and structured securities (8%), and noninv. grade bonds (2%).

Investments in Affiliates: None

Group Affiliation: Tokio Marine Holdings Inc

Licensed in: DC, DE, NY

Commenced Business: October 1984

Address: 590 Madison Avenue 29th Floor, New York, NY 10022

Phone: (215) 787-4000 **Domicile State:** NY **NAIC Code:** 71005

Data Date	Rating	RACR #1	RACR #2	Total Assets ($mil)	Capital ($mil)	Net Premium ($mil)	Net Income ($mil)
2021	A-	6.20	4.29	259.1	100.9	98.6	13.7
2020	A-	5.78	3.83	243.0	85.1	86.3	15.2
2019	A-	5.04	3.32	227.3	70.0	83.1	8.8
2018	A-	4.81	3.19	212.1	61.0	74.7	-0.5
2017	A	5.19	3.33	199.1	61.2	61.8	-5.8

Tokio Marine Holdings Inc Composite Group Rating: C+ Largest Group Members	Assets ($mil)	Rating
RELIANCE STANDARD LIFE INS CO	17529	C+
SAFETY NATIONAL CASUALTY CORP	9990	B
PHILADELPHIA INDEMNITY INS CO	9935	B-
HOUSTON CASUALTY CO	3912	B-
US SPECIALTY INS CO	2203	C

FIRST SECURITY BENEFIT LIFE & ANN   B   Good

Major Rating Factors: Good overall results on stability tests (5.4 on a scale of 0 to 10) despite negative cash flow from operations for 2021, fair risk adjusted capital in prior years. Strengths include good financial support from affiliation with NZC Capital LLC, excellent operational trends and excellent risk diversification. Fair quality investment portfolio (3.5) with large holdings of BBB rated bonds in addition to moderate junk bond exposure. Fair profitability (3.4) with operating losses during 2021.

Other Rating Factors: Strong capitalization (7.1) based on excellent risk adjusted capital (severe loss scenario). Excellent liquidity (9.1).

Principal Business: Group retirement contracts (63%) and individual annuities (37%).

Principal Investments: CMOs and structured securities (50%), nonCMO investment grade bonds (39%), noninv. grade bonds (4%), cash (4%), and common & preferred stock (1%).

Investments in Affiliates: None

Group Affiliation: NZC Capital LLC

Licensed in: KS, NY

Commenced Business: July 1995

Address: 350 Park Avenue 14th Floor, Albany, NY 12207

Phone: (785) 431-3000 **Domicile State:** NY **NAIC Code:** 60084

Data Date	Rating	RACR #1	RACR #2	Total Assets ($mil)	Capital ($mil)	Net Premium ($mil)	Net Income ($mil)
2021	B	2.35	1.04	556.7	31.3	8.8	-3.8
2020	B	2.68	1.19	536.8	35.7	7.6	2.4
2019	B	2.69	1.20	494.4	33.5	9.2	1.1
2018	B	2.22	1.02	533.5	32.1	18.3	3.1
2017	B	1.49	0.70	675.0	30.2	14.1	1.4

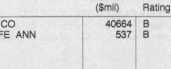

NZC Capital LLC Composite Group Rating: B Largest Group Members	Assets ($mil)	Rating
SECURITY BENEFIT LIFE INS CO	40664	B
FIRST SECURITY BENEFIT LIFE ANN	537	B

FIRST SYMETRA NATL LIFE INS CO OF NY   C+   Fair

Major Rating Factors: Fair quality investment portfolio (4.1 on a scale of 0 to 10) with large holdings of BBB rated bonds in addition to moderate junk bond exposure. Exposure to mortgages is significant, but the mortgage default rate has been low. Fair profitability (3.0) with investment income below regulatory standards in relation to interest assumptions of reserves. Fair liquidity (4.9).

Other Rating Factors: Fair overall results on stability tests (4.7) including fair risk adjusted capital in prior years. Good capitalization (5.7) based on good risk adjusted capital (moderate loss scenario).

Principal Business: Individual annuities (91%), group health insurance (7%), and group life insurance (2%).

Principal Investments: NonCMO investment grade bonds (61%), CMOs and structured securities (18%), mortgages in good standing (17%), noninv. grade bonds (2%), and cash (1%).

Investments in Affiliates: None

Group Affiliation: Sumitomo Life Ins Company

Licensed in: NY

Commenced Business: January 1990

Address: 420 LEXINGTON AVE SUITE 300, NEW YORK, NY 10170

Phone: (425) 256-8000 **Domicile State:** NY **NAIC Code:** 78417

Data Date	Rating	RACR #1	RACR #2	Total Assets ($mil)	Capital ($mil)	Net Premium ($mil)	Net Income ($mil)
2021	C+	1.44	0.72	3,477.6	179.2	601.6	12.2
2020	C+	1.23	0.62	3,048.6	138.5	532.0	-4.7
2019	B	1.42	0.73	2,707.6	142.3	619.5	2.7
2018	B+	1.79	0.92	2,246.7	139.2	553.5	1.0
2017	B+	1.87	0.95	1,803.0	114.7	355.8	9.3

Rating Indexes

Ranges | Cap. | Stab. | Inv. | Prof. | Liq.

■ Weak ■ Fair ▨ Good □ Strong

FIRST UNUM LIFE INS CO   C+   Fair

Major Rating Factors: Fair overall results on stability tests (4.8 on a scale of 0 to 10) including fair financial strength of affiliated Unum Group. Fair quality investment portfolio (4.8) with large holdings of BBB rated bonds in addition to junk bond exposure equal to 60% of capital. Good overall profitability (6.5). Return on equity has been fair, averaging 7.7%.

Other Rating Factors: Strong capitalization (7.7) based on excellent risk adjusted capital (severe loss scenario). Excellent liquidity (7.3).

Principal Business: Group health insurance (62%), group life insurance (20%), individual health insurance (16%), and individual life insurance (2%).

Principal Investments: NonCMO investment grade bonds (82%), mortgages in good standing (9%), noninv. grade bonds (6%), and CMOs and structured securities (2%).

Investments in Affiliates: None
Group Affiliation: Unum Group
Licensed in: NY
Commenced Business: January 1960
Address: 666 THIRD AVENUE SUITE 301, GARDEN CITY, NY 11530
Phone: (207) 575-2211   **Domicile State:** NY   **NAIC Code:** 64297

Data Date	Rating	RACR #1	RACR #2	Total Assets ($mil)	Capital ($mil)	Net Premium ($mil)	Net Income ($mil)
2021	C+	2.80	1.48	4,405.9	392.4	530.0	46.9
2020	C+	2.38	1.25	4,248.5	310.1	487.6	47.4
2019	C+	2.47	1.30	4,068.5	307.9	469.2	21.9
2018	C+	2.33	1.21	3,760.8	274.4	453.9	-13.6
2017	C+	2.66	1.36	3,457.4	299.1	392.7	27.4

Unum Group Composite Group Rating: C+ Largest Group Members	Assets ($mil)	Rating
UNUM LIFE INS CO OF AMERICA	21791	C+
PROVIDENT LIFE ACCIDENT INS CO	6172	C+
FIRST UNUM LIFE INS CO	4249	C+
COLONIAL LIFE ACCIDENT INS CO	3760	C+
PAUL REVERE LIFE INS CO	1280	C+

FIVE STAR LIFE INS CO   C   Fair

Major Rating Factors: Fair profitability (3.6 on a scale of 0 to 10) with investment income below regulatory standards in relation to interest assumptions of reserves. Fair overall results on stability tests (3.4) including negative cash flow from operations for 2021. Weak liquidity (1.4) as a spike in claims or a run on policy withdrawals may stretch capacity.

Other Rating Factors: Strong capitalization (7.4) based on excellent risk adjusted capital (severe loss scenario). High quality investment portfolio (7.2).

Principal Business: Group life insurance (76%), individual life insurance (20%), and group health insurance (3%).

Principal Investments: NonCMO investment grade bonds (83%), CMOs and structured securities (10%), policy loans (3%), noninv. grade bonds (1%), and cash (1%).

Investments in Affiliates: None
Group Affiliation: 5 Star Financial LLC
Licensed in: All states except NY
Commenced Business: May 1943
Address: 8440 Jefferson Highway Ste 301, Lincoln, NE 68516
Phone: (800) 776-2322   **Domicile State:** NE   **NAIC Code:** 77879

Data Date	Rating	RACR #1	RACR #2	Total Assets ($mil)	Capital ($mil)	Net Premium ($mil)	Net Income ($mil)
2021	C	2.07	1.29	324.2	30.3	165.2	2.0
2020	C	1.93	1.18	313.5	28.0	135.7	1.2
2019	C	2.13	1.32	310.6	30.8	124.3	2.4
2018	C	1.97	1.22	302.2	28.1	130.0	-0.3
2017	C	1.86	1.16	291.2	28.9	126.1	-10.0

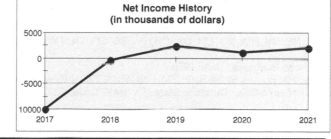

Net Income History
(in thousands of dollars)

FORETHOUGHT LIFE INS CO   B   Good

Major Rating Factors: Good overall results on stability tests (5.8 on a scale of 0 to 10) despite fair financial strength of affiliated Global Atlantic Financial Group. Other stability subfactors include excellent operational trends and excellent risk diversification. Good capitalization (6.2) based on good risk adjusted capital (moderate loss scenario). Moreover, capital levels have been consistent over the last five years. Good liquidity (6.4).

Other Rating Factors: Fair quality investment portfolio (4.4). Excellent profitability (7.8) despite modest operating losses during 2020.

Principal Business: Individual annuities (92%), group retirement contracts (4%), group life insurance (2%), individual health insurance (1%), and individual life insurance (1%).

Principal Investments: CMOs and structured securities (43%), mortgages in good standing (25%), nonCMO investment grade bonds (24%), noninv. grade bonds (3%), and common & preferred stock (1%).

Investments in Affiliates: 3%
Group Affiliation: Global Atlantic Financial Group
Licensed in: All states except NY
Commenced Business: September 1980
Address: 300 NORTH MERIDIAN ST STE 1800, INDIANAPOLIS, IN 46204
Phone: (317) 223-2700   **Domicile State:** IN   **NAIC Code:** 91642

Data Date	Rating	RACR #1	RACR #2	Total Assets ($mil)	Capital ($mil)	Net Premium ($mil)	Net Income ($mil)
2021	B	1.78	0.86	47,725.7	2,372.4	4,546.3	84.2
2020	B	1.65	0.85	39,499.2	1,956.7	3,877.7	-56.6
2019	B	2.06	0.98	36,338.3	1,889.0	4,810.3	189.3
2018	B	1.86	0.90	31,172.9	1,688.6	4,820.4	112.0
2017	B	2.03	0.96	31,431.3	1,595.9	-4,463.2	352.1

Global Atlantic Financial Group Composite Group Rating: C+ Largest Group Members	Assets ($mil)	Rating
COMMONWEALTH ANNUITY LIFE INS CO	42764	C
FORETHOUGHT LIFE INS CO	39499	B
ACCORDIA LIFE ANNUITY CO	11882	C+
FIRST ALLMERICA FINANCIAL LIFE INS	3062	C+

FRANDISCO LIFE INS CO *

A   Excellent

Major Rating Factors: Excellent overall results on stability tests (7.1 on a scale of 0 to 10). Strengths that enhance stability include excellent operational trends and excellent risk diversification. Strong capitalization (10.0) based on excellent risk adjusted capital (severe loss scenario). Furthermore, this high level of risk adjusted capital has been consistently maintained over the last five years. High quality investment portfolio (8.9).

Other Rating Factors: Excellent profitability (9.3) with operating gains in each of the last five years. Excellent liquidity (8.4).

Principal Business: Reinsurance (100%).

Principal Investments: NonCMO investment grade bonds (92%).

Investments in Affiliates: None

Group Affiliation: 1st Franklin Financial Corp

Licensed in: GA

Commenced Business: November 1977

Address: 135 East Tugalo Street, Toccoa, GA 30577

Phone: (706) 886-7571   **Domicile State:** GA   **NAIC Code:** 89079

Data Date	Rating	RACR #1	RACR #2	Total Assets ($mil)	Capital ($mil)	Net Premium ($mil)	Net Income ($mil)
2021	A	10.49	9.44	121.9	96.2	24.3	4.5
2020	A	10.07	9.06	113.6	91.6	19.4	4.9
2019	A	9.59	8.63	106.5	86.6	20.4	5.6
2018	A	9.17	8.25	96.9	81.0	18.9	4.8
2017	A	9.06	8.16	87.0	76.1	13.9	4.3

Adverse Trends in Operations

Decrease in premium volume from 2019 to 2020 (5%)
Change in asset mix during 2019 (4%)

FREEDOM LIFE INS CO OF AMERICA *

B+   Good

Major Rating Factors: Good overall results on stability tests (6.5 on a scale of 0 to 10) despite excessive premium growth. Other stability subfactors include excellent operational trends, good risk adjusted capital for prior years and excellent risk diversification. Strong current capitalization (7.3) based on excellent risk adjusted capital (severe loss scenario) reflecting improvement over results in 2017. High quality investment portfolio (7.3).

Other Rating Factors: Excellent profitability (8.3) with operating gains in each of the last five years. Excellent liquidity (7.4).

Principal Business: Group health insurance (67%), individual health insurance (24%), and individual life insurance (9%).

Principal Investments: NonCMO investment grade bonds (39%), common & preferred stock (22%), cash (22%), and CMOs and structured securities (16%).

Investments in Affiliates: 22%

Group Affiliation: Credit Suisse Group

Licensed in: AL, AZ, AR, CO, DE, FL, GA, IL, IN, IA, KS, KY, LA, MD, MI, MN, MS, MO, NE, NV, NM, NC, OH, OK, OR, PA, SC, SD, TN, TX, UT, VA, WA, WV, WY

Commenced Business: June 1956

Address: 300 Burnett Street Suite 200, Fort Worth, TX 76102-2734

Phone: (817) 878-3300   **Domicile State:** TX   **NAIC Code:** 62324

Data Date	Rating	RACR #1	RACR #2	Total Assets ($mil)	Capital ($mil)	Net Premium ($mil)	Net Income ($mil)
2021	B+	1.40	1.23	462.4	280.1	834.7	141.8
2020	B+	1.41	1.26	421.3	266.6	664.8	85.8
2019	B+	1.48	1.33	321.1	221.8	533.7	62.8
2018	B+	1.18	1.03	211.5	122.8	422.3	37.6
2017	C+	1.11	0.96	148.3	76.4	282.2	19.4

Adverse Trends in Operations

Change in asset mix during 2019 (6%)
Change in asset mix during 2017 (5.5%)

FUNERAL DIRECTORS LIFE INS CO

B   Good

Major Rating Factors: Good current capitalization (6.9 on a scale of 0 to 10) based on good risk adjusted capital (severe loss scenario), although results have slipped from the excellent range over the last year. Good liquidity (6.1) with sufficient resources to handle a spike in claims as well as a significant increase in policy surrenders. Good overall results on stability tests (5.8) despite excessive premium growth excellent operational trends and excellent risk diversification.

Other Rating Factors: Fair quality investment portfolio (4.7). Excellent profitability (7.7) with operating gains in each of the last five years.

Principal Business: Individual annuities (62%), group life insurance (31%), and individual life insurance (8%).

Principal Investments: NonCMO investment grade bonds (63%), CMOs and structured securities (16%), mortgages in good standing (12%), noninv. grade bonds (6%), and misc. investments (2%).

Investments in Affiliates: 1%

Group Affiliation: Directors Investment Group

Licensed in: All states except DC, ME, MA, NH, NY, WY, PR

Commenced Business: April 1981

Address: 6550 Directors Parkway, Abilene, TX 79606

Phone: (915) 695-3412   **Domicile State:** TX   **NAIC Code:** 99775

Data Date	Rating	RACR #1	RACR #2	Total Assets ($mil)	Capital ($mil)	Net Premium ($mil)	Net Income ($mil)
2021	B	1.94	0.99	1,718.8	155.2	338.7	14.9
2020	B	1.96	1.03	1,583.3	140.7	246.5	5.1
2019	B	2.06	1.11	1,512.5	134.2	257.3	14.3
2018	B-	2.29	1.23	1,409.8	130.0	231.9	14.2
2017	B-	2.30	1.24	1,320.3	116.3	212.4	8.4

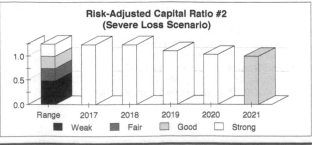

Risk-Adjusted Capital Ratio #2 (Severe Loss Scenario)

Legend: Weak (Range), Fair, Good, Strong — years 2017, 2018, 2019, 2020, 2021

GARDEN STATE LIFE INS CO *   A   Excellent

Major Rating Factors: Good quality investment portfolio (6.9 on a scale of 0 to 10) despite mixed results such as: no exposure to mortgages and large holdings of BBB rated bonds but minimal holdings in junk bonds. Excellent overall results on stability tests (7.8). Strengths that enhance stability include excellent operational trends and excellent risk diversification. Strong capitalization (10.0) based on excellent risk adjusted capital (severe loss scenario).

Other Rating Factors: Excellent profitability (9.0) with operating gains in each of the last five years. Excellent liquidity (7.2).

Principal Business: Reinsurance (56%), individual life insurance (32%), individual health insurance (11%), and group health insurance (1%).

Principal Investments: NonCMO investment grade bonds (94%), policy loans (2%), CMOs and structured securities (1%), and cash (1%).

Investments in Affiliates: None

Group Affiliation: American National Group Inc

Licensed in: All states except PR

Commenced Business: November 1956

Address: 2450 SOUTH SHORE BOULEVARD, GALVESTON, TX 77550

Phone: (409) 763-4661   **Domicile State:** TX   **NAIC Code:** 63657

Data Date	Rating	RACR #1	RACR #2	Total Assets ($mil)	Capital ($mil)	Net Premium ($mil)	Net Income ($mil)
2021	A	9.97	8.97	143.5	92.2	25.6	5.0
2020	A	9.91	8.92	143.9	91.7	22.7	5.4
2019	A	9.69	8.72	145.2	89.8	23.6	10.2
2018	A	8.87	7.98	136.3	81.4	21.9	9.2
2017	A-	8.04	7.23	131.3	73.4	21.3	5.7

Adverse Trends in Operations

Decrease in premium volume from 2019 to 2020 (4%)
Decrease in premium volume from 2016 to 2017 (2%)

GENERAL RE LIFE CORP   C   Fair

Major Rating Factors: Fair overall results on stability tests (4.1 on a scale of 0 to 10). Good quality investment portfolio (6.9) with no exposure to mortgages and minimal holdings in junk bonds. Weak profitability (2.0) with operating losses during 2021.

Other Rating Factors: Strong capitalization (7.9) based on excellent risk adjusted capital (severe loss scenario). Excellent liquidity (9.0).

Principal Business: Reinsurance (100%).

Principal Investments: NonCMO investment grade bonds (74%), common & preferred stock (6%), and cash (1%).

Investments in Affiliates: 18%

Group Affiliation: Berkshire-Hathaway

Licensed in: All states except PR

Commenced Business: August 1967

Address: 120 Long Ridge Rd, Stamford, CT 6902

Phone: (203) 352-3000   **Domicile State:** CT   **NAIC Code:** 86258

Data Date	Rating	RACR #1	RACR #2	Total Assets ($mil)	Capital ($mil)	Net Premium ($mil)	Net Income ($mil)
2021	C	2.41	1.62	5,020.2	878.1	1,485.6	-89.6
2020	C	2.91	1.94	4,851.7	955.2	1,335.1	322.7
2019	C	2.07	1.33	4,593.3	802.5	1,307.0	211.9
2018	C	1.84	1.32	4,071.4	848.7	1,335.9	212.8
2017	C+	4.62	2.45	4,066.3	746.8	60.4	608.3

Rating Indexes

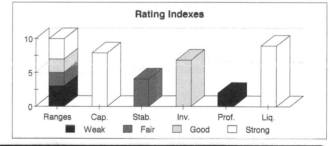

Ranges   Cap.   Stab.   Inv.   Prof.   Liq.
■ Weak   ■ Fair   □ Good   □ Strong

GENWORTH LIFE & ANNUITY INS CO   C   Fair

Major Rating Factors: Fair overall results on stability tests (3.6 on a scale of 0 to 10) including negative cash flow from operations for 2021. Good overall capitalization (6.0) based on mixed results -- excessive policy leverage mitigated by good risk adjusted capital (severe loss scenario). Nevertheless, capital levels have fluctuated during prior years. Good quality investment portfolio (5.0).

Other Rating Factors: Good liquidity (5.0). Weak profitability (1.8) with operating losses during 2021.

Principal Business: Individual life insurance (76%), reinsurance (20%), individual health insurance (3%), and individual annuities (1%).

Principal Investments: NonCMO investment grade bonds (63%), mortgages in good standing (13%), CMOs and structured securities (12%), policy loans (4%), and misc. investments (6%).

Investments in Affiliates: 1%

Group Affiliation: Genworth Financial

Licensed in: All states except NY, PR

Commenced Business: April 1871

Address: 6610 WEST BROAD STREET, RICHMOND, VA 23230

Phone: (804) 662-2400   **Domicile State:** VA   **NAIC Code:** 65536

Data Date	Rating	RACR #1	RACR #2	Total Assets ($mil)	Capital ($mil)	Net Premium ($mil)	Net Income ($mil)
2021	C	1.56	0.87	19,843.6	864.6	-1,249.1	-179.3
2020	C-	1.44	0.84	21,136.4	991.8	175.2	-182.1
2019	C-	1.53	0.97	21,575.1	1,368.5	-901.0	185.8
2018	C-	1.65	0.94	21,184.1	1,153.9	6.4	-209.5
2017	C	1.82	1.05	22,444.5	1,288.8	520.7	-32.1

Rating Indexes

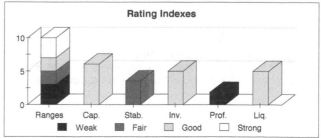

Ranges   Cap.   Stab.   Inv.   Prof.   Liq.
■ Weak   ■ Fair   □ Good   □ Strong

GENWORTH LIFE INS CO

B-   Good

Major Rating Factors: Good quality investment portfolio (5.1 on a scale of 0 to 10) despite large holdings of BBB rated bonds in addition to junk bond exposure equal to 80% of capital. Exposure to mortgages is significant, but the mortgage default rate has been low. Good overall profitability (5.4) although investment income, in comparison to reserve requirements, is below regulatory standards. Good liquidity (6.9).

Other Rating Factors: Good overall results on stability tests (5.0) despite fair risk adjusted capital in prior years excellent operational trends and excellent risk diversification. Strong capitalization (7.1) based on excellent risk adjusted capital (severe loss scenario).

Principal Business: Individual health insurance (72%), reinsurance (10%), group health insurance (10%), and individual life insurance (8%).

Principal Investments: NonCMO investment grade bonds (64%), mortgages in good standing (11%), CMOs and structured securities (7%), noninv. grade bonds (5%), and misc. investments (13%).

Investments in Affiliates: 3%

Group Affiliation: Genworth Financial

Licensed in: All states except NY

Commenced Business: October 1956

Address: 2711 CENTERVILLE ROAD STE 400, WILMINGTON, DE 19808

Phone: (800) 255-7836 **Domicile State:** DE **NAIC Code:** 70025

Data Date	Rating	RACR #1	RACR #2	Total Assets ($mil)	Capital ($mil)	Net Premium ($mil)	Net Income ($mil)
2021	B-	1.70	1.09	41,321.0	2,937.1	2,350.0	828.8
2020	C	1.19	0.78	41,144.1	2,123.0	2,379.4	432.7
2019	C	0.98	0.70	40,635.1	2,179.8	2,323.1	89.0
2018	C	0.94	0.65	39,995.4	1,871.0	2,287.8	-625.0
2017	C+	1.20	0.86	40,012.0	2,727.7	2,308.7	-39.1

Rating Indexes

GENWORTH LIFE INS CO OF NEW YORK

C   Fair

Major Rating Factors: Fair quality investment portfolio (3.4 on a scale of 0 to 10) with large holdings of BBB rated bonds in addition to significant exposure to junk bonds. Fair overall results on stability tests (3.8) including negative cash flow from operations for 2021, fair risk adjusted capital in prior years. Good capitalization (5.5) based on good risk adjusted capital (moderate loss scenario).

Other Rating Factors: Good liquidity (5.9). Weak profitability (2.3).

Principal Business: Individual health insurance (63%), reinsurance (16%), individual life insurance (16%), group health insurance (4%), and individual annuities (1%).

Principal Investments: NonCMO investment grade bonds (67%), CMOs and structured securities (17%), mortgages in good standing (8%), and noninv. grade bonds (3%).

Investments in Affiliates: None

Group Affiliation: Genworth Financial

Licensed in: CT, DC, DE, FL, IL, NJ, NY, RI, VA

Commenced Business: October 1988

Address: 600 THIRD AVENUE SUITE 2400, NEW YORK, NY 10016

Phone: (800) 357-1066 **Domicile State:** NY **NAIC Code:** 72990

Data Date	Rating	RACR #1	RACR #2	Total Assets ($mil)	Capital ($mil)	Net Premium ($mil)	Net Income ($mil)
2021	C	1.35	0.68	7,569.5	224.2	240.9	7.5
2020	C	1.28	0.63	7,656.4	219.5	245.7	-50.2
2019	C	1.73	0.89	7,604.8	316.6	247.6	82.0
2018	C	1.26	0.64	7,664.4	233.8	251.8	-56.0
2017	C	1.41	0.72	7,985.9	288.4	260.0	-168.1

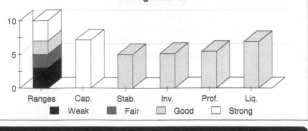

Junk Bonds as a % of Capital

Capital — $224 mil.
Junk Bonds — $231 mil.

GERBER LIFE INS CO *

B+   Good

Major Rating Factors: Good overall results on stability tests (6.4 on a scale of 0 to 10). Stability strengths include excellent operational trends and excellent risk diversification. Good quality investment portfolio (5.8) despite mixed results such as: large holdings of BBB rated bonds but junk bond exposure equal to 62% of capital. Good overall profitability (6.0) although investment income, in comparison to reserve requirements, is below regulatory standards.

Other Rating Factors: Good liquidity (5.2). Strong capitalization (7.5) based on excellent risk adjusted capital (severe loss scenario).

Principal Business: Individual life insurance (52%), group health insurance (35%), individual health insurance (7%), and reinsurance (6%).

Principal Investments: NonCMO investment grade bonds (70%), CMOs and structured securities (13%), noninv. grade bonds (7%), policy loans (4%), and misc. investments (6%).

Investments in Affiliates: None

Group Affiliation: Nestle SA

Licensed in: All states, the District of Columbia and Puerto Rico

Commenced Business: September 1968

Address: 1311 Mamaroneck Avenue, White Plains, NY 10605

Phone: (914) 272-4000 **Domicile State:** NY **NAIC Code:** 70939

Data Date	Rating	RACR #1	RACR #2	Total Assets ($mil)	Capital ($mil)	Net Premium ($mil)	Net Income ($mil)
2021	B+	2.45	1.36	5,146.7	540.1	863.6	26.4
2020	B+	2.42	1.36	4,805.9	511.8	880.7	0.9
2019	B+	2.47	1.42	4,509.0	512.1	817.9	4.5
2018	B+	1.81	1.05	3,992.2	311.7	745.1	-1.1
2017	B+	1.83	1.07	3,703.2	300.7	727.1	-2.7

Adverse Trends in Operations

Decrease in capital during 2017 (2%)

GLOBE LIFE & ACCIDENT INS CO   C   Fair

Major Rating Factors: Fair current capitalization (4.7 on a scale of 0 to 10) based on fair risk adjusted capital (moderate loss scenario), although results have slipped from the good range over the last year. Fair quality investment portfolio (4.0) with large holdings of BBB rated bonds in addition to junk bond exposure equal to 72% of capital. Fair overall results on stability tests (3.1) including fair risk adjusted capital in prior years.

Other Rating Factors: Weak liquidity (1.1). Excellent profitability (7.9) with operating gains in each of the last five years.

Principal Business: Individual life insurance (61%), group life insurance (33%), individual health insurance (4%), and reinsurance (2%).

Principal Investments: NonCMO investment grade bonds (82%), noninv. grade bonds (5%), common & preferred stock (3%), policy loans (2%), and misc. investments (8%).

Investments in Affiliates: 5%

Group Affiliation: Torchmark Corp

Licensed in: All states except NY, PR

Commenced Business: September 1980

Address: 10306 REGENCY PARKWAY DRIVE, OMAHA, NE 68114-3743

Phone: (972) 569-3744 **Domicile State:** NE **NAIC Code:** 91472

Data Date	Rating	RACR #1	RACR #2	Total Assets ($mil)	Capital ($mil)	Net Premium ($mil)	Net Income ($mil)
2021	C	0.96	0.63	5,236.5	343.8	799.5	57.3
2020	C+	1.03	0.66	5,074.2	342.1	739.4	91.6
2019	C+	1.16	0.74	4,831.9	347.2	698.5	110.6
2018	C+	1.17	0.77	4,726.2	371.8	713.4	98.4
2017	C+	1.00	0.63	4,485.1	280.2	694.0	51.8

Risk-Adjusted Capital Ratio #1
(Moderate Loss Scenario)

■ Weak ▨ Fair ☐ Good

GLOBE LIFE INSURANCE CO OF NY   B   Good

Major Rating Factors: Good overall results on stability tests (5.9 on a scale of 0 to 10) despite fair financial strength of affiliated Torchmark Corp. Other stability subfactors include excellent operational trends and excellent risk diversification. Good quality investment portfolio (5.1) despite mixed results such as: large holdings of BBB rated bonds but moderate junk bond exposure. Fair liquidity (4.7).

Other Rating Factors: Strong capitalization (7.4) based on excellent risk adjusted capital (severe loss scenario). Excellent profitability (7.2) with operating gains in each of the last five years.

Principal Business: Individual health insurance (55%), individual life insurance (40%), individual annuities (3%), and group health insurance (2%).

Principal Investments: NonCMO investment grade bonds (87%), noninv. grade bonds (5%), policy loans (4%), and CMOs and structured securities (2%).

Investments in Affiliates: None

Group Affiliation: Torchmark Corp

Licensed in: NY

Commenced Business: December 1984

Address: 1020 SEVENTH NORTH ST STE 130, LIVERPOOL, NY 13212

Phone: (315) 451-2544 **Domicile State:** NY **NAIC Code:** 74101

Data Date	Rating	RACR #1	RACR #2	Total Assets ($mil)	Capital ($mil)	Net Premium ($mil)	Net Income ($mil)
2021	B	2.02	1.24	266.6	36.6	73.7	1.8
2020	B	2.36	1.45	258.5	43.0	71.7	7.4
2019	B-	2.38	1.48	250.2	41.8	70.9	13.3
2018	B	1.75	1.08	246.4	29.3	70.2	1.9
2017	B	1.87	1.16	238.8	30.3	68.6	0.2

Torchmark Corp
Composite Group Rating: C+

Largest Group Members	Assets ($mil)	Rating
LIBERTY NATIONAL LIFE INS CO	8308	B-
GLOBE LIFE ACCIDENT INS CO	5074	C
AMERICAN INCOME LIFE INS CO	4675	B-
FAMILY HERITAGE LIFE INS CO OF AMER	1436	B-
UNITED AMERICAN INS CO	729	B

GOLDEN RULE INS CO   B   Good

Major Rating Factors: Good overall results on stability tests (5.2 on a scale of 0 to 10) despite fair financial strength of affiliated UnitedHealth Group Inc. Other stability subfactors include excellent operational trends and excellent risk diversification. Good current capitalization (5.2) based on mixed results -- excessive policy leverage mitigated by excellent risk adjusted capital (severe loss scenario) reflecting improvement over results in 2016. Good liquidity (6.7).

Other Rating Factors: High quality investment portfolio (8.0). Excellent profitability (9.2) with operating gains in each of the last five years.

Principal Business: Group health insurance (68%), individual health insurance (31%), and individual life insurance (1%).

Principal Investments: NonCMO investment grade bonds (60%) and CMOs and structured securities (21%).

Investments in Affiliates: None

Group Affiliation: UnitedHealth Group Inc

Licensed in: All states except NY, PR

Commenced Business: June 1961

Address: 7440 WOODLAND DRIVE, INDIANAPOLIS, IN 46278

Phone: (317) 290-8100 **Domicile State:** IN **NAIC Code:** 62286

Data Date	Rating	RACR #1	RACR #2	Total Assets ($mil)	Capital ($mil)	Net Premium ($mil)	Net Income ($mil)
3-21	B	1.44	1.14	632.3	318.3	428.8	64.5
3-20	B	1.46	1.14	633.5	292.7	386.7	38.7
2020	B	1.19	0.94	0.0	0.0	0.0	0.0
2019	B	1.32	1.04	0.0	0.0	0.0	0.0
2018	B	1.44	1.12	0.0	0.0	0.0	0.0
2017	B	1.14	0.89	0.0	0.0	0.0	0.0
2016	B	0.99	0.78	0.0	0.0	0.0	0.0

UnitedHealth Group Inc
Composite Group Rating: C

Largest Group Members	Assets ($mil)	Rating
UNITED HEALTHCARE INS CO	21587	C
UHC OF CALIFORNIA INC	793	C-
GOLDEN RULE INS CO	629	B
UNIMERICA INS CO	450	B-
OPTUM INS OF OH INC	424	B-

GOVERNMENT PERSONNEL MUTUAL L I C   B-   Good

Major Rating Factors: Good quality investment portfolio (5.7 on a scale of 0 to 10) despite significant exposure to mortgages . Mortgage default rate has been low. large holdings of BBB rated bonds in addition to small junk bond holdings. Good liquidity (5.4) with sufficient resources to handle a spike in claims as well as a significant increase in policy surrenders. Fair overall results on stability tests (4.9) including negative cash flow from operations for 2021.

Other Rating Factors: Weak profitability (1.9) with operating losses during 2021. Strong capitalization (7.4) based on excellent risk adjusted capital (severe loss scenario).

Principal Business: Individual life insurance (82%) and individual health insurance (18%).

Principal Investments: NonCMO investment grade bonds (53%), mortgages in good standing (19%), policy loans (7%), cash (6%), and misc. investments (11%).

Investments in Affiliates: 3%

Group Affiliation: GPM Life Group

Licensed in: All states except NJ, NY, PR

Commenced Business: October 1934

Address: 2211 NE Loop 410, San Antonio, TX 78217

Phone: (800) 938-9765 **Domicile State:** TX **NAIC Code:** 63967

Data Date	Rating	RACR #1	RACR #2	Total Assets ($mil)	Capital ($mil)	Net Premium ($mil)	Net Income ($mil)
2021	B-	1.95	1.27	799.8	96.5	59.0	-12.0
2020	B-	2.02	1.30	809.0	99.3	59.4	-6.5
2019	B-	1.86	1.24	812.1	105.5	51.9	-5.9
2018	B	2.68	1.70	820.2	114.8	46.1	-0.9
2017	B+	2.64	1.69	825.7	116.8	44.2	5.3

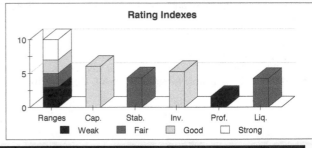

Rating Indexes

Ranges | Cap. | Stab. | Inv. | Prof. | Liq.
■ Weak ■ Fair ▨ Good □ Strong

GRANGE LIFE INS CO   C+   Fair

Major Rating Factors: Fair liquidity (4.2 on a scale of 0 to 10) as cash from operations and sale of marketable assets may not be adequate to cover a spike in claims or a run on policy withdrawals. Fair overall results on stability tests (4.4). Good capitalization (6.0) based on good risk adjusted capital (severe loss scenario).

Other Rating Factors: Good quality investment portfolio (5.2). Weak profitability (1.6) with operating losses during 2021.

Principal Business: Individual life insurance (96%), reinsurance (3%), and individual annuities (1%).

Principal Investments: NonCMO investment grade bonds (74%), CMOs and structured securities (21%), and policy loans (3%).

Investments in Affiliates: None

Group Affiliation: Grange Mutual Casualty Group

Licensed in: GA, IL, IN, IA, KS, KY, MI, MN, MO, OH, PA, SC, TN, VA, WI

Commenced Business: July 1968

Address: 671 South High Street, Columbus, OH 43206-1066

Phone: (800) 399-3797 **Domicile State:** OH **NAIC Code:** 71218

Data Date	Rating	RACR #1	RACR #2	Total Assets ($mil)	Capital ($mil)	Net Premium ($mil)	Net Income ($mil)
2021	C+	1.52	0.87	470.1	29.9	46.8	-7.4
2020	C+	1.94	1.13	463.8	37.5	51.2	2.6
2019	C+	1.80	1.06	443.8	34.2	47.6	1.3
2018	C	1.99	1.18	450.1	37.3	110.1	-3.9
2017	C	4.34	2.42	412.2	72.5	1.8	-1.3

Rating Indexes

Ranges | Cap. | Stab. | Inv. | Prof. | Liq.
■ Weak ■ Fair ▨ Good □ Strong

GRANULAR INSURANCE CO   D   Weak

Major Rating Factors: Weak profitability (1.0 on a scale of 0 to 10) with operating losses during 2021. Return on equity has been low, averaging -2.7%. Weak overall results on stability tests (1.7) including weak results on operational trends. Strong overall capitalization (10.0) based on excellent risk adjusted capital (severe loss scenario). Nevertheless, capital levels have fluctuated during prior years.

Other Rating Factors: High quality investment portfolio (8.5). Excellent liquidity (7.2).

Principal Business: Group health insurance (98%) and reinsurance (2%).

Principal Investments: NonCMO investment grade bonds (63%) and cash (30%).

Investments in Affiliates: None

Group Affiliation: Bank of America Corp

Licensed in: All states except ME, NY, PR

Commenced Business: July 1981

Address: 150 N College Street 22nd Fl, Charleston, SC 29401

Phone: (800) 456-2133 **Domicile State:** SC **NAIC Code:** 93521

Data Date	Rating	RACR #1	RACR #2	Total Assets ($mil)	Capital ($mil)	Net Premium ($mil)	Net Income ($mil)
2021	D	5.60	4.20	69.3	43.6	43.9	-18.6
2020	C-	8.42	7.58	64.4	61.9	0.4	-6.4
2019	U	3.95	3.56	8.1	7.8	0.1	3.2
2018	C	4.34	3.91	21.9	15.7	0.2	-0.6
2017	D+	4.32	3.89	23.4	16.4	0.3	-0.1

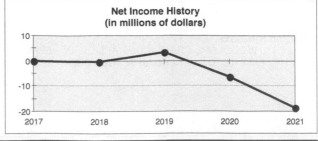

**Net Income History
(in millions of dollars)**

GREAT AMERICAN LIFE INS CO

B- | **Good**

Major Rating Factors: Fair current capitalization (4.0 on a scale of 0 to 10) based on excellent risk adjusted capital (severe loss scenario) reflecting improvement over results in 2017. Fair overall results on stability tests (4.0). Good quality investment portfolio (5.1) despite mixed results such as: large holdings of BBB rated bonds but moderate junk bond exposure.

Other Rating Factors: Good liquidity (6.2). Excellent profitability (7.1) with operating gains in each of the last five years.

Principal Business: Individual annuities (97%) and group retirement contracts (2%).

Principal Investments: NonCMO investment grade bonds (51%), CMOs and structured securities (30%), mortgages in good standing (6%), noninv. grade bonds (4%), and misc. investments (7%).

Investments in Affiliates: 1%

Group Affiliation: American Financial Group Inc

Licensed in: All states except NY, PR

Commenced Business: August 1963

Address: 301 East Fourth Street, Cincinnati, OH 45202

Phone: (800) 854-3649 **Domicile State:** OH **NAIC Code:** 63312

Data Date	Rating	RACR #1	RACR #2	Total Assets ($mil)	Capital ($mil)	Net Premium ($mil)	Net Income ($mil)
2021	B-	1.85	1.01	38,448.9	2,878.1	5,027.0	329.0
2020	B-	1.92	1.06	35,797.2	2,897.2	-2,716.0	184.1
2019	B-	1.82	1.02	40,018.8	2,868.1	4,704.4	13.6
2018	B-	1.80	1.00	35,802.4	2,701.4	5,216.4	768.0
2017	B-	1.66	0.93	32,576.6	2,131.5	4,134.9	263.2

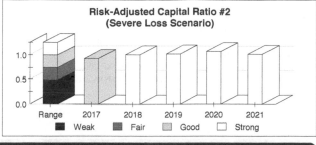

Risk-Adjusted Capital Ratio #2
(Severe Loss Scenario)

Range | 2017 | 2018 | 2019 | 2020 | 2021
■ Weak ■ Fair ▢ Good ☐ Strong

GREAT SOUTHERN LIFE INS CO

C | **Fair**

Major Rating Factors: Fair overall results on stability tests (3.7 on a scale of 0 to 10) including negative cash flow from operations for 2021 and excessive premium growth. Good liquidity (6.7) with sufficient resources to handle a spike in claims. Weak profitability (1.7) with operating losses during 2021. Return on equity has been low, averaging -8.4%.

Other Rating Factors: Strong capitalization (8.1) based on excellent risk adjusted capital (severe loss scenario). High quality investment portfolio (7.5).

Principal Business: Individual life insurance (50%), individual health insurance (43%), group life insurance (3%), individual annuities (2%), and group health insurance (1%).

Principal Investments: NonCMO investment grade bonds (80%), common & preferred stock (12%), CMOs and structured securities (4%), and noninv. grade bonds (2%).

Investments in Affiliates: None

Group Affiliation: Americo Life Inc

Licensed in: All states except NY, VT, PR

Commenced Business: November 1909

Address: PO Box 139061, Dallas, TX 75313-9061

Phone: (816) 391-2000 **Domicile State:** TX **NAIC Code:** 90212

Data Date	Rating	RACR #1	RACR #2	Total Assets ($mil)	Capital ($mil)	Net Premium ($mil)	Net Income ($mil)
2021	C	2.82	1.73	191.1	36.2	36.7	-8.8
2020	C+	4.05	2.42	197.4	43.4	26.3	-10.7
2019	B	5.69	3.75	207.2	52.2	5.4	-2.6
2018	A-	5.78	4.41	212.9	53.5	0.2	2.4
2017	B	5.59	2.93	211.9	51.5	0.2	3.2

Rating Indexes

Ranges | Cap. | Stab. | Inv. | Prof. | Liq.
■ Weak ■ Fair ▢ Good ☐ Strong

GREAT WESTERN INS CO

C- | **Fair**

Major Rating Factors: Fair capitalization for the current period (4.0 on a scale of 0 to 10) based on mixed results -- excessive policy leverage mitigated by good risk adjusted capital (moderate loss scenario) reflecting some improvement over results in 2018. Low quality investment portfolio (2.1) containing large holdings of BBB rated bonds in addition to significant exposure to junk bonds. Weak profitability (1.8) with investment income below regulatory standards in relation to interest assumptions of reserves.

Other Rating Factors: Weak overall results on stability tests (2.9) including weak risk adjusted capital in prior years, negative cash flow from operations for 2021. Excellent liquidity (7.4).

Principal Business: Group life insurance (67%), individual life insurance (31%), individual annuities (1%), and reinsurance (1%).

Principal Investments: NonCMO investment grade bonds (76%), CMOs and structured securities (10%), mortgages in good standing (6%), and noninv. grade bonds (5%).

Investments in Affiliates: None

Group Affiliation: JAMEL Ltd

Licensed in: All states except AK, HI, NY, PR

Commenced Business: May 1983

Address: 3434 Washington Blvd Ste 300, Des Moines, IA 50309

Phone: (801) 621-5688 **Domicile State:** UT **NAIC Code:** 71480

Data Date	Rating	RACR #1	RACR #2	Total Assets ($mil)	Capital ($mil)	Net Premium ($mil)	Net Income ($mil)
2021	C-	1.43	0.70	1,191.0	47.5	-2.3	0.0
2020	C-	1.28	0.62	1,343.9	45.0	-4.4	3.5
2019	C-	0.99	0.50	1,369.6	32.0	-4.4	0.8
2018	C-	0.53	0.26	1,394.2	23.4	-9.7	-4.0
2017	D	0.61	0.31	1,388.0	32.4	213.4	-99.6

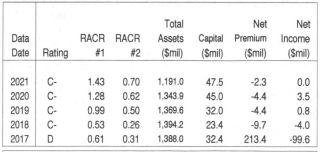

Junk Bonds as a % of Capital

Capital | $47 mil.
Junk Bonds | $54 mil.

0% 20% 40% 60% 80% 100% 120%
■ BB ■ B ▢ CCC ☐ In default

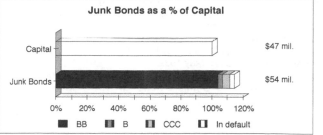

GREAT-WEST LIFE & ANNUITY INS CO   C   Fai

Major Rating Factors: Fair quality investment portfolio (4.8 on a scale of 0 to 10) with significant exposure to mortgages . Mortgage default rate has been low. Fair liquidity (4.5) as cash from operations and sale of marketable assets may not be adequate to cover a spike in claims or a run on policy withdrawals. Good capitalization (6.8) based on good risk adjusted capital (severe loss scenario).
Other Rating Factors: Weak profitability (1.9). Weak overall results on stability tests (2.4) including weak results on operational trends and negative cash flow from operations for 2021.
Principal Business: Reinsurance (50%), group retirement contracts (43%), individual life insurance (4%), and group life insurance (1%).
Principal Investments: NonCMO investment grade bonds (53%), CMOs and structured securities (18%), mortgages in good standing (11%), policy loans (10%), and misc. investments (6%).
Investments in Affiliates: 3%
Group Affiliation: Great West Life Asr
Licensed in: All states, the District of Columbia and Puerto Rico
Commenced Business: April 1907
Address: 8515 East Orchard Road, Greenwood Village, CO 80111
Phone: (800) 537-2033 **Domicile State:** CO **NAIC Code:** 68322

Data Date	Rating	RACR #1	RACR #2	Total Assets ($mil)	Capital ($mil)	Net Premium ($mil)	Net Income ($mil)
2021	C	1.79	0.98	75,889.8	2,915.6	6,298.4	297.9
2020	C	1.69	0.94	75,084.7	2,161.3	12,860.4	-1,695.0
2019	B-	1.99	1.09	48,781.4	1,441.8	-5,366.4	382.8
2018	B-	1.37	0.74	55,785.5	1,326.9	7,592.6	315.5
2017	B-	1.23	0.67	58,010.2	1,129.5	5,270.5	170.0

Rating Indexes

GREAT-WEST LIFE & ANNUITY INS OF NY   C   Fai

Major Rating Factors: Good quality investment portfolio (5.7 on a scale of 0 to 10) despite mixed results such as: minimal exposure to mortgages and large holdings of BBB rated bonds but small junk bond holdings. Good liquidity (5.8) with sufficient resources to handle a spike in claims as well as a significant increase in policy surrenders. Weak profitability (1.8).
Other Rating Factors: Weak overall results on stability tests (2.1) including weak results on operational trends, negative cash flow from operations for 2021. Strong capitalization (7.6) based on excellent risk adjusted capital (severe loss scenario).
Principal Business: Reinsurance (66%), group retirement contracts (26%), and individual life insurance (7%).
Principal Investments: NonCMO investment grade bonds (75%), CMOs and structured securities (12%), mortgages in good standing (7%), and cash (1%).
Investments in Affiliates: None
Group Affiliation: Great West Life Asr
Licensed in: IL, NY
Commenced Business: January 1972
Address: 489 5th Avenue 28th Floor, New York, NY 10017
Phone: (303) 737-3000 **Domicile State:** NY **NAIC Code:** 79359

Data Date	Rating	RACR #1	RACR #2	Total Assets ($mil)	Capital ($mil)	Net Premium ($mil)	Net Income ($mil)
2021	C	2.84	1.43	4,138.8	193.3	524.1	14.3
2020	C	3.18	1.69	3,618.6	189.3	1,653.5	-144.5
2019	B-	4.11	2.18	1,635.4	110.2	-395.9	25.8
2018	B-	1.97	1.06	2,199.9	81.4	268.0	-5.6
2017	B	2.16	1.16	2,198.5	87.5	328.5	3.1

Rating Indexes

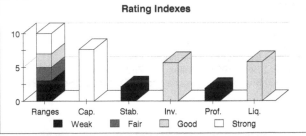

GREATER GEORGIA LIFE INS CO   B   Good

Major Rating Factors: Good quality investment portfolio (6.7 on a scale of 0 to 10) despite mixed results such as: no exposure to mortgages and large holdings of BBB rated bonds but minimal holdings in junk bonds. Good liquidity (6.5) with sufficient resources to handle a spike in claims. Good overall results on stability tests (6.3) despite negative cash flow from operations for 2021 excellent operational trends, good risk adjusted capital for prior years and excellent risk diversification.
Other Rating Factors: Weak profitability (1.7) with operating losses during 2021. Strong capitalization (7.9) based on excellent risk adjusted capital (severe loss scenario).
Principal Business: Group life insurance (51%), group health insurance (49%), and individual life insurance (1%).
Principal Investments: NonCMO investment grade bonds (57%), CMOs and structured securities (8%), and noninv. grade bonds (6%).
Investments in Affiliates: None
Group Affiliation: Anthem Inc
Licensed in: AL, GA, MS, NC, SC, TN, VA
Commenced Business: May 1982
Address: 3350 PEACHTREE ROAD, ATLANTA, GA 30308
Phone: (317) 488-6716 **Domicile State:** GA **NAIC Code:** 97217

Data Date	Rating	RACR #1	RACR #2	Total Assets ($mil)	Capital ($mil)	Net Premium ($mil)	Net Income ($mil)
2021	B	2.25	1.57	106.1	30.9	46.8	-16.5
2020	B	1.24	0.92	78.5	26.6	46.7	-7.7
2019	B	1.31	0.98	71.4	24.7	46.6	1.2
2018	B	1.33	0.99	62.6	23.8	36.2	2.5
2017	B	1.17	0.87	59.2	20.5	34.6	-0.6

Adverse Trends in Operations

Decrease in capital during 2017 (4%)

GUARANTEE TRUST LIFE INS CO

B   **Good**

Major Rating Factors: Good quality investment portfolio (6.5 on a scale of 0 to 10) despite significant exposure to mortgages . Mortgage default rate has been low. large holdings of BBB rated bonds in addition to small junk bond holdings. Good overall results on stability tests (5.8). Stability strengths include excellent operational trends and excellent risk diversification. Strong capitalization (8.1) based on excellent risk adjusted capital (severe loss scenario).

Other Rating Factors: Excellent profitability (7.7) with operating gains in each of the last five years. Excellent liquidity (7.2).

Principal Business: Individual health insurance (76%), group health insurance (14%), and individual life insurance (10%).

Principal Investments: NonCMO investment grade bonds (49%), CMOs and structured securities (29%), mortgages in good standing (10%), noninv. grade bonds (6%), and misc. investments (5%).

Investments in Affiliates: 2%

Group Affiliation: Guarantee Trust

Licensed in: All states except NY

Commenced Business: June 1936

Address: 1275 Milwaukee Avenue, Glenview, IL 60025

Phone: (847) 699-0600 **Domicile State:** IL **NAIC Code:** 64211

Data Date	Rating	RACR #1	RACR #2	Total Assets ($mil)	Capital ($mil)	Net Premium ($mil)	Net Income ($mil)
2021	B	2.77	1.75	791.2	153.5	255.5	24.6
2020	B	2.47	1.59	738.5	127.5	234.3	21.5
2019	B	2.22	1.45	679.9	106.3	232.4	16.0
2018	B	2.01	1.32	638.9	92.3	229.6	20.3
2017	B	1.84	1.21	594.8	79.2	218.7	12.4

Adverse Trends in Operations

Increase in policy surrenders from 2016 to 2017 (32%)

GUARANTY INCOME LIFE INS CO

B   **Good**

Major Rating Factors: Good capitalization (6.7 on a scale of 0 to 10) based on good risk adjusted capital (severe loss scenario). Moreover, capital has steadily grown over the last five years. Good overall results on stability tests (5.4). Stability strengths include excellent operational trends and excellent risk diversification. Fair quality investment portfolio (4.5).

Other Rating Factors: Excellent profitability (8.2) with operating gains in each of the last five years. Excellent liquidity (7.1).

Principal Business: N/A

Principal Investments: NonCMO investment grade bonds (42%), CMOs and structured securities (23%), common & preferred stock (17%), noninv. grade bonds (6%), and misc. investments (11%).

Investments in Affiliates: 10%

Group Affiliation: Kuvare US Holdings Inc

Licensed in: All states except AK, HI, ME, NY, PR

Commenced Business: February 1926

Address: 929 Government Street, Cedar Rapids, IA 52401

Phone: (225) 383-0355 **Domicile State:** IA **NAIC Code:** 64238

Data Date	Rating	RACR #1	RACR #2	Total Assets ($mil)	Capital ($mil)	Net Premium ($mil)	Net Income ($mil)
2021	B	1.18	0.96	3,458.1	631.7	552.4	25.5
2020	B	1.09	0.92	2,572.0	545.2	443.3	6.7
2019	B	1.09	0.96	1,790.7	455.9	517.1	10.2
2018	B	3.51	1.51	902.4	73.0	231.7	9.8
2017	C+	3.39	1.52	664.5	56.6	116.9	3.0

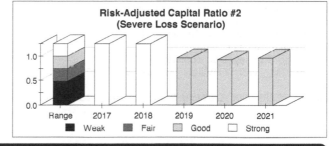

Risk-Adjusted Capital Ratio #2 (Severe Loss Scenario)

Range 2017 2018 2019 2020 2021
■ Weak ■ Fair ▨ Good □ Strong

GUARDIAN INS & ANNUITY CO INC

B   **Good**

Major Rating Factors: Good quality investment portfolio (5.7 on a scale of 0 to 10) despite significant exposure to mortgages . Mortgage default rate has been low. large holdings of BBB rated bonds in addition to small junk bond holdings. Good liquidity (6.1) with sufficient resources to handle a spike in claims as well as a significant increase in policy surrenders. Fair overall results on stability tests (4.8).

Other Rating Factors: Strong capitalization (7.6) based on excellent risk adjusted capital (severe loss scenario). Excellent profitability (7.5) despite operating losses during 2021.

Principal Business: Individual annuities (82%) and individual life insurance (17%).

Principal Investments: NonCMO investment grade bonds (75%), mortgages in good standing (14%), policy loans (2%), noninv. grade bonds (2%), and CMOs and structured securities (2%).

Investments in Affiliates: None

Group Affiliation: Guardian Group

Licensed in: All states except PR

Commenced Business: December 1971

Address: 2711 CENTERVILLE ROAD STE 400, WILMINGTON, DE 19808

Phone: (212) 598-8000 **Domicile State:** DE **NAIC Code:** 78778

Data Date	Rating	RACR #1	RACR #2	Total Assets ($mil)	Capital ($mil)	Net Premium ($mil)	Net Income ($mil)
2021	B	2.66	1.39	14,206.8	548.9	151.5	-83.5
2020	B	2.69	1.39	14,235.4	527.0	133.3	-100.3
2019	B	2.87	1.46	14,070.1	515.5	407.3	-48.9
2018	B	2.60	1.32	13,308.1	455.3	2,154.0	147.9
2017	B	1.72	0.88	17,357.0	310.2	449.4	26.3

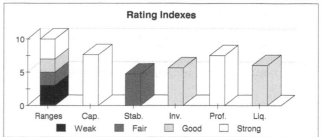

Rating Indexes

Ranges Cap. Stab. Inv. Prof. Liq.
■ Weak ■ Fair ▨ Good □ Strong

GUARDIAN LIFE INS CO OF AMERICA *   A   Excellent

Major Rating Factors: Good quality investment portfolio (6.7 on a scale of 0 to 10) despite mixed results such as: large holdings of BBB rated bonds but moderate junk bond exposure. Good liquidity (5.7) with sufficient resources to handle a spike in claims as well as a significant increase in policy surrenders. Strong capitalization (8.4) based on excellent risk adjusted capital (severe loss scenario).

Other Rating Factors: Excellent profitability (7.6) with operating gains in each of the last five years. Excellent overall results on stability tests (7.5) excellent operational trends and excellent risk diversification.

Principal Business: Individual life insurance (49%), group health insurance (36%), group life insurance (7%), reinsurance (6%), and individual health insurance (2%).

Principal Investments: NonCMO investment grade bonds (67%), mortgages in good standing (8%), policy loans (6%), noninv. grade bonds (5%), and misc. investments (14%).

Investments in Affiliates: 2%
Group Affiliation: Guardian Group
Licensed in: All states except PR
Commenced Business: July 1860
Address: 7 HANOVER SQUARE, NEW YORK, NY 10001
Phone: (212) 598-8000 **Domicile State:** NY **NAIC Code:** 64246

Data Date	Rating	RACR #1	RACR #2	Total Assets ($mil)	Capital ($mil)	Net Premium ($mil)	Net Income ($mil)
2021	A	3.06	1.92	72,127.3	8,589.0	9,452.9	223.2
2020	A	2.79	1.76	68,044.4	7,759.7	8,957.4	147.0
2019	A	2.83	1.84	62,204.0	7,615.6	8,742.0	548.5
2018	A	2.77	1.80	58,488.7	7,171.8	8,387.5	310.4
2017	A	2.84	1.83	55,568.8	6,683.7	8,116.1	423.1

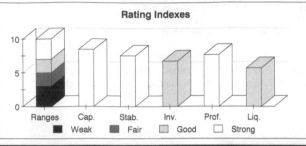

Rating Indexes (Ranges, Cap., Stab., Inv., Prof., Liq.) — Weak, Fair, Good, Strong

GUGGENHEIM LIFE & ANNUITY CO   B-   Good

Major Rating Factors: Good overall results on stability tests (5.1 on a scale of 0 to 10) despite fair financial strength of affiliated Sammons Enterprises Inc. Other stability subfactors include excellent operational trends, good risk adjusted capital for prior years and excellent risk diversification. Good liquidity (6.1) with sufficient resources to handle a spike in claims as well as a significant increase in policy surrenders. Fair quality investment portfolio (4.5).

Other Rating Factors: Strong capitalization (7.7) based on excellent risk adjusted capital (severe loss scenario). Excellent profitability (8.1) with operating gains in each of the last five years.

Principal Business: Individual annuities (97%) and reinsurance (3%).

Principal Investments: NonCMO investment grade bonds (58%), CMOs and structured securities (21%), common & preferred stock (3%), mortgages in good standing (3%), and noninv. grade bonds (2%).

Investments in Affiliates: 7%
Group Affiliation: Sammons Enterprises Inc
Licensed in: All states except NY
Commenced Business: October 1985
Address: 2711 CENTERVILLE ROAD STE 400, WILMINGTON, DE 19808-1645
Phone: (317) 396-9960 **Domicile State:** DE **NAIC Code:** 83607

Data Date	Rating	RACR #1	RACR #2	Total Assets ($mil)	Capital ($mil)	Net Premium ($mil)	Net Income ($mil)
2021	B-	2.79	1.48	14,709.5	1,163.3	954.1	29.8
2020	B-	1.86	0.99	13,825.2	745.6	890.9	67.4
2019	B-	1.89	1.01	13,885.3	714.1	949.7	76.7
2018	B-	1.89	1.00	13,820.1	698.8	680.6	99.1
2017	B-	1.61	0.82	14,353.5	608.6	804.5	155.5

Sammons Enterprises Inc
Composite Group Rating: C+

Largest Group Members	Assets ($mil)	Rating
DELAWARE LIFE INS CO	41747	C
CLEAR SPRING LIFE ANNTY CO	13825	B-
DELAWARE LIFE INS CO OF NEW YORK	2244	B
LACKAWANNA CASUALTY CO	515	C
CLEAR SPRING PC CO	328	E-

HANNOVER LIFE REASSURANCE CO OF AMER   B   Good

Major Rating Factors: Good capitalization (6.5 on a scale of 0 to 10) based on good risk adjusted capital (severe loss scenario). Moreover, capital levels have been consistent over the last five years. Good liquidity (6.7) with sufficient resources to handle a spike in claims as well as a significant increase in policy surrenders. Fair overall results on stability tests (4.0) including excessive premium growth.

Other Rating Factors: High quality investment portfolio (7.4). Excellent profitability (8.0) with operating gains in each of the last five years.

Principal Business: Reinsurance (100%).

Principal Investments: NonCMO investment grade bonds (86%), common & preferred stock (5%), CMOs and structured securities (5%), noninv. grade bonds (2%), and cash (1%).

Investments in Affiliates: 4%
Group Affiliation: Haftpflichtverband der Deutschen Ind
Licensed in: All states, the District of Columbia and Puerto Rico
Commenced Business: October 1988
Address: 200 S Orange Ave Ste 1900, Orlando, FL 32801
Phone: (407) 649-8411 **Domicile State:** FL **NAIC Code:** 88340

Data Date	Rating	RACR #1	RACR #2	Total Assets ($mil)	Capital ($mil)	Net Premium ($mil)	Net Income ($mil)
2021	B	1.43	0.94	17,746.6	625.2	477.3	88.6
2020	B	1.45	0.88	18,226.1	573.4	314.2	19.8
2019	B	1.58	0.89	17,527.2	552.8	444.3	70.1
2018	B+	2.84	1.71	16,953.4	549.9	410.6	36.3
2017	B+	2.10	1.14	15,439.3	411.2	232.7	45.6

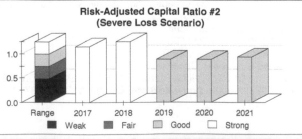

Risk-Adjusted Capital Ratio #2 (Severe Loss Scenario) (Range, 2017, 2018, 2019, 2020, 2021) — Weak, Fair, Good, Strong

HARLEYSVILLE LIFE INS CO
B — Good

Major Rating Factors: Good overall results on stability tests (5.4 on a scale of 0 to 10) despite fair financial strength of affiliated Nationwide Corp. Other stability subfactors include good operational trends and excellent risk diversification. Good quality investment portfolio (6.2) despite mixed results such as: no exposure to mortgages and large holdings of BBB rated bonds but small junk bond holdings. Good liquidity (5.9).

Other Rating Factors: Fair profitability (4.7) with investment income below regulatory standards in relation to interest assumptions of reserves. Strong capitalization (8.3) based on excellent risk adjusted capital (severe loss scenario).

Principal Business: Individual life insurance (88%) and individual annuities (12%).

Principal Investments: NonCMO investment grade bonds (84%), CMOs and structured securities (5%), noninv. grade bonds (3%), and policy loans (1%).

Investments in Affiliates: None

Group Affiliation: Nationwide Corp

Licensed in: AL, AZ, AR, CT, DC, DE, FL, GA, IL, IN, IA, KY, MD, MA, MI, MN, NE, NH, NJ, NM, NC, ND, OH, PA, RI, SC, SD, TN, TX, UT, VA, WV, WI

Commenced Business: June 1961

Address: 355 MAPLE AVENUE, COLUMBUS, OH 43215-2220

Phone: (800) 882-2822 **Domicile State:** OH **NAIC Code:** 64327

Data Date	Rating	RACR #1	RACR #2	Total Assets ($mil)	Capital ($mil)	Net Premium ($mil)	Net Income ($mil)
2020	B	3.65	1.89	0.0	0.0	0.0	0.0
2019	B	3.56	1.88	0.0	0.0	0.0	0.0
2018	B	3.33	1.77	0.0	0.0	0.0	0.0
2017	B	3.04	1.64	0.0	0.0	0.0	0.0
2016	B	2.86	1.55	0.0	0.0	0.0	0.0

Nationwide Corp
Composite Group Rating: C+

Largest Group Members	Assets ($mil)	Rating
NATIONWIDE LIFE INS CO	166217	B-
NATIONWIDE MUTUAL INS CO	37596	B
NATIONWIDE LIFE ANNUITY INS CO	37563	C
JEFFERSON NATIONAL LIFE INS CO	8968	C+
NATIONWIDE AGRIBUSINESS INS CO	1578	B-

HARTFORD LIFE & ACCIDENT INS CO
B- — Good

Major Rating Factors: Good quality investment portfolio (6.5 on a scale of 0 to 10) despite significant exposure to mortgages . Mortgage default rate has been low. large holdings of BBB rated bonds in addition to small junk bond holdings. Good liquidity (6.8) with sufficient resources to handle a spike in claims as well as a significant increase in policy surrenders. Good overall results on stability tests (5.3) good operational trends and excellent risk diversification.

Other Rating Factors: Fair profitability (3.7). Strong capitalization (8.7) based on excellent risk adjusted capital (severe loss scenario).

Principal Business: Group health insurance (59%), group life insurance (37%), and reinsurance (3%).

Principal Investments: NonCMO investment grade bonds (54%), CMOs and structured securities (17%), mortgages in good standing (12%), noninv. grade bonds (4%), and common & preferred stock (2%).

Investments in Affiliates: None

Group Affiliation: Hartford Financial Services Inc

Licensed in: All states, the District of Columbia and Puerto Rico

Commenced Business: February 1967

Address: One Hartford Plaza, Hartford, CT 06155-0001

Phone: (860) 547-5000 **Domicile State:** CT **NAIC Code:** 70815

Data Date	Rating	RACR #1	RACR #2	Total Assets ($mil)	Capital ($mil)	Net Premium ($mil)	Net Income ($mil)
2021	B-	3.49	2.16	13,021.6	2,410.1	3,658.2	34.5
2020	B-	3.93	2.45	12,824.5	2,601.5	3,993.4	289.4
2019	B-	4.24	2.69	12,877.7	2,643.9	4,083.1	514.7
2018	C	3.70	2.40	12,909.5	2,407.4	4,130.8	398.1
2017	C	3.42	2.19	12,935.8	2,020.5	5,777.5	1,066.7

Adverse Trends in Operations

Decrease in capital during 2020 (2%)
Decrease in premium volume from 2017 to 2018 (22%)
Increase in policy surrenders from 2017 to 2018 (738%)
Change in premium mix from 2016 to 2017 (10.2%)
Increase in policy surrenders from 2016 to 2017 (188%)

HAYMARKET INS CO
D- — Weak

Major Rating Factors: Poor capitalization (1.6 on a scale of 0 to 10) based on weak risk adjusted capital (moderate loss scenario). Low quality investment portfolio (0.8) containing large holdings of BBB rated bonds in addition to significant exposure to junk bonds. Weak profitability (2.7). Excellent expense controls. Return on equity has been low, averaging -1.6%.

Other Rating Factors: Weak overall results on stability tests (0.9) including weak risk adjusted capital in prior years. Excellent liquidity (9.1).

Principal Business: Reinsurance (100%).

Principal Investments: NonCMO investment grade bonds (38%), CMOs and structured securities (18%), mortgages in good standing (9%), cash (7%), and misc. investments (24%).

Investments in Affiliates: 9%

Group Affiliation: Advantage Capital Partners LLC

Licensed in: NE, SC, UT

Commenced Business: September 2015

Address: 222 South 15th Street 1202S, Omaha, NE 68114

Phone: (801) 618-0937 **Domicile State:** NE **NAIC Code:** 15828

Data Date	Rating	RACR #1	RACR #2	Total Assets ($mil)	Capital ($mil)	Net Premium ($mil)	Net Income ($mil)
2021	D-	0.57	0.27	2,707.8	54.2	55.6	4.7
2020	D-	0.47	0.24	2,514.7	49.4	122.4	3.8
2019	D-	0.37	0.18	1,788.0	32.8	227.0	-11.3
2018	D	0.44	0.23	1,245.9	31.7	141.3	-3.3
2017	D	1.01	0.58	858.8	27.9	69.1	1.6

Junk Bonds as a % of Capital

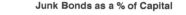
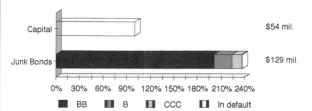

Capital — $54 mil.
Junk Bonds — $129 mil.

0% 30% 60% 90% 120% 150% 180% 210% 240%

■ BB   ▨ B   ▨ CCC   ▢ In default

HCC LIFE INS CO
B | **Good**

Major Rating Factors: Good overall results on stability tests (5.8 on a scale of 0 to 10) despite fair financial strength of affiliated HCC Ins Holdings Inc. Other stability subfactors include excellent operational trends and excellent risk diversification. Good liquidity (6.8) with sufficient resources to handle a spike in claims. Strong capitalization (9.9) based on excellent risk adjusted capital (severe loss scenario).

Other Rating Factors: High quality investment portfolio (7.8). Excellent profitability (9.2) with operating gains in each of the last five years.

Principal Business: Group health insurance (95%), individual health insurance (3%), and reinsurance (2%).

Principal Investments: CMOs and structured securities (50%) and nonCMO investment grade bonds (49%).

Investments in Affiliates: None

Group Affiliation: HCC Ins Holdings Inc

Licensed in: All states except PR

Commenced Business: March 1981

Address: 150 West Market Street Ste 800, Indianapolis, IN 46204-2814

Phone: (770) 973-9851 **Domicile State:** IN **NAIC Code:** 92711

Data Date	Rating	RACR #1	RACR #2	Total Assets ($mil)	Capital ($mil)	Net Premium ($mil)	Net Income ($mil)
2021	B	3.96	2.96	1,491.3	750.0	1,501.8	177.1
2020	B	4.23	3.19	1,346.5	743.4	1,399.0	165.8
2019	B	4.14	3.15	1,182.6	644.8	1,248.7	85.9
2018	B	3.35	2.56	1,097.0	561.5	1,365.8	121.4
2017	B	3.06	2.40	994.8	406.2	1,095.5	90.9

HCC Ins Holdings Inc
Composite Group Rating: C+

Largest Group Members	Assets ($mil)	Rating
RELIANCE STANDARD LIFE INS CO	17529	C+
SAFETY NATIONAL CASUALTY CORP	9990	B
PHILADELPHIA INDEMNITY INS CO	9935	B-
HOUSTON CASUALTY CO	3912	B-
US SPECIALTY INS CO	2203	C

HEALTH NET LIFE INS CO
B | **Good**

Major Rating Factors: Fair profitability (4.8 on a scale of 0 to 10) with operating losses during 2021. Fair overall results on stability tests (4.0). Strong overall capitalization (10.0) based on excellent risk adjusted capital (severe loss scenario). Nevertheless, capital levels have fluctuated during prior years.

Other Rating Factors: High quality investment portfolio (8.1). Excellent liquidity (7.0).

Principal Business: Individual health insurance (69%) and group health insurance (31%).

Principal Investments: NonCMO investment grade bonds (50%), cash (24%), CMOs and structured securities (18%), and noninv. grade bonds (1%).

Investments in Affiliates: None

Group Affiliation: Centene Corporation

Licensed in: All states except MI, NY, PR

Commenced Business: January 1987

Address: 21281 Burbank Boulevard B3, Woodland Hills, CA 91367

Phone: (314) 725-4477 **Domicile State:** CA **NAIC Code:** 66141

Data Date	Rating	RACR #1	RACR #2	Total Assets ($mil)	Capital ($mil)	Net Premium ($mil)	Net Income ($mil)
2021	B	3.91	3.07	616.8	353.3	524.2	-27.3
2020	B-	2.59	2.08	700.7	394.8	887.3	238.7
2019	C	3.06	2.42	606.1	375.6	739.9	66.6
2018	C	2.98	2.36	704.7	363.0	752.6	-53.1
2017	C	3.44	2.79	691.4	399.9	763.3	-16.4

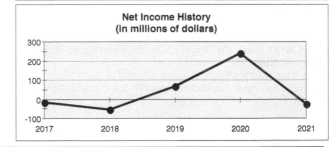

Net Income History
(in millions of dollars)

HERITAGE LIFE INS CO
C+ | **Fair**

Major Rating Factors: Fair quality investment portfolio (3.6 on a scale of 0 to 10) with large holdings of BBB rated bonds in addition to junk bond exposure equal to 54% of capital. Fair overall results on stability tests (4.5). Good overall profitability (6.9). Excellent expense controls. Return on equity has been fair, averaging 6.1%.

Other Rating Factors: Good liquidity (6.5). Strong capitalization (7.0) based on excellent risk adjusted capital (severe loss scenario).

Principal Business: Reinsurance (100%).

Principal Investments: NonCMO investment grade bonds (55%), CMOs and structured securities (16%), noninv. grade bonds (7%), common & preferred stock (6%), and policy loans (1%).

Investments in Affiliates: 5%

Group Affiliation: Calton Holdings LLC

Licensed in: All states except NY

Commenced Business: August 1957

Address: 8601 N SCOTTSDALE RD STE 300, SCOTTSDALE, AZ 85253

Phone: (312) 977-0904 **Domicile State:** AZ **NAIC Code:** 64394

Data Date	Rating	RACR #1	RACR #2	Total Assets ($mil)	Capital ($mil)	Net Premium ($mil)	Net Income ($mil)
2021	C+	1.64	1.00	7,707.6	960.7	212.0	70.2
2020	C+	1.56	0.97	7,314.5	914.0	1,770.9	-7.8
2019	C+	2.87	1.58	4,860.3	958.7	558.8	63.6
2018	C+	4.52	2.19	3,930.8	1,007.1	35.2	97.1
2017	C+	3.75	1.72	4,212.9	958.7	105.7	87.5

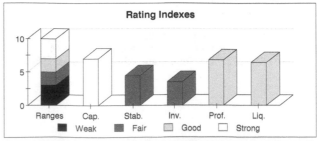

Rating Indexes

HM LIFE INS CO *　　　　　　　　　　　　　　　　　　　　B+　　　　Good

Major Rating Factors: Good quality investment portfolio (5.0 on a scale of 0 to 10) with no exposure to mortgages and minimal holdings in junk bonds. Good overall profitability (6.8). Return on equity has been fair, averaging 6.8%. Good liquidity (6.9) with sufficient resources to handle a spike in claims.

Other Rating Factors: Good overall results on stability tests (6.5) excellent operational trends and excellent risk diversification. Strong capitalization (10.0) based on excellent risk adjusted capital (severe loss scenario).

Principal Business: Group health insurance (97%) and reinsurance (3%).

Principal Investments: NonCMO investment grade bonds (43%), common & preferred stock (19%), CMOs and structured securities (16%), and noninv. grade bonds (7%).

Investments in Affiliates: None

Group Affiliation: Highmark Inc

Licensed in: All states except NY, PR

Commenced Business: May 1981

Address: Fifth AvePlace 120 Fifth Ave, Pittsburgh, PA 15222-3099

Phone: (800) 328-5433 **Domicile State:** PA **NAIC Code:** 93440

Data Date	Rating	RACR #1	RACR #2	Total Assets ($mil)	Capital ($mil)	Net Premium ($mil)	Net Income ($mil)
2021	B+	4.84	3.20	881.3	498.1	450.2	46.5
2020	B+	5.36	3.52	810.2	471.0	384.1	44.4
2019	B	4.74	3.11	727.2	431.5	398.3	44.4
2018	B	4.28	2.84	677.8	391.3	421.9	56.1
2017	B-	3.20	2.29	674.0	360.1	720.9	-23.8

Rating Indexes

(Bar chart with categories: Ranges, Cap., Stab., Inv., Prof., Liq.; legend: Weak, Fair, Good, Strong)

HM LIFE INS CO OF NEW YORK　　　　　　　　　　　　　B　　　　Good

Major Rating Factors: Good overall results on stability tests (5.9 on a scale of 0 to 10). Stability strengths include excellent operational trends and excellent risk diversification. Good overall profitability (5.2). Return on equity has been fair, averaging 5.9%. Strong capitalization (10.0) based on excellent risk adjusted capital (severe loss scenario).

Other Rating Factors: High quality investment portfolio (8.6). Excellent liquidity (7.7).

Principal Business: Group health insurance (100%).

Principal Investments: NonCMO investment grade bonds (59%), CMOs and structured securities (23%), cash (16%), and noninv. grade bonds (1%).

Investments in Affiliates: None

Group Affiliation: Highmark Inc

Licensed in: DC, NY, RI

Commenced Business: March 1997

Address: 420 Fifth Avenue 3rd Floor, New York, NY 10119

Phone: (800) 328-5433 **Domicile State:** NY **NAIC Code:** 60213

Data Date	Rating	RACR #1	RACR #2	Total Assets ($mil)	Capital ($mil)	Net Premium ($mil)	Net Income ($mil)
2021	B	6.83	5.76	81.4	55.6	35.7	3.5
2020	B-	6.65	4.57	73.1	51.6	36.9	10.9
2019	B-	4.95	3.43	61.0	41.2	39.2	-2.8
2018	B	5.77	3.94	66.2	43.8	36.2	-1.1
2017	B	3.64	2.90	67.3	45.1	72.8	5.1

Adverse Trends in Operations

Decrease in capital during 2019 (6%)
Decrease in asset base during 2019 (8%)
Decrease in asset base during 2018 (2%)
Change in asset mix during 2018 (4.4%)
Decrease in premium volume from 2017 to 2018 (50%)

HOMESTEADERS LIFE CO　　　　　　　　　　　　　　　　B　　　　Good

Major Rating Factors: Good current capitalization (6.4 on a scale of 0 to 10) based on good risk adjusted capital (severe loss scenario), although results have slipped from the excellent range over the last year. Good overall results on stability tests (5.5). Stability strengths include excellent operational trends and excellent risk diversification. Fair quality investment portfolio (4.7).

Other Rating Factors: Fair profitability (4.6) with investment income below regulatory standards in relation to interest assumptions of reserves. Excellent liquidity (7.0).

Principal Business: Group life insurance (92%), individual life insurance (6%), and individual annuities (2%).

Principal Investments: NonCMO investment grade bonds (66%), CMOs and structured securities (22%), mortgages in good standing (6%), noninv. grade bonds (3%), and cash (1%).

Investments in Affiliates: None

Group Affiliation: None

Licensed in: All states except NY, PR

Commenced Business: February 1906

Address: 5700 Westown Parkway, West Des Moines, IA 50266-8221

Phone: (515) 440-7777 **Domicile State:** IA **NAIC Code:** 64505

Data Date	Rating	RACR #1	RACR #2	Total Assets ($mil)	Capital ($mil)	Net Premium ($mil)	Net Income ($mil)
2021	B	1.79	0.93	3,451.6	194.7	561.7	5.5
2020	B	1.98	1.00	3,249.4	209.9	449.8	10.4
2019	B	2.15	1.13	3,213.2	215.3	490.0	15.6
2018	B	2.21	1.16	3,068.8	207.0	492.2	16.5
2017	B	2.27	1.21	2,921.3	193.2	480.0	16.3

**Risk-Adjusted Capital Ratio #2
(Severe Loss Scenario)**

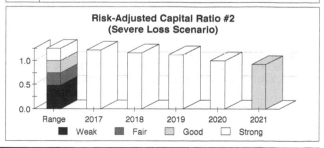

(Bar chart with categories: Range, 2017, 2018, 2019, 2020, 2021; legend: Weak, Fair, Good, Strong)

HORACE MANN LIFE INS CO   B   Good

Major Rating Factors: Good overall capitalization (6.8 on a scale of 0 to 10) based on good risk adjusted capital (severe loss scenario). However, capital levels have fluctuated somewhat during past years. Good quality investment portfolio (5.0) despite mixed results such as: large holdings of BBB rated bonds but moderate junk bond exposure. Good liquidity (5.0).

Other Rating Factors: Good overall results on stability tests (5.3) good operational trends and excellent risk diversification. Excellent profitability (7.4) with operating gains in each of the last five years.

Principal Business: Individual annuities (68%), individual life insurance (18%), group retirement contracts (9%), and reinsurance (4%).

Principal Investments: NonCMO investment grade bonds (54%), CMOs and structured securities (24%), noninv. grade bonds (4%), common & preferred stock (3%), and misc. investments (13%).

Investments in Affiliates: 1%

Group Affiliation: Horace Mann Educators Corp

Licensed in: All states except NY, PR

Commenced Business: September 1949

Address: #1 HORACE MANN PLAZA, SPRINGFIELD, IL 62715

Phone: (800) 999-1030 **Domicile State:** IL **NAIC Code:** 64513

Data Date	Rating	RACR #1	RACR #2	Total Assets ($mil)	Capital ($mil)	Net Premium ($mil)	Net Income ($mil)
2021	B	1.90	0.97	9,032.1	472.6	571.3	40.2
2020	B	1.91	0.98	8,177.4	430.7	542.7	23.5
2019	B	1.65	0.85	7,419.9	318.4	-1,827.1	20.3
2018	B	1.82	0.93	9,285.7	466.1	551.9	63.1
2017	B	1.77	0.91	9,262.8	473.2	562.4	59.0

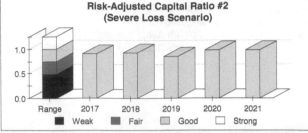

Risk-Adjusted Capital Ratio #2 (Severe Loss Scenario)

HUMANA INS CO OF KENTUCKY   C   Fair

Major Rating Factors: Fair profitability (4.2 on a scale of 0 to 10) with operating losses during 2021. Return on equity has been fair, averaging 5.1%. Weak liquidity (0.8) as a spike in claims may stretch capacity. Weak overall results on stability tests (2.9) including excessive premium growth.

Other Rating Factors: Strong capitalization (7.1) based on excellent risk adjusted capital (severe loss scenario). High quality investment portfolio (7.3).

Principal Business: Individual health insurance (88%), reinsurance (9%), and group life insurance (3%).

Principal Investments: NonCMO investment grade bonds (47%), CMOs and structured securities (33%), noninv. grade bonds (4%), and cash (1%).

Investments in Affiliates: None

Group Affiliation: Humana Inc

Licensed in: CA, CO, KY, MI, OR, PA, TX, UT, WA, WI

Commenced Business: January 2001

Address: 500 WEST MAIN STREET, LOUISVILLE, KY 40202

Phone: (502) 580-1000 **Domicile State:** KY **NAIC Code:** 60219

Data Date	Rating	RACR #1	RACR #2	Total Assets ($mil)	Capital ($mil)	Net Premium ($mil)	Net Income ($mil)
2021	C	1.34	1.07	234.1	131.6	518.3	-7.7
2020	B-	2.45	1.94	212.5	151.0	316.9	11.5
2019	B-	3.29	2.54	182.6	139.2	212.2	2.6
2018	B+	6.78	4.98	216.7	185.0	135.4	20.9
2017	B-	6.34	4.65	215.3	164.9	126.5	17.3

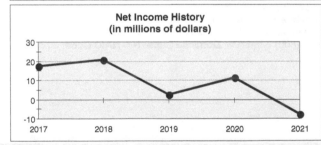

Net Income History (in millions of dollars)

HUMANA INS CO OF PUERTO RICO INC   C   Fair

Major Rating Factors: Fair overall results on stability tests (4.2 on a scale of 0 to 10). Good quality investment portfolio (6.7) despite mixed results such as: no exposure to mortgages and substantial holdings of BBB bonds but minimal holdings in junk bonds. Good liquidity (6.6) with sufficient resources to handle a spike in claims.

Other Rating Factors: Weak profitability (2.6) with operating losses during 2021. Strong capitalization (7.9) based on excellent risk adjusted capital (severe loss scenario).

Principal Business: Group health insurance (90%) and individual health insurance (10%).

Principal Investments: NonCMO investment grade bonds (38%), CMOs and structured securities (32%), cash (7%), and noninv. grade bonds (4%).

Investments in Affiliates: None

Group Affiliation: Humana Inc

Licensed in: PR

Commenced Business: September 1971

Address: 383 FD ROOSEVELT AVENUE, SAN JUAN, PR 00918-2131

Phone: (787) 282-7900 **Domicile State:** PR **NAIC Code:** 84603

Data Date	Rating	RACR #1	RACR #2	Total Assets ($mil)	Capital ($mil)	Net Premium ($mil)	Net Income ($mil)
2021	C	2.08	1.57	79.6	45.0	119.6	-2.9
2020	C+	2.15	1.62	79.0	48.0	122.2	5.0
2019	C+	N/A	N/A	77.4	43.1	137.5	-6.1
2018	C+	2.06	1.58	83.4	48.7	133.2	-2.3
2017	B-	2.18	1.74	77.0	49.4	130.9	4.4

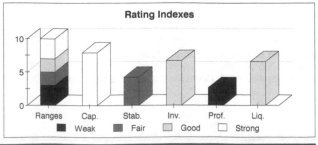

Rating Indexes

IA AMERICAN LIFE INS CO   C   Fair

Major Rating Factors: Fair overall results on stability tests (4.1 on a scale of 0 to 10) including fair financial strength of affiliated Industrial Alliance Ins & Financial. Fair quality investment portfolio (4.5). Good capitalization (6.8) based on good risk adjusted capital (severe loss scenario). Moreover, capital levels have been consistent over the last five years.

Other Rating Factors: Good liquidity (6.7). Weak profitability (2.8) with investment income below regulatory standards in relation to interest assumptions of reserves.

Principal Business: Individual life insurance (85%), individual annuities (10%), reinsurance (5%), and individual health insurance (1%).

Principal Investments: Common & preferred stock (55%), nonCMO investment grade bonds (39%), policy loans (2%), and cash (2%).

Investments in Affiliates: 55%

Group Affiliation: Industrial Alliance Ins & Financial

Licensed in: All states except NY, PR

Commenced Business: May 1980

Address: 425 AUSTIN AVENUE, WACO, TX 76701

Phone: (254) 297-2777 **Domicile State:** TX **NAIC Code:** 91693

Data Date	Rating	RACR #1	RACR #2	Total Assets ($mil)	Capital ($mil)	Net Premium ($mil)	Net Income ($mil)
2021	C	1.00	0.97	267.4	143.4	48.0	2.7
2020	C	0.97	0.93	210.8	98.0	39.9	-0.8
2019	C	0.93	0.88	167.9	64.7	29.9	0.0
2018	C	0.89	0.85	159.7	62.4	16.2	1.3
2017	C+	0.82	0.79	148.4	50.1	21.6	0.8

Industrial Alliance Ins Financial
Composite Group Rating: C
Largest Group Members

	Assets ($mil)	Rating
AMERICAN-AMICABLE LIFE INS CO OF TX	407	C
INDUSTRIAL ALLIANCE INS FIN SERV	281	C
OCCIDENTAL LIFE INS CO OF NC	277	C
IA AMERICAN LIFE INS CO	211	C
DEALERS ASR CO	199	B-

ILLINOIS MUTUAL LIFE INS CO *   B+   Good

Major Rating Factors: Good quality investment portfolio (5.9 on a scale of 0 to 10) despite mixed results such as: large holdings of BBB rated bonds but moderate junk bond exposure. Good liquidity (6.5) with sufficient resources to handle a spike in claims as well as a significant increase in policy surrenders. Good overall results on stability tests (6.7) despite negative cash flow from operations for 2021 excellent operational trends and excellent risk diversification.

Other Rating Factors: Strong capitalization (8.5) based on excellent risk adjusted capital (severe loss scenario). Excellent profitability (7.0) despite modest operating losses during 2020.

Principal Business: Individual life insurance (54%), individual health insurance (43%), group health insurance (3%), and individual annuities (1%).

Principal Investments: NonCMO investment grade bonds (63%), CMOs and structured securities (14%), common & preferred stock (7%), mortgages in good standing (6%), and misc. investments (9%).

Investments in Affiliates: None

Group Affiliation: None

Licensed in: All states except AK, DC, HI, NY, PR

Commenced Business: July 1912

Address: 300 SW Adams Street, Peoria, IL 61634

Phone: (309) 674-8255 **Domicile State:** IL **NAIC Code:** 64580

Data Date	Rating	RACR #1	RACR #2	Total Assets ($mil)	Capital ($mil)	Net Premium ($mil)	Net Income ($mil)
2021	B+	3.70	2.01	1,595.0	277.6	98.0	24.1
2020	B+	3.59	1.94	1,561.0	250.1	98.3	-0.6
2019	B+	3.75	2.05	1,530.7	255.4	100.9	0.5
2018	B+	3.75	2.09	1,460.5	240.1	101.5	27.4
2017	B	3.74	2.12	1,442.0	229.0	105.4	12.7

Adverse Trends in Operations

Decrease in capital during 2020 (2%)
Decrease in premium volume from 2019 to 2020 (3%)
Decrease in premium volume from 2017 to 2018 (4%)
Increase in policy surrenders from 2016 to 2017 (52%)

INDEPENDENCE LIFE & ANNUITY CO   D+   Weak

Major Rating Factors: Weak overall results on stability tests (2.6 on a scale of 0 to 10) including potential financial drain due to affiliation with Sun Life Assurance Group. Strong capitalization (4.0) based on excellent risk adjusted capital (severe loss scenario). Moreover, capital levels have been consistently high over the last five years. Good liquidity (6.8).

Other Rating Factors: High quality investment portfolio (7.5). Excellent profitability (7.4) with operating gains in each of the last five years.

Principal Business: N/A

Principal Investments: NonCMO investment grade bonds (60%), CMOs and structured securities (34%), and policy loans (4%).

Investments in Affiliates: None

Group Affiliation: Sun Life Assurance Group

Licensed in: All states except NY, PR

Commenced Business: November 1945

Address: 1209 Orange Street, Wilmington, DE 19801

Phone: (781) 237-6030 **Domicile State:** DE **NAIC Code:** 64602

Data Date	Rating	RACR #1	RACR #2	Total Assets ($mil)	Capital ($mil)	Net Premium ($mil)	Net Income ($mil)
2021	D+	4.88	3.73	3,445.7	189.5	2.4	2.0
2020	C-	4.47	3.30	3,426.9	172.7	0.0	2.5
2019	C	4.31	3.33	3,529.0	170.2	-0.4	4.9
2018	D+	4.55	3.24	3,169.9	165.4	-0.4	4.1
2017	D	4.47	3.19	3,144.3	161.3	-0.4	3.8

Sun Life Assurance Group
Composite Group Rating: D
Largest Group Members

	Assets ($mil)	Rating
SUN LIFE ASR CO OF CANADA	19738	D
INDEPENDENCE LIFE ANNUITY CO	3427	D+
SUN LIFE HEALTH INS CO	986	D+
PROFESSIONAL INS CO	85	D+

INDEPENDENT LIFE INSURANCE CO   D   Weak

Major Rating Factors: Weak profitability (1.8 on a scale of 0 to 10) with operating losses during 2021. Weak overall results on stability tests (2.2) including lack of operational experience. Strong capitalization (4.0) based on excellent risk adjusted capital (severe loss scenario).
Other Rating Factors: Fair quality investment portfolio (4.4). Excellent liquidity (7.7).
Principal Business: Individual annuities (100%).
Principal Investments: NonCMO investment grade bonds (68%), noninv. grade bonds (6%), common & preferred stock (5%), CMOs and structured securities (4%), and cash (2%).
Investments in Affiliates: None
Group Affiliation: Independent Life Insurance Company
Licensed in: TX
Commenced Business: April 2018
Address: Dallas, TX 75267-9053
Phone: (800) 793-0848 **Domicile State:** TX **NAIC Code:** 16354

Data Date	Rating	RACR #1	RACR #2	Total Assets ($mil)	Capital ($mil)	Net Premium ($mil)	Net Income ($mil)
2021	D	4.61	2.16	468.3	80.9	18.6	-6.6
2020	D	3.02	1.60	260.5	29.8	-37.9	-4.2
2019	D	4.26	3.83	173.1	40.8	67.5	-3.3
2018	D	5.52	4.97	75.2	43.4	12.4	-1.1
2017	N/A	N/A	N/A	0.0	0.0	0.0	0.0

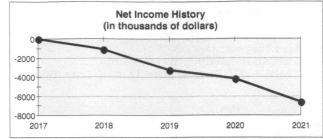

Net Income History
(in thousands of dollars)

INDUSTRIAL ALLIANCE INS & FIN SERV   C   Fair

Major Rating Factors: Fair liquidity (3.5 on a scale of 0 to 10) as cash from operations and sale of marketable assets may not be adequate to cover a spike in claims or a run on policy withdrawals. Fair overall results on stability tests (3.6). Weak profitability (1.4) with operating losses during 2021.
Other Rating Factors: Strong capitalization (7.9) based on excellent risk adjusted capital (severe loss scenario). High quality investment portfolio (7.4).
Principal Business: Reinsurance (94%), individual life insurance (4%), and individual annuities (1%).
Principal Investments: NonCMO investment grade bonds (95%), noninv. grade bonds (1%), policy loans (1%), and cash (1%).
Investments in Affiliates: None
Group Affiliation: Industrial Alliance Ins & Financial
Licensed in: AK, AZ, AR, CA, CO, GA, HI, ID, IL, IN, IA, KS, KY, LA, ME, MD, MI, MS, MO, MT, NE, NV, NH, NJ, NM, OH, OK, OR, PA, SC, TN, TX, UT, VA, WA, WV, WI, WY
Commenced Business: June 1967
Address: 425 AUSTIN AVENUE, WACO, TX 76701
Phone: (254) 297-2777 **Domicile State:** TX **NAIC Code:** 14406

Data Date	Rating	RACR #1	RACR #2	Total Assets ($mil)	Capital ($mil)	Net Premium ($mil)	Net Income ($mil)
2021	C	2.65	1.59	295.2	38.4	119.0	-9.7
2020	C	3.55	2.09	281.3	48.2	96.7	-16.2
2019	C	5.10	3.04	274.1	64.6	81.7	-5.1
2018	C	6.17	3.65	261.0	70.3	43.0	19.0
2017	C-	4.15	2.44	246.9	52.0	70.2	7.4

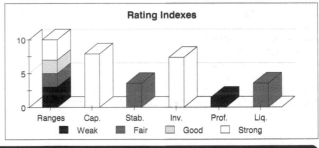

Rating Indexes

Ranges Cap. Stab. Inv. Prof. Liq.
■ Weak ■ Fair ▢ Good □ Strong

INTEGRITY LIFE INS CO   C+   Fair

Major Rating Factors: Fair overall results on stability tests (4.7 on a scale of 0 to 10). Good quality investment portfolio (5.0) despite mixed results such as: large holdings of BBB rated bonds but moderate junk bond exposure. Good liquidity (6.6) with sufficient resources to handle a spike in claims as well as a significant increase in policy surrenders.
Other Rating Factors: Weak profitability (2.8) with investment income below regulatory standards in relation to interest assumptions of reserves. Strong capitalization (7.4) based on excellent risk adjusted capital (severe loss scenario).
Principal Business: Individual annuities (100%).
Principal Investments: NonCMO investment grade bonds (40%), CMOs and structured securities (22%), common & preferred stock (15%), mortgages in good standing (10%), and misc. investments (10%).
Investments in Affiliates: 8%
Group Affiliation: Western & Southern Group
Licensed in: All states except NY, PR
Commenced Business: May 1966
Address: 400 BROADWAY, CINCINNATI, OH 45202
Phone: (513) 629-1800 **Domicile State:** OH **NAIC Code:** 74780

Data Date	Rating	RACR #1	RACR #2	Total Assets ($mil)	Capital ($mil)	Net Premium ($mil)	Net Income ($mil)
2021	C+	1.89	1.28	9,956.3	1,481.4	373.2	51.4
2020	C+	1.92	1.27	9,814.7	1,302.3	340.1	86.3
2019	C+	1.83	1.23	9,914.4	1,271.3	477.2	13.1
2018	B-	1.76	1.18	9,415.1	1,131.3	661.0	59.2
2017	B-	1.58	1.05	9,210.2	875.8	845.7	21.1

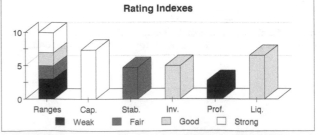

Rating Indexes

Ranges Cap. Stab. Inv. Prof. Liq.
■ Weak ■ Fair ▢ Good □ Strong

INVESTORS HERITAGE LIFE INS CO   C   Fair

Major Rating Factors: Fair quality investment portfolio (3.9 on a scale of 0 to 10) with large holdings of BBB rated bonds in addition to moderate junk bond exposure. Fair profitability (3.3). Return on equity has been low, averaging -1.2%. Fair overall results on stability tests (3.3).
Other Rating Factors: Good liquidity (6.9). Strong capitalization (7.6) based on excellent risk adjusted capital (severe loss scenario).
Principal Business: Individual annuities (89%), group life insurance (7%), and individual life insurance (4%).
Principal Investments: NonCMO investment grade bonds (41%), CMOs and structured securities (20%), noninv. grade bonds (7%), mortgages in good standing (6%), and misc. investments (15%).
Investments in Affiliates: None
Group Affiliation: Investors Heritage Capital Corp
Licensed in: All states except CT, DC, NJ, NY, PR
Commenced Business: March 1961
Address: 200 CAPITAL AVENUE, FRANKFORT, KY 40601
Phone: (502) 223-2361 **Domicile State:** KY **NAIC Code:** 64904

Data Date	Rating	RACR #1	RACR #2	Total Assets ($mil)	Capital ($mil)	Net Premium ($mil)	Net Income ($mil)
2021	C	2.84	1.40	1,398.4	170.8	455.9	3.9
2020	C	2.31	1.13	921.0	93.4	74.5	0.3
2019	C-	1.78	0.88	833.3	58.5	265.2	-7.4
2018	C+	2.46	1.33	559.3	40.9	97.4	7.3
2017	C	1.22	0.79	454.2	29.4	42.7	1.3

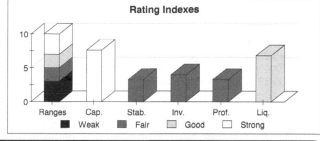

Rating Indexes

INVESTORS LIFE INS CO NORTH AMERICA   B-   Good

Major Rating Factors: Fair current capitalization (4.0 on a scale of 0 to 10) based on good risk adjusted capital (severe loss scenario), although results have slipped from the excellent range over the last year. Fair quality investment portfolio (3.5) with large holdings of BBB rated bonds in addition to junk bond exposure equal to 63% of capital. Fair overall results on stability tests (3.5) including negative cash flow from operations for 2021, weak results on operational trends.
Other Rating Factors: Good overall profitability (6.2). Good liquidity (5.2).
Principal Business: Individual life insurance (97%), individual annuities (1%), and reinsurance (1%).
Principal Investments: NonCMO investment grade bonds (64%), common & preferred stock (13%), CMOs and structured securities (13%), noninv. grade bonds (5%), and policy loans (3%).
Investments in Affiliates: 2%
Group Affiliation: Americo Life Inc
Licensed in: All states except NY, PR
Commenced Business: December 1963
Address: PO Box 139061, Dallas, TX 75313-9061
Phone: (816) 391-2000 **Domicile State:** TX **NAIC Code:** 63487

Data Date	Rating	RACR #1	RACR #2	Total Assets ($mil)	Capital ($mil)	Net Premium ($mil)	Net Income ($mil)
2021	B-	1.87	0.99	512.5	25.7	3.2	2.5
2020	B	2.13	1.09	519.6	25.5	0.0	1.8
2019	B	2.08	1.07	535.8	24.7	-0.1	2.9
2018	B	3.19	1.74	569.0	56.5	-0.1	0.3
2017	B	2.07	1.60	600.4	56.1	0.1	1.0

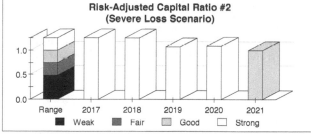

Risk-Adjusted Capital Ratio #2
(Severe Loss Scenario)

JACKSON NATIONAL LIFE INS CO   C+   Fair

Major Rating Factors: Fair current capitalization (4.0 on a scale of 0 to 10) based on excellent risk adjusted capital (severe loss scenario) reflecting improvement over results in 2017. Fair overall results on stability tests (4.0). Good quality investment portfolio (5.8) despite large holdings of BBB rated bonds in addition to moderate junk bond exposure. Exposure to mortgages is significant, but the mortgage default rate has been low.
Other Rating Factors: Excellent profitability (8.0). Excellent liquidity (7.3).
Principal Business: Individual annuities (87%), reinsurance (7%), individual life insurance (3%), and group retirement contracts (2%).
Principal Investments: NonCMO investment grade bonds (48%), CMOs and structured securities (18%), mortgages in good standing (17%), policy loans (6%), and misc. investments (8%).
Investments in Affiliates: 2%
Group Affiliation: Prudential plc
Licensed in: All states except NY, PR
Commenced Business: August 1961
Address: 1 CORPORATE WAY, LANSING, MI 48951
Phone: (517) 381-5500 **Domicile State:** MI **NAIC Code:** 65056

Data Date	Rating	RACR #1	RACR #2	Total Assets ($mil)	Capital ($mil)	Net Premium ($mil)	Net Income ($mil)
2021	C+	2.07	1.15	303,000	6,098.2	19,845.3	135.9
2020	B	1.83	0.98	281,000	4,780.5	-8,369.9	-1,933.5
2019	B	1.80	0.99	255,000	4,759.6	20,569.2	-263.5
2018	B	1.95	1.08	225,000	4,788.4	22,986.4	1,896.3
2017	B	1.60	0.88	229,000	3,884.1	19,004.5	168.4

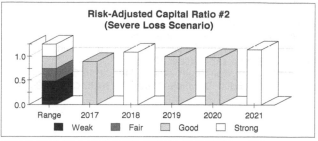

Risk-Adjusted Capital Ratio #2
(Severe Loss Scenario)

JACKSON NATIONAL LIFE INS CO OF NY B Good

Major Rating Factors: Good overall results on stability tests (5.5 on a scale of 0 to 10) despite fair financial strength of affiliated Prudential plc and negative cash flow from operations for 2021. Other stability subfactors include excellent operational trends and excellent risk diversification. Good quality investment portfolio (5.4) despite mixed results such as: no exposure to mortgages and large holdings of BBB rated bonds but minimal holdings in junk bonds. Strong capitalization (9.4) based on excellent risk adjusted capital (severe loss scenario).

Other Rating Factors: Excellent profitability (8.2) with operating gains in each of the last five years. Excellent liquidity (7.0).
Principal Business: Individual annuities (100%).
Principal Investments: NonCMO investment grade bonds (72%), CMOs and structured securities (22%), and noninv. grade bonds (3%).
Investments in Affiliates: None
Group Affiliation: Prudential plc
Licensed in: DE, MI, NY
Commenced Business: August 1996
Address: 2900 WESTCHESTER AVE STE 305, PURCHASE, NY 10577
Phone: (517) 381-5500 **Domicile State:** NY **NAIC Code:** 60140

Data Date	Rating	RACR #1	RACR #2	Total Assets ($mil)	Capital ($mil)	Net Premium ($mil)	Net Income ($mil)
2021	B	3.74	2.58	19,048.2	661.9	148.7	48.4
2020	B	3.91	2.59	16,606.0	607.8	141.7	19.9
2019	B	4.41	3.08	14,745.2	612.7	130.3	27.1
2018	B	4.97	3.20	12,307.5	583.2	140.4	31.5
2017	B	4.54	2.98	12,922.1	557.1	142.6	69.8

Prudential plc
Composite Group Rating: C+
Largest Group Members

	Assets ($mil)	Rating
JACKSON NATIONAL LIFE INS CO	280802	C+
JACKSON NATIONAL LIFE INS CO OF NY	16606	C+

JEFFERSON NATIONAL LIFE INS CO C+ Fair

Major Rating Factors: Fair overall results on stability tests (4.8 on a scale of 0 to 10) including excessive premium growth and fair risk adjusted capital in prior years. Good current capitalization (5.7) based on good risk adjusted capital (severe loss scenario) reflecting some improvement over results in 2017. Good quality investment portfolio (6.3).

Other Rating Factors: Excellent profitability (8.9). Excellent liquidity (10.0).
Principal Business: Individual annuities (99%) and individual life insurance (1%).
Principal Investments: NonCMO investment grade bonds (54%), CMOs and structured securities (17%), cash (17%), common & preferred stock (4%), and misc. investments (5%).
Investments in Affiliates: 1%
Group Affiliation: Nationwide Mutual Group
Licensed in: All states except NY, PR
Commenced Business: February 1937
Address: 350 NORTH ST PAUL STREET, DALLAS, TX 75201
Phone: (866) 667-0561 **Domicile State:** TX **NAIC Code:** 64017

Data Date	Rating	RACR #1	RACR #2	Total Assets ($mil)	Capital ($mil)	Net Premium ($mil)	Net Income ($mil)
2021	C+	1.13	0.84	10,807.0	102.6	1,387.5	18.0
2020	C	1.10	0.77	8,968.0	81.8	985.9	15.1
2019	C	0.89	0.59	7,674.7	52.3	1,024.6	8.6
2018	C	0.92	0.58	6,172.2	42.7	1,145.8	6.8
2017	C	0.84	0.52	5,816.9	34.7	1,049.4	-0.2

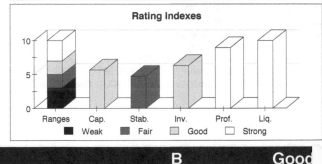

Rating Indexes

JOHN HANCOCK LIFE & HEALTH INS CO B Good

Major Rating Factors: Good overall results on stability tests (6.2 on a scale of 0 to 10). Stability strengths include excellent operational trends and excellent risk diversification. Good quality investment portfolio (6.2) despite mixed results such as: minimal exposure to mortgages and substantial holdings of BBB bonds but minimal holdings in junk bonds. Strong capitalization (9.8) based on excellent risk adjusted capital (severe loss scenario).

Other Rating Factors: Excellent profitability (9.4) with operating gains in each of the last five years. Excellent liquidity (9.0).
Principal Business: Group health insurance (74%), individual health insurance (22%), and reinsurance (4%).
Principal Investments: NonCMO investment grade bonds (64%), mortgages in good standing (8%), CMOs and structured securities (4%), real estate (3%), and misc. investments (12%).
Investments in Affiliates: None
Group Affiliation: Manulife Financial Group
Licensed in: All states, the District of Columbia and Puerto Rico
Commenced Business: October 1981
Address: 197 Clarendon Street, Boston, MA 02116-5010
Phone: (617) 572-6000 **Domicile State:** MA **NAIC Code:** 93610

Data Date	Rating	RACR #1	RACR #2	Total Assets ($mil)	Capital ($mil)	Net Premium ($mil)	Net Income ($mil)
2021	B	5.38	2.87	19,441.1	1,448.4	677.5	182.2
2020	C	4.84	2.64	19,136.7	1,284.1	688.3	158.7
2019	B	4.36	2.36	16,068.0	1,108.8	682.1	91.7
2018	B	3.87	2.11	13,819.8	992.8	690.3	144.7
2017	B	3.56	1.95	14,006.8	891.9	686.5	104.6

Adverse Trends in Operations

Increase in policy surrenders from 2019 to 2020 (565%)
Decrease in premium volume from 2018 to 2019 (1%)
Decrease in asset base during 2018 (1%)
Change in premium mix from 2016 to 2017 (15.1%)

JOHN HANCOCK LIFE INS CO (USA)

B-   **Good**

Major Rating Factors: Good quality investment portfolio (5.1 on a scale of 0 to 10) despite substantial holdings of BBB bonds in addition to moderate junk bond exposure. Exposure to mortgages is significant, but the mortgage default rate has been low. Good profitability (5.0). Return on equity has been fair, averaging 7.0%. Good liquidity (6.8).

Other Rating Factors: Good overall results on stability tests (5.2) despite excessive premium growth good operational trends, good risk adjusted capital for prior years and excellent risk diversification. Strong capitalization (7.3) based on excellent risk adjusted capital (severe loss scenario).

Principal Business: Group retirement contracts (68%), individual life insurance (23%), individual health insurance (5%), reinsurance (2%), and group health insurance (2%).

Principal Investments: NonCMO investment grade bonds (47%), mortgages in good standing (11%), CMOs and structured securities (6%), real estate (4%), and misc. investments (21%).

Investments in Affiliates: 6%

Group Affiliation: Manulife Financial Group

Licensed in: All states except NY

Commenced Business: January 1956

Address: 201 Townsend Street Suite 900, Lansing, MI 48933

Phone: (617) 572-6000 **Domicile State:** MI **NAIC Code:** 65838

Data Date	Rating	RACR #1	RACR #2	Total Assets ($mil)	Capital ($mil)	Net Premium ($mil)	Net Income ($mil)
2021	B-	1.88	1.20	273,000	10,411.6	15,930.9	2,263.9
2020	B-	1.83	1.15	266,000	9,007.8	11,667.1	609.9
2019	B-	1.72	1.09	243,000	8,475.8	14,948.1	1,216.0
2018	B-	1.67	1.06	220,000	8,869.3	5,815.6	1,033.7
2017	B	1.60	0.98	243,000	8,109.4	18,286.5	1,898.9

Rating Indexes

JOHN HANCOCK LIFE INS CO OF NY

C+   **Fair**

Major Rating Factors: Fair profitability (3.0 on a scale of 0 to 10). Return on equity has been low, averaging 2.2%. Fair overall results on stability tests (4.5). Good quality investment portfolio (6.0) with minimal exposure to mortgages and minimal holdings in junk bonds.

Other Rating Factors: Good liquidity (5.9). Strong capitalization (8.5) based on excellent risk adjusted capital (severe loss scenario).

Principal Business: Group retirement contracts (62%), individual life insurance (25%), reinsurance (12%), and individual annuities (1%).

Principal Investments: NonCMO investment grade bonds (62%), mortgages in good standing (7%), real estate (3%), CMOs and structured securities (3%), and misc. investments (13%).

Investments in Affiliates: None

Group Affiliation: Manulife Financial Group

Licensed in: MI, NY

Commenced Business: July 1992

Address: 100 Summit Lake Drive 2nd Fl, Valhalla, NY 10595

Phone: (800) 344 1029 **Domicile State:** NY **NAIC Code:** 86375

Data Date	Rating	RACR #1	RACR #2	Total Assets ($mil)	Capital ($mil)	Net Premium ($mil)	Net Income ($mil)
2021	C+	3.87	2.00	19,494.3	1,320.4	1,005.6	141.9
2020	C+	3.68	1.91	19,339.5	1,213.7	962.2	-287.1
2019	B	4.26	2.21	17,663.3	1,423.8	515.9	-196.6
2018	B	4.56	2.36	16,452.3	1,662.7	1,051.5	375.4
2017	B	4.08	2.10	17,574.1	1,482.5	1,072.9	84.7

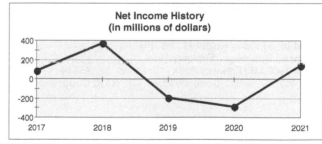

Net Income History
(in millions of dollars)

KANSAS CITY LIFE INS CO

B   **Good**

Major Rating Factors: Good overall capitalization (6.3 on a scale of 0 to 10) based on good risk adjusted capital (severe loss scenario). Nevertheless, capital levels have fluctuated during prior years. Good liquidity (5.0) with sufficient resources to handle a spike in claims as well as a significant increase in policy surrenders. Good overall results on stability tests (5.5) despite negative cash flow from operations for 2021 good operational trends and excellent risk diversification.

Other Rating Factors: Fair quality investment portfolio (4.9). Fair profitability (3.4) with investment income below regulatory standards in relation to interest assumptions of reserves.

Principal Business: Individual life insurance (43%), individual annuities (23%), group health insurance (17%), reinsurance (11%), and group life insurance (5%).

Principal Investments: NonCMO investment grade bonds (65%), mortgages in good standing (18%), CMOs and structured securities (7%), real estate (4%), and misc. investments (5%).

Investments in Affiliates: 2%

Group Affiliation: Kansas City Life Group

Licensed in: All states except NY, PR

Commenced Business: May 1895

Address: 3520 Broadway, Kansas City, MO 64111-2565

Phone: (816) 753-7000 **Domicile State:** MO **NAIC Code:** 65129

Data Date	Rating	RACR #1	RACR #2	Total Assets ($mil)	Capital ($mil)	Net Premium ($mil)	Net Income ($mil)
2021	B	1.57	0.91	3,770.7	245.3	265.2	24.2
2020	B	1.42	0.87	3,723.8	265.3	528.2	11.6
2019	B	1.47	0.90	3,399.9	260.8	286.8	6.9
2018	B	1.50	0.93	3,333.2	278.2	286.9	15.5
2017	B	1.88	1.07	3,411.3	307.5	300.7	16.0

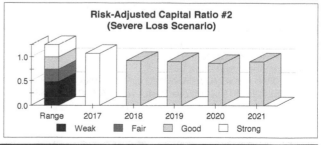

Risk-Adjusted Capital Ratio #2
(Severe Loss Scenario)

LAFAYETTE LIFE INS CO   B   Good

Major Rating Factors: Good overall results on stability tests (5.6 on a scale of 0 to 10). Stability strengths include excellent operational trends, good risk adjusted capital for prior years and excellent risk diversification. Good liquidity (5.5) with sufficient resources to handle a spike in claims as well as a significant increase in policy surrenders. Fair quality investment portfolio (4.2).

Other Rating Factors: Fair profitability (4.2) with operating losses during 2021. Strong capitalization (7.0) based on excellent risk adjusted capital (severe loss scenario).

Principal Business: Individual life insurance (84%), individual annuities (12%), and group retirement contracts (4%).

Principal Investments: NonCMO investment grade bonds (45%), CMOs and structured securities (16%), policy loans (11%), mortgages in good standing (10%), and misc. investments (15%).

Investments in Affiliates: 2%

Group Affiliation: Western & Southern Group

Licensed in: All states except NY, PR

Commenced Business: December 1905

Address: 301 EAST 4TH STREET, CINCINNATI, OH 45202

Phone: (513) 362-4900 **Domicile State:** OH **NAIC Code:** 65242

Data Date	Rating	RACR #1	RACR #2	Total Assets ($mil)	Capital ($mil)	Net Premium ($mil)	Net Income ($mil)
2021	B	1.98	1.00	6,345.5	404.3	643.5	-14.8
2020	B	1.73	0.85	5,964.1	363.1	589.2	2.8
2019	B	1.84	0.91	5,797.5	358.9	575.4	0.5
2018	B	1.81	0.90	5,493.5	334.4	575.6	28.2
2017	B	1.80	0.90	5,435.9	318.0	558.4	3.3

Adverse Trends in Operations

Decrease in premium volume from 2016 to 2017 (2%)

LIBERTY BANKERS LIFE INS CO   B-   Good

Major Rating Factors: Good capitalization (5.6 on a scale of 0 to 10) based on good risk adjusted capital (severe loss scenario). Moreover, capital levels have been consistent over the last five years. Good liquidity (6.7) with sufficient resources to handle a spike in claims as well as a significant increase in policy surrenders. Good overall results on stability tests (5.1) despite excessive premium growth excellent operational trends and excellent risk diversification.

Other Rating Factors: Fair quality investment portfolio (4.2). Excellent profitability (8.7) with operating gains in each of the last five years.

Principal Business: Individual annuities (85%), individual life insurance (12%), and individual health insurance (2%).

Principal Investments: NonCMO investment grade bonds (42%), mortgages in good standing (24%), common & preferred stock (9%), CMOs and structured securities (9%), and misc. investments (16%).

Investments in Affiliates: 8%

Group Affiliation: Liberty Life Group Trust

Licensed in: All states except AL, NY, PR

Commenced Business: February 1958

Address: 1605 LBJ Freeway Suite 710, Dallas, TX 75234

Phone: (469) 522-4400 **Domicile State:** OK **NAIC Code:** 68543

Data Date	Rating	RACR #1	RACR #2	Total Assets ($mil)	Capital ($mil)	Net Premium ($mil)	Net Income ($mil)
2021	B-	1.16	0.83	2,323.6	278.4	548.1	23.5
2020	B-	1.26	0.91	2,044.9	257.0	320.3	23.4
2019	C	1.28	0.89	2,006.2	242.1	460.4	12.1
2018	C	1.20	0.85	1,846.9	231.7	315.9	10.8
2017	D+	1.14	0.80	1,711.6	201.9	305.5	9.2

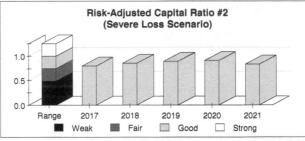

Risk-Adjusted Capital Ratio #2
(Severe Loss Scenario)

Range / Weak / Fair / Good / Strong — 2017 2018 2019 2020 2021

LIBERTY NATIONAL LIFE INS CO   B-   Good

Major Rating Factors: Good overall results on stability tests (5.0 on a scale of 0 to 10) despite fair financial strength of affiliated Torchmark Corp. Other stability subfactors include excellent operational trends and excellent risk diversification. Good overall capitalization (6.6) based on good risk adjusted capital (severe loss scenario). However, capital levels have fluctuated somewhat during past years. Good overall profitability (5.8) although investment income, in comparison to reserve requirements, is below regulatory standards.

Other Rating Factors: Fair quality investment portfolio (4.7). Fair liquidity (3.0).

Principal Business: Reinsurance (49%), individual life insurance (29%), individual health insurance (13%), group life insurance (9%), and individual annuities (1%).

Principal Investments: NonCMO investment grade bonds (76%), noninv. grade bonds (5%), common & preferred stock (4%), policy loans (3%), and misc. investments (11%).

Investments in Affiliates: 7%

Group Affiliation: Torchmark Corp

Licensed in: All states except NY, PR

Commenced Business: July 1929

Address: 10306 REGENCY PARKWAY DR, OMAHA, NE 68114

Phone: (205) 325-4918 **Domicile State:** NE **NAIC Code:** 65331

Data Date	Rating	RACR #1	RACR #2	Total Assets ($mil)	Capital ($mil)	Net Premium ($mil)	Net Income ($mil)
2021	B-	1.78	0.95	8,756.8	579.7	1,148.5	104.5
2020	B-	1.66	0.89	8,307.6	518.0	1,039.3	95.3
2019	B	1.89	1.01	8,043.5	555.9	939.8	133.9
2018	B	1.93	1.02	7,793.0	570.1	982.5	107.9
2017	B	1.91	1.00	7,411.6	542.3	819.7	132.8

Torchmark Corp
Composite Group Rating: C+
Largest Group Members

	Assets ($mil)	Rating
LIBERTY NATIONAL LIFE INS CO	8308	B-
GLOBE LIFE ACCIDENT INS CO	5074	C
AMERICAN INCOME LIFE INS CO	4675	B-
FAMILY HERITAGE LIFE INS CO OF AMER	1436	B-
UNITED AMERICAN INS CO	729	B

LIFE INS CO OF ALABAMA   C+   Fair

Major Rating Factors: Fair profitability (4.6 on a scale of 0 to 10). Return on equity has been low, averaging 1.9%. Fair overall results on stability tests (4.6). Good quality investment portfolio (5.6) despite mixed results such as: no exposure to mortgages and large holdings of BBB rated bonds but no exposure to junk bonds.

Other Rating Factors: Good liquidity (6.7). Strong capitalization (8.0) based on excellent risk adjusted capital (severe loss scenario).

Principal Business: Individual health insurance (70%), individual life insurance (22%), and group health insurance (8%).

Principal Investments: NonCMO investment grade bonds (62%), CMOs and structured securities (17%), common & preferred stock (10%), policy loans (4%), and misc. investments (8%).

Investments in Affiliates: None

Group Affiliation: None

Licensed in: AL, AR, FL, GA, KY, LA, MS, NC, OK, SC, TN

Commenced Business: August 1952

Address: 302 Broad Street, Gadsden, AL 35901

Phone: (256) 543-2022 **Domicile State:** AL **NAIC Code:** 65412

Data Date	Rating	RACR #1	RACR #2	Total Assets ($mil)	Capital ($mil)	Net Premium ($mil)	Net Income ($mil)
2021	C+	2.58	1.65	130.7	33.2	36.5	0.7
2020	C+	3.09	1.98	130.3	40.6	37.1	1.9
2019	C+	3.82	2.50	126.8	40.4	37.5	0.1
2018	B	4.03	2.69	123.9	41.4	37.2	-0.3
2017	B	3.52	2.17	124.8	42.5	36.7	2.2

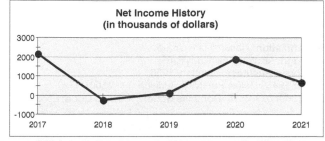

Net Income History (in thousands of dollars)

LIFE INS CO OF BOSTON & NEW YORK *   B+   Good

Major Rating Factors: Good quality investment portfolio (6.4 on a scale of 0 to 10) despite mixed results such as: no exposure to mortgages and large holdings of BBB rated bonds but small junk bond holdings. Good overall profitability (5.3) although investment income, in comparison to reserve requirements, is below regulatory standards. Good liquidity (6.6).

Other Rating Factors: Good overall results on stability tests (6.4) excellent operational trends and good risk diversification. Strong capitalization (8.7) based on excellent risk adjusted capital (severe loss scenario).

Principal Business: Individual life insurance (69%), individual health insurance (16%), and group health insurance (15%).

Principal Investments: NonCMO investment grade bonds (62%), policy loans (19%), common & preferred stock (7%), CMOs and structured securities (6%), and misc. investments (6%).

Investments in Affiliates: None

Group Affiliation: Boston Mutual Group

Licensed in: NY

Commenced Business: March 1990

Address: 4300 Camp Road PO Box 331, Athol Springs, NY 14010

Phone: (212) 684-2000 **Domicile State:** NY **NAIC Code:** 78140

Data Date	Rating	RACR #1	RACR #2	Total Assets ($mil)	Capital ($mil)	Net Premium ($mil)	Net Income ($mil)
2021	B+	3.67	2.13	193.4	38.3	22.5	3.4
2020	A-	3.70	2.15	183.4	37.0	23.6	-0.1
2019	A-	3.80	2.20	172.8	35.6	24.3	2.6
2018	A-	3.48	2.14	160.1	32.3	23.5	2.7
2017	A-	3.30	2.36	150.4	30.1	22.6	1.5

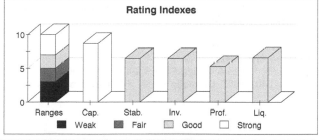

Rating Indexes

Ranges | Cap. | Stab. | Inv. | Prof. | Liq.
■ Weak   ■ Fair   ☐ Good   ☐ Strong

LIFE INS CO OF NORTH AMERICA   B   Good

Major Rating Factors: Good quality investment portfolio (5.4 on a scale of 0 to 10) despite mixed results such as: minimal exposure to mortgages and large holdings of BBB rated bonds but minimal holdings in junk bonds. Good liquidity (6.9) with sufficient resources to handle a spike in claims as well as a significant increase in policy surrenders. Good overall results on stability tests (5.3) good operational trends and excellent risk diversification.

Other Rating Factors: Fair profitability (4.2) with operating losses during 2021. Strong capitalization (9.4) based on excellent risk adjusted capital (severe loss scenario).

Principal Business: Group health insurance (60%), group life insurance (37%), and reinsurance (3%).

Principal Investments: NonCMO investment grade bonds (78%), mortgages in good standing (9%), CMOs and structured securities (8%), and noninv. grade bonds (6%).

Investments in Affiliates: None

Group Affiliation: CIGNA Corp

Licensed in: All states, the District of Columbia and Puerto Rico

Commenced Business: September 1957

Address: 2 LIBERTY PLC 1601 CHESTNUT ST, PHILADELPHIA, PA 19192-2362

Phone: (212) 576-7000 **Domicile State:** PA **NAIC Code:** 65498

Data Date	Rating	RACR #1	RACR #2	Total Assets ($mil)	Capital ($mil)	Net Premium ($mil)	Net Income ($mil)
2021	B	4.43	2.59	9,002.2	1,670.2	2,661.9	-74.5
2020	B+	5.48	3.48	8,874.2	2,056.5	4,055.4	298.8
2019	B	3.13	2.04	9,469.3	2,303.9	3,931.0	330.3
2018	B	2.62	1.69	8,667.9	1,776.2	3,730.7	299.0
2017	B	2.62	1.69	8,900.7	1,798.2	3,730.5	334.4

Adverse Trends in Operations

Decrease in capital during 2020 (11%)
Increase in policy surrenders from 2019 to 2020 (92%)
Decrease in asset base during 2020 (6%)
Decrease in asset base during 2018 (3%)
Decrease in capital during 2018 (1%)

LIFE INS CO OF THE SOUTHWEST   B   Good

Major Rating Factors: Good overall profitability (5.9 on a scale of 0 to 10). Return on equity has been low, averaging 4.3%. Good liquidity (5.5) with sufficient resources to handle a spike in claims as well as a significant increase in policy surrenders. Good overall results on stability tests (5.5) excellent operational trends, good risk adjusted capital for prior years and excellent risk diversification.

Other Rating Factors: Fair quality investment portfolio (4.7). Strong capitalization (7.4) based on excellent risk adjusted capital (severe loss scenario).

Principal Business: Individual life insurance (56%), individual annuities (42%), and group retirement contracts (1%).

Principal Investments: NonCMO investment grade bonds (52%), mortgages in good standing (17%), CMOs and structured securities (14%), noninv. grade bonds (3%), and policy loans (2%).

Investments in Affiliates: None

Group Affiliation: National Life Group

Licensed in: All states except NY, PR

Commenced Business: January 1956

Address: 15455 Dallas Parkway, Addison, TX 75001

Phone: (800) 579-2878 **Domicile State:** TX **NAIC Code:** 65528

Data Date	Rating	RACR #1	RACR #2	Total Assets ($mil)	Capital ($mil)	Net Premium ($mil)	Net Income ($mil)
2021	B	2.50	1.25	27,512.1	1,973.9	3,275.6	307.7
2020	B	2.19	1.08	25,868.5	1,659.4	2,639.4	162.3
2019	B	2.16	1.07	22,877.6	1,515.6	2,629.5	289.2
2018	B	1.97	0.97	19,775.6	1,241.1	2,103.4	-193.8
2017	B	2.33	1.14	18,743.4	1,207.6	1,769.3	61.2

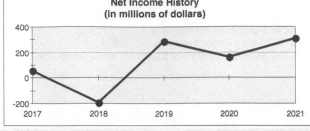

Net Income History
(in millions of dollars)

LIFE OF THE SOUTH INS CO   C-   Fair

Major Rating Factors: Fair capitalization for the current period (4.8 on a scale of 0 to 10) based on fair risk adjusted capital (severe loss scenario) reflecting some improvement over results in 2017. Fair overall results on stability tests (3.2) including negative cash flow from operations for 2021, weak risk adjusted capital in prior years and excessive premium growth. Weak profitability (2.9) with investment income below regulatory standards in relation to interest assumptions of reserves.

Other Rating Factors: Good quality investment portfolio (5.8). Excellent liquidity (7.8).

Principal Business: Credit health insurance (45%), credit life insurance (40%), and individual health insurance (14%).

Principal Investments: NonCMO investment grade bonds (35%), common & preferred stock (28%), CMOs and structured securities (25%), and cash (4%).

Investments in Affiliates: 20%

Group Affiliation: Tiptree Inc

Licensed in: All states except CA, NY, WI, PR

Commenced Business: January 1982

Address: 2350 Prince Ave Bldg 1 Ste 4, Athens, GA 30603

Phone: (904) 407-1097 **Domicile State:** GA **NAIC Code:** 97691

Data Date	Rating	RACR #1	RACR #2	Total Assets ($mil)	Capital ($mil)	Net Premium ($mil)	Net Income ($mil)
2021	C-	0.85	0.72	143.9	31.3	79.6	0.4
2020	C	0.68	0.56	146.1	22.9	62.5	1.9
2019	C	0.75	0.60	131.2	21.7	72.3	0.7
2018	C	0.79	0.63	111.0	22.8	65.2	2.3
2017	C	0.66	0.48	103.0	19.3	62.5	4.6

Risk-Adjusted Capital Ratio #2
(Severe Loss Scenario)

LIFECARE ASSURANCE CO   C   Fair

Major Rating Factors: Fair quality investment portfolio (3.2 on a scale of 0 to 10) with large holdings of BBB rated bonds in addition to significant exposure to junk bonds. Fair profitability (3.9) with investment income below regulatory standards in relation to interest assumptions of reserves. Fair overall results on stability tests (4.2) including fair risk adjusted capital in prior years.

Other Rating Factors: Good capitalization (5.7) based on good risk adjusted capital (moderate loss scenario). Excellent liquidity (8.7).

Principal Business: Reinsurance (100%).

Principal Investments: NonCMO investment grade bonds (67%), CMOs and structured securities (24%), noninv. grade bonds (3%), and mortgages in good standing (2%).

Investments in Affiliates: None

Group Affiliation: 21st Century Life & Health Co Inc

Licensed in: All states except CT, FL, MN, NH, NY, RI, SC, WY, PR

Commenced Business: July 1980

Address: 8601 N Scottsdale Road Ste 300, Scottsdale, AZ 85253

Phone: (818) 887-4436 **Domicile State:** AZ **NAIC Code:** 91898

Data Date	Rating	RACR #1	RACR #2	Total Assets ($mil)	Capital ($mil)	Net Premium ($mil)	Net Income ($mil)
2021	C	1.48	0.75	2,933.0	100.0	198.5	7.2
2020	C	1.62	0.80	2,813.5	109.0	185.4	33.4
2019	C	1.26	0.65	2,673.9	73.6	178.4	12.4
2018	C	1.14	0.58	2,544.6	61.9	170.4	-2.1
2017	C	1.07	0.57	2,438.4	64.5	238.4	-18.7

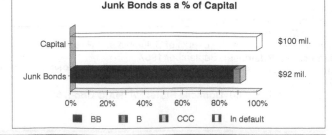

Junk Bonds as a % of Capital

LIFEMAP ASR CO   B-   Good

Major Rating Factors: Good liquidity (6.7 on a scale of 0 to 10) with sufficient resources to handle a spike in claims. Good overall results on stability tests (5.3) despite negative cash flow from operations for 2021. Strengths include good financial support from affiliation with Regence Group, excellent operational trends and excellent risk diversification. Fair quality investment portfolio (4.9).

Other Rating Factors: Fair profitability (4.0) with operating losses during 2021. Strong capitalization (8.5) based on excellent risk adjusted capital (severe loss scenario).

Principal Business: Group health insurance (57%), group life insurance (38%), individual health insurance (4%), and reinsurance (1%).

Principal Investments: NonCMO investment grade bonds (39%), CMOs and structured securities (32%), common & preferred stock (26%), and cash (2%).

Investments in Affiliates: 2%

Group Affiliation: Regence Group

Licensed in: AK, AZ, CA, ID, MT, OR, RI, UT, WA, WY

Commenced Business: July 1966

Address: 100 SW MARKET STREET, PORTLAND, OR 97201

Phone: (503) 225-6069 **Domicile State:** OR **NAIC Code:** 97985

Data Date	Rating	RACR #1	RACR #2	Total Assets ($mil)	Capital ($mil)	Net Premium ($mil)	Net Income ($mil)
2021	B-	2.83	2.02	107.2	61.7	68.9	-0.2
2020	B-	2.68	1.92	106.6	60.0	72.5	2.2
2019	B-	2.38	1.72	103.6	55.7	76.5	3.9
2018	B-	1.96	1.44	94.2	48.0	80.1	-0.6
2017	B-	1.92	1.40	97.2	47.6	84.3	-0.2

Regence Group Composite Group Rating: B Largest Group Members	Assets ($mil)	Rating
USABLE LIFE	503	B+
LIFEMAP ASR CO	107	B-

LIFESECURE INS CO   B-   Good

Major Rating Factors: Good overall results on stability tests (5.1 on a scale of 0 to 10). Stability strengths include excellent operational trends and excellent risk diversification. Good profitability (5.0) although investment income, in comparison to reserve requirements, is below regulatory standards. Fair quality investment portfolio (4.3).

Other Rating Factors: Strong capitalization (7.4) based on excellent risk adjusted capital (severe loss scenario). Excellent liquidity (9.1).

Principal Business: Individual health insurance (67%), reinsurance (28%), individual life insurance (4%), and group health insurance (1%).

Principal Investments: NonCMO investment grade bonds (86%), CMOs and structured securities (7%), noninv. grade bonds (5%), and cash (2%).

Investments in Affiliates: None

Group Affiliation: Blue Cross Blue Shield of Michigan

Licensed in: All states except NY, PR

Commenced Business: July 1954

Address: 10559 Citation Drive Suite 300, Brighton, MI 48116

Phone: (810) 220-7700 **Domicile State:** MI **NAIC Code:** 77720

Data Date	Rating	RACR #1	RACR #2	Total Assets ($mil)	Capital ($mil)	Net Premium ($mil)	Net Income ($mil)
2021	B-	2.25	1.28	582.7	55.4	93.3	2.9
2020	C	2.57	1.61	523.4	53.1	85.7	1.0
2019	D+	2.46	1.59	467.1	48.0	82.3	0.8
2018	D	2.47	1.60	416.0	46.9	81.5	0.9
2017	D	2.00	1.75	366.3	46.3	72.5	-3.4

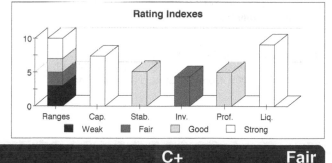

Rating Indexes

LINCOLN BENEFIT LIFE CO   C+   Fair

Major Rating Factors: Fair overall capitalization (4.9 on a scale of 0 to 10) based on mixed results -- excessive policy leverage mitigated by fair risk adjusted capital (moderate loss scenario). Fair quality investment portfolio (3.6) with large holdings of BBB rated bonds in addition to moderate junk bond exposure. Fair overall results on stability tests (4.8) including negative cash flow from operations for 2021, fair risk adjusted capital in prior years.

Other Rating Factors: Good liquidity (5.6). Excellent profitability (8.4) with operating gains in each of the last five years.

Principal Business: Individual life insurance (87%), individual health insurance (4%), individual annuities (3%), reinsurance (3%), and group life insurance (2%).

Principal Investments: NonCMO investment grade bonds (57%), CMOs and structured securities (21%), mortgages in good standing (8%), common & preferred stock (4%), and misc. investments (7%).

Investments in Affiliates: 2%

Group Affiliation: Resolution Life Holdings Inc

Licensed in: All states except NY, PR

Commenced Business: October 1938

Address: 1221 N STREET SUITE 200, LINCOLN, NE 68508

Phone: (888) 503-8110 **Domicile State:** NE **NAIC Code:** 65595

Data Date	Rating	RACR #1	RACR #2	Total Assets ($mil)	Capital ($mil)	Net Premium ($mil)	Net Income ($mil)
2021	C+	0.99	0.56	12,067.4	436.8	-156.4	56.5
2020	C+	0.99	0.57	11,631.9	416.3	277.7	45.2
2019	C+	1.02	0.61	9,172.9	352.6	-913.4	34.1
2018	C+	0.96	0.57	10,462.5	379.9	80.1	35.7
2017	C+	1.04	0.60	11,231.3	425.8	111.0	64.5

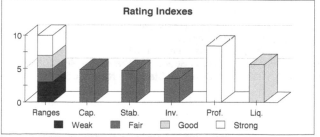

Rating Indexes

LINCOLN HERITAGE LIFE INS CO   B-   Good

Major Rating Factors: Good quality investment portfolio (6.6 on a scale of 0 to 10) despite mixed results such as: minimal exposure to mortgages and substantial holdings of BBB bonds but minimal holdings in junk bonds. Good liquidity (5.3) with sufficient resources to handle a spike in claims as well as a significant increase in policy surrenders. Good overall results on stability tests (5.1) excellent operational trends and excellent risk diversification.

Other Rating Factors: Weak profitability (2.7) with investment income below regulatory standards in relation to interest assumptions of reserves. Strong capitalization (7.2) based on excellent risk adjusted capital (severe loss scenario).

Principal Business: Individual life insurance (98%) and reinsurance (1%).

Principal Investments: NonCMO investment grade bonds (42%), CMOs and structured securities (31%), cash (8%), policy loans (7%), and misc. investments (8%).

Investments in Affiliates: None
Group Affiliation: Londen Ins Group
Licensed in: All states except NY, PR
Commenced Business: October 1963
Address: 920 S Spring St, Springfield, IL 62704
Phone: (602) 957-1650 **Domicile State:** IL **NAIC Code:** 65927

Data Date	Rating	RACR #1	RACR #2	Total Assets ($mil)	Capital ($mil)	Net Premium ($mil)	Net Income ($mil)
2021	B-	2.07	1.13	1,118.1	89.9	374.2	12.4
2020	B-	2.11	1.14	1,144.6	91.5	375.0	-2.1
2019	B-	2.21	1.20	1,092.3	94.3	360.8	8.0
2018	B-	2.21	1.19	1,033.9	89.6	348.7	4.0
2017	B-	2.24	1.22	970.0	88.0	340.5	1.8

Adverse Trends In Operations

Decrease in capital during 2020 (3%)
Decrease in capital during 2017 (21%)

LINCOLN LIFE & ANNUITY CO OF NY   B   Good

Major Rating Factors: Good quality investment portfolio (6.1 on a scale of 0 to 10) despite significant exposure to mortgages . Mortgage default rate has been low. large holdings of BBB rated bonds in addition to small junk bond holdings. Good overall profitability (5.3). Return on equity has been fair, averaging 8.2%. Good liquidity (5.3).

Other Rating Factors: Good overall results on stability tests (5.5) excellent operational trends and excellent risk diversification. Strong capitalization (8.2) based on excellent risk adjusted capital (severe loss scenario).

Principal Business: Individual annuities (29%), group retirement contracts (29%), individual life insurance (22%), reinsurance (9%), and other lines (11%).

Principal Investments: NonCMO investment grade bonds (77%), mortgages in good standing (11%), CMOs and structured securities (7%), policy loans (2%), and noninv. grade bonds (2%).

Investments in Affiliates: None
Group Affiliation: Lincoln National Corp
Licensed in: All states except PR
Commenced Business: December 1897
Address: 100 Madison Street Suite 1860, Syracuse, NY 13202-2802
Phone: (336) 691-3000 **Domicile State:** NY **NAIC Code:** 62057

Data Date	Rating	RACR #1	RACR #2	Total Assets ($mil)	Capital ($mil)	Net Premium ($mil)	Net Income ($mil)
2021	B	3.54	1.83	17,305.7	991.3	824.6	41.1
2020	B	3.67	1.88	16,478.3	996.5	696.1	23.4
2019	B	4.14	2.11	15,653.8	1,105.6	741.8	98.9
2018	B	4.26	2.16	14,482.2	1,117.6	738.6	80.2
2017	B	4.41	2.20	14,783.9	1,187.3	1,338.2	236.7

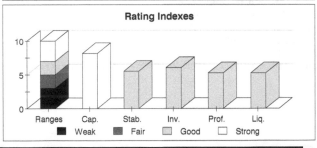

Rating Indexes

LINCOLN NATIONAL LIFE INS CO   C+   Fair

Major Rating Factors: Fair overall results on stability tests (4.6 on a scale of 0 to 10) including negative cash flow from operations for 2021. Good overall capitalization (6.4) based on good risk adjusted capital (severe loss scenario). However, capital levels have fluctuated somewhat during past years. Good quality investment portfolio (6.3).

Other Rating Factors: Good liquidity (5.6). Weak profitability (2.3) with operating losses during 2021.

Principal Business: Individual annuities (42%), individual life insurance (23%), group retirement contracts (15%), group health insurance (10%), and other lines (10%).

Principal Investments: NonCMO investment grade bonds (64%), mortgages in good standing (12%), CMOs and structured securities (8%), common & preferred stock (4%), and misc. investments (7%).

Investments in Affiliates: 7%
Group Affiliation: Lincoln National Corp
Licensed in: All states except NY
Commenced Business: September 1905
Address: 1300 South Clinton Street, Fort Wayne, IN 46802-3425
Phone: (800) 237-3813 **Domicile State:** IN **NAIC Code:** 65676

Data Date	Rating	RACR #1	RACR #2	Total Assets ($mil)	Capital ($mil)	Net Premium ($mil)	Net Income ($mil)
2021	C+	1.33	0.92	317,000	8,447.1	17,319.5	-576.4
2020	B	1.21	0.87	295,000	8,503.4	23,004.1	104.9
2019	B	1.12	0.83	267,000	8,154.5	25,549.2	398.9
2018	B	1.07	0.80	238,000	8,079.7	25,384.3	1,019.6
2017	B	1.32	0.92	240,000	7,845.4	17,337.1	1,390.1

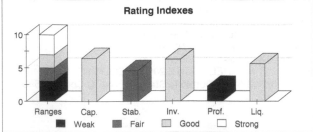

Rating Indexes

LOCOMOTIVE ENGRS&COND MUT PROT ASSN   B   Good

Major Rating Factors: Good overall profitability (6.7 on a scale of 0 to 10). Good overall results on stability tests (5.7). Stability strengths include excellent operational trends and good risk diversification. Fair quality investment portfolio (3.4).
Other Rating Factors: Strong capitalization (10.0) based on excellent risk adjusted capital (severe loss scenario). Excellent liquidity (7.4).
Principal Business: Individual life insurance (100%).
Principal Investments: Common & preferred stock (46%), nonCMO investment grade bonds (46%), and cash (1%).
Investments in Affiliates: None
Group Affiliation: None
Licensed in: MI, NE, NM, TX
Commenced Business: July 1910
Address: 4000 Town Center Suite 1250, Southfield, MI 48075-1407
Phone: (800) 514-0010 **Domicile State:** MI **NAIC Code:** 87920

Data Date	Rating	RACR #1	RACR #2	Total Assets ($mil)	Capital ($mil)	Net Premium ($mil)	Net Income ($mil)
2021	B	6.78	4.05	100.1	85.7	17.9	4.8
2020	B	6.85	4.08	88.5	75.2	18.5	5.4
2019	B+	8.79	5.20	83.4	70.4	19.6	5.4
2018	B+	8.25	5.32	73.2	61.9	19.6	3.4
2017	B+	7.98	4.90	72.2	59.3	19.4	0.7

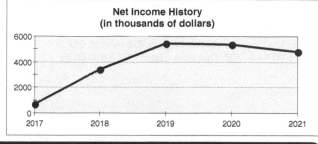

Net Income History
(in thousands of dollars)

LOYAL AMERICAN LIFE INS CO   B   Good

Major Rating Factors: Good overall results on stability tests (5.6 on a scale of 0 to 10). Stability strengths include excellent operational trends and excellent risk diversification. Good current capitalization (6.4) based on good risk adjusted capital (severe loss scenario), although results have slipped from the excellent range over the last year. Good quality investment portfolio (6.1).
Other Rating Factors: Good overall profitability (6.4). Good liquidity (6.8).
Principal Business: Individual health insurance (76%), reinsurance (21%), individual life insurance (2%), and group health insurance (1%).
Principal Investments: NonCMO investment grade bonds (77%), common & preferred stock (21%), and noninv. grade bonds (1%).
Investments in Affiliates: 21%
Group Affiliation: CIGNA Corp
Licensed in: All states except NY, PR
Commenced Business: July 1955
Address: 1300 East Ninth Street, Cleveland, OH 44114
Phone: (512) 451-2224 **Domicile State:** OH **NAIC Code:** 65722

Data Date	Rating	RACR #1	RACR #2	Total Assets ($mil)	Capital ($mil)	Net Premium ($mil)	Net Income ($mil)
2021	B	1.07	0.93	403.0	133.6	363.3	18.9
2020	B	1.19	1.04	411.5	160.0	374.0	26.9
2019	B-	1.14	0.99	367.9	134.9	371.9	14.0
2018	B-	1.07	0.92	338.7	116.8	345.3	8.5
2017	B-	0.95	0.82	310.6	96.6	311.5	9.1

Adverse Trends in Operations

Increase in policy surrenders from 2019 to 2020 (124%)
Increase in policy surrenders from 2018 to 2019 (196%)
Increase in policy surrenders from 2017 to 2018 (494%)
Increase in policy surrenders from 2016 to 2017 (5060%)

LUMICO LIFE INSURANCE CO   C   Fair

Major Rating Factors: Weak profitability (1.9 on a scale of 0 to 10) with operating losses during 2021. Return on equity has been low, averaging -4.9%. Weak overall results on stability tests (2.7) including weak results on operational trends and negative cash flow from operations for 2021. Strong capitalization (10.0) based on excellent risk adjusted capital (severe loss scenario).
Other Rating Factors: High quality investment portfolio (7.5). Excellent liquidity (7.4).
Principal Business: Individual life insurance (61%) and individual health insurance (38%).
Principal Investments: NonCMO investment grade bonds (76%), CMOs and structured securities (18%), and common & preferred stock (5%).
Investments in Affiliates: None
Group Affiliation: Swiss Re Limited
Licensed in: All states except NY, PR
Commenced Business: May 1966
Address: 5025 N CENTRAL AVE SUITE 546, JEFFERSON CITY, MO 65101
Phone: (877) 794-7773 **Domicile State:** MO **NAIC Code:** 73504

Data Date	Rating	RACR #1	RACR #2	Total Assets ($mil)	Capital ($mil)	Net Premium ($mil)	Net Income ($mil)
2021	C	8.75	6.35	201.9	85.3	21.3	-10.7
2020	C	10.28	9.25	152.4	97.1	16.2	3.9
2019	C	10.57	9.51	127.5	97.5	9.5	-12.8
2018	C	6.43	5.79	60.3	46.1	5.5	-0.1
2017	C	6.15	5.53	53.1	42.2	3.6	-1.2

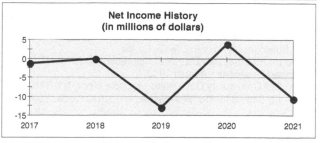

Net Income History
(in millions of dollars)

M LIFE INS CO *   B+   Good

Major Rating Factors: Good overall results on stability tests (6.8 on a scale of 0 to 10) despite excessive premium growth. Other stability subfactors include excellent operational trends and excellent risk diversification. Fair profitability (4.4) with investment income below regulatory standards in relation to interest assumptions of reserves. Strong capitalization (10.0) based on excellent risk adjusted capital (severe loss scenario).

Other Rating Factors: High quality investment portfolio (8.5). Excellent liquidity (9.0).

Principal Business: Reinsurance (100%).

Principal Investments: NonCMO investment grade bonds (80%), CMOs and structured securities (15%), and cash (2%).

Investments in Affiliates: None

Group Affiliation: M Financial Holdings Inc

Licensed in: AZ, CO, DE, IA, MI, NE, NJ, OH

Commenced Business: December 1981

Address: The Corp Co 1675 Broadway, Centennial, CO 80112

Phone: (503) 414-7336 **Domicile State:** CO **NAIC Code:** 93580

Data Date	Rating	RACR #1	RACR #2	Total Assets ($mil)	Capital ($mil)	Net Premium ($mil)	Net Income ($mil)
2021	B+	7.64	5.06	479.6	168.1	539.9	39.6
2020	B+	8.61	5.61	382.5	161.3	340.2	42.7
2019	B+	7.79	5.11	395.4	141.4	426.2	45.5
2018	B+	6.86	4.44	487.4	131.9	421.1	48.6
2017	B	6.48	4.29	330.4	107.0	473.0	37.9

Adverse Trends in Operations

Decrease in asset base during 2020 (3%)
Decrease in premium volume from 2019 to 2020 (20%)
Decrease in asset base during 2019 (19%)
Decrease in premium volume from 2017 to 2018 (11%)
Increase in policy surrenders from 2016 to 2017 (109%)

MADISON NATIONAL LIFE INS CO INC   B   Good

Major Rating Factors: Good overall profitability (5.3 on a scale of 0 to 10). Return on equity has been good over the last five years, averaging 12.6%. Fair overall results on stability tests (4.1). Strong overall capitalization (10.0) based on excellent risk adjusted capital (severe loss scenario). Nevertheless, capital levels have fluctuated during prior years.

Other Rating Factors: High quality investment portfolio (8.6). Excellent liquidity (9.0).

Principal Business: Group health insurance (62%), group life insurance (24%), individual life insurance (5%), individual annuities (5%), and reinsurance (3%).

Principal Investments: NonCMO investment grade bonds (87%) and cash (3%).

Investments in Affiliates: None

Group Affiliation: Geneve Holdings Inc

Licensed in: All states except NY, PR

Commenced Business: March 1962

Address: 1241 John Q Hammons Drive, Madison, WI 53717-1929

Phone: (800) 356-9601 **Domicile State:** WI **NAIC Code:** 65781

Data Date	Rating	RACR #1	RACR #2	Total Assets ($mil)	Capital ($mil)	Net Premium ($mil)	Net Income ($mil)
2021	B	4.40	3.28	236.9	92.9	112.5	12.4
2020	C+	4.13	3.01	210.0	86.1	108.0	14.4
2019	C+	4.32	3.14	201.9	83.3	100.4	16.5
2018	B	1.44	1.37	337.4	196.0	93.9	16.0
2017	B-	1.48	1.41	326.3	179.6	87.9	12.8

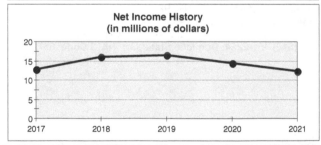

Net Income History
(in millions of dollars)

MANHATTAN LIFE INS CO   B   Good

Major Rating Factors: Good quality investment portfolio (6.1 on a scale of 0 to 10) despite mixed results such as: minimal exposure to mortgages and large holdings of BBB rated bonds but small junk bond holdings. Good overall profitability (5.4) although investment income, in comparison to reserve requirements, is below regulatory standards. Good liquidity (6.2).

Other Rating Factors: Fair overall results on stability tests (4.0) including negative cash flow from operations for 2021. Strong capitalization (7.3) based on excellent risk adjusted capital (severe loss scenario).

Principal Business: Individual health insurance (69%), individual annuities (22%), individual life insurance (5%), group health insurance (3%), and reinsurance (1%).

Principal Investments: NonCMO investment grade bonds (67%), CMOs and structured securities (11%), common & preferred stock (7%), mortgages in good standing (6%), and misc. investments (6%).

Investments in Affiliates: 5%

Group Affiliation: Manhattan Life Group Inc

Licensed in: All states, the District of Columbia and Puerto Rico

Commenced Business: August 1850

Address: 225 Community Drive Suite 11, Great Neck, NY 11021

Phone: (713) 529-0045 **Domicile State:** NY **NAIC Code:** 65870

Data Date	Rating	RACR #1	RACR #2	Total Assets ($mil)	Capital ($mil)	Net Premium ($mil)	Net Income ($mil)
2021	B	1.74	1.21	632.6	77.6	68.5	10.1
2020	B	1.49	1.02	692.7	68.2	144.5	8.2
2019	B	1.55	1.08	647.3	66.0	93.7	13.0
2018	B	1.39	0.98	633.3	59.0	79.8	12.3
2017	B	1.30	0.94	581.1	54.1	90.1	8.6

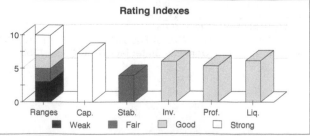

Rating Indexes

MANHATTANLIFE INSURANCE AND ANNUITY COMPANY   C+   Fair

Major Rating Factors: Fair overall results on stability tests (4.8 on a scale of 0 to 10) including fair risk adjusted capital in prior years. Good current capitalization (5.5) based on good risk adjusted capital (severe loss scenario) reflecting some improvement over results in 2017. Good quality investment portfolio (5.2).
Other Rating Factors: Good overall profitability (6.7). Good liquidity (6.5).
Principal Business: Individual health insurance (60%), reinsurance (17%), group health insurance (16%), and individual life insurance (7%).
Principal Investments: NonCMO investment grade bonds (55%), common & preferred stock (27%), mortgages in good standing (5%), real estate (3%), and misc. investments (5%).
Investments in Affiliates: 27%
Group Affiliation: Manhattan Life Group Inc
Licensed in: All states except NY, PR
Commenced Business: September 1963
Address: 425 W Capitol Ave Ste 1800, Houston, TX 77092
Phone: (713) 529-0045 **Domicile State:** AR **NAIC Code:** 61883

Data Date	Rating	RACR #1	RACR #2	Total Assets ($mil)	Capital ($mil)	Net Premium ($mil)	Net Income ($mil)
2021	C+	0.91	0.81	792.0	219.4	280.7	9.6
2020	C+	0.89	0.79	761.1	195.5	249.1	16.9
2019	C	0.92	0.82	737.8	179.4	237.7	7.2
2018	C	0.82	0.73	700.5	153.7	251.4	19.3
2017	C	0.62	0.57	390.8	102.4	113.8	4.3

Rating Indexes

(Chart: Ranges, Cap., Stab., Inv., Prof., Liq. — Weak, Fair, Good, Strong)

MAPFRE LIFE INS CO OF PR   B   Good

Major Rating Factors: Good overall results on stability tests (5.1 on a scale of 0 to 10) despite fair financial strength of affiliated MAPFRE Ins Group and negative cash flow from operations for 2021. Other stability subfactors include good operational trends and excellent risk diversification. Good overall profitability (5.7) despite operating losses during 2021. Good liquidity (6.6).
Other Rating Factors: Strong capitalization (8.6) based on excellent risk adjusted capital (severe loss scenario). High quality investment portfolio (8.3).
Principal Business: Group health insurance (89%), individual health insurance (10%), individual life insurance (1%), group life insurance (1%), and credit life insurance (1%).
Principal Investments: NonCMO investment grade bonds (89%), cash (8%), and common & preferred stock (3%).
Investments in Affiliates: None
Group Affiliation: MAPFRE Ins Group
Licensed in: PR
Commenced Business: February 1984
Address: Urb Ind Tres Monjitas 297 Ave, San Juan, PR 00918-1410
Phone: (787) 250-6500 **Domicile State:** PR **NAIC Code:** 77054

Data Date	Rating	RACR #1	RACR #2	Total Assets ($mil)	Capital ($mil)	Net Premium ($mil)	Net Income ($mil)
2021	B	2.63	2.04	59.3	29.9	51.7	-1.2
2020	C+	2.71	2.07	64.6	34.2	57.2	6.0
2019	C-	N/A	N/A	59.2	29.0	65.6	0.3
2018	C-	1.78	1.41	59.3	28.5	80.1	1.8
2017	D+	N/A	N/A	61.6	26.2	90.7	4.3

MAPFRE Ins Group
Composite Group Rating: C+
Largest Group Members

	Assets ($mil)	Rating
COMMERCE INS CO	2207	B-
MAPFRE PRAICO INS CO	429	C-
AMERICAN COMMERCE INS CO	346	B-
CITATION INS CO (MA)	217	C+
COMMERCE WEST INS CO	176	C

MASSACHUSETTS MUTUAL LIFE INS CO   B   Good

Major Rating Factors: Good quality investment portfolio (6.0 on a scale of 0 to 10) despite large holdings of BBB rated bonds in addition to moderate junk bond exposure. Exposure to mortgages is significant, but the mortgage default rate has been low. Good liquidity (6.4) with sufficient resources to handle a spike in claims as well as a significant increase in policy surrenders. Fair overall results on stability tests (4.2) including excessive premium growth.
Other Rating Factors: Strong capitalization (7.1) based on excellent risk adjusted capital (severe loss scenario). Excellent profitability (7.3) despite operating losses during 2021.
Principal Business: Group retirement contracts (39%), individual life insurance (36%), individual annuities (19%), reinsurance (3%), and individual health insurance (2%).
Principal Investments: NonCMO investment grade bonds (42%), common & preferred stock (12%), mortgages in good standing (11%), CMOs and structured securities (9%), and misc. investments (19%).
Investments in Affiliates: 16%
Group Affiliation: Massachusetts Mutual Group
Licensed in: All states, the District of Columbia and Puerto Rico
Commenced Business: August 1851
Address: 1295 STATE STREET, SPRINGFIELD, MA 1111
Phone: (Phone number unavailable) **Domicile State:** MA **NAIC Code:** 65935

Data Date	Rating	RACR #1	RACR #2	Total Assets ($mil)	Capital ($mil)	Net Premium ($mil)	Net Income ($mil)
2021	B	1.41	1.09	315,000	26,979.3	19,868.0	-216.4
2020	B	1.60	1.19	300,000	24,327.4	10,275.0	215.9
2019	A-	1.61	1.17	268,000	18,892.9	22,752.2	424.2
2018	A-	1.69	1.19	244,000	15,609.8	22,905.7	-821.3
2017	A-	1.42	1.05	240,000	15,705.2	17,461.6	52.1

Rating Indexes

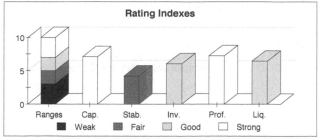

(Chart: Ranges, Cap., Stab., Inv., Prof., Liq. — Weak, Fair, Good, Strong)

MCS LIFE INS CO
D-   **Weak**

Major Rating Factors: Weak liquidity (1.4 on a scale of 0 to 10) as a spike in claims may stretch capacity. Weak overall results on stability tests (1.0) including negative cash flow from operations for 2021. Fair current capitalization (3.2) based on mixed results -- excessive policy leverage mitigated by fair risk adjusted capital (severe loss scenario), although results have slipped from the excellent range over the last year.

Other Rating Factors: Good overall profitability (5.6). High quality investment portfolio (9.5).

Principal Business: Group health insurance (92%), individual health insurance (7%), and group life insurance (1%).

Principal Investments: Cash (51%) and nonCMO investment grade bonds (49%).

Investments in Affiliates: None

Group Affiliation: Medical Card System Inc

Licensed in: PR

Commenced Business: January 1996

Address: Ste 900 255 Ponce de Leon Ave, San Juan, PR 917

Phone: (787) 758-2500   **Domicile State:** PR   **NAIC Code:** 60030

Data Date	Rating	RACR #1	RACR #2	Total Assets ($mil)	Capital ($mil)	Net Premium ($mil)	Net Income ($mil)
2021	D-	0.65	0.53	90.5	36.1	290.0	2.2
2020	D-	1.40	1.15	109.4	59.4	282.6	18.2
2019	D-	N/A	N/A	108.4	51.1	277.0	13.5
2018	D-	N/A	N/A	94.6	45.2	290.4	4.2
2017	D-	0.89	0.73	97.5	43.3	310.0	22.1

Rating Indexes

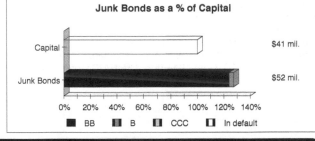

MEDAMERICA INS CO
C   **Fair**

Major Rating Factors: Fair capitalization for the current period (4.0 on a scale of 0 to 10) based on mixed results -- excessive policy leverage mitigated by good risk adjusted capital (moderate loss scenario) reflecting some improvement over results in 2018. Fair overall results on stability tests (3.8) including weak risk adjusted capital in prior years, negative cash flow from operations for 2021. Good liquidity (6.9).

Other Rating Factors: Low quality investment portfolio (2.6). Weak profitability (0.9) with operating losses during 2021.

Principal Business: N/A

Principal Investments: NonCMO investment grade bonds (69%), common & preferred stock (6%), noninv. grade bonds (5%), mortgages in good standing (4%), and CMOs and structured securities (4%).

Investments in Affiliates: 1%

Group Affiliation: Lifetime Healthcare Inc

Licensed in: All states except FL, NY, PR

Commenced Business: August 1966

Address: 651 Holiday Drive Foster Plaza, Pittsburgh, PA 15520-2740

Phone: (585) 238-4464   **Domicile State:** PA   **NAIC Code:** 69515

Data Date	Rating	RACR #1	RACR #2	Total Assets ($mil)	Capital ($mil)	Net Premium ($mil)	Net Income ($mil)
2021	C	1.18	0.63	1,146.3	40.5	-41.2	-70.1
2020	C	1.25	0.62	1,156.9	38.3	-45.6	-34.2
2019	C	0.98	0.49	1,126.9	28.8	-52.5	-102.8
2018	C	0.85	0.47	1,199.8	31.0	57.3	-134.6
2017	C	0.99	0.54	960.2	31.2	62.2	-8.7

Junk Bonds as a % of Capital

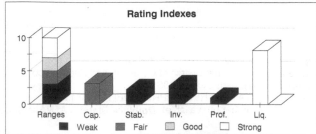

Capital — $41 mil.

Junk Bonds — $52 mil.

MEDAMERICA INS CO OF NEW YORK
D+   **Weak**

Major Rating Factors: Low quality investment portfolio (2.7 on a scale of 0 to 10) containing substantial holdings of BBB bonds in addition to moderate junk bond exposure. Weak profitability (0.9) with operating losses during 2021. Return on equity has been low, averaging -137.7%. Weak overall results on stability tests (2.2) including weak risk adjusted capital in prior years.

Other Rating Factors: Fair capitalization (3.2) based on fair risk adjusted capital (moderate loss scenario). Excellent liquidity (8.1).

Principal Business: Individual health insurance (80%) and group health insurance (20%).

Principal Investments: NonCMO investment grade bonds (72%), common & preferred stock (16%), mortgages in good standing (3%), noninv. grade bonds (2%), and misc. investments (7%).

Investments in Affiliates: None

Group Affiliation: Lifetime Healthcare Inc

Licensed in: NY

Commenced Business: November 1987

Address: 165 Court Street, Rochester, NY 14647

Phone: (585) 238-4351   **Domicile State:** NY   **NAIC Code:** 83437

Data Date	Rating	RACR #1	RACR #2	Total Assets ($mil)	Capital ($mil)	Net Premium ($mil)	Net Income ($mil)
2021	D+	0.77	0.45	1,128.1	28.1	44.2	-22.7
2020	D+	0.77	0.45	1,062.3	26.7	46.5	-21.0
2019	C	0.69	0.41	996.9	24.2	47.8	-23.3
2018	C	1.22	0.71	931.0	22.0	44.7	-110.8
2017	D-	1.22	0.73	788.9	18.1	43.8	-18.4

Rating Indexes

MEDICO CORP LIFE INS CO   B-   Good

Major Rating Factors: Fair overall results on stability tests (4.9 on a scale of 0 to 10) including fair financial strength of affiliated American Enterprise Mutual Holding. Strong capitalization (8.0) based on excellent risk adjusted capital (severe loss scenario). Moreover, capital levels have been consistently high over the last five years. High quality investment portfolio (7.6).

Other Rating Factors: Excellent profitability (8.1) with operating gains in each of the last five years. Excellent liquidity (7.5).

Principal Business: Individual health insurance (100%).

Principal Investments: NonCMO investment grade bonds (68%), CMOs and structured securities (14%), cash (13%), noninv. grade bonds (2%), and common & preferred stock (1%).

Investments in Affiliates: None

Group Affiliation: American Enterprise Mutual Holding

Licensed in: All states except CA, CT, MA, NH, NJ, NY, PR

Commenced Business: May 1960

Address: 1010 North 102nd St Ste 201, Des Moines, IA 50309

Phone: (804) 354-7000 **Domicile State:** NE **NAIC Code:** 79987

Data Date	Rating	RACR #1	RACR #2	Total Assets ($mil)	Capital ($mil)	Net Premium ($mil)	Net Income ($mil)
2021	B-	3.60	3.24	72.9	27.8	0.0	0.5
2020	B-	4.27	3.84	47.0	27.1	0.0	0.6
2019	B-	3.96	3.57	48.4	25.8	0.0	0.4
2018	B-	3.22	2.89	73.5	25.0	0.0	0.3
2017	A-	3.01	2.71	65.6	22.3	0.0	0.3

American Enterprise Mutual Holding Composite Group Rating: C Largest Group Members	Assets ($mil)	Rating
GREAT WESTERN INS CO	1344	C-
AMERICAN REPUBLIC INS CO	1267	B-
MEDICO INS CO	57	B-
MEDICO CORP LIFE INS CO	47	B-
AMERICAN REPUBLIC CORP INS CO	15	C

MEDICO INS CO   B-   Good

Major Rating Factors: Fair overall results on stability tests (4.0 on a scale of 0 to 10) including fair financial strength of affiliated American Enterprise Mutual Holding. Fair overall capitalization (4.0) based on excellent risk adjusted capital (severe loss scenario). Nevertheless, capital levels have fluctuated during prior years. Fair profitability (4.8).

Other Rating Factors: High quality investment portfolio (7.7). Excellent liquidity (7.1).

Principal Business: Individual health insurance (86%), group health insurance (13%), and individual life insurance (1%).

Principal Investments: NonCMO investment grade bonds (73%), CMOs and structured securities (19%), cash (6%), and common & preferred stock (1%).

Investments in Affiliates: None

Group Affiliation: American Enterprise Mutual Holding

Licensed in: All states except CT, NJ, NY, PR

Commenced Business: April 1930

Address: 1010 North 102nd St Ste 201, Des Moines, IA 50309

Phone: (800) 228-6080 **Domicile State:** NE **NAIC Code:** 31119

Data Date	Rating	RACR #1	RACR #2	Total Assets ($mil)	Capital ($mil)	Net Premium ($mil)	Net Income ($mil)
2021	B-	4.14	3.73	75.0	32.4	0.0	1.4
2020	B-	4.93	4.44	56.7	34.5	-5.5	1.3
2019	B-	4.80	4.32	52.7	32.8	0.4	1.3
2018	B-	4.59	4.13	83.7	37.7	0.5	7.1
2017	B	4.28	3.85	81.9	34.8	0.5	1.3

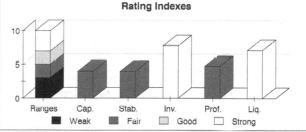

Rating Indexes

MEDMUTUAL LIFE INS CO   B-   Good

Major Rating Factors: Good liquidity (6.0 on a scale of 0 to 10) with sufficient resources to handle a spike in claims. Good overall results on stability tests (5.3) despite negative cash flow from operations for 2021 and excessive premium growth. Other stability subfactors include good operational trends and good risk diversification. Weak profitability (1.8) with operating losses during 2021. Return on equity has been low, averaging -1.6%.

Other Rating Factors: Strong capitalization (7.6) based on excellent risk adjusted capital (severe loss scenario). High quality investment portfolio (9.3).

Principal Business: Group life insurance (78%), group health insurance (19%), and individual health insurance (2%).

Principal Investments: NonCMO investment grade bonds (57%) and cash (11%).

Investments in Affiliates: None

Group Affiliation: Medical Mutual of Ohio

Licensed in: AZ, AR, CO, DC, DE, GA, IL, IN, IA, KS, KY, LA, MD, MI, MN, MS, MO, MT, NE, NV, NJ, NM, ND, OH, OK, OR, PA, SC, SD, TX, UT, VA, WV, WI, WY

Commenced Business: October 1955

Address: 2060 East Ninth Street, Cleveland, OH 44115-1355

Phone: (216) 687-7000 **Domicile State:** OH **NAIC Code:** 62375

Data Date	Rating	RACR #1	RACR #2	Total Assets ($mil)	Capital ($mil)	Net Premium ($mil)	Net Income ($mil)
2021	B-	1.81	1.39	60.0	33.2	39.9	-16.3
2020	B	2.26	1.73	45.9	34.6	31.2	1.0
2019	B	2.37	1.81	48.1	34.7	27.2	2.9
2018	B	2.51	1.92	44.9	31.8	27.2	3.9
2017	B	1.61	1.25	44.9	27.6	47.3	4.9

Adverse Trends in Operations
Decrease in asset base during 2020 (4%)
Change in premium mix from 2017 to 2018 (7.3%)
Decrease in premium volume from 2017 to 2018 (42%)
Change in premium mix from 2016 to 2017 (5.3%)

MEMBERS LIFE INS CO   B   Good

Major Rating Factors: Good overall results on stability tests (6.2 on a scale of 0 to 10). Stability strengths include excellent operational trends and excellent risk diversification. Good overall profitability (5.7) despite operating losses during 2021. Return on equity has been low, averaging 2.5%. Good liquidity (6.8) with sufficient resources to handle a spike in claims.

Other Rating Factors: Strong capitalization (8.0) based on excellent risk adjusted capital (severe loss scenario). High quality investment portfolio (9.0).

Principal Business: Individual annuities (99%) and individual life insurance (1%).

Principal Investments: NonCMO investment grade bonds (35%), CMOs and structured securities (6%), and cash (1%).

Investments in Affiliates: None

Group Affiliation: CUNA Mutual Ins Group

Licensed in: All states except NY, PR

Commenced Business: March 1976

Address: 2000 HERITAGE WAY, WAVERLY, IA 50677

Phone: (800) 356-2644 **Domicile State:** IA **NAIC Code:** 86126

Data Date	Rating	RACR #1	RACR #2	Total Assets ($mil)	Capital ($mil)	Net Premium ($mil)	Net Income ($mil)
2021	B	3.08	2.77	386.6	35.6	0.0	-0.7
2020	B	3.76	3.38	303.8	40.7	0.0	0.2
2019	B	3.89	3.50	244.5	40.0	0.0	1.2
2018	C+	4.12	3.71	164.7	39.4	0.0	0.4
2017	C	2.03	1.82	120.4	18.6	0.0	1.9

Adverse Trends in Operations

Decrease in capital during 2017 (20%)

MERIT LIFE INS CO   C   Fair

Major Rating Factors: Fair overall results on stability tests (4.1 on a scale of 0 to 10) including fair financial strength of affiliated Fortress Investment Group LLC and negative cash flow from operations for 2021. Fair quality investment portfolio (3.8) with large holdings of BBB rated bonds in addition to moderate junk bond exposure. Good liquidity (6.6).

Other Rating Factors: Weak profitability (2.4) with operating losses during 2021. Strong capitalization (8.0) based on excellent risk adjusted capital (severe loss scenario).

Principal Business: Individual life insurance (319%), credit life insurance (142%), credit health insurance (73%), group health insurance (5%), and individual annuities (1%).

Principal Investments: NonCMO investment grade bonds (62%), CMOs and structured securities (17%), noninv. grade bonds (13%), cash (3%), and common & preferred stock (2%).

Investments in Affiliates: None

Group Affiliation: Fortress Investment Group LLC

Licensed in: All states except AK, MA, NH, NY, VT, PR

Commenced Business: October 1957

Address: 601 NW 2ND ST, AUSTIN, TX 78701-3218

Phone: (800) 325-2147 **Domicile State:** TX **NAIC Code:** 65951

Data Date	Rating	RACR #1	RACR #2	Total Assets ($mil)	Capital ($mil)	Net Premium ($mil)	Net Income ($mil)
2021	C	3.67	3.31	56.9	25.0	0.0	-5.5
2020	C	3.58	3.23	60.2	25.0	0.0	-7.7
2019	C	2.93	1.83	59.2	20.2	-179.2	23.4
2018	B	8.57	4.85	351.4	94.1	-20.5	53.3
2017	B	4.95	2.70	442.2	79.1	49.6	36.6

Fortress Investment Group LLC
Composite Group Rating: C
Largest Group Members

	Assets ($mil)	Rating
ATHENE ANNUITY LIFE CO	76556	C
VENERABLE INS AND ANNTY CO	49488	C
ATHENE ANNUITY LIFE ASR CO	34398	C
ATHENE ANNUITY LIFE ASR CO OF NY	3532	B-
ASPEN AMERICAN INS CO	1248	C+

METROPOLITAN LIFE INS CO   B   Good

Major Rating Factors: Good quality investment portfolio (5.3 on a scale of 0 to 10) despite substantial holdings of BBB bonds in addition to junk bond exposure equal to 85% of capital. Exposure to mortgages is significant, but the mortgage default rate has been low. Good liquidity (6.8) with sufficient resources to handle a spike in claims as well as a significant increase in policy surrenders. Good overall results on stability tests (5.9) good operational trends, good risk adjusted capital for prior years and excellent risk diversification.

Other Rating Factors: Strong capitalization (7.4) based on excellent risk adjusted capital (severe loss scenario). Excellent profitability (8.4) with operating gains in each of the last five years.

Principal Business: Group life insurance (40%), group health insurance (28%), group retirement contracts (18%), individual life insurance (9%), and other lines (6%).

Principal Investments: NonCMO investment grade bonds (41%), mortgages in good standing (21%), CMOs and structured securities (17%), noninv. grade bonds (4%), and misc. investments (15%).

Investments in Affiliates: 4%

Group Affiliation: MetLife Inc

Licensed in: All states, the District of Columbia and Puerto Rico

Commenced Business: May 1867

Address: 200 Park Avenue, New York, NY 10166-0188

Phone: (212) 578-9000 **Domicile State:** NY **NAIC Code:** 65978

Data Date	Rating	RACR #1	RACR #2	Total Assets ($mil)	Capital ($mil)	Net Premium ($mil)	Net Income ($mil)
2021	B	2.48	1.26	404,000	11,803.8	22,761.2	3,512.7
2020	B	2.15	1.13	409,000	11,315.5	26,331.7	3,394.0
2019	B-	2.20	1.14	390,000	10,914.8	25,210.4	3,859.2
2018	B-	2.14	1.10	378,000	11,098.1	31,708.6	3,656.7
2017	B-	1.17	0.77	397,000	10,384.5	18,256.1	1,982.0

Adverse Trends in Operations

Decrease in premium volume from 2018 to 2019 (20%)
Increase in policy surrenders from 2017 to 2018 (35%)
Change in premium mix from 2016 to 2017 (5.4%)
Increase in policy surrenders from 2016 to 2017 (43%)
Decrease in premium volume from 2016 to 2017 (27%)

METROPOLITAN TOWER LIFE INS CO | C+ | Fair

Major Rating Factors: Fair profitability (3.9 on a scale of 0 to 10). Excellent expense controls. Return on equity has been low, averaging 1.1%. Fair overall results on stability tests (4.8). Good quality investment portfolio (5.4) despite substantial holdings of BBB bonds in addition to moderate junk bond exposure. Exposure to mortgages is significant, but the mortgage default rate has been low.
Other Rating Factors: Good liquidity (6.4). Strong capitalization (7.2) based on excellent risk adjusted capital (severe loss scenario).
Principal Business: Group retirement contracts (65%), reinsurance (21%), individual life insurance (7%), individual annuities (5%), and group life insurance (2%).
Principal Investments: NonCMO investment grade bonds (47%), CMOs and structured securities (21%), mortgages in good standing (17%), policy loans (6%), and noninv. grade bonds (3%).
Investments in Affiliates: 1%
Group Affiliation: MetLife Inc
Licensed in: All states, the District of Columbia and Puerto Rico
Commenced Business: February 1983
Address: 1209 Orange Street, Lincoln, NE 68516
Phone: (212) 578-2211 **Domicile State:** NE **NAIC Code:** 97136

Data Date	Rating	RACR #1	RACR #2	Total Assets ($mil)	Capital ($mil)	Net Premium ($mil)	Net Income ($mil)
2021	C+	2.29	1.11	43,883.0	1,638.2	2,528.2	184.6
2020	C+	2.19	1.08	35,277.2	1,388.0	6,249.3	-236.8
2019	B-	2.50	1.23	26,314.7	1,502.5	4,865.3	-13.2
2018	B-	2.70	1.31	20,617.2	1,549.4	1,868.6	76.3
2017	B-	3.39	1.53	4,921.8	733.3	200.3	73.9

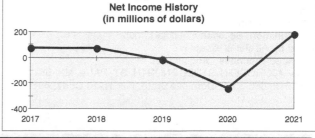

Net Income History
(in millions of dollars)

MIDLAND NATIONAL LIFE INS CO | B | Good

Major Rating Factors: Good liquidity (5.6 on a scale of 0 to 10) with sufficient resources to handle a spike in claims as well as a significant increase in policy surrenders. Fair quality investment portfolio (4.5) with large holdings of BBB rated bonds in addition to junk bond exposure equal to 61% of capital. Fair overall results on stability tests (4.5).
Other Rating Factors: Strong capitalization (7.3) based on excellent risk adjusted capital (severe loss scenario). Excellent profitability (9.2) with operating gains in each of the last five years.
Principal Business: Individual annuities (56%), individual life insurance (42%), and group retirement contracts (2%).
Principal Investments: NonCMO investment grade bonds (49%), CMOs and structured securities (26%), noninv. grade bonds (6%), mortgages in good standing (6%), and misc. investments (12%).
Investments in Affiliates: 3%
Group Affiliation: Sammons Enterprises Inc
Licensed in: All states except NY
Commenced Business: September 1906
Address: 4350 Westown Parkway, West Des Moines, IA 50266
Phone: (605) 335-5700 **Domicile State:** IA **NAIC Code:** 66044

Data Date	Rating	RACR #1	RACR #2	Total Assets ($mil)	Capital ($mil)	Net Premium ($mil)	Net Income ($mil)
2021	B	2.32	1.18	74,313.6	5,248.4	4,077.7	956.6
2020	B+	1.97	1.00	67,262.5	4,205.1	6,449.8	152.6
2019	B+	2.03	1.08	60,416.3	3,852.4	3,256.0	371.2
2018	B+	2.07	1.05	57,914.7	3,571.2	3,681.1	401.6
2017	B+	1.97	1.00	56,496.2	3,414.1	4,043.4	545.8

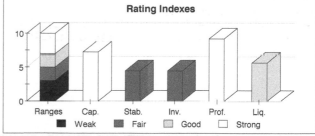

Rating Indexes

Ranges Cap. Stab. Inv. Prof. Liq.
■ Weak ■ Fair ▨ Good □ Strong

MIDWESTERN UNITED LIFE INS CO | B | Good

Major Rating Factors: Good overall results on stability tests (6.0 on a scale of 0 to 10). Stability strengths include excellent operational trends and excellent risk diversification. Good overall profitability (5.5) despite operating losses during 2021. Return on equity has been low, averaging 2.0%. Strong capitalization (10.0) based on excellent risk adjusted capital (severe loss scenario).
Other Rating Factors: High quality investment portfolio (7.7). Excellent liquidity (7.0).
Principal Business: Individual life insurance (100%).
Principal Investments: NonCMO investment grade bonds (70%), CMOs and structured securities (19%), mortgages in good standing (4%), cash (3%), and misc. investments (4%).
Investments in Affiliates: None
Group Affiliation: Voya Financial Inc
Licensed in: All states except NY, PR
Commenced Business: August 1948
Address: 8761 BUFFETT PARKWAY, INDIANAPOLIS, IN 46204
Phone: (303) 860-1290 **Domicile State:** IN **NAIC Code:** 66109

Data Date	Rating	RACR #1	RACR #2	Total Assets ($mil)	Capital ($mil)	Net Premium ($mil)	Net Income ($mil)
2021	B	14.40	12.96	248.1	145.3	2.3	-0.7
2020	B+	14.71	12.69	230.2	146.4	2.3	2.9
2019	B	14.42	12.98	231.4	143.2	2.7	14.4
2018	B	12.97	11.67	231.6	128.2	2.8	3.9
2017	B	12.57	11.17	232.4	124.2	2.9	-6.0

Adverse Trends in Operations

Decrease in premium volume from 2019 to 2020 (14%)
Increase in policy surrenders from 2018 to 2019 (44%)
Decrease in premium volume from 2017 to 2018 (6%)
Decrease in capital during 2017 (5%)
Decrease in premium volume from 2016 to 2017 (6%)

MINNESOTA LIFE INS CO
C+   **Fair**

Major Rating Factors: Fair overall results on stability tests (4.4 on a scale of 0 to 10). Good quality investment portfolio (5.8) despite large holdings of BBB rated bonds in addition to moderate junk bond exposure. Exposure to mortgages is significant, but the mortgage default rate has been low. Good liquidity (6.0) with sufficient resources to handle a spike in claims as well as a significant increase in policy surrenders.

Other Rating Factors: Weak profitability (1.9) with operating losses during 2021. Strong capitalization (7.5) based on excellent risk adjusted capital (severe loss scenario).

Principal Business: Group retirement contracts (44%), individual life insurance (22%), group life insurance (15%), reinsurance (9%), and other lines (11%).

Principal Investments: NonCMO investment grade bonds (53%), mortgages in good standing (15%), CMOs and structured securities (15%), common & preferred stock (4%), and misc. investments (9%).

Investments in Affiliates: 2%

Group Affiliation: Securian Financial Group

Licensed in: All states except NY

Commenced Business: August 1880

Address: 400 ROBERT STREET NORTH, ST. PAUL, MN 55101-2098

Phone: (612) 665-3500   **Domicile State:** MN   **NAIC Code:** 66168

Data Date	Rating	RACR #1	RACR #2	Total Assets ($mil)	Capital ($mil)	Net Premium ($mil)	Net Income ($mil)
2021	C+	2.15	1.32	66,996.4	3,402.9	7,746.6	-25.1
2020	B-	2.26	1.39	60,201.9	3,363.6	7,663.7	-9.2
2019	B	2.09	1.32	56,377.3	3,148.9	8,622.1	-156.2
2018	B+	2.11	1.32	46,519.4	2,849.0	7,546.6	74.7
2017	B+	2.31	1.46	46,433.6	3,059.9	7,586.6	277.9

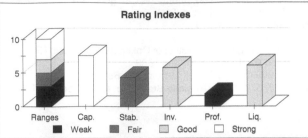

Rating Indexes

MML BAY STATE LIFE INS CO
B-   **Good**

Major Rating Factors: Fair overall capitalization (4.0 on a scale of 0 to 10) based on excellent risk adjusted capital (severe loss scenario). Nevertheless, capital levels have fluctuated during prior years. Fair overall results on stability tests (4.0). Good quality investment portfolio (6.7).

Other Rating Factors: Good overall profitability (5.8). Excellent liquidity (7.2).

Principal Business: Individual life insurance (99%) and group life insurance (1%).

Principal Investments: NonCMO investment grade bonds (57%), policy loans (21%), CMOs and structured securities (18%), noninv. grade bonds (2%), and cash (2%).

Investments in Affiliates: None

Group Affiliation: Massachusetts Mutual Group

Licensed in: All states except NY, PR

Commenced Business: July 1894

Address: 100 BRIGHT MEADOW BOULEVARD, ENFIELD, CT 6082

Phone: (413) 788-8411   **Domicile State:** CT   **NAIC Code:** 70416

Data Date	Rating	RACR #1	RACR #2	Total Assets ($mil)	Capital ($mil)	Net Premium ($mil)	Net Income ($mil)
2021	B-	4.74	3.46	5,462.8	265.4	11.4	18.5
2020	B-	5.01	3.58	5,352.1	274.5	-4.3	12.4
2019	B	5.54	3.99	5,117.8	293.5	2.9	13.7
2018	B	6.09	4.42	4,859.7	309.9	0.9	18.3
2017	B	5.70	4.06	4,960.5	295.3	1.6	14.8

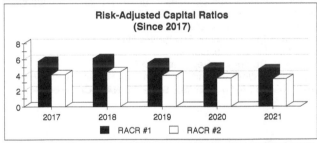

Risk-Adjusted Capital Ratios
(Since 2017)

MONY LIFE INS CO
B-   **Good**

Major Rating Factors: Good current capitalization (6.9 on a scale of 0 to 10) based on good risk adjusted capital (severe loss scenario), although results have slipped from the excellent range over the last year. Good quality investment portfolio (5.3) despite mixed results such as: large holdings of BBB rated bonds but junk bond exposure equal to 65% of capital. Good overall results on stability tests (5.0) despite negative cash flow from operations for 2021 excellent operational trends and excellent risk diversification.

Other Rating Factors: Fair liquidity (4.2). Weak profitability (2.9) with investment income below regulatory standards in relation to interest assumptions of reserves.

Principal Business: Individual life insurance (89%), individual health insurance (7%), and individual annuities (3%).

Principal Investments: NonCMO investment grade bonds (67%), CMOs and structured securities (11%), policy loans (9%), mortgages in good standing (6%), and noninv. grade bonds (2%).

Investments in Affiliates: None

Group Affiliation: Dai-ichi Life Holdings Inc

Licensed in: All states, the District of Columbia and Puerto Rico

Commenced Business: February 1843

Address: 5788 WIDEWATERS PARKWAY 2ND FL, SYRACUSE, NY 13214

Phone: (800) 487-6669   **Domicile State:** NY   **NAIC Code:** 66370

Data Date	Rating	RACR #1	RACR #2	Total Assets ($mil)	Capital ($mil)	Net Premium ($mil)	Net Income ($mil)
2021	B-	1.88	0.99	6,597.6	334.5	190.1	21.0
2020	B-	1.98	1.03	6,705.5	371.4	197.8	7.5
2019	B-	2.06	1.08	6,887.2	389.5	209.5	28.7
2018	B-	2.33	1.23	7,062.7	421.8	217.2	43.2
2017	B-	2.39	1.26	7,224.2	433.8	231.1	60.1

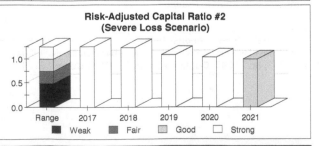

Risk-Adjusted Capital Ratio #2
(Severe Loss Scenario)

MULTINATIONAL LIFE INS CO   C-   Fair

Major Rating Factors: Fair overall results on stability tests (3.3 on a scale of 0 to 10) including fair financial strength of affiliated Ancon Investment Corp. Weak profitability (2.9) with investment income below regulatory standards in relation to interest assumptions of reserves. Good quality investment portfolio (5.5).
Other Rating Factors: Strong capitalization (7.5) based on excellent risk adjusted capital (severe loss scenario). Excellent liquidity (7.2).
Principal Business: Individual health insurance (52%), individual life insurance (29%), group health insurance (10%), and group life insurance (9%).
Principal Investments: NonCMO investment grade bonds (59%), cash (15%), CMOs and structured securities (10%), real estate (8%), and misc. investments (9%).
Investments in Affiliates: None
Group Affiliation: Ancon Investment Corp
Licensed in: PR
Commenced Business: July 1969
Address: 470 Ponce de Leon Ave, Hato Rey, PR 918
Phone: (787) 758-8080 **Domicile State:** PR **NAIC Code:** 72087

Data Date	Rating	RACR #1	RACR #2	Total Assets ($mil)	Capital ($mil)	Net Premium ($mil)	Net Income ($mil)
2021	C-	2.26	1.30	132.4	25.8	31.2	3.0
2020	C-	2.59	1.45	130.9	24.6	31.7	2.9
2019	C-	N/A	N/A	123.3	23.8	33.3	2.7
2018	C-	2.22	1.22	121.2	21.5	31.2	3.1
2017	C-	2.01	1.13	115.0	19.5	31.8	2.7

Ancon Investment Corp Composite Group Rating: C- Largest Group Members	Assets ($mil)	Rating
MULTINATIONAL INS CO	148	C-
MULTINATIONAL LIFE INS CO	131	C-

MUNICH AMERICAN REASSURANCE CO   C   Fair

Major Rating Factors: Fair overall results on stability tests (3.0 on a scale of 0 to 10) including negative cash flow from operations for 2021. Good liquidity (6.1) with sufficient resources to handle a spike in claims as well as a significant increase in policy surrenders. Weak profitability (1.5) with operating losses during 2021.
Other Rating Factors: Strong capitalization (8.0) based on excellent risk adjusted capital (severe loss scenario). High quality investment portfolio (7.1).
Principal Business: Reinsurance (100%).
Principal Investments: NonCMO investment grade bonds (95%), CMOs and structured securities (1%), and noninv. grade bonds (1%).
Investments in Affiliates: None
Group Affiliation: Munchener R-G AG
Licensed in: All states, the District of Columbia and Puerto Rico
Commenced Business: November 1959
Address: 56 Perimeter Center East NE, Atlanta, GA 30326
Phone: (770) 350-3200 **Domicile State:** GA **NAIC Code:** 66346

Data Date	Rating	RACR #1	RACR #2	Total Assets ($mil)	Capital ($mil)	Net Premium ($mil)	Net Income ($mil)
2021	C	2.67	1.64	9,176.0	607.7	35.7	-254.9
2020	C	1.42	0.97	8,353.5	593.3	1,987.5	-92.6
2019	C	2.51	1.59	8,006.8	655.9	661.6	8.9
2018	C	2.43	1.53	8,138.2	638.6	1,111.4	69.1
2017	C	2.61	1.76	7,822.7	718.5	849.3	-48.4

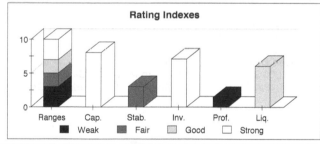

Rating Indexes

MUTUAL OF AMERICA LIFE INS CO   B   Good

Major Rating Factors: Good current capitalization (6.2 on a scale of 0 to 10) based on good risk adjusted capital (severe loss scenario), although results have slipped from the excellent range over the last year. Good quality investment portfolio (5.7) despite mixed results such as: large holdings of BBB rated bonds but junk bond exposure equal to 63% of capital. Good liquidity (6.7).
Other Rating Factors: Fair overall results on stability tests (4.6) including negative cash flow from operations for 2021. Weak profitability (2.4).
Principal Business: Group retirement contracts (82%) and individual annuities (17%).
Principal Investments: NonCMO investment grade bonds (61%), CMOs and structured securities (27%), noninv. grade bonds (3%), common & preferred stock (3%), and policy loans (1%).
Investments in Affiliates: 3%
Group Affiliation: None
Licensed in: All states except PR
Commenced Business: October 1945
Address: 320 Park Avenue, New York, NY 10022
Phone: (212) 224-1600 **Domicile State:** NY **NAIC Code:** 88668

Data Date	Rating	RACR #1	RACR #2	Total Assets ($mil)	Capital ($mil)	Net Premium ($mil)	Net Income ($mil)
2021	B	1.46	0.90	28,283.4	762.1	2,372.9	46.0
2020	B	2.28	1.06	25,908.1	729.9	1,095.7	-116.3
2019	B	2.19	1.07	23,658.1	837.2	2,560.6	-21.3
2018	B+	2.57	1.23	20,380.8	927.2	2,597.3	16.0
2017	A-	3.03	1.43	21,184.9	983.3	2,710.1	25.7

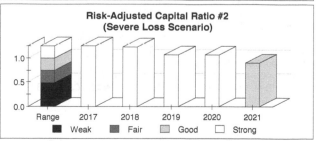

Risk-Adjusted Capital Ratio #2 (Severe Loss Scenario)

MUTUAL OF OMAHA INS CO
B **Good**

Major Rating Factors: Good overall profitability (5.7 on a scale of 0 to 10). Excellent expense controls. Good overall results on stability tests (5.5). Stability strengths include excellent operational trends, good risk adjusted capital for prior years and excellent risk diversification. Fair quality investment portfolio (4.9).

Other Rating Factors: Strong capitalization (7.2) based on excellent risk adjusted capital (severe loss scenario). Excellent liquidity (7.0).

Principal Business: Reinsurance (59%), individual health insurance (36%), and group health insurance (5%).

Principal Investments: NonCMO investment grade bonds (45%), common & preferred stock (29%), CMOs and structured securities (9%), mortgages in good standing (5%), and noninv. grade bonds (2%).

Investments in Affiliates: 31%

Group Affiliation: Mutual Of Omaha Group

Licensed in: All states, the District of Columbia and Puerto Rico

Commenced Business: January 1910

Address: MUTUAL OF OMAHA PLAZA, OMAHA, NE 68175

Phone: (800) 775-6000 **Domicile State:** NE **NAIC Code:** 71412

Data Date	Rating	RACR #1	RACR #2	Total Assets ($mil)	Capital ($mil)	Net Premium ($mil)	Net Income ($mil)
2021	B	1.25	1.13	10,341.8	3,996.6	3,779.1	219.9
2020	C+	1.15	1.05	9,440.5	3,623.5	3,715.1	766.8
2019	C+	0.88	0.82	9,107.4	3,140.0	3,538.5	-130.6
2018	B-	0.98	0.92	8,084.0	3,172.7	3,282.6	-157.4
2017	B+	1.03	0.96	7,824.4	3,189.6	3,036.5	-7.1

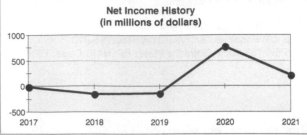

Net Income History
(in millions of dollars)

MUTUAL TRUST LIFE INS CO
B **Good**

Major Rating Factors: Good overall profitability (5.4 on a scale of 0 to 10) despite operating losses during 2021. Good liquidity (5.2) with sufficient resources to handle a spike in claims as well as a significant increase in policy surrenders. Good overall results on stability tests (5.9). Stability strengths include excellent operational trends and excellent risk diversification.

Other Rating Factors: Fair quality investment portfolio (4.3). Strong capitalization (7.1) based on excellent risk adjusted capital (severe loss scenario).

Principal Business: Individual life insurance (95%), reinsurance (4%), and individual annuities (1%).

Principal Investments: NonCMO investment grade bonds (60%), CMOs and structured securities (18%), policy loans (13%), noninv. grade bonds (4%), and common & preferred stock (1%).

Investments in Affiliates: None

Group Affiliation: Pan-American Life

Licensed in: All states except NY, PR

Commenced Business: April 1905

Address: 1200 Jorie Boulevard, Oak Brook, IL 60523-2269

Phone: (800) 323-7320 **Domicile State:** IL **NAIC Code:** 66427

Data Date	Rating	RACR #1	RACR #2	Total Assets ($mil)	Capital ($mil)	Net Premium ($mil)	Net Income ($mil)
2021	B	2.07	1.04	2,259.5	165.1	212.1	-2.4
2020	B	2.08	1.03	2,191.5	163.8	193.4	1.0
2019	B	2.22	1.11	2,116.0	162.3	189.6	10.9
2018	B	2.19	1.10	2,044.0	152.9	176.5	7.7
2017	B	2.10	1.05	2,015.5	145.0	186.1	5.7

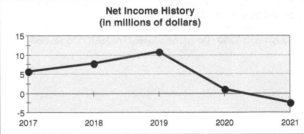

Net Income History
(in millions of dollars)

NASSAU LIFE & ANNUITY CO
D **Weak**

Major Rating Factors: Weak overall results on stability tests (1.8 on a scale of 0 to 10) including potential financial drain due to affiliation with Nassau Reinsurance Group Holdings LP. Weak profitability (1.6) with operating losses during 2021. Return on equity has been low, averaging -17.6%. Fair quality investment portfolio (4.0).

Other Rating Factors: Good capitalization (6.0) based on good risk adjusted capital (moderate loss scenario). Excellent liquidity (8.9).

Principal Business: Individual annuities (90%), individual health insurance (5%), individual life insurance (3%), reinsurance (2%), and group health insurance (1%).

Principal Investments: NonCMO investment grade bonds (45%), CMOs and structured securities (29%), mortgages in good standing (10%), noninv. grade bonds (5%), and misc. investments (9%).

Investments in Affiliates: 1%

Group Affiliation: Nassau Reinsurance Group Holdings LP

Licensed in: All states except NY, PR

Commenced Business: December 1981

Address: One American Row, Hartford, CT 6103

Phone: (860) 403-5000 **Domicile State:** CT **NAIC Code:** 93734

Data Date	Rating	RACR #1	RACR #2	Total Assets ($mil)	Capital ($mil)	Net Premium ($mil)	Net Income ($mil)
2021	D	1.69	0.85	1,935.6	116.5	196.0	-123.8
2020	D+	1.85	0.98	1,211.1	107.2	181.0	1.6
2019	D+	3.70	2.35	275.9	37.8	54.0	-2.6
2018	D	2.24	2.01	35.3	10.6	5.7	0.3
2017	E+	2.38	2.15	31.1	10.2	-0.4	-0.7

Nassau Reinsurance Group Holdings LP Composite Group Rating: E+ Largest Group Members	Assets ($mil)	Rating
NASSAU LIFE INSURANCE CO	14022	D-
PHL VARIABLE INS CO	5626	E
NASSAU LIFE ANNUITY CO	1211	D
NASSAU LIFE INS CO OF KS	71	D-
NATIONAL SERVICE CONTRACT INS CO RRG	4	C-

NASSAU LIFE INSURANCE CO   D-   Weak

Major Rating Factors: Weak overall results on stability tests (1.3 on a scale of 0 to 10) including negative cash flow from operations for 2021. Fair quality investment portfolio (4.8) with large holdings of BBB rated bonds in addition to significant exposure to junk bonds. Fair liquidity (3.6) as cash from operations and sale of marketable assets may not be adequate to cover a spike in claims or a run on policy withdrawals.

Other Rating Factors: Good capitalization (5.5) based on good risk adjusted capital (moderate loss scenario). Good profitability (5.0).

Principal Business: Individual life insurance (89%), reinsurance (9%), and individual annuities (2%).

Principal Investments: NonCMO investment grade bonds (49%), policy loans (23%), CMOs and structured securities (14%), mortgages in good standing (5%), and misc. investments (9%).

Investments in Affiliates: None

Group Affiliation: Nassau Reinsurance Group Holdings LP

Licensed in: All states, the District of Columbia and Puerto Rico

Commenced Business: May 1851

Address: 15 Tech Valley Drive, East Greenbush, NY 12061-4137

Phone: (860) 403-5000 **Domicile State:** NY **NAIC Code:** 67814

Data Date	Rating	RACR #1	RACR #2	Total Assets ($mil)	Capital ($mil)	Net Premium ($mil)	Net Income ($mil)
2021	D-	1.33	0.67	14,014.5	376.4	285.8	87.4
2020	D-	1.10	0.55	14,021.8	295.3	300.7	-11.7
2019	D-	1.65	0.82	11,733.9	448.3	244.6	-14.7
2018	D-	1.71	0.86	11,959.8	514.9	246.0	94.2
2017	D-	1.55	0.78	12,478.2	449.2	289.7	68.4

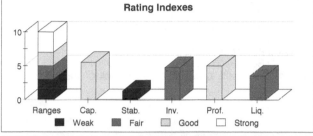

NATIONAL BENEFIT LIFE INS CO *   A-   Excellent

Major Rating Factors: Good quality investment portfolio (6.6 on a scale of 0 to 10) despite mixed results such as: no exposure to mortgages and large holdings of BBB rated bonds but small junk bond holdings. Good overall profitability (6.2). Excellent expense controls. Return on equity has been good over the last five years, averaging 14.0%. Good liquidity (6.8).

Other Rating Factors: Excellent overall results on stability tests (7.1) excellent operational trends and excellent risk diversification. Strong capitalization (9.3) based on excellent risk adjusted capital (severe loss scenario).

Principal Business: Individual life insurance (99%).

Principal Investments: NonCMO investment grade bonds (64%), CMOs and structured securities (24%), noninv. grade bonds (4%), common & preferred stock (1%), and policy loans (1%).

Investments in Affiliates: None

Group Affiliation: Primerica Inc

Licensed in: All states except PR

Commenced Business: May 1963

Address: One Court Square, Long Island City, NY 11101-3433

Phone: (718) 361-3636 **Domicile State:** NY **NAIC Code:** 61409

Data Date	Rating	RACR #1	RACR #2	Total Assets ($mil)	Capital ($mil)	Net Premium ($mil)	Net Income ($mil)
2021	A-	4.69	2.52	675.0	133.6	116.0	25.9
2020	A-	5.00	2.71	636.0	134.1	106.8	19.3
2019	A-	5.74	3.13	592.4	144.7	98.0	19.6
2018	B+	6.43	3.46	566.9	153.9	91.2	21.5
2017	B+	6.61	3.53	539.5	155.3	82.8	14.9

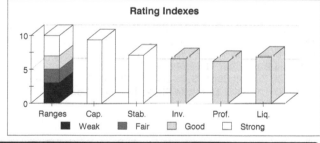

NATIONAL FARM LIFE INS CO   B   Good

Major Rating Factors: Good quality investment portfolio (6.5 on a scale of 0 to 10) despite mixed results such as: minimal exposure to mortgages and substantial holdings of BBB bonds but small junk bond holdings. Good overall profitability (5.1) although investment income, in comparison to reserve requirements, is below regulatory standards. Good liquidity (6.1).

Other Rating Factors: Good overall results on stability tests (5.5) excellent operational trends and good risk diversification. Strong capitalization (7.9) based on excellent risk adjusted capital (severe loss scenario).

Principal Business: Individual life insurance (96%) and individual annuities (4%).

Principal Investments: NonCMO investment grade bonds (81%), common & preferred stock (5%), policy loans (5%), CMOs and structured securities (3%), and misc. investments (4%).

Investments in Affiliates: None

Group Affiliation: National Farm Group

Licensed in: TX

Commenced Business: May 1946

Address: 6001 Bridge Street, Fort Worth, TX 76112

Phone: (817) 451-9550 **Domicile State:** TX **NAIC Code:** 66532

Data Date	Rating	RACR #1	RACR #2	Total Assets ($mil)	Capital ($mil)	Net Premium ($mil)	Net Income ($mil)
2021	B	2.72	1.63	443.8	51.7	26.6	1.4
2020	B	3.01	1.80	435.9	51.1	26.5	2.5
2019	B	3.16	1.91	428.5	50.2	25.7	3.9
2018	B	3.07	1.85	420.4	46.6	25.4	2.8
2017	B	2.87	1.71	410.1	43.1	25.3	3.3

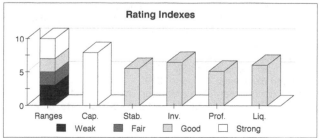

NATIONAL FARMERS UNION LIFE INS CO * B+ Good

Major Rating Factors: Good overall results on stability tests (6.2 on a scale of 0 to 10). Stability strengths include good operational trends and excellent risk diversification. Good quality investment portfolio (5.4) despite mixed results such as: large holdings of BBB rated bonds but moderate junk bond exposure. Good overall profitability (5.6).
Other Rating Factors: Good liquidity (6.2). Strong capitalization (8.4) based on excellent risk adjusted capital (severe loss scenario).
Principal Business: Individual life insurance (75%), reinsurance (24%), and group life insurance (1%).
Principal Investments: NonCMO investment grade bonds (60%), CMOs and structured securities (13%), common & preferred stock (11%), noninv. grade bonds (5%), and misc. investments (11%).
Investments in Affiliates: 3%
Group Affiliation: Americo Life Inc
Licensed in: AK, AZ, AR, CA, CO, DC, ID, IL, IN, IA, KS, KY, MI, MN, MS, MO, MT, NE, NV, NM, ND, OH, OK, OR, PA, SD, TX, UT, VA, WA, WI, WY
Commenced Business: April 1938
Address: PO Box 139061, Dallas, TX 75313-9061
Phone: (816) 391-2000 **Domicile State:** TX **NAIC Code:** 66540

Data Date	Rating	RACR #1	RACR #2	Total Assets ($mil)	Capital ($mil)	Net Premium ($mil)	Net Income ($mil)
2021	B+	3.38	1.90	158.8	29.5	4.7	3.0
2020	B+	3.40	2.14	163.0	30.1	5.1	4.9
2019	B+	3.62	2.13	169.8	32.0	5.4	7.8
2018	B+	5.19	2.75	191.1	48.3	5.7	6.1
2017	B+	4.45	2.34	199.0	44.6	6.3	4.9

Adverse Trends in Operations

Decrease in asset base during 2020 (4%)
Decrease in capital during 2019 (34%)
Decrease in asset base during 2019 (11%)
Decrease in premium volume from 2016 to 2017 (11%)
Decrease in asset base during 2017 (2%)

NATIONAL FOUNDATION LIFE INS CO * A Excellent

Major Rating Factors: Excellent overall results on stability tests (7.1 on a scale of 0 to 10). Strengths that enhance stability include excellent operational trends and excellent risk diversification. Strong capitalization (8.2) based on excellent risk adjusted capital (severe loss scenario). Furthermore, this high level of risk adjusted capital has been consistently maintained over the last five years. High quality investment portfolio (8.8).
Other Rating Factors: Excellent profitability (9.1) with operating gains in each of the last five years. Excellent liquidity (7.5).
Principal Business: Individual health insurance (64%), group health insurance (28%), individual life insurance (7%), and reinsurance (1%).
Principal Investments: NonCMO investment grade bonds (60%), cash (22%), and CMOs and structured securities (16%).
Investments in Affiliates: None
Group Affiliation: Credit Suisse Group
Licensed in: AL, AK, AZ, AR, CA, CO, DC, DE, GA, ID, IN, IA, KS, KY, LA, ME, MS, MO, MT, NE, NV, NM, NC, ND, OH, OK, OR, PA, SC, SD, TN, TX, UT, VA, WA, WY
Commenced Business: November 1983
Address: 300 Burnett Street Suite 200, Fort Worth, TX 76102-2734
Phone: (817) 878-3300 **Domicile State:** TX **NAIC Code:** 98205

Data Date	Rating	RACR #1	RACR #2	Total Assets ($mil)	Capital ($mil)	Net Premium ($mil)	Net Income ($mil)
2021	A	2.31	1.81	94.2	55.6	149.7	21.7
2020	A	2.56	1.99	86.9	56.7	120.8	23.2
2019	B+	2.23	1.74	70.8	46.8	96.2	13.8
2018	B+	1.66	1.28	53.8	33.0	78.6	10.7
2017	B	1.61	1.25	38.9	21.7	53.7	5.4

Adverse Trends in Operations

Change in asset mix during 2019 (5%)
Change in asset mix during 2018 (4.1%)

NATIONAL GUARDIAN LIFE INS CO B- Good

Major Rating Factors: Good quality investment portfolio (5.3 on a scale of 0 to 10) despite mixed results such as: minimal exposure to mortgages and large holdings of BBB rated bonds but small junk bond holdings. Good liquidity (6.6) with sufficient resources to handle a spike in claims as well as a significant increase in policy surrenders. Fair overall results on stability tests (3.5) including weak results on operational trends.
Other Rating Factors: Strong capitalization (7.6) based on excellent risk adjusted capital (severe loss scenario). Excellent profitability (7.3) with operating gains in each of the last five years.
Principal Business: Group life insurance (37%), group health insurance (31%), individual life insurance (21%), individual health insurance (5%), and other lines (6%).
Principal Investments: NonCMO investment grade bonds (75%), CMOs and structured securities (9%), noninv. grade bonds (5%), mortgages in good standing (3%), and misc. investments (8%).
Investments in Affiliates: 1%
Group Affiliation: NGL Ins Group
Licensed in: All states except NY, PR
Commenced Business: October 1910
Address: 2 East Gilman Street, Madison, WI 53703-1494
Phone: (608) 257-5611 **Domicile State:** WI **NAIC Code:** 66583

Data Date	Rating	RACR #1	RACR #2	Total Assets ($mil)	Capital ($mil)	Net Premium ($mil)	Net Income ($mil)
2021	B-	2.52	1.41	4,698.1	495.1	60.2	73.7
2020	B	1.84	1.18	4,419.3	417.5	190.8	23.3
2019	B	1.59	1.03	4,301.6	367.4	659.9	31.2
2018	B-	1.52	0.98	4,080.0	333.2	653.9	30.0
2017	B-	1.53	0.98	3,884.4	322.6	603.4	28.8

Adverse Trends in Operations

Change in premium mix from 2019 to 2020 (26.7%)
Decrease in premium volume from 2019 to 2020 (71%)

NATIONAL HEALTH INS CO *
B+ **Good**

Major Rating Factors: Good overall results on stability tests (6.5 on a scale of 0 to 10) despite negative cash flow from operations for 2021. Other stability subfactors include good operational trends, good risk adjusted capital for prior years and excellent risk diversification. Strong current capitalization (8.5) based on excellent risk adjusted capital (severe loss scenario) reflecting improvement over results in 2018. High quality investment portfolio (8.5).

Other Rating Factors: Excellent profitability (7.2) despite modest operating losses during 2019. Excellent liquidity (7.3).

Principal Business: Group health insurance (80%), individual health insurance (18%), and individual life insurance (1%).

Principal Investments: NonCMO investment grade bonds (82%) and cash (16%).

Investments in Affiliates: None

Group Affiliation: AmTrust Financial Services Inc

Licensed in: All states except NY, PR

Commenced Business: January 1966

Address: 4455 LBJ Freeway Suite 375, Dallas, TX 75244

Phone: (800) 237-1900 **Domicile State:** TX **NAIC Code:** 82538

Data Date	Rating	RACR #1	RACR #2	Total Assets ($mil)	Capital ($mil)	Net Premium ($mil)	Net Income ($mil)
2021	B+	4.79	1.98	181.1	79.9	12.0	2.0
2020	B	3.36	1.40	129.6	52.2	12.0	2.6
2019	C+	2.38	1.00	87.2	31.0	10.3	-0.1
2018	C-	1.99	0.84	59.4	18.9	13.2	1.1
2017	C+	2.08	0.88	50.8	14.6	9.6	3.0

Adverse Trends in Operations

Decrease in premium volume from 2018 to 2019 (22%)
Change in asset mix during 2019 (15%)

NATIONAL INCOME LIFE INS CO
B **Good**

Major Rating Factors: Good overall results on stability tests (5.9 on a scale of 0 to 10) doopito fair financial strength of affiliated Torchmark Corp. Other stability subfactors include excellent operational trends and excellent risk diversification. Good quality investment portfolio (6.3) despite mixed results such as: no exposure to mortgages and large holdings of BBB rated bonds but small junk bond holdings. Fair profitability (4.3) with investment income below regulatory standards in relation to interest assumptions of reserves.

Other Rating Factors: Fair liquidity (4.5). Strong capitalization (7.4) based on excellent risk adjusted capital (severe loss scenario).

Principal Business: Individual life insurance (93%) and individual health insurance (7%).

Principal Investments: NonCMO investment grade bonds (86%), policy loans (4%), noninv. grade bonds (2%), CMOs and structured securities (1%), and cash (1%).

Investments in Affiliates: None

Group Affiliation: Torchmark Corp

Licensed in: NY

Commenced Business: November 2000

Address: 1020 SEVENTH NORTH ST STE 130, SYRACUSE, NY 13212

Phone: (315) 451-8180 **Domicile State:** NY **NAIC Code:** 10093

Data Date	Rating	RACR #1	RACR #2	Total Assets ($mil)	Capital ($mil)	Net Premium ($mil)	Net Income ($mil)
2021	B	2.14	1.25	390.6	41.7	106.5	12.7
2020	B	2.23	1.30	344.0	39.1	95.4	14.9
2019	B+	2.54	1.50	305.9	40.5	92.3	13.7
2018	B+	2.78	1.65	270.5	40.2	85.8	11.6
2017	B	2.85	1.72	203.3	37.0	80.7	9.1

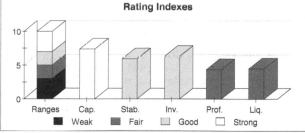

Rating Indexes — Ranges, Cap., Stab., Inv., Prof., Liq. — Weak, Fair, Good, Strong

NATIONAL INTEGRITY LIFE INS CO
C+ **Fair**

Major Rating Factors: Fair overall results on stability tests (4.8 on a scale of 0 to 10) including excessive premium growth. Good quality investment portfolio (5.7) despite mixed results such as: large holdings of BBB rated bonds but junk bond exposure equal to 53% of capital. Good liquidity (6.3) with sufficient resources to handle a spike in claims as well as a significant increase in policy surrenders.

Other Rating Factors: Weak profitability (2.6) with investment income below regulatory standards in relation to interest assumptions of reserves. Strong capitalization (8.4) based on excellent risk adjusted capital (severe loss scenario).

Principal Business: Individual annuities (90%), individual life insurance (6%), and group retirement contracts (4%).

Principal Investments: NonCMO investment grade bonds (55%), CMOs and structured securities (25%), mortgages in good standing (7%), noninv. grade bonds (6%), and misc. investments (6%).

Investments in Affiliates: 3%

Group Affiliation: Western & Southern Group

Licensed in: CT, DC, FL, ME, NH, NY, OH, RI, VT

Commenced Business: December 1968

Address: 14 MAIN STREET SUITE 100, GREENWICH, NY 12834

Phone: (513) 629-1402 **Domicile State:** NY **NAIC Code:** 75264

Data Date	Rating	RACR #1	RACR #2	Total Assets ($mil)	Capital ($mil)	Net Premium ($mil)	Net Income ($mil)
2021	C+	4.18	1.96	4,580.3	426.3	359.3	85.9
2020	C+	3.43	1.61	4,481.4	343.7	179.7	-42.4
2019	C+	3.93	1.87	4,484.1	377.1	209.9	35.6
2018	B-	3.70	1.77	4,492.6	339.0	249.2	25.4
2017	B-	2.71	1.36	4,640.5	315.9	224.4	-14.1

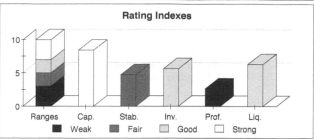

Rating Indexes — Ranges, Cap., Stab., Inv., Prof., Liq. — Weak, Fair, Good, Strong

NATIONAL LIFE INS CO

B   **Good**

Major Rating Factors: Good overall results on stability tests (5.8 on a scale of 0 to 10). Stability strengths include excellent operational trends and excellent risk diversification. Good quality investment portfolio (6.0) despite mixed results such as: minimal exposure to mortgages and large holdings of BBB rated bonds but small junk bond holdings. Good liquidity (6.9).

Other Rating Factors: Strong capitalization (7.1) based on excellent risk adjusted capital (severe loss scenario). Excellent profitability (7.9) despite modest operating losses during 2018.

Principal Business: Individual life insurance (95%), individual annuities (5%), individual health insurance (2%), and group retirement contracts (2%).

Principal Investments: NonCMO investment grade bonds (49%), common & preferred stock (21%), CMOs and structured securities (12%), policy loans (5%), and misc. investments (12%).

Investments in Affiliates: 21%

Group Affiliation: National Life Group

Licensed in: All states except PR

Commenced Business: January 1850

Address: 1 National Life Drive, Montpelier, VT 5604

Phone: (802) 229-3333 **Domicile State:** VT **NAIC Code:** 66680

Data Date	Rating	RACR #1	RACR #2	Total Assets ($mil)	Capital ($mil)	Net Premium ($mil)	Net Income ($mil)
2021	B	1.22	1.09	11,011.8	2,878.8	418.0	10.8
2020	B-	1.25	1.10	10,516.9	2,566.8	375.1	25.9
2019	B-	1.21	1.06	10,102.7	2,289.3	338.7	39.9
2018	B-	1.38	1.18	9,502.8	2,131.1	373.1	-22.8
2017	B	1.45	1.25	9,500.0	2,015.6	-43.2	14.9

Adverse Trends in Operations

Decrease in premium volume from 2018 to 2019 (9%)
Change in premium mix from 2017 to 2018 (30.1%)
Increase in policy surrenders from 2017 to 2018 (33%)
Decrease in premium volume from 2016 to 2017 (113%)

NATIONAL SECURITY LIFE & ANNUITY CO

B-   **Good**

Major Rating Factors: Fair overall results on stability tests (4.0 on a scale of 0 to 10) including fair financial strength of affiliated Ohio Natonal Mutual Inc. Fair overall capitalization (4.0) based on mixed results -- excessive policy leverage mitigated by excellent risk adjusted capital (severe loss scenario). Moreover, capital has steadily grown over the last five years. High quality investment portfolio (7.4).

Other Rating Factors: Excellent profitability (7.7) with operating gains in each of the last five years. Excellent liquidity (7.3).

Principal Business: Reinsurance (79%), individual annuities (20%), and individual life insurance (1%).

Principal Investments: NonCMO investment grade bonds (78%), CMOs and structured securities (11%), cash (9%), and noninv. grade bonds (3%).

Investments in Affiliates: None

Group Affiliation: Ohio Natonal Mutual Inc

Licensed in: AZ, AR, DC, IL, IN, IA, KS, LA, NE, NH, NJ, NY, OH, OK, OR, PA, SC, SD, TX, UT

Commenced Business: July 1975

Address: 810 Seventh Avenue Suite 3600, Melville, NY 11747

Phone: (303) 860-1290 **Domicile State:** NY **NAIC Code:** 85472

Data Date	Rating	RACR #1	RACR #2	Total Assets ($mil)	Capital ($mil)	Net Premium ($mil)	Net Income ($mil)
2021	B-	2.98	2.68	482.6	36.6	-2.8	6.1
2020	B-	2.51	2.26	464.8	30.4	-0.7	3.0
2019	B-	2.23	2.01	463.3	26.9	-2.3	4.4
2018	B-	1.95	1.76	434.1	23.0	3.2	1.9
2017	B	1.71	1.54	498.9	21.1	12.2	2.0

Ohio Natonal Mutual Inc
Composite Group Rating: C+

Largest Group Members	Assets ($mil)	Rating
OHIO NATIONAL LIFE INS CO	28400	C+
OHIO NATIONAL LIFE ASR CORP	3033	B
NATIONAL SECURITY LIFE ANNUITY CO	465	B-

NATIONAL TEACHERS ASSOCIATES L I C

B-   **Good**

Major Rating Factors: Good current capitalization (6.4 on a scale of 0 to 10) based on good risk adjusted capital (severe loss scenario), although results have slipped from the excellent range over the last year. Good overall profitability (5.4) although investment income, in comparison to reserve requirements, is below regulatory standards. Fair quality investment portfolio (4.8).

Other Rating Factors: Fair overall results on stability tests (4.9). Excellent liquidity (7.7).

Principal Business: Individual health insurance (98%) and individual life insurance (2%).

Principal Investments: NonCMO investment grade bonds (48%), CMOs and structured securities (35%), noninv. grade bonds (3%), and common & preferred stock (2%).

Investments in Affiliates: None

Group Affiliation: Ellard Family Holdings Inc

Licensed in: All states except NY, PR

Commenced Business: July 1938

Address: 4949 Keller Springs Rd, Addison, TX 75001-5910

Phone: (972) 532-2100 **Domicile State:** TX **NAIC Code:** 87963

Data Date	Rating	RACR #1	RACR #2	Total Assets ($mil)	Capital ($mil)	Net Premium ($mil)	Net Income ($mil)
2021	B-	1.64	0.92	657.1	49.5	94.4	27.2
2020	B-	1.85	1.08	589.6	51.2	93.8	30.9
2019	B-	2.56	1.67	541.0	68.4	130.3	-15.7
2018	B	3.46	2.29	583.6	138.7	130.2	28.9
2017	B	2.89	1.95	544.9	115.9	130.7	20.3

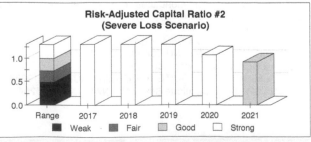

Risk-Adjusted Capital Ratio #2 (Severe Loss Scenario)

■ Weak ■ Fair ■ Good □ Strong

NATIONAL WESTERN LIFE INS CO
B   Good

Major Rating Factors: Good quality investment portfolio (6.4 on a scale of 0 to 10) despite mixed results such as: minimal exposure to mortgages and large holdings of BBB rated bonds but small junk bond holdings. Good liquidity (6.7) with sufficient resources to handle a spike in claims as well as a significant increase in policy surrenders. Strong capitalization (4.0) based on excellent risk adjusted capital (severe loss scenario).

Other Rating Factors: Fair overall results on stability tests (4.2). Excellent profitability (7.2) with operating gains in each of the last five years.

Principal Business: Individual annuities (62%) and individual life insurance (38%).

Principal Investments: NonCMO investment grade bonds (67%), CMOs and structured securities (14%), common & preferred stock (5%), mortgages in good standing (4%), and misc. investments (4%).

Investments in Affiliates: 5%

Group Affiliation: None

Licensed in: All states except NY

Commenced Business: June 1957

Address: 1675 Broadway #1200, Centennial, CO 80112

Phone: (512) 719-2240 **Domicile State:** CO **NAIC Code:** 66850

Data Date	Rating	RACR #1	RACR #2	Total Assets ($mil)	Capital ($mil)	Net Premium ($mil)	Net Income ($mil)
2021	B	2.64	1.71	10,771.7	1,580.2	725.4	63.5
2020	B	2.62	1.68	10,701.3	1,505.2	-1,084.9	6.5
2019	B-	3.02	1.83	10,792.6	1,529.5	527.3	151.3
2018	B-	4.03	2.10	10,991.0	1,419.0	687.9	31.3
2017	A	4.09	2.16	11,149.8	1,374.6	863.1	126.9

Rating Indexes

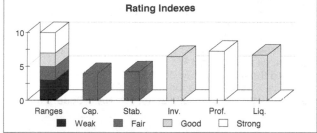

NATIONWIDE LIFE & ANNUITY INS CO
C   Fair

Major Rating Factors: Fair quality investment portfolio (4.7 on a scale of 0 to 10) with large holdings of BBB rated bonds in addition to junk bond exposure equal to 67% of capital. Exposure to mortgages is significant, but the mortgage default rate has been low. Fair overall results on stability tests (4.2). Good liquidity (5.1).

Other Rating Factors: Weak profitability (1.9). Strong capitalization (7.5) based on excellent risk adjusted capital (severe loss scenario).

Principal Business: Individual annuities (52%), individual life insurance (41%), and group retirement contracts (7%).

Principal Investments: NonCMO investment grade bonds (61%), mortgages in good standing (19%), CMOs and structured securities (6%), and noninv. grade bonds (4%).

Investments in Affiliates: 2%

Group Affiliation: Nationwide Corp

Licensed in: All states except NY, PR

Commenced Business: May 1981

Address: ONE WEST NATIONWIDE BLVD, COLUMBUS, OH 43215-2220

Phone: (614) 249-5227 **Domicile State:** OH **NAIC Code:** 92657

Data Date	Rating	RACR #1	RACR #2	Total Assets ($mil)	Capital ($mil)	Net Premium ($mil)	Net Income ($mil)
2021	C	2.79	1.34	42,615.4	2,553.4	5,254.6	2.4
2020	C	2.84	1.35	37,502.0	2,414.0	4,626.9	99.0
2019	C	3.03	1.48	34,069.7	2,215.8	6,727.4	-623.5
2018	C	2.58	1.25	25,929.2	1,467.7	6,338.5	230.0
2017	C	3.06	1.57	20,608.3	1,339.6	5,655.3	-276.3

Rating Indexes

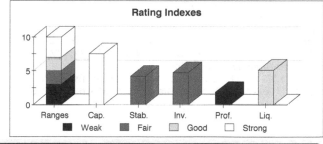

NATIONWIDE LIFE INS CO
B-   Good

Major Rating Factors: Good quality investment portfolio (6.3 on a scale of 0 to 10) despite significant exposure to mortgages . Mortgage default rate has been low. large holdings of BBB rated bonds in addition to small junk bond holdings. Good liquidity (6.6) with sufficient resources to handle a spike in claims as well as a significant increase in policy surrenders. Good overall results on stability tests (5.1) excellent operational trends and excellent risk diversification.

Other Rating Factors: Strong capitalization (7.8) based on excellent risk adjusted capital (severe loss scenario). Excellent profitability (8.3) with operating gains in each of the last five years.

Principal Business: Individual annuities (51%), group retirement contracts (34%), group life insurance (7%), individual life insurance (5%), and group health insurance (3%).

Principal Investments: NonCMO investment grade bonds (58%), mortgages in good standing (16%), CMOs and structured securities (11%), common & preferred stock (6%), and misc. investments (8%).

Investments in Affiliates: 6%

Group Affiliation: Nationwide Corp

Licensed in: All states, the District of Columbia and Puerto Rico

Commenced Business: January 1931

Address: ONE WEST NATIONWIDE BLVD, COLUMBUS, OH 43215-2220

Phone: (614) 249-5227 **Domicile State:** OH **NAIC Code:** 66869

Data Date	Rating	RACR #1	RACR #2	Total Assets ($mil)	Capital ($mil)	Net Premium ($mil)	Net Income ($mil)
2021	B-	2.16	1.53	179,000	9,091.4	12,663.4	810.8
2020	B-	2.25	1.59	166,000	9,105.4	10,635.4	486.9
2019	B-	2.36	1.67	155,000	8,821.6	10,167.6	629.0
2018	B-	2.40	1.61	139,000	6,845.1	9,828.0	711.0
2017	B-	2.19	1.46	146,000	5,949.3	10,402.4	1,038.7

Adverse Trends in Operations

Decrease in asset base during 2018 (4%)
Decrease in premium volume from 2017 to 2018 (6%)

NEW ENGLAND LIFE INS CO
B-   **Good**

Major Rating Factors: Good capitalization (5.6 on a scale of 0 to 10) based on good risk adjusted capital (moderate loss scenario). Good quality investment portfolio (6.4) despite mixed results such as: large holdings of BBB rated bonds but junk bond exposure equal to 58% of capital. Good liquidity (5.0) with sufficient resources to handle a spike in claims as well as a significant increase in policy surrenders.

Other Rating Factors: Good overall results on stability tests (5.0) despite fair risk adjusted capital in prior years good operational trends and excellent risk diversification. Weak profitability (2.9) with investment income below regulatory standards in relation to interest assumptions of reserves.

Principal Business: Individual life insurance (92%), individual annuities (5%), and individual health insurance (3%).

Principal Investments: NonCMO investment grade bonds (47%), policy loans (26%), CMOs and structured securities (11%), noninv. grade bonds (5%), and misc. investments (10%).

Investments in Affiliates: None

Group Affiliation: Brighthouse Financial Inc

Licensed In: All states except PR

Commenced Business: December 1980

Address: One Financial Plaza, Boston, MA 2111

Phone: (800) 882-1292   **Domicile State:** MA   **NAIC Code:** 91626

Data Date	Rating	RACR #1	RACR #2	Total Assets ($mil)	Capital ($mil)	Net Premium ($mil)	Net Income ($mil)
2021	B-	1.40	0.72	9,856.9	138.7	90.6	40.3
2020	C+	1.48	0.76	9,649.5	150.6	125.7	105.3
2019	B	1.18	0.61	9,118.5	115.8	150.6	61.1
2018	B	1.99	1.03	8,500.7	213.1	132.3	130.3
2017	B	4.27	2.15	10,160.6	482.5	153.8	68.0

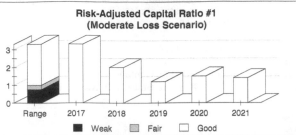

Risk-Adjusted Capital Ratio #1 (Moderate Loss Scenario)

Weak · Fair · Good

NEW ERA LIFE INS CO
B-   **Good**

Major Rating Factors: Good current capitalization (6.0 on a scale of 0 to 10) based on good risk adjusted capital (severe loss scenario) reflecting some improvement over results in 2017. Good liquidity (6.6) with sufficient resources to handle a spike in claims as well as a significant increase in policy surrenders. Fair quality investment portfolio (3.8).

Other Rating Factors: Fair overall results on stability tests (4.9) including fair risk adjusted capital in prior years. Excellent profitability (8.6) with operating gains in each of the last five years.

Principal Business: Individual annuities (55%), individual health insurance (43%), and individual life insurance (2%).

Principal Investments: NonCMO investment grade bonds (41%), common & preferred stock (18%), mortgages in good standing (18%), noninv. grade bonds (13%), and misc. investments (9%).

Investments in Affiliates: 18%

Group Affiliation: New Era Life Group

Licensed In: AL, AZ, AR, CA, CO, DE, FL, GA, IN, KS, KY, LA, MI, MS, MO, MT, NE, NM, NC, ND, OH, OK, PA, SC, SD, TN, TX, UT, WA, WV

Commenced Business: June 1924

Address: 11720 Katy Freeway Suite 1700, Houston, TX 77079

Phone: (281) 368-7200   **Domicile State:** TX   **NAIC Code:** 78743

Data Date	Rating	RACR #1	RACR #2	Total Assets ($mil)	Capital ($mil)	Net Premium ($mil)	Net Income ($mil)
2021	B-	1.07	0.88	641.7	150.6	199.1	12.8
2020	C	0.91	0.75	592.9	123.6	167.7	6.4
2019	C	0.95	0.78	552.5	100.9	180.0	2.0
2018	C	0.97	0.77	543.1	90.2	152.3	2.8
2017	C	0.94	0.73	538.3	79.3	181.4	3.5

Risk-Adjusted Capital Ratio #2 (Severe Loss Scenario)

Weak · Fair · Good · Strong

NEW YORK LIFE INS & ANNUITY CORP *
B+   **Good**

Major Rating Factors: Good quality investment portfolio (6.0 on a scale of 0 to 10) despite large holdings of BBB rated bonds in addition to moderate junk bond exposure. Exposure to mortgages is significant, but the mortgage default rate has been low. Good liquidity (5.6) with sufficient resources to handle a spike in claims as well as a significant increase in policy surrenders. Good overall results on stability tests (6.8) excellent operational trends and excellent risk diversification.

Other Rating Factors: Strong capitalization (8.1) based on excellent risk adjusted capital (severe loss scenario). Excellent profitability (7.2) with operating gains in each of the last five years.

Principal Business: Individual annuities (70%), individual life insurance (22%), and reinsurance (8%).

Principal Investments: NonCMO investment grade bonds (53%), CMOs and structured securities (25%), mortgages in good standing (13%), noninv. grade bonds (4%), and misc. investments (5%).

Investments in Affiliates: 4%

Group Affiliation: New York Life Group

Licensed In: All states except PR

Commenced Business: December 1980

Address: 200 CONTINENTAL DRIVE STE 306, WILMINGTON, DE 19801

Phone: (212) 576-7000   **Domicile State:** DE   **NAIC Code:** 91596

Data Date	Rating	RACR #1	RACR #2	Total Assets ($mil)	Capital ($mil)	Net Premium ($mil)	Net Income ($mil)
2021	B+	3.41	1.72	183,000	9,734.4	13,964.3	329.3
2020	B+	3.37	1.70	175,000	9,447.9	12,599.1	183.4
2019	B+	3.67	1.82	165,000	9,354.6	13,267.9	631.4
2018	B+	3.52	1.74	153,000	8,586.1	12,235.2	266.8
2017	B+	3.81	1.87	153,000	9,186.9	13,315.8	652.2

Adverse Trends in Operations

Decrease in premium volume from 2019 to 2020 (5%)
Decrease in capital during 2018 (7%)
Decrease in premium volume from 2017 to 2018 (8%)
Increase in policy surrenders from 2017 to 2018 (28%)

NEW YORK LIFE INS CO *   A-   Excellent

Major Rating Factors: Good quality investment portfolio (6.8 on a scale of 0 to 10) despite large holdings of BBB rated bonds in addition to moderate junk bond exposure. Exposure to mortgages is significant, but the mortgage default rate has been low. Good liquidity (5.8) with sufficient resources to handle a spike in claims as well as a significant increase in policy surrenders. Strong capitalization (7.1) based on excellent risk adjusted capital (severe loss scenario).

Other Rating Factors: Excellent profitability (7.8). Excellent overall results on stability tests (7.0) excellent operational trends, good risk adjusted capital for prior years and excellent risk diversification.

Principal Business: Individual life insurance (49%), group retirement contracts (30%), group life insurance (11%), reinsurance (5%), and other lines (6%).

Principal Investments: NonCMO investment grade bonds (46%), CMOs and structured securities (16%), mortgages in good standing (11%), common & preferred stock (8%), and misc. investments (18%).

Investments in Affiliates: 13%

Group Affiliation: New York Life Group

Licensed In: All states, the District of Columbia and Puerto Rico

Commenced Business: April 1845

Address: 51 MADISON AVENUE, NEW YORK, NY 10010

Phone: (212) 576-7000 **Domicile State:** NY **NAIC Code:** 66915

Data Date	Rating	RACR #1	RACR #2	Total Assets ($mil)	Capital ($mil)	Net Premium ($mil)	Net Income ($mil)
2021	A-	1.36	1.09	214,000	24,566.4	17,733.8	949.2
2020	A-	1.19	0.97	201,000	21,728.4	20,570.7	-76.0
2019	A-	1.73	1.32	189,000	22,032.3	15,962.5	377.6
2018	A-	1.78	1.34	180,000	21,006.5	17,084.3	1,210.4
2017	A-	1.70	1.30	177,000	20,357.0	15,070.0	1,479.9

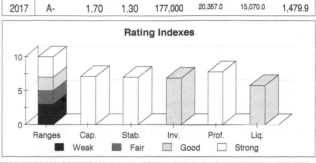

Rating Indexes

NORTH AMERICAN CO FOR LIFE & H INS   B   Good

Major Rating Factors: Good capitalization (6.3 on a scale of 0 to 10) based on good risk adjusted capital (moderate loss scenario). Moreover, capital levels have been consistent over the last five years. Fair quality investment portfolio (3.6) with large holdings of BBB rated bonds in addition to junk bond exposure equal to 91% of capital. Fair liquidity (4.5).

Other Rating Factors: Fair overall results on stability tests (4.4). Excellent profitability (8.6).

Principal Business: Individual annuities (68%), individual life insurance (30%), reinsurance (1%), and group life insurance (1%).

Principal Investments: NonCMO investment grade bonds (48%), CMOs and structured securities (28%), noninv. grade bonds (6%), mortgages in good standing (6%), and misc. investments (11%).

Investments in Affiliates: 2%

Group Affiliation: Sammons Enterprises Inc

Licensed In: All states except NY

Commenced Business: June 1886

Address: 4350 Westown Parkway, West Des Moines, IA 50266

Phone: (515) 440-5500 **Domicile State:** IA **NAIC Code:** 66974

Data Date	Rating	RACR #1	RACR #2	Total Assets ($mil)	Capital ($mil)	Net Premium ($mil)	Net Income ($mil)
2021	B	1.86	0.88	35,313.3	1,930.9	2,637.4	361.6
2020	B	1.68	0.78	32,392.3	1,584.7	2,545.3	-43.7
2019	B	1.88	0.89	29,479.1	1,539.7	2,485.2	45.6
2018	B	1.79	0.85	27,330.5	1,431.2	2,686.5	128.5
2017	D	1.77	0.83	25,007.5	1,361.4	2,443.5	147.4

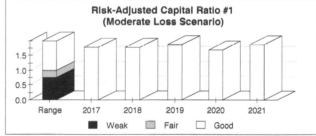

Risk-Adjusted Capital Ratio #1
(Moderate Loss Scenario)

NORTHWESTERN LONG TERM CARE INS CO *   B+   Good

Major Rating Factors: Good overall results on stability tests (6.8 on a scale of 0 to 10). Stability strengths include excellent operational trends and excellent risk diversification. Strong capitalization (8.0) based on excellent risk adjusted capital (severe loss scenario). Moreover, capital has steadily grown over the last five years. High quality investment portfolio (8.2).

Other Rating Factors: Excellent profitability (7.7) with operating gains in each of the last five years. Excellent liquidity (7.3).

Principal Business: Individual health insurance (100%).

Principal Investments: NonCMO investment grade bonds (101%).

Investments in Affiliates: None

Group Affiliation: Northwestern Mutual Group

Licensed In: All states except PR

Commenced Business: October 1953

Address: 720 EAST WISCONSIN AVENUE, MILWAUKEE, WI 53202

Phone: (414) 271-1444 **Domicile State:** WI **NAIC Code:** 69000

Data Date	Rating	RACR #1	RACR #2	Total Assets ($mil)	Capital ($mil)	Net Premium ($mil)	Net Income ($mil)
2021	B+	11.75	4.74	320.0	218.3	0.0	9.4
2020	B+	10.79	4.35	293.3	195.0	0.0	7.4
2019	B+	10.19	4.12	283.2	173.5	0.0	7.0
2018	B	9.04	3.65	240.4	141.8	0.0	2.9
2017	B	8.03	3.23	200.6	104.1	-0.1	7.5

Adverse Trends in Operations

Decrease in premium volume from 2016 to 2017 (145%)

NORTHWESTERN MUTUAL LIFE INS CO *   B+   Good

Major Rating Factors: Good quality investment portfolio (6.0 on a scale of 0 to 10) despite large holdings of BBB rated bonds in addition to junk bond exposure equal to 60% of capital. Exposure to mortgages is significant, but the mortgage default rate has been low. Good overall profitability (5.1) although investment income, in comparison to reserve requirements, is below regulatory standards. Good liquidity (5.8).

Other Rating Factors: Good overall results on stability tests (6.7) excellent operational trends and excellent risk diversification. Strong capitalization (8.3) based on excellent risk adjusted capital (severe loss scenario).

Principal Business: Individual life insurance (80%), individual annuities (9%), individual health insurance (6%), reinsurance (4%), and group retirement contracts (1%).

Principal Investments: NonCMO investment grade bonds (46%), mortgages in good standing (17%), CMOs and structured securities (13%), policy loans (6%), and misc. investments (17%).

Investments in Affiliates: 7%

Group Affiliation: Northwestern Mutual Group

Licensed in: All states except PR

Commenced Business: November 1858

Address: 720 EAST WISCONSIN AVENUE, MILWAUKEE, WI 53202-4797

Phone: (414) 271-1444 **Domicile State:** WI **NAIC Code:** 67091

Data Date	Rating	RACR #1	RACR #2	Total Assets ($mil)	Capital ($mil)	Net Premium ($mil)	Net Income ($mil)
2021	B+	3.73	1.89	335,000	29,283.2	22,551.3	977.8
2020	B+	3.44	1.73	309,000	24,957.5	19,148.8	425.3
2019	B+	3.51	1.78	290,000	24,216.2	18,796.8	1,267.5
2018	B+	3.32	1.69	272,000	22,134.2	17,822.9	783.0
2017	B+	3.27	1.66	265,000	20,850.2	17,698.7	1,017.0

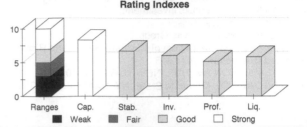

Rating Indexes

NY LIFE GROUP INS CO OF NY   B   Good

Major Rating Factors: Good quality investment portfolio (5.6 on a scale of 0 to 10) despite mixed results such as: minimal exposure to mortgages and large holdings of BBB rated bonds but minimal holdings in junk bonds. Good overall profitability (6.3). Excellent expense controls. Return on equity has been good over the last five years, averaging 11.4%. Good liquidity (6.5).

Other Rating Factors: Good overall results on stability tests (6.3) excellent operational trends and excellent risk diversification. Strong capitalization (7.8) based on excellent risk adjusted capital (severe loss scenario).

Principal Business: Group health insurance (78%) and group life insurance (21%).

Principal Investments: NonCMO investment grade bonds (80%), CMOs and structured securities (9%), noninv. grade bonds (6%), and mortgages in good standing (5%).

Investments in Affiliates: None

Group Affiliation: CIGNA Corp

Licensed in: AL, DC, MO, NY, PA, TN

Commenced Business: December 1965

Address: 140 EAST 45TH STREET, NEW YORK, NY 10010

Phone: (212) 576-7000 **Domicile State:** NY **NAIC Code:** 64548

Data Date	Rating	RACR #1	RACR #2	Total Assets ($mil)	Capital ($mil)	Net Premium ($mil)	Net Income ($mil)
2021	B	2.31	1.56	503.4	111.9	257.3	17.1
2020	B	2.11	1.48	461.5	98.7	233.3	-7.4
2019	A-	2.38	1.66	424.4	104.9	217.1	15.1
2018	A-	2.49	1.65	408.7	108.8	202.0	17.8
2017	A-	2.71	1.77	403.7	109.0	178.7	22.9

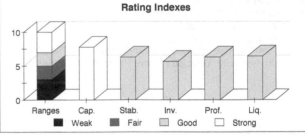

Rating Indexes

NYLIFE INS CO OF ARIZONA *   B+   Good

Major Rating Factors: Good overall profitability (5.4 on a scale of 0 to 10) despite operating losses during 2021. Return on equity has been low, averaging 4.1%. Good overall results on stability tests (5.5). Stability strengths include good operational trends and excellent risk diversification. Strong capitalization (10.0) based on excellent risk adjusted capital (severe loss scenario).

Other Rating Factors: High quality investment portfolio (8.5). Excellent liquidity (7.5).

Principal Business: Individual life insurance (100%).

Principal Investments: NonCMO investment grade bonds (80%) and CMOs and structured securities (19%).

Investments in Affiliates: None

Group Affiliation: New York Life Group

Licensed in: All states except ME, NY, PR

Commenced Business: December 1987

Address: 14850 N SCOTTSDALE RD STE 400, SCOTTSDALE, AZ 85254

Phone: (212) 576-7000 **Domicile State:** AZ **NAIC Code:** 81353

Data Date	Rating	RACR #1	RACR #2	Total Assets ($mil)	Capital ($mil)	Net Premium ($mil)	Net Income ($mil)
2021	B+	11.51	10.36	159.0	109.1	3.7	-2.0
2020	B+	11.57	10.41	158.2	109.7	8.8	7.3
2019	B+	11.34	10.21	163.8	108.1	11.4	4.7
2018	B+	11.76	10.58	176.6	113.4	13.7	2.9
2017	B	11.43	9.28	177.2	110.3	14.8	9.9

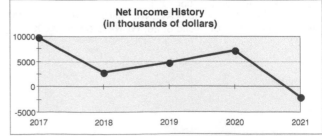

Net Income History
(in thousands of dollars)

OCCIDENTAL LIFE INS CO OF NC — C — Fair

Major Rating Factors: Fair overall results on stability tests (4.2 on a scale of 0 to 10) including fair financial strength of affiliated Industrial Alliance Ins & Financial. Fair profitability (4.0) with investment income below regulatory standards in relation to interest assumptions of reserves. Fair liquidity (3.5).
Other Rating Factors: Strong capitalization (8.2) based on excellent risk adjusted capital (severe loss scenario). High quality investment portfolio (7.4).
Principal Business: Individual life insurance (82%), individual annuities (17%), and group life insurance (1%).
Principal Investments: NonCMO investment grade bonds (87%), mortgages in good standing (5%), policy loans (4%), and CMOs and structured securities (1%).
Investments in Affiliates: None
Group Affiliation: Industrial Alliance Ins & Financial
Licensed in: All states except NY
Commenced Business: November 1906
Address: 425 AUSTIN AVENUE, WACO, TX 76701
Phone: (254) 297-2777 **Domicile State:** TX **NAIC Code:** 67148

Data Date	Rating	RACR #1	RACR #2	Total Assets ($mil)	Capital ($mil)	Net Premium ($mil)	Net Income ($mil)
2021	C	3.17	1.83	295.3	36.6	68.7	4.4
2020	C	3.07	1.77	277.5	33.6	62.4	2.3
2019	C	2.86	1.67	259.9	29.2	53.9	4.8
2018	C	2.76	1.60	253.1	27.7	34.4	4.8
2017	C	2.70	1.61	257.6	27.0	43.2	0.5

Industrial Alliance Ins Financial
Composite Group Rating: C
Largest Group Members

	Assets ($mil)	Rating
AMERICAN-AMICABLE LIFE INS CO OF TX	407	C
INDUSTRIAL ALLIANCE INS FIN SERV	281	C
OCCIDENTAL LIFE INS CO OF NC	277	C
IA AMERICAN LIFE INS CO	211	C
DEALERS ASR CO	199	B-

OCEANVIEW LIFE AND ANNUITY CO — C — Fair

Major Rating Factors: Fair current capitalization (3.6 on a scale of 0 to 10) based on fair risk adjusted capital (moderate loss scenario), although results have slipped from the good range over the last year. Fair overall results on stability tests (3.6) including excessive premium growth and fair risk adjusted capital in prior years. Low quality investment portfolio (1.9).
Other Rating Factors: Weak profitability (1.9) with operating losses during 2021. Excellent liquidity (7.9).
Principal Business: Individual annuities (100%).
Principal Investments: Mortgages in good standing (40%), CMOs and structured securities (27%), nonperforming mortgages (13%), cash (9%), and misc. investments (9%).
Investments in Affiliates: None
Group Affiliation: Penn Mutual Life Ins Company
Licensed in: All states except NY, VT, PR
Commenced Business: October 1965
Address: 16479 Dallas Parkway Suite 850, DENVER, CO 80202-1233
Phone: (833) 656 7455 **Domicile State:** TX **NAIC Code:** 68446

Data Date	Rating	RACR #1	RACR #2	Total Assets ($mil)	Capital ($mil)	Net Premium ($mil)	Net Income ($mil)
2021	C	0.83	0.57	3,661.7	308.5	1,620.8	-23.1
2020	C+	3.45	1.79	1,883.5	206.2	975.0	-40.8
2019	C+	9.65	8.07	646.1	134.1	0.0	-1.1
2018	B	3.81	3.43	7.7	7.7	0.0	-0.1
2017	B	3.83	3.45	7.8	7.8	0.0	-0.1

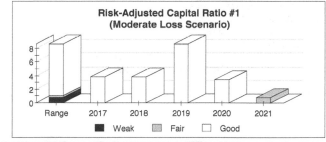

Risk-Adjusted Capital Ratio #1
(Moderate Loss Scenario)

Range 2017 2018 2019 2020 2021
■ Weak ▨ Fair ☐ Good

OHIO NATIONAL LIFE ASR CORP — B — Good

Major Rating Factors: Good overall results on stability tests (5.6 on a scale of 0 to 10) despite fair financial strength of affiliated Ohio Natonal Mutual Inc. Other stability subfactors include excellent operational trends and excellent risk diversification. Good quality investment portfolio (5.6) despite large holdings of BBB rated bonds in addition to moderate junk bond exposure. Exposure to mortgages is significant, but the mortgage default rate has been low. Good overall profitability (5.2) although investment income, in comparison to reserve requirements, is below regulatory standards.
Other Rating Factors: Good liquidity (5.4). Strong capitalization (7.1) based on excellent risk adjusted capital (severe loss scenario).
Principal Business: Individual life insurance (90%) and individual health insurance (10%).
Principal Investments: NonCMO investment grade bonds (58%), mortgages in good standing (16%), CMOs and structured securities (10%), policy loans (5%), and misc. investments (7%).
Investments in Affiliates: None
Group Affiliation: Ohio Natonal Mutual Inc
Licensed in: All states except NY
Commenced Business: August 1979
Address: One Financial Way, Cincinnati, OH 45242
Phone: (513) 794-6100 **Domicile State:** OH **NAIC Code:** 89206

Data Date	Rating	RACR #1	RACR #2	Total Assets ($mil)	Capital ($mil)	Net Premium ($mil)	Net Income ($mil)
2021	B	2.00	1.05	3,181.4	246.8	153.8	14.7
2020	B	1.95	1.03	3,032.6	232.7	136.2	10.6
2019	B	2.27	1.19	2,998.6	257.4	141.2	62.9
2018	B+	2.08	1.09	4,054.3	290.4	152.1	35.9
2017	B+	2.03	1.06	3,978.3	283.9	158.3	43.7

Ohio Natonal Mutual Inc
Composite Group Rating: C+
Largest Group Members

	Assets ($mil)	Rating
OHIO NATIONAL LIFE INS CO	28400	C+
OHIO NATIONAL LIFE ASR CORP	3033	B
NATIONAL SECURITY LIFE ANNUITY CO	465	B-

OHIO NATIONAL LIFE INS CO

C+   **Fair**

Major Rating Factors: Fair overall results on stability tests (4.2 on a scale of 0 to 10). Good quality investment portfolio (5.7) despite significant exposure to mortgages . Mortgage default rate has been low. large holdings of BBB rated bonds in addition to small junk bond holdings. Good overall profitability (6.1). Return on equity has been fair, averaging 6.3%.

Other Rating Factors: Good liquidity (6.2). Strong overall capitalization (7.2) based on mixed results -- excessive policy leverage mitigated by excellent risk adjusted capital (severe loss scenario).

Principal Business: Individual life insurance (70%), individual annuities (11%), reinsurance (11%), group retirement contracts (7%), and individual health insurance (1%).

Principal Investments: NonCMO investment grade bonds (51%), mortgages in good standing (11%), policy loans (10%), CMOs and structured securities (9%), and misc. investments (13%).

Investments in Affiliates: 7%

Group Affiliation: Ohio Natonal Mutual Inc

Licensed in: All states except NY

Commenced Business: October 1910

Address: One Financial Way, Cincinnati, OH 45242

Phone: (513) 794-6100   **Domicile State:** OH   **NAIC Code:** 67172

Data Date	Rating	RACR #1	RACR #2	Total Assets ($mil)	Capital ($mil)	Net Premium ($mil)	Net Income ($mil)
2021	C+	1.63	1.13	28,854.3	1,455.5	-17,687.3	419.1
2020	C+	1.48	0.94	28,400.3	1,078.5	519.7	134.9
2019	C+	1.42	0.93	28,224.8	1,019.9	272.0	-83.8
2018	B-	1.29	0.85	29,084.4	1,019.1	1,420.8	-55.4
2017	B	1.41	0.93	31,676.7	1,101.6	1,841.2	71.0

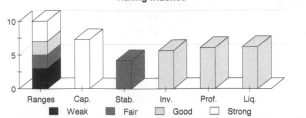

Rating Indexes

Ranges   Cap.   Stab.   Inv.   Prof.   Liq.

■ Weak   ■ Fair   ▨ Good   ☐ Strong

OLD REPUBLIC LIFE INS CO *

B+   **Good**

Major Rating Factors: Good overall results on stability tests (6.6 on a scale of 0 to 10). Stability strengths include excellent operational trends and excellent risk diversification. Good quality investment portfolio (5.5) despite mixed results such as: no exposure to mortgages and substantial holdings of BBB bonds but minimal holdings in junk bonds. Good overall profitability (5.8) although investment income, in comparison to reserve requirements, is below regulatory standards.

Other Rating Factors: Strong capitalization (10.0) based on excellent risk adjusted capital (severe loss scenario). Excellent liquidity (7.6).

Principal Business: Group health insurance (57%), individual life insurance (26%), and reinsurance (17%).

Principal Investments: NonCMO investment grade bonds (66%), common & preferred stock (18%), and cash (2%).

Investments in Affiliates: None

Group Affiliation: Old Republic Group

Licensed in: All states except NY

Commenced Business: April 1923

Address: 307 NORTH MICHIGAN AVENUE, CHICAGO, IL 60601

Phone: (312) 346-8100   **Domicile State:** IL   **NAIC Code:** 67261

Data Date	Rating	RACR #1	RACR #2	Total Assets ($mil)	Capital ($mil)	Net Premium ($mil)	Net Income ($mil)
2021	B+	5.94	3.84	106.8	48.0	10.8	3.8
2020	B-	5.34	3.53	105.0	43.7	10.7	3.5
2019	B-	5.06	3.09	107.8	40.1	13.0	3.7
2018	B-	4.05	2.48	109.0	33.6	14.3	0.8
2017	B-	3.66	2.28	122.7	34.8	18.2	1.7

Adverse Trends in Operations

Increase in policy surrenders from 2019 to 2020 (193%)
Decrease in premium volume from 2019 to 2020 (18%)
Decrease in asset base during 2018 (11%)
Decrease in premium volume from 2017 to 2018 (21%)
Decrease in premium volume from 2016 to 2017 (6%)

OLD UNITED LIFE INS CO

B   **Good**

Major Rating Factors: Good overall results on stability tests (5.6 on a scale of 0 to 10) despite fair financial strength of affiliated Berkshire Hathaway Inc and excessive premium growth. Other stability subfactors include excellent operational trends and excellent risk diversification. Fair quality investment portfolio (3.9). Strong capitalization (10.0) based on excellent risk adjusted capital (severe loss scenario).

Other Rating Factors: Excellent profitability (7.4) with operating gains in each of the last five years. Excellent liquidity (10.0).

Principal Business: Credit health insurance (56%) and credit life insurance (44%).

Principal Investments: NonCMO investment grade bonds (57%), common & preferred stock (41%), cash (1%), and CMOs and structured securities (1%).

Investments in Affiliates: None

Group Affiliation: Berkshire Hathaway Inc

Licensed in: All states except ME, NH, NY, PR

Commenced Business: January 1964

Address: 3800 N Central Ave Ste 460, Phoenix, AZ 85012

Phone: (913) 895-0200   **Domicile State:** AZ   **NAIC Code:** 76007

Data Date	Rating	RACR #1	RACR #2	Total Assets ($mil)	Capital ($mil)	Net Premium ($mil)	Net Income ($mil)
2021	B	5.69	3.50	129.8	89.4	12.0	0.6
2020	B	6.64	4.06	113.3	78.7	8.1	3.0
2019	B	6.39	3.89	95.9	65.1	6.4	4.1
2018	B	6.96	4.21	88.8	52.5	5.6	7.6
2017	B	6.47	4.50	84.7	47.8	6.1	2.9

Berkshire Hathaway Inc
Composite Group Rating: C+
Largest Group Members

	Assets ($mil)	Rating
NATIONAL INDEMNITY CO	317406	C+
GOVERNMENT EMPLOYEES INS CO	44674	B
COLUMBIA INS CO	32046	C+
BERKSHIRE HATHAWAY LIFE INS CO OF NE	23422	C+
GENERAL REINS CORP	18513	C+

OMAHA INS CO   B-   Good

Major Rating Factors: Good capitalization (6.1 on a scale of 0 to 10) based on good risk adjusted capital (severe loss scenario). Good liquidity (6.2) with sufficient resources to handle a spike in claims. Fair overall results on stability tests (4.9).
Other Rating Factors: Weak profitability (1.9) with operating losses during 2021. High quality investment portfolio (7.1).
Principal Business: Individual health insurance (100%).
Principal Investments: CMOs and structured securities (60%) and nonCMO investment grade bonds (41%).
Investments in Affiliates: None
Group Affiliation: Mutual Of Omaha Group
Licensed in: All states except FL, NH, NY, PR
Commenced Business: November 2006
Address: MUTUAL OF OMAHA PLAZA, OMAHA, NE 68175
Phone: (402) 342-7600 **Domicile State:** NE **NAIC Code:** 13100

Data Date	Rating	RACR #1	RACR #2	Total Assets ($mil)	Capital ($mil)	Net Premium ($mil)	Net Income ($mil)
2021	B-	1.71	0.89	114.7	52.7	79.7	-2.2
2020	B-	1.87	0.96	122.5	56.0	78.7	-1.9
2019	B-	1.97	1.02	109.5	54.9	73.6	-9.0
2018	B-	1.81	0.95	98.9	49.3	65.5	-6.7
2017	B-	1.84	0.97	98.3	45.2	56.2	-5.3

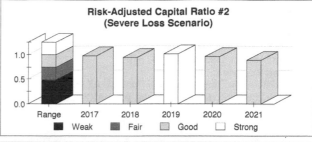

Risk-Adjusted Capital Ratio #2 (Severe Loss Scenario)

OPTIMUM RE INS CO   C+   Fair

Major Rating Factors: Fair overall results on stability tests (4.6 on a scale of 0 to 10) including negative cash flow from operations for 2021. Weak profitability (2.4) with investment income below regulatory standards in relation to interest assumptions of reserves. Strong capitalization (7.8) based on excellent risk adjusted capital (severe loss scenario).
Other Rating Factors: High quality investment portfolio (7.1). Excellent liquidity (7.0).
Principal Business: Reinsurance (100%).
Principal Investments: NonCMO investment grade bonds (73%), cash (19%), common & preferred stock (5%), and real estate (2%).
Investments in Affiliates: 2%
Group Affiliation: Optimum Group Inc
Licensed in: All states except NY
Commenced Business: June 1978
Address: 1345 River Bend Drive Ste 100, DALLAS, TX 75247
Phone: (214) 528-2020 **Domicile State:** TX **NAIC Code:** 88099

Data Date	Rating	RACR #1	RACR #2	Total Assets ($mil)	Capital ($mil)	Net Premium ($mil)	Net Income ($mil)
2021	C+	2.48	1.52	282.9	48.7	71.5	2.7
2020	C+	2.61	1.60	273.4	49.3	65.7	5.6
2019	C+	2.67	1.64	211.5	45.2	62.1	4.7
2018	C+	2.51	1.54	196.7	41.1	47.7	5.8
2017	C+	2.53	1.57	183.4	37.5	42.7	5.2

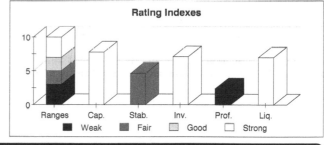

Rating Indexes

OPTUM INS OF OH INC   B-   Good

Major Rating Factors: Good overall profitability (5.2 on a scale of 0 to 10). Return on equity has been excellent over the last five years averaging 49.0%. Fair overall results on stability tests (4.5) including fair financial strength of affiliated UnitedHealth Group Inc and negative cash flow from operations for 2021. Strong capitalization (8.0) based on excellent risk adjusted capital (severe loss scenario).
Other Rating Factors: High quality investment portfolio (9.8). Excellent liquidity (9.1).
Principal Business: Individual life insurance (99%).
Principal Investments: Cash (97%) and nonCMO investment grade bonds (2%).
Investments in Affiliates: None
Group Affiliation: UnitedHealth Group Inc
Licensed in: All states except ME, NY, PR
Commenced Business: December 1978
Address: 50 W Broad Street Suite 1800, Columbus, OH 43215
Phone: (952) 979-7329 **Domicile State:** OH **NAIC Code:** 69647

Data Date	Rating	RACR #1	RACR #2	Total Assets ($mil)	Capital ($mil)	Net Premium ($mil)	Net Income ($mil)
2021	B-	3.87	3.48	251.7	39.5	0.0	27.3
2020	B-	5.69	5.12	424.2	67.2	0.0	32.0
2019	B	5.28	4.75	506.8	66.2	0.0	31.3
2018	B	6.13	5.52	356.2	68.7	0.0	35.2
2017	B	4.96	4.47	185.9	47.9	0.0	14.4

UnitedHealth Group Inc Composite Group Rating: C Largest Group Members	Assets ($mil)	Rating
UNITED HEALTHCARE INS CO	21587	C
UHC OF CALIFORNIA INC	793	C-
GOLDEN RULE INS CO	629	B
UNIMERICA INS CO	450	B-
OPTUM INS OF OH INC	424	B-

OXFORD LIFE INS CO *

B+   **Good**

Major Rating Factors: Good quality investment portfolio (5.7 on a scale of 0 to 10) despite significant exposure to mortgages . Mortgage default rate has been low. large holdings of BBB rated bonds in addition to small junk bond holdings. Good liquidity (5.5) with sufficient resources to handle a spike in claims as well as a significant increase in policy surrenders. Good overall results on stability tests (5.9) good operational trends and excellent risk diversification.

Other Rating Factors: Strong capitalization (7.3) based on excellent risk adjusted capital (severe loss scenario). Excellent profitability (8.1) with operating gains in each of the last five years.

Principal Business: Individual annuities (80%), individual life insurance (13%), individual health insurance (6%), and reinsurance (1%).

Principal Investments: NonCMO investment grade bonds (67%), CMOs and structured securities (14%), mortgages in good standing (12%), common & preferred stock (2%), and misc. investments (3%).

Investments in Affiliates: 1%

Group Affiliation: Amerco Corp

Licensed in: All states except NY, VT, PR

Commenced Business: June 1968

Address: 2721 North Central Avenue, Phoenix, AZ 85004

Phone: (602) 263-6666 **Domicile State:** AZ **NAIC Code:** 76112

Data Date	Rating	RACR #1	RACR #2	Total Assets ($mil)	Capital ($mil)	Net Premium ($mil)	Net Income ($mil)
2021	B+	2.20	1.21	2,955.5	230.2	417.9	23.2
2020	B+	1.93	1.14	2,750.7	218.3	563.4	5.8
2019	B+	2.13	1.33	2,377.1	223.3	314.7	20.1
2018	B+	2.00	1.24	2,213.9	203.7	391.7	11.4
2017	B+	2.01	1.27	1,954.6	195.9	405.0	10.4

Adverse Trends in Operations

Decrease in premium volume from 2018 to 2019 (20%)
Increase in policy surrenders from 2018 to 2019 (35%)
Change in premium mix from 2018 to 2019 (5%)
Change in premium mix from 2017 to 2018 (4.7%)
Increase in policy surrenders from 2016 to 2017 (65%)

OZARK NATIONAL LIFE INS CO

C+   **Fair**

Major Rating Factors: Fair overall results on stability tests (4.5 on a scale of 0 to 10). Good liquidity (6.1) with sufficient resources to handle a spike in claims as well as a significant increase in policy surrenders. Weak profitability (2.9) with investment income below regulatory standards in relation to interest assumptions of reserves.

Other Rating Factors: Strong capitalization (8.6) based on excellent risk adjusted capital (severe loss scenario). High quality investment portfolio (7.2).

Principal Business: Individual life insurance (99%).

Principal Investments: NonCMO investment grade bonds (84%), CMOs and structured securities (11%), policy loans (2%), noninv. grade bonds (1%), and cash (1%).

Investments in Affiliates: None

Group Affiliation: CNS Corp

Licensed in: AL, AZ, AR, CA, CO, FL, GA, IL, IN, IA, KS, KY, LA, MI, MN, MS, MO, MT, NE, NV, NM, ND, OH, OK, SD, TN, TX, UT, WI, WY

Commenced Business: June 1964

Address: 500 East Ninth Street, Kansas City, MO 64106-2627

Phone: (816) 842-6300 **Domicile State:** MO **NAIC Code:** 67393

Data Date	Rating	RACR #1	RACR #2	Total Assets ($mil)	Capital ($mil)	Net Premium ($mil)	Net Income ($mil)
2021	C+	3.71	2.07	849.9	105.8	77.0	28.2
2020	C+	2.80	1.57	810.3	78.0	77.7	21.0
2019	C+	2.17	1.22	774.0	58.4	80.8	-0.9
2018	B-	5.01	2.81	838.4	142.8	81.9	20.4
2017	B-	4.82	2.69	820.9	138.8	82.6	15.8

Rating Indexes

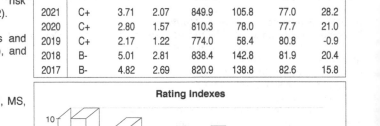

PACIFIC GUARDIAN LIFE INS CO LTD

B   **Good**

Major Rating Factors: Good quality investment portfolio (6.6 on a scale of 0 to 10) despite large exposure to mortgages . Mortgage default rate has been low. substantial holdings of BBB bonds in addition to minimal holdings in junk bonds. Good liquidity (5.6) with sufficient resources to handle a spike in claims as well as a significant increase in policy surrenders. Good overall results on stability tests (5.9) excellent operational trends and excellent risk diversification.

Other Rating Factors: Fair profitability (3.0) with operating losses during 2021. Strong capitalization (8.3) based on excellent risk adjusted capital (severe loss scenario).

Principal Business: Group health insurance (50%), individual life insurance (36%), group life insurance (7%), and individual annuities (6%).

Principal Investments: NonCMO investment grade bonds (43%), mortgages in good standing (37%), CMOs and structured securities (9%), policy loans (5%), and misc. investments (4%).

Investments in Affiliates: None

Group Affiliation: Meiji Yasuda Life Ins Co

Licensed in: All states except CT, FL, GA, IL, KS, MA, MN, NJ, NY, PR

Commenced Business: June 1962

Address: 1440 Kapiolani Blvd Ste 1600, Honolulu, HI 96814-3698

Phone: (808) 955-2236 **Domicile State:** HI **NAIC Code:** 64343

Data Date	Rating	RACR #1	RACR #2	Total Assets ($mil)	Capital ($mil)	Net Premium ($mil)	Net Income ($mil)
2021	B	3.32	1.88	594.9	86.3	72.3	-0.8
2020	B+	3.24	1.88	573.6	83.7	65.1	-0.9
2019	B+	2.96	1.76	565.5	86.5	77.1	1.4
2018	A-	3.47	2.03	556.9	94.0	77.7	4.8
2017	A-	3.96	2.31	553.9	102.4	74.4	4.0

Adverse Trends in Operations

Decrease in capital during 2020 (3%)
Decrease in premium volume from 2019 to 2020 (16%)
Decrease in capital during 2019 (8%)
Decrease in capital during 2018 (8%)
Decrease in capital during 2017 (4%)

PACIFIC LIFE & ANNUITY CO *   B+   Good

Major Rating Factors: Good quality investment portfolio (6.4 on a scale of 0 to 10) despite mixed results such as: large holdings of BBB rated bonds but moderate junk bond exposure. Good overall profitability (6.6). Return on equity has been fair, averaging 10.0%. Good liquidity (6.0) with sufficient resources to handle a spike in claims as well as a significant increase in policy surrenders.

Other Rating Factors: Good overall results on stability tests (6.5) despite excessive premium growth good operational trends and excellent risk diversification. Strong capitalization (8.4) based on excellent risk adjusted capital (severe loss scenario).

Principal Business: Individual annuities (72%), group retirement contracts (25%), and individual life insurance (3%).

Principal Investments: NonCMO investment grade bonds (84%), mortgages in good standing (7%), CMOs and structured securities (4%), and noninv. grade bonds (2%).

Investments in Affiliates: None
Group Affiliation: Pacific LifeCorp
Licensed In: All states except PR
Commenced Business: July 1983
Address: 3800 N CENTRAL AVE STE 460, PHOENIX, AZ 85021
Phone: (714) 640-3011 **Domicile State:** AZ **NAIC Code:** 97268

Data Date	Rating	RACR #1	RACR #2	Total Assets ($mil)	Capital ($mil)	Net Premium ($mil)	Net Income ($mil)
2021	B+	4.09	1.94	8,615.1	536.9	583.0	32.1
2020	B+	4.41	2.08	8,218.5	554.8	452.8	7.4
2019	B+	4.62	2.20	7,786.1	545.6	566.5	32.8
2018	B+	5.10	2.42	7,132.8	550.4	544.9	59.2
2017	B+	4.61	2.24	7,125.3	540.6	520.6	46.0

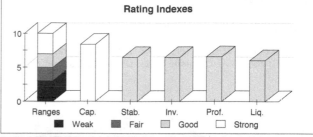

Rating Indexes

Ranges   Cap.   Stab.   Inv.   Prof.   Liq.
■ Weak   ■ Fair   ▨ Good   ☐ Strong

PACIFIC LIFE INS CO *   A-   Excellent

Major Rating Factors: Good quality investment portfolio (5.6 on a scale of 0 to 10) despite large holdings of BBB rated bonds in addition to moderate junk bond exposure. Exposure to mortgages is significant, but the mortgage default rate has been low. Good liquidity (6.0) with sufficient resources to handle a spike in claims as well as a significant increase in policy surrenders. Good overall results on stability tests (6.9) excellent operational trends and excellent risk diversification.

Other Rating Factors: Weak profitability (2.8) with investment income below regulatory standards in relation to interest assumptions of reserves. Strong capitalization (8.5) based on excellent risk adjusted capital (severe loss scenario).

Principal Business: Individual annuities (40%), individual life insurance (29%), reinsurance (16%), and group retirement contracts (10%).

Principal Investments: NonCMO investment grade bonds (52%), mortgages in good standing (15%), CMOs and structured securities (9%), policy loans (7%), and misc. investments (12%).

Investments in Affiliates: 5%
Group Affiliation: Pacific LifeCorp
Licensed In: All states except NY, PR
Commenced Business: May 1868
Address: 6750 MERCY ROAD, OMAHA, NE 68106
Phone: (714) 630-3011 **Domicile State:** NE **NAIC Code:** 67466

Data Date	Rating	RACR #1	RACR #2	Total Assets ($mil)	Capital ($mil)	Net Premium ($mil)	Net Income ($mil)
2021	A-	3.63	1.99	178,000	11,353.2	13,984.3	861.0
2020	A-	3.69	2.05	169,000	11,364.2	11,759.8	-98.7
2019	A-	3.69	2.08	146,000	10,509.6	13,440.7	1,715.9
2018	A-	3.68	2.04	129,000	9,691.4	12,254.2	868.7
2017	A-	3.57	2.00	129,000	9,312.9	9,267.9	1,201.4

Adverse Trends in Operations

Decrease in premium volume from 2019 to 2020 (13%)

PAN-AMERICAN LIFE INS CO   B   Good

Major Rating Factors: Good overall results on stability tests (5.6 on a scale of 0 to 10) despite negative cash flow from operations for 2021. Other stability subfactors include good operational trends and excellent risk diversification. Good quality investment portfolio (5.4) despite mixed results such as: large holdings of BBB rated bonds but moderate junk bond exposure. Good liquidity (6.4).

Other Rating Factors: Strong capitalization (8.1) based on excellent risk adjusted capital (severe loss scenario). Excellent profitability (7.1) with operating gains in each of the last five years.

Principal Business: Group health insurance (74%), reinsurance (14%), individual life insurance (6%), individual health insurance (5%), and group life insurance (2%).

Principal Investments: NonCMO investment grade bonds (52%), CMOs and structured securities (23%), noninv. grade bonds (7%), policy loans (5%), and misc. investments (12%).

Investments in Affiliates: 2%
Group Affiliation: Pan-American Life
Licensed In: All states except ME, NY, VT
Commenced Business: March 1912
Address: PAN-AMERICAN LIFE CENTER, NEW ORLEANS, LA 70130-6060
Phone: (504) 566-1300 **Domicile State:** LA **NAIC Code:** 67539

Data Date	Rating	RACR #1	RACR #2	Total Assets ($mil)	Capital ($mil)	Net Premium ($mil)	Net Income ($mil)
2021	B	2.81	1.76	1,236.0	267.9	262.3	10.8
2020	B	2.41	1.50	1,289.0	251.4	278.9	11.7
2019	B	2.26	1.46	1,276.3	231.6	344.6	5.1
2018	B	2.48	1.61	1,205.2	243.6	217.1	15.5
2017	B	2.41	1.53	1,221.1	234.1	212.9	14.5

Adverse Trends in Operations

Decrease in premium volume from 2019 to 2020 (19%)
Change in premium mix from 2018 to 2019 (6%)
Decrease in capital during 2019 (5%)
Decrease in premium volume from 2016 to 2017 (6%)
Decrease in asset base during 2017 (3%)

PARK AVENUE LIFE INS CO   B   Good

Major Rating Factors: Good current capitalization (6.9 on a scale of 0 to 10) based on good risk adjusted capital (severe loss scenario), although results have slipped from the excellent range over the last year. Good quality investment portfolio (6.2) despite mixed results such as: no exposure to mortgages and large holdings of BBB rated bonds but small junk bond holdings. Good liquidity (6.5).

Other Rating Factors: Good overall results on stability tests (5.2) despite negative cash flow from operations for 2021 good operational trends and excellent risk diversification. Excellent profitability (8.1) with operating gains in each of the last five years.

Principal Business: Reinsurance (70%) and individual life insurance (30%).

Principal Investments: NonCMO investment grade bonds (77%), common & preferred stock (19%), noninv. grade bonds (2%), and policy loans (1%).

Investments in Affiliates: 19%

Group Affiliation: Guardian Group

Licensed in: All states except HI, NY, PR

Commenced Business: April 1965

Address: 2711 CENTERVILLE ROAD STE 400, WILMINGTON, DE 19808

Phone: (866) 766-6599 **Domicile State:** DE **NAIC Code:** 60003

Data Date	Rating	RACR #1	RACR #2	Total Assets ($mil)	Capital ($mil)	Net Premium ($mil)	Net Income ($mil)
2021	B	1.11	0.99	199.4	46.7	1.1	5.0
2020	B	1.18	1.04	215.2	52.9	1.3	5.2
2019	B	1.07	0.95	220.6	45.5	1.4	5.4
2018	B	1.24	1.08	233.8	50.4	1.6	6.4
2017	B	1.09	0.93	236.5	41.2	1.8	5.0

Risk-Adjusted Capital Ratio #2 (Severe Loss Scenario)

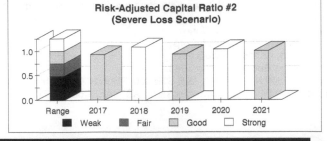

PARKER CENTENNIAL ASR CO *   A-   Excellent

Major Rating Factors: Good liquidity (6.8 on a scale of 0 to 10) with sufficient resources to handle a spike in claims. Excellent overall results on stability tests (7.1). Strengths that enhance stability include excellent operational trends and excellent risk diversification. Strong capitalization (10.0) based on excellent risk adjusted capital (severe loss scenario). Furthermore, this high level of risk adjusted capital has been consistently maintained over the last five years.

Other Rating Factors: High quality investment portfolio (8.4). Excellent profitability (7.6) with operating gains in each of the last five years.

Principal Business: Group retirement contracts (100%).

Principal Investments: NonCMO investment grade bonds (97%) and noninv. grade bonds (2%).

Investments in Affiliates: None

Group Affiliation: Sentry Ins Group

Licensed in: All states except NY, PR

Commenced Business: August 1973

Address: 1800 NORTH POINT DRIVE, STEVENS POINT, WI 54481

Phone: (715) 346-6000 **Domicile State:** WI **NAIC Code:** 71099

Data Date	Rating	RACR #1	RACR #2	Total Assets ($mil)	Capital ($mil)	Net Premium ($mil)	Net Income ($mil)
2021	A-	5.37	4.84	99.1	47.9	4.9	1.8
2020	A-	5.43	4.88	96.0	47.7	1.9	1.6
2019	A	5.41	4.87	96.2	47.4	2.3	1.9
2018	A	5.40	4.86	94.9	47.1	4.8	1.6
2017	A	5.46	4.92	91.8	46.8	2.3	1.9

Adverse Trends in Operations

Decrease in premium volume from 2019 to 2020 (17%)
Decrease in premium volume from 2018 to 2019 (51%)

PARTNERRE LIFE RE CO OF AM   C   Fair

Major Rating Factors: Fair overall results on stability tests (3.8 on a scale of 0 to 10) including excessive premium growth. Good liquidity (6.6) with sufficient resources to handle a spike in claims. Weak profitability (1.7) with operating losses during 2021. Return on equity has been low, averaging -21.1%.

Other Rating Factors: Strong capitalization (8.3) based on excellent risk adjusted capital (severe loss scenario). High quality investment portfolio (8.5).

Principal Business: Reinsurance (100%).

Principal Investments: NonCMO investment grade bonds (56%), CMOs and structured securities (33%), and cash (5%).

Investments in Affiliates: None

Group Affiliation: Giovanni Agnelli BV

Licensed in: All states except NY, PR

Commenced Business: July 1964

Address: 425 WEST CAPITOL AVE STE 1, LITTLE ROCK, AR 72201

Phone: (203) 485-4200 **Domicile State:** AR **NAIC Code:** 74900

Data Date	Rating	RACR #1	RACR #2	Total Assets ($mil)	Capital ($mil)	Net Premium ($mil)	Net Income ($mil)
2021	C	2.79	1.87	417.3	48.8	19.5	-15.9
2020	C	2.40	1.62	105.1	39.7	15.2	-8.6
2019	C	2.21	1.50	89.3	35.3	11.6	-9.3
2018	C	2.00	1.36	72.1	32.2	8.6	-3.1
2017	C	1.59	1.09	53.2	23.4	5.8	-3.7

Rating Indexes

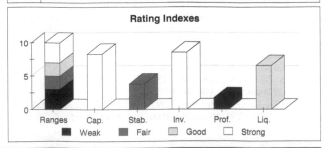

PAUL REVERE LIFE INS CO   C+   Fair

Major Rating Factors: Fair overall results on stability tests (4.0 on a scale of 0 to 10) including fair financial strength of affiliated Unum Group and negative cash flow from operations for 2021. Fair current capitalization (4.0) based on mixed results -- excessive policy leverage mitigated by excellent risk adjusted capital (severe loss scenario) reflecting improvement over results in 2017. Fair quality investment portfolio (4.9).

Other Rating Factors: Good liquidity (6.6). Excellent profitability (7.4) with operating gains in each of the last five years.

Principal Business: Individual health insurance (67%), reinsurance (22%), individual life insurance (5%), group health insurance (5%), and group life insurance (1%).

Principal Investments: NonCMO investment grade bonds (92%), mortgages in good standing (3%), CMOs and structured securities (2%), and noninv. grade bonds (1%).

Investments in Affiliates: None
Group Affiliation: Unum Group
Licensed in: All states except PR
Commenced Business: July 1930
Address: 1 MERCANTILE STREET, WORCESTER, MA 1608
Phone: (423) 294-1011 **Domicile State:** MA **NAIC Code:** 67598

Data Date	Rating	RACR #1	RACR #2	Total Assets ($mil)	Capital ($mil)	Net Premium ($mil)	Net Income ($mil)
2021	C+	18.78	16.90	745.4	270.0	-318.8	122.6
2020	C+	18.88	16.99	1,280.3	353.7	-1,966.0	170.6
2019	C+	1.45	0.90	3,213.5	173.2	90.2	63.8
2018	C+	1.55	0.94	3,410.2	191.1	93.2	70.4
2017	C+	1.40	0.82	3,570.6	177.3	93.8	55.4

Unum Group
Composite Group Rating: C+

Largest Group Members	Assets ($mil)	Rating
UNUM LIFE INS CO OF AMERICA	21791	C+
PROVIDENT LIFE ACCIDENT INS CO	6172	C+
FIRST UNUM LIFE INS CO	4249	C+
COLONIAL LIFE ACCIDENT INS CO	3760	C+
PAUL REVERE LIFE INS CO	1280	C+

PAVONIA LIFE INS CO OF MICHIGAN   C   Fair

Major Rating Factors: Fair quality investment portfolio (4.7 on a scale of 0 to 10). Fair overall results on stability tests (3.5) including negative cash flow from operations for 2021, fair risk adjusted capital in prior years. Good current capitalization (5.7) based on good risk adjusted capital (moderate loss scenario) reflecting some improvement over results in 2020.

Other Rating Factors: Weak profitability (2.4) with investment income below regulatory standards in relation to interest assumptions of reserves. Weak liquidity (2.3).

Principal Business: Reinsurance (49%), individual life insurance (36%), credit life insurance (11%), and credit health insurance (4%).

Principal Investments: NonCMO investment grade bonds (77%), CMOs and structured securities (18%), cash (2%), noninv. grade bonds (1%), and policy loans (1%).

Investments in Affiliates: None
Group Affiliation: SNA Capital LLC
Licensed in: All states except NY, PR
Commenced Business: January 1981
Address: 500 Woodward Avenue Suite 4000, Southfield, MI 48034
Phone: (800) 323-1317 **Domicile State:** MI **NAIC Code:** 93777

Data Date	Rating	RACR #1	RACR #2	Total Assets ($mil)	Capital ($mil)	Net Premium ($mil)	Net Income ($mil)
2021	C	1.46	0.79	1,005.1	54.8	33.2	13.7
2020	C	1.16	0.63	1,027.6	45.5	34.2	-19.5
2019	E	1.71	0.93	1,061.3	70.9	39.4	-6.6
2018	C	1.73	0.95	1,101.5	73.8	45.3	94.6
2017	C	1.63	0.91	1,034.5	66.6	51.6	2.5

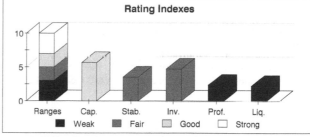

Rating Indexes

Ranges | Cap. | Stab. | Inv. | Prof. | Liq.
■ Weak   ■ Fair   ▨ Good   ☐ Strong

PEKIN LIFE INS CO   B   Good

Major Rating Factors: Good overall capitalization (6.8 on a scale of 0 to 10) based on good risk adjusted capital (severe loss scenario). Nevertheless, capital levels have fluctuated during prior years. Good quality investment portfolio (5.5) despite mixed results such as: large holdings of BBB rated bonds but junk bond exposure equal to 54% of capital. Good liquidity (5.1).

Other Rating Factors: Good overall results on stability tests (5.7) excellent operational trends and excellent risk diversification. Fair profitability (3.7) with operating losses during 2021.

Principal Business: Individual life insurance (46%), group life insurance (23%), individual health insurance (18%), individual annuities (4%), and other lines (10%).

Principal Investments: NonCMO investment grade bonds (64%), CMOs and structured securities (21%), mortgages in good standing (7%), noninv. grade bonds (4%), and misc. investments (3%).

Investments in Affiliates: None
Group Affiliation: Farmers Automobile Ins Assn
Licensed in: AL, AZ, AR, GA, IL, IN, IA, KS, KY, LA, MI, MN, MS, MO, NE, NV, NC, OH, PA, TN, TX, UT, VA, WI
Commenced Business: September 1965
Address: 2505 COURT STREET, PEKIN, IL 61558-0001
Phone: (309) 346-1161 **Domicile State:** IL **NAIC Code:** 67628

Data Date	Rating	RACR #1	RACR #2	Total Assets ($mil)	Capital ($mil)	Net Premium ($mil)	Net Income ($mil)
2021	B	1.72	0.97	1,626.3	122.0	197.3	-3.8
2020	B	1.77	0.99	1,576.7	121.8	186.8	1.2
2019	B	1.90	1.08	1,548.4	125.9	185.4	1.5
2018	B	2.09	1.23	1,503.9	129.2	184.5	3.4
2017	B	2.03	1.20	1,475.0	127.6	199.3	7.4

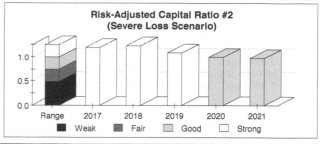

Risk-Adjusted Capital Ratio #2
(Severe Loss Scenario)

Range | 2017 | 2018 | 2019 | 2020 | 2021
■ Weak   ■ Fair   ▨ Good   ☐ Strong

PENN INS & ANNTY CO OF NY   B   Good

Major Rating Factors: Good liquidity (5.5 on a scale of 0 to 10) with sufficient resources to handle a spike in claims as well as a significant increase in policy surrenders. Fair current capitalization (3.0) based on excellent risk adjusted capital (severe loss scenario) reflecting improvement over results in 2020. Fair quality investment portfolio (4.8).

Other Rating Factors: Fair overall results on stability tests (4.0) including weak results on operational trends. Weak profitability (2.6) with investment income below regulatory standards in relation to interest assumptions of reserves.

Principal Business: Reinsurance (76%) and individual life insurance (24%).

Principal Investments: NonCMO investment grade bonds (56%), CMOs and structured securities (36%), noninv. grade bonds (2%), common & preferred stock (1%), and cash (1%).

Investments in Affiliates: None

Group Affiliation: Penn Mutual Life Insurance Company

Licensed in: NY

Commenced Business: January 2009

Address: 162 Prospect Hill Road, Brewster, NY 10509

Phone: (860) 298-6000 **Domicile State:** NY **NAIC Code:** 13588

Data Date	Rating	RACR #1	RACR #2	Total Assets ($mil)	Capital ($mil)	Net Premium ($mil)	Net Income ($mil)
2021	B	2.48	1.29	385.7	37.9	29.8	10.5
2020	B	1.77	0.90	352.4	23.0	869.6	-1.0
2019	B	2.08	1.49	174.6	19.4	8.8	-0.3
2018	B	2.11	1.66	168.8	19.8	22.8	-1.1
2017	B	2.28	2.06	150.3	21.3	123.6	-2.9

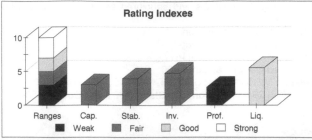

Rating Indexes

PENN INS & ANNUITY CO   C+   Fair

Major Rating Factors: Fair overall results on stability tests (4.8 on a scale of 0 to 10). Good quality investment portfolio (5.5) despite mixed results such as: large holdings of BBB rated bonds but moderate junk bond exposure. Good liquidity (5.7) with sufficient resources to handle a spike in claims as well as a significant increase in policy surrenders.

Other Rating Factors: Weak profitability (2.8) with operating losses during 2021. Strong capitalization (7.2) based on excellent risk adjusted capital (severe loss scenario).

Principal Business: Individual life insurance (77%), reinsurance (21%), and individual annuities (2%).

Principal Investments: NonCMO investment grade bonds (45%), CMOs and structured securities (28%), policy loans (7%), noninv. grade bonds (3%), and common & preferred stock (2%).

Investments in Affiliates: 1%

Group Affiliation: Penn Mutual Group

Licensed in: All states except NY, PR

Commenced Business: April 1981

Address: 1209 Orange Street, Wilmington, DE 19801

Phone: (215) 956-8086 **Domicile State:** DE **NAIC Code:** 93262

Data Date	Rating	RACR #1	RACR #2	Total Assets ($mil)	Capital ($mil)	Net Premium ($mil)	Net Income ($mil)
2021	C+	1.99	1.16	9,532.6	669.0	845.4	-10.1
2020	C+	2.00	1.18	8,358.5	671.4	785.4	-22.2
2019	C+	2.03	1.22	7,173.5	625.3	768.6	-21.9
2018	C+	1.80	1.10	6,110.1	472.6	758.8	40.2
2017	C+	1.85	1.16	5,321.0	431.5	701.2	-15.9

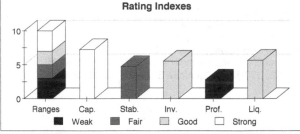

Rating Indexes

PENN MUTUAL LIFE INS CO   B   Good

Major Rating Factors: Good quality investment portfolio (5.8 on a scale of 0 to 10) despite mixed results such as: large holdings of BBB rated bonds but moderate junk bond exposure. Good liquidity (6.6) with sufficient resources to handle a spike in claims as well as a significant increase in policy surrenders. Strong capitalization (4.0) based on excellent risk adjusted capital (severe loss scenario).

Other Rating Factors: Fair profitability (3.8) with operating losses during 2021. Fair overall results on stability tests (4.2).

Principal Business: Individual life insurance (80%) and individual annuities (19%).

Principal Investments: NonCMO investment grade bonds (42%), CMOs and structured securities (26%), common & preferred stock (5%), policy loans (3%), and noninv. grade bonds (3%).

Investments in Affiliates: 6%

Group Affiliation: Penn Mutual Group

Licensed in: All states except NY, PR

Commenced Business: May 1847

Address: The Penn Mutual Life Ins Co, Philadelphia, PA 19172

Phone: (215) 956-8000 **Domicile State:** PA **NAIC Code:** 67644

Data Date	Rating	RACR #1	RACR #2	Total Assets ($mil)	Capital ($mil)	Net Premium ($mil)	Net Income ($mil)
2021	B	1.88	1.28	27,994.9	2,571.6	1,245.9	-150.1
2020	B	1.78	1.23	24,930.3	2,261.0	-605.3	6.1
2019	B	1.62	1.12	23,326.9	1,998.7	1,148.6	57.6
2018	B	1.77	1.21	21,048.5	1,853.6	988.8	37.5
2017	B	1.80	1.22	20,669.4	1,697.4	821.8	-40.5

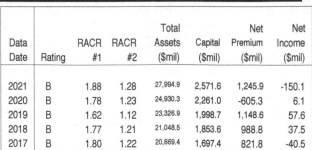

Rating Indexes

PHILADELPHIA AMERICAN LIFE INS CO   B   Good

Major Rating Factors: Good overall results on stability tests (5.8 on a scale of 0 to 10). Stability strengths include excellent operational trends, good risk adjusted capital for prior years and excellent risk diversification. Good liquidity (5.8) with sufficient resources to handle a spike in claims as well as a significant increase in policy surrenders. Fair quality investment portfolio (3.7).

Other Rating Factors: Strong capitalization (7.1) based on excellent risk adjusted capital (severe loss scenario). Excellent profitability (9.1) with operating gains in each of the last five years.

Principal Business: Individual health insurance (89%), individual annuities (10%), and individual life insurance (1%).

Principal Investments: NonCMO investment grade bonds (52%), noninv. grade bonds (25%), mortgages in good standing (14%), and CMOs and structured securities (8%).

Investments in Affiliates: None

Group Affiliation: New Era Life Group

Licensed in: All states except NY, RI, PR

Commenced Business: March 1978

Address: 11720 Katy Freeway Suite 1700, Houston, TX 77079

Phone: (281) 368-7200 **Domicile State:** TX **NAIC Code:** 67784

Data Date	Rating	RACR #1	RACR #2	Total Assets ($mil)	Capital ($mil)	Net Premium ($mil)	Net Income ($mil)
2021	B	1.70	1.05	390.4	84.6	336.8	11.2
2020	B	1.64	1.05	372.3	75.7	282.3	21.1
2019	B	1.75	1.20	326.1	58.3	239.9	14.8
2018	B	1.56	1.06	303.3	44.3	190.3	8.1
2017	B	1.51	0.97	284.8	35.5	157.2	3.9

Adverse Trends in Operations

Increase in policy surrenders from 2018 to 2019 (63%)
Increase in policy surrenders from 2017 to 2018 (37%)

PHL VARIABLE INS CO   E+   Very Weak

Major Rating Factors: Poor capitalization (1.4 on a scale of 0 to 10) based on weak risk adjusted capital (moderate loss scenario). Low quality investment portfolio (0.8) containing large holdings of BBB rated bonds in addition to significant exposure to junk bonds. Weak profitability (1.2) with operating losses during 2021. Return on equity has been low, averaging -28.1%.

Other Rating Factors: Weak overall results on stability tests (0.7) including weak risk adjusted capital in prior years, weak results on operational trends. Excellent liquidity (10.0).

Principal Business: Individual life insurance (97%), reinsurance (2%), and individual annuities (1%).

Principal Investments: NonCMO investment grade bonds (50%), CMOs and structured securities (27%), policy loans (5%), noninv. grade bonds (4%), and misc. investments (10%).

Investments in Affiliates: None

Group Affiliation: Nassau Reinsurance Group Holdings LP

Licensed in: All states except ME, NY

Commenced Business: July 1981

Address: One American Row, Hartford, CT 6103

Phone: (860) 403-5000 **Domicile State:** CT **NAIC Code:** 93548

Data Date	Rating	RACR #1	RACR #2	Total Assets ($mil)	Capital ($mil)	Net Premium ($mil)	Net Income ($mil)
2021	E+	0.55	0.25	5,173.0	53.0	0.0	-31.6
2020	E	0.35	0.16	5,625.5	30.6	0.0	-4.1
2019	E-	0.57	0.26	5,931.1	53.2	-1,111.3	-109.1
2018	D	1.00	0.51	5,914.1	117.8	379.2	-101.7
2017	D-	1.62	0.86	6,319.3	184.1	320.9	-56.2

Junk Bonds as a % of Capital

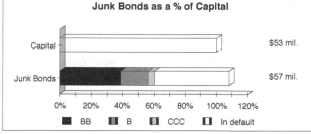

Capital	$53 mil.
Junk Bonds	$57 mil.

BB B CCC In default

PHYSICIANS LIFE INS CO *   B+   Good

Major Rating Factors: Good quality investment portfolio (5.6 on a scale of 0 to 10) despite mixed results such as: large holdings of BBB rated bonds but junk bond exposure equal to 72% of capital. Good overall profitability (5.9). Return on equity has been low, averaging 3.7%. Good liquidity (5.5).

Other Rating Factors: Good overall results on stability tests (6.4) despite negative cash flow from operations for 2021 excellent operational trends and excellent risk diversification. Strong capitalization (7.6) based on excellent risk adjusted capital (severe loss scenario).

Principal Business: Individual life insurance (53%), individual health insurance (31%), group life insurance (14%), individual annuities (1%), and reinsurance (1%).

Principal Investments: NonCMO investment grade bonds (61%), CMOs and structured securities (26%), noninv. grade bonds (7%), common & preferred stock (3%), and policy loans (1%).

Investments in Affiliates: None

Group Affiliation: Physicians Mutual Group

Licensed in: All states except NY, PR

Commenced Business: January 1970

Address: 2600 Dodge Street, Omaha, NE 68131-2671

Phone: (402) 633-1000 **Domicile State:** NE **NAIC Code:** 72125

Data Date	Rating	RACR #1	RACR #2	Total Assets ($mil)	Capital ($mil)	Net Premium ($mil)	Net Income ($mil)
2021	B+	2.86	1.42	1,783.0	172.5	242.1	1.6
2020	A-	2.87	1.43	1,752.2	172.3	260.4	-2.0
2019	A-	2.98	1.51	1,726.3	172.8	284.0	16.0
2018	A-	2.83	1.44	1,678.2	158.6	268.8	7.2
2017	A-	3.01	1.53	1,632.1	151.4	268.1	8.7

Rating Indexes

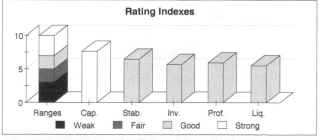

Ranges Cap. Stab. Inv. Prof. Liq.

Weak Fair Good Strong

PHYSICIANS MUTUAL INS CO *   A+   Excellent

Major Rating Factors: Good quality investment portfolio (5.6 on a scale of 0 to 10) despite mixed results such as: no exposure to mortgages and large holdings of BBB rated bonds but small junk bond holdings. Strong capitalization (9.2) based on excellent risk adjusted capital (severe loss scenario). Furthermore, this high level of risk adjusted capital has been consistently maintained over the last five years. Excellent profitability (9.0) with operating gains in each of the last five years.

Other Rating Factors: Excellent liquidity (7.3). Excellent overall results on stability tests (7.9) excellent operational trends and excellent risk diversification.

Principal Business: Individual health insurance (64%), reinsurance (21%), and group health insurance (15%).

Principal Investments: NonCMO investment grade bonds (48%), CMOs and structured securities (23%), common & preferred stock (18%), noninv. grade bonds (7%), and real estate (1%).

Investments in Affiliates: 6%

Group Affiliation: Physicians Mutual Group

Licensed in: All states except PR

Commenced Business: February 1902

Address: 2600 Dodge Street, Omaha, NE 68131-2671

Phone: (402) 633-1000 **Domicile State:** NE **NAIC Code:** 80578

Data Date	Rating	RACR #1	RACR #2	Total Assets ($mil)	Capital ($mil)	Net Premium ($mil)	Net Income ($mil)
2021	A+	3.42	2.47	2,785.1	1,161.7	519.8	65.7
2020	A+	3.37	2.47	2,599.1	1,102.1	495.5	71.5
2019	A+	3.27	2.44	2,480.5	1,037.4	485.8	47.3
2018	A+	3.40	2.56	2,356.3	993.4	463.5	52.1
2017	A+	3.43	2.56	2,291.9	951.2	436.2	39.8

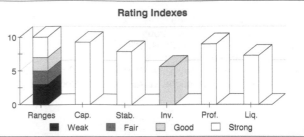

Rating Indexes

Ranges | Cap. | Stab. | Inv. | Prof. | Liq.
■ Weak   ■ Fair   ▨ Good   ☐ Strong

PIONEER AMERICAN INS CO   C-   Fair

Major Rating Factors: Fair overall results on stability tests (3.2 on a scale of 0 to 10). Weak profitability (1.8) with operating losses during 2021. Good liquidity (6.3) with sufficient resources to handle a spike in claims as well as a significant increase in policy surrenders.

Other Rating Factors: Strong capitalization (10.0) based on excellent risk adjusted capital (severe loss scenario). High quality investment portfolio (8.4).

Principal Business: Individual life insurance (96%) and individual annuities (3%).

Principal Investments: NonCMO investment grade bonds (90%), policy loans (3%), mortgages in good standing (2%), and cash (1%).

Investments in Affiliates: None

Group Affiliation: Industrial Alliance Ins & Financial

Licensed in: AL, AK, AZ, AR, CA, CO, DC, FL, GA, HI, ID, IL, IN, KS, KY, LA, MD, MA, MS, MO, MT, NV, NJ, NM, NC, OH, OK, OR, RI, SC, TN, TX, UT, VA, WA, WV, WY, PR

Commenced Business: May 1946

Address: 425 AUSTIN AVENUE, WACO, TX 76701

Phone: (254) 297-2777 **Domicile State:** TX **NAIC Code:** 67873

Data Date	Rating	RACR #1	RACR #2	Total Assets ($mil)	Capital ($mil)	Net Premium ($mil)	Net Income ($mil)
2021	C-	4.96	4.47	122.3	45.3	52.2	-3.7
2020	C-	5.18	4.66	111.8	46.9	42.9	-5.9
2019	C-	3.82	3.43	87.0	31.8	35.5	-2.6
2018	C-	4.39	3.95	85.2	36.3	18.1	-3.3
2017	C	2.83	2.54	68.7	21.3	24.0	-3.0

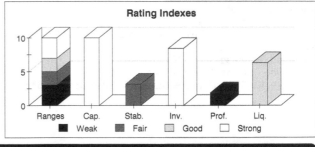

Rating Indexes

Ranges | Cap. | Stab. | Inv. | Prof. | Liq.
■ Weak   ■ Fair   ▨ Good   ☐ Strong

PIONEER MUTUAL LIFE INS CO   C   Fair

Major Rating Factors: Fair profitability (3.8 on a scale of 0 to 10). Excellent expense controls. Return on equity has been low, averaging -1.2%. Fair overall results on stability tests (3.7) including negative cash flow from operations for 2021. Good quality investment portfolio (6.9) despite large holdings of BBB rated bonds in addition to moderate junk bond exposure. Exposure to mortgages is significant, but the mortgage default rate has been low.

Other Rating Factors: Strong capitalization (10.0) based on excellent risk adjusted capital (severe loss scenario). Excellent liquidity (7.8).

Principal Business: Individual life insurance (94%) and individual annuities (6%).

Principal Investments: NonCMO investment grade bonds (77%), mortgages in good standing (11%), noninv. grade bonds (4%), CMOs and structured securities (2%), and cash (1%).

Investments in Affiliates: None

Group Affiliation: American United Life Group

Licensed in: All states except AK, NY, PR

Commenced Business: November 1947

Address: P O BOX 2167, FARGO, ND 58104

Phone: (701) 277-2300 **Domicile State:** ND **NAIC Code:** 67911

Data Date	Rating	RACR #1	RACR #2	Total Assets ($mil)	Capital ($mil)	Net Premium ($mil)	Net Income ($mil)
2021	C	8.31	6.71	63.9	52.4	5.0	26.8
2020	B-	1.98	1.00	509.5	28.2	11.8	-15.1
2019	B	2.80	1.44	510.7	43.6	13.3	-4.5
2018	B	3.26	1.78	509.6	46.9	14.2	9.1
2017	B	2.44	1.28	517.9	37.5	19.1	-6.6

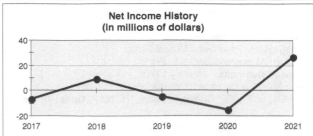

Net Income History
(in millions of dollars)

2017 | 2018 | 2019 | 2020 | 2021

PIONEER SECURITY LIFE INS CO   C-   Fair

Major Rating Factors: Fair overall results on stability tests (3.3 on a scale of 0 to 10). Low quality investment portfolio (2.9). Weak profitability (2.7) with operating losses during 2021.
Other Rating Factors: Good liquidity (6.8) with sufficient resources to handle a spike in claims. Strong capitalization (7.0) based on excellent risk adjusted capital (severe loss scenario).
Principal Business: Individual life insurance (100%).
Principal Investments: Common & preferred stock (73%), nonCMO investment grade bonds (23%), and policy loans (2%).
Investments in Affiliates: 73%
Group Affiliation: Industrial Alliance Ins & Financial
Licensed in: AL, AR, CA, CO, DC, DE, FL, GA, HI, ID, IL, IN, KS, KY, LA, MD, MN, MS, MO, MT, NE, NM, NC, ND, OK, OR, PA, SC, SD, TN, TX, UT, VA, WA, WV, WI
Commenced Business: November 1956
Address: 425 AUSTIN AVENUE, WACO, TX 76701
Phone: (254) 297-2777 **Domicile State:** TX **NAIC Code:** 67946

Data Date	Rating	RACR #1	RACR #2	Total Assets ($mil)	Capital ($mil)	Net Premium ($mil)	Net Income ($mil)
2021	C-	1.03	1.01	192.0	144.0	24.9	-0.8
2020	C-	0.97	0.95	145.2	102.4	23.3	-1.4
2019	C-	0.95	0.93	104.4	66.4	23.6	0.3
2018	C-	0.95	0.93	95.8	62.5	12.0	-3.2
2017	C	1.00	0.97	80.6	49.0	19.3	-2.2

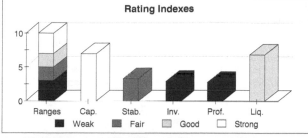

Rating Indexes

POPULAR LIFE RE *   B+   Good

Major Rating Factors: Good overall results on stability tests (5.0 on a scale of 0 to 10). Stability strengths include good risk diversification. Strong capitalization (10.0) based on excellent risk adjusted capital (severe loss scenario). High quality investment portfolio (8.9) with no exposure to mortgages and no exposure to junk bonds.
Other Rating Factors: Excellent profitability (8.0) with operating gains in each of the last five years. Excellent liquidity (9.2).
Principal Business: Reinsurance (100%).
Principal Investments: CMOs and structured securities (57%), nonCMO investment grade bonds (38%), and cash (5%).
Investments in Affiliates: None
Group Affiliation: Popular Inc
Licensed in: (No states)
Commenced Business: December 2003
Address: CORPORATE OFFICE PARK SOLAR A, GUAYNABO, PR 966
Phone: (787) 706-4111 **Domicile State:** PR **NAIC Code:** 11876

Data Date	Rating	RACR #1	RACR #2	Total Assets ($mil)	Capital ($mil)	Net Premium ($mil)	Net Income ($mil)
2021	B+	5.71	5.14	70.2	43.7	16.5	5.2
2020	B	6.48	5.84	83.5	53.6	13.6	8.0
2019	B	5.79	5.21	74.8	45.6	18.0	6.6
2018	B	5.37	4.83	70.6	41.2	18.5	5.3
2017	B	5.05	4.54	67.0	37.9	17.3	4.7

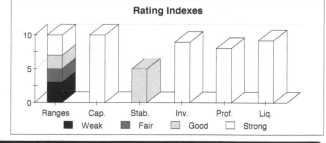

Rating Indexes

PRIMERICA LIFE INS CO   B   Good

Major Rating Factors: Good overall results on stability tests (5.8 on a scale of 0 to 10) despite excessive premium growth. Other stability subfactors include excellent operational trends and excellent risk diversification. Fair quality investment portfolio (4.3). Strong capitalization (7.8) based on excellent risk adjusted capital (severe loss scenario).
Other Rating Factors: Excellent profitability (8.5) with operating gains in each of the last five years. Excellent liquidity (7.4).
Principal Business: Individual life insurance (100%).
Principal Investments: NonCMO investment grade bonds (50%), CMOs and structured securities (23%), common & preferred stock (18%), and noninv. grade bonds (4%).
Investments in Affiliates: 17%
Group Affiliation: Primerica Inc
Licensed in: All states except NY
Commenced Business: January 1903
Address: 33 Arch Street - 26th Floor, Nashville, TN 37201
Phone: (770) 381-1000 **Domicile State:** TN **NAIC Code:** 65919

Data Date	Rating	RACR #1	RACR #2	Total Assets ($mil)	Capital ($mil)	Net Premium ($mil)	Net Income ($mil)
2021	B	1.88	1.55	2,064.3	779.6	721.6	255.2
2020	B	1.47	1.24	1,732.6	650.1	531.0	392.4
2019	B	1.36	1.18	1,594.6	666.0	357.1	507.8
2018	B	1.45	1.25	1,595.5	674.2	339.1	505.9
2017	B	1.32	1.13	1,493.8	598.0	291.0	398.2

Adverse Trends in Operations

Decrease in capital during 2020 (2%)
Decrease in capital during 2019 (1%)

PRINCIPAL LIFE INS CO *
B+   Good

Major Rating Factors: Good quality investment portfolio (5.7 on a scale of 0 to 10) despite large holdings of BBB rated bonds in addition to junk bond exposure equal to 77% of capital. Exposure to mortgages is significant, but the mortgage default rate has been low. Good overall profitability (6.5). Return on equity has been excellent over the last five years averaging 16.5%. Good liquidity (5.4).

Other Rating Factors: Good overall results on stability tests (5.5) good operational trends and excellent risk diversification. Strong capitalization (7.2) based on excellent risk adjusted capital (severe loss scenario).

Principal Business: Group retirement contracts (25%), group health insurance (22%), reinsurance (16%), individual life insurance (13%), and other lines (25%).

Principal Investments: NonCMO investment grade bonds (46%), CMOs and structured securities (20%), mortgages in good standing (19%), noninv. grade bonds (5%), and misc. investments (8%).

Investments in Affiliates: 5%

Group Affiliation: Principal Financial Group

Licensed in: All states, the District of Columbia and Puerto Rico

Commenced Business: September 1879

Address: 711 HIGH STREET, DES MOINES, IA 50392-2300

Phone: (800) 986-3343 **Domicile State:** IA **NAIC Code:** 61271

Data Date	Rating	RACR #1	RACR #2	Total Assets ($mil)	Capital ($mil)	Net Premium ($mil)	Net Income ($mil)
2021	B+	2.01	1.13	239,000	5,375.2	5,946.4	864.0
2020	B+	2.10	1.18	224,000	5,682.4	7,376.4	915.9
2019	B+	2.04	1.16	210,000	5,193.4	10,407.1	989.3
2018	B+	2.15	1.23	185,000	5,319.6	9,702.9	1,017.6
2017	B+	2.19	1.22	189,000	4,946.8	8,339.6	1,976.7

Rating Indexes

Ranges   Cap.   Stab.   Inv.   Prof.   Liq.

■ Weak   ■ Fair   □ Good   □ Strong

PRINCIPAL NATIONAL LIFE INS CO
B   Good

Major Rating Factors: Good overall results on stability tests (5.7 on a scale of 0 to 10). Strengths include good financial support from affiliation with Principal Financial Group, excellent operational trends and excellent risk diversification. Weak profitability (2.9) with operating losses during 2021. Return on equity has been low, averaging -1.3%. Strong capitalization (9.7) based on excellent risk adjusted capital (severe loss scenario).

Other Rating Factors: High quality investment portfolio (7.3). Excellent liquidity (10.0).

Principal Business: Individual life insurance (100%).

Principal Investments: NonCMO investment grade bonds (77%), CMOs and structured securities (12%), cash (9%), and noninv. grade bonds (1%).

Investments in Affiliates: None

Group Affiliation: Principal Financial Group

Licensed in: All states except NY, PR

Commenced Business: March 1968

Address: 711 HIGH STREET, DES MOINES, IA 50392-2300

Phone: (515) 247-5111 **Domicile State:** IA **NAIC Code:** 71161

Data Date	Rating	RACR #1	RACR #2	Total Assets ($mil)	Capital ($mil)	Net Premium ($mil)	Net Income ($mil)
2021	B	5.63	2.78	832.4	269.5	0.0	-2.0
2020	B	6.01	2.95	622.0	250.7	0.0	-2.0
2019	B	6.15	3.03	476.4	220.9	0.0	-1.7
2018	B	6.76	3.34	387.2	205.2	0.0	-3.6
2017	B	5.70	2.82	316.9	148.9	0.0	-3.9

Principal Financial Group
Composite Group Rating: B+
Largest Group Members

	Assets ($mil)	Rating
PRINCIPAL LIFE INS CO	224366	B+
PRINCIPAL NATIONAL LIFE INS CO	622	B

PROFESSIONAL INS CO
D+   Weak

Major Rating Factors: Weak overall results on stability tests (2.6 on a scale of 0 to 10) including potential financial drain due to affiliation with Sun Life Assurance Group. Good quality investment portfolio (6.7) despite mixed results such as: no exposure to mortgages and large holdings of BBB rated bonds but small junk bond holdings. Good overall profitability (6.3). Excellent expense controls.

Other Rating Factors: Good liquidity (6.9). Strong capitalization (10.0) based on excellent risk adjusted capital (severe loss scenario).

Principal Business: Individual health insurance (94%) and individual life insurance (6%).

Principal Investments: NonCMO investment grade bonds (71%), CMOs and structured securities (18%), noninv. grade bonds (5%), policy loans (3%), and cash (2%).

Investments in Affiliates: None

Group Affiliation: Sun Life Assurance Group

Licensed in: All states except AK, DE, ME, NH, NJ, NY, RI, VT, PR

Commenced Business: September 1937

Address: 350 North St Paul Street, Dallas, TX 75201

Phone: (781) 237-6030 **Domicile State:** TX **NAIC Code:** 68047

Data Date	Rating	RACR #1	RACR #2	Total Assets ($mil)	Capital ($mil)	Net Premium ($mil)	Net Income ($mil)
2021	D+	3.36	3.03	84.5	27.2	12.9	3.5
2020	C-	3.02	2.62	84.7	24.3	15.0	5.0
2019	C	6.10	5.49	113.7	54.9	17.0	4.8
2018	D+	5.59	5.03	111.2	50.2	19.2	5.1
2017	D	5.02	4.51	109.6	45.0	21.6	4.4

Sun Life Assurance Group
Composite Group Rating: D
Largest Group Members

	Assets ($mil)	Rating
SUN LIFE ASR CO OF CANADA	19738	D
INDEPENDENCE LIFE ANNUITY CO	3427	D+
SUN LIFE HEALTH INS CO	986	D+
PROFESSIONAL INS CO	85	D+

PROTECTIVE LIFE & ANNUITY INS CO

C+ **Fair**

Major Rating Factors: Fair profitability (3.0 on a scale of 0 to 10) with investment income below regulatory standards in relation to interest assumptions of reserves. Fair overall results on stability tests (3.3) including weak results on operational trends, negative cash flow from operations for 2021. Good quality investment portfolio (6.0).

Other Rating Factors: Good liquidity (5.3). Strong capitalization (7.6) based on excellent risk adjusted capital (severe loss scenario).

Principal Business: Individual life insurance (44%), reinsurance (36%), and individual annuities (20%).

Principal Investments: NonCMO investment grade bonds (66%), CMOs and structured securities (21%), mortgages in good standing (6%), noninv. grade bonds (3%), and policy loans (1%).

Investments in Affiliates: None

Group Affiliation: Dai-ichi Life Holdings Inc

Licensed in: All states except MN, PR

Commenced Business: December 1978

Address: 2801 HIGHWAY 280 SOUTH, BIRMINGHAM, AL 35223

Phone: (205) 268-1000 **Domicile State:** AL **NAIC Code:** 88536

Data Date	Rating	RACR #1	RACR #2	Total Assets ($mil)	Capital ($mil)	Net Premium ($mil)	Net Income ($mil)
2021	C+	2.63	1.37	6,210.6	505.4	181.9	42.7
2020	C+	2.40	1.25	6,322.5	471.9	414.1	31.3
2019	C+	1.83	0.96	5,998.8	345.5	1,339.2	24.4
2018	C+	1.61	0.84	5,108.7	268.3	3,190.5	-118.7
2017	B	2.28	1.15	2,076.5	155.9	248.7	23.3

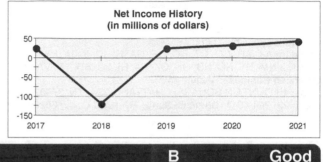

Net Income History
(in millions of dollars)

PROTECTIVE LIFE INS CO

B **Good**

Major Rating Factors: Good quality investment portfolio (6.4 on a scale of 0 to 10) despite large holdings of BBB rated bonds in addition to moderate junk bond exposure. Exposure to mortgages is significant, but the mortgage default rate has been low. Good overall profitability (5.1) although investment income, in comparison to reserve requirements, is below regulatory standards. Good liquidity (5.4).

Other Rating Factors: Good overall results on stability tests (5.8) despite excessive premium growth good operational trends, good risk adjusted capital for prior years and excellent risk diversification. Strong capitalization (7.1) based on excellent risk adjusted capital (severe loss scenario).

Principal Business: Individual life insurance (47%), individual annuities (38%), and reinsurance (15%).

Principal Investments: NonCMO investment grade bonds (58%), mortgages in good standing (15%), CMOs and structured securities (14%), common & preferred stock (4%), and misc. investments (6%).

Investments in Affiliates: 3%

Group Affiliation: Dai-ichi Life Holdings Inc

Licensed in: All states except NY

Commenced Business: September 1907

Address: 1620 WESTGATE CIRCLE SUITE 200, NASHVILLE, TN 37201-2043

Phone: (205) 268-1000 **Domicile State:** TN **NAIC Code:** 68136

Data Date	Rating	RACR #1	RACR #2	Total Assets ($mil)	Capital ($mil)	Net Premium ($mil)	Net Income ($mil)
2021	B	1.52	1.05	80,820.8	5,318.6	5,094.2	426.3
2020	B	1.46	1.02	74,296.9	5,083.3	3,766.7	710.4
2019	B	1.38	0.99	70,360.9	4,915.7	23,428.7	-619.9
2018	B	1.34	0.98	57,811.8	4,340.3	12,612.4	321.1
2017	D	1.54	1.19	47,662.8	4,282.3	2,409.9	731.2

Rating Indexes

Ranges | Cap. | Stab. | Inv. | Prof. | Liq.

■ Weak ▨ Fair ▢ Good ☐ Strong

PROVIDENT LIFE & ACCIDENT INS CO

C+ **Fair**

Major Rating Factors: Fair overall results on stability tests (4.0 on a scale of 0 to 10) including fair financial strength of affiliated Unum Group. Strong capitalization (4.0) based on excellent risk adjusted capital (severe loss scenario). Moreover, capital levels have been consistently high over the last five years. Good quality investment portfolio (5.2).

Other Rating Factors: Good overall profitability (6.5). Good liquidity (6.7).

Principal Business: Individual health insurance (70%), individual life insurance (29%), and reinsurance (1%).

Principal Investments: NonCMO investment grade bonds (76%), mortgages in good standing (10%), noninv. grade bonds (5%), policy loans (3%), and misc. investments (6%).

Investments in Affiliates: None

Group Affiliation: Unum Group

Licensed in: All states except NY

Commenced Business: May 1887

Address: 1 FOUNTAIN SQUARE, CHATTANOOGA, TN 37402-1330

Phone: (423) 294-1011 **Domicile State:** TN **NAIC Code:** 68195

Data Date	Rating	RACR #1	RACR #2	Total Assets ($mil)	Capital ($mil)	Net Premium ($mil)	Net Income ($mil)
2021	C+	3.97	2.11	6,214.2	971.3	644.8	340.3
2020	C+	12.26	11.03	6,172.2	705.2	-1,318.1	-177.5
2019	C+	2.75	1.38	7,893.4	658.9	763.6	219.4
2018	C+	2.50	1.26	7,994.0	607.3	771.0	204.8
2017	C+	2.44	1.22	8,034.0	605.0	769.3	163.5

Unum Group Composite Group Rating: C+ Largest Group Members	Assets ($mil)	Rating
UNUM LIFE INS CO OF AMERICA	21791	C+
PROVIDENT LIFE ACCIDENT INS CO	6172	C+
FIRST UNUM LIFE INS CO	4249	C+
COLONIAL LIFE ACCIDENT INS CO	3760	C+
PAUL REVERE LIFE INS CO	1280	C+

PROVIDENT LIFE & CAS INS CO — B — Good

Major Rating Factors: Good overall results on stability tests (5.4 on a scale of 0 to 10) despite fair financial strength of affiliated Unum Group. Other stability subfactors include excellent operational trends and excellent risk diversification. Good quality investment portfolio (5.3) despite mixed results such as: minimal exposure to mortgages and large holdings of BBB rated bonds but small junk bond holdings. Strong capitalization (10.0) based on excellent risk adjusted capital (severe loss scenario).

Other Rating Factors: Excellent profitability (8.1) with operating gains in each of the last five years. Excellent liquidity (7.1).

Principal Business: Individual health insurance (84%), group health insurance (13%), reinsurance (2%), and individual life insurance (1%).

Principal Investments: NonCMO investment grade bonds (89%), noninv. grade bonds (4%), mortgages in good standing (2%), and CMOs and structured securities (2%).

Investments in Affiliates: None

Group Affiliation: Unum Group

Licensed in: AK, AR, CO, CT, DC, DE, GA, HI, ID, IL, IA, KY, LA, MA, MS, MO, NE, NH, NJ, NM, NY, NC, ND, OH, OK, PA, RI, SC, SD, TN, VA, WA

Commenced Business: January 1952

Address: 1 FOUNTAIN SQUARE, CHATTANOOGA, TN 37402-1330

Phone: (423) 294-1011 **Domicile State:** TN **NAIC Code:** 68209

Data Date	Rating	RACR #1	RACR #2	Total Assets ($mil)	Capital ($mil)	Net Premium ($mil)	Net Income ($mil)
2021	B	5.13	2.98	861.9	173.5	112.6	30.8
2020	B-	5.24	3.06	830.6	164.6	103.8	20.9
2019	B-	4.10	2.39	739.3	124.4	99.7	2.1
2018	B-	4.30	2.47	736.0	131.2	94.8	6.1
2017	B-	4.75	2.63	746.7	150.2	92.2	26.0

Unum Group
Composite Group Rating: C+
Largest Group Members

	Assets ($mil)	Rating
UNUM LIFE INS CO OF AMERICA	21791	C+
PROVIDENT LIFE ACCIDENT INS CO	6172	C+
FIRST UNUM LIFE INS CO	4249	C+
COLONIAL LIFE ACCIDENT INS CO	3760	C+
PAUL REVERE LIFE INS CO	1280	C+

PRUCO LIFE INS CO — C — Fair

Major Rating Factors: Fair profitability (3.0 on a scale of 0 to 10) with investment income below regulatory standards in relation to interest assumptions of reserves. Good quality investment portfolio (5.7) despite mixed results such as: minimal exposure to mortgages and substantial holdings of BBB bonds but minimal holdings in junk bonds. Good liquidity (6.7).

Other Rating Factors: Weak overall results on stability tests (2.8) including weak results on operational trends and negative cash flow from operations for 2021. Strong capitalization (7.9) based on excellent risk adjusted capital (severe loss scenario).

Principal Business: Individual life insurance (56%), reinsurance (32%), and individual annuities (12%).

Principal Investments: NonCMO investment grade bonds (34%), mortgages in good standing (8%), CMOs and structured securities (6%), noninv. grade bonds (4%), and misc. investments (28%).

Investments in Affiliates: 4%

Group Affiliation: Prudential of America

Licensed in: All states except NY, PR

Commenced Business: December 1971

Address: 2929 N CENTRAL AVE STE 1700, PHOENIX, AZ 85253-2738

Phone: (860) 534-8057 **Domicile State:** AZ **NAIC Code:** 79227

Data Date	Rating	RACR #1	RACR #2	Total Assets ($mil)	Capital ($mil)	Net Premium ($mil)	Net Income ($mil)
2021	C	2.74	1.57	167,000	5,954.6	12,934.2	780.6
2020	C	1.10	0.63	138,000	1,461.3	2,344.0	-600.9
2019	C+	1.30	0.75	130,000	1,665.4	1,137.2	223.8
2018	C+	1.30	0.73	113,000	1,460.9	1,521.8	158.7
2017	C+	1.22	0.68	122,000	1,364.9	1,770.7	-457.4

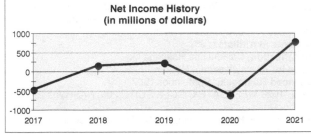

Net Income History (in millions of dollars)

PRUCO LIFE INS CO OF NEW JERSEY — B- — Good

Major Rating Factors: Good quality investment portfolio (5.7 on a scale of 0 to 10) despite mixed results such as: minimal exposure to mortgages and large holdings of BBB rated bonds but small junk bond holdings. Good liquidity (6.6) with sufficient resources to handle a spike in claims as well as a significant increase in policy surrenders. Good overall results on stability tests (5.0) despite fair risk adjusted capital in prior years excellent operational trends and excellent risk diversification.

Other Rating Factors: Weak profitability (2.8) with investment income below regulatory standards in relation to interest assumptions of reserves. Strong capitalization (7.8) based on excellent risk adjusted capital (severe loss scenario).

Principal Business: Individual life insurance (89%) and individual annuities (11%).

Principal Investments: NonCMO investment grade bonds (56%), CMOs and structured securities (17%), policy loans (9%), mortgages in good standing (5%), and noninv. grade bonds (3%).

Investments in Affiliates: 2%

Group Affiliation: Prudential of America

Licensed in: NJ, NY

Commenced Business: December 1982

Address: 213 WASHINGTON STREET, NEWARK, NJ 07102-2917

Phone: (973) 802-6000 **Domicile State:** NJ **NAIC Code:** 97195

Data Date	Rating	RACR #1	RACR #2	Total Assets ($mil)	Capital ($mil)	Net Premium ($mil)	Net Income ($mil)
2021	B-	2.96	1.50	20,574.7	591.6	321.9	52.0
2020	B-	1.74	0.88	19,448.3	337.1	364.1	-70.3
2019	B-	1.87	0.95	17,949.1	338.6	297.0	38.3
2018	B-	1.46	0.74	15,224.3	233.6	257.3	32.6
2017	B-	1.42	0.71	15,975.5	223.0	219.8	33.3

Adverse Trends in Operations

Decrease in asset base during 2018 (5%)
Change in premium mix from 2016 to 2017 (45.3%)
Decrease in capital during 2017 (29%)

PRUDENTIAL ANNUITIES LIFE ASR CORP | B- | Good

Major Rating Factors: Fair quality investment portfolio (4.9 on a scale of 0 to 10) with substantial holdings of BBB bonds in addition to junk bond exposure equal to 69% of capital. Fair profitability (4.8). Fair overall results on stability tests (3.8) including weak results on operational trends.

Other Rating Factors: Strong overall capitalization (8.5) based on mixed results -- excessive policy leverage mitigated by excellent risk adjusted capital (severe loss scenario). Excellent liquidity (9.9).

Principal Business: N/A

Principal Investments: NonCMO investment grade bonds (64%), CMOs and structured securities (19%), and cash (3%).

Investments in Affiliates: None

Group Affiliation: Prudential of America

Licensed in: All states except NY

Commenced Business: May 1988

Address: 2929 N CENTRAL AVE STE 1700, PHOENIX, AZ 85253-2738

Phone: (203) 926-1888 **Domicile State:** AZ **NAIC Code:** 86630

Data Date	Rating	RACR #1	RACR #2	Total Assets ($mil)	Capital ($mil)	Net Premium ($mil)	Net Income ($mil)
2021	B-	2.60	2.02	48,354.5	1,013.9	-4,050.5	2,045.4
2020	B-	9.71	5.57	70,536.2	6,130.9	5,999.8	-767.7
2019	B-	8.97	5.55	59,047.3	4,748.5	7,944.1	-2,051.6
2018	B-	13.18	8.54	54,107.4	6,396.1	7,075.7	-851.5
2017	B-	15.11	11.06	58,738.7	8,058.9	5,247.4	3,910.5

Adverse Trends in Operations

Decrease in premium volume from 2019 to 2020 (24%)
Decrease in capital during 2019 (26%)
Decrease in capital during 2018 (21%)
Increase in policy surrenders from 2016 to 2017 (44%)
Decrease in premium volume from 2016 to 2017 (66%)

PRUDENTIAL INS CO OF AMERICA | B | Good

Major Rating Factors: Good quality investment portfolio (6.3 on a scale of 0 to 10) despite large holdings of BBB rated bonds in addition to moderate junk bond exposure. Exposure to mortgages is significant, but the mortgage default rate has been low. Good overall profitability (6.9). Return on equity has been fair, averaging 6.3%. Good liquidity (6.7).

Other Rating Factors: Good overall results on stability tests (5.8) despite excessive premium growth good operational trends and excellent risk diversification. Strong capitalization (7.3) based on excellent risk adjusted capital (severe loss scenario).

Principal Business: Group retirement contracts (44%), reinsurance (33%), group life insurance (13%), individual life insurance (5%), and group health insurance (4%).

Principal Investments: NonCMO investment grade bonds (47%), CMOs and structured securities (15%), mortgages in good standing (14%), common & preferred stock (9%), and misc. investments (13%).

Investments in Affiliates: 12%

Group Affiliation: Prudential of America

Licensed in: All states, the District of Columbia and Puerto Rico

Commenced Business: October 1875

Address: 751 BROAD STREET, NEWARK, NJ 07102-3777

Phone: (973) 802-6000 **Domicile State:** NJ **NAIC Code:** 68241

Data Date	Rating	RACR #1	RACR #2	Total Assets ($mil)	Capital ($mil)	Net Premium ($mil)	Net Income ($mil)
2021	B	1.49	1.17	324,000	19,122.9	33,229.1	965.7
2020	B	1.54	1.10	311,000	11,507.0	25,161.8	1,770.4
2019	B	1.54	1.11	292,000	11,483.3	29,746.0	-169.3
2018	B	1.54	1.10	271,000	10,694.8	30,479.2	1,324.5
2017	B	1.45	1.04	266,000	9,948.3	25,303.8	-216.7

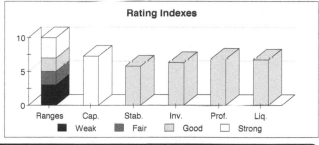

Rating Indexes

PRUDENTIAL LEGACY INS CO OF NJ | C | Fair

Major Rating Factors: Fair current capitalization (3.8 on a scale of 0 to 10) based on fair risk adjusted capital (severe loss scenario), although results have slipped from the good range over the last year. Good overall profitability (5.4). Return on equity has been excellent over the last five years averaging 59.6%. Weak liquidity (0.0).

Other Rating Factors: Weak overall results on stability tests (2.8) including weak risk adjusted capital in prior years. High quality investment portfolio (9.1).

Principal Business: Reinsurance (100%).

Principal Investments: NonCMO investment grade bonds (79%).

Investments in Affiliates: 25%

Group Affiliation: Prudential of America

Licensed in: NJ

Commenced Business: October 2010

Address: 751 Broad St, Newark, NJ 07102-3777

Phone: (877) 301-1212 **Domicile State:** NJ **NAIC Code:** 13809

Data Date	Rating	RACR #1	RACR #2	Total Assets ($mil)	Capital ($mil)	Net Premium ($mil)	Net Income ($mil)
2021	C	0.69	0.60	55,451.9	400.0	1,781.9	39.3
2020	C	0.95	0.83	55,911.1	685.2	1,972.7	63.6
2019	C	0.58	0.48	57,249.4	351.7	2,196.2	153.4
2018	D+	0.49	0.40	57,291.3	255.1	2,291.0	152.3
2017	D+	0.47	0.39	59,813.8	258.1	2,513.3	427.7

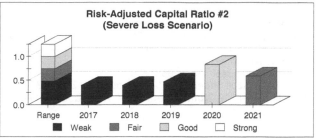

Risk-Adjusted Capital Ratio #2
(Severe Loss Scenario)

PRUDENTIAL RETIREMENT INS & ANNUITY — B- — Good

Major Rating Factors: Good overall profitability (5.1 on a scale of 0 to 10) although investment income, in comparison to reserve requirements, is below regulatory standards. Good overall results on stability tests (5.1) despite excessive premium growth. Other stability subfactors include excellent operational trends, good risk adjusted capital for prior years and excellent risk diversification. Fair quality investment portfolio (4.7).

Other Rating Factors: Strong capitalization (7.1) based on excellent risk adjusted capital (severe loss scenario). Excellent liquidity (10.0).

Principal Business: Group retirement contracts (52%) and reinsurance (48%).

Principal Investments: NonCMO investment grade bonds (59%), mortgages in good standing (18%), CMOs and structured securities (18%), and noninv. grade bonds (3%).

Investments in Affiliates: None

Group Affiliation: Prudential of America

Licensed in: All states, the District of Columbia and Puerto Rico

Commenced Business: October 1981

Address: 280 TRUMBULL STREET, HARTFORD, CT 06103-3509

Phone: (303) 737-3000 **Domicile State:** CT **NAIC Code:** 93629

Data Date	Rating	RACR #1	RACR #2	Total Assets ($mil)	Capital ($mil)	Net Premium ($mil)	Net Income ($mil)
2021	B-	1.90	1.08	100,000.0	1,495.2	1,744.2	470.2
2020	B-	1.77	0.87	88,908.6	1,157.0	1,383.3	19.9
2019	B-	1.92	0.95	80,985.8	1,178.0	1,209.3	37.2
2018	B-	2.06	0.90	69,883.2	1,082.3	1,082.4	135.3
2017	B-	1.88	0.86	75,337.8	1,056.8	884.3	100.5

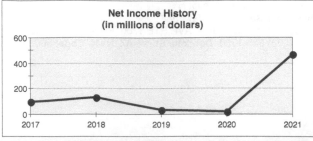

Net Income History
(in millions of dollars)

PURITAN LIFE INS CO — C- — Fair

Major Rating Factors: Fair current capitalization (4.0 on a scale of 0 to 10) based on mixed results -- excessive policy leverage mitigated by fair risk adjusted capital (severe loss scenario), although results have slipped from the good range over the last year. Low quality investment portfolio (2.8). Weak profitability (2.3) with operating losses during 2021.

Other Rating Factors: Weak overall results on stability tests (2.9) including negative cash flow from operations for 2021. Good liquidity (6.8).

Principal Business: N/A.

Principal Investments: Common & preferred stock (91%) and nonCMO investment grade bonds (2%).

Investments in Affiliates: 91%

Group Affiliation: Verde Investments Inc

Licensed in: AZ, TX

Commenced Business: January 1984

Address: 701 Brazos Street Suite 720, Scottsdale, AZ 85253

Phone: (602) 385-3629 **Domicile State:** TX **NAIC Code:** 68071

Data Date	Rating	RACR #1	RACR #2	Total Assets ($mil)	Capital ($mil)	Net Premium ($mil)	Net Income ($mil)
2021	C-	0.74	0.67	31.1	29.1	-0.1	-1.4
2020	U	0.96	0.85	23.2	21.3	-0.1	-1.2
2019	U	1.02	0.91	25.3	24.2	-0.1	0.1
2018	U	0.99	0.88	23.4	22.1	-0.1	-0.3
2017	C-	0.94	0.85	20.9	19.3	0.2	-0.3

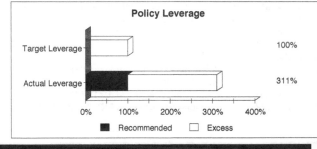

Policy Leverage

PURITAN LIFE INS CO OF AMERICA — C — Fair

Major Rating Factors: Fair quality investment portfolio (4.6 on a scale of 0 to 10). Fair overall results on stability tests (3.5). Good liquidity (6.0) with sufficient resources to handle a spike in claims as well as a significant increase in policy surrenders.

Other Rating Factors: Weak profitability (1.9) with operating losses during 2021. Return on equity has been low, averaging -6.3%. Strong capitalization (7.5) based on excellent risk adjusted capital (severe loss scenario).

Principal Business: Individual annuities (74%), individual health insurance (22%), individual life insurance (2%), and group life insurance (2%).

Principal Investments: NonCMO investment grade bonds (53%), CMOs and structured securities (19%), cash (4%), mortgages in good standing (4%), and misc. investments (12%).

Investments in Affiliates: None

Group Affiliation: Verde Capital Partners LLC

Licensed in: AL, AZ, AR, CA, CO, CT, FL, GA, HI, ID, IL, IN, IA, KS, KY, LA, MD, MI, MN, MS, MO, MT, NE, NV, NH, NM, NC, ND, OH, OK, OR, PA, SD, TN, TX, UT, WA, WV, WI, WY

Commenced Business: June 1958

Address: 701 Brazos Street Suite 720, Scottsdale, AZ 85253

Phone: (888) 474-9519 **Domicile State:** TX **NAIC Code:** 71390

Data Date	Rating	RACR #1	RACR #2	Total Assets ($mil)	Capital ($mil)	Net Premium ($mil)	Net Income ($mil)
2021	C	2.64	1.34	271.6	27.5	48.4	-1.2
2020	C	2.56	1.32	230.1	20.8	49.5	-1.3
2019	C	2.86	1.96	188.1	22.9	71.2	-0.2
2018	D+	1.78	1.31	133.2	21.6	25.3	1.1
2017	D+	2.57	2.28	119.4	18.3	23.4	-0.8

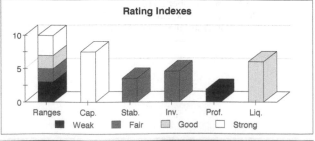

Rating Indexes

REINSURANCE CO OF MO INC   C   Fair

Major Rating Factors: Fair profitability (3.5 on a scale of 0 to 10) with operating losses during 2021. Return on equity has been low, averaging -2.0%. Fair overall results on stability tests (4.2) including negative cash flow from operations for 2021. Good capitalization (6.3) based on good risk adjusted capital (severe loss scenario). Moreover, capital levels have been consistent over the last five years.
Other Rating Factors: Low quality investment portfolio (1.4). Excellent liquidity (7.0).
Principal Business: Reinsurance (100%).
Principal Investments: Common & preferred stock (88%), nonCMO investment grade bonds (7%), and CMOs and structured securities (1%).
Investments in Affiliates: 88%
Group Affiliation: Reinsurance Group of America Inc
Licensed in: MO
Commenced Business: December 1998
Address: 16600 Swingley Ridge Road, Chesterfield, MO 63017-1706
Phone: (636) 736-7000 **Domicile State:** MO **NAIC Code:** 89004

Data Date	Rating	RACR #1	RACR #2	Total Assets ($mil)	Capital ($mil)	Net Premium ($mil)	Net Income ($mil)
2021	C	1.01	0.91	2,697.7	2,361.7	31.5	-13.3
2020	C	1.05	0.93	2,343.1	2,135.8	30.3	4.1
2019	C	1.01	0.90	2,421.8	2,124.7	34.9	75.1
2018	C	1.04	0.92	2,262.1	2,053.4	32.3	-24.9
2017	C	0.98	0.87	1,765.8	1,557.5	16.3	-183.1

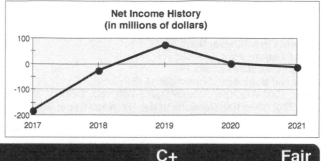

Net Income History
(in millions of dollars)

RELIANCE STANDARD LIFE INS CO   C+   Fair

Major Rating Factors: Fair overall results on stability tests (4.5 on a scale of 0 to 10) including fair risk adjusted capital in prior years. Good current capitalization (6.1) based on good risk adjusted capital (severe loss scenario) reflecting some improvement over results in 2020. Good liquidity (6.1) with sufficient resources to handle a spike in claims as well as a significant increase in policy surrenders.
Other Rating Factors: Low quality investment portfolio (2.6). Excellent profitability (7.6) with operating gains in each of the last five years.
Principal Business: Individual annuities (40%), group health insurance (37%), group life insurance (19%), and group retirement contracts (5%).
Principal Investments: Mortgages in good standing (34%), CMOs and structured securities (24%), nonCMO investment grade bonds (20%), noninv. grade bonds (11%), and misc. investments (9%).
Investments in Affiliates: 2%
Group Affiliation: Tokio Marine Holdings Inc
Licensed in: All states except NY
Commenced Business: April 1907
Address: 1100 East Woodfield Road, Schaumburg, IL 60173
Phone: (215) 787-4000 **Domicile State:** IL **NAIC Code:** 68381

Data Date	Rating	RACR #1	RACR #2	Total Assets ($mil)	Capital ($mil)	Net Premium ($mil)	Net Income ($mil)
2021	C+	1.56	0.89	18,943.6	1,843.1	2,057.3	289.8
2020	C+	1.26	0.73	17,528.5	1,577.2	2,291.9	84.3
2019	C+	1.43	0.85	15,902.9	1,517.1	2,356.0	220.5
2018	C+	1.88	1.01	13,875.0	1,278.3	3,160.5	245.1
2017	B	1.87	1.06	12,172.5	1,152.0	2,202.8	118.3

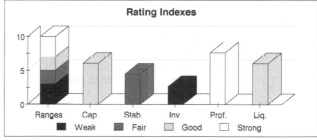

Rating Indexes

RELIASTAR LIFE INS CO   B-   Good

Major Rating Factors: Good quality investment portfolio (5.9 on a scale of 0 to 10) despite large holdings of BBB rated bonds in addition to moderate junk bond exposure. Exposure to mortgages is significant, but the mortgage default rate has been low. Good liquidity (6.0) with sufficient resources to handle a spike in claims as well as a significant increase in policy surrenders. Fair overall results on stability tests (3.9).
Other Rating Factors: Weak profitability (1.8) with operating losses during 2021. Strong overall capitalization (7.5) based on mixed results -- excessive policy leverage mitigated by excellent risk adjusted capital (severe loss scenario).
Principal Business: Group health insurance (52%), individual life insurance (25%), group life insurance (16%), individual annuities (4%), and reinsurance (3%).
Principal Investments: NonCMO investment grade bonds (46%), CMOs and structured securities (21%), mortgages in good standing (11%), common & preferred stock (6%), and misc. investments (14%).
Investments in Affiliates: 6%
Group Affiliation: Voya Financial Inc
Licensed in: All states, the District of Columbia and Puerto Rico
Commenced Business: September 1885
Address: 20 WASHINGTON AVENUE SOUTH, MINNEAPOLIS, MN 55401
Phone: (770) 980-5100 **Domicile State:** MN **NAIC Code:** 67105

Data Date	Rating	RACR #1	RACR #2	Total Assets ($mil)	Capital ($mil)	Net Premium ($mil)	Net Income ($mil)
2021	B-	1.96	1.34	15,173.4	1,781.7	-4,852.1	-1,210.7
2020	B-	2.02	1.19	19,614.9	1,596.2	1,124.5	205.4
2019	B-	1.93	1.16	19,707.3	1,536.3	666.8	35.5
2018	B-	2.05	1.21	20,238.5	1,632.9	1,122.5	100.6
2017	C+	1.98	1.18	19,910.1	1,483.1	633.1	234.3

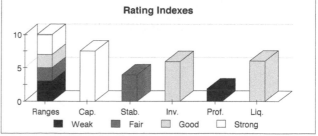

Rating Indexes

RELIASTAR LIFE INS CO OF NEW YORK — B- — Good

Major Rating Factors: Good quality investment portfolio (6.5 on a scale of 0 to 10) despite mixed results such as: minimal exposure to mortgages and large holdings of BBB rated bonds but small junk bond holdings. Good overall profitability (5.6). Excellent expense controls. Return on equity has been low, averaging 4.9%. Good liquidity (6.5).

Other Rating Factors: Fair overall results on stability tests (4.0) including negative cash flow from operations for 2021. Strong overall capitalization (10.0) based on mixed results -- excessive policy leverage mitigated by excellent risk adjusted capital (severe loss scenario).

Principal Business: Individual life insurance (67%), group health insurance (27%), group life insurance (3%), individual annuities (2%), and individual health insurance (1%).

Principal Investments: NonCMO investment grade bonds (56%), CMOs and structured securities (22%), mortgages in good standing (8%), policy loans (4%), and misc. investments (7%).

Investments in Affiliates: None
Group Affiliation: Voya Financial Inc
Licensed in: All states except PR
Commenced Business: September 1917
Address: 1000 WOODBURY ROAD STE 208, WOODBURY, NY 11797
Phone: (770) 980-5100 **Domicile State:** NY **NAIC Code:** 61360

Data Date	Rating	RACR #1	RACR #2	Total Assets ($mil)	Capital ($mil)	Net Premium ($mil)	Net Income ($mil)
2021	B-	6.25	3.33	2,258.6	433.0	-928.8	109.3
2020	B-	2.83	1.51	2,782.4	243.1	132.0	-19.1
2019	B	3.60	1.92	2,848.6	303.4	130.7	13.6
2018	B	3.31	1.78	2,815.2	278.7	138.3	17.5
2017	B	3.08	1.67	3,016.7	272.7	146.1	-32.1

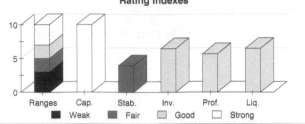

Rating Indexes

Ranges, Cap., Stab., Inv., Prof., Liq.
■ Weak ■ Fair ▨ Good □ Strong

RENAISSANCE L&H INS CO OF AMERICA — B — Good

Major Rating Factors: Good current capitalization (6.9 on a scale of 0 to 10) based on good risk adjusted capital (severe loss scenario), although results have slipped from the excellent range over the last year. Good liquidity (5.2) with sufficient resources to handle a spike in claims. Good overall results on stability tests (5.4) despite negative cash flow from operations for 2021 excellent operational trends and good risk diversification.

Other Rating Factors: Fair quality investment portfolio (4.8). Fair profitability (3.8) with operating losses during 2021.

Principal Business: Individual health insurance (51%), group health insurance (34%), reinsurance (12%), and group life insurance (3%).

Principal Investments: NonCMO investment grade bonds (43%), CMOs and structured securities (28%), common & preferred stock (23%), and noninv. grade bonds (2%).

Investments in Affiliates: None
Group Affiliation: Renaissance Health Service Corp
Licensed in: All states except NY, PR
Commenced Business: June 1953
Address: 1209 Orange St, Indianapolis, IN 46202
Phone: (517) 349-6000 **Domicile State:** DE **NAIC Code:** 61700

Data Date	Rating	RACR #1	RACR #2	Total Assets ($mil)	Capital ($mil)	Net Premium ($mil)	Net Income ($mil)
2021	B	1.33	0.99	97.9	48.9	181.9	-1.4
2020	B	1.42	1.06	94.7	49.5	171.1	9.5
2019	C+	1.63	1.21	92.6	56.2	170.5	3.3
2018	N/A	N/A	N/A	95.3	67.8	0.0	3.2
2017	N/A	N/A	N/A	91.9	66.3	0.0	3.7

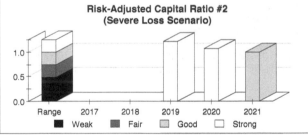

**Risk-Adjusted Capital Ratio #2
(Severe Loss Scenario)**

Range, 2017, 2018, 2019, 2020, 2021
■ Weak ■ Fair ▨ Good □ Strong

RESOLUTION LIFE COLORADO INC — C — Fair

Major Rating Factors: Good capitalization (3.0 on a scale of 0 to 10) based on good risk adjusted capital (severe loss scenario). Fair overall results on stability tests (3.0) including negative cash flow from operations for 2021, lack of operational experience. Low quality investment portfolio (1.0).

Other Rating Factors: Weak profitability (2.9) with operating losses during 2021. Excellent liquidity (7.0).

Principal Business: Reinsurance (100%).

Principal Investments: Common & preferred stock (94%), nonCMO investment grade bonds (2%), CMOs and structured securities (2%), and policy loans (1%).

Investments in Affiliates: 94%
Group Affiliation: Resolution Life Group Holdings LP
Licensed in: CO
Commenced Business: March 2020
Address: 5770 Powers Ferry Road, NW Atlanta, GA 30327
Phone: (770) 980-5100 **Domicile State:** CO **NAIC Code:** 16920

Data Date	Rating	RACR #1	RACR #2	Total Assets ($mil)	Capital ($mil)	Net Premium ($mil)	Net Income ($mil)
2021	C	0.98	0.90	1,510.0	1,339.8	153.4	-9.7
2020	N/A	N/A	N/A	0.0	0.0	0.0	0.0
2019	N/A	N/A	N/A	0.0	0.0	0.0	0.0
2018	N/A	N/A	N/A	0.0	0.0	0.0	0.0
2017	N/A	N/A	N/A	0.0	0.0	0.0	0.0

**Risk-Adjusted Capital Ratio #2
(Severe Loss Scenario)**

Range, 2017, 2018, 2019, 2020, 2021
■ Weak ■ Fair ▨ Good □ Strong

RGA REINSURANCE CO   B-   Good

Major Rating Factors: Good capitalization (5.8 on a scale of 0 to 10) based on good risk adjusted capital (moderate loss scenario). Capital levels have been relatively consistent over the last five years. Good overall profitability (6.2) despite operating losses during 2021. Return on equity has been fair, averaging 8.8%. Good overall results on stability tests (5.3) good operational trends and excellent risk diversification.

Other Rating Factors: Fair quality investment portfolio (4.1). Fair liquidity (4.4).
Principal Business: Reinsurance (100%).
Principal Investments: NonCMO investment grade bonds (51%), mortgages in good standing (16%), CMOs and structured securities (13%), noninv. grade bonds (7%), and misc. investments (11%).

Investments in Affiliates: 2%
Group Affiliation: Reinsurance Group of America Inc
Licensed in: All states, the District of Columbia and Puerto Rico
Commenced Business: October 1982
Address: 16600 Swingley Ridge Road, Chesterfield, MO 63017-1706
Phone: (636) 736-7000 **Domicile State:** MO **NAIC Code:** 93572

Data Date	Rating	RACR #1	RACR #2	Total Assets ($mil)	Capital ($mil)	Net Premium ($mil)	Net Income ($mil)
2021	B-	1.54	0.83	49,440.5	2,367.9	6,598.5	-98.3
2020	B-	1.62	0.85	42,010.0	2,130.9	3,199.7	-132.5
2019	B-	1.65	0.87	41,587.9	2,150.1	3,377.3	280.4
2018	B-	1.70	0.93	36,983.5	2,078.7	4,488.1	659.9
2017	B-	1.63	0.87	33,356.1	1,584.0	4,286.4	138.4

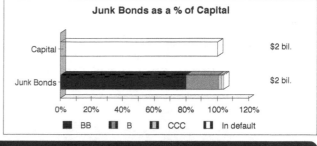

Junk Bonds as a % of Capital

RIVERSOURCE LIFE INS CO   B   Good

Major Rating Factors: Good quality investment portfolio (5.9 on a scale of 0 to 10) despite mixed results such as: substantial holdings of BBB bonds but moderate junk bond exposure. Good overall profitability (5.2) although investment income, in comparison to reserve requirements, is below regulatory standards. Fair overall results on stability tests (4.8).

Other Rating Factors: Strong overall capitalization (7.5) based on mixed results -- excessive policy leverage mitigated by excellent risk adjusted capital (severe loss scenario). Excellent liquidity (8.1).
Principal Business: Individual annuities (79%), individual life insurance (16%), individual health insurance (4%), and group retirement contracts (1%).
Principal Investments: NonCMO investment grade bonds (27%), CMOs and structured securities (15%), mortgages in good standing (7%), policy loans (4%), and misc. investments (10%).

Investments in Affiliates: 5%
Group Affiliation: Ameriprise Financial Inc
Licensed in: All states except NY, PR
Commenced Business: October 1957
Address: 227 AMERIPRISE FINANCIAL CNTR, MINNEAPOLIS, MN 55474
Phone: (612) 671-3131 **Domicile State:** MN **NAIC Code:** 65005

Data Date	Rating	RACR #1	RACR #2	Total Assets ($mil)	Capital ($mil)	Net Premium ($mil)	Net Income ($mil)
2021	B	2.09	1.35	116,000	3,412.5	-1,346.3	252.7
2020	B	2.68	1.65	118,000	4,790.0	5,044.4	1,581.5
2019	C+	1.77	1.09	107,000	2,914.1	3,293.0	786.2
2018	C+	1.90	1.18	98,013.8	3,280.1	5,242.3	1,627.8
2017	C	1.40	0.86	107,000	2,390.0	5,082.8	222.0

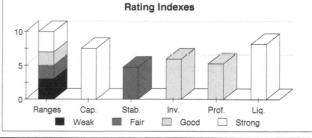

Rating Indexes

RIVERSOURCE LIFE INS CO OF NY   C   Fair

Major Rating Factors: Fair overall results on stability tests (4.3 on a scale of 0 to 10). Good quality investment portfolio (5.7) despite mixed results such as: large holdings of BBB rated bonds but moderate junk bond exposure. Weak profitability (2.8) with investment income below regulatory standards in relation to interest assumptions of reserves.

Other Rating Factors: Strong capitalization (7.7) based on excellent risk adjusted capital (severe loss scenario). Excellent liquidity (7.8).
Principal Business: Individual annuities (69%), individual life insurance (23%), individual health insurance (5%), and group retirement contracts (3%).
Principal Investments: NonCMO investment grade bonds (43%), CMOs and structured securities (26%), mortgages in good standing (6%), noninv. grade bonds (4%), and misc. investments (5%).

Investments in Affiliates: None
Group Affiliation: Ameriprise Financial Inc
Licensed in: NY
Commenced Business: October 1972
Address: 20 MADISON AVENUE EXTENSION, ALBANY, NY 12203-5326
Phone: (612) 671-3131 **Domicile State:** NY **NAIC Code:** 80594

Data Date	Rating	RACR #1	RACR #2	Total Assets ($mil)	Capital ($mil)	Net Premium ($mil)	Net Income ($mil)
2021	C	2.93	1.46	8,277.9	309.1	300.7	6.1
2020	C	3.10	1.54	7,802.9	305.4	297.1	-46.2
2019	C	2.44	1.24	7,112.0	234.3	349.2	-82.8
2018	C	2.86	1.44	6,406.0	264.9	367.0	31.2
2017	C	2.82	1.42	6,911.3	269.1	372.1	1.7

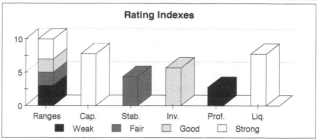

Rating Indexes

S USA LIFE INS CO INC

B- **Good**

Major Rating Factors: Fair overall results on stability tests (3.5 on a scale of 0 to 10) including fair financial strength of affiliated SBLI USA Group and weak results on operational trends. Fair quality investment portfolio (3.8) with significant exposure to mortgages . Mortgage default rate has been low. Weak profitability (1.7) with operating losses during 2021.

Other Rating Factors: Strong capitalization (7.3) based on excellent risk adjusted capital (severe loss scenario). Excellent liquidity (8.1).

Principal Business: Individual annuities (91%), individual life insurance (7%), and individual health insurance (2%).

Principal Investments: CMOs and structured securities (54%), nonCMO investment grade bonds (24%), mortgages in good standing (16%), cash (1%), and common & preferred stock (1%).

Investments in Affiliates: None

Group Affiliation: SBLI USA Group

Licensed in: All states except CT, NH, NY, PR

Commenced Business: July 1995

Address: 3800 N CENTRAL AVE STE 460, PHOENIX, AZ 85021

Phone: (212) 356-0300 **Domicile State:** AZ **NAIC Code:** 60183

Data Date	Rating	RACR #1	RACR #2	Total Assets ($mil)	Capital ($mil)	Net Premium ($mil)	Net Income ($mil)
2021	B-	2.66	1.19	1,514.6	139.1	454.2	-24.3
2020	B-	2.98	1.30	582.8	45.9	55.6	-5.8
2019	B-	1.44	1.30	78.4	11.4	13.3	-7.5
2018	B	3.88	3.49	28.7	17.2	7.7	-6.9
2017	B	2.49	2.24	17.5	8.0	4.2	-0.2

SBLI USA Group
Composite Group Rating: C+
Largest Group Members

	Assets ($mil)	Rating
SBLI USA MUT LIFE INS CO INC	2156	B-
SHENANDOAH LIFE INS CO	1421	C
S USA LIFE INS CO INC	583	B-

SAGICOR LIFE INS CO

D- **Weak**

Major Rating Factors: Low quality investment portfolio (2.5 on a scale of 0 to 10) containing large holdings of BBB rated bonds in addition to junk bond exposure equal to 51% of capital. Weak profitability (1.6) with operating losses during 2021. Weak overall results on stability tests (1.3) including weak risk adjusted capital in prior years.

Other Rating Factors: Fair capitalization (4.1) based on fair risk adjusted capital (moderate loss scenario). Fair liquidity (4.5).

Principal Business: Individual annuities (94%) and individual life insurance (6%).

Principal Investments: NonCMO investment grade bonds (49%), CMOs and structured securities (24%), common & preferred stock (10%), noninv. grade bonds (4%), and misc. investments (7%).

Investments in Affiliates: None

Group Affiliation: Sagicor Financial Corp

Licensed in: All states except AK, NY, PR

Commenced Business: April 1954

Address: 900 CONGRESS AVE SUITE 300, AUSTIN, TX 78731

Phone: (480) 425-5100 **Domicile State:** TX **NAIC Code:** 60445

Data Date	Rating	RACR #1	RACR #2	Total Assets ($mil)	Capital ($mil)	Net Premium ($mil)	Net Income ($mil)
2021	D-	0.89	0.45	2,997.6	169.7	471.6	-62.9
2020	D	0.55	0.28	2,332.3	90.4	594.6	-40.6
2019	D+	0.70	0.36	2,037.3	98.8	443.2	-48.6
2018	C-	0.82	0.42	1,594.5	102.5	388.8	6.7
2017	C-	1.14	0.59	1,115.0	72.5	84.5	-1.4

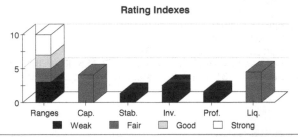

Rating Indexes

SB MUTL LIFE INS CO OF MA

B **Good**

Major Rating Factors: Good quality investment portfolio (5.5 on a scale of 0 to 10) despite mixed results such as: large holdings of BBB rated bonds but junk bond exposure equal to 64% of capital. Good overall profitability (5.9). Excellent expense controls. Return on equity has been good over the last five years, averaging 13.6%. Good liquidity (5.7).

Other Rating Factors: Fair overall results on stability tests (4.7). Strong capitalization (7.0) based on excellent risk adjusted capital (severe loss scenario).

Principal Business: Individual life insurance (96%) and individual annuities (4%).

Principal Investments: NonCMO investment grade bonds (72%), CMOs and structured securities (13%), noninv. grade bonds (3%), common & preferred stock (2%), and policy loans (2%).

Investments in Affiliates: None

Group Affiliation: Savings Bank Life Group

Licensed in: All states except NY, PR

Commenced Business: January 1992

Address: One Linscott Road, Woburn, MA 1801

Phone: (781) 938-3500 **Domicile State:** MA **NAIC Code:** 70435

Data Date	Rating	RACR #1	RACR #2	Total Assets ($mil)	Capital ($mil)	Net Premium ($mil)	Net Income ($mil)
2021	B	1.99	1.03	3,563.5	206.6	130.6	33.7
2020	B	1.82	0.94	3,486.8	187.0	146.4	38.6
2019	B	2.14	1.10	3,407.6	193.9	310.5	24.3
2018	B+	2.43	1.27	3,066.5	201.8	128.1	39.1
2017	B+	1.96	1.14	3,032.4	202.5	140.5	46.8

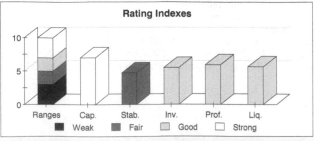

Rating Indexes

SBLI USA MUT LIFE INS CO INC | B- | Good

Major Rating Factors: Good capitalization (5.6 on a scale of 0 to 10) based on good risk adjusted capital (moderate loss scenario). Good overall profitability (6.7). Excellent expense controls. Return on equity has been good over the last five years, averaging 11.8%. Good liquidity (5.2) with sufficient resources to handle a spike in claims as well as a significant increase in policy surrenders.

Other Rating Factors: Good overall results on stability tests (5.2) despite fair risk adjusted capital in prior years good operational trends and excellent risk diversification. Fair quality investment portfolio (3.8).

Principal Business: Individual annuities (84%), individual life insurance (12%), group life insurance (2%), and individual health insurance (1%).

Principal Investments: NonCMO investment grade bonds (47%), CMOs and structured securities (44%), policy loans (3%), and noninv. grade bonds (1%).

Investments in Affiliates: None

Group Affiliation: Reservoir Capital Group LLC

Licensed in: All states except CA, CT, FL, ID, KS, LA, ME, MA

Commenced Business: January 2000

Address: 100 WEST 33RD STREET STE 1007, NEW YORK, NY 10001-2900

Phone: (212) 356-0300 **Domicile State:** NY **NAIC Code:** 60176

Data Date	Rating	RACR #1	RACR #2	Total Assets ($mil)	Capital ($mil)	Net Premium ($mil)	Net Income ($mil)
2021	B-	1.37	0.68	2,554.3	134.7	506.1	5.6
2020	B-	1.59	0.80	2,155.5	131.4	436.9	-37.9
2019	B-	1.34	0.75	1,716.7	96.1	209.6	15.9
2018	B-	1.29	0.79	1,557.9	89.1	173.6	17.1
2017	B	1.70	0.98	1,474.0	95.4	81.2	16.8

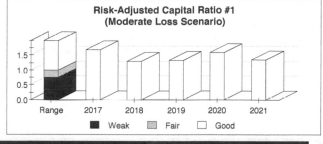

Risk-Adjusted Capital Ratio #1
(Moderate Loss Scenario)

SCOR GLOBAL LIFE AMERICAS REIN CO | C- | Fair

Major Rating Factors: Fair capitalization (4.6 on a scale of 0 to 10) based on fair risk adjusted capital (moderate loss scenario). Fair overall results on stability tests (3.3) including negative cash flow from operations for 2021, fair risk adjusted capital in prior years. Weak profitability (1.2) with operating losses during 2021.

Other Rating Factors: Good liquidity (5.8). High quality investment portfolio (7.9).

Principal Business: Reinsurance (100%).

Principal Investments: NonCMO investment grade bonds (68%), common & preferred stock (12%), CMOs and structured securities (6%), cash (3%), and policy loans (2%).

Investments in Affiliates: 20%

Group Affiliation: SCOR Reinsurance Group

Licensed in: All states except NY, PR

Commenced Business: April 1945

Address: 2711 CENTERVILLE ROAD STE 400, WILMINGTON, DE 19808

Phone: (704) 344-2700 **Domicile State:** DE **NAIC Code:** 64688

Data Date	Rating	RACR #1	RACR #2	Total Assets ($mil)	Capital ($mil)	Net Premium ($mil)	Net Income ($mil)
2021	C-	0.95	0.68	738.5	142.6	225.9	-49.5
2020	C-	0.82	0.61	957.4	170.3	228.4	-58.2
2019	C	0.96	0.70	1,065.3	206.8	225.2	2.2
2018	C	0.84	0.63	1,037.4	208.0	196.6	-52.8
2017	C+	1.14	0.84	1,112.0	208.0	130.5	8.9

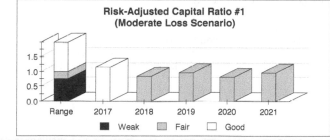

Risk-Adjusted Capital Ratio #1
(Moderate Loss Scenario)

SCOR GLOBAL LIFE REINS CO OF DE | C- | Fair

Major Rating Factors: Fair overall results on stability tests (3.3 on a scale of 0 to 10) including negative cash flow from operations for 2021. Weak profitability (0.9) with operating losses during 2021. Good liquidity (5.7) with sufficient resources to handle a spike in claims as well as a significant increase in policy surrenders.

Other Rating Factors: Strong capitalization (9.1) based on excellent risk adjusted capital (severe loss scenario). High quality investment portfolio (8.5).

Principal Business: Reinsurance (100%).

Principal Investments: NonCMO investment grade bonds (45%), CMOs and structured securities (22%), policy loans (5%), and cash (2%).

Investments in Affiliates: None

Group Affiliation: SCOR Reinsurance Group

Licensed in: All states except AL, PR

Commenced Business: May 1977

Address: 2711 CENTERVILLE ROAD STE 400, WILMINGTON, DE 19808

Phone: (704) 344-2700 **Domicile State:** DE **NAIC Code:** 87017

Data Date	Rating	RACR #1	RACR #2	Total Assets ($mil)	Capital ($mil)	Net Premium ($mil)	Net Income ($mil)
2021	C-	3.74	2.41	347.8	63.3	70.6	-41.0
2020	C	4.35	2.61	347.8	104.2	88.3	10.7
2019	C	3.69	2.23	446.2	99.2	67.8	-30.4
2018	C	4.60	2.78	473.3	127.1	103.7	37.8
2017	C	3.42	2.07	375.4	97.4	75.9	-1.5

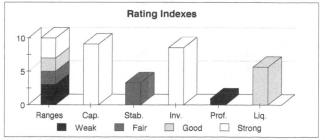

Rating Indexes

SCOR GLOBAL LIFE USA RE CO   C+   Fair

Major Rating Factors: Good quality investment portfolio (6.8 on a scale of 0 to 10) despite mixed results such as: no exposure to mortgages and substantial holdings of BBB bonds but no exposure to junk bonds. Weak overall results on stability tests (2.9) including fair financial strength of affiliated SCOR Reinsurance Group and negative cash flow from operations for 2021. Weak profitability (1.9) with operating losses during 2021.

Other Rating Factors: Weak liquidity (0.3). Strong capitalization (7.6) based on excellent risk adjusted capital (severe loss scenario).

Principal Business: Reinsurance (100%).

Principal Investments: NonCMO investment grade bonds (57%), CMOs and structured securities (13%), and cash (4%).

Investments in Affiliates: 23%

Group Affiliation: SCOR Reinsurance Group

Licensed In: All states except PR

Commenced Business: October 1982

Address: 2711 Centerville Road Ste 400, Wilmington, DE 19808

Phone: (913) 901-4600 **Domicile State:** DE **NAIC Code:** 97071

Data Date	Rating	RACR #1	RACR #2	Total Assets ($mil)	Capital ($mil)	Net Premium ($mil)	Net Income ($mil)
2021	C+	2.29	1.40	787.5	184.1	302.4	-10.9
2020	C+	2.20	1.35	828.9	176.4	311.3	-29.8
2019	B-	3.24	1.95	764.5	237.8	318.7	8.1
2018	B-	3.38	2.06	764.6	264.4	249.3	14.2
2017	B-	4.13	2.46	817.3	277.1	133.8	-15.8

SCOR Reinsurance Group Composite Group Rating: C Largest Group Members	Assets ($mil)	Rating
SCOR REINS CO	5337	C
SCOR GLOBAL LIFE AMERICAS REIN CO	957	C-
SCOR GLOBAL LIFE USA RE CO	829	C+
GENERAL SECURITY NATIONAL INS CO	431	C-
SCOR GLOBAL LIFE REINS CO OF DE	348	C

SECU LIFE INS CO   B-   Good

Major Rating Factors: Fair overall results on stability tests (3.8 on a scale of 0 to 10) including excessive premium growth. Strong capitalization (10.0) based on excellent risk adjusted capital (severe loss scenario). Capital levels have been relatively consistent over the last five years. High quality investment portfolio (7.9) despite large exposure to mortgages . Mortgage default rate has been low. substantial holdings of BBB bonds in addition to no exposure to junk bonds.

Other Rating Factors: Excellent profitability (8.6) with operating gains in each of the last five years. Excellent liquidity (7.0).

Principal Business: Individual life insurance (61%), individual annuities (26%), and group life insurance (13%).

Principal Investments: NonCMO investment grade bonds (55%), mortgages in good standing (38%), and cash (7%).

Investments in Affiliates: None

Group Affiliation: State Employees Credit Union

Licensed In: NC

Commenced Business: January 2013

Address: 119 N Salisbury St Floor 10, Raleigh, NC 27603

Phone: (919) 839-5084 **Domicile State:** NC **NAIC Code:** 14924

Data Date	Rating	RACR #1	RACR #2	Total Assets ($mil)	Capital ($mil)	Net Premium ($mil)	Net Income ($mil)
2021	B-	4.11	3.23	75.7	32.2	14.2	0.6
2020	B	4.20	3.55	69.2	31.9	10.9	1.5
2019	B	4.10	3.69	63.0	30.0	15.9	0.8
2018	B	4.27	3.84	50.3	28.8	10.1	1.1
2017	B-	4.56	4.10	43.3	27.4	7.7	1.0

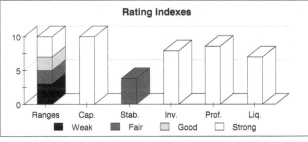

Rating Indexes

Ranges Cap. Stab. Inv. Prof. Liq.
■ Weak ■ Fair ▨ Good □ Strong

SECURIAN LIFE INS CO   B-   Good

Major Rating Factors: Good liquidity (6.4 on a scale of 0 to 10) with sufficient resources to handle a spike in claims as well as a significant increase in policy surrenders. Fair overall results on stability tests (4.9) including fair financial strength of affiliated Securian Financial Group. Weak profitability (2.9) with operating losses during 2021.

Other Rating Factors: Strong capitalization (9.5) based on excellent risk adjusted capital (severe loss scenario). High quality investment portfolio (7.4).

Principal Business: Group life insurance (77%), group retirement contracts (10%), group health insurance (8%), individual life insurance (3%), and credit health insurance (1%).

Principal Investments: NonCMO investment grade bonds (62%), CMOs and structured securities (19%), mortgages in good standing (15%), noninv. grade bonds (1%), and common & preferred stock (1%).

Investments in Affiliates: None

Group Affiliation: Securian Financial Group

Licensed In: All states, the District of Columbia and Puerto Rico

Commenced Business: December 1981

Address: 400 ROBERT STREET NORTH, ST. PAUL, MN 55101-2098

Phone: (651) 665-3500 **Domicile State:** MN **NAIC Code:** 93742

Data Date	Rating	RACR #1	RACR #2	Total Assets ($mil)	Capital ($mil)	Net Premium ($mil)	Net Income ($mil)
2021	B-	4.26	2.65	2,066.0	476.1	532.3	-30.3
2020	B	4.36	2.76	1,780.1	446.8	510.3	6.3
2019	B	5.11	3.31	1,437.2	447.3	450.1	19.3
2018	B	5.40	3.45	1,094.9	360.8	445.1	9.9
2017	B	5.67	3.77	775.7	305.3	238.9	0.9

Securian Financial Group Composite Group Rating: C+ Largest Group Members	Assets ($mil)	Rating
MINNESOTA LIFE INS CO	60202	C+
SECURIAN LIFE INS CO	1780	B
SECURIAN CASUALTY CO	458	B

SECURICO LIFE INS CO   D   Weak

Major Rating Factors: Weak profitability (1.9 on a scale of 0 to 10). Return on equity has been low, averaging -7.8%. Weak overall results on stability tests (2.0) including negative cash flow from operations for 2021. Good quality investment portfolio (6.1) with no exposure to mortgages and no exposure to junk bonds.
Other Rating Factors: Strong capitalization (10.0) based on excellent risk adjusted capital (severe loss scenario). Excellent liquidity (7.0).
Principal Business: Reinsurance (89%) and individual life insurance (11%).
Principal Investments: NonCMO investment grade bonds (17%) and common & preferred stock (8%).
Investments in Affiliates: None
Group Affiliation: NAP Group Inc
Licensed in: TX
Commenced Business: August 1984
Address: PO Box 341364, Richardson, TX 75080
Phone: (855) 877-5433 **Domicile State:** TX **NAIC Code:** 66516

Data Date	Rating	RACR #1	RACR #2	Total Assets ($mil)	Capital ($mil)	Net Premium ($mil)	Net Income ($mil)
2021	D	5.42	4.87	29.3	26.8	1.3	1.2
2020	D	3.18	2.86	12.3	11.1	1.0	-1.2
2019	D	2.14	1.93	7.3	6.7	0.7	-0.3
2018	D	2.48	2.23	2.3	2.0	0.5	-0.3
2017	D	2.72	2.44	2.4	2.3	0.4	-0.2

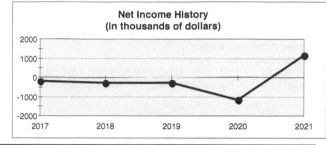

Net Income History
(in thousands of dollars)

SECURITY BENEFIT LIFE INS CO   B   Good

Major Rating Factors: Good overall results on stability tests (5.5 on a scale of 0 to 10). Stability strengths include good operational trends and excellent risk diversification. Fair quality investment portfolio (4.3) with large holdings of BBB rated bonds in addition to moderate junk bond exposure. Strong overall capitalization (7.7) based on mixed results -- excessive policy leverage mitigated by excellent risk adjusted capital (severe loss scenario).
Other Rating Factors: Excellent profitability (8.3) with operating gains in each of the last five years. Excellent liquidity (7.2).
Principal Business: Individual annuities (92%), reinsurance (6%), and group retirement contracts (1%).
Principal Investments: CMOs and structured securities (33%), nonCMO investment grade bonds (17%), noninv. grade bonds (7%), mortgages in good standing (3%), and misc. investments (32%).
Investments in Affiliates: 35%
Group Affiliation: NZC Captial LLC
Licensed in: All states except NY, PR
Commenced Business: February 1892
Address: One Security Benefit Place, Topeka, KS 66636-0001
Phone: (785) 431-3000 **Domicile State:** KS **NAIC Code:** 68675

Data Date	Rating	RACR #1	RACR #2	Total Assets ($mil)	Capital ($mil)	Net Premium ($mil)	Net Income ($mil)
2021	B	3.10	1.46	46,517.4	4,436.3	-855.0	987.8
2020	B	2.76	1.29	40,663.8	3,509.7	4,450.7	426.3
2019	B	2.91	1.32	36,450.7	3,031.8	2,767.3	216.5
2018	B	2.55	1.21	33,538.6	2,398.1	1,985.9	272.2
2017	B	2.49	1.11	33,099.5	1,900.6	2,951.4	181.0

Adverse Trends in Operations

Decrease in premium volume from 2017 to 2018 (33%)
Increase in policy surrenders from 2017 to 2018 (70%)
Decrease in premium volume from 2016 to 2017 (19%)

SECURITY LIFE OF DENVER INS CO   B-   Good

Major Rating Factors: Good overall capitalization (5.5 on a scale of 0 to 10) based on mixed results -- excessive policy leverage mitigated by good risk adjusted capital (moderate loss scenario). Fair quality investment portfolio (3.7) with large holdings of BBB rated bonds in addition to moderate junk bond exposure. Fair overall results on stability tests (3.6) including negative cash flow from operations for 2021 and fair risk adjusted capital in prior years.
Other Rating Factors: Weak profitability (1.8) with operating losses during 2021. Weak liquidity (0.6).
Principal Business: Reinsurance (96%) and individual life insurance (4%).
Principal Investments: NonCMO investment grade bonds (63%), CMOs and structured securities (16%), mortgages in good standing (8%), policy loans (5%), and misc. investments (7%).
Investments in Affiliates: None
Group Affiliation: Voya Financial Inc
Licensed in: All states, the District of Columbia and Puerto Rico
Commenced Business: May 1950
Address: 8055 EAST TUFTS AVENUE STE 710, DENVER, CO 80231
Phone: (770) 618-3885 **Domicile State:** CO **NAIC Code:** 68713

Data Date	Rating	RACR #1	RACR #2	Total Assets ($mil)	Capital ($mil)	Net Premium ($mil)	Net Income ($mil)
2021	B-	1.33	0.71	34,605.0	1,213.6	16,469.5	-598.7
2020	B-	1.24	0.69	15,475.1	794.3	385.3	-46.7
2019	B-	1.38	0.79	15,511.3	881.1	-1,021.8	-226.5
2018	B-	1.46	0.83	15,351.7	965.4	1,578.4	-61.8
2017	C+	1.60	0.92	14,548.2	950.5	693.4	58.2

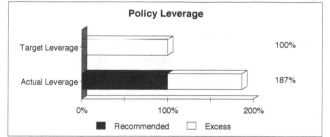

Policy Leverage

Target Leverage — 100%
Actual Leverage — 187%

0%   100%   200%

■ Recommended   □ Excess

SECURITY MUTUAL LIFE INS CO OF NY　　　　　　　　C　　　　Fair

Major Rating Factors: Good capitalization (6.5 on a scale of 0 to 10) based on good risk adjusted capital (severe loss scenario). Moreover, capital levels have been consistent over the last five years. Good quality investment portfolio (6.1) despite mixed results such as: minimal exposure to mortgages and large holdings of BBB rated bonds but minimal holdings in junk bonds. Good overall profitability (5.9).

Other Rating Factors: Weak liquidity (0.6). Weak overall results on stability tests (2.9).

Principal Business: Individual life insurance (97%) and individual annuities (3%).

Principal Investments: NonCMO investment grade bonds (66%), policy loans (18%), mortgages in good standing (8%), cash (1%), and CMOs and structured securities (1%).

Investments in Affiliates: None

Group Affiliation: None

Licensed in: All states except PR

Commenced Business: January 1887

Address: 100 COURT STREET, BINGHAMTON, NY 13901-3479

Phone: (607) 723-3551　**Domicile State:** NY　**NAIC Code:** 68772

Data Date	Rating	RACR #1	RACR #2	Total Assets ($mil)	Capital ($mil)	Net Premium ($mil)	Net Income ($mil)
2021	C	1.76	0.94	2,996.8	188.4	241.5	7.9
2020	C	1.72	0.92	2,903.6	180.7	225.4	10.3
2019	C	1.74	0.92	2,830.1	173.2	216.2	9.4
2018	C	1.68	0.89	2,767.4	164.9	205.5	7.1
2017	C	1.62	0.88	2,751.9	155.9	204.7	4.4

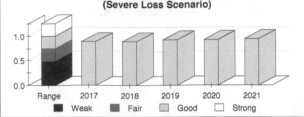

Risk-Adjusted Capital Ratio #2 (Severe Loss Scenario)

SECURITY NATIONAL LIFE INS CO　　　　　　　　　　　D　　　Weak

Major Rating Factors: Low quality investment portfolio (2.7 on a scale of 0 to 10) containing significant exposure to mortgages . Mortgage default rate has been low. Weak overall results on stability tests (1.4) including weak risk adjusted capital in prior years. Good capitalization (5.0) based on good risk adjusted capital (moderate loss scenario).

Other Rating Factors: Excellent profitability (8.2). Excellent liquidity (8.1).

Principal Business: Individual life insurance (90%), individual annuities (8%), and reinsurance (1%).

Principal Investments: NonCMO investment grade bonds (18%), real estate (17%), mortgages in good standing (13%), common & preferred stock (6%), and misc. investments (9%).

Investments in Affiliates: 5%

Group Affiliation: Security National Life

Licensed in: AL, AK, AZ, AR, CA, CO, DC, DE, FL, GA, HI, ID, IL, IN, IA, KS, KY, LA, MD, MI, MN, MS, MO, MT, NE, NV, NM, ND, OH, OK, OR, PA, SC, SD, TN, TX, UT, VA, WI, WY

Commenced Business: July 1967

Address: 5300 SOUTH 360 WEST, SALT LAKE CITY, UT 84123

Phone: (801) 264-1060　**Domicile State:** UT　**NAIC Code:** 69485

Data Date	Rating	RACR #1	RACR #2	Total Assets ($mil)	Capital ($mil)	Net Premium ($mil)	Net Income ($mil)
2021	D	1.01	0.61	702.8	57.4	92.9	5.6
2020	D	0.70	0.46	678.2	53.1	87.1	6.1
2019	D	0.95	0.63	645.2	49.4	89.9	3.6
2018	D	1.08	0.64	666.7	47.2	85.5	18.0
2017	D-	0.80	0.48	584.7	36.3	81.3	-3.0

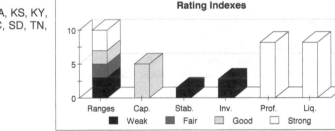

Rating Indexes

SELECTED FUNERAL AND LIFE INSURANCE COMPANY　　C+　　Fair

Major Rating Factors: Fair quality investment portfolio (4.5 on a scale of 0 to 10) with large holdings of BBB rated bonds in addition to junk bond exposure equal to 70% of capital. Fair profitability (4.2). Return on equity has been low, averaging 1.2%. Fair overall results on stability tests (4.4).

Other Rating Factors: Good liquidity (5.2). Strong capitalization (7.7) based on excellent risk adjusted capital (severe loss scenario).

Principal Business: Individual life insurance (56%) and individual annuities (44%).

Principal Investments: NonCMO investment grade bonds (75%), noninv. grade bonds (10%), common & preferred stock (6%), CMOs and structured securities (6%), and misc. investments (3%).

Investments in Affiliates: None

Group Affiliation: Superior Funeral and Life Insurance

Licensed in: AR, LA, MS, OK

Commenced Business: October 1960

Address: 119 CONVENTION BOULEVARD, HOT SPRINGS, AR 71901

Phone: (501) 624-2172　**Domicile State:** AR　**NAIC Code:** 83836

Data Date	Rating	RACR #1	RACR #2	Total Assets ($mil)	Capital ($mil)	Net Premium ($mil)	Net Income ($mil)
2021	C+	2.88	1.45	194.3	29.2	18.3	2.0
2020	C+	2.66	1.32	187.6	25.3	16.0	0.2
2019	C+	2.87	1.42	189.2	27.5	14.9	0.7
2018	C+	2.76	1.40	185.3	25.5	15.8	0.8
2017	C+	2.67	1.36	181.7	24.5	15.2	0.6

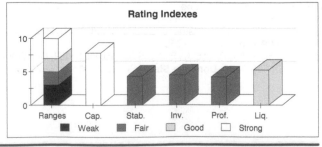

Rating Indexes

SENTINEL SECURITY LIFE INS CO

D   Weak

Major Rating Factors: Weak overall results on stability tests (1.5 on a scale of 0 to 10) including potential financial drain due to affiliation with Advantage Captial Partners LLC and weak risk adjusted capital in prior years. Weak profitability (2.4) with investment income below regulatory standards in relation to interest assumptions of reserves. Fair capitalization (4.2) based on fair risk adjusted capital (moderate loss scenario).

Other Rating Factors: Fair quality investment portfolio (3.4). Excellent liquidity (7.8).

Principal Business: Individual annuities (85%), group health insurance (10%), individual health insurance (3%), and individual life insurance (2%).

Principal Investments: NonCMO investment grade bonds (36%), CMOs and structured securities (25%), cash (12%), mortgages in good standing (11%), and misc. investments (11%).

Investments in Affiliates: 2%

Group Affiliation: Advantage Captial Partners LLC

Licensed in: AL, AZ, AR, CA, CO, DE, FL, GA, HI, ID, IL, IN, IA, KS, KY, LA, MD, MN, MS, MT, NE, NV, NM, NC, ND, OH, OK, OR, PA, RI, SC, SD, TX, UT, WA, WY

Commenced Business: September 1948

Address: 1405 WEST 2200 SOUTH, SALT LAKE CITY, UT 84111

Phone: (801) 484-8514 **Domicile State:** UT **NAIC Code:** 68802

Data Date	Rating	RACR #1	RACR #2	Total Assets ($mil)	Capital ($mil)	Net Premium ($mil)	Net Income ($mil)
2021	D	0.90	0.48	858.0	63.0	205.4	5.2
2020	D	1.21	0.59	693.8	59.2	92.3	7.6
2019	D	1.15	0.55	690.4	56.3	60.0	8.7
2018	D	0.69	0.32	1,255.2	39.6	50.1	1.8
2017	C-	1.00	0.46	798.9	39.4	28.8	3.5

Advantage Captial Partners LLC
Composite Group Rating: D

Largest Group Members	Assets ($mil)	Rating
HAYMARKET INS CO	2515	D-
ATLANTIC COAST LIFE INS CO	758	C-
SENTINEL SECURITY LIFE INS CO	694	D

SENTRY LIFE INS CO *

A   Excellent

Major Rating Factors: Good liquidity (6.1 on a scale of 0 to 10) with sufficient resources to handle a spike in claims as well as a significant increase in policy surrenders. Excellent overall results on stability tests (7.4). Strengths that enhance stability include excellent operational trends and excellent risk diversification. Strong capitalization (8.4) based on excellent risk adjusted capital (severe loss scenario).

Other Rating Factors: High quality investment portfolio (7.2). Excellent profitability (7.9) with operating gains in each of the last five years.

Principal Business: Group retirement contracts (96%), individual life insurance (3%), and individual annuities (1%).

Principal Investments: NonCMO investment grade bonds (92%), CMOs and structured securities (5%), and noninv. grade bonds (2%).

Investments in Affiliates: None

Group Affiliation: Sentry Ins Group

Licensed in: All states except NY, PR

Commenced Business: November 1958

Address: 1800 NORTH POINT DRIVE, STEVENS POINT, WI 54481

Phone: (715) 346-6000 **Domicile State:** WI **NAIC Code:** 68810

Data Date	Rating	RACR #1	RACR #2	Total Assets ($mil)	Capital ($mil)	Net Premium ($mil)	Net Income ($mil)
2021	A	3.40	1.90	9,857.5	335.1	862.0	38.3
2020	A	3.32	1.87	9,061.2	323.8	701.0	21.5
2019	A	3.41	1.90	8,168.8	308.9	764.6	35.7
2018	A	3.45	1.97	7,018.9	295.8	795.7	32.3
2017	A	3.24	1.89	6,958.1	272.9	751.9	28.0

Adverse Trends in Operations

Decrease in premium volume from 2019 to 2020 (8%)
Decrease in premium volume from 2018 to 2019 (4%)

SETTLERS LIFE INS CO

B-   Good

Major Rating Factors: Fair quality investment portfolio (4.4 on a scale of 0 to 10) with large holdings of BBB rated bonds in addition to junk bond exposure equal to 51% of capital. Fair profitability (3.5) with investment income below regulatory standards in relation to interest assumptions of reserves. Fair overall results on stability tests (4.5).

Other Rating Factors: Weak liquidity (2.7). Strong capitalization (7.3) based on excellent risk adjusted capital (severe loss scenario).

Principal Business: Individual life insurance (90%) and group life insurance (9%).

Principal Investments: NonCMO investment grade bonds (94%) and policy loans (2%).

Investments in Affiliates: None

Group Affiliation: NGL Ins Group

Licensed in: All states except NY, PR

Commenced Business: September 1982

Address: 2 East Gilman Street, Madison, WI 53703-1494

Phone: (608) 257-5611 **Domicile State:** WI **NAIC Code:** 97241

Data Date	Rating	RACR #1	RACR #2	Total Assets ($mil)	Capital ($mil)	Net Premium ($mil)	Net Income ($mil)
2021	B-	2.15	1.19	413.8	25.9	39.3	5.7
2020	B	4.25	2.23	450.6	64.7	39.0	8.0
2019	B	3.41	1.85	443.7	58.7	47.7	10.6
2018	D	2.87	1.56	426.4	46.5	54.1	3.4
2017	B	2.67	1.44	415.5	44.3	53.2	2.5

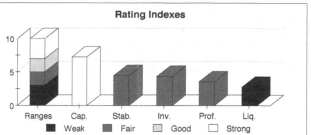

Rating Indexes

SHELTER LIFE INS CO

B **Good**

Major Rating Factors: Good quality investment portfolio (6.8 on a scale of 0 to 10) despite mixed results such as: minimal exposure to mortgages and substantial holdings of BBB bonds but minimal holdings in junk bonds. Good liquidity (6.2) with sufficient resources to handle a spike in claims as well as a significant increase in policy surrenders. Good overall results on stability tests (5.4) excellent operational trends and excellent risk diversification.

Other Rating Factors: Fair profitability (4.7) with investment income below regulatory standards in relation to interest assumptions of reserves. Strong capitalization (8.9) based on excellent risk adjusted capital (severe loss scenario).

Principal Business: Individual life insurance (86%), group health insurance (9%), individual annuities (3%), and group life insurance (1%).

Principal Investments: NonCMO investment grade bonds (47%), CMOs and structured securities (35%), mortgages in good standing (4%), policy loans (2%), and noninv. grade bonds (1%).

Investments in Affiliates: 1%

Group Affiliation: Shelter Ins Companies

Licensed in: AR, CO, IL, IN, IA, KS, KY, LA, MS, MO, NE, NV, OH, OK, TN

Commenced Business: March 1959

Address: 1817 WEST BROADWAY, COLUMBIA, MO 65218-0001

Phone: (573) 445-8441 **Domicile State:** MO **NAIC Code:** 65757

Data Date	Rating	RACR #1	RACR #2	Total Assets ($mil)	Capital ($mil)	Net Premium ($mil)	Net Income ($mil)
2021	B	3.87	2.25	1,404.6	266.0	152.0	14.2
2020	B	3.75	2.21	1,361.3	248.8	145.0	14.0
2019	B	3.71	2.25	1,308.8	237.1	140.4	14.6
2018	B	3.85	2.42	1,273.9	231.0	136.9	18.7
2017	B	3.70	2.35	1,236.6	206.5	130.8	11.6

Rating Indexes

SHELTERPOINT LIFE INS CO *

A **Excellent**

Major Rating Factors: Strong capitalization (8.5 on a scale of 0 to 10) based on excellent risk adjusted capital (severe loss scenario). Furthermore, this high level of risk adjusted capital has been consistently maintained over the last five years. High quality investment portfolio (7.5) with no exposure to mortgages and minimal holdings in junk bonds. Excellent profitability (8.1) with operating gains in each of the last five years.

Other Rating Factors: Excellent liquidity (7.5). Excellent overall results on stability tests (7.3) excellent operational trends and excellent risk diversification.

Principal Business: Group health insurance (97%) and reinsurance (2%).

Principal Investments: NonCMO investment grade bonds (25%), CMOs and structured securities (9%), cash (5%), and common & preferred stock (3%).

Investments in Affiliates: 3%

Group Affiliation: ShelterPoint Group Inc

Licensed in: CO, CT, DC, DE, FL, IL, MD, MA, MI, MN, NJ, NY, NC, PA, RI, SC, TN

Commenced Business: November 1972

Address: 600 NORTHERN BLVD, GREAT NECK, NY 11530

Phone: (516) 829-8100 **Domicile State:** NY **NAIC Code:** 81434

Data Date	Rating	RACR #1	RACR #2	Total Assets ($mil)	Capital ($mil)	Net Premium ($mil)	Net Income ($mil)
2021	A	2.36	1.97	392.4	162.9	478.5	99.7
2020	A	1.98	1.66	277.6	94.8	307.5	32.5
2019	A	1.75	1.47	189.4	63.2	213.1	5.4
2018	A	2.08	1.75	156.0	68.4	187.6	8.8
2017	A	2.63	2.23	114.9	61.0	97.2	3.5

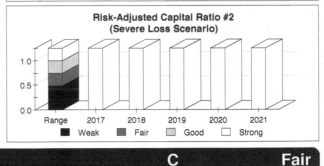

Risk-Adjusted Capital Ratio #2 (Severe Loss Scenario)

SHENANDOAH LIFE INS CO

C **Fair**

Major Rating Factors: Fair quality investment portfolio (4.8 on a scale of 0 to 10) with large holdings of BBB rated bonds in addition to moderate junk bond exposure. Good overall capitalization (6.0) based on good risk adjusted capital (severe loss scenario). However, capital levels have fluctuated somewhat during past years. Weak profitability (2.8) with operating losses during 2021.

Other Rating Factors: Weak liquidity (0.3). Weak overall results on stability tests (2.5) including negative cash flow from operations for 2021.

Principal Business: Reinsurance (89%), individual life insurance (6%), individual health insurance (3%), and group health insurance (1%).

Principal Investments: NonCMO investment grade bonds (46%), CMOs and structured securities (40%), mortgages in good standing (4%), policy loans (2%), and misc. investments (6%).

Investments in Affiliates: 2%

Group Affiliation: Reservoir Capital Group LLC

Licensed in: All states except CA, CT, ID, ME, NY, PR

Commenced Business: February 1916

Address: 4415 PHEASANT RIDGE RD STE 300, ROANOKE, VA 24014

Phone: (540) 985-4400 **Domicile State:** VA **NAIC Code:** 68845

Data Date	Rating	RACR #1	RACR #2	Total Assets ($mil)	Capital ($mil)	Net Premium ($mil)	Net Income ($mil)
2021	C	1.61	0.87	1,850.5	101.0	493.0	-1.3
2020	C	1.62	0.84	1,421.2	92.3	486.2	-2.5
2019	B-	2.39	1.27	1,001.2	99.4	90.7	8.1
2018	B-	2.84	1.55	994.7	108.6	42.8	15.0
2017	B-	2.52	1.37	1,036.4	94.6	40.4	27.4

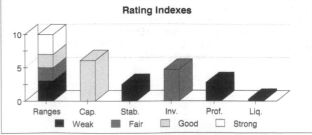

Rating Indexes

SILAC INSURANCE CO   C-   Fair

Major Rating Factors: Fair current capitalization (3.3 on a scale of 0 to 10) based on fair risk adjusted capital (moderate loss scenario), although results have slipped from the good range over the last year. Fair overall results on stability tests (3.3) including excessive premium growth and weak risk adjusted capital in prior years. Low quality investment portfolio (1.3).
Other Rating Factors: Good overall profitability (6.2). Excellent liquidity (8.4).
Principal Business: Individual annuities (97%) and individual health insurance (3%).
Principal Investments: NonCMO investment grade bonds (47%), CMOs and structured securities (20%), noninv. grade bonds (9%), mortgages in good standing (9%), and misc. investments (13%).
Investments in Affiliates: None
Group Affiliation: SILAC LLC
Licensed in: All states except MN, NJ, NY, PR
Commenced Business: June 1935
Address: 3 TRIAD CENTER, SALT LAKE CITY, UT 84111
Phone: (801) 579-3400 **Domicile State:** UT **NAIC Code:** 62952

Data Date	Rating	RACR #1	RACR #2	Total Assets ($mil)	Capital ($mil)	Net Premium ($mil)	Net Income ($mil)
2021	C-	0.79	0.42	6,778.9	271.4	1,299.7	62.6
2020	C	1.45	0.73	2,987.8	201.5	776.0	52.4
2019	D+	1.42	0.78	1,636.2	121.3	278.2	11.9
2018	C	1.11	0.83	485.3	57.7	100.3	-4.2
2017	C+	0.98	0.80	351.6	43.3	59.7	-6.7

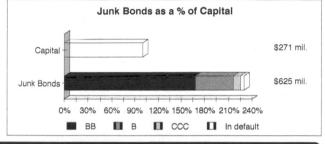

Junk Bonds as a % of Capital

Capital — $271 mil.
Junk Bonds — $625 mil.

0% 30% 60% 90% 120% 150% 180% 210% 240%

■ BB   ■ B   ▨ CCC   ☐ In default

SOUTHERN FARM BUREAU LIFE INS CO *   A   Excellent

Major Rating Factors: Good quality investment portfolio (5.7 on a scale of 0 to 10) despite significant exposure to mortgages. Mortgage default rate has been low. large holdings of BBB rated bonds in addition to small junk bond holdings. Good liquidity (6.4) with sufficient resources to handle a spike in claims as well as a significant increase in policy surrenders. Strong capitalization (9.0) based on excellent risk adjusted capital (severe loss scenario).
Other Rating Factors: Excellent profitability (7.7) with operating gains in each of the last five years. Excellent overall results on stability tests (7.4) excellent operational trends and excellent risk diversification.
Principal Business: Individual life insurance (87%), individual annuities (9%), individual health insurance (2%), and group life insurance (1%).
Principal Investments: NonCMO investment grade bonds (52%), mortgages in good standing (13%), CMOs and structured securities (13%), common & preferred stock (7%), and misc. investments (14%).
Investments in Affiliates: 7%
Group Affiliation: Southern Farm Bureau Group
Licensed in: AL, AR, CO, FL, GA, KY, LA, MS, NC, SC, TN, TX, VA
Commenced Business: December 1946
Address: 1401 Livingston Lane, Jackson, MS 39213
Phone: (601) 981-7422 **Domicile State:** MS **NAIC Code:** 68896

Data Date	Rating	RACR #1	RACR #2	Total Assets ($mil)	Capital ($mil)	Net Premium ($mil)	Net Income ($mil)
2021	A	4.38	2.36	15,730.7	3,074.3	945.6	156.4
2020	A	4.46	2.37	15,189.7	2,862.3	906.8	75.2
2019	A	4.31	2.31	14,731.0	2,721.7	891.7	145.1
2018	A	4.47	2.40	14,285.8	2,594.2	865.3	118.1
2017	A	4.47	2.40	14,191.7	2,558.7	882.3	115.6

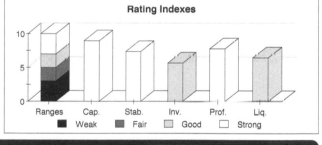

Rating Indexes

10

5

0
Ranges   Cap.   Stab.   Inv.   Prof.   Liq.
■ Weak   ■ Fair   ▨ Good   ☐ Strong

SOUTHERN FINANCIAL LIFE INS CO   D+   Weak

Major Rating Factors: Low quality investment portfolio (2.7 on a scale of 0 to 10). Weak overall results on stability tests (2.8). Good liquidity (6.7) with sufficient resources to handle a spike in claims.
Other Rating Factors: Strong capitalization (7.9) based on excellent risk adjusted capital (severe loss scenario). Moreover, capital levels have been consistently high over the last five years. Excellent profitability (8.6) with operating gains in each of the last five years.
Principal Business: Reinsurance (99%) and credit life insurance (1%).
Principal Investments: NonCMO investment grade bonds (44%), common & preferred stock (41%), noninv. grade bonds (7%), and cash (1%).
Investments in Affiliates: None
Group Affiliation: None
Licensed in: LA, TX
Commenced Business: June 1984
Address: 111 MATRIX LOOP, LAFAYETTE, LA 70507
Phone: (470) 639-8576 **Domicile State:** LA **NAIC Code:** 69418

Data Date	Rating	RACR #1	RACR #2	Total Assets ($mil)	Capital ($mil)	Net Premium ($mil)	Net Income ($mil)
2021	D+	2.71	1.58	169.4	60.9	19.8	3.4
2020	D+	2.63	1.52	150.8	50.3	21.7	3.8
2019	D+	2.77	1.60	137.0	43.7	20.2	2.4
2018	D+	2.89	1.62	126.7	36.9	16.2	0.8
2017	D+	2.98	1.64	123.6	37.1	17.4	4.1

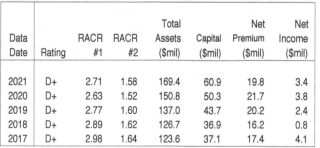

Rating Indexes

10

5

0
Ranges   Cap.   Stab.   Inv.   Prof.   Liq.
■ Weak   ■ Fair   ▨ Good   ☐ Strong

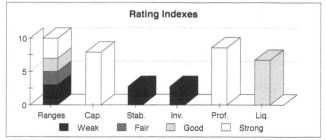

STANDARD INS CO *   B+   Good

Major Rating Factors: Good quality investment portfolio (5.1 on a scale of 0 to 10) despite substantial holdings of BBB bonds in addition to moderate junk bond exposure. Exposure to mortgages is large, but the mortgage default rate has been low. Good liquidity (6.4) with sufficient resources to handle a spike in claims as well as a significant increase in policy surrenders. Good overall results on stability tests (6.5) excellent operational trends and excellent risk diversification.

Other Rating Factors: Strong capitalization (7.1) based on excellent risk adjusted capital (severe loss scenario). Excellent profitability (7.3) with operating gains in each of the last five years.

Principal Business: Group retirement contracts (50%), group health insurance (21%), group life insurance (14%), individual annuities (10%), and other lines (5%).

Principal Investments: NonCMO investment grade bonds (44%), mortgages in good standing (39%), CMOs and structured securities (9%), noninv. grade bonds (4%), and cash (1%).

Investments in Affiliates: None

Group Affiliation: Meiji Yasuda Life Ins Company

Licensed in: All states except NY

Commenced Business: April 1906

Address: 1100 SOUTHWEST SIXTH AVENUE, PORTLAND, OR 97204-1093

Phone: (503) 321-7000 **Domicile State:** OR **NAIC Code:** 69019

Data Date	Rating	RACR #1	RACR #2	Total Assets ($mil)	Capital ($mil)	Net Premium ($mil)	Net Income ($mil)
2021	B+	2.09	1.07	32,461.1	1,433.2	6,353.4	131.2
2020	B+	2.43	1.25	29,581.9	1,540.4	6,350.6	203.8
2019	B+	2.48	1.29	26,665.4	1,443.7	5,161.6	197.9
2018	B+	2.32	1.21	23,862.6	1,294.0	4,459.1	201.6
2017	B+	2.02	1.06	23,952.0	1,108.4	4,300.3	178.2

Adverse Trends in Operations

Increase in policy surrenders from 2018 to 2019 (26%)

STANDARD LIFE & ACCIDENT INS CO   B   Good

Major Rating Factors: Good overall results on stability tests (5.4 on a scale of 0 to 10) despite negative cash flow from operations for 2021. Other stability subfactors include good operational trends and excellent risk diversification. Fair quality investment portfolio (4.9). Fair profitability (4.1).

Other Rating Factors: Strong capitalization (10.0) based on excellent risk adjusted capital (severe loss scenario). Excellent liquidity (8.7).

Principal Business: Individual health insurance (38%), group health insurance (32%), reinsurance (19%), individual life insurance (9%), and group life insurance (2%).

Principal Investments: NonCMO investment grade bonds (86%), mortgages in good standing (5%), noninv. grade bonds (2%), and policy loans (1%).

Investments in Affiliates: None

Group Affiliation: American National Group Inc

Licensed in: All states except ME, NH, NJ, NY, PR

Commenced Business: June 1976

Address: ONE MOODY PLAZA, GALVESTON, TX 77550

Phone: (409) 763-4661 **Domicile State:** TX **NAIC Code:** 86355

Data Date	Rating	RACR #1	RACR #2	Total Assets ($mil)	Capital ($mil)	Net Premium ($mil)	Net Income ($mil)
2021	B	16.35	9.94	488.4	307.0	66.0	59.0
2020	B	6.91	4.15	483.5	292.2	78.6	7.9
2019	A-	6.93	4.21	500.4	293.7	81.4	12.4
2018	A-	6.05	3.79	516.9	291.9	107.6	10.9
2017	A-	5.78	3.59	521.6	289.5	98.3	10.7

Adverse Trends in Operations

Decrease in premium volume from 2019 to 2020 (3%)
Decrease in asset base during 2020 (3%)
Decrease in asset base during 2019 (3%)
Decrease in premium volume from 2018 to 2019 (24%)

STANDARD LIFE INS CO OF NY *   A   Excellent

Major Rating Factors: Excellent overall results on stability tests (7.7 on a scale of 0 to 10). Strengths that enhance stability include excellent operational trends and excellent risk diversification. Strong capitalization (10.0) based on excellent risk adjusted capital (severe loss scenario). Furthermore, this high level of risk adjusted capital has been consistently maintained over the last five years. High quality investment portfolio (7.4).

Other Rating Factors: Excellent profitability (8.3) with operating gains in each of the last five years. Excellent liquidity (7.4).

Principal Business: Group health insurance (67%), group life insurance (26%), and individual health insurance (7%).

Principal Investments: NonCMO investment grade bonds (50%), mortgages in good standing (40%), and cash (10%).

Investments in Affiliates: None

Group Affiliation: Meiji Yasuda Life Ins Company

Licensed in: NY

Commenced Business: January 2001

Address: 360 HAMILTON AVENUE SUITE 210, WHITE PLAINS, NY 10604-2911

Phone: (914) 989-4400 **Domicile State:** NY **NAIC Code:** 89009

Data Date	Rating	RACR #1	RACR #2	Total Assets ($mil)	Capital ($mil)	Net Premium ($mil)	Net Income ($mil)
2021	A	6.14	4.21	325.0	142.5	118.3	21.3
2020	A	5.57	3.76	316.6	128.7	113.7	18.9
2019	A-	5.71	3.82	305.9	123.2	103.9	23.5
2018	A-	4.56	3.05	303.0	99.0	104.0	1.2
2017	A-	4.90	3.20	292.2	96.2	90.0	11.9

Adverse Trends in Operations

Increase in policy surrenders from 2019 to 2020 (420%)
Increase in policy surrenders from 2016 to 2017 (375%)

STANDARD SECURITY LIFE INS CO OF NY * A- Excellent

Major Rating Factors: Good overall results on stability tests (6.3 on a scale of 0 to 10) despite excessive premium growth. Strengths that enhance stability include good operational trends and excellent risk diversification. Strong capitalization (10.0) based on excellent risk adjusted capital (severe loss scenario). Furthermore, this high level of risk adjusted capital has been consistently maintained over the last five years. High quality investment portfolio (8.2).

Other Rating Factors: Excellent profitability (8.0) with operating gains in each of the last five years. Excellent liquidity (8.5).

Principal Business: Group health insurance (99%).

Principal Investments: NonCMO investment grade bonds (96%) and cash (1%).

Investments in Affiliates: None

Group Affiliation: Geneve Holdings Inc

Licensed in: All states, the District of Columbia and Puerto Rico

Commenced Business: December 1958

Address: 485 Madison Avenue 14th Floor, New York, NY 10022-5872

Phone: (212) 355-4141 **Domicile State:** NY **NAIC Code:** 69078

Data Date	Rating	RACR #1	RACR #2	Total Assets ($mil)	Capital ($mil)	Net Premium ($mil)	Net Income ($mil)
2021	A-	4.41	3.60	152.8	73.6	173.7	44.8
2020	B+	5.51	4.32	134.7	64.6	114.6	12.9
2019	B+	6.84	5.30	114.5	57.1	81.2	5.2
2018	B+	6.86	5.24	129.1	70.8	89.0	8.3
2017	B	6.77	5.23	131.5	65.6	80.3	3.6

Adverse Trends in Operations

Increase in policy surrenders from 2019 to 2020 (522%)
Decrease in asset base during 2019 (11%)
Decrease in capital during 2019 (19%)
Increase in policy surrenders from 2017 to 2018 (1284%)
Decrease in asset base during 2017 (15%)

STARMOUNT LIFE INS CO C Fair

Major Rating Factors: Fair overall results on stability tests (3.3 on a scale of 0 to 10) including negative cash flow from operations for 2021. Weak profitability (1.8) with operating losses during 2021. Return on equity has been low, averaging -14.0%. Weak liquidity (1.3) as a spike in claims may stretch capacity.

Other Rating Factors: Strong capitalization (7.8) based on excellent risk adjusted capital (severe loss scenario). High quality investment portfolio (7.4).

Principal Business: Group health insurance (94%), individual health insurance (4%), and individual life insurance (2%).

Principal Investments: NonCMO investment grade bonds (81%), real estate (5%), and policy loans (1%).

Investments in Affiliates: None

Group Affiliation: Unum Group

Licensed in: All states except NY, PR

Commenced Business: August 1983

Address: 8485 Goodwood Blvd, PORTLAND, ME 4122

Phone: (225) 926-2888 **Domicile State:** ME **NAIC Code:** 68985

Data Date	Rating	RACR #1	RACR #2	Total Assets ($mil)	Capital ($mil)	Net Premium ($mil)	Net Income ($mil)
2021	C	1.93	1.50	132.1	66.9	272.9	-19.7
2020	C	2.24	1.74	131.7	74.3	258.2	10.6
2019	C	1.36	1.06	110.2	49.0	250.6	-14.3
2018	C	1.37	1.08	94.0	45.3	209.9	-9.5
2017	B	1.18	0.92	79.9	37.4	179.7	-2.8

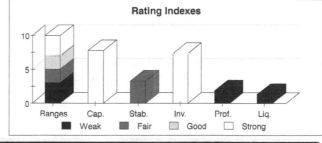

Rating Indexes

Ranges | Cap. | Stab. | Inv. | Prof. | Liq.
■ Weak ■ Fair ▨ Good ☐ Strong

STATE FARM LIFE & ACCIDENT ASR CO * A+ Excellent

Major Rating Factors: Good quality investment portfolio (6.3 on a scale of 0 to 10) despite mixed results such as: no exposure to mortgages and large holdings of BBB rated bonds but minimal holdings in junk bonds. Good liquidity (6.4) with sufficient resources to handle a spike in claims as well as a significant increase in policy surrenders. Fair profitability (3.0) with investment income below regulatory standards in relation to interest assumptions of reserves.

Other Rating Factors: Excellent overall results on stability tests (7.9) excellent operational trends and excellent risk diversification. Strong capitalization (8.8) based on excellent risk adjusted capital (severe loss scenario).

Principal Business: Individual life insurance (97%) and individual annuities (3%).

Principal Investments: NonCMO investment grade bonds (65%), CMOs and structured securities (20%), common & preferred stock (7%), policy loans (5%), and noninv. grade bonds (1%).

Investments in Affiliates: 1%

Group Affiliation: State Farm Group

Licensed in: CT, IL, NY, WI

Commenced Business: July 1961

Address: One State Farm Plaza, Bloomington, IL 61710

Phone: (309) 766-2311 **Domicile State:** IL **NAIC Code:** 69094

Data Date	Rating	RACR #1	RACR #2	Total Assets ($mil)	Capital ($mil)	Net Premium ($mil)	Net Income ($mil)
2021	A+	3.82	2.21	3,528.9	611.4	266.7	15.0
2020	A+	4.23	2.43	3,349.6	584.3	255.1	11.4
2019	A+	4.83	2.72	3,183.5	574.8	256.7	41.8
2018	A+	5.54	3.14	3,035.3	540.2	245.3	29.5
2017	A+	5.39	3.07	2,915.8	503.2	239.5	25.8

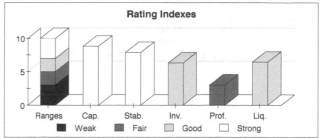

Rating Indexes

Ranges | Cap. | Stab. | Inv. | Prof. | Liq.
■ Weak ■ Fair ▨ Good ☐ Strong

STATE FARM LIFE INS CO *

A+   **Excellent**

Major Rating Factors: Good quality investment portfolio (6.2 on a scale of 0 to 10) despite significant exposure to mortgages . Mortgage default rate has been low. substantial holdings of BBB bonds in addition to minimal holdings in junk bonds. Good liquidity (6.5) with sufficient resources to handle a spike in claims as well as a significant increase in policy surrenders. Excellent overall results on stability tests (7.9) excellent operational trends and excellent risk diversification.

Other Rating Factors: Strong capitalization (9.7) based on excellent risk adjusted capital (severe loss scenario). Excellent profitability (7.4) with operating gains in each of the last five years.

Principal Business: Individual life insurance (95%), individual annuities (3%), and group life insurance (2%).

Principal Investments: NonCMO investment grade bonds (49%), CMOs and structured securities (15%), mortgages in good standing (14%), common & preferred stock (9%), and misc. investments (12%).

Investments in Affiliates: 3%
Group Affiliation: State Farm Group
Licensed in: All states except MA, NY, WI, PR
Commenced Business: April 1929
Address: One State Farm Plaza, Bloomington, IL 61710
Phone: (309) 766-2311 **Domicile State:** IL **NAIC Code:** 69108

Data Date	Rating	RACR #1	RACR #2	Total Assets ($mil)	Capital ($mil)	Net Premium ($mil)	Net Income ($mil)
2021	A+	4.96	2.78	86,273.0	14,931.3	5,479.3	913.7
2020	A+	4.77	2.67	81,784.4	13,167.2	5,225.8	328.0
2019	A+	4.73	2.63	78,649.7	12,360.4	5,283.7	631.3
2018	A+	4.69	2.62	74,990.7	11,524.0	5,118.6	676.7
2017	A+	4.47	2.52	73,080.0	10,904.7	5,018.7	466.4

Adverse Trends In Operations

Decrease in premium volume from 2019 to 2020 (1%)
Decrease in premium volume from 2016 to 2017 (7%)

STATE LIFE INS CO

B   **Good**

Major Rating Factors: Good overall results on stability tests (5.4 on a scale of 0 to 10) despite excessive premium growth. Other stability subfactors include good operational trends and excellent risk diversification. Good capitalization (6.1) based on good risk adjusted capital (severe loss scenario). Moreover, capital levels have been consistent over the last five years. Good overall profitability (5.5) although investment income, in comparison to reserve requirements, is below regulatory standards.

Other Rating Factors: Fair quality investment portfolio (4.4). Fair liquidity (3.6).

Principal Business: Individual life insurance (68%), individual annuities (27%), individual health insurance (2%), and reinsurance (2%).

Principal Investments: NonCMO investment grade bonds (63%), mortgages in good standing (15%), CMOs and structured securities (14%), noninv. grade bonds (3%), and cash (1%).

Investments in Affiliates: None
Group Affiliation: American United Life Group
Licensed in: All states except NY, PR
Commenced Business: September 1894
Address: ONE AMERICAN SQUARE, INDIANAPOLIS, IN 46282-0001
Phone: (317) 285-2300 **Domicile State:** IN **NAIC Code:** 69116

Data Date	Rating	RACR #1	RACR #2	Total Assets ($mil)	Capital ($mil)	Net Premium ($mil)	Net Income ($mil)
2021	B	1.76	0.89	10,441.4	581.6	691.0	23.0
2020	B	1.70	0.86	10,045.6	559.5	465.1	26.6
2019	B	1.77	0.91	9,334.5	545.0	625.9	61.1
2018	B	1.72	0.88	8,490.2	496.0	705.3	48.1
2017	B	1.63	0.82	7,828.0	438.8	31.3	20.0

Adverse Trends In Operations

Decrease in premium volume from 2019 to 2020 (26%)
Decrease in premium volume from 2018 to 2019 (11%)
Change in premium mix from 2016 to 2017 (221.0%)
Decrease in capital during 2017 (5%)
Decrease in premium volume from 2016 to 2017 (96%)

STATE MUTUAL INS CO

D   **Weak**

Major Rating Factors: Weak profitability (1.9 on a scale of 0 to 10) with operating losses during 2021. Weak overall results on stability tests (1.8). Fair current capitalization (4.6) based on fair risk adjusted capital (moderate loss scenario), although results have slipped from the good range over the last year.

Other Rating Factors: Fair quality investment portfolio (3.8). Excellent liquidity (7.4).

Principal Business: Individual health insurance (84%), individual life insurance (12%), and reinsurance (4%).

Principal Investments: NonCMO investment grade bonds (39%), common & preferred stock (14%), CMOs and structured securities (11%), real estate (8%), and misc. investments (21%).

Investments in Affiliates: 13%
Group Affiliation: None
Licensed in: All states except CA, CT, ME, NH, NJ, NY, PR
Commenced Business: October 1890
Address: 210 E Second Avenue Suite 301, Rome, GA 30161-1714
Phone: (706) 291-1054 **Domicile State:** GA **NAIC Code:** 69132

Data Date	Rating	RACR #1	RACR #2	Total Assets ($mil)	Capital ($mil)	Net Premium ($mil)	Net Income ($mil)
2021	D	0.90	0.70	217.6	26.7	101.9	-2.4
2020	D	1.34	0.87	194.5	24.8	30.7	9.9
2019	D	0.94	0.62	180.1	20.3	39.5	-5.9
2018	D	1.14	0.73	189.5	26.3	25.5	-15.4
2017	C-	1.19	0.77	267.3	29.1	-33.1	-7.8

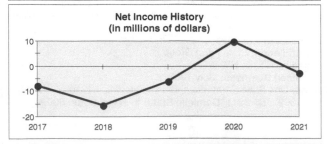

Net Income History
(in millions of dollars)

SUN LIFE & HEALTH INS CO   D+   Weak

Major Rating Factors: Weak overall results on stability tests (2.6 on a scale of 0 to 10) including potential financial drain due to affiliation with Sun Life Assurance Group. Weak profitability (2.4) with operating losses during 2021. Good quality investment portfolio (6.8) despite mixed results such as: minimal exposure to mortgages and large holdings of BBB rated bonds but small junk bond holdings.

Other Rating Factors: Good liquidity (6.0). Strong capitalization (7.6) based on excellent risk adjusted capital (severe loss scenario).

Principal Business: Group health insurance (70%), group life insurance (23%), and reinsurance (7%).

Principal Investments: NonCMO investment grade bonds (73%), CMOs and structured securities (17%), mortgages in good standing (5%), noninv. grade bonds (1%), and cash (1%).

Investments in Affiliates: None

Group Affiliation: Sun Life Assurance Group

Licensed in: All states, the District of Columbia and Puerto Rico

Commenced Business: January 1975

Address: 201 Townsend Street Ste 900, Lansing, MI 48933

Phone: (781) 237-6030 **Domicile State:** MI **NAIC Code:** 80926

Data Date	Rating	RACR #1	RACR #2	Total Assets ($mil)	Capital ($mil)	Net Premium ($mil)	Net Income ($mil)
2021	D+	2.39	1.43	1,078.5	133.9	152.2	-6.7
2020	D	2.11	1.25	985.6	106.9	125.4	1.3
2019	D	2.26	1.35	964.9	107.9	120.6	2.7
2018	D	2.34	1.39	930.6	105.4	116.9	7.2
2017	D	2.95	1.74	943.2	129.9	644.6	-68.3

Sun Life Assurance Group Composite Group Rating: D Largest Group Members	Assets ($mil)	Rating
SUN LIFE ASR CO OF CANADA	19738	D
INDEPENDENCE LIFE ANNUITY CO	3427	D+
SUN LIFE HEALTH INS CO	986	D+
PROFESSIONAL INS CO	85	D+

SUN LIFE ASR CO OF CANADA   D   Weak

Major Rating Factors: Poor capitalization (1.2 on a scale of 0 to 10) based on weak risk adjusted capital (moderate loss scenario). Low quality investment portfolio (1.1) containing large holdings of BBB rated bonds in addition to junk bond exposure equal to 59% of capital. Exposure to mortgages is significant, but the mortgage default rate has been low. Weak overall results on stability tests (1.2) including weak risk adjusted capital in prior years, negative cash flow from operations for 2021.

Other Rating Factors: Fair liquidity (3.7). Good overall profitability (5.2).

Principal Business: Group health insurance (71%), group life insurance (14%), individual life insurance (9%), and reinsurance (6%).

Principal Investments: NonCMO investment grade bonds (57%), mortgages in good standing (15%), CMOs and structured securities (15%), real estate (4%), and misc. investments (8%).

Investments in Affiliates: 1%

Group Affiliation: Sun Life Assurance Group

Licensed in: All states except NY

Commenced Business: May 1871

Address: 150 King Street West, Toronto Ontario, MI 2481

Phone: (781) 237-6030 **Domicile State:** MI **NAIC Code:** 80802

Data Date	Rating	RACR #1	RACR #2	Total Assets ($mil)	Capital ($mil)	Net Premium ($mil)	Net Income ($mil)
2021	D	0.53	0.31	19,675.7	798.3	2,339.4	152.2
2020	D	0.54	0.30	19,738.2	711.8	2,173.1	173.8
2019	D+	0.67	0.38	19,515.5	987.7	2,751.4	156.0
2018	D	0.72	0.42	18,836.1	1,323.9	3,434.0	581.8
2017	D-	0.62	0.35	19,086.1	916.9	1,789.4	259.6

Risk-Adjusted Capital Ratio #1 (Moderate Loss Scenario)

SUNSET LIFE INS CO OF AMERICA   C   Fair

Major Rating Factors: Strong capitalization (4.0 on a scale of 0 to 10) based on excellent risk adjusted capital (severe loss scenario). Capital levels have been relatively consistent over the last five years. Fair profitability (4.3) with operating losses during 2021. Return on equity has been low, averaging 0.3%. Fair overall results on stability tests (3.5).

Other Rating Factors: Good quality investment portfolio (5.9). Excellent liquidity (10.0).

Principal Business: Individual life insurance (78%) and individual annuities (22%).

Principal Investments: NonCMO investment grade bonds (35%), cash (5%), and CMOs and structured securities (4%).

Investments in Affiliates: None

Group Affiliation: Kansas City Life Group

Licensed in: All states except AL, NH, NJ, NY, TN, VT, WI, PR

Commenced Business: May 1937

Address: 3520 Broadway, Kansas City, MO 64111-2565

Phone: (561) 713-0269 **Domicile State:** MO **NAIC Code:** 69272

Data Date	Rating	RACR #1	RACR #2	Total Assets ($mil)	Capital ($mil)	Net Premium ($mil)	Net Income ($mil)
2021	C	7.47	6.73	49.0	47.1	0.0	-0.8
2020	C+	5.28	4.32	36.2	25.0	-243.7	-0.3
2019	B-	2.68	1.40	297.8	24.9	6.7	2.5
2018	B-	2.58	1.35	304.7	24.7	8.2	2.1
2017	B-	2.51	1.31	316.3	25.2	9.1	-3.7

Risk-Adjusted Capital Ratio #2 (Severe Loss Scenario)

SURETY LIFE INS CO
D   Weak

Major Rating Factors: Weak profitability (2.8 on a scale of 0 to 10). Excellent expense controls. Return on equity has been low, averaging -1.8%. Weak overall results on stability tests (2.0). Good quality investment portfolio (5.6) despite mixed results such as: no exposure to mortgages and substantial holdings of BBB bonds but no exposure to junk bonds.

Other Rating Factors: Strong capitalization (8.4) based on excellent risk adjusted capital (severe loss scenario). Excellent liquidity (9.7).

Principal Business: Individual life insurance (97%), individual annuities (2%), and individual health insurance (2%).

Principal Investments: NonCMO investment grade bonds (74%), common & preferred stock (24%), and CMOs and structured securities (7%).

Investments in Affiliates: None

Group Affiliation: Government Employees Health Assn Inc

Licensed in: All states except PR

Commenced Business: March 1936

Address: 12925 West Dodge Road, Omaha, NE 68154

Phone: (816) 257-5500 **Domicile State:** NE **NAIC Code:** 69310

Data Date	Rating	RACR #1	RACR #2	Total Assets ($mil)	Capital ($mil)	Net Premium ($mil)	Net Income ($mil)
2021	D	3.55	1.90	29.5	27.4	0.4	0.3
2020	D	4.70	2.31	29.2	27.2	0.6	-0.6
2019	D	4.77	2.31	29.0	27.6	0.0	-0.6
2018	D	3.21	1.56	19.7	18.2	0.0	-0.4
2017	D	3.17	1.54	19.1	18.5	0.0	-0.4

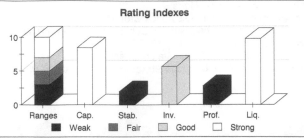

Rating Indexes

Ranges, Cap., Stab., Inv., Prof., Liq.

■ Weak   ■ Fair   ▨ Good   □ Strong

SWBC LIFE INS CO *
A-   Excellent

Major Rating Factors: Good quality investment portfolio (6.2 on a scale of 0 to 10) with no exposure to mortgages and minimal holdings in junk bonds. Good overall results on stability tests (6.2). Strengths that enhance stability include excellent operational trends and good risk diversification. Strong capitalization (9.5) based on excellent risk adjusted capital (severe loss scenario).

Other Rating Factors: Excellent profitability (7.8) with operating gains in each of the last five years. Excellent liquidity (9.0).

Principal Business: Credit health insurance (38%), reinsurance (32%), and credit life insurance (28%).

Principal Investments: NonCMO investment grade bonds (47%), cash (28%), common & preferred stock (14%), and noninv. grade bonds (1%).

Investments in Affiliates: None

Group Affiliation: Southwest Business Corp

Licensed in: GA, LA, MI, OK, TN, TX, UT, VA

Commenced Business: December 1980

Address: 9311 San Pedro Ste 600, San Antonio, TX 78216

Phone: (210) 321-7361 **Domicile State:** TX **NAIC Code:** 99538

Data Date	Rating	RACR #1	RACR #2	Total Assets ($mil)	Capital ($mil)	Net Premium ($mil)	Net Income ($mil)
2021	A-	3.95	2.67	42.4	25.4	17.6	2.7
2020	A-	4.19	2.88	37.9	26.6	17.4	2.7
2019	A-	3.87	2.69	34.9	24.3	17.3	2.0
2018	A-	3.73	2.61	32.7	23.2	17.7	2.9
2017	B+	3.44	2.34	31.0	21.0	16.2	2.6

Adverse Trends in Operations

Decrease in premium volume from 2018 to 2019 (3%)
Increase in policy surrenders from 2017 to 2018 (103%)

SWISS RE LIFE & HEALTH AMER INC
C+   Fair

Major Rating Factors: Fair overall results on stability tests (4.7 on a scale of 0 to 10) including fair financial strength of affiliated Swiss Reinsurance Group, excessive premium growth and negative cash flow from operations for 2021. Good quality investment portfolio (6.6) despite significant exposure to mortgages . Mortgage default rate has been low. large holdings of BBB rated bonds in addition to small junk bond holdings. Good profitability (5.0) despite operating losses during 2021.

Other Rating Factors: Good liquidity (5.0). Strong capitalization (7.4) based on excellent risk adjusted capital (severe loss scenario).

Principal Business: Reinsurance (100%).

Principal Investments: NonCMO investment grade bonds (70%), mortgages in good standing (11%), CMOs and structured securities (8%), noninv. grade bonds (2%), and common & preferred stock (1%).

Investments in Affiliates: 8%

Group Affiliation: Swiss Reinsurance Group

Licensed in: All states, the District of Columbia and Puerto Rico

Commenced Business: September 1967

Address: 237 EAST HIGH STREET, JEFFERSON CITY, MO 65101

Phone: (877) 794-7773 **Domicile State:** MO **NAIC Code:** 82627

Data Date	Rating	RACR #1	RACR #2	Total Assets ($mil)	Capital ($mil)	Net Premium ($mil)	Net Income ($mil)
2021	C+	1.91	1.25	13,957.8	1,556.0	3,509.7	-403.2
2020	C+	1.94	1.26	12,892.8	1,467.8	1,818.6	10.3
2019	C+	2.01	1.30	12,728.9	1,531.6	596.5	1,497.7
2018	C	2.00	1.28	15,932.4	2,035.8	6,288.5	-1,164.9
2017	C	1.36	0.86	14,134.1	1,157.4	2,548.5	139.9

Swiss Reinsurance Group
Composite Group Rating: C+
Largest Group Members

	Assets ($mil)	Rating
SWISS REINS AMERICA CORP	18192	C
SWISS RE LIFE HEALTH AMER INC	12893	C+
WESTPORT INS CORP	4594	B-
SWISS RE (NOT RE) PPTY CAS A	2909	A+
SWISS RE CORPORATE SOLUTIONS AMERICA	498	C

SYMETRA LIFE INS CO

B-   **Good**

Major Rating Factors: Good liquidity (5.6 on a scale of 0 to 10) with sufficient resources to handle a spike in claims as well as a significant increase in policy surrenders. Fair quality investment portfolio (4.7) with large holdings of BBB rated bonds in addition to moderate junk bond exposure. Exposure to mortgages is significant, but the mortgage default rate has been low. Fair overall results on stability tests (4.8).

Other Rating Factors: Weak profitability (1.9) with investment income below regulatory standards in relation to interest assumptions of reserves. Strong capitalization (7.0) based on excellent risk adjusted capital (severe loss scenario).

Principal Business: Individual annuities (67%), group health insurance (17%), individual life insurance (13%), and group life insurance (3%).

Principal Investments: NonCMO investment grade bonds (51%), CMOs and structured securities (22%), mortgages in good standing (18%), noninv. grade bonds (3%), and misc. investments (5%).

Investments in Affiliates: 1%

Group Affiliation: Sumitomo Life Ins Company

Licensed In: All states except NY

Commenced Business: April 1957

Address: 4125 WESTOWN PARKWAY SUITE 102, WEST DES MOINES, IA 50266

Phone: (425) 256-8000   **Domicile State:** IA   **NAIC Code:** 68608

Data Date	Rating	RACR #1	RACR #2	Total Assets ($mil)	Capital ($mil)	Net Premium ($mil)	Net Income ($mil)
2021	B-	1.89	1.01	46,627.5	2,331.6	4,609.0	136.8
2020	B-	1.99	1.06	44,263.4	2,316.1	4,234.0	-59.8
2019	B	1.96	1.05	42,241.9	2,141.6	4,138.5	170.6
2018	B	1.98	1.07	37,859.9	2,126.6	268.7	-118.7
2017	B	1.80	0.98	36,482.8	2,218.9	4,116.2	267.8

Rating Indexes

TALCOTT RESOLUTION LIFE

B-   **Good**

Major Rating Factors: Good quality investment portfolio (5.6 on a scale of 0 to 10) despite significant exposure to mortgages . Mortgage default rate has been low. large holdings of BBB rated bonds in addition to small junk bond holdings. Good overall profitability (5.4). Return on equity has been excellent over the last five years averaging 35.0%. Good liquidity (6.5).

Other Rating Factors: Good overall results on stability tests (5.0) good operational trends, good risk adjusted capital for prior years and excellent risk diversification. Strong overall capitalization (7.1) based on mixed results -- excessive policy leverage mitigated by excellent risk adjusted capital (severe loss scenario).

Principal Business: Individual life insurance (72%), individual annuities (19%), and reinsurance (8%).

Principal Investments: NonCMO investment grade bonds (51%), CMOs and structured securities (18%), mortgages in good standing (12%), noninv. grade bonds (2%), and misc. investments (11%).

Investments in Affiliates: None

Group Affiliation: Hartford Financial Services Inc

Licensed In: All states except NY

Commenced Business: July 1965

Address: One Hartford Plaza, Windsor, CT 06095-1512

Phone: (800) 862-6668   **Domicile State:** CT   **NAIC Code:** 71153

Data Date	Rating	RACR #1	RACR #2	Total Assets ($mil)	Capital ($mil)	Net Premium ($mil)	Net Income ($mil)
2021	B-	2.07	1.04	36,351.0	772.4	-13,324.6	134.6
2020	B-	1.77	0.89	35,237.4	621.7	135.5	47.1
2019	B-	2.58	1.31	34,277.7	979.3	120.0	396.2
2018	B-	2.82	1.44	32,808.8	1,160.8	-1,618.5	65.0
2017	B-	3.40	1.71	36,378.6	1,139.0	229.9	170.8

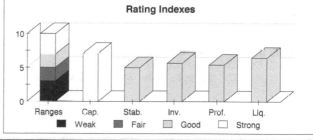

Rating Indexes

TALCOTT RESOLUTION LIFE INS CO

B-   **Good**

Major Rating Factors: Fair current capitalization (4.0 on a scale of 0 to 10) based on good risk adjusted capital (severe loss scenario), although results have slipped from the excellent range over the last year. Fair overall results on stability tests (4.0) including negative cash flow from operations for 2021. Good quality investment portfolio (5.5).

Other Rating Factors: Good liquidity (6.1). Weak profitability (2.9) with operating losses during 2021.

Principal Business: Reinsurance (88%), group retirement contracts (9%), individual annuities (2%), and individual life insurance (1%).

Principal Investments: NonCMO investment grade bonds (57%), CMOs and structured securities (16%), policy loans (7%), mortgages in good standing (6%), and misc. investments (11%).

Investments in Affiliates: 4%

Group Affiliation: Hartford Financial Services Inc

Licensed In: All states except PR

Commenced Business: January 1979

Address: One Hartford Plaza, Windsor, CT 06095-1512

Phone: (800) 862-6668   **Domicile State:** CT   **NAIC Code:** 88072

Data Date	Rating	RACR #1	RACR #2	Total Assets ($mil)	Capital ($mil)	Net Premium ($mil)	Net Income ($mil)
2021	B-	1.39	0.90	101,000	2,153.5	1,161.0	-562.7
2020	B-	2.39	1.54	92,345.5	3,142.2	-49.8	596.8
2019	C+	1.97	1.38	88,716.2	3,194.4	-5.8	198.6
2018	C+	2.03	1.46	86,253.3	3,712.7	-5,343.5	-11.2
2017	C+	1.88	1.28	109,000	3,552.5	433.0	1,197.6

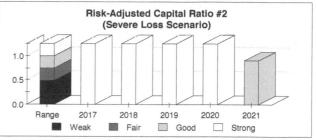

Risk-Adjusted Capital Ratio #2
(Severe Loss Scenario)

TEACHERS INS & ANNUITY ASN OF AM *   A+   Excellent

Major Rating Factors: Good quality investment portfolio (6.4 on a scale of 0 to 10) despite large holdings of BBB rated bonds in addition to moderate junk bond exposure. Exposure to mortgages is significant, but the mortgage default rate has been low. Good liquidity (6.1) with sufficient resources to handle a spike in claims as well as a significant increase in policy surrenders. Strong capitalization (8.9) based on excellent risk adjusted capital (severe loss scenario).

Other Rating Factors: Excellent profitability (8.9) with operating gains in each of the last five years. Excellent overall results on stability tests (7.0) excellent operational trends and excellent risk diversification.

Principal Business: Group retirement contracts (60%), individual annuities (39%), and individual life insurance (1%).

Principal Investments: NonCMO investment grade bonds (45%), CMOs and structured securities (18%), mortgages in good standing (13%), noninv. grade bonds (6%), and misc. investments (16%).

Investments in Affiliates: 10%

Group Affiliation: TIAA

Licensed in: All states, the District of Columbia and Puerto Rico

Commenced Business: May 1918

Address: 730 THIRD AVENUE, NEW YORK, NY 10017

Phone: (212) 490-9000 **Domicile State:** NY **NAIC Code:** 69345

Data Date	Rating	RACR #1	RACR #2	Total Assets ($mil)	Capital ($mil)	Net Premium ($mil)	Net Income ($mil)
2021	A+	3.88	2.26	343,000	42,972.7	13,772.5	3,872.0
2020	A+	3.82	2.24	326,000	40,001.3	17,232.1	603.7
2019	A+	3.77	2.26	316,000	38,871.8	14,910.0	1,617.9
2018	A+	3.78	2.23	303,000	38,126.3	15,034.0	1,453.1
2017	A+	3.83	2.26	295,000	36,336.1	15,386.5	1,020.4

Rating Indexes

Ranges Cap. Stab. Inv. Prof. Liq.
■ Weak ■ Fair ▨ Good □ Strong

TENNESSEE FARMERS LIFE INS CO *   B+   Good

Major Rating Factors: Good overall results on stability tests (6.6 on a scale of 0 to 10). Stability strengths include excellent operational trends and excellent risk diversification. Good quality investment portfolio (5.1) despite mixed results such as: large holdings of BBB rated bonds but moderate junk bond exposure. Good liquidity (6.5).

Other Rating Factors: Strong capitalization (8.1) based on excellent risk adjusted capital (severe loss scenario). Excellent profitability (7.0) with operating gains in each of the last five years.

Principal Business: Individual life insurance (79%), individual annuities (20%), and reinsurance (2%).

Principal Investments: NonCMO investment grade bonds (77%), common & preferred stock (15%), noninv. grade bonds (5%), policy loans (1%), and real estate (1%).

Investments in Affiliates: 3%

Group Affiliation: Tennessee Farmers Ins Companies

Licensed in: TN

Commenced Business: September 1973

Address: 147 Bear Creek Pike, Columbia, TN 38401-2266

Phone: (931) 388-7872 **Domicile State:** TN **NAIC Code:** 82759

Data Date	Rating	RACR #1	RACR #2	Total Assets ($mil)	Capital ($mil)	Net Premium ($mil)	Net Income ($mil)
2021	B+	2.65	1.72	2,599.1	590.9	205.9	26.1
2020	B+	2.58	1.65	2,487.3	549.0	181.8	28.4
2019	B+	2.58	1.68	2,398.8	505.0	174.0	38.3
2018	B+	2.53	1.64	2,299.8	461.9	168.4	46.7
2017	B+	3.18	1.88	2,276.8	442.1	175.4	28.7

Adverse Trends in Operations

Decrease in premium volume from 2017 to 2018 (4%)
Decrease in premium volume from 2016 to 2017 (11%)

TEXAS LIFE INS CO   C+   Fair

Major Rating Factors: Fair overall results on stability tests (4.4 on a scale of 0 to 10) including fair financial strength of affiliated Wilton Re Holdings Ltd. Fair quality investment portfolio (3.5) with large holdings of BBB rated bonds in addition to significant exposure to junk bonds. Good capitalization (5.9) based on good risk adjusted capital (moderate loss scenario).

Other Rating Factors: Good overall profitability (6.5). Good liquidity (5.4).

Principal Business: Individual life insurance (100%).

Principal Investments: CMOs and structured securities (30%), nonCMO investment grade bonds (22%), noninv. grade bonds (14%), common & preferred stock (5%), and misc. investments (27%).

Investments in Affiliates: None

Group Affiliation: Wilton Re Holdings Ltd

Licensed in: All states except NY, PR

Commenced Business: April 1901

Address: P O BOX 830, WACO, TX 76703-0830

Phone: (254) 752-6521 **Domicile State:** TX **NAIC Code:** 69396

Data Date	Rating	RACR #1	RACR #2	Total Assets ($mil)	Capital ($mil)	Net Premium ($mil)	Net Income ($mil)
2021	C+	1.59	0.83	1,632.4	114.5	314.9	19.0
2020	C+	1.59	0.82	1,471.0	117.0	301.2	-4.0
2019	C+	1.85	0.95	1,351.3	125.5	279.1	37.2
2018	B-	1.60	0.83	1,232.2	95.0	263.0	38.8
2017	B	1.60	0.90	1,158.1	74.4	254.9	37.0

Wilton Re Holdings Ltd
Composite Group Rating: C
Largest Group Members

	Assets ($mil)	Rating
WILTON REASSURANCE CO	18452	C
WILCAC LIFE INS CO	5499	C-
TEXAS LIFE INS CO	1471	C+
WILTON REASSURANCE LIFE CO OF NY	875	C+

THE UNION LABOR LIFE INS CO   B   Good

Major Rating Factors: Good liquidity (6.6 on a scale of 0 to 10) with sufficient resources to handle a spike in claims. Good overall results on stability tests (5.5). Stability strengths include excellent operational trends and excellent risk diversification. Strong capitalization (7.7) based on excellent risk adjusted capital (severe loss scenario). Moreover, capital has steadily grown over the last five years.

Other Rating Factors: High quality investment portfolio (7.1). Excellent profitability (8.2) with operating gains in each of the last five years.

Principal Business: Group health insurance (77%), group life insurance (20%), and group retirement contracts (2%).

Principal Investments: NonCMO investment grade bonds (50%), CMOs and structured securities (23%), common & preferred stock (9%), and mortgages in good standing (8%).

Investments in Affiliates: 5%

Group Affiliation: ULLICO Inc

Licensed in: All states except PR

Commenced Business: May 1927

Address: 8403 COLESVILLE ROAD, SILVER SPRING, MD 20910

Phone: (202) 682-0900 **Domicile State:** MD **NAIC Code:** 69744

Data Date	Rating	RACR #1	RACR #2	Total Assets ($mil)	Capital ($mil)	Net Premium ($mil)	Net Income ($mil)
2021	B	2.18	1.46	4,752.2	154.7	190.4	11.2
2020	B	2.20	1.47	4,306.6	141.6	185.5	12.7
2019	B	2.18	1.44	4,284.8	129.9	165.5	19.7
2018	B	2.11	1.37	3,892.6	108.7	150.2	13.3
2017	B	2.03	1.31	3,614.2	94.2	138.1	9.3

Rating Indexes

Ranges Cap. Stab. Inv. Prof. Liq.
■ Weak ■ Fair □ Good □ Strong

TIAA-CREF LIFE INS CO   B   Good

Major Rating Factors: Good quality investment portfolio (6.3 on a scale of 0 to 10) despite mixed results such as: no exposure to mortgages and large holdings of BBB rated bonds but minimal holdings in junk bonds. Good overall profitability (5.8). Excellent expense controls. Return on equity has been low, averaging 3.5%. Good overall results on stability tests (5.0) good operational trends, good risk adjusted capital for prior years and excellent risk diversification.

Other Rating Factors: Fair liquidity (3.0). Strong capitalization (7.4) based on excellent risk adjusted capital (severe loss scenario).

Principal Business: Individual annuities (52%), individual life insurance (37%), group life insurance (9%), and individual health insurance (1%).

Principal Investments: NonCMO investment grade bonds (87%) and CMOs and structured securities (13%).

Investments in Affiliates: None

Group Affiliation: TIAA

Licensed in: All states except PR

Commenced Business: December 1996

Address: 730 THIRD AVENUE, NEW YORK, NY 10017

Phone: (212) 490-9000 **Domicile State:** NY **NAIC Code:** 60142

Data Date	Rating	RACR #1	RACR #2	Total Assets ($mil)	Capital ($mil)	Net Premium ($mil)	Net Income ($mil)
2021	B	2.39	1.27	17,626.1	841.7	433.6	121.8
2020	B	2.53	1.34	15,760.7	818.8	368.3	311.5
2019	B	1.95	1.04	13,137.8	510.5	624.5	-207.8
2018	B	2.00	1.05	13,267.2	500.9	689.0	-14.6
2017	B	1.81	0.96	12,558.7	411.5	734.6	29.2

Adverse Trends in Operations

Decrease in premium volume from 2019 to 2020 (41%)
Decrease in premium volume from 2018 to 2019 (9%)
Increase in policy surrenders from 2017 to 2018 (36%)
Decrease in premium volume from 2017 to 2018 (6%)

TIER ONE INSURANCE CO   B   Good

Major Rating Factors: Fair overall results on stability tests (4.4 on a scale of 0 to 10) including negative cash flow from operations for 2021. Weak profitability (1.6) with operating losses during 2021. Return on equity has been low, averaging -20.3%. Strong overall capitalization (8.0) based on excellent risk adjusted capital (severe loss scenario). However, capital levels have fluctuated somewhat during past years.

Other Rating Factors: High quality investment portfolio (9.3). Excellent liquidity (7.0).

Principal Business: Individual health insurance (100%).

Principal Investments: NonCMO investment grade bonds (55%) and cash (31%).

Investments in Affiliates: None

Group Affiliation: Aflac Incorporated

Licensed in: All states except NY, PR

Commenced Business: August 1981

Address: 1833 SOUTH MORGAN ROAD, Omaha, NE 68114-3743

Phone: (706) 243-8708 **Domicile State:** NE **NAIC Code:** 92908

Data Date	Rating	RACR #1	RACR #2	Total Assets ($mil)	Capital ($mil)	Net Premium ($mil)	Net Income ($mil)
2021	B	7.30	6.57	73.6	57.0	3.4	-26.8
2020	U	7.73	6.96	75.9	61.2	0.0	-24.5
2019	U	4.12	3.71	14.7	12.1	0.0	-1.9
2018	U	4.12	3.70	10.0	10.0	0.0	0.1
2017	U	4.03	3.63	9.2	9.2	0.0	0.1

Rating Indexes

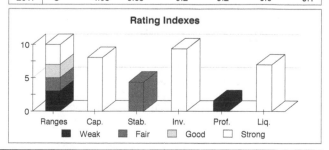

Ranges Cap. Stab. Inv. Prof. Liq.
■ Weak ■ Fair □ Good □ Strong

TRANS OCEANIC LIFE INS CO *   B+   Good

Major Rating Factors: Good overall results on stability tests (6.4 on a scale of 0 to 10). Stability strengths include excellent operational trends and good risk diversification. Fair quality investment portfolio (4.9). Strong capitalization (7.6) based on excellent risk adjusted capital (severe loss scenario). Capital levels have been relatively consistent over the last five years.

Other Rating Factors: Excellent profitability (8.8) with operating gains in each of the last five years. Excellent liquidity (7.7).

Principal Business: Individual annuities (86%) and individual health insurance (14%).

Principal Investments: NonCMO investment grade bonds (42%), common & preferred stock (18%), cash (13%), real estate (11%), and CMOs and structured securities (7%).

Investments in Affiliates: 5%

Group Affiliation: Trans-Oceanic Group Inc

Licensed in: FL, PR

Commenced Business: December 1959

Address: # 121 ONEILL, SAN JUAN, PR 00918-2404

Phone: (787) 620-2680   **Domicile State:** PR   **NAIC Code:** 69523

Data Date	Rating	RACR #1	RACR #2	Total Assets ($mil)	Capital ($mil)	Net Premium ($mil)	Net Income ($mil)
2021	B+	2.17	1.42	407.4	39.3	32.3	6.2
2020	B+	1.83	1.26	198.9	33.4	32.1	3.3
2019	B+	1.97	1.34	77.3	32.4	30.7	2.0
2018	A-	2.54	1.61	74.2	32.8	29.5	1.9
2017	A-	2.59	1.65	72.5	33.3	30.1	1.9

Adverse Trends in Operations

Decrease in capital during 2019 (2%)
Increase in policy surrenders from 2017 to 2018 (3207%)
Decrease in capital during 2018 (1%)
Decrease in premium volume from 2017 to 2018 (2%)
Decrease in premium volume from 2016 to 2017 (2%)

TRANS WORLD ASR CO *   B+   Good

Major Rating Factors: Good overall results on stability tests (6.7 on a scale of 0 to 10). Stability strengths include excellent operational trends and good risk diversification. Good quality investment portfolio (5.6) despite mixed results such as: large holdings of BBB rated bonds but moderate junk bond exposure. Good overall profitability (6.1).

Other Rating Factors: Strong capitalization (8.7) based on excellent risk adjusted capital (severe loss scenario). Excellent liquidity (8.0).

Principal Business: Individual life insurance (74%), reinsurance (16%), and individual annuities (10%).

Principal Investments: NonCMO investment grade bonds (74%), noninv. grade bonds (7%), mortgages in good standing (6%), common & preferred stock (5%), and misc. investments (9%).

Investments in Affiliates: 10%

Group Affiliation: TWA Corp

Licensed in: All states except NH, NY, VT, PR

Commenced Business: December 1963

Address: 885 S El Camino Real, San Mateo, CA 94402

Phone: (850) 456-7401   **Domicile State:** CA   **NAIC Code:** 69566

Data Date	Rating	RACR #1	RACR #2	Total Assets ($mil)	Capital ($mil)	Net Premium ($mil)	Net Income ($mil)
2021	B+	3.33	2.16	341.0	85.3	12.4	2.3
2020	B+	2.92	1.99	343.3	86.8	12.6	3.7
2019	B+	2.82	2.05	342.2	85.8	13.6	2.0
2018	B+	2.71	2.01	343.7	86.3	12.3	3.2
2017	B+	2.50	1.91	346.8	86.3	11.4	3.1

Adverse Trends in Operations

Decrease in premium volume from 2019 to 2020 (7%)
Increase in policy surrenders from 2016 to 2017 (44%)
Decrease in asset base during 2017 (2%)

TRANSAMERICA FINANCIAL LIFE INS CO   B   Good

Major Rating Factors: Good overall results on stability tests (5.6 on a scale of 0 to 10). Stability strengths include excellent operational trends and excellent risk diversification. Good quality investment portfolio (5.3) despite large holdings of BBB rated bonds in addition to moderate junk bond exposure. Exposure to mortgages is significant, but the mortgage default rate has been low. Good overall profitability (6.5).

Other Rating Factors: Strong capitalization (7.7) based on excellent risk adjusted capital (severe loss scenario). Excellent liquidity (7.7).

Principal Business: Group retirement contracts (87%), reinsurance (5%), individual life insurance (3%), individual annuities (2%), and individual health insurance (1%).

Principal Investments: NonCMO investment grade bonds (51%), mortgages in good standing (19%), CMOs and structured securities (12%), noninv. grade bonds (3%), and misc. investments (7%).

Investments in Affiliates: 2%

Group Affiliation: AEGON USA Group

Licensed in: All states except PR

Commenced Business: October 1947

Address: 440 Mamaroneck Avenue, Harrison, NY 10528

Phone: (914) 627-3630   **Domicile State:** NY   **NAIC Code:** 70688

Data Date	Rating	RACR #1	RACR #2	Total Assets ($mil)	Capital ($mil)	Net Premium ($mil)	Net Income ($mil)
2021	B	3.04	1.49	35,545.8	1,088.6	5,206.8	188.8
2020	B	2.95	1.44	33,514.5	1,077.6	5,225.0	78.6
2019	B	2.89	1.39	31,907.5	1,018.0	5,702.0	351.1
2018	B	3.10	1.49	29,480.6	1,090.5	5,742.7	200.4
2017	B	2.97	1.45	34,192.5	1,050.4	5,150.0	158.7

Adverse Trends in Operations

Decrease in capital during 2019 (7%)
Increase in policy surrenders from 2017 to 2018 (47%)
Decrease in asset base during 2018 (14%)
Decrease in capital during 2017 (4%)
Decrease in premium volume from 2016 to 2017 (11%)

TRANSAMERICA LIFE INS CO

B **Good**

Major Rating Factors: Good quality investment portfolio (6.3 on a scale of 0 to 10) despite large holdings of BBB rated bonds in addition to moderate junk bond exposure. Exposure to mortgages is significant, but the mortgage default rate has been low. Good liquidity (6.3) with sufficient resources to handle a spike in claims as well as a significant increase in policy surrenders. Good overall results on stability tests (5.4) good operational trends and excellent risk diversification.

Other Rating Factors: Fair profitability (4.8). Strong capitalization (7.1) based on excellent risk adjusted capital (severe loss scenario).

Principal Business: Group retirement contracts (53%), individual life insurance (24%), individual annuities (8%), reinsurance (7%), and other lines (9%).

Principal Investments: NonCMO investment grade bonds (57%), mortgages in good standing (12%), CMOs and structured securities (8%), common & preferred stock (5%), and misc. investments (10%).

Investments in Affiliates: 6%

Group Affiliation: AEGON USA Group

Licensed in: All states except NY

Commenced Business: March 1962

Address: 4333 Edgewood Rd NE, Cedar Rapids, IA 52499

Phone: (319) 355-8511 **Domicile State:** IA **NAIC Code:** 86231

Data Date	Rating	RACR #1	RACR #2	Total Assets ($mil)	Capital ($mil)	Net Premium ($mil)	Net Income ($mil)
2021	B	1.48	1.05	203,000	7,276.9	14,263.3	154.2
2020	B	1.59	1.14	200,000	8,109.6	16,526.8	1,291.4
2019	B	1.55	1.17	130,000	6,560.7	12,669.4	3,335.3
2018	B	1.47	1.08	117,000	5,778.3	11,321.6	-1,338.6
2017	B	1.47	1.07	125,000	5,411.7	-3,259.8	381.4

Adverse Trends in Operations

Change in premium mix from 2017 to 2018 (73.1%)
Decrease in asset base during 2018 (7%)
Decrease in asset base during 2017 (5%)
Increase in policy surrenders from 2016 to 2017 (28%)
Decrease in premium volume from 2016 to 2017 (123%)

TRANSAMERICA PACIFIC RE INC

C **Fair**

Major Rating Factors: Strong capitalization (3.0 on a scale of 0 to 10) based on excellent risk adjusted capital (severe loss scenario). Fair quality investment portfolio (4.9). Fair overall results on stability tests (3.0) including lack of operational experience.

Other Rating Factors: Weak profitability (0.9) with operating losses during 2020. Excellent liquidity (7.0).

Principal Business: Reinsurance (100%).

Principal Investments: NonCMO investment grade bonds (77%) and CMOs and structured securities (13%).

Investments in Affiliates: None

Group Affiliation: AEGON N V

Licensed in: VT

Commenced Business: June 2020

Address: Burlington, VT 5401

Phone: (319) 355-8511 **Domicile State:** VT **NAIC Code:** 16815

Data Date	Rating	RACR #1	RACR #2	Total Assets ($mil)	Capital ($mil)	Net Premium ($mil)	Net Income ($mil)
2020	C	5.44	3.14	0.0	0.0	0.0	0.0
2019	N/A	N/A	N/A	0.0	0.0	0.0	0.0
2018	N/A	N/A	N/A	0.0	0.0	0.0	0.0
2017	N/A	N/A	N/A	0.0	0.0	0.0	0.0
2016	N/A	N/A	N/A	0.0	0.0	0.0	0.0

Risk-Adjusted Capital Ratios (Since 2016)

TRIPLE S VIDA INC

C+ **Fair**

Major Rating Factors: Fair capitalization (4.8 on a scale of 0 to 10) based on fair risk adjusted capital (moderate loss scenario). Fair quality investment portfolio (3.3). Fair overall results on stability tests (4.6) including fair risk adjusted capital in prior years.

Other Rating Factors: Good profitability (5.0) although investment income, in comparison to reserve requirements, is below regulatory standards. Good liquidity (6.0).

Principal Business: Individual life insurance (54%), individual health insurance (35%), group life insurance (5%), group health insurance (5%), and individual annuities (2%).

Principal Investments: NonCMO investment grade bonds (53%), common & preferred stock (21%), CMOs and structured securities (20%), policy loans (1%), and cash (1%).

Investments in Affiliates: None

Group Affiliation: Triple-S Management Corp

Licensed in: PR

Commenced Business: September 1964

Address: 1052 Munoz Rivera, San Juan, PR 927

Phone: (787) 777-8432 **Domicile State:** PR **NAIC Code:** 73814

Data Date	Rating	RACR #1	RACR #2	Total Assets ($mil)	Capital ($mil)	Net Premium ($mil)	Net Income ($mil)
2021	C+	0.98	0.62	810.1	58.3	227.7	5.9
2020	C+	0.92	0.59	750.6	63.4	212.9	11.2
2019	B-	N/A	N/A	735.4	55.7	205.0	3.6
2018	B-	1.18	0.77	655.1	60.3	182.4	6.4
2017	B-	1.27	0.83	637.9	67.1	169.6	10.9

Risk-Adjusted Capital Ratio #1 (Moderate Loss Scenario)

TRUSTMARK INS CO
B   **Good**

Major Rating Factors: Good overall results on stability tests (5.4 on a scale of 0 to 10). Stability strengths include excellent operational trends and excellent risk diversification. Fair quality investment portfolio (4.8). Fair profitability (3.2) with investment income below regulatory standards in relation to interest assumptions of reserves.

Other Rating Factors: Strong capitalization (7.9) based on excellent risk adjusted capital (severe loss scenario). Excellent liquidity (7.0).

Principal Business: Group life insurance (54%), group health insurance (27%), individual life insurance (10%), individual health insurance (9%), and reinsurance (1%).

Principal Investments: NonCMO investment grade bonds (43%), CMOs and structured securities (21%), mortgages in good standing (8%), common & preferred stock (7%), and misc. investments (15%).

Investments in Affiliates: None

Group Affiliation: Trustmark Group Inc

Licensed in: All states, the District of Columbia and Puerto Rico

Commenced Business: January 1913

Address: 400 FIELD DRIVE, LAKE FOREST, IL 60045-2581

Phone: (847) 615-1500   **Domicile State:** IL   **NAIC Code:** 61425

Data Date	Rating	RACR #1	RACR #2	Total Assets ($mil)	Capital ($mil)	Net Premium ($mil)	Net Income ($mil)
2021	B	2.83	1.59	1,807.8	320.4	389.7	40.2
2020	B	2.95	1.65	1,742.4	314.4	365.9	39.8
2019	B+	3.02	1.73	1,654.1	330.9	366.2	12.2
2018	B+	3.12	1.80	1,585.5	335.0	366.5	13.8
2017	B+	3.12	1.77	1,548.0	323.8	343.3	22.6

Adverse Trends in Operations

Decrease in capital during 2020 (5%)
Decrease in capital during 2019 (1%)

TRUSTMARK LIFE INS CO *
A-   **Excellent**

Major Rating Factors: Good overall results on stability tests (5.5 on a scale of 0 to 10). Strengths that enhance stability include good operational trends and excellent risk diversification. Good overall profitability (6.2). Return on equity has been good over the last five years, averaging 10.2%. Good liquidity (6.8) with sufficient resources to handle a spike in claims.

Other Rating Factors: Strong capitalization (10.0) based on excellent risk adjusted capital (severe loss scenario). High quality investment portfolio (7.1).

Principal Business: Group health insurance (94%) and group life insurance (6%).

Principal Investments: NonCMO investment grade bonds (64%), CMOs and structured securities (19%), common & preferred stock (4%), and mortgages in good standing (4%).

Investments in Affiliates: None

Group Affiliation: Trustmark Group Inc

Licensed in: All states except PR

Commenced Business: February 1925

Address: 400 FIELD DRIVE, LAKE FOREST, IL 60045-2581

Phone: (847) 615-1500   **Domicile State:** IL   **NAIC Code:** 62863

Data Date	Rating	RACR #1	RACR #2	Total Assets ($mil)	Capital ($mil)	Net Premium ($mil)	Net Income ($mil)
2021	A-	7.01	4.80	249.3	152.4	119.6	7.8
2020	A-	7.12	4.88	269.9	166.9	131.8	17.8
2019	B+	8.46	5.87	276.7	172.8	119.4	24.1
2018	B+	8.38	5.94	319.9	175.5	124.6	25.7
2017	B+	7.49	4.70	303.0	164.4	112.6	17.4

Adverse Trends in Operations

Decrease in asset base during 2020 (2%)
Decrease in capital during 2019 (2%)
Decrease in asset base during 2019 (14%)
Decrease in premium volume from 2016 to 2017 (18%)
Decrease in asset base during 2017 (2%)

UNICARE LIFE & HEALTH INS CO
B   **Good**

Major Rating Factors: Good overall profitability (6.7 on a scale of 0 to 10). Return on equity has been fair, averaging 9.3%. Fair quality investment portfolio (3.7). Fair overall results on stability tests (4.9) including weak results on operational trends.

Other Rating Factors: Weak liquidity (0.0) as a spike in claims may stretch capacity. Strong capitalization (10.0) based on excellent risk adjusted capital (severe loss scenario).

Principal Business: Reinsurance (96%), group health insurance (2%), group life insurance (1%), and individual health insurance (1%).

Principal Investments: NonCMO investment grade bonds (69%), noninv. grade bonds (16%), and cash (2%).

Investments in Affiliates: None

Group Affiliation: Anthem Inc

Licensed in: All states, the District of Columbia and Puerto Rico

Commenced Business: December 1980

Address: 120 MONUMENT CIRCLE, INDIANAPOLIS, IN 46204

Phone: (877) 864-2273   **Domicile State:** IN   **NAIC Code:** 80314

Data Date	Rating	RACR #1	RACR #2	Total Assets ($mil)	Capital ($mil)	Net Premium ($mil)	Net Income ($mil)
2021	B	5.03	3.54	957.9	289.4	404.3	67.3
2020	B	5.39	3.55	1,033.2	266.3	332.7	45.3
2019	B-	3.33	2.59	894.8	222.1	531.7	14.6
2018	B-	1.71	1.31	310.6	60.5	353.9	-7.2
2017	B-	2.12	1.60	283.9	70.1	312.7	8.8

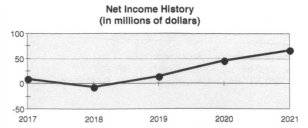

Net Income History
(in millions of dollars)

UNIMERICA INS CO   B-   Good

Major Rating Factors: Good overall results on stability tests (5.0 on a scale of 0 to 10) despite fair financial strength of affiliated UnitedHealth Group Inc. Other stability subfactors include good operational trends and excellent risk diversification. Strong capitalization (10.0) based on excellent risk adjusted capital (severe loss scenario). Capital levels have been relatively consistent over the last five years. High quality investment portfolio (8.5).

Other Rating Factors: Excellent profitability (9.0) with operating gains in each of the last five years. Excellent liquidity (7.1).

Principal Business: Group health insurance (94%), group life insurance (3%), and reinsurance (3%).

Principal Investments: NonCMO investment grade bonds (70%) and CMOs and structured securities (16%).

Investments in Affiliates: None
Group Affiliation: UnitedHealth Group Inc
Licensed in: All states except NY, PR
Commenced Business: December 1980
Address: 10701 WEST RESEARCH DRIVE, MILWAUKEE, WI 53214
Phone: (952) 251-9723 **Domicile State:** WI **NAIC Code:** 91529

Data Date	Rating	RACR #1	RACR #2	Total Assets ($mil)	Capital ($mil)	Net Premium ($mil)	Net Income ($mil)
2021	B-	6.25	4.81	427.6	260.2	312.0	68.7
2020	B-	4.65	3.63	450.0	241.4	400.0	57.7
2019	B	3.88	3.02	396.0	204.8	404.0	47.0
2018	B	4.14	3.24	436.7	230.7	431.8	62.5
2017	B	1.73	1.39	502.5	186.1	874.3	31.4

UnitedHealth Group Inc Composite Group Rating: C Largest Group Members	Assets ($mil)	Rating
UNITED HEALTHCARE INS CO	21587	C
UHC OF CALIFORNIA INC	793	C-
GOLDEN RULE INS CO	629	B
UNIMERICA INS CO	450	B-
OPTUM INS OF OH INC	424	B-

UNION FIDELITY LIFE INS CO   C   Fair

Major Rating Factors: Fair overall results on stability tests (3.6 on a scale of 0 to 10) including fair financial strength of affiliated General Electric Corp Group and negative cash flow from operations for 2021, fair risk adjusted capital in prior years. Fair quality investment portfolio (3.7) with large holdings of BBB rated bonds in addition to junk bond exposure equal to 95% of capital. Fair liquidity (4.4).

Other Rating Factors: Good capitalization (6.4) based on good risk adjusted capital (severe loss scenario). Weak profitability (1.8) with investment income below regulatory standards in relation to interest assumptions of reserves.

Principal Business: Reinsurance (92%), group health insurance (4%), group life insurance (2%), individual life insurance (1%), and individual health insurance (1%).

Principal Investments: NonCMO investment grade bonds (83%), CMOs and structured securities (6%), mortgages in good standing (5%), and noninv. grade bonds (3%).

Investments in Affiliates: 1%
Group Affiliation: General Electric Corp Group
Licensed in: All states except NY, PR
Commenced Business: February 1926
Address: 7101 College Blvd Ste 1400, Overland Park, KS 66211
Phone: (913) 982-3700 **Domicile State:** KS **NAIC Code:** 62596

Data Date	Rating	RACR #1	RACR #2	Total Assets ($mil)	Capital ($mil)	Net Premium ($mil)	Net Income ($mil)
2021	C	1.83	0.92	19,882.4	862.7	225.3	139.9
2020	D-	1.62	0.81	20,130.0	776.8	239.4	37.0
2019	E	1.57	0.80	20,382.8	728.6	245.0	-32.0
2018	E	1.44	0.73	20,505.2	667.8	253.5	-298.8
2017	E	1.14	0.57	20,435.4	536.6	263.9	-1,210.0

General Electric Corp Group Composite Group Rating: C- Largest Group Members	Assets ($mil)	Rating
UNION FIDELITY LIFE INS CO	20130	C
EMPLOYERS REASSURANCE CORP	19964	C-
ELECTRIC INS CO	1170	C-

UNION SECURITY INS CO   B   Good

Major Rating Factors: Good quality investment portfolio (5.4 on a scale of 0 to 10) despite mixed results such as: minimal exposure to mortgages and large holdings of BBB rated bonds but small junk bond holdings. Good liquidity (6.3) with sufficient resources to handle a spike in claims as well as a significant increase in policy surrenders. Fair overall results on stability tests (4.8) including negative cash flow from operations for 2021 and excessive premium growth.

Other Rating Factors: Strong capitalization (9.3) based on excellent risk adjusted capital (severe loss scenario). Excellent profitability (8.3) with operating gains in each of the last five years.

Principal Business: Individual health insurance (56%), individual life insurance (28%), individual annuities (9%), group health insurance (4%), and other lines (4%).

Principal Investments: NonCMO investment grade bonds (68%), CMOs and structured securities (18%), mortgages in good standing (5%), noninv. grade bonds (3%), and misc. investments (5%).

Investments in Affiliates: None
Group Affiliation: Assurant Inc
Licensed in: All states except NY, PR
Commenced Business: September 1910
Address: 2323 GRAND BOULEVARD, TOPEKA, KS 66614
Phone: (651) 361-4000 **Domicile State:** KS **NAIC Code:** 70408

Data Date	Rating	RACR #1	RACR #2	Total Assets ($mil)	Capital ($mil)	Net Premium ($mil)	Net Income ($mil)
2021	B	4.92	2.50	3,149.8	205.6	4.1	84.9
2020	B	2.90	1.48	2,908.0	127.9	3.1	34.7
2019	B	2.81	1.46	2,608.5	123.6	3.9	48.1
2018	B	2.86	1.48	2,448.4	126.3	3.8	90.0
2017	B	2.37	1.23	2,698.7	113.9	4.1	106.2

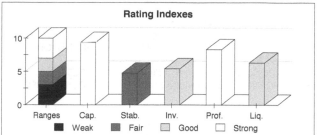

Rating Indexes

Ranges Cap. Stab. Inv. Prof. Liq.

■ Weak ■ Fair ☐ Good ☐ Strong

UNION SECURITY LIFE INS CO OF NY   B   Good

Major Rating Factors: Good overall results on stability tests (6.2 on a scale of 0 to 10). Stability strengths include good operational trends and excellent risk diversification. Good overall profitability (5.2). Return on equity has been fair, averaging 6.6%. Strong capitalization (10.0) based on excellent risk adjusted capital (severe loss scenario).

Other Rating Factors: High quality investment portfolio (8.1). Excellent liquidity (10.0).

Principal Business: Individual health insurance (86%), individual annuities (7%), group health insurance (4%), individual life insurance (1%), and other lines (2%).

Principal Investments: NonCMO investment grade bonds (54%), CMOs and structured securities (16%), and cash (1%).

Investments in Affiliates: None

Group Affiliation: Assurant Inc

Licensed in: NY

Commenced Business: April 1974

Address: 212 HIGHBRIDGE STREET SUITE D, NEW YORK, NY 10006

Phone: (315) 637-4232 **Domicile State:** NY **NAIC Code:** 81477

Data Date	Rating	RACR #1	RACR #2	Total Assets ($mil)	Capital ($mil)	Net Premium ($mil)	Net Income ($mil)
2021	B	6.12	5.50	55.8	42.7	0.5	1.1
2020	B-	6.16	5.55	56.0	43.1	0.5	1.2
2019	C+	6.38	5.74	56.6	44.7	0.7	2.5
2018	C+	6.72	6.05	59.9	48.2	0.8	5.0
2017	C+	7.06	6.36	66.7	52.7	1.0	6.3

Adverse Trends in Operations

Decrease in asset base during 2018 (10%)
Decrease in premium volume from 2017 to 2018 (22%)
Decrease in capital during 2017 (22%)
Change in asset mix during 2017 (10.5%)
Decrease in asset base during 2017 (18%)

UNITED AMERICAN INS CO   B   Good

Major Rating Factors: Good overall results on stability tests (5.9 on a scale of 0 to 10) despite fair financial strength of affiliated Torchmark Corp. Other stability subfactors include excellent operational trends, good risk adjusted capital for prior years and excellent risk diversification. Good quality investment portfolio (6.2) despite mixed results such as: no exposure to mortgages and large holdings of BBB rated bonds but small junk bond holdings. Good liquidity (5.7).

Other Rating Factors: Strong capitalization (7.4) based on excellent risk adjusted capital (severe loss scenario). Excellent profitability (8.0) with operating gains in each of the last five years.

Principal Business: Individual health insurance (62%), group health insurance (29%), individual annuities (4%), reinsurance (4%), and individual life insurance (2%).

Principal Investments: NonCMO investment grade bonds (82%), common & preferred stock (6%), noninv. grade bonds (3%), CMOs and structured securities (2%), and policy loans (1%).

Investments in Affiliates: 10%

Group Affiliation: Torchmark Corp

Licensed in: All states except NY, PR

Commenced Business: August 1981

Address: 10306 REGENCY PARKWAY DR, OMAHA, NE 68114

Phone: (972) 529-5085 **Domicile State:** NE **NAIC Code:** 92916

Data Date	Rating	RACR #1	RACR #2	Total Assets ($mil)	Capital ($mil)	Net Premium ($mil)	Net Income ($mil)
2021	B	1.63	1.24	714.5	191.6	547.4	33.6
2020	B	1.68	1.29	729.1	209.3	541.0	64.0
2019	B-	1.25	0.96	707.6	147.8	515.1	5.4
2018	B-	1.52	1.14	743.3	158.3	488.5	30.4
2017	B-	1.56	1.17	766.7	162.0	481.4	88.1

Torchmark Corp
Composite Group Rating: C+
Largest Group Members

Largest Group Members	Assets ($mil)	Rating
LIBERTY NATIONAL LIFE INS CO	8308	B-
GLOBE LIFE ACCIDENT INS CO	5074	C
AMERICAN INCOME LIFE INS CO	4675	B
FAMILY HERITAGE LIFE INS CO OF AMER	1436	B-
UNITED AMERICAN INS CO	729	B

UNITED FARM FAMILY LIFE INS CO *   B+   Good

Major Rating Factors: Good liquidity (5.9 on a scale of 0 to 10) with sufficient resources to handle a spike in claims as well as a significant increase in policy surrenders. Good overall results on stability tests (6.5). Stability strengths include excellent operational trends and excellent risk diversification. Fair profitability (4.2) with investment income below regulatory standards in relation to interest assumptions of reserves.

Other Rating Factors: Strong capitalization (8.5) based on excellent risk adjusted capital (severe loss scenario). High quality investment portfolio (7.0).

Principal Business: Individual life insurance (88%), individual annuities (7%), and reinsurance (5%).

Principal Investments: NonCMO investment grade bonds (68%), mortgages in good standing (16%), CMOs and structured securities (5%), policy loans (4%), and misc. investments (5%).

Investments in Affiliates: 2%

Group Affiliation: Indiana Farm Bureau

Licensed in: AZ, CA, IL, IN, IA, MD, MA, NH, NJ, NC, ND, OH, PA

Commenced Business: May 1964

Address: 225 South East Street, Indianapolis, IN 46202

Phone: (317) 692-7200 **Domicile State:** IN **NAIC Code:** 69892

Data Date	Rating	RACR #1	RACR #2	Total Assets ($mil)	Capital ($mil)	Net Premium ($mil)	Net Income ($mil)
2021	B+	3.30	2.02	2,457.7	363.7	118.8	9.9
2020	B+	3.34	2.01	2,474.9	357.5	128.6	12.2
2019	B+	3.38	2.03	2,417.1	347.2	134.7	9.6
2018	A	3.39	2.02	2,359.3	335.2	134.0	14.3
2017	A	3.43	2.01	2,321.9	326.3	136.5	18.2

Adverse Trends in Operations

Decrease in premium volume from 2019 to 2020 (4%)
Decrease in premium volume from 2017 to 2018 (2%)

UNITED FIDELITY LIFE INS CO
C   **Fair**

Major Rating Factors: Fair overall results on stability tests (4.1 on a scale of 0 to 10). Good capitalization (5.8) based on good risk adjusted capital (severe loss scenario). Capital levels have been relatively consistent over the last five years. Good liquidity (6.9) with sufficient resources to handle a spike in claims as well as a significant increase in policy surrenders.

Other Rating Factors: Low quality investment portfolio (2.8). Excellent profitability (7.2) with operating gains in each of the last five years.

Principal Business: Individual life insurance (92%), individual annuities (4%), reinsurance (2%), and individual health insurance (2%).

Principal Investments: Common & preferred stock (81%), nonCMO investment grade bonds (11%), CMOs and structured securities (5%), policy loans (1%), and mortgages in good standing (1%).

Investments in Affiliates: 79%

Group Affiliation: Americo Life Inc

Licensed in: All states except CT, FL, HI, ME, MI, MN, NH, NJ, NY, VT, PR

Commenced Business: September 1977

Address: PO Box 139061, Dallas, TX 75313-9061

Phone: (816) 391-2000 **Domicile State:** TX **NAIC Code:** 87645

Data Date	Rating	RACR #1	RACR #2	Total Assets ($mil)	Capital ($mil)	Net Premium ($mil)	Net Income ($mil)
2021	C	0.86	0.85	1,121.1	879.8	4.8	10.1
2020	C	0.85	0.84	867.6	620.6	5.2	30.8
2019	C	0.84	0.83	859.5	600.3	5.5	56.6
2018	C	0.76	0.75	755.9	488.3	6.0	48.7
2017	C	0.77	0.75	802.9	520.0	6.3	29.6

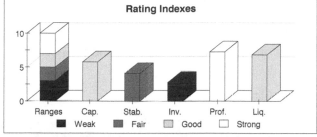

Rating Indexes (Ranges, Cap., Stab., Inv., Prof., Liq.) — Weak, Fair, Good, Strong

UNITED HEALTHCARE INS CO
C   **Fair**

Major Rating Factors: Fair overall capitalization (4.8 on a scale of 0 to 10) based on mixed results -- excessive policy leverage mitigated by good risk adjusted capital (severe loss scenario). Nevertheless, capital levels have fluctuated during prior years. Fair overall results on stability tests (3.3). Good quality investment portfolio (6.4).

Other Rating Factors: Weak liquidity (1.3). Excellent profitability (7.5) with operating gains in each of the last five years.

Principal Business: Group health insurance (87%), individual health insurance (8%), and reinsurance (5%).

Principal Investments: NonCMO investment grade bonds (39%), common & preferred stock (25%), CMOs and structured securities (20%), noninv. grade bonds (7%), and real estate (2%).

Investments in Affiliates: 24%

Group Affiliation: UnitedHealth Group Inc

Licensed in: All states except NY

Commenced Business: April 1972

Address: 185 ASYLUM STREET, HARTFORD, CT 06103-3408

Phone: (877) 832-7734 **Domicile State:** CT **NAIC Code:** 79413

Data Date	Rating	RACR #1	RACR #2	Total Assets ($mil)	Capital ($mil)	Net Premium ($mil)	Net Income ($mil)
2021	C	0.88	0.76	22,699.4	7,379.6	52,670.9	1,981.5
2020	C	0.94	0.80	21,687.3	7,611.2	54,386.8	2,748.4
2019	C	1.05	0.89	20,997.1	8,535.5	55,642.1	3,177.4
2018	C	1.05	0.88	20,752.5	8,128.2	54,442.0	3,080.5
2017	C	0.89	0.75	19,617.5	6,355.2	50,538.6	2,599.6

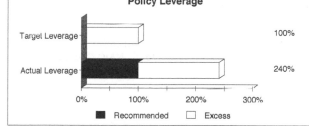

Policy Leverage — Target Leverage 100%, Actual Leverage 240% — Recommended, Excess

UNITED HERITAGE LIFE INS CO
B   **Good**

Major Rating Factors: Good overall results on stability tests (5.7 on a scale of 0 to 10) despite excessive premium growth. Other stability subfactors include excellent operational trends and excellent risk diversification. Fair quality investment portfolio (3.9) with large holdings of BBB rated bonds in addition to junk bond exposure equal to 86% of capital. Fair liquidity (4.7).

Other Rating Factors: Strong capitalization (7.2) based on excellent risk adjusted capital (severe loss scenario). Excellent profitability (7.8) with operating gains in each of the last five years.

Principal Business: Individual life insurance (51%), individual annuities (35%), group health insurance (8%), and group life insurance (7%).

Principal Investments: NonCMO investment grade bonds (71%), common & preferred stock (8%), CMOs and structured securities (7%), noninv. grade bonds (6%), and misc. investments (7%).

Investments in Affiliates: None

Group Affiliation: United Heritage Mutual Holding Co

Licensed in: All states except NY, PR

Commenced Business: September 1935

Address: 707 E UNITED HERITAGE COURT, MERIDIAN, ID 83642-7785

Phone: (208) 466-7856 **Domicile State:** ID **NAIC Code:** 63983

Data Date	Rating	RACR #1	RACR #2	Total Assets ($mil)	Capital ($mil)	Net Premium ($mil)	Net Income ($mil)
2021	B	2.21	1.14	682.2	76.1	100.1	5.2
2020	B	2.15	1.07	635.1	72.5	77.8	5.1
2019	B	2.45	1.21	626.9	70.8	87.6	5.1
2018	B	2.41	1.18	603.8	67.3	84.0	6.3
2017	B	2.54	1.26	574.2	63.3	75.4	5.6

Adverse Trends in Operations

Decrease in premium volume from 2019 to 2020 (11%)
Increase in policy surrenders from 2018 to 2019 (40%)

UNITED HOME LIFE INS CO
B **Good**

Major Rating Factors: Good overall profitability (5.8 on a scale of 0 to 10). Return on equity has been fair, averaging 5.7%. Good liquidity (6.1) with sufficient resources to handle a spike in claims as well as a significant increase in policy surrenders. Good overall results on stability tests (5.4) despite excessive premium growth excellent operational trends and excellent risk diversification.

Other Rating Factors: Strong capitalization (9.7) based on excellent risk adjusted capital (severe loss scenario). High quality investment portfolio (7.8).

Principal Business: Individual life insurance (99%) and reinsurance (1%).

Principal Investments: NonCMO investment grade bonds (87%), CMOs and structured securities (3%), policy loans (3%), cash (3%), and misc. investments (2%).

Investments in Affiliates: None

Group Affiliation: Indiana Farm Bureau

Licensed in: All states except AK, MA, NH, NY, PR

Commenced Business: December 1948

Address: 225 South East Street, Indianapolis, IN 46202

Phone: (800) 428-3001 **Domicile State:** IN **NAIC Code:** 69922

Data Date	Rating	RACR #1	RACR #2	Total Assets ($mil)	Capital ($mil)	Net Premium ($mil)	Net Income ($mil)
2021	B	3.16	2.77	193.7	30.1	32.5	7.1
2020	B	2.73	2.46	111.1	23.7	23.8	1.1
2019	B	2.45	2.20	104.0	21.1	22.1	1.2
2018	B	2.35	2.11	97.6	19.9	22.0	-0.1
2017	B	2.35	2.12	92.8	19.5	20.9	0.2

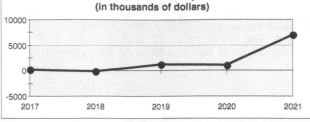

Net Income History (in thousands of dollars)

UNITED INS CO OF AMERICA
B- **Good**

Major Rating Factors: Good overall results on stability tests (5.3 on a scale of 0 to 10) despite fair financial strength of affiliated Kemper Corporation. Other stability subfactors include good operational trends and excellent risk diversification. Good overall capitalization (6.5) based on good risk adjusted capital (severe loss scenario). However, capital levels have fluctuated somewhat during past years. Good overall profitability (6.5).

Other Rating Factors: Fair quality investment portfolio (4.4). Fair liquidity (4.7).

Principal Business: Reinsurance (70%), individual life insurance (28%), and individual health insurance (2%).

Principal Investments: NonCMO investment grade bonds (57%), CMOs and structured securities (16%), common & preferred stock (9%), policy loans (6%), and misc. investments (10%).

Investments in Affiliates: 2%

Group Affiliation: Kemper Corporation

Licensed in: All states except AK, NY, PR

Commenced Business: April 1928

Address: ONE EAST WACKER DRIVE, CHICAGO, IL 60601

Phone: (314) 819-4300 **Domicile State:** IL **NAIC Code:** 69930

Data Date	Rating	RACR #1	RACR #2	Total Assets ($mil)	Capital ($mil)	Net Premium ($mil)	Net Income ($mil)
2021	B-	1.58	0.94	5,067.0	445.0	599.7	22.2
2020	B-	1.22	0.77	4,991.3	436.6	977.2	-3.6
2019	B-	1.63	0.98	4,149.5	411.1	367.4	92.3
2018	B-	1.87	1.10	3,906.9	450.9	362.0	140.7
2017	B-	1.82	1.04	3,833.6	421.8	362.5	84.8

Kemper Corporation
Composite Group Rating: C+

Largest Group Members	Assets ($mil)	Rating
UNITED INS CO OF AMERICA	4991	B-
TRINITY UNIVERSAL INS CO	4236	B
INFINITY INS CO	1080	C-
ALLIANCE UNITED INS CO	959	C
AMERICAN ACCESS CASUALTY CO	523	D

UNITED LIFE INS CO
B- **Good**

Major Rating Factors: Fair quality investment portfolio (3.8 on a scale of 0 to 10) with large holdings of BBB rated bonds in addition to junk bond exposure equal to 77% of capital. Fair profitability (4.1) with operating losses during 2021. Return on equity has been low, averaging 1.4%. Fair overall results on stability tests (3.9).

Other Rating Factors: Strong capitalization (7.1) based on excellent risk adjusted capital (severe loss scenario). Excellent liquidity (8.2).

Principal Business: Individual annuities (78%) and individual life insurance (22%).

Principal Investments: NonCMO investment grade bonds (43%), CMOs and structured securities (32%), noninv. grade bonds (7%), common & preferred stock (4%), and misc. investments (12%).

Investments in Affiliates: None

Group Affiliation: United Fire & Casualty Group

Licensed in: All states except AK, HI, ME, NY, VT, PR

Commenced Business: October 1962

Address: 118 SECOND AVENUE SE, CEDAR RAPIDS, IA 52401-1429

Phone: (800) 553-7937 **Domicile State:** IA **NAIC Code:** 69973

Data Date	Rating	RACR #1	RACR #2	Total Assets ($mil)	Capital ($mil)	Net Premium ($mil)	Net Income ($mil)
2021	B-	2.23	1.04	2,915.1	256.8	279.1	-2.9
2020	B	2.05	0.94	2,084.6	156.4	29.8	2.1
2019	B	2.37	1.15	1,763.5	157.6	241.0	7.7
2018	B	2.59	1.27	1,514.4	142.8	178.2	20.3
2017	B	2.95	1.58	1,498.0	144.5	123.3	5.5

Rating Indexes

Ranges — Cap. — Stab. — Inv. — Prof. — Liq.
■ Weak ■ Fair □ Good □ Strong

UNITED OF OMAHA LIFE INS CO
B   Good

Major Rating Factors: Good quality investment portfolio (5.1 on a scale of 0 to 10) despite large holdings of BBB rated bonds in addition to moderate junk bond exposure. Exposure to mortgages is significant, but the mortgage default rate has been low. Good liquidity (5.4) with sufficient resources to handle a spike in claims as well as a significant increase in policy surrenders. Good overall results on stability tests (6.0) good operational trends and excellent risk diversification.

Other Rating Factors: Strong capitalization (7.2) based on excellent risk adjusted capital (severe loss scenario). Excellent profitability (7.1) despite modest operating losses during 2021.

Principal Business: Individual life insurance (36%), group health insurance (18%), group retirement contracts (16%), individual health insurance (15%), and other lines (15%).

Principal Investments: NonCMO investment grade bonds (58%), CMOs and structured securities (16%), mortgages in good standing (14%), noninv. grade bonds (3%), and misc. investments (6%).

Investments in Affiliates: 4%

Group Affiliation: Mutual Of Omaha Group

Licensed in: All states except NY

Commenced Business: November 1926

Address: 3300 MUTUAL OF OMAHA PLAZA, OMAHA, NE 68175

Phone: (402) 342-7600 **Domicile State:** NE **NAIC Code:** 69868

Data Date	Rating	RACR #1	RACR #2	Total Assets ($mil)	Capital ($mil)	Net Premium ($mil)	Net Income ($mil)
2021	B	1.96	1.12	31,183.6	1,924.8	4,840.6	-29.0
2020	B	1.99	1.12	28,649.9	1,870.8	4,575.4	78.0
2019	B	2.08	1.18	26,246.4	1,761.9	3,717.4	136.2
2018	B	2.06	1.18	23,038.8	1,639.4	3,263.6	55.4
2017	B	2.00	1.14	22,803.2	1,605.7	4,024.6	61.7

Adverse Trends in Operations

Change in premium mix from 2019 to 2020 (5.3%)
Decrease in premium volume from 2017 to 2018 (19%)
Change in premium mix from 2017 to 2018 (7.0%)

UNITED STATES LIFE INS CO IN NYC
C+   Fair

Major Rating Factors: Fair quality investment portfolio (4.9 on a scale of 0 to 10) with large holdings of BBB rated bonds in addition to junk bond exposure equal to 81% of capital. Exposure to mortgages is significant, but the mortgage default rate has been low. Fair overall results on stability tests (4.8) including excessive premium growth and negative cash flow from operations for 2021. Good overall profitability (5.5).

Other Rating Factors: Good liquidity (5.2). Strong capitalization (7.3) based on excellent risk adjusted capital (severe loss scenario).

Principal Business: Individual annuities (55%), group retirement contracts (34%), individual life insurance (10%), and group health insurance (1%).

Principal Investments: NonCMO investment grade bonds (54%), CMOs and structured securities (18%), mortgages in good standing (12%), noninv. grade bonds (6%), and policy loans (1%).

Investments in Affiliates: 1%

Group Affiliation: American International Group

Licensed in: All states except PR

Commenced Business: March 1850

Address: 175 Water Street, New York, NY 10005-1400

Phone: (713) 522-1111 **Domicile State:** NY **NAIC Code:** 70106

Data Date	Rating	RACR #1	RACR #2	Total Assets ($mil)	Capital ($mil)	Net Premium ($mil)	Net Income ($mil)
2021	C+	2.51	1.21	32,282.1	2,020.0	2,436.8	178.5
2020	C+	2.32	1.10	30,307.8	1,789.8	1,653.7	253.7
2019	C+	2.10	0.99	29,540.0	1,571.0	1,832.9	253.0
2018	C+	1.81	0.83	28,200.3	1,278.1	-3,594.2	-214.8
2017	D	2.28	1.11	29,430.5	1,756.4	1,297.7	89.4

Rating Indexes

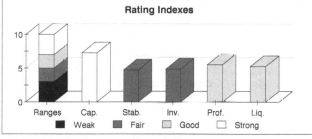

UNITED WORLD LIFE INS CO *
B+   Good

Major Rating Factors: Good overall results on stability tests (6.7 on a scale of 0 to 10). Stability strengths include excellent operational trends and excellent risk diversification. Good liquidity (6.6) with sufficient resources to handle a spike in claims. Strong capitalization (7.6) based on excellent risk adjusted capital (severe loss scenario).

Other Rating Factors: High quality investment portfolio (7.4). Excellent profitability (7.3) with operating gains in each of the last five years.

Principal Business: Individual health insurance (100%).

Principal Investments: CMOs and structured securities (54%) and nonCMO investment grade bonds (39%).

Investments in Affiliates: None

Group Affiliation: Mutual Of Omaha Group

Licensed in: All states except CT, NY, PR

Commenced Business: April 1970

Address: MUTUAL OF OMAHA PLAZA, OMAHA, NE 68175

Phone: (402) 342-7600 **Domicile State:** NE **NAIC Code:** 72850

Data Date	Rating	RACR #1	RACR #2	Total Assets ($mil)	Capital ($mil)	Net Premium ($mil)	Net Income ($mil)
2021	B+	3.36	1.38	160.3	59.5	0.9	2.7
2020	B+	3.23	1.33	154.3	53.8	1.0	2.8
2019	B+	3.20	1.33	147.3	46.1	1.1	1.4
2018	B+	3.95	1.66	128.5	44.6	1.2	2.8
2017	B+	4.96	2.11	122.8	48.7	1.3	1.9

Adverse Trends in Operations

Decrease in premium volume from 2019 to 2020 (7%)
Decrease in premium volume from 2017 to 2018 (6%)
Decrease in capital during 2018 (9%)
Decrease in capital during 2017 (5%)
Decrease in premium volume from 2016 to 2017 (6%)

UNIVERSAL GUARANTY LIFE INS CO   C+   Fair

Major Rating Factors: Fair overall results on stability tests (4.4 on a scale of 0 to 10) including negative cash flow from operations for 2021. Good liquidity (6.4) with sufficient resources to handle a spike in claims as well as a significant increase in policy surrenders. Low quality investment portfolio (2.4).

Other Rating Factors: Weak profitability (2.9). Strong capitalization (7.1) based on excellent risk adjusted capital (severe loss scenario).

Principal Business: N/A

Principal Investments: NonCMO investment grade bonds (36%), common & preferred stock (29%), mortgages in good standing (7%), real estate (4%), and misc. investments (23%).

Investments in Affiliates: 4%

Group Affiliation: UTG Inc

Licensed in: AL, AZ, AR, CO, DE, GA, ID, IL, IN, IA, KS, KY, LA, MA, MN, MS, MO, MT, NE, NV, NM, NC, ND, OH, OK, OR, PA, RI, SC, SD, TN, TX, UT, VA, WA, WV, WI

Commenced Business: December 1966

Address: 65 East State Street Ste 2100, Columbus, OH 43215-4260

Phone: (877) 881-1777 **Domicile State:** OH **NAIC Code:** 70130

Data Date	Rating	RACR #1	RACR #2	Total Assets ($mil)	Capital ($mil)	Net Premium ($mil)	Net Income ($mil)
2021	C+	1.79	1.04	360.0	64.7	4.6	0.5
2020	C+	2.18	1.28	349.3	70.6	4.6	6.3
2019	C+	2.22	1.28	349.0	66.0	5.2	8.3
2018	C+	1.93	1.12	346.2	60.0	5.3	6.2
2017	C+	1.82	1.03	343.3	54.7	5.6	5.4

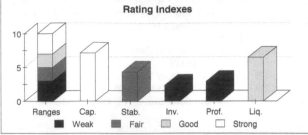

Rating Indexes

UNIVERSAL LIFE INS CO   B   Good

Major Rating Factors: Good current capitalization (6.8 on a scale of 0 to 10) based on good risk adjusted capital (severe loss scenario), although results have slipped from the excellent range over the last year. Good overall results on stability tests (5.8) despite excessive premium growth. Other stability subfactors include good operational trends and excellent risk diversification. Fair quality investment portfolio (3.8).

Other Rating Factors: Excellent profitability (8.2) with operating gains in each of the last five years. Excellent liquidity (7.5).

Principal Business: Individual annuities (94%), group life insurance (2%), group health insurance (2%), and credit life insurance (1%).

Principal Investments: NonCMO investment grade bonds (30%), CMOs and structured securities (28%), common & preferred stock (18%), noninv. grade bonds (14%), and cash (4%).

Investments in Affiliates: None

Group Affiliation: Universal Ins Co Group

Licensed in: PR

Commenced Business: September 1994

Address: Calle Bolivia #33 6to Piso, Guaynabo, PR 969

Phone: (787) 641-7171 **Domicile State:** PR **NAIC Code:** 60041

Data Date	Rating	RACR #1	RACR #2	Total Assets ($mil)	Capital ($mil)	Net Premium ($mil)	Net Income ($mil)
2021	B	2.01	0.97	2,445.4	165.9	112.5	30.2
2020	B+	2.03	1.05	2,112.8	148.5	83.3	23.7
2019	B+	2.11	1.14	1,950.0	137.0	159.5	38.9
2018	B+	2.62	1.39	1,591.1	117.7	112.5	33.4
2017	B+	2.76	1.45	1,403.0	98.6	97.4	26.8

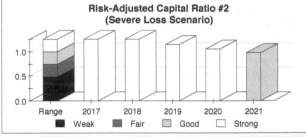

Risk-Adjusted Capital Ratio #2 (Severe Loss Scenario)

UNUM INS CO   C   Fair

Major Rating Factors: Fair overall results on stability tests (3.8 on a scale of 0 to 10). Weak profitability (2.2) with investment income below regulatory standards in relation to interest assumptions of reserves. Strong capitalization (9.4) based on excellent risk adjusted capital (severe loss scenario). Moreover, capital levels have been consistently high over the last five years.

Other Rating Factors: High quality investment portfolio (7.1). Excellent liquidity (7.8).

Principal Business: Group health insurance (99%) and individual life insurance (1%).

Principal Investments: NonCMO investment grade bonds (74%) and CMOs and structured securities (4%).

Investments in Affiliates: None

Group Affiliation: Unum Group

Licensed in: All states except NY, PR

Commenced Business: February 1966

Address: 2211 CONGRESS STREET, PORTLAND, ME 4122

Phone: (423) 294-1011 **Domicile State:** ME **NAIC Code:** 67601

Data Date	Rating	RACR #1	RACR #2	Total Assets ($mil)	Capital ($mil)	Net Premium ($mil)	Net Income ($mil)
2021	C	3.54	2.61	117.9	74.2	140.7	31.6
2020	C	4.30	2.78	79.0	48.9	48.0	1.8
2019	C	6.06	3.55	67.3	47.3	21.5	1.0
2018	C	6.92	4.51	62.8	46.9	4.8	1.2
2017	C	6.93	4.58	60.0	46.1	0.0	1.9

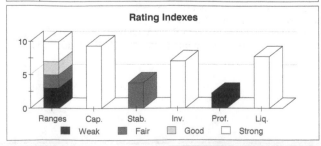

Rating Indexes

UNUM LIFE INS CO OF AMERICA

C+   **Fair**

Major Rating Factors: Fair quality investment portfolio (3.4 on a scale of 0 to 10) with large holdings of BBB rated bonds in addition to significant exposure to junk bonds. Fair profitability (4.6) with operating losses during 2021. Fair overall results on stability tests (3.4) including excessive premium growth.

Other Rating Factors: Good liquidity (6.9). Strong capitalization (7.1) based on excellent risk adjusted capital (severe loss scenario).

Principal Business: Group health insurance (64%), group life insurance (31%), individual health insurance (5%), and reinsurance (1%).

Principal Investments: NonCMO investment grade bonds (77%), noninv. grade bonds (10%), mortgages in good standing (5%), and CMOs and structured securities (2%).

Investments in Affiliates: None

Group Affiliation: Unum Group

Licensed in: All states except NY

Commenced Business: September 1966

Address: 2211 CONGRESS STREET, PORTLAND, ME 4122

Phone: (207) 575-2211   **Domicile State:** ME   **NAIC Code:** 62235

Data Date	Rating	RACR #1	RACR #2	Total Assets ($mil)	Capital ($mil)	Net Premium ($mil)	Net Income ($mil)
2021	C+	2.08	1.06	22,629.7	1,296.7	3,162.7	-27.9
2020	C+	3.30	1.46	21,791.5	1,598.7	1,996.1	332.7
2019	C+	2.29	1.22	22,429.8	1,765.8	3,755.0	454.8
2018	C+	2.41	1.28	22,022.4	1,834.2	3,616.2	493.2
2017	C+	2.35	1.24	21,455.0	1,728.0	3,486.2	378.2

Junk Bonds as a % of Capital

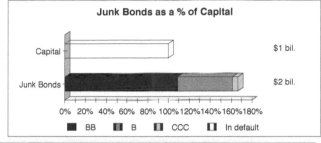

US FINANCIAL LIFE INS CO

B   **Good**

Major Rating Factors: Fair overall results on stability tests (4.2 on a scale of 0 to 10) including fair financial strength of affiliated AXA Financial Inc and negative cash flow from operations for 2021. Strong capitalization (10.0) based on excellent risk adjusted capital (severe loss scenario). Moreover, capital levels have been consistently high over the last five years. High quality investment portfolio (7.0).

Other Rating Factors: Excellent profitability (8.3) despite modest operating losses during 2018. Excellent liquidity (9.0).

Principal Business: Individual life insurance (100%).

Principal Investments: NonCMO investment grade bonds (63%), CMOs and structured securities (26%), noninv. grade bonds (5%), and common & preferred stock (3%).

Investments in Affiliates: None

Group Affiliation: AXA Financial Inc

Licensed in: All states except NY, PR

Commenced Business: September 1974

Address: 4000 Smith Road Suite 300, SCOTTSDALE, AZ 85253

Phone: (312) 220 0655   **Domicile State:** OH   **NAIC Code:** 84530

Data Date	Rating	RACR #1	RACR #2	Total Assets ($mil)	Capital ($mil)	Net Premium ($mil)	Net Income ($mil)
2021	B	11.12	5.24	373.7	124.5	0.0	5.8
2020	B	8.88	4.06	497.6	111.0	6.7	24.6
2019	B	4.25	2.29	529.3	91.1	29.7	4.8
2018	B	2.93	1.58	537.9	87.0	32.7	13.5
2017	B	3.09	1.67	541.4	73.4	36.0	9.0

AXA Financial Inc
Composite Group Rating: C+

Largest Group Members	Assets ($mil)	Rating
HERITAGE LIFE INS CO	7314	C+
US FINANCIAL LIFE INS CO	498	B
PROFESSIONAL LIFE CAS CO	12	C+

USAA LIFE INS CO *

B+   **Good**

Major Rating Factors: Good overall results on stability tests (5.2 on a scale of 0 to 10) despite negative cash flow from operations for 2021. Other stability subfactors include excellent risk diversification. Good quality investment portfolio (6.7) despite mixed results such as: large holdings of BBB rated bonds but moderate junk bond exposure. Good overall profitability (5.9) despite operating losses during 2021.

Other Rating Factors: Good liquidity (5.7). Strong capitalization (8.6) based on excellent risk adjusted capital (severe loss scenario).

Principal Business: Individual annuities (64%), individual life insurance (26%), and individual health insurance (10%).

Principal Investments: NonCMO investment grade bonds (72%), CMOs and structured securities (11%), mortgages in good standing (9%), noninv. grade bonds (3%), and misc. investments (3%).

Investments in Affiliates: None

Group Affiliation: USAA Group

Licensed in: All states except NY, PR

Commenced Business: August 1963

Address: 9800 Fredericksburg Rd, San Antonio, TX 78288

Phone: (210) 531-8722   **Domicile State:** TX   **NAIC Code:** 69663

Data Date	Rating	RACR #1	RACR #2	Total Assets ($mil)	Capital ($mil)	Net Premium ($mil)	Net Income ($mil)
2021	B+	3.83	2.09	26,197.9	2,583.2	-3,771.0	-32.1
2020	A	3.42	1.85	27,476.7	2,448.0	2,116.7	-37.6
2019	A	3.74	2.06	26,401.6	2,672.0	1,907.5	197.6
2018	A	3.78	2.06	25,390.9	2,537.3	1,816.4	245.5
2017	A	3.83	2.06	24,666.8	2,466.7	1,530.2	245.3

Rating Indexes

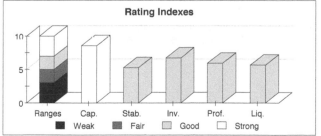

USAA LIFE INS CO OF NEW YORK | B | Good

Major Rating Factors: Good quality investment portfolio (6.2 on a scale of 0 to 10) despite mixed results such as: large holdings of BBB rated bonds but moderate junk bond exposure. Good liquidity (5.4) with sufficient resources to handle a spike in claims as well as a significant increase in policy surrenders. Fair profitability (3.9).

Other Rating Factors: Fair overall results on stability tests (4.1) including negative cash flow from operations for 2021. Strong overall capitalization (8.0) based on mixed results -- excessive policy leverage mitigated by excellent risk adjusted capital (severe loss scenario).

Principal Business: Individual annuities (63%) and individual life insurance (37%).

Principal Investments: NonCMO investment grade bonds (78%), CMOs and structured securities (13%), mortgages in good standing (3%), noninv. grade bonds (2%), and misc. investments (3%).

Investments in Affiliates: None

Group Affiliation: USAA Group

Licensed in: NY

Commenced Business: November 1997

Address: 529 Main Street, Highland Falls, NY 10928

Phone: (210) 531-8722 **Domicile State:** NY **NAIC Code:** 60228

Data Date	Rating	RACR #1	RACR #2	Total Assets ($mil)	Capital ($mil)	Net Premium ($mil)	Net Income ($mil)
2021	B	3.03	1.65	665.9	85.5	-159.2	10.0
2020	B	2.21	1.18	831.6	75.6	38.6	-12.5
2019	B+	2.35	1.25	793.5	78.2	33.8	-7.7
2018	B+	2.64	1.39	780.1	85.6	37.9	7.7
2017	B+	2.50	1.31	757.9	78.5	36.8	2.5

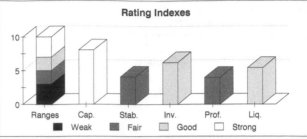

Rating Indexes

Ranges | Cap. | Stab. | Inv. | Prof. | Liq.
■ Weak ▨ Fair ▦ Good □ Strong

USABLE LIFE * | B+ | Good

Major Rating Factors: Good quality investment portfolio (6.3 on a scale of 0 to 10) despite mixed results such as: no exposure to mortgages and large holdings of BBB rated bonds but minimal holdings in junk bonds. Good liquidity (6.3) with sufficient resources to handle a spike in claims. Good overall results on stability tests (6.4) despite negative cash flow from operations for 2021 excellent operational trends and excellent risk diversification.

Other Rating Factors: Fair profitability (4.7) with operating losses during 2021. Strong capitalization (8.3) based on excellent risk adjusted capital (severe loss scenario).

Principal Business: Reinsurance (48%), group life insurance (24%), group health insurance (22%), individual health insurance (6%), and individual life insurance (1%).

Principal Investments: NonCMO investment grade bonds (79%), common & preferred stock (11%), CMOs and structured securities (9%), and policy loans (1%).

Investments in Affiliates: None

Group Affiliation: Arkansas Bl Cross Bl Shield Group

Licensed in: All states except NY, PR

Commenced Business: December 1980

Address: 320 W Capitol Suite 700, Little Rock, AR 72201

Phone: (501) 375-7200 **Domicile State:** AR **NAIC Code:** 94358

Data Date	Rating	RACR #1	RACR #2	Total Assets ($mil)	Capital ($mil)	Net Premium ($mil)	Net Income ($mil)
2021	B+	2.53	1.84	505.6	229.2	498.8	-5.1
2020	B+	2.74	2.00	502.6	235.0	467.4	10.3
2019	B+	2.81	2.07	476.2	230.5	458.5	17.6
2018	A-	2.84	2.13	514.7	273.8	572.6	142.5
2017	A-	2.80	2.10	535.3	278.1	586.1	37.8

Adverse Trends in Operations

Decrease in asset base during 2019 (7%)
Decrease in capital during 2019 (16%)
Decrease in premium volume from 2018 to 2019 (20%)
Decrease in premium volume from 2017 to 2018 (2%)
Decrease in asset base during 2018 (4%)

UTIC INS CO | B | Good

Major Rating Factors: Good overall results on stability tests (5.9 on a scale of 0 to 10). Stability strengths include excellent operational trends and good risk diversification. Fair quality investment portfolio (3.8). Fair profitability (4.5). Return on equity has been low, averaging 3.0%.

Other Rating Factors: Strong capitalization (8.6) based on excellent risk adjusted capital (severe loss scenario). Excellent liquidity (7.8).

Principal Business: Individual health insurance (53%) and reinsurance (47%).

Principal Investments: NonCMO investment grade bonds (61%), common & preferred stock (23%), cash (4%), CMOs and structured securities (2%), and noninv. grade bonds (1%).

Investments in Affiliates: None

Group Affiliation: Bl Cross & Bl Shield of AL Group

Licensed in: AL, PA, TN

Commenced Business: February 1964

Address: 450 Riverchase Parkway East, Birmingham, AL 35244

Phone: (205) 220-2100 **Domicile State:** AL **NAIC Code:** 81531

Data Date	Rating	RACR #1	RACR #2	Total Assets ($mil)	Capital ($mil)	Net Premium ($mil)	Net Income ($mil)
2021	B	3.51	2.07	165.0	46.7	15.2	7.9
2020	B	3.28	1.97	145.3	35.4	15.6	-2.4
2019	B	2.34	1.42	116.3	20.4	16.0	-2.2
2018	B+	2.64	1.66	101.4	22.8	20.0	1.3
2017	B+	2.60	1.66	94.4	22.8	21.0	2.5

Adverse Trends in Operations

Decrease in premium volume from 2019 to 2020 (2%)
Decrease in premium volume from 2018 to 2019 (20%)
Decrease in capital during 2019 (11%)
Decrease in premium volume from 2017 to 2018 (5%)
Decrease in premium volume from 2016 to 2017 (8%)

VANTIS LIFE INS CO   C+   Fair

Major Rating Factors: Fair quality investment portfolio (4.6 on a scale of 0 to 10) with large holdings of BBB rated bonds in addition to junk bond exposure equal to 84% of capital. Fair overall results on stability tests (3.1) including excessive premium growth, weak results on operational trends and negative cash flow from operations for 2021. Good liquidity (5.5).
Other Rating Factors: Weak profitability (1.9) with operating losses during 2021. Strong capitalization (7.6) based on excellent risk adjusted capital (severe loss scenario).
Principal Business: Individual life insurance (56%), individual annuities (38%), and group life insurance (6%).
Principal Investments: NonCMO investment grade bonds (70%), CMOs and structured securities (14%), noninv. grade bonds (8%), common & preferred stock (1%), and misc. investments (4%).
Investments in Affiliates: None
Group Affiliation: Penn Mutual Life Insurance Company
Licensed in: All states except NY, PR
Commenced Business: January 1964
Address: 200 Day Hill Road, Windsor, CT 6095
Phone: (860) 298-6000 **Domicile State:** CT **NAIC Code:** 68632

Data Date	Rating	RACR #1	RACR #2	Total Assets ($mil)	Capital ($mil)	Net Premium ($mil)	Net Income ($mil)
2021	C+	2.83	1.41	542.5	60.5	26.7	-7.1
2020	C+	3.00	1.47	544.1	68.4	17.1	-1.6
2019	C+	2.28	1.46	565.1	91.0	32.9	-1.9
2018	C+	1.71	1.14	523.8	63.7	120.7	-6.1
2017	C+	1.35	0.94	421.9	45.0	184.8	-1.8

Adverse Trends in Operations

Decrease in premium volume from 2019 to 2020 (48%)
Decrease in capital during 2020 (25%)
Decrease in premium volume from 2018 to 2019 (73%)
Increase in policy surrenders from 2017 to 2018 (141%)
Decrease in premium volume from 2017 to 2018 (35%)

VARIABLE ANNUITY LIFE INS CO   B   Good

Major Rating Factors: Good overall results on stability tests (5.8 on a scale of 0 to 10). Stability strengths include excellent operational trends and excellent risk diversification. Good quality investment portfolio (5.5) despite large holdings of BBB rated bonds in addition to junk bond exposure equal to 87% of capital. Exposure to mortgages is significant, but the mortgage default rate has been low. Good liquidity (5.3).
Other Rating Factors: Strong capitalization (7.5) based on excellent risk adjusted capital (severe loss scenario). Excellent profitability (7.9) with operating gains in each of the last five years.
Principal Business: Individual annuities (56%) and group retirement contracts (44%).
Principal Investments: NonCMO investment grade bonds (53%), CMOs and structured securities (21%), mortgages in good standing (14%), noninv. grade bonds (5%), and policy loans (1%).
Investments in Affiliates: 1%
Group Affiliation: American International Group
Licensed in: All states except PR
Commenced Business: May 1969
Address: 2929 Allen Parkway, Houston, TX 77019
Phone: (800) 448-2542 **Domicile State:** TX **NAIC Code:** 70238

Data Date	Rating	RACR #1	RACR #2	Total Assets ($mil)	Capital ($mil)	Net Premium ($mil)	Net Income ($mil)
2021	B	2.63	1.30	95,249.3	3,280.6	3,931.3	687.9
2020	B	2.47	1.21	91,110.5	2,905.6	3,999.2	563.0
2019	B	2.37	1.14	85,830.0	2,600.3	4,607.1	431.5
2018	B	2.39	1.12	78,453.7	2,689.6	4,844.4	682.1
2017	B	2.49	1.19	81,665.0	2,800.0	4,179.0	639.7

Adverse Trends in Operations

Decrease in premium volume from 2019 to 2020 (13%)
Decrease in capital during 2019 (3%)
Decrease in premium volume from 2018 to 2019 (5%)
Decrease in asset base during 2018 (4%)
Decrease in premium volume from 2016 to 2017 (9%)

VENERABLE INS AND ANNTY CO   C   Fair

Major Rating Factors: Fair current capitalization (4.4 on a scale of 0 to 10) based on mixed results -- excessive policy leverage mitigated by fair risk adjusted capital (moderate loss scenario), although results have slipped from the good range over the last year. Fair quality investment portfolio (4.8) with large holdings of BBB rated bonds in addition to moderate junk bond exposure. Exposure to mortgages is significant, but the mortgage default rate has been low. Good liquidity (5.7).
Other Rating Factors: Weak overall results on stability tests (2.6) including fair financial strength of affiliated Voya Financial Inc and weak results on operational trends. Weak profitability (1.9) with operating losses during 2021.
Principal Business: Individual annuities (58%), individual life insurance (26%), and group retirement contracts (16%).
Principal Investments: NonCMO investment grade bonds (43%), CMOs and structured securities (19%), mortgages in good standing (17%), common & preferred stock (13%), and noninv. grade bonds (3%).
Investments in Affiliates: 16%
Group Affiliation: Voya Financial Inc
Licensed in: All states except NY, PR
Commenced Business: October 1973
Address: 909 LOCUST STREET, DES MOINES, IA 50309-3942
Phone: (610) 425-4310 **Domicile State:** IA **NAIC Code:** 80942

Data Date	Rating	RACR #1	RACR #2	Total Assets ($mil)	Capital ($mil)	Net Premium ($mil)	Net Income ($mil)
2021	C	0.88	0.68	38,977.6	2,087.2	-4,618.6	-1,268.9
2020	B-	1.31	0.93	49,487.8	2,685.8	3.1	128.8
2019	B-	1.16	0.82	50,251.8	2,441.4	7.9	99.8
2018	B-	1.11	0.78	50,810.6	2,221.2	-18,517.7	-225.0
2017	B-	1.70	0.84	58,725.1	1,835.2	1,806.7	513.7

Policy Leverage

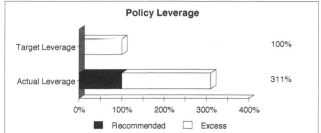

Target Leverage — 100%
Actual Leverage — 311%

0% 100% 200% 300% 400%

■ Recommended □ Excess

VOYA RETIREMENT INS & ANNUITY CO *   B+   Good

Major Rating Factors: Good quality investment portfolio (5.6 on a scale of 0 to 10) despite large holdings of BBB rated bonds in addition to junk bond exposure equal to 61% of capital. Exposure to mortgages is significant, but the mortgage default rate has been low. Good liquidity (6.1) with sufficient resources to handle a spike in claims as well as a significant increase in policy surrenders. Good overall results on stability tests (5.1) good historical risk adjusted capital and excellent risk diversification.

Other Rating Factors: Strong capitalization (7.1) based on excellent risk adjusted capital (severe loss scenario). Excellent profitability (7.4) with operating gains in each of the last five years.

Principal Business: Group retirement contracts (99%) and individual life insurance (1%).

Principal Investments: NonCMO investment grade bonds (51%), CMOs and structured securities (21%), mortgages in good standing (14%), noninv. grade bonds (3%), and misc. investments (6%).

Investments in Affiliates: 2%

Group Affiliation: Voya Financial Inc

Licensed in: All states, the District of Columbia and Puerto Rico

Commenced Business: April 1976

Address: ONE ORANGE WAY, WINDSOR, CT 06095-4774

Phone: (860) 580-4646 **Domicile State:** CT **NAIC Code:** 86509

Data Date	Rating	RACR #1	RACR #2	Total Assets ($mil)	Capital ($mil)	Net Premium ($mil)	Net Income ($mil)
2021	B+	2.13	1.08	129,000	2,232.0	7,984.3	794.1
2020	B+	2.02	0.98	122,000	2,040.3	16,099.9	299.3
2019	B+	2.11	1.03	112,000	2,004.9	12,351.6	325.5
2018	B+	2.18	1.06	100,000.0	2,000.0	12,253.6	377.0
2017	B+	2.05	1.00	105,000	1,792.7	12,592.5	194.9

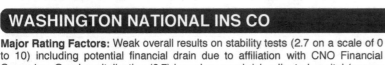

Rating Indexes

Ranges | Cap. | Stab. | Inv. | Prof. | Liq.
■ Weak   ■ Fair   ▨ Good   ☐ Strong

WASHINGTON NATIONAL INS CO   D+   Weak

Major Rating Factors: Weak overall results on stability tests (2.7 on a scale of 0 to 10) including potential financial drain due to affiliation with CNO Financial Group Inc. Good capitalization (6.7) based on good risk adjusted capital (severe loss scenario). Good quality investment portfolio (5.3).

Other Rating Factors: Good liquidity (6.4). Excellent profitability (7.0) with operating gains in each of the last five years.

Principal Business: Individual health insurance (58%), group health insurance (31%), individual life insurance (7%), reinsurance (3%), and individual annuities (1%).

Principal Investments: NonCMO investment grade bonds (72%), CMOs and structured securities (15%), noninv. grade bonds (3%), common & preferred stock (2%), and misc. investments (8%).

Investments in Affiliates: 1%

Group Affiliation: CNO Financial Group Inc

Licensed in: All states except NY

Commenced Business: September 1923

Address: 11825 NORTH PENNSYLVANIA STREE, CARMEL, IN 46032

Phone: (317) 817-6100 **Domicile State:** IN **NAIC Code:** 70319

Data Date	Rating	RACR #1	RACR #2	Total Assets ($mil)	Capital ($mil)	Net Premium ($mil)	Net Income ($mil)
2021	D+	1.66	0.96	5,828.8	361.0	731.3	57.3
2020	D+	1.65	0.95	5,742.1	361.7	731.2	65.2
2019	D+	1.56	0.93	5,604.2	347.6	717.0	59.5
2018	D+	1.52	0.89	5,466.1	365.8	703.3	61.2
2017	D+	1.71	0.95	5,418.5	373.2	688.9	26.7

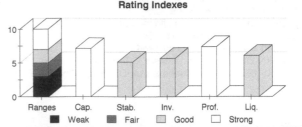

CNO Financial Group Inc Composite Group Rating: D+ Largest Group Members	Assets ($mil)	Rating
BANKERS LIFE CAS CO	17025	D+
WASHINGTON NATIONAL INS CO	5742	D+
COLONIAL PENN LIFE INS CO	894	D+
BANKERS CONSECO LIFE INS CO	537	D

WEA INS CORP   C   Fair

Major Rating Factors: Fair quality investment portfolio (3.7 on a scale of 0 to 10). Fair overall results on stability tests (3.7) including negative cash flow from operations for 2021. Good current capitalization (6.0) based on good risk adjusted capital (severe loss scenario), although results have slipped from the excellent range over the last year.

Other Rating Factors: Good liquidity (5.8). Weak profitability (1.8) with operating losses during 2021.

Principal Business: Group health insurance (100%).

Principal Investments: NonCMO investment grade bonds (48%), common & preferred stock (27%), CMOs and structured securities (16%), and cash (2%).

Investments in Affiliates: 3%

Group Affiliation: Wisconsin Education Assn Ins Trust

Licensed in: WI

Commenced Business: July 1985

Address: 45 NOB HILL ROAD, Madison, WI 53713-0000

Phone: (608) 276-4000 **Domicile State:** WI **NAIC Code:** 72273

Data Date	Rating	RACR #1	RACR #2	Total Assets ($mil)	Capital ($mil)	Net Premium ($mil)	Net Income ($mil)
2021	C	1.22	0.88	786.8	163.2	651.3	-34.4
2020	C	1.53	1.08	790.8	197.8	641.7	11.0
2019	C	1.47	1.05	701.8	170.2	585.2	-31.5
2018	C	1.52	1.10	661.5	170.7	603.8	20.2
2017	C	1.85	1.27	661.0	167.0	466.6	1.4

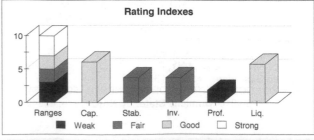

Rating Indexes

Ranges | Cap. | Stab. | Inv. | Prof. | Liq.
■ Weak   ■ Fair   ▨ Good   ☐ Strong

WEST COAST LIFE INS CO   B   Good

Major Rating Factors: Good liquidity (5.8 on a scale of 0 to 10) with sufficient resources to handle a spike in claims as well as a significant increase in policy surrenders. Fair overall results on stability tests (4.3) including negative cash flow from operations for 2021. Fair quality investment portfolio (4.4).

Other Rating Factors: Strong capitalization (7.6) based on excellent risk adjusted capital (severe loss scenario). Excellent profitability (7.5) with operating gains in each of the last five years.

Principal Business: Individual life insurance (98%) and reinsurance (2%).

Principal Investments: NonCMO investment grade bonds (70%), mortgages in good standing (11%), noninv. grade bonds (7%), CMOs and structured securities (4%), and misc. investments (8%).

Investments in Affiliates: None

Group Affiliation: Dai-ichi Life Holdings Inc

Licensed in: All states except NY, PR

Commenced Business: February 1915

Address: 10306 REGENCY PARKWAY DRIVE, OMAHA, NE 68114

Phone: (205) 268-1000 **Domicile State:** NE **NAIC Code:** 70335

Data Date	Rating	RACR #1	RACR #2	Total Assets ($mil)	Capital ($mil)	Net Premium ($mil)	Net Income ($mil)
2021	B	2.91	1.42	4,377.3	403.8	2.2	122.5
2020	B-	2.46	1.20	4,374.6	370.4	3.0	337.1
2019	B-	2.77	1.35	5,348.0	442.2	-81.5	30.8
2018	B-	2.60	1.26	5,336.5	411.9	-26.3	63.7
2017	B-	2.65	1.29	5,244.8	400.9	-21.1	70.5

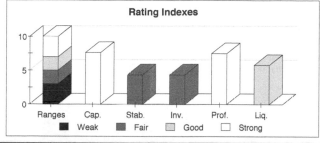

Rating Indexes

WESTERN & SOUTHERN LIFE INS CO   B   Good

Major Rating Factors: Good overall results on stability tests (5.7 on a scale of 0 to 10). Stability strengths include excellent operational trends and excellent risk diversification. Fair quality investment portfolio (3.4). Strong capitalization (7.4) based on excellent risk adjusted capital (severe loss scenario). Capital levels have been relatively consistent over the last five years.

Other Rating Factors: Excellent profitability (7.7) with operating gains in each of the last five years. Excellent liquidity (7.0).

Principal Business: Individual life insurance (88%), individual health insurance (10%), group life insurance (2%), and reinsurance (1%).

Principal Investments: Common & preferred stock (49%), nonCMO investment grade bonds (24%), CMOs and structured securities (3%), policy loans (1%), and misc. investments (22%).

Investments in Affiliates: 59%

Group Affiliation: Western & Southern Group

Licensed in: All states except AK, ME, MA, NY, PR

Commenced Business: April 1888

Address: 400 BROADWAY, CINCINNATI, OH 45202

Phone: (513) 357-4000 **Domicile State:** OH **NAIC Code:** 70483

Data Date	Rating	RACR #1	RACR #2	Total Assets ($mil)	Capital ($mil)	Net Premium ($mil)	Net Income ($mil)
2021	B	1.36	1.24	12,681.6	6,756.1	220.3	98.7
2020	B	1.33	1.23	11,180.1	5,657.7	226.2	100.6
2019	B	1.31	1.21	10,903.1	5,428.0	231.8	158.8
2018	B	1.38	1.28	10,112.6	4,937.1	237.1	415.1
2017	B	2.03	1.70	10,551.5	5,099.3	246.7	269.7

Adverse Trends in Operations

Decrease in premium volume from 2019 to 2020 (2%)
Decrease in premium volume from 2017 to 2018 (4%)
Decrease in asset base during 2018 (4%)
Decrease in capital during 2018 (3%)
Decrease in premium volume from 2016 to 2017 (3%)

WESTERN UNITED LIFE ASR CO   B-   Good

Major Rating Factors: Good capitalization (5.8 on a scale of 0 to 10) based on good risk adjusted capital (moderate loss scenario). Moreover, capital levels have been consistent over the last five years. Good liquidity (6.0) with sufficient resources to handle a spike in claims as well as a significant increase in policy surrenders. Good overall results on stability tests (5.0) despite excessive premium growth excellent operational trends and excellent risk diversification.

Other Rating Factors: Fair quality investment portfolio (4.0). Fair profitability (4.8) with investment income below regulatory standards in relation to interest assumptions of reserves.

Principal Business: Individual annuities (90%) and individual health insurance (10%).

Principal Investments: NonCMO investment grade bonds (63%), mortgages in good standing (13%), CMOs and structured securities (13%), noninv. grade bonds (2%), and misc. investments (6%).

Investments in Affiliates: 1%

Group Affiliation: Manhattan Life Group Inc

Licensed in: All states except NY, PR

Commenced Business: February 1975

Address: 929 West Sprague Ave, Spokane, WA 99201

Phone: (713) 529-0045 **Domicile State:** WA **NAIC Code:** 85189

Data Date	Rating	RACR #1	RACR #2	Total Assets ($mil)	Capital ($mil)	Net Premium ($mil)	Net Income ($mil)
2021	B-	1.55	0.81	1,473.0	102.0	352.9	3.1
2020	B-	1.64	0.86	1,283.4	95.5	246.1	6.0
2019	B-	1.65	0.80	1,225.1	80.2	203.5	3.5
2018	B-	1.66	0.80	1,223.1	79.4	157.7	5.1
2017	B-	1.70	0.82	1,201.0	78.0	138.5	7.8

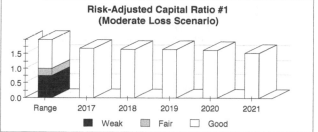

Risk-Adjusted Capital Ratio #1
(Moderate Loss Scenario)

WESTERN-SOUTHERN LIFE ASR CO
| | B | Good |

Major Rating Factors: Good overall results on stability tests (5.9 on a scale of 0 to 10). Stability strengths include good operational trends, good risk adjusted capital for prior years and excellent risk diversification. Good liquidity (6.4) with sufficient resources to handle a spike in claims as well as a significant increase in policy surrenders. Fair quality investment portfolio (4.3).
Other Rating Factors: Strong capitalization (7.0) based on excellent risk adjusted capital (severe loss scenario). Excellent profitability (7.4).
Principal Business: Individual annuities (86%), individual life insurance (8%), and group retirement contracts (6%).
Principal Investments: NonCMO investment grade bonds (36%), CMOs and structured securities (32%), mortgages in good standing (15%), noninv. grade bonds (8%), and common & preferred stock (5%).
Investments in Affiliates: 3%
Group Affiliation: Western & Southern Group
Licensed in: All states except NY, PR
Commenced Business: March 1981
Address: 400 BROADWAY, CINCINNATI, OH 45202
Phone: (513) 357-4000 **Domicile State:** OH **NAIC Code:** 92622

Data Date	Rating	RACR #1	RACR #2	Total Assets ($mil)	Capital ($mil)	Net Premium ($mil)	Net Income ($mil)
2021	B	1.90	1.03	19,537.6	1,539.3	2,988.2	118.4
2020	B	1.78	0.94	17,043.5	1,196.8	2,878.6	82.3
2019	B	1.89	1.01	14,808.2	1,068.7	2,293.7	81.6
2018	B	1.93	1.05	13,029.4	939.8	1,420.1	16.1
2017	B	1.99	1.11	12,452.5	980.6	1,177.9	69.8

Adverse Trends in Operations

Change in premium mix from 2018 to 2019 (6%)
Decrease in capital during 2018 (4%)
Change in premium mix from 2017 to 2018 (8.6%)
Change in premium mix from 2016 to 2017 (7.3%)
Decrease in capital during 2017 (10%)

WILCAC LIFE INS CO
| | C | Fair |

Major Rating Factors: Fair overall results on stability tests (4.0 on a scale of 0 to 10) including fair financial strength of affiliated Wilton Re Holdings Ltd and negative cash flow from operations for 2021. Fair quality investment portfolio (4.2) with large holdings of BBB rated bonds in addition to significant exposure to junk bonds. Good overall profitability (5.1).
Other Rating Factors: Good liquidity (5.6). Strong capitalization (7.1) based on excellent risk adjusted capital (severe loss scenario).
Principal Business: N/A
Principal Investments: NonCMO investment grade bonds (47%), CMOs and structured securities (20%), noninv. grade bonds (7%), common & preferred stock (5%), and misc. investments (19%).
Investments in Affiliates: None
Group Affiliation: Wilton Re Holdings Ltd
Licensed in: All states except NY
Commenced Business: August 1911
Address: 1275A SANDUSKY ROAD, JACKSONVILLE, IL 62650
Phone: (203) 762-4400 **Domicile State:** IL **NAIC Code:** 62413

Data Date	Rating	RACR #1	RACR #2	Total Assets ($mil)	Capital ($mil)	Net Premium ($mil)	Net Income ($mil)
2021	C	2.14	1.05	5,581.8	238.6	108.6	3.9
2020	C-	1.97	0.95	5,498.9	210.1	120.7	-10.6
2019	C	3.28	1.57	2,975.8	90.9	696.1	-21.9
2018	C	4.93	2.25	2,289.2	120.5	-5.6	13.1
2017	C	5.41	2.47	2,378.3	143.2	-1,561.9	10.3

Wilton Re Holdings Ltd Composite Group Rating: C Largest Group Members	Assets ($mil)	Rating
WILTON REASSURANCE CO	18452	C
WILCAC LIFE INS CO	5499	C-
TEXAS LIFE INS CO	1471	C+
WILTON REASSURANCE LIFE CO OF NY	875	C+

WILLIAM PENN LIFE INS CO OF NEW YORK
| | C | Fair |

Major Rating Factors: Fair overall results on stability tests (3.6 on a scale of 0 to 10) including fair financial strength of affiliated Legal & General America Inc. Fair overall capitalization (4.0) based on excellent risk adjusted capital (severe loss scenario). However, capital levels have fluctuated somewhat during past years. Fair profitability (4.7) with investment income below regulatory standards in relation to interest assumptions of reserves.
Other Rating Factors: Good quality investment portfolio (5.9). Good liquidity (6.7).
Principal Business: Individual life insurance (96%) and group retirement contracts (3%).
Principal Investments: NonCMO investment grade bonds (56%), mortgages in good standing (14%), noninv. grade bonds (8%), CMOs and structured securities (6%), and policy loans (2%).
Investments in Affiliates: None
Group Affiliation: Legal & General America Inc
Licensed in: AZ, CT, DC, FL, ID, IA, KS, KY, MD, MS, MT, NJ, NY, OK, OR, PA, RI, SC, SD, TX, VT
Commenced Business: February 1963
Address: 70 EAST SUNRISE HWY STE 500, VALLEY STREAM, NY 11581
Phone: (301) 279-4800 **Domicile State:** NY **NAIC Code:** 66230

Data Date	Rating	RACR #1	RACR #2	Total Assets ($mil)	Capital ($mil)	Net Premium ($mil)	Net Income ($mil)
2021	C	2.77	1.35	1,356.2	123.8	71.9	48.9
2020	C	2.90	1.40	1,325.0	130.8	-133.9	50.6
2019	C	2.44	1.18	1,317.5	104.5	24.8	31.0
2018	C	2.23	1.08	1,194.1	102.8	-316.9	-216.5
2017	C-	2.53	1.20	1,185.2	110.1	24.0	35.4

Legal General America Inc Composite Group Rating: C- Largest Group Members	Assets ($mil)	Rating
BANNER LIFE INS CO	6462	C-
WILLIAM PENN LIFE INS CO OF NEW YORK	1325	C

WILTON REASSURANCE CO
C   Fair

Major Rating Factors: Fair capitalization for the current period (4.0 on a scale of 0 to 10) based on good risk adjusted capital (moderate loss scenario) reflecting some improvement over results in 2017. Fair quality investment portfolio (4.8) with large holdings of BBB rated bonds in addition to junk bond exposure equal to 60% of capital. Fair overall results on stability tests (3.4) including weak risk adjusted capital in prior years, negative cash flow from operations for 2021.

Other Rating Factors: Good overall profitability (5.7). Good liquidity (5.9).

Principal Business: Reinsurance (100%).

Principal Investments: NonCMO investment grade bonds (58%), CMOs and structured securities (16%), common & preferred stock (7%), noninv. grade bonds (6%), and misc. investments (14%).

Investments in Affiliates: 5%

Group Affiliation: Wilton Re Holdings Ltd

Licensed in: All states except PR

Commenced Business: February 1901

Address: 5TH AVE TOWERS 100 S 5TH ST, MINNEAPOLIS, MN 55402

Phone: (203) 762-4400 **Domicile State:** MN **NAIC Code:** 66133

Data Date	Rating	RACR #1	RACR #2	Total Assets ($mil)	Capital ($mil)	Net Premium ($mil)	Net Income ($mil)
2021	C	1.01	0.71	22,558.5	1,372.7	4,356.0	256.9
2020	C	0.92	0.51	18,452.1	644.5	-1,224.4	-38.1
2019	C	0.83	0.54	18,346.6	843.6	340.6	86.4
2018	D+	0.68	0.47	18,607.3	950.2	3,849.6	44.8
2017	C	0.68	0.46	15,004.1	655.7	190.1	21.4

Risk-Adjusted Capital Ratio #1 (Moderate Loss Scenario)

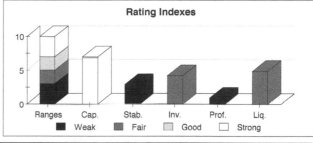

WILTON REASSURANCE LIFE CO OF NY
C-   Fair

Major Rating Factors: Fair quality investment portfolio (4.2 on a scale of 0 to 10) with large holdings of BBB rated bonds in addition to moderate junk bond exposure. Fair liquidity (4.9) as cash from operations and sale of marketable assets may not be adequate to cover a spike in claims or a run on policy withdrawals. Weak profitability (0.9) with operating losses during 2021.

Other Rating Factors: Weak overall results on stability tests (2.9) including negative cash flow from operations for 2021. Strong overall capitalization (7.0) based on mixed results -- excessive policy leverage mitigated by excellent risk adjusted capital (severe loss scenario).

Principal Business: Individual life insurance (88%), individual health insurance (7%), individual annuities (4%), group retirement contracts (1%), and group health insurance (1%).

Principal Investments: NonCMO investment grade bonds (72%), mortgages in good standing (7%), noninv. grade bonds (6%), CMOs and structured securities (6%), and misc. investments (9%).

Investments in Affiliates: None

Group Affiliation: Wilton Re Holdings Ltd

Licensed in: All states except PR

Commenced Business: November 1956

Address: 800 WESTCHESTER AVE STE 641 N, RYE BROOK, NY 10573

Phone: (203) 762-4400 **Domicile State:** NY **NAIC Code:** 60704

Data Date	Rating	RACR #1	RACR #2	Total Assets ($mil)	Capital ($mil)	Net Premium ($mil)	Net Income ($mil)
2021	C-	2.09	1.00	7,515.8	327.6	-4,000.0	-931.2
2020	C+	1.92	0.91	874.9	81.2	10.6	-11.7
2019	C+	2.42	1.16	871.9	103.2	11.0	12.9
2018	C+	2.53	1.25	875.3	100.0	12.2	8.7
2017	B-	2.58	1.30	895.8	92.9	14.2	7.8

Rating Indexes

ZURICH AMERICAN LIFE INS CO
C-   Fair

Major Rating Factors: Fair overall results on stability tests (3.1 on a scale of 0 to 10) including excessive premium growth and negative cash flow from operations for 2021. Weak profitability (1.7) with operating losses during 2021. Return on equity has been low, averaging -29.4%. Good capitalization (6.9) based on good risk adjusted capital (severe loss scenario).

Other Rating Factors: High quality investment portfolio (7.9). Excellent liquidity (7.1).

Principal Business: Group life insurance (29%), group retirement contracts (26%), individual annuities (21%), individual life insurance (19%), and group health insurance (5%).

Principal Investments: NonCMO investment grade bonds (65%), policy loans (14%), CMOs and structured securities (13%), and common & preferred stock (2%).

Investments in Affiliates: 2%

Group Affiliation: Zurich Financial Services Group

Licensed in: All states except NY, PR

Commenced Business: September 1947

Address: 1400 AMERICAN LANE, SCHAUMBURG, IL 60196-1056

Phone: (877) 301-5376 **Domicile State:** IL **NAIC Code:** 90557

Data Date	Rating	RACR #1	RACR #2	Total Assets ($mil)	Capital ($mil)	Net Premium ($mil)	Net Income ($mil)
2021	C-	1.66	0.99	16,900.4	163.6	862.8	-0.9
2020	C-	1.76	1.03	15,906.9	164.3	614.1	-79.1
2019	C-	1.85	1.07	15,201.3	166.2	1,059.8	-48.6
2018	C	1.69	0.96	14,048.2	126.0	-88.9	-55.7
2017	C	1.62	0.92	14,226.5	119.6	1,579.9	-33.4

Rating Indexes

Section III

Weiss Ratings
Recommended Companies

A compilation of those
U.S. Life and Annuity Insurers
receiving a Weiss Safety Rating
of A+, A, A- or B+.

Companies are listed in alphabetical order.

Section III Contents

This section provides a list of recommended carriers along with additional information you should have when shopping for insurance. It contains all insurers receiving a Weiss Safety Rating of A+, A, A-, or B+. If an insurer is not on this list, it should not be automatically assumed that the firm is weak. Indeed, there are many firms that have not achieved a B+ or better rating but are in relatively good condition with adequate resources to cover their risk during an average recession. Not being included in this list should not be construed as a recommendation to surrender policies.

Left Pages

1. **Safety Rating**
   Our rating is measured on a scale from A to F and considers a wide range of factors. Highly-rated companies are, in our opinion, less likely to experience financial difficulties than lower rated firms. See *About Weiss Safety Ratings* for more information.

2. **Insurance Company Name**
   The legally registered name, which can sometimes differ from the name that the company uses for advertising. An insurer's name can be very similar to the name of other companies which may not be on our Recommended List, so make sure you note the exact name before contacting your agent.

3. **Address**
   The address of the main office where you can contact the firm for additional financial data or for the location of local branches and/or registered agents.

4. **Telephone Number**
   The number to call for additional financial data or for the phone numbers of local branches and/or registered agents.

Right Pages

The right-side pages present the percentage of the company's business that is involved in each type of insurance. Specifically, the numbers shown are the amounts of premium (including certain annuity payments and other deposit funds not technically called premiums) for each line of business as a percent of total premiums. The amounts shown are net premiums and, therefore, include only policies for which the company carries risk.

1. **Domicile State**
   The state which has primary regulatory responsibility for the company. It may differ from the location of the company's corporate headquarters. You do not have to be living in the domicile state to purchase insurance from this firm, provided it is licensed to do business in your state.

2. **Individual Life**
   Life insurance policies offered to individual customers where a single contract covers a single person.

3. **Individual Health**
   Health insurance policies for individual customers that are acquired by a person on his/her own, not through an employer.

4. **Individual Annuities** A retirement investment vehicle for individual customers which may be fixed and/or variable annuity contracts.

5. **Group Life** Life insurance policies that can only be acquired through an employer, a public institution, or a union.

6. **Group Health** Health insurance policies for groups such as the employees of a corporation, public institution or union.

7. **Group Annuities** Annuity contracts for groups such as the employees of a corporation, public institution or union.

8. **Credit Life** Life insurance policies designed to protect lenders against the eventual death of the borrower. Typically, if the borrower dies, the policy guarantees repayment of the loan balance.

9. **Credit Health** Health insurance policies designed to protect lenders against the sickness of the borrower. Typically, if the borrower becomes ill, the policy guarantees repayment of the loan balance.

10. **Supplemental Contracts** Policies in which the premium is paid from the benefits of another contract.

Weiss Safety Ratings are not deemed to be a recommendation concerning the purchase or sale of the securities of any insurance company that is publicly owned.

RATING	INSURANCE COMPANY NAME	ADDRESS	CITY	STATE	ZIP	PHONE
B+	ADVANCE INS CO OF KANSAS	1133 SW TOPEKA BLVD	TOPEKA	KS	66629	(800) 530-5989
B+	AMERICAN CONTINENTAL INS CO	1021 REAMS FLEMING BOULEVARD	FRANKLIN	TN	37064	(800) 264-4000
A	AMERICAN FAMILY LIFE ASR CO OF NY	22 CORPORATE WOODS BOULEVARD S	ALBANY	NY	12211	(800) 992-3522
A+	AMERICAN FAMILY LIFE INS CO	6000 AMERICAN PARKWAY	MADISON	WI	53783	(800) 692-6326
B+	AMERICAN FIDELITY ASR CO	9000 CAMERON PARKWAY	OKLAHOMA CITY	OK	73114	(800) 654-8489
B+	AMERICAN HEALTH & LIFE INS CO	3001 MEACHAM BOULEVARD SUITE 1	FORT WORTH	TX	76137	(800) 307-0048
A-	AMICA LIFE INS CO	100 AMICA WAY	LINCOLN	RI	02865	(800) 652-6422
A-	ANNUITY INVESTORS LIFE INS CO	301 EAST FOURTH STREET	CINCINNATI	OH	45202	(888) 497-8556
B+	ASSURITY LIFE INS CO	2000 Q STREET	LINCOLN	NE	68503	(800) 869-0355
A	BERKLEY LIFE & HEALTH INS CO	11201 DOUGLAS AVE	URBANDALE	IA	50322	(800) 866-2308
B+	BEST LIFE & HEALTH INS CO	AUSTIN	AUSTIN	TX	78752	(800) 433-0088
A-	BLUEBONNET LIFE INS CO	3545 LAKELAND DR	FLOWOOD	MS	39232	(800) 222-8046
B+	BOSTON MUTUAL LIFE INS CO	120 ROYALL STREET	CANTON	MA	02021	(800) 669-2668
A-	CENTRAL STATES H & L CO OF OMAHA	1212 NORTH 96TH STREET	OMAHA	NE	68114	(800) 826-6587
A+	CHESAPEAKE LIFE INS CO	1833 SOUTH MORGAN ROAD	OKLAHOMA CITY	OK	73128	(800) 733-1110
B+	CHRISTIAN FIDELITY LIFE INS CO	1999 BRYAN STREET SUITE 900	DALLAS	TX	75201	(866) 361-1634
B+	CM LIFE INS CO	100 BRIGHT MEADOW BOULEVARD	ENFIELD	CT	6082	(800) 272-2216
B+	COMPANION LIFE INS CO	2501 FARAWAY DRIVE	COLUMBIA	SC	29219	(800) 753-0404
B+	COMPANION LIFE INS CO OF CA	731 SANSOME STREET 2ND FLOOR	SAN FRANCISCO	CA	94111	(800) 421-2368
A-	COUNTRY INVESTORS LIFE ASR CO	1701 TOWANDA AVENUE	BLOOMINGTON	IL	61701	(866) 268-6879
A+	COUNTRY LIFE INS CO	1701 TOWANDA AVENUE	BLOOMINGTON	IL	61701	(866) 268-6879
A-	DELAWARE AMERICAN LIFE INS CO	1209 ORANGE STREET	WILMINGTON	DE	19801	(302) 594-2000
A	DIRECT GENERAL LIFE INS CO	911 CHESTNUT STREET	ORANGEBURG	SC	29115	(877) 463-4732
A	EMPIRE FIDELITY INVESTMENTS L I C	640 FIFTH AVENUE 5TH FLOOR	NEW YORK	NY	10019	(800) 634-9361
B+	ENTERPRISE LIFE INS CO	300 BURNETT STREET SUITE 200	FORT WORTH	TX	76102	(817) 878-3300
B+	FARM BUREAU LIFE INS CO	5400 UNIVERSITY AVENUE	WEST DES MOINES	IA	50266	(800) 247-4170
A-	FARM BUREAU LIFE INS CO OF MICHIGAN	7373 WEST SAGINAW HIGHWAY	LANSING	MI	48917	(800) 292-2680
A	FEDERATED LIFE INS CO	121 EAST PARK SQUARE	OWATONNA	MN	55060	(888) 333-4949
A	FIDELITY INVESTMENTS LIFE INS CO	49 NORTH 400 WEST 6TH FLOOR	SALT LAKE CITY	UT	84101	(800) 634-9361
A-	FIDELITY SECURITY LIFE INS CO	3130 BROADWAY	KANSAS CITY	MO	64111	(816) 756-1060
A-	FIDELITY SECURITY LIFE INS CO OF NY	162 PROSPECT HILL ROAD SUITE 1	BREWSTER	NY	10509	(800) 821-7303
A-	FIRST RELIANCE STANDARD LIFE INS CO	590 MADISON AVENUE 29TH FLOOR	NEW YORK	NY	10022	(800) 353-3986
A	FRANDISCO LIFE INS CO	135 EAST TUGALO STREET	TOCCOA	GA	30577	(706) 886-7571
B+	FREEDOM LIFE INS CO OF AMERICA	300 BURNETT STREET SUITE 200	FORT WORTH	TX	76102	(817) 878-3300
A	GARDEN STATE LIFE INS CO	ONE MOODY PLAZA	GALVESTON	TX	77550	(800) 638-8565
B+	GERBER LIFE INS CO	1311 MAMARONECK AVENUE SUITE 3	WHITE PLAINS	NY	10605	(800) 704-2180
A	GUARDIAN LIFE INS CO OF AMERICA	10 HUDSON YARDS	NEW YORK	NY	10001	(800) 441-6455
B+	HM LIFE INS CO	120 FIFTH AVENUE	PITTSBURGH	PA	15222	(800) 328-5433
B+	ILLINOIS MUTUAL LIFE INS CO	300 SW ADAMS STREET	PEORIA	IL	61634	(800) 437-7355
B+	LIFE INS CO OF BOSTON & NEW YORK	4300 CAMP ROAD PO BOX 331	ATHOL SPRINGS	NY	14010	(800) 645-2317
B+	M LIFE INS CO	THE CORPORATION COMPANY 7700 E	CENTENNIAL	CO	80112	(503) 414-7336
A-	NATIONAL BENEFIT LIFE INS CO	30-30 47TH AVENUE SUITE 625	LONG ISLAND CITY	NY	11101	(800) 222-2062
B+	NATIONAL FARMERS UNION LIFE INS CO	PO BOX 139061	DALLAS	TX	75313	(800) 366-6565
A	NATIONAL FOUNDATION LIFE INS CO	300 BURNETT STREET SUITE 200	FORT WORTH	TX	76102	(800) 221-9039
B+	NATIONAL HEALTH INS CO	4455 LBJ FREEWAY SUITE 375	DALLAS	TX	75244	(888) 781-0580
A-	NEW YORK LIFE INS CO	51 MADISON AVENUE	NEW YORK	NY	10010	(212) 576-7000
B+	NIAGARA LIFE & HEALTH INS CO	300 INTERNATIONAL DRIVE SUITE	WILLIAMSVILLE	NY	14221	(803) 735-1251
B+	NORTHWESTERN LONG TERM CARE INS CO	720 EAST WISCONSIN AVENUE	MILWAUKEE	WI	53202	(414) 271-1444
B+	NORTHWESTERN MUTUAL LIFE INS CO	720 EAST WISCONSIN AVENUE	MILWAUKEE	WI	53202	(414) 271-1444
B+	NY LIFE INS & ANNUITY CORP	1209 ORANGE STREET	WILMINGTON	DE	19801	(212) 576-7000
B+	NYLIFE INS CO OF ARIZONA	14850 N SCOTTSDALE ROAD SUITE	SCOTTSDALE	AZ	85254	(212) 576-7000
B+	OLD REPUBLIC LIFE INS CO	307 NORTH MICHIGAN AVENUE	CHICAGO	IL	60601	(312) 346-8100
B+	OXFORD LIFE INS CO	2721 NORTH CENTRAL AVENUE	PHOENIX	AZ	85004	(800) 308-2318
B+	PACIFIC LIFE & ANNUITY CO	8825 NORTH 23RD AVENUE SUITE 1	PHOENIX	AZ	85021	(800) 800-7646
A-	PACIFIC LIFE INS CO	6750 MERCY ROAD	OMAHA	NE	68106	(800) 800-7646
B+	PAN AMERICAN ASR CO	PAN-AMERICAN LIFE CENTER 601 P	NEW ORLEANS	LA	70130	(877) 939-4550

DOM. STATE	IND. LIFE	IND. HEALTH	IND. ANNU.	GROUP LIFE	GROUP HEALTH	GROUP ANNU	CREDIT LIFE	CREDIT HEALTH	SUP. CONTR.	OTHER	INSURANCE COMPANY NAME
KS	12	0	0	58	30	0	0	0	0	0	ADVANCE INS CO OF KANSAS
TN	9	91	0	0	0	0	0	0	0	0	AMERICAN CONTINENTAL INS CO
NY	4	92	0	0	4	0	0	0	0	0	AMERICAN FAMILY LIFE ASR CO OF NY
WI	94	1	3	2	0	0	0	0	0	0	AMERICAN FAMILY LIFE INS CO
OK	13	27	18	0	42	1	0	0	0	0	AMERICAN FIDELITY ASR CO
TX	10	1	0	4	1	0	40	44	0	0	AMERICAN HEALTH & LIFE INS CO
RI	83	0	8	10	0	0	0	0	0	0	AMICA LIFE INS CO
OH	0	0	79	0	0	21	0	0	0	0	ANNUITY INVESTORS LIFE INS CO
NE	48	28	1	4	20	0	0	0	0	0	ASSURITY LIFE INS CO
IA	0	0	0	0	100	0	0	0	0	0	BERKLEY LIFE & HEALTH INS CO
TX	0	62	0	1	36	0	0	0	0	0	BEST LIFE & HEALTH INS CO
MS	2	0	0	97	0	0	0	0	0	0	BLUEBONNET LIFE INS CO
MA	65	2	0	20	14	0	0	0	0	0	BOSTON MUTUAL LIFE INS CO
NE	1	72	0	0	0	0	18	9	0	0	CENTRAL STATES H & L CO OF OMAHA
OK	2	98	0	0	0	0	0	0	0	0	CHESAPEAKE LIFE INS CO
TX	12	81	0	0	7	0	0	0	0	0	CHRISTIAN FIDELITY LIFE INS CO
CT	20	0	80	0	0	0	0	0	0	0	CM LIFE INS CO
SC	0	1	0	9	90	0	0	0	0	0	COMPANION LIFE INS CO
CA	0	0	0	0	100	0	0	0	0	0	COMPANION LIFE INS CO OF CA
IL	0	0	0	0	0	0	0	0	0	0	COUNTRY INVESTORS LIFE ASR CO
IL	71	16	2	1	11	0	0	0	0	0	COUNTRY LIFE INS CO
DE	0	1	0	17	82	0	0	0	0	0	DELAWARE AMERICAN LIFE INS CO
SC	100	0	0	0	0	0	0	0	0	0	DIRECT GENERAL LIFE INS CO
NY	0	0	100	0	0	0	0	0	0	0	EMPIRE FIDELITY INVESTMENTS L I C
TX	0	6	0	0	94	0	0	0	0	0	ENTERPRISE LIFE INS CO
IA	58	0	41	0	0	1	0	0	0	0	FARM BUREAU LIFE INS CO
MI	76	0	22	1	0	2	0	0	0	0	FARM BUREAU LIFE INS CO OF MICHIGAN
MN	73	14	12	1	0	0	0	0	0	0	FEDERATED LIFE INS CO
UT	0	0	100	0	0	0	0	0	0	0	FIDELITY INVESTMENTS LIFE INS CO
MO	1	4	8	2	82	4	0	0	0	0	FIDELITY SECURITY LIFE INS CO
NY	0	2	1	0	97	0	0	0	0	0	FIDELITY SECURITY LIFE INS CO OF NY
NY	0	0	0	9	91	0	0	0	0	0	FIRST RELIANCE STANDARD LIFE INS CO
GA	0	0	0	0	0	0	43	57	0	0	FRANDISCO LIFE INS CO
TX	12	30	0	0	58	0	0	0	0	0	FREEDOM LIFE INS CO OF AMERICA
TX	66	27	0	0	8	0	0	0	0	0	GARDEN STATE LIFE INS CO
NY	66	2	0	0	31	0	0	0	0	0	GERBER LIFE INS CO
NY	50	6	0	7	37	0	0	0	0	0	GUARDIAN LIFE INS CO OF AMERICA
PA	0	0	0	0	100	0	0	0	0	0	HM LIFE INS CO
IL	52	44	1	0	3	0	0	0	0	0	ILLINOIS MUTUAL LIFE INS CO
NY	79	19	0	0	2	0	0	0	0	0	LIFE INS CO OF BOSTON & NEW YORK
CO	99	1	0	0	0	0	0	0	0	0	M LIFE INS CO
NY	99	0	0	0	1	0	0	0	0	0	NATIONAL BENEFIT LIFE INS CO
TX	98	0	1	1	0	0	0	0	0	0	NATIONAL FARMERS UNION LIFE INS CO
TX	7	64	0	0	29	0	0	0	0	0	NATIONAL FOUNDATION LIFE INS CO
TX	100	0	0	0	0	0	0	0	0	0	NATIONAL HEALTH INS CO
NY	49	2	3	14	1	31	0	0	0	0	NEW YORK LIFE INS CO
NY	0	19	0	0	81	0	0	0	0	0	NIAGARA LIFE & HEALTH INS CO
WI	0	0	0	0	0	0	0	0	0	0	NORTHWESTERN LONG TERM CARE INS CO
WI	80	10	10	0	0	1	0	0	0	0	NORTHWESTERN MUTUAL LIFE INS CO
DE	19	0	73	8	0	0	0	0	0	0	NY LIFE INS & ANNUITY CORP
AZ	100	0	0	0	0	0	0	0	0	0	NYLIFE INS CO OF ARIZONA
IL	60	0	0	0	40	0	0	0	0	0	OLD REPUBLIC LIFE INS CO
AZ	14	6	80	0	0	0	0	0	0	0	OXFORD LIFE INS CO
AZ	2	0	73	0	0	25	0	0	0	0	PACIFIC LIFE & ANNUITY CO
NE	28	0	49	0	0	23	0	0	0	0	PACIFIC LIFE INS CO
LA	100	0	0	0	0	0	0	0	0	0	PAN AMERICAN ASR CO

RATING	INSURANCE COMPANY NAME	ADDRESS	CITY	STATE	ZIP	PHONE
A-	PARKER CENTENNIAL ASR CO	1800 NORTH POINT DRIVE	STEVENS POINT	WI	54481	(800) 373-6879
B+	PHYSICIANS LIFE INS CO	2600 DODGE STREET	OMAHA	NE	68131	(800) 228-9100
A+	PHYSICIANS MUTUAL INS CO	2600 DODGE STREET	OMAHA	NE	68131	(800) 228-9100
B+	POPULAR LIFE RE	CORPORATE OFFICE PARK SOLAR A	GUAYNABO	PR	966	(787) 706-4111
B+	PRINCIPAL LIFE INS CO	711 HIGH STREET	DES MOINES	IA	50392	(800) 986-3343
A	SENTRY LIFE INS CO	1800 NORTH POINT DRIVE	STEVENS POINT	WI	54481	(800) 373-6879
A	SHELTERPOINT LIFE INS CO	1225 FRANKLIN AVENUE - SUITE 4	GARDEN CITY	NY	11530	(800) 365-4999
A	SOUTHERN FARM BUREAU LIFE INS CO	1401 LIVINGSTON LANE	JACKSON	MS	39213	(800) 457-9611
B+	STANDARD INS CO	1100 SOUTHWEST SIXTH AVENUE	PORTLAND	OR	97204	(503) 321-7000
A	STANDARD LIFE INS CO OF NY	333 WESTCHESTER AVENUE WEST BU	WHITE PLAINS	NY	10604	(914) 989-4400
A-	STANDARD SECURITY LIFE INS CO OF NY	485 MADISON AVENUE 14TH FLOOR	NEW YORK	NY	10022	(212) 355-4141
A+	STATE FARM LIFE & ACCIDENT ASR CO	ONE STATE FARM PLAZA	BLOOMINGTON	IL	61710	(855) 733-7333
A+	STATE FARM LIFE INS CO	ONE STATE FARM PLAZA	BLOOMINGTON	IL	61710	(855) 733-7333
A-	SWBC LIFE INS CO	9311 SAN PEDRO STE 600	SAN ANTONIO	TX	78216	(866) 252-1920
B+	SYMETRA NATIONAL LIFE INS CO	4350 WESTOWN PARKWAY SUITE 180	WEST DES MOINES	IA	50266	(800) 796-3872
A+	TEACHERS INS & ANNUITY ASN OF AM	730 THIRD AVENUE	NEW YORK	NY	10017	(800) 842-2252
B+	TENNESSEE FARMERS LIFE INS CO	147 BEAR CREEK PIKE	COLUMBIA	TN	38401	(931) 388-7872
B+	TRANS OCEANIC LIFE INS CO	#121 ONEILL	SAN JUAN	PR	00918	(787) 620-2680
B+	TRANS WORLD ASR CO	885 S EL CAMINO REAL	SAN MATEO	CA	94402	(866) 997-6349
A-	TRUSTMARK LIFE INS CO	400 FIELD DRIVE	LAKE FOREST	IL	60045	(800) 366-6663
B+	UNITED FARM FAMILY LIFE INS CO	225 SOUTH EAST STREET	INDIANAPOLIS	IN	46202	(800) 723-3276
B+	UNITED NATIONAL LIFE INS CO OF AM	1275 MILWAUKEE AVENUE	GLENVIEW	IL	60025	(800) 207-8050
B+	UNITED WORLD LIFE INS CO	MUTUAL OF OMAHA PLAZA	OMAHA	NE	68175	(800) 228-7104
B+	USAA LIFE INS CO	9800 FREDERICKSBURG ROAD	SAN ANTONIO	TX	78288	(210) 498-8000
B+	USABLE LIFE	320 W CAPITOL SUITE 700	LITTLE ROCK	AR	72201	(800) 370-5856
B+	VOYA RETIREMENT INS & ANNUITY CO	ONE ORANGE WAY	WINDSOR	CT	06095	(877) 886-5050

DOM. STATE	IND. LIFE	IND. HEALTH	IND. ANNU.	GROUP LIFE	GROUP HEALTH	GROUP ANNU	CREDIT LIFE	CREDIT HEALTH	SUP. CONTR.	OTHER	INSURANCE COMPANY NAME
WI	0	0	0	0	0	100	0	0	0	0	PARKER CENTENNIAL ASR CO
NE	78	0	1	20	0	1	0	0	0	0	PHYSICIANS LIFE INS CO
NE	0	87	0	0	13	0	0	0	0	0	PHYSICIANS MUTUAL INS CO
PR	0	0	0	1	24	0	41	34	0	0	POPULAR LIFE RE
IA	15	8	13	8	27	30	0	0	0	0	PRINCIPAL LIFE INS CO
WI	2	0	1	0	0	97	0	0	0	0	SENTRY LIFE INS CO
NY	0	0	0	0	100	0	0	0	0	0	SHELTERPOINT LIFE INS CO
MS	88	1	10	1	0	0	0	0	0	0	SOUTHERN FARM BUREAU LIFE INS CO
OR	0	4	11	2	23	59	0	0	0	0	STANDARD INS CO
NY	0	5	0	26	68	0	0	0	0	0	STANDARD LIFE INS CO OF NY
NY	0	0	0	0	99	0	0	0	0	0	STANDARD SECURITY LIFE INS CO OF NY
IL	97	0	3	0	0	0	0	0	0	0	STATE FARM LIFE & ACCIDENT ASR CO
IL	95	0	3	2	0	0	0	0	0	0	STATE FARM LIFE INS CO
TX	11	0	0	0	4	0	37	47	0	1	SWBC LIFE INS CO
IA	100	0	0	0	0	0	0	0	0	0	SYMETRA NATIONAL LIFE INS CO
NY	1	0	39	0	0	60	0	0	0	0	TEACHERS INS & ANNUITY ASN OF AM
TN	77	0	21	0	2	0	0	0	0	0	TENNESSEE FARMERS LIFE INS CO
PR	1	99	0	0	0	0	0	0	0	0	TRANS OCEANIC LIFE INS CO
CA	75	0	10	16	0	0	0	0	0	0	TRANS WORLD ASR CO
IL	0	0	0	6	94	0	0	0	0	0	TRUSTMARK LIFE INS CO
IN	91	0	9	0	0	0	0	0	0	0	UNITED FARM FAMILY LIFE INS CO
IL	2	94	0	0	4	0	0	0	0	0	UNITED NATIONAL LIFE INS CO OF AM
NE	100	0	0	0	0	0	0	0	0	0	UNITED WORLD LIFE INS CO
TX	0	0	0	0	0	0	0	0	0	0	USAA LIFE INS CO
AR	1	28	0	25	46	0	0	0	0	0	USABLE LIFE
CT	0	0	-33	0	0	133	0	0	0	0	VOYA RETIREMENT INS & ANNUITY CO

Section IV

Weiss Ratings
Recommended Companies
by State

A compilation of those

U.S. Life and Annuity Insurers

receiving a Weiss Safety Rating
of A+, A, A- or B+.

Companies are ranked by Safety Rating
in each state where they are licensed to do business.

Section IV Contents

This section provides a list of the recommended carriers licensed to do business in each state. It contains all insurers receiving a Weiss Safety Rating of A+, A, A-, or B+. If an insurer is not on this list, it should not be automatically assumed that the firm is weak. Indeed, there are many firms that have not achieved a B+ or better rating but are in relatively good condition with adequate resources to cover their risk during an average recession. Not being included in this list should not be construed as a recommendation to surrender policies.

Companies are ranked within each state by their Safety Rating. However, companies with the same rating should be viewed as having the same relative strength regardless of their ranking in this table. While the specific order in which they appear on the page is based upon differences in our underlying indexes, you can assume that companies with the same rating have differences that are only minor and relatively inconsequential.

1. **Safety Rating**   Our rating is measured on a scale from A to F and considers a wide range of factors. Highly rated companies are, in our opinion, less likely to experience financial difficulties than lower rated firms. See *About Weiss Safety Ratings* for more information.

2. **Insurance Company Name**   The legally registered name, which can sometimes differ from the name that the company uses for advertising. An insurer's name can be very similar to the name of other companies which may not be on our Recommended List, so make sure you note the exact name before contacting your agent.

3. **Domicile State**   The state which has primary regulatory responsibility for the company. It may differ from the location of the company's corporate headquarters. You do not have to be living in the domicile state to purchase insurance from this firm, provided it is licensed to do business in your state.

4. **Total Assets**   All assets admitted by state insurance regulators in millions of dollars. This includes investments, current business assets, and separate accounts.

Weiss Safety Ratings are not deemed to be a recommendation concerning the purchase or sale of the securities of any insurance company that is publicly owned.

Alabama

INSURANCE COMPANY NAME	DOM. STATE	TOTAL ASSETS ($MIL)
Rating: A+		
AMERICAN FAMILY LIFE INS CO	WI	5,473.4
CHESAPEAKE LIFE INS CO	OK	251.1
COUNTRY LIFE INS CO	IL	9,442.8
PHYSICIANS MUTUAL INS CO	NE	2,785.1
STATE FARM LIFE INS CO	IL	86,273.0
TEACHERS INS & ANNUITY ASN OF AM	NY	343,000.0
Rating: A		
BERKLEY LIFE & HEALTH INS CO	IA	478.2
DIRECT GENERAL LIFE INS CO	SC	33.5
FEDERATED LIFE INS CO	MN	2,427.1
FIDELITY INVESTMENTS LIFE INS CO	UT	44,295.4
GARDEN STATE LIFE INS CO	TX	143.5
GUARDIAN LIFE INS CO OF AMERICA	NY	72,127.3
NATIONAL FOUNDATION LIFE INS CO	TX	94.2
SENTRY LIFE INS CO	WI	9,857.5
SOUTHERN FARM BUREAU LIFE INS CO	MS	15,730.7
Rating: A-		
AMICA LIFE INS CO	RI	1,465.4
ANNUITY INVESTORS LIFE INS CO	OH	3,225.7
BLUEBONNET LIFE INS CO	MS	71.5
CENTRAL STATES H & L CO OF OMAHA	NE	386.9
COUNTRY INVESTORS LIFE ASR CO	IL	323.0
DELAWARE AMERICAN LIFE INS CO	DE	106.3
FIDELITY SECURITY LIFE INS CO	MO	982.0
NATIONAL BENEFIT LIFE INS CO	NY	675.0
NEW YORK LIFE INS CO	NY	214,000.0
PACIFIC LIFE INS CO	NE	178,000.0
PARKER CENTENNIAL ASR CO	WI	99.1
STANDARD SECURITY LIFE INS CO OF NY	NY	152.8
TRUSTMARK LIFE INS CO	IL	249.3
Rating: B+		
AMERICAN CONTINENTAL INS CO	TN	439.4
AMERICAN FIDELITY ASR CO	OK	7,628.5
AMERICAN HEALTH & LIFE INS CO	TX	1,264.4
ASSURITY LIFE INS CO	NE	2,660.6
BEST LIFE & HEALTH INS CO	TX	31.3
BOSTON MUTUAL LIFE INS CO	MA	1,634.0
CHRISTIAN FIDELITY LIFE INS CO	TX	44.0
CM LIFE INS CO	CT	9,072.1
COMPANION LIFE INS CO	SC	689.7
FREEDOM LIFE INS CO OF AMERICA	TX	462.4
GERBER LIFE INS CO	NY	5,146.7
HM LIFE INS CO	PA	881.3
ILLINOIS MUTUAL LIFE INS CO	IL	1,595.0
NATIONAL HEALTH INS CO	TX	181.1
NORTHWESTERN LONG TERM CARE INS CO	WI	320.0
NORTHWESTERN MUTUAL LIFE INS CO	WI	335,000.0
NY LIFE INS & ANNUITY CORP	DE	183,000.0
NYLIFE INS CO OF ARIZONA	AZ	159.0
OLD REPUBLIC LIFE INS CO	IL	106.8
OXFORD LIFE INS CO	AZ	2,955.5
PACIFIC LIFE & ANNUITY CO	AZ	8,615.1

INSURANCE COMPANY NAME	DOM. STATE	TOTAL ASSETS ($MIL)
PAN AMERICAN ASR CO	LA	26.7
PHYSICIANS LIFE INS CO	NE	1,783.0
PRINCIPAL LIFE INS CO	IA	239,000.0
STANDARD INS CO	OR	32,461.1
SYMETRA NATIONAL LIFE INS CO	IA	24.4
TRANS WORLD ASR CO	CA	341.0
UNITED NATIONAL LIFE INS CO OF AM	IL	52.1
UNITED WORLD LIFE INS CO	NE	160.3
USAA LIFE INS CO	TX	26,197.9
USABLE LIFE	AR	505.6
VOYA RETIREMENT INS & ANNUITY CO	CT	129,000.0

Alaska

INSURANCE COMPANY NAME	DOM. STATE	TOTAL ASSETS ($MIL)
USABLE LIFE	AR	505.6
VOYA RETIREMENT INS & ANNUITY CO	CT	129,000.0

Rating: A+

INSURANCE COMPANY NAME	DOM. STATE	TOTAL ASSETS ($MIL)
AMERICAN FAMILY LIFE INS CO	WI	5,473.4
CHESAPEAKE LIFE INS CO	OK	251.1
COUNTRY LIFE INS CO	IL	9,442.8
PHYSICIANS MUTUAL INS CO	NE	2,785.1
STATE FARM LIFE INS CO	IL	86,273.0
TEACHERS INS & ANNUITY ASN OF AM	NY	343,000.0

Rating: A

INSURANCE COMPANY NAME	DOM. STATE	TOTAL ASSETS ($MIL)
BERKLEY LIFE & HEALTH INS CO	IA	478.2
DIRECT GENERAL LIFE INS CO	SC	33.5
FIDELITY INVESTMENTS LIFE INS CO	UT	44,295.4
GARDEN STATE LIFE INS CO	TX	143.5
GUARDIAN LIFE INS CO OF AMERICA	NY	72,127.3
NATIONAL FOUNDATION LIFE INS CO	TX	94.2
SENTRY LIFE INS CO	WI	9,857.5

Rating: A-

INSURANCE COMPANY NAME	DOM. STATE	TOTAL ASSETS ($MIL)
AMICA LIFE INS CO	RI	1,465.4
ANNUITY INVESTORS LIFE INS CO	OH	3,225.7
CENTRAL STATES H & L CO OF OMAHA	NE	386.9
COUNTRY INVESTORS LIFE ASR CO	IL	323.0
DELAWARE AMERICAN LIFE INS CO	DE	106.3
FIDELITY SECURITY LIFE INS CO	MO	982.0
NATIONAL BENEFIT LIFE INS CO	NY	675.0
NEW YORK LIFE INS CO	NY	214,000.0
PACIFIC LIFE INS CO	NE	178,000.0
PARKER CENTENNIAL ASR CO	WI	99.1
STANDARD SECURITY LIFE INS CO OF NY	NY	152.8
TRUSTMARK LIFE INS CO	IL	249.3

Rating: B+

INSURANCE COMPANY NAME	DOM. STATE	TOTAL ASSETS ($MIL)
AMERICAN FIDELITY ASR CO	OK	7,628.5
AMERICAN HEALTH & LIFE INS CO	TX	1,264.4
ASSURITY LIFE INS CO	NE	2,660.6
BEST LIFE & HEALTH INS CO	TX	31.3
BOSTON MUTUAL LIFE INS CO	MA	1,634.0
CM LIFE INS CO	CT	9,072.1
COMPANION LIFE INS CO	SC	689.7
GERBER LIFE INS CO	NY	5,146.7
HM LIFE INS CO	PA	881.3
NATIONAL FARMERS UNION LIFE INS CO	TX	158.8
NATIONAL HEALTH INS CO	TX	181.1
NORTHWESTERN LONG TERM CARE INS CO	WI	320.0
NORTHWESTERN MUTUAL LIFE INS CO	WI	335,000.0
NY LIFE INS & ANNUITY CORP	DE	183,000.0
NYLIFE INS CO OF ARIZONA	AZ	159.0
OLD REPUBLIC LIFE INS CO	IL	106.8
OXFORD LIFE INS CO	AZ	2,955.5
PACIFIC LIFE & ANNUITY CO	AZ	8,615.1
PHYSICIANS LIFE INS CO	NE	1,783.0
PRINCIPAL LIFE INS CO	IA	239,000.0
STANDARD INS CO	OR	32,461.1
TRANS WORLD ASR CO	CA	341.0
UNITED WORLD LIFE INS CO	NE	160.3
USAA LIFE INS CO	TX	26,197.9

Arizona

INSURANCE COMPANY NAME	DOM. STATE	TOTAL ASSETS ($MIL)
Rating: A+		
AMERICAN FAMILY LIFE INS CO	WI	5,473.4
CHESAPEAKE LIFE INS CO	OK	251.1
COUNTRY LIFE INS CO	IL	9,442.8
PHYSICIANS MUTUAL INS CO	NE	2,785.1
STATE FARM LIFE INS CO	IL	86,273.0
TEACHERS INS & ANNUITY ASN OF AM	NY	343,000.0
Rating: A		
BERKLEY LIFE & HEALTH INS CO	IA	478.2
DIRECT GENERAL LIFE INS CO	SC	33.5
FEDERATED LIFE INS CO	MN	2,427.1
FIDELITY INVESTMENTS LIFE INS CO	UT	44,295.4
GARDEN STATE LIFE INS CO	TX	143.5
GUARDIAN LIFE INS CO OF AMERICA	NY	72,127.3
NATIONAL FOUNDATION LIFE INS CO	TX	94.2
SENTRY LIFE INS CO	WI	9,857.5
Rating: A-		
AMICA LIFE INS CO	RI	1,465.4
ANNUITY INVESTORS LIFE INS CO	OH	3,225.7
CENTRAL STATES H & L CO OF OMAHA	NE	386.9
COUNTRY INVESTORS LIFE ASR CO	IL	323.0
DELAWARE AMERICAN LIFE INS CO	DE	106.3
FIDELITY SECURITY LIFE INS CO	MO	982.0
NATIONAL BENEFIT LIFE INS CO	NY	675.0
NEW YORK LIFE INS CO	NY	214,000.0
PACIFIC LIFE INS CO	NE	178,000.0
PARKER CENTENNIAL ASR CO	WI	99.1
STANDARD SECURITY LIFE INS CO OF NY	NY	152.8
TRUSTMARK LIFE INS CO	IL	249.3
Rating: B+		
AMERICAN CONTINENTAL INS CO	TN	439.4
AMERICAN FIDELITY ASR CO	OK	7,628.5
AMERICAN HEALTH & LIFE INS CO	TX	1,264.4
ASSURITY LIFE INS CO	NE	2,660.6
BEST LIFE & HEALTH INS CO	TX	31.3
BOSTON MUTUAL LIFE INS CO	MA	1,634.0
CHRISTIAN FIDELITY LIFE INS CO	TX	44.0
CM LIFE INS CO	CT	9,072.1
COMPANION LIFE INS CO	SC	689.7
COMPANION LIFE INS CO OF CA	CA	34.1
ENTERPRISE LIFE INS CO	TX	159.9
FARM BUREAU LIFE INS CO	IA	9,888.5
FREEDOM LIFE INS CO OF AMERICA	TX	462.4
GERBER LIFE INS CO	NY	5,146.7
HM LIFE INS CO	PA	881.3
ILLINOIS MUTUAL LIFE INS CO	IL	1,595.0
M LIFE INS CO	CO	479.6
NATIONAL FARMERS UNION LIFE INS CO	TX	158.8
NATIONAL HEALTH INS CO	TX	181.1
NORTHWESTERN LONG TERM CARE INS CO	WI	320.0
NORTHWESTERN MUTUAL LIFE INS CO	WI	335,000.0
NY LIFE INS & ANNUITY CORP	DE	183,000.0
NYLIFE INS CO OF ARIZONA	AZ	159.0

INSURANCE COMPANY NAME	DOM. STATE	TOTAL ASSETS ($MIL)
OLD REPUBLIC LIFE INS CO	IL	106.8
OXFORD LIFE INS CO	AZ	2,955.5
PACIFIC LIFE & ANNUITY CO	AZ	8,615.1
PAN AMERICAN ASR CO	LA	26.7
PHYSICIANS LIFE INS CO	NE	1,783.0
PRINCIPAL LIFE INS CO	IA	239,000.0
STANDARD INS CO	OR	32,461.1
SYMETRA NATIONAL LIFE INS CO	IA	24.4
TRANS WORLD ASR CO	CA	341.0
UNITED FARM FAMILY LIFE INS CO	IN	2,457.7
UNITED NATIONAL LIFE INS CO OF AM	IL	52.1
UNITED WORLD LIFE INS CO	NE	160.3
USAA LIFE INS CO	TX	26,197.9
USABLE LIFE	AR	505.6
VOYA RETIREMENT INS & ANNUITY CO	CT	129,000.0

Arkansas

INSURANCE COMPANY NAME	DOM. STATE	TOTAL ASSETS ($MIL)

Rating: A+

INSURANCE COMPANY NAME	DOM. STATE	TOTAL ASSETS ($MIL)
AMERICAN FAMILY LIFE INS CO	WI	5,473.4
CHESAPEAKE LIFE INS CO	OK	251.1
COUNTRY LIFE INS CO	IL	9,442.8
PHYSICIANS MUTUAL INS CO	NE	2,785.1
STATE FARM LIFE INS CO	IL	86,273.0
TEACHERS INS & ANNUITY ASN OF AM	NY	343,000.0

Rating: A

INSURANCE COMPANY NAME	DOM. STATE	TOTAL ASSETS ($MIL)
BERKLEY LIFE & HEALTH INS CO	IA	478.2
DIRECT GENERAL LIFE INS CO	SC	33.5
FEDERATED LIFE INS CO	MN	2,427.1
FIDELITY INVESTMENTS LIFE INS CO	UT	44,295.4
GARDEN STATE LIFE INS CO	TX	143.5
GUARDIAN LIFE INS CO OF AMERICA	NY	72,127.3
NATIONAL FOUNDATION LIFE INS CO	TX	94.2
SENTRY LIFE INS CO	WI	9,857.5
SOUTHERN FARM BUREAU LIFE INS CO	MS	15,730.7

Rating: A-

INSURANCE COMPANY NAME	DOM. STATE	TOTAL ASSETS ($MIL)
AMICA LIFE INS CO	RI	1,465.4
ANNUITY INVESTORS LIFE INS CO	OH	3,225.7
BLUEBONNET LIFE INS CO	MS	71.5
CENTRAL STATES H & L CO OF OMAHA	NE	386.9
COUNTRY INVESTORS LIFE ASR CO	IL	323.0
DELAWARE AMERICAN LIFE INS CO	DE	106.3
FIDELITY SECURITY LIFE INS CO	MO	982.0
NATIONAL BENEFIT LIFE INS CO	NY	675.0
NEW YORK LIFE INS CO	NY	214,000.0
PACIFIC LIFE INS CO	NE	178,000.0
PARKER CENTENNIAL ASR CO	WI	99.1
STANDARD SECURITY LIFE INS CO OF NY	NY	152.8
TRUSTMARK LIFE INS CO	IL	249.3

Rating: B+

INSURANCE COMPANY NAME	DOM. STATE	TOTAL ASSETS ($MIL)
AMERICAN CONTINENTAL INS CO	TN	439.4
AMERICAN FIDELITY ASR CO	OK	7,628.5
AMERICAN HEALTH & LIFE INS CO	TX	1,264.4
ASSURITY LIFE INS CO	NE	2,660.6
BEST LIFE & HEALTH INS CO	TX	31.3
BOSTON MUTUAL LIFE INS CO	MA	1,634.0
CHRISTIAN FIDELITY LIFE INS CO	TX	44.0
CM LIFE INS CO	CT	9,072.1
COMPANION LIFE INS CO	SC	689.7
ENTERPRISE LIFE INS CO	TX	159.9
FREEDOM LIFE INS CO OF AMERICA	TX	462.4
GERBER LIFE INS CO	NY	5,146.7
HM LIFE INS CO	PA	881.3
ILLINOIS MUTUAL LIFE INS CO	IL	1,595.0
NATIONAL FARMERS UNION LIFE INS CO	TX	158.8
NATIONAL HEALTH INS CO	TX	181.1
NORTHWESTERN LONG TERM CARE INS CO	WI	320.0
NORTHWESTERN MUTUAL LIFE INS CO	WI	335,000.0
NY LIFE INS & ANNUITY CORP	DE	183,000.0
NYLIFE INS CO OF ARIZONA	AZ	159.0
OLD REPUBLIC LIFE INS CO	IL	106.8

INSURANCE COMPANY NAME	DOM. STATE	TOTAL ASSETS ($MIL)
OXFORD LIFE INS CO	AZ	2,955.5
PACIFIC LIFE & ANNUITY CO	AZ	8,615.1
PAN AMERICAN ASR CO	LA	26.7
PHYSICIANS LIFE INS CO	NE	1,783.0
PRINCIPAL LIFE INS CO	IA	239,000.0
STANDARD INS CO	OR	32,461.1
SYMETRA NATIONAL LIFE INS CO	IA	24.4
TRANS WORLD ASR CO	CA	341.0
UNITED NATIONAL LIFE INS CO OF AM	IL	52.1
UNITED WORLD LIFE INS CO	NE	160.3
USAA LIFE INS CO	TX	26,197.9
USABLE LIFE	AR	505.6
VOYA RETIREMENT INS & ANNUITY CO	CT	129,000.0

California

INSURANCE COMPANY NAME	DOM. STATE	TOTAL ASSETS ($MIL)

Rating: A+

INSURANCE COMPANY NAME	DOM. STATE	TOTAL ASSETS ($MIL)
AMERICAN FAMILY LIFE INS CO	WI	5,473.4
CHESAPEAKE LIFE INS CO	OK	251.1
PHYSICIANS MUTUAL INS CO	NE	2,785.1
STATE FARM LIFE INS CO	IL	86,273.0
TEACHERS INS & ANNUITY ASN OF AM	NY	343,000.0

Rating: A

INSURANCE COMPANY NAME	DOM. STATE	TOTAL ASSETS ($MIL)
BERKLEY LIFE & HEALTH INS CO	IA	478.2
DIRECT GENERAL LIFE INS CO	SC	33.5
FEDERATED LIFE INS CO	MN	2,427.1
FIDELITY INVESTMENTS LIFE INS CO	UT	44,295.4
GARDEN STATE LIFE INS CO	TX	143.5
GUARDIAN LIFE INS CO OF AMERICA	NY	72,127.3
NATIONAL FOUNDATION LIFE INS CO	TX	94.2
SENTRY LIFE INS CO	WI	9,857.5

Rating: A-

INSURANCE COMPANY NAME	DOM. STATE	TOTAL ASSETS ($MIL)
AMICA LIFE INS CO	RI	1,465.4
ANNUITY INVESTORS LIFE INS CO	OH	3,225.7
CENTRAL STATES H & L CO OF OMAHA	NE	386.9
DELAWARE AMERICAN LIFE INS CO	DE	106.3
FIDELITY SECURITY LIFE INS CO	MO	982.0
NATIONAL BENEFIT LIFE INS CO	NY	675.0
NEW YORK LIFE INS CO	NY	214,000.0
PACIFIC LIFE INS CO	NE	178,000.0
PARKER CENTENNIAL ASR CO	WI	99.1
STANDARD SECURITY LIFE INS CO OF NY	NY	152.8
TRUSTMARK LIFE INS CO	IL	249.3

Rating: B+

INSURANCE COMPANY NAME	DOM. STATE	TOTAL ASSETS ($MIL)
AMERICAN FIDELITY ASR CO	OK	7,628.5
AMERICAN HEALTH & LIFE INS CO	TX	1,264.4
ASSURITY LIFE INS CO	NE	2,660.6
BEST LIFE & HEALTH INS CO	TX	31.3
BOSTON MUTUAL LIFE INS CO	MA	1,634.0
CM LIFE INS CO	CT	9,072.1
COMPANION LIFE INS CO OF CA	CA	34.1
GERBER LIFE INS CO	NY	5,146.7
HM LIFE INS CO	PA	881.3
ILLINOIS MUTUAL LIFE INS CO	IL	1,595.0
NATIONAL FARMERS UNION LIFE INS CO	TX	158.8
NATIONAL HEALTH INS CO	TX	181.1
NORTHWESTERN LONG TERM CARE INS CO	WI	320.0
NORTHWESTERN MUTUAL LIFE INS CO	WI	335,000.0
NY LIFE INS & ANNUITY CORP	DE	183,000.0
NYLIFE INS CO OF ARIZONA	AZ	159.0
OLD REPUBLIC LIFE INS CO	IL	106.8
OXFORD LIFE INS CO	AZ	2,955.5
PACIFIC LIFE & ANNUITY CO	AZ	8,615.1
PAN AMERICAN ASR CO	LA	26.7
PHYSICIANS LIFE INS CO	NE	1,783.0
PRINCIPAL LIFE INS CO	IA	239,000.0
STANDARD INS CO	OR	32,461.1
SYMETRA NATIONAL LIFE INS CO	IA	24.4
TRANS WORLD ASR CO	CA	341.0

INSURANCE COMPANY NAME	DOM. STATE	TOTAL ASSETS ($MIL)
UNITED FARM FAMILY LIFE INS CO	IN	2,457.7
UNITED WORLD LIFE INS CO	NE	160.3
USAA LIFE INS CO	TX	26,197.9
USABLE LIFE	AR	505.6
VOYA RETIREMENT INS & ANNUITY CO	CT	129,000.0

Colorado

INSURANCE COMPANY NAME	DOM. STATE	TOTAL ASSETS ($MIL)

Rating: A+

INSURANCE COMPANY NAME	DOM. STATE	TOTAL ASSETS ($MIL)
AMERICAN FAMILY LIFE INS CO	WI	5,473.4
CHESAPEAKE LIFE INS CO	OK	251.1
COUNTRY LIFE INS CO	IL	9,442.8
PHYSICIANS MUTUAL INS CO	NE	2,785.1
STATE FARM LIFE INS CO	IL	86,273.0
TEACHERS INS & ANNUITY ASN OF AM	NY	343,000.0

Rating: A

INSURANCE COMPANY NAME	DOM. STATE	TOTAL ASSETS ($MIL)
BERKLEY LIFE & HEALTH INS CO	IA	478.2
DIRECT GENERAL LIFE INS CO	SC	33.5
FEDERATED LIFE INS CO	MN	2,427.1
FIDELITY INVESTMENTS LIFE INS CO	UT	44,295.4
GARDEN STATE LIFE INS CO	TX	143.5
GUARDIAN LIFE INS CO OF AMERICA	NY	72,127.3
NATIONAL FOUNDATION LIFE INS CO	TX	94.2
SENTRY LIFE INS CO	WI	9,857.5
SHELTERPOINT LIFE INS CO	NY	392.4
SOUTHERN FARM BUREAU LIFE INS CO	MS	15,730.7

Rating: A-

INSURANCE COMPANY NAME	DOM. STATE	TOTAL ASSETS ($MIL)
AMICA LIFE INS CO	RI	1,465.4
ANNUITY INVESTORS LIFE INS CO	OH	3,225.7
CENTRAL STATES H & L CO OF OMAHA	NE	386.9
COUNTRY INVESTORS LIFE ASR CO	IL	323.0
DELAWARE AMERICAN LIFE INS CO	DE	106.3
FIDELITY SECURITY LIFE INS CO	MO	982.0
NATIONAL BENEFIT LIFE INS CO	NY	675.0
NEW YORK LIFE INS CO	NY	214,000.0
PACIFIC LIFE INS CO	NE	178,000.0
PARKER CENTENNIAL ASR CO	WI	99.1
STANDARD SECURITY LIFE INS CO OF NY	NY	152.8
TRUSTMARK LIFE INS CO	IL	249.3

Rating: B+

INSURANCE COMPANY NAME	DOM. STATE	TOTAL ASSETS ($MIL)
AMERICAN CONTINENTAL INS CO	TN	439.4
AMERICAN FIDELITY ASR CO	OK	7,628.5
AMERICAN HEALTH & LIFE INS CO	TX	1,264.4
ASSURITY LIFE INS CO	NE	2,660.6
BEST LIFE & HEALTH INS CO	TX	31.3
BOSTON MUTUAL LIFE INS CO	MA	1,634.0
CHRISTIAN FIDELITY LIFE INS CO	TX	44.0
CM LIFE INS CO	CT	9,072.1
COMPANION LIFE INS CO	SC	689.7
FARM BUREAU LIFE INS CO	IA	9,888.5
FREEDOM LIFE INS CO OF AMERICA	TX	462.4
GERBER LIFE INS CO	NY	5,146.7
HM LIFE INS CO	PA	881.3
ILLINOIS MUTUAL LIFE INS CO	IL	1,595.0
M LIFE INS CO	CO	479.6
NATIONAL FARMERS UNION LIFE INS CO	TX	158.8
NATIONAL HEALTH INS CO	TX	181.1
NORTHWESTERN LONG TERM CARE INS CO	WI	320.0
NORTHWESTERN MUTUAL LIFE INS CO	WI	335,000.0
NY LIFE INS & ANNUITY CORP	DE	183,000.0
NYLIFE INS CO OF ARIZONA	AZ	159.0

INSURANCE COMPANY NAME	DOM. STATE	TOTAL ASSETS ($MIL)
OLD REPUBLIC LIFE INS CO	IL	106.8
OXFORD LIFE INS CO	AZ	2,955.5
PACIFIC LIFE & ANNUITY CO	AZ	8,615.1
PAN AMERICAN ASR CO	LA	26.7
PHYSICIANS LIFE INS CO	NE	1,783.0
PRINCIPAL LIFE INS CO	IA	239,000.0
STANDARD INS CO	OR	32,461.1
SYMETRA NATIONAL LIFE INS CO	IA	24.4
TRANS WORLD ASR CO	CA	341.0
UNITED NATIONAL LIFE INS CO OF AM	IL	52.1
UNITED WORLD LIFE INS CO	NE	160.3
USAA LIFE INS CO	TX	26,197.9
USABLE LIFE	AR	505.6
VOYA RETIREMENT INS & ANNUITY CO	CT	129,000.0

Connecticut

INSURANCE COMPANY NAME	DOM. STATE	TOTAL ASSETS ($MIL)
Rating: A+		
AMERICAN FAMILY LIFE INS CO	WI	5,473.4
CHESAPEAKE LIFE INS CO	OK	251.1
COUNTRY LIFE INS CO	IL	9,442.8
PHYSICIANS MUTUAL INS CO	NE	2,785.1
STATE FARM LIFE & ACCIDENT ASR CO	IL	3,528.9
STATE FARM LIFE INS CO	IL	86,273.0
TEACHERS INS & ANNUITY ASN OF AM	NY	343,000.0
Rating: A		
AMERICAN FAMILY LIFE ASR CO OF NY	NY	1,108.3
BERKLEY LIFE & HEALTH INS CO	IA	478.2
DIRECT GENERAL LIFE INS CO	SC	33.5
FEDERATED LIFE INS CO	MN	2,427.1
FIDELITY INVESTMENTS LIFE INS CO	UT	44,295.4
GARDEN STATE LIFE INS CO	TX	143.5
GUARDIAN LIFE INS CO OF AMERICA	NY	72,127.3
SENTRY LIFE INS CO	WI	9,857.5
SHELTERPOINT LIFE INS CO	NY	392.4
Rating: A-		
AMICA LIFE INS CO	RI	1,465.4
ANNUITY INVESTORS LIFE INS CO	OH	3,225.7
CENTRAL STATES H & L CO OF OMAHA	NE	386.9
COUNTRY INVESTORS LIFE ASR CO	IL	323.0
DELAWARE AMERICAN LIFE INS CO	DE	106.3
FIDELITY SECURITY LIFE INS CO	MO	982.0
NATIONAL BENEFIT LIFE INS CO	NY	675.0
NEW YORK LIFE INS CO	NY	214,000.0
PACIFIC LIFE INS CO	NE	178,000.0
PARKER CENTENNIAL ASR CO	WI	99.1
STANDARD SECURITY LIFE INS CO OF NY	NY	152.8
TRUSTMARK LIFE INS CO	IL	249.3
Rating: B+		
AMERICAN FIDELITY ASR CO	OK	7,628.5
AMERICAN HEALTH & LIFE INS CO	TX	1,264.4
ASSURITY LIFE INS CO	NE	2,660.6
BOSTON MUTUAL LIFE INS CO	MA	1,634.0
CM LIFE INS CO	CT	9,072.1
GERBER LIFE INS CO	NY	5,146.7
HM LIFE INS CO	PA	881.3
ILLINOIS MUTUAL LIFE INS CO	IL	1,595.0
NATIONAL HEALTH INS CO	TX	181.1
NIAGARA LIFE & HEALTH INS CO	NY	20.4
NORTHWESTERN LONG TERM CARE INS CO	WI	320.0
NORTHWESTERN MUTUAL LIFE INS CO	WI	335,000.0
NY LIFE INS & ANNUITY CORP	DE	183,000.0
NYLIFE INS CO OF ARIZONA	AZ	159.0
OLD REPUBLIC LIFE INS CO	IL	106.8
OXFORD LIFE INS CO	AZ	2,955.5
PACIFIC LIFE & ANNUITY CO	AZ	8,615.1
PAN AMERICAN ASR CO	LA	26.7
PHYSICIANS LIFE INS CO	NE	1,783.0
PRINCIPAL LIFE INS CO	IA	239,000.0
STANDARD INS CO	OR	32,461.1

INSURANCE COMPANY NAME	DOM. STATE	TOTAL ASSETS ($MIL)
SYMETRA NATIONAL LIFE INS CO	IA	24.4
TRANS WORLD ASR CO	CA	341.0
USAA LIFE INS CO	TX	26,197.9
USABLE LIFE	AR	505.6
VOYA RETIREMENT INS & ANNUITY CO	CT	129,000.0

Delaware

INSURANCE COMPANY NAME	DOM. STATE	TOTAL ASSETS ($MIL)

Rating: A+

INSURANCE COMPANY NAME	DOM. STATE	TOTAL ASSETS ($MIL)
AMERICAN FAMILY LIFE INS CO	WI	5,473.4
CHESAPEAKE LIFE INS CO	OK	251.1
COUNTRY LIFE INS CO	IL	9,442.8
PHYSICIANS MUTUAL INS CO	NE	2,785.1
STATE FARM LIFE INS CO	IL	86,273.0
TEACHERS INS & ANNUITY ASN OF AM	NY	343,000.0

Rating: A

INSURANCE COMPANY NAME	DOM. STATE	TOTAL ASSETS ($MIL)
BERKLEY LIFE & HEALTH INS CO	IA	478.2
DIRECT GENERAL LIFE INS CO	SC	33.5
FEDERATED LIFE INS CO	MN	2,427.1
FIDELITY INVESTMENTS LIFE INS CO	UT	44,295.4
GARDEN STATE LIFE INS CO	TX	143.5
GUARDIAN LIFE INS CO OF AMERICA	NY	72,127.3
NATIONAL FOUNDATION LIFE INS CO	TX	94.2
SENTRY LIFE INS CO	WI	9,857.5
SHELTERPOINT LIFE INS CO	NY	392.4

Rating: A-

INSURANCE COMPANY NAME	DOM. STATE	TOTAL ASSETS ($MIL)
AMICA LIFE INS CO	RI	1,465.4
ANNUITY INVESTORS LIFE INS CO	OH	3,225.7
CENTRAL STATES H & L CO OF OMAHA	NE	386.9
COUNTRY INVESTORS LIFE ASR CO	IL	323.0
DELAWARE AMERICAN LIFE INS CO	DE	106.3
FIDELITY SECURITY LIFE INS CO	MO	982.0
FIRST RELIANCE STANDARD LIFE INS CO	NY	259.1
NATIONAL BENEFIT LIFE INS CO	NY	675.0
NEW YORK LIFE INS CO	NY	214,000.0
PACIFIC LIFE INS CO	NE	178,000.0
PARKER CENTENNIAL ASR CO	WI	99.1
STANDARD SECURITY LIFE INS CO OF NY	NY	152.8
TRUSTMARK LIFE INS CO	IL	249.3

Rating: B+

INSURANCE COMPANY NAME	DOM. STATE	TOTAL ASSETS ($MIL)
AMERICAN FIDELITY ASR CO	OK	7,628.5
AMERICAN HEALTH & LIFE INS CO	TX	1,264.4
ASSURITY LIFE INS CO	NE	2,660.6
BOSTON MUTUAL LIFE INS CO	MA	1,634.0
CM LIFE INS CO	CT	9,072.1
COMPANION LIFE INS CO	SC	689.7
FREEDOM LIFE INS CO OF AMERICA	TX	462.4
GERBER LIFE INS CO	NY	5,146.7
HM LIFE INS CO	PA	881.3
ILLINOIS MUTUAL LIFE INS CO	IL	1,595.0
M LIFE INS CO	CO	479.6
NATIONAL HEALTH INS CO	TX	181.1
NORTHWESTERN LONG TERM CARE INS CO	WI	320.0
NORTHWESTERN MUTUAL LIFE INS CO	WI	335,000.0
NY LIFE INS & ANNUITY CORP	DE	183,000.0
NYLIFE INS CO OF ARIZONA	AZ	159.0
OLD REPUBLIC LIFE INS CO	IL	106.8
OXFORD LIFE INS CO	AZ	2,955.5
PACIFIC LIFE & ANNUITY CO	AZ	8,615.1
PAN AMERICAN ASR CO	LA	26.7
PHYSICIANS LIFE INS CO	NE	1,783.0

INSURANCE COMPANY NAME	DOM. STATE	TOTAL ASSETS ($MIL)
PRINCIPAL LIFE INS CO	IA	239,000.0
STANDARD INS CO	OR	32,461.1
SYMETRA NATIONAL LIFE INS CO	IA	24.4
TRANS WORLD ASR CO	CA	341.0
UNITED WORLD LIFE INS CO	NE	160.3
USAA LIFE INS CO	TX	26,197.9
USABLE LIFE	AR	505.6
VOYA RETIREMENT INS & ANNUITY CO	CT	129,000.0

District Of Columbia

INSURANCE COMPANY NAME	DOM. STATE	TOTAL ASSETS ($MIL)

Rating: A+

INSURANCE COMPANY NAME	DOM. STATE	TOTAL ASSETS ($MIL)
AMERICAN FAMILY LIFE INS CO	WI	5,473.4
CHESAPEAKE LIFE INS CO	OK	251.1
PHYSICIANS MUTUAL INS CO	NE	2,785.1
STATE FARM LIFE INS CO	IL	86,273.0
TEACHERS INS & ANNUITY ASN OF AM	NY	343,000.0

Rating: A

INSURANCE COMPANY NAME	DOM. STATE	TOTAL ASSETS ($MIL)
BERKLEY LIFE & HEALTH INS CO	IA	478.2
DIRECT GENERAL LIFE INS CO	SC	33.5
FIDELITY INVESTMENTS LIFE INS CO	UT	44,295.4
GARDEN STATE LIFE INS CO	TX	143.5
GUARDIAN LIFE INS CO OF AMERICA	NY	72,127.3
NATIONAL FOUNDATION LIFE INS CO	TX	94.2
SENTRY LIFE INS CO	WI	9,857.5
SHELTERPOINT LIFE INS CO	NY	392.4

Rating: A-

INSURANCE COMPANY NAME	DOM. STATE	TOTAL ASSETS ($MIL)
AMICA LIFE INS CO	RI	1,465.4
ANNUITY INVESTORS LIFE INS CO	OH	3,225.7
CENTRAL STATES H & L CO OF OMAHA	NE	386.9
DELAWARE AMERICAN LIFE INS CO	DE	106.3
FIDELITY SECURITY LIFE INS CO	MO	982.0
FIRST RELIANCE STANDARD LIFE INS CO	NY	259.1
NATIONAL BENEFIT LIFE INS CO	NY	675.0
NEW YORK LIFE INS CO	NY	214,000.0
PACIFIC LIFE INS CO	NE	178,000.0
PARKER CENTENNIAL ASR CO	WI	99.1
STANDARD SECURITY LIFE INS CO OF NY	NY	152.8
TRUSTMARK LIFE INS CO	IL	249.3

Rating: B+

INSURANCE COMPANY NAME	DOM. STATE	TOTAL ASSETS ($MIL)
AMERICAN FIDELITY ASR CO	OK	7,628.5
AMERICAN HEALTH & LIFE INS CO	TX	1,264.4
ASSURITY LIFE INS CO	NE	2,660.6
BEST LIFE & HEALTH INS CO	TX	31.3
BOSTON MUTUAL LIFE INS CO	MA	1,634.0
CM LIFE INS CO	CT	9,072.1
COMPANION LIFE INS CO	SC	689.7
GERBER LIFE INS CO	NY	5,146.7
HM LIFE INS CO	PA	881.3
NATIONAL FARMERS UNION LIFE INS CO	TX	158.8
NATIONAL HEALTH INS CO	TX	181.1
NORTHWESTERN LONG TERM CARE INS CO	WI	320.0
NORTHWESTERN MUTUAL LIFE INS CO	WI	335,000.0
NY LIFE INS & ANNUITY CORP	DE	183,000.0
NYLIFE INS CO OF ARIZONA	AZ	159.0
OLD REPUBLIC LIFE INS CO	IL	106.8
OXFORD LIFE INS CO	AZ	2,955.5
PACIFIC LIFE & ANNUITY CO	AZ	8,615.1
PAN AMERICAN ASR CO	LA	26.7
PHYSICIANS LIFE INS CO	NE	1,783.0
PRINCIPAL LIFE INS CO	IA	239,000.0
STANDARD INS CO	OR	32,461.1
SYMETRA NATIONAL LIFE INS CO	IA	24.4
TRANS WORLD ASR CO	CA	341.0

INSURANCE COMPANY NAME	DOM. STATE	TOTAL ASSETS ($MIL)
UNITED WORLD LIFE INS CO	NE	160.3
USAA LIFE INS CO	TX	26,197.9
USABLE LIFE	AR	505.6
VOYA RETIREMENT INS & ANNUITY CO	CT	129,000.0

Florida

INSURANCE COMPANY NAME	DOM. STATE	TOTAL ASSETS ($MIL)

Rating: A+

INSURANCE COMPANY NAME	DOM. STATE	TOTAL ASSETS ($MIL)
AMERICAN FAMILY LIFE INS CO	WI	5,473.4
CHESAPEAKE LIFE INS CO	OK	251.1
COUNTRY LIFE INS CO	IL	9,442.8
PHYSICIANS MUTUAL INS CO	NE	2,785.1
STATE FARM LIFE INS CO	IL	86,273.0
TEACHERS INS & ANNUITY ASN OF AM	NY	343,000.0

Rating: A

INSURANCE COMPANY NAME	DOM. STATE	TOTAL ASSETS ($MIL)
BERKLEY LIFE & HEALTH INS CO	IA	478.2
DIRECT GENERAL LIFE INS CO	SC	33.5
FEDERATED LIFE INS CO	MN	2,427.1
FIDELITY INVESTMENTS LIFE INS CO	UT	44,295.4
GARDEN STATE LIFE INS CO	TX	143.5
GUARDIAN LIFE INS CO OF AMERICA	NY	72,127.3
SENTRY LIFE INS CO	WI	9,857.5
SHELTERPOINT LIFE INS CO	NY	392.4
SOUTHERN FARM BUREAU LIFE INS CO	MS	15,730.7

Rating: A-

INSURANCE COMPANY NAME	DOM. STATE	TOTAL ASSETS ($MIL)
AMICA LIFE INS CO	RI	1,465.4
ANNUITY INVESTORS LIFE INS CO	OH	3,225.7
CENTRAL STATES H & L CO OF OMAHA	NE	386.9
COUNTRY INVESTORS LIFE ASR CO	IL	323.0
DELAWARE AMERICAN LIFE INS CO	DE	106.3
FIDELITY SECURITY LIFE INS CO	MO	982.0
NATIONAL BENEFIT LIFE INS CO	NY	675.0
NEW YORK LIFE INS CO	NY	214,000.0
PACIFIC LIFE INS CO	NE	178,000.0
PARKER CENTENNIAL ASR CO	WI	99.1
STANDARD SECURITY LIFE INS CO OF NY	NY	152.8
TRUSTMARK LIFE INS CO	IL	249.3

Rating: B+

INSURANCE COMPANY NAME	DOM. STATE	TOTAL ASSETS ($MIL)
AMERICAN CONTINENTAL INS CO	TN	439.4
AMERICAN FIDELITY ASR CO	OK	7,628.5
AMERICAN HEALTH & LIFE INS CO	TX	1,264.4
ASSURITY LIFE INS CO	NE	2,660.6
BEST LIFE & HEALTH INS CO	TX	31.3
BOSTON MUTUAL LIFE INS CO	MA	1,634.0
CHRISTIAN FIDELITY LIFE INS CO	TX	44.0
CM LIFE INS CO	CT	9,072.1
COMPANION LIFE INS CO	SC	689.7
FREEDOM LIFE INS CO OF AMERICA	TX	462.4
GERBER LIFE INS CO	NY	5,146.7
HM LIFE INS CO	PA	881.3
ILLINOIS MUTUAL LIFE INS CO	IL	1,595.0
NATIONAL HEALTH INS CO	TX	181.1
NORTHWESTERN LONG TERM CARE INS CO	WI	320.0
NORTHWESTERN MUTUAL LIFE INS CO	WI	335,000.0
NY LIFE INS & ANNUITY CORP	DE	183,000.0
NYLIFE INS CO OF ARIZONA	AZ	159.0
OLD REPUBLIC LIFE INS CO	IL	106.8
OXFORD LIFE INS CO	AZ	2,955.5
PACIFIC LIFE & ANNUITY CO	AZ	8,615.1
PAN AMERICAN ASR CO	LA	26.7

INSURANCE COMPANY NAME	DOM. STATE	TOTAL ASSETS ($MIL)
PHYSICIANS LIFE INS CO	NE	1,783.0
PRINCIPAL LIFE INS CO	IA	239,000.0
STANDARD INS CO	OR	32,461.1
SYMETRA NATIONAL LIFE INS CO	IA	24.4
TRANS OCEANIC LIFE INS CO	PR	407.4
TRANS WORLD ASR CO	CA	341.0
UNITED WORLD LIFE INS CO	NE	160.3
USAA LIFE INS CO	TX	26,197.9
USABLE LIFE	AR	505.6
VOYA RETIREMENT INS & ANNUITY CO	CT	129,000.0

Georgia

INSURANCE COMPANY NAME	DOM. STATE	TOTAL ASSETS ($MIL)

Rating: A+

INSURANCE COMPANY NAME	DOM. STATE	TOTAL ASSETS ($MIL)
AMERICAN FAMILY LIFE INS CO	WI	5,473.4
CHESAPEAKE LIFE INS CO	OK	251.1
COUNTRY LIFE INS CO	IL	9,442.8
PHYSICIANS MUTUAL INS CO	NE	2,785.1
STATE FARM LIFE INS CO	IL	86,273.0
TEACHERS INS & ANNUITY ASN OF AM	NY	343,000.0

Rating: A

INSURANCE COMPANY NAME	DOM. STATE	TOTAL ASSETS ($MIL)
BERKLEY LIFE & HEALTH INS CO	IA	478.2
DIRECT GENERAL LIFE INS CO	SC	33.5
FEDERATED LIFE INS CO	MN	2,427.1
FIDELITY INVESTMENTS LIFE INS CO	UT	44,295.4
FRANDISCO LIFE INS CO	GA	121.9
GARDEN STATE LIFE INS CO	TX	143.5
GUARDIAN LIFE INS CO OF AMERICA	NY	72,127.3
NATIONAL FOUNDATION LIFE INS CO	TX	94.2
SENTRY LIFE INS CO	WI	9,857.5
SOUTHERN FARM BUREAU LIFE INS CO	MS	15,730.7

Rating: A-

INSURANCE COMPANY NAME	DOM. STATE	TOTAL ASSETS ($MIL)
AMICA LIFE INS CO	RI	1,465.4
ANNUITY INVESTORS LIFE INS CO	OH	3,225.7
CENTRAL STATES H & L CO OF OMAHA	NE	386.9
COUNTRY INVESTORS LIFE ASR CO	IL	323.0
DELAWARE AMERICAN LIFE INS CO	DE	106.3
FIDELITY SECURITY LIFE INS CO	MO	982.0
NATIONAL BENEFIT LIFE INS CO	NY	675.0
NEW YORK LIFE INS CO	NY	214,000.0
PACIFIC LIFE INS CO	NE	178,000.0
PARKER CENTENNIAL ASR CO	WI	99.1
STANDARD SECURITY LIFE INS CO OF NY	NY	152.8
SWBC LIFE INS CO	TX	42.4
TRUSTMARK LIFE INS CO	IL	249.3

Rating: B+

INSURANCE COMPANY NAME	DOM. STATE	TOTAL ASSETS ($MIL)
AMERICAN CONTINENTAL INS CO	TN	439.4
AMERICAN FIDELITY ASR CO	OK	7,628.5
AMERICAN HEALTH & LIFE INS CO	TX	1,264.4
ASSURITY LIFE INS CO	NE	2,660.6
BEST LIFE & HEALTH INS CO	TX	31.3
BOSTON MUTUAL LIFE INS CO	MA	1,634.0
CHRISTIAN FIDELITY LIFE INS CO	TX	44.0
CM LIFE INS CO	CT	9,072.1
COMPANION LIFE INS CO	SC	689.7
FREEDOM LIFE INS CO OF AMERICA	TX	462.4
GERBER LIFE INS CO	NY	5,146.7
HM LIFE INS CO	PA	881.3
ILLINOIS MUTUAL LIFE INS CO	IL	1,595.0
NATIONAL HEALTH INS CO	TX	181.1
NORTHWESTERN LONG TERM CARE INS CO	WI	320.0
NORTHWESTERN MUTUAL LIFE INS CO	WI	335,000.0
NY LIFE INS & ANNUITY CORP	DE	183,000.0
NYLIFE INS CO OF ARIZONA	AZ	159.0
OLD REPUBLIC LIFE INS CO	IL	106.8
OXFORD LIFE INS CO	AZ	2,955.5

INSURANCE COMPANY NAME	DOM. STATE	TOTAL ASSETS ($MIL)
PACIFIC LIFE & ANNUITY CO	AZ	8,615.1
PAN AMERICAN ASR CO	LA	26.7
PHYSICIANS LIFE INS CO	NE	1,783.0
PRINCIPAL LIFE INS CO	IA	239,000.0
STANDARD INS CO	OR	32,461.1
SYMETRA NATIONAL LIFE INS CO	IA	24.4
TRANS WORLD ASR CO	CA	341.0
UNITED NATIONAL LIFE INS CO OF AM	IL	52.1
UNITED WORLD LIFE INS CO	NE	160.3
USAA LIFE INS CO	TX	26,197.9
USABLE LIFE	AR	505.6
VOYA RETIREMENT INS & ANNUITY CO	CT	129,000.0

Hawaii

INSURANCE COMPANY NAME	DOM. STATE	TOTAL ASSETS ($MIL)
### Rating: A+		
AMERICAN FAMILY LIFE INS CO	WI	5,473.4
CHESAPEAKE LIFE INS CO	OK	251.1
PHYSICIANS MUTUAL INS CO	NE	2,785.1
STATE FARM LIFE INS CO	IL	86,273.0
TEACHERS INS & ANNUITY ASN OF AM	NY	343,000.0
### Rating: A		
BERKLEY LIFE & HEALTH INS CO	IA	478.2
FIDELITY INVESTMENTS LIFE INS CO	UT	44,295.4
GARDEN STATE LIFE INS CO	TX	143.5
GUARDIAN LIFE INS CO OF AMERICA	NY	72,127.3
SENTRY LIFE INS CO	WI	9,857.5
### Rating: A-		
AMICA LIFE INS CO	RI	1,465.4
ANNUITY INVESTORS LIFE INS CO	OH	3,225.7
CENTRAL STATES H & L CO OF OMAHA	NE	386.9
DELAWARE AMERICAN LIFE INS CO	DE	106.3
FIDELITY SECURITY LIFE INS CO	MO	982.0
NATIONAL BENEFIT LIFE INS CO	NY	675.0
NEW YORK LIFE INS CO	NY	214,000.0
PACIFIC LIFE INS CO	NE	178,000.0
PARKER CENTENNIAL ASR CO	WI	99.1
STANDARD SECURITY LIFE INS CO OF NY	NY	152.8
TRUSTMARK LIFE INS CO	IL	249.3
### Rating: B+		
AMERICAN FIDELITY ASR CO	OK	7,628.5
AMERICAN HEALTH & LIFE INS CO	TX	1,264.4
ASSURITY LIFE INS CO	NE	2,660.6
BEST LIFE & HEALTH INS CO	TX	31.3
BOSTON MUTUAL LIFE INS CO	MA	1,634.0
CM LIFE INS CO	CT	9,072.1
COMPANION LIFE INS CO OF CA	CA	34.1
GERBER LIFE INS CO	NY	5,146.7
HM LIFE INS CO	PA	881.3
NATIONAL HEALTH INS CO	TX	181.1
NORTHWESTERN LONG TERM CARE INS CO	WI	320.0
NORTHWESTERN MUTUAL LIFE INS CO	WI	335,000.0
NY LIFE INS & ANNUITY CORP	DE	183,000.0
NYLIFE INS CO OF ARIZONA	AZ	159.0
OLD REPUBLIC LIFE INS CO	IL	106.8
OXFORD LIFE INS CO	AZ	2,955.5
PACIFIC LIFE & ANNUITY CO	AZ	8,615.1
PAN AMERICAN ASR CO	LA	26.7
PHYSICIANS LIFE INS CO	NE	1,783.0
PRINCIPAL LIFE INS CO	IA	239,000.0
STANDARD INS CO	OR	32,461.1
TRANS WORLD ASR CO	CA	341.0
UNITED WORLD LIFE INS CO	NE	160.3
USAA LIFE INS CO	TX	26,197.9
USABLE LIFE	AR	505.6
VOYA RETIREMENT INS & ANNUITY CO	CT	129,000.0

Idaho

INSURANCE COMPANY NAME	DOM. STATE	TOTAL ASSETS ($MIL)
Rating: A+		
AMERICAN FAMILY LIFE INS CO	WI	5,473.4
CHESAPEAKE LIFE INS CO	OK	251.1
COUNTRY LIFE INS CO	IL	9,442.8
PHYSICIANS MUTUAL INS CO	NE	2,785.1
STATE FARM LIFE INS CO	IL	86,273.0
TEACHERS INS & ANNUITY ASN OF AM	NY	343,000.0
Rating: A		
BERKLEY LIFE & HEALTH INS CO	IA	478.2
DIRECT GENERAL LIFE INS CO	SC	33.5
FEDERATED LIFE INS CO	MN	2,427.1
FIDELITY INVESTMENTS LIFE INS CO	UT	44,295.4
GARDEN STATE LIFE INS CO	TX	143.5
GUARDIAN LIFE INS CO OF AMERICA	NY	72,127.3
NATIONAL FOUNDATION LIFE INS CO	TX	94.2
SENTRY LIFE INS CO	WI	9,857.5
Rating: A-		
AMICA LIFE INS CO	RI	1,465.4
ANNUITY INVESTORS LIFE INS CO	OH	3,225.7
CENTRAL STATES H & L CO OF OMAHA	NE	386.9
COUNTRY INVESTORS LIFE ASR CO	IL	323.0
DELAWARE AMERICAN LIFE INS CO	DE	106.3
FIDELITY SECURITY LIFE INS CO	MO	982.0
NATIONAL BENEFIT LIFE INS CO	NY	675.0
NEW YORK LIFE INS CO	NY	214,000.0
PACIFIC LIFE INS CO	NE	178,000.0
PARKER CENTENNIAL ASR CO	WI	99.1
STANDARD SECURITY LIFE INS CO OF NY	NY	152.8
TRUSTMARK LIFE INS CO	IL	249.3
Rating: B+		
AMERICAN FIDELITY ASR CO	OK	7,628.5
AMERICAN HEALTH & LIFE INS CO	TX	1,264.4
ASSURITY LIFE INS CO	NE	2,660.6
BEST LIFE & HEALTH INS CO	TX	31.3
BOSTON MUTUAL LIFE INS CO	MA	1,634.0
CHRISTIAN FIDELITY LIFE INS CO	TX	44.0
CM LIFE INS CO	CT	9,072.1
COMPANION LIFE INS CO	SC	689.7
FARM BUREAU LIFE INS CO	IA	9,888.5
GERBER LIFE INS CO	NY	5,146.7
HM LIFE INS CO	PA	881.3
ILLINOIS MUTUAL LIFE INS CO	IL	1,595.0
NATIONAL FARMERS UNION LIFE INS CO	TX	158.8
NATIONAL HEALTH INS CO	TX	181.1
NORTHWESTERN LONG TERM CARE INS CO	WI	320.0
NORTHWESTERN MUTUAL LIFE INS CO	WI	335,000.0
NY LIFE INS & ANNUITY CORP	DE	183,000.0
NYLIFE INS CO OF ARIZONA	AZ	159.0
OLD REPUBLIC LIFE INS CO	IL	106.8
OXFORD LIFE INS CO	AZ	2,955.5
PACIFIC LIFE & ANNUITY CO	AZ	8,615.1
PAN AMERICAN ASR CO	LA	26.7
PHYSICIANS LIFE INS CO	NE	1,783.0

INSURANCE COMPANY NAME	DOM. STATE	TOTAL ASSETS ($MIL)
PRINCIPAL LIFE INS CO	IA	239,000.0
STANDARD INS CO	OR	32,461.1
SYMETRA NATIONAL LIFE INS CO	IA	24.4
TRANS WORLD ASR CO	CA	341.0
UNITED NATIONAL LIFE INS CO OF AM	IL	52.1
UNITED WORLD LIFE INS CO	NE	160.3
USAA LIFE INS CO	TX	26,197.9
USABLE LIFE	AR	505.6
VOYA RETIREMENT INS & ANNUITY CO	CT	129,000.0

Illinois

INSURANCE COMPANY NAME	DOM. STATE	TOTAL ASSETS ($MIL)	INSURANCE COMPANY NAME	DOM. STATE	TOTAL ASSETS ($MIL)
Rating: A+			PACIFIC LIFE & ANNUITY CO	AZ	8,615.1
			PAN AMERICAN ASR CO	LA	26.7
AMERICAN FAMILY LIFE INS CO	WI	5,473.4	PHYSICIANS LIFE INS CO	NE	1,783.0
CHESAPEAKE LIFE INS CO	OK	251.1	PRINCIPAL LIFE INS CO	IA	239,000.0
COUNTRY LIFE INS CO	IL	9,442.8	STANDARD INS CO	OR	32,461.1
PHYSICIANS MUTUAL INS CO	NE	2,785.1	SYMETRA NATIONAL LIFE INS CO	IA	24.4
STATE FARM LIFE & ACCIDENT ASR CO	IL	3,528.9	TRANS WORLD ASR CO	CA	341.0
STATE FARM LIFE INS CO	IL	86,273.0	UNITED FARM FAMILY LIFE INS CO	IN	2,457.7
TEACHERS INS & ANNUITY ASN OF AM	NY	343,000.0	UNITED NATIONAL LIFE INS CO OF AM	IL	52.1
			UNITED WORLD LIFE INS CO	NE	160.3
Rating: A			USAA LIFE INS CO	TX	26,197.9
			USABLE LIFE	AR	505.6
BERKLEY LIFE & HEALTH INS CO	IA	478.2	VOYA RETIREMENT INS & ANNUITY CO	CT	129,000.0
DIRECT GENERAL LIFE INS CO	SC	33.5			
FEDERATED LIFE INS CO	MN	2,427.1			
FIDELITY INVESTMENTS LIFE INS CO	UT	44,295.4			
GARDEN STATE LIFE INS CO	TX	143.5			
GUARDIAN LIFE INS CO OF AMERICA	NY	72,127.3			
SENTRY LIFE INS CO	WI	9,857.5			
SHELTERPOINT LIFE INS CO	NY	392.4			
Rating: A-					
AMICA LIFE INS CO	RI	1,465.4			
ANNUITY INVESTORS LIFE INS CO	OH	3,225.7			
CENTRAL STATES H & L CO OF OMAHA	NE	386.9			
COUNTRY INVESTORS LIFE ASR CO	IL	323.0			
DELAWARE AMERICAN LIFE INS CO	DE	106.3			
FIDELITY SECURITY LIFE INS CO	MO	982.0			
NATIONAL BENEFIT LIFE INS CO	NY	675.0			
NEW YORK LIFE INS CO	NY	214,000.0			
PACIFIC LIFE INS CO	NE	178,000.0			
PARKER CENTENNIAL ASR CO	WI	99.1			
STANDARD SECURITY LIFE INS CO OF NY	NY	152.8			
TRUSTMARK LIFE INS CO	IL	249.3			
Rating: B+					
AMERICAN CONTINENTAL INS CO	TN	439.4			
AMERICAN FIDELITY ASR CO	OK	7,628.5			
AMERICAN HEALTH & LIFE INS CO	TX	1,264.4			
ASSURITY LIFE INS CO	NE	2,660.6			
BEST LIFE & HEALTH INS CO	TX	31.3			
BOSTON MUTUAL LIFE INS CO	MA	1,634.0			
CHRISTIAN FIDELITY LIFE INS CO	TX	44.0			
CM LIFE INS CO	CT	9,072.1			
COMPANION LIFE INS CO	SC	689.7			
ENTERPRISE LIFE INS CO	TX	159.9			
FREEDOM LIFE INS CO OF AMERICA	TX	462.4			
GERBER LIFE INS CO	NY	5,146.7			
HM LIFE INS CO	PA	881.3			
ILLINOIS MUTUAL LIFE INS CO	IL	1,595.0			
NATIONAL FARMERS UNION LIFE INS CO	TX	158.8			
NATIONAL HEALTH INS CO	TX	181.1			
NORTHWESTERN LONG TERM CARE INS CO	WI	320.0			
NORTHWESTERN MUTUAL LIFE INS CO	WI	335,000.0			
NY LIFE INS & ANNUITY CORP	DE	183,000.0			
NYLIFE INS CO OF ARIZONA	AZ	159.0			
OLD REPUBLIC LIFE INS CO	IL	106.8			
OXFORD LIFE INS CO	AZ	2,955.5			

Indiana

INSURANCE COMPANY NAME	DOM. STATE	TOTAL ASSETS ($MIL)
### Rating: A+		
AMERICAN FAMILY LIFE INS CO	WI	5,473.4
CHESAPEAKE LIFE INS CO	OK	251.1
COUNTRY LIFE INS CO	IL	9,442.8
PHYSICIANS MUTUAL INS CO	NE	2,785.1
STATE FARM LIFE INS CO	IL	86,273.0
TEACHERS INS & ANNUITY ASN OF AM	NY	343,000.0
### Rating: A		
BERKLEY LIFE & HEALTH INS CO	IA	478.2
DIRECT GENERAL LIFE INS CO	SC	33.5
FEDERATED LIFE INS CO	MN	2,427.1
FIDELITY INVESTMENTS LIFE INS CO	UT	44,295.4
GARDEN STATE LIFE INS CO	TX	143.5
GUARDIAN LIFE INS CO OF AMERICA	NY	72,127.3
NATIONAL FOUNDATION LIFE INS CO	TX	94.2
SENTRY LIFE INS CO	WI	9,857.5
### Rating: A-		
AMICA LIFE INS CO	RI	1,465.4
ANNUITY INVESTORS LIFE INS CO	OH	3,225.7
CENTRAL STATES H & L CO OF OMAHA	NE	386.9
COUNTRY INVESTORS LIFE ASR CO	IL	323.0
DELAWARE AMERICAN LIFE INS CO	DE	106.3
FIDELITY SECURITY LIFE INS CO	MO	982.0
NATIONAL BENEFIT LIFE INS CO	NY	675.0
NEW YORK LIFE INS CO	NY	214,000.0
PACIFIC LIFE INS CO	NE	178,000.0
PARKER CENTENNIAL ASR CO	WI	99.1
STANDARD SECURITY LIFE INS CO OF NY	NY	152.8
TRUSTMARK LIFE INS CO	IL	249.3
### Rating: B+		
AMERICAN CONTINENTAL INS CO	TN	439.4
AMERICAN FIDELITY ASR CO	OK	7,628.5
AMERICAN HEALTH & LIFE INS CO	TX	1,264.4
ASSURITY LIFE INS CO	NE	2,660.6
BEST LIFE & HEALTH INS CO	TX	31.3
BOSTON MUTUAL LIFE INS CO	MA	1,634.0
CHRISTIAN FIDELITY LIFE INS CO	TX	44.0
CM LIFE INS CO	CT	9,072.1
COMPANION LIFE INS CO	SC	689.7
FREEDOM LIFE INS CO OF AMERICA	TX	462.4
GERBER LIFE INS CO	NY	5,146.7
HM LIFE INS CO	PA	881.3
ILLINOIS MUTUAL LIFE INS CO	IL	1,595.0
NATIONAL FARMERS UNION LIFE INS CO	TX	158.8
NATIONAL HEALTH INS CO	TX	181.1
NORTHWESTERN LONG TERM CARE INS CO	WI	320.0
NORTHWESTERN MUTUAL LIFE INS CO	WI	335,000.0
NY LIFE INS & ANNUITY CORP	DE	183,000.0
NYLIFE INS CO OF ARIZONA	AZ	159.0
OLD REPUBLIC LIFE INS CO	IL	106.8
OXFORD LIFE INS CO	AZ	2,955.5
PACIFIC LIFE & ANNUITY CO	AZ	8,615.1
PAN AMERICAN ASR CO	LA	26.7

INSURANCE COMPANY NAME	DOM. STATE	TOTAL ASSETS ($MIL)
PHYSICIANS LIFE INS CO	NE	1,783.0
PRINCIPAL LIFE INS CO	IA	239,000.0
STANDARD INS CO	OR	32,461.1
SYMETRA NATIONAL LIFE INS CO	IA	24.4
TRANS WORLD ASR CO	CA	341.0
UNITED FARM FAMILY LIFE INS CO	IN	2,457.7
UNITED NATIONAL LIFE INS CO OF AM	IL	52.1
UNITED WORLD LIFE INS CO	NE	160.3
USAA LIFE INS CO	TX	26,197.9
USABLE LIFE	AR	505.6
VOYA RETIREMENT INS & ANNUITY CO	CT	129,000.0

Iowa

INSURANCE COMPANY NAME	DOM. STATE	TOTAL ASSETS ($MIL)

Rating: A+

INSURANCE COMPANY NAME	DOM. STATE	TOTAL ASSETS ($MIL)
AMERICAN FAMILY LIFE INS CO	WI	5,473.4
CHESAPEAKE LIFE INS CO	OK	251.1
COUNTRY LIFE INS CO	IL	9,442.8
PHYSICIANS MUTUAL INS CO	NE	2,785.1
STATE FARM LIFE INS CO	IL	86,273.0
TEACHERS INS & ANNUITY ASN OF AM	NY	343,000.0

Rating: A

INSURANCE COMPANY NAME	DOM. STATE	TOTAL ASSETS ($MIL)
BERKLEY LIFE & HEALTH INS CO	IA	478.2
FEDERATED LIFE INS CO	MN	2,427.1
FIDELITY INVESTMENTS LIFE INS CO	UT	44,295.4
GARDEN STATE LIFE INS CO	TX	143.5
GUARDIAN LIFE INS CO OF AMERICA	NY	72,127.3
NATIONAL FOUNDATION LIFE INS CO	TX	94.2
SENTRY LIFE INS CO	WI	9,857.5

Rating: A-

INSURANCE COMPANY NAME	DOM. STATE	TOTAL ASSETS ($MIL)
AMICA LIFE INS CO	RI	1,465.4
ANNUITY INVESTORS LIFE INS CO	OH	3,225.7
CENTRAL STATES H & L CO OF OMAHA	NE	386.9
COUNTRY INVESTORS LIFE ASR CO	IL	323.0
DELAWARE AMERICAN LIFE INS CO	DE	106.3
FIDELITY SECURITY LIFE INS CO	MO	982.0
NATIONAL BENEFIT LIFE INS CO	NY	675.0
NEW YORK LIFE INS CO	NY	214,000.0
PACIFIC LIFE INS CO	NE	178,000.0
PARKER CENTENNIAL ASR CO	WI	99.1
STANDARD SECURITY LIFE INS CO OF NY	NY	152.8
TRUSTMARK LIFE INS CO	IL	249.3

Rating: B+

INSURANCE COMPANY NAME	DOM. STATE	TOTAL ASSETS ($MIL)
AMERICAN CONTINENTAL INS CO	TN	439.4
AMERICAN FIDELITY ASR CO	OK	7,628.5
AMERICAN HEALTH & LIFE INS CO	TX	1,264.4
ASSURITY LIFE INS CO	NE	2,660.6
BEST LIFE & HEALTH INS CO	TX	31.3
BOSTON MUTUAL LIFE INS CO	MA	1,634.0
CM LIFE INS CO	CT	9,072.1
COMPANION LIFE INS CO	SC	689.7
FARM BUREAU LIFE INS CO	IA	9,888.5
FREEDOM LIFE INS CO OF AMERICA	TX	462.4
GERBER LIFE INS CO	NY	5,146.7
HM LIFE INS CO	PA	881.3
ILLINOIS MUTUAL LIFE INS CO	IL	1,595.0
M LIFE INS CO	CO	479.6
NATIONAL FARMERS UNION LIFE INS CO	TX	158.8
NATIONAL HEALTH INS CO	TX	181.1
NORTHWESTERN LONG TERM CARE INS CO	WI	320.0
NORTHWESTERN MUTUAL LIFE INS CO	WI	335,000.0
NY LIFE INS & ANNUITY CORP	DE	183,000.0
NYLIFE INS CO OF ARIZONA	AZ	159.0
OLD REPUBLIC LIFE INS CO	IL	106.8
OXFORD LIFE INS CO	AZ	2,955.5
PACIFIC LIFE & ANNUITY CO	AZ	8,615.1
PHYSICIANS LIFE INS CO	NE	1,783.0

INSURANCE COMPANY NAME	DOM. STATE	TOTAL ASSETS ($MIL)
PRINCIPAL LIFE INS CO	IA	239,000.0
STANDARD INS CO	OR	32,461.1
SYMETRA NATIONAL LIFE INS CO	IA	24.4
TRANS WORLD ASR CO	CA	341.0
UNITED FARM FAMILY LIFE INS CO	IN	2,457.7
UNITED NATIONAL LIFE INS CO OF AM	IL	52.1
UNITED WORLD LIFE INS CO	NE	160.3
USAA LIFE INS CO	TX	26,197.9
USABLE LIFE	AR	505.6
VOYA RETIREMENT INS & ANNUITY CO	CT	129,000.0

Kansas

INSURANCE COMPANY NAME	DOM. STATE	TOTAL ASSETS ($MIL)

Rating: A+

INSURANCE COMPANY NAME	DOM. STATE	TOTAL ASSETS ($MIL)
AMERICAN FAMILY LIFE INS CO	WI	5,473.4
CHESAPEAKE LIFE INS CO	OK	251.1
COUNTRY LIFE INS CO	IL	9,442.8
PHYSICIANS MUTUAL INS CO	NE	2,785.1
STATE FARM LIFE INS CO	IL	86,273.0
TEACHERS INS & ANNUITY ASN OF AM	NY	343,000.0

Rating: A

INSURANCE COMPANY NAME	DOM. STATE	TOTAL ASSETS ($MIL)
BERKLEY LIFE & HEALTH INS CO	IA	478.2
DIRECT GENERAL LIFE INS CO	SC	33.5
FEDERATED LIFE INS CO	MN	2,427.1
FIDELITY INVESTMENTS LIFE INS CO	UT	44,295.4
GARDEN STATE LIFE INS CO	TX	143.5
GUARDIAN LIFE INS CO OF AMERICA	NY	72,127.3
NATIONAL FOUNDATION LIFE INS CO	TX	94.2
SENTRY LIFE INS CO	WI	9,857.5

Rating: A-

INSURANCE COMPANY NAME	DOM. STATE	TOTAL ASSETS ($MIL)
AMICA LIFE INS CO	RI	1,465.4
ANNUITY INVESTORS LIFE INS CO	OH	3,225.7
CENTRAL STATES H & L CO OF OMAHA	NE	386.9
COUNTRY INVESTORS LIFE ASR CO	IL	323.0
DELAWARE AMERICAN LIFE INS CO	DE	106.3
FIDELITY SECURITY LIFE INS CO	MO	982.0
NATIONAL BENEFIT LIFE INS CO	NY	675.0
NEW YORK LIFE INS CO	NY	214,000.0
PACIFIC LIFE INS CO	NE	178,000.0
PARKER CENTENNIAL ASR CO	WI	99.1
STANDARD SECURITY LIFE INS CO OF NY	NY	152.8
TRUSTMARK LIFE INS CO	IL	249.3

Rating: B+

INSURANCE COMPANY NAME	DOM. STATE	TOTAL ASSETS ($MIL)
ADVANCE INS CO OF KANSAS	KS	78.4
AMERICAN CONTINENTAL INS CO	TN	439.4
AMERICAN FIDELITY ASR CO	OK	7,628.5
AMERICAN HEALTH & LIFE INS CO	TX	1,264.4
ASSURITY LIFE INS CO	NE	2,660.6
BEST LIFE & HEALTH INS CO	TX	31.3
BOSTON MUTUAL LIFE INS CO	MA	1,634.0
CHRISTIAN FIDELITY LIFE INS CO	TX	44.0
CM LIFE INS CO	CT	9,072.1
COMPANION LIFE INS CO	SC	689.7
ENTERPRISE LIFE INS CO	TX	159.9
FARM BUREAU LIFE INS CO	IA	9,888.5
FREEDOM LIFE INS CO OF AMERICA	TX	462.4
GERBER LIFE INS CO	NY	5,146.7
HM LIFE INS CO	PA	881.3
ILLINOIS MUTUAL LIFE INS CO	IL	1,595.0
NATIONAL FARMERS UNION LIFE INS CO	TX	158.8
NATIONAL HEALTH INS CO	TX	181.1
NORTHWESTERN LONG TERM CARE INS CO	WI	320.0
NORTHWESTERN MUTUAL LIFE INS CO	WI	335,000.0
NY LIFE INS & ANNUITY CORP	DE	183,000.0
NYLIFE INS CO OF ARIZONA	AZ	159.0
OLD REPUBLIC LIFE INS CO	IL	106.8

INSURANCE COMPANY NAME	DOM. STATE	TOTAL ASSETS ($MIL)
OXFORD LIFE INS CO	AZ	2,955.5
PACIFIC LIFE & ANNUITY CO	AZ	8,615.1
PAN AMERICAN ASR CO	LA	26.7
PHYSICIANS LIFE INS CO	NE	1,783.0
PRINCIPAL LIFE INS CO	IA	239,000.0
STANDARD INS CO	OR	32,461.1
SYMETRA NATIONAL LIFE INS CO	IA	24.4
TRANS WORLD ASR CO	CA	341.0
UNITED NATIONAL LIFE INS CO OF AM	IL	52.1
UNITED WORLD LIFE INS CO	NE	160.3
USAA LIFE INS CO	TX	26,197.9
USABLE LIFE	AR	505.6
VOYA RETIREMENT INS & ANNUITY CO	CT	129,000.0

Kentucky

INSURANCE COMPANY NAME	DOM. STATE	TOTAL ASSETS ($MIL)

Rating: A+

INSURANCE COMPANY NAME	DOM. STATE	TOTAL ASSETS ($MIL)
AMERICAN FAMILY LIFE INS CO	WI	5,473.4
CHESAPEAKE LIFE INS CO	OK	251.1
COUNTRY LIFE INS CO	IL	9,442.8
PHYSICIANS MUTUAL INS CO	NE	2,785.1
STATE FARM LIFE INS CO	IL	86,273.0
TEACHERS INS & ANNUITY ASN OF AM	NY	343,000.0

Rating: A

INSURANCE COMPANY NAME	DOM. STATE	TOTAL ASSETS ($MIL)
BERKLEY LIFE & HEALTH INS CO	IA	478.2
DIRECT GENERAL LIFE INS CO	SC	33.5
FEDERATED LIFE INS CO	MN	2,427.1
FIDELITY INVESTMENTS LIFE INS CO	UT	44,295.4
GARDEN STATE LIFE INS CO	TX	143.5
GUARDIAN LIFE INS CO OF AMERICA	NY	72,127.3
NATIONAL FOUNDATION LIFE INS CO	TX	94.2
SENTRY LIFE INS CO	WI	9,857.5
SOUTHERN FARM BUREAU LIFE INS CO	MS	15,730.7

Rating: A-

INSURANCE COMPANY NAME	DOM. STATE	TOTAL ASSETS ($MIL)
AMICA LIFE INS CO	RI	1,465.4
ANNUITY INVESTORS LIFE INS CO	OH	3,225.7
CENTRAL STATES H & L CO OF OMAHA	NE	386.9
COUNTRY INVESTORS LIFE ASR CO	IL	323.0
DELAWARE AMERICAN LIFE INS CO	DE	106.3
FIDELITY SECURITY LIFE INS CO	MO	982.0
NATIONAL BENEFIT LIFE INS CO	NY	675.0
NEW YORK LIFE INS CO	NY	214,000.0
PACIFIC LIFE INS CO	NE	178,000.0
PARKER CENTENNIAL ASR CO	WI	99.1
STANDARD SECURITY LIFE INS CO OF NY	NY	152.8
TRUSTMARK LIFE INS CO	IL	249.3

Rating: B+

INSURANCE COMPANY NAME	DOM. STATE	TOTAL ASSETS ($MIL)
AMERICAN CONTINENTAL INS CO	TN	439.4
AMERICAN FIDELITY ASR CO	OK	7,628.5
AMERICAN HEALTH & LIFE INS CO	TX	1,264.4
ASSURITY LIFE INS CO	NE	2,660.6
BEST LIFE & HEALTH INS CO	TX	31.3
BOSTON MUTUAL LIFE INS CO	MA	1,634.0
CHRISTIAN FIDELITY LIFE INS CO	TX	44.0
CM LIFE INS CO	CT	9,072.1
COMPANION LIFE INS CO	SC	689.7
FREEDOM LIFE INS CO OF AMERICA	TX	462.4
GERBER LIFE INS CO	NY	5,146.7
HM LIFE INS CO	PA	881.3
ILLINOIS MUTUAL LIFE INS CO	IL	1,595.0
NATIONAL FARMERS UNION LIFE INS CO	TX	158.8
NATIONAL HEALTH INS CO	TX	181.1
NORTHWESTERN LONG TERM CARE INS CO	WI	320.0
NORTHWESTERN MUTUAL LIFE INS CO	WI	335,000.0
NY LIFE INS & ANNUITY CORP	DE	183,000.0
NYLIFE INS CO OF ARIZONA	AZ	159.0
OLD REPUBLIC LIFE INS CO	IL	106.8
OXFORD LIFE INS CO	AZ	2,955.5
PACIFIC LIFE & ANNUITY CO	AZ	8,615.1

INSURANCE COMPANY NAME	DOM. STATE	TOTAL ASSETS ($MIL)
PAN AMERICAN ASR CO	LA	26.7
PHYSICIANS LIFE INS CO	NE	1,783.0
PRINCIPAL LIFE INS CO	IA	239,000.0
STANDARD INS CO	OR	32,461.1
SYMETRA NATIONAL LIFE INS CO	IA	24.4
TRANS WORLD ASR CO	CA	341.0
UNITED NATIONAL LIFE INS CO OF AM	IL	52.1
UNITED WORLD LIFE INS CO	NE	160.3
USAA LIFE INS CO	TX	26,197.9
USABLE LIFE	AR	505.6
VOYA RETIREMENT INS & ANNUITY CO	CT	129,000.0

Louisiana

INSURANCE COMPANY NAME	DOM. STATE	TOTAL ASSETS ($MIL)

Rating: A+

INSURANCE COMPANY NAME	DOM. STATE	TOTAL ASSETS ($MIL)
AMERICAN FAMILY LIFE INS CO	WI	5,473.4
CHESAPEAKE LIFE INS CO	OK	251.1
COUNTRY LIFE INS CO	IL	9,442.8
PHYSICIANS MUTUAL INS CO	NE	2,785.1
STATE FARM LIFE INS CO	IL	86,273.0
TEACHERS INS & ANNUITY ASN OF AM	NY	343,000.0

Rating: A

INSURANCE COMPANY NAME	DOM. STATE	TOTAL ASSETS ($MIL)
BERKLEY LIFE & HEALTH INS CO	IA	478.2
DIRECT GENERAL LIFE INS CO	SC	33.5
FEDERATED LIFE INS CO	MN	2,427.1
FIDELITY INVESTMENTS LIFE INS CO	UT	44,295.4
GARDEN STATE LIFE INS CO	TX	143.5
GUARDIAN LIFE INS CO OF AMERICA	NY	72,127.3
NATIONAL FOUNDATION LIFE INS CO	TX	94.2
SENTRY LIFE INS CO	WI	9,857.5
SOUTHERN FARM BUREAU LIFE INS CO	MS	15,730.7

Rating: A-

INSURANCE COMPANY NAME	DOM. STATE	TOTAL ASSETS ($MIL)
AMICA LIFE INS CO	RI	1,465.4
ANNUITY INVESTORS LIFE INS CO	OH	3,225.7
BLUEBONNET LIFE INS CO	MS	71.5
CENTRAL STATES H & L CO OF OMAHA	NE	386.9
COUNTRY INVESTORS LIFE ASR CO	IL	323.0
DELAWARE AMERICAN LIFE INS CO	DE	106.3
FIDELITY SECURITY LIFE INS CO	MO	982.0
NATIONAL BENEFIT LIFE INS CO	NY	675.0
NEW YORK LIFE INS CO	NY	214,000.0
PACIFIC LIFE INS CO	NE	178,000.0
PARKER CENTENNIAL ASR CO	WI	99.1
STANDARD SECURITY LIFE INS CO OF NY	NY	152.8
SWBC LIFE INS CO	TX	42.4
TRUSTMARK LIFE INS CO	IL	249.3

Rating: B+

INSURANCE COMPANY NAME	DOM. STATE	TOTAL ASSETS ($MIL)
AMERICAN CONTINENTAL INS CO	TN	439.4
AMERICAN FIDELITY ASR CO	OK	7,628.5
AMERICAN HEALTH & LIFE INS CO	TX	1,264.4
ASSURITY LIFE INS CO	NE	2,660.6
BEST LIFE & HEALTH INS CO	TX	31.3
BOSTON MUTUAL LIFE INS CO	MA	1,634.0
CHRISTIAN FIDELITY LIFE INS CO	TX	44.0
CM LIFE INS CO	CT	9,072.1
COMPANION LIFE INS CO	SC	689.7
ENTERPRISE LIFE INS CO	TX	159.9
FREEDOM LIFE INS CO OF AMERICA	TX	462.4
GERBER LIFE INS CO	NY	5,146.7
HM LIFE INS CO	PA	881.3
ILLINOIS MUTUAL LIFE INS CO	IL	1,595.0
NATIONAL HEALTH INS CO	TX	181.1
NORTHWESTERN LONG TERM CARE INS CO	WI	320.0
NORTHWESTERN MUTUAL LIFE INS CO	WI	335,000.0
NY LIFE INS & ANNUITY CORP	DE	183,000.0
NYLIFE INS CO OF ARIZONA	AZ	159.0
OLD REPUBLIC LIFE INS CO	IL	106.8

INSURANCE COMPANY NAME	DOM. STATE	TOTAL ASSETS ($MIL)
OXFORD LIFE INS CO	AZ	2,955.5
PACIFIC LIFE & ANNUITY CO	AZ	8,615.1
PAN AMERICAN ASR CO	LA	26.7
PHYSICIANS LIFE INS CO	NE	1,783.0
PRINCIPAL LIFE INS CO	IA	239,000.0
STANDARD INS CO	OR	32,461.1
SYMETRA NATIONAL LIFE INS CO	IA	24.4
TRANS WORLD ASR CO	CA	341.0
UNITED NATIONAL LIFE INS CO OF AM	IL	52.1
UNITED WORLD LIFE INS CO	NE	160.3
USAA LIFE INS CO	TX	26,197.9
USABLE LIFE	AR	505.6
VOYA RETIREMENT INS & ANNUITY CO	CT	129,000.0

Maine

INSURANCE COMPANY NAME	DOM. STATE	TOTAL ASSETS ($MIL)
VOYA RETIREMENT INS & ANNUITY CO	CT	129,000.0

Rating: A+

INSURANCE COMPANY NAME	DOM. STATE	TOTAL ASSETS ($MIL)
AMERICAN FAMILY LIFE INS CO	WI	5,473.4
CHESAPEAKE LIFE INS CO	OK	251.1
COUNTRY LIFE INS CO	IL	9,442.8
PHYSICIANS MUTUAL INS CO	NE	2,785.1
STATE FARM LIFE INS CO	IL	86,273.0
TEACHERS INS & ANNUITY ASN OF AM	NY	343,000.0

Rating: A

INSURANCE COMPANY NAME	DOM. STATE	TOTAL ASSETS ($MIL)
BERKLEY LIFE & HEALTH INS CO	IA	478.2
DIRECT GENERAL LIFE INS CO	SC	33.5
FEDERATED LIFE INS CO	MN	2,427.1
FIDELITY INVESTMENTS LIFE INS CO	UT	44,295.4
GARDEN STATE LIFE INS CO	TX	143.5
GUARDIAN LIFE INS CO OF AMERICA	NY	72,127.3
NATIONAL FOUNDATION LIFE INS CO	TX	94.2
SENTRY LIFE INS CO	WI	9,857.5

Rating: A-

INSURANCE COMPANY NAME	DOM. STATE	TOTAL ASSETS ($MIL)
AMICA LIFE INS CO	RI	1,465.4
ANNUITY INVESTORS LIFE INS CO	OH	3,225.7
CENTRAL STATES H & L CO OF OMAHA	NE	386.9
COUNTRY INVESTORS LIFE ASR CO	IL	323.0
DELAWARE AMERICAN LIFE INS CO	DE	106.3
FIDELITY SECURITY LIFE INS CO	MO	982.0
NATIONAL BENEFIT LIFE INS CO	NY	675.0
NEW YORK LIFE INS CO	NY	214,000.0
PACIFIC LIFE INS CO	NE	178,000.0
PARKER CENTENNIAL ASR CO	WI	99.1
STANDARD SECURITY LIFE INS CO OF NY	NY	152.8
TRUSTMARK LIFE INS CO	IL	249.3

Rating: B+

INSURANCE COMPANY NAME	DOM. STATE	TOTAL ASSETS ($MIL)
AMERICAN FIDELITY ASR CO	OK	7,628.5
AMERICAN HEALTH & LIFE INS CO	TX	1,264.4
ASSURITY LIFE INS CO	NE	2,660.6
BOSTON MUTUAL LIFE INS CO	MA	1,634.0
CM LIFE INS CO	CT	9,072.1
COMPANION LIFE INS CO	SC	689.7
GERBER LIFE INS CO	NY	5,146.7
HM LIFE INS CO	PA	881.3
ILLINOIS MUTUAL LIFE INS CO	IL	1,595.0
NATIONAL HEALTH INS CO	TX	181.1
NORTHWESTERN LONG TERM CARE INS CO	WI	320.0
NORTHWESTERN MUTUAL LIFE INS CO	WI	335,000.0
NY LIFE INS & ANNUITY CORP	DE	183,000.0
OLD REPUBLIC LIFE INS CO	IL	106.8
OXFORD LIFE INS CO	AZ	2,955.5
PACIFIC LIFE & ANNUITY CO	AZ	8,615.1
PHYSICIANS LIFE INS CO	NE	1,783.0
PRINCIPAL LIFE INS CO	IA	239,000.0
STANDARD INS CO	OR	32,461.1
TRANS WORLD ASR CO	CA	341.0
UNITED WORLD LIFE INS CO	NE	160.3
USAA LIFE INS CO	TX	26,197.9
USABLE LIFE	AR	505.6

Maryland

INSURANCE COMPANY NAME	DOM. STATE	TOTAL ASSETS ($MIL)

Rating: A+

INSURANCE COMPANY NAME	DOM. STATE	TOTAL ASSETS ($MIL)
AMERICAN FAMILY LIFE INS CO	WI	5,473.4
CHESAPEAKE LIFE INS CO	OK	251.1
COUNTRY LIFE INS CO	IL	9,442.8
PHYSICIANS MUTUAL INS CO	NE	2,785.1
STATE FARM LIFE INS CO	IL	86,273.0
TEACHERS INS & ANNUITY ASN OF AM	NY	343,000.0

Rating: A

INSURANCE COMPANY NAME	DOM. STATE	TOTAL ASSETS ($MIL)
BERKLEY LIFE & HEALTH INS CO	IA	478.2
DIRECT GENERAL LIFE INS CO	SC	33.5
FEDERATED LIFE INS CO	MN	2,427.1
FIDELITY INVESTMENTS LIFE INS CO	UT	44,295.4
GARDEN STATE LIFE INS CO	TX	143.5
GUARDIAN LIFE INS CO OF AMERICA	NY	72,127.3
SENTRY LIFE INS CO	WI	9,857.5
SHELTERPOINT LIFE INS CO	NY	392.4

Rating: A-

INSURANCE COMPANY NAME	DOM. STATE	TOTAL ASSETS ($MIL)
AMICA LIFE INS CO	RI	1,465.4
ANNUITY INVESTORS LIFE INS CO	OH	3,225.7
CENTRAL STATES H & L CO OF OMAHA	NE	386.9
COUNTRY INVESTORS LIFE ASR CO	IL	323.0
DELAWARE AMERICAN LIFE INS CO	DE	106.3
FIDELITY SECURITY LIFE INS CO	MO	982.0
NATIONAL BENEFIT LIFE INS CO	NY	675.0
NEW YORK LIFE INS CO	NY	214,000.0
PACIFIC LIFE INS CO	NE	178,000.0
PARKER CENTENNIAL ASR CO	WI	99.1
STANDARD SECURITY LIFE INS CO OF NY	NY	152.8
TRUSTMARK LIFE INS CO	IL	249.3

Rating: B+

INSURANCE COMPANY NAME	DOM. STATE	TOTAL ASSETS ($MIL)
AMERICAN FIDELITY ASR CO	OK	7,628.5
AMERICAN HEALTH & LIFE INS CO	TX	1,264.4
ASSURITY LIFE INS CO	NE	2,660.6
BEST LIFE & HEALTH INS CO	TX	31.3
BOSTON MUTUAL LIFE INS CO	MA	1,634.0
CM LIFE INS CO	CT	9,072.1
COMPANION LIFE INS CO	SC	689.7
FREEDOM LIFE INS CO OF AMERICA	TX	462.4
GERBER LIFE INS CO	NY	5,146.7
HM LIFE INS CO	PA	881.3
ILLINOIS MUTUAL LIFE INS CO	IL	1,595.0
NATIONAL HEALTH INS CO	TX	181.1
NORTHWESTERN LONG TERM CARE INS CO	WI	320.0
NORTHWESTERN MUTUAL LIFE INS CO	WI	335,000.0
NY LIFE INS & ANNUITY CORP	DE	183,000.0
NYLIFE INS CO OF ARIZONA	AZ	159.0
OLD REPUBLIC LIFE INS CO	IL	106.8
OXFORD LIFE INS CO	AZ	2,955.5
PACIFIC LIFE & ANNUITY CO	AZ	8,615.1
PAN AMERICAN ASR CO	LA	26.7
PHYSICIANS LIFE INS CO	NE	1,783.0
PRINCIPAL LIFE INS CO	IA	239,000.0
STANDARD INS CO	OR	32,461.1

INSURANCE COMPANY NAME	DOM. STATE	TOTAL ASSETS ($MIL)
SYMETRA NATIONAL LIFE INS CO	IA	24.4
TRANS WORLD ASR CO	CA	341.0
UNITED FARM FAMILY LIFE INS CO	IN	2,457.7
UNITED WORLD LIFE INS CO	NE	160.3
USAA LIFE INS CO	TX	26,197.9
USABLE LIFE	AR	505.6
VOYA RETIREMENT INS & ANNUITY CO	CT	129,000.0

Massachusetts

INSURANCE COMPANY NAME	DOM. STATE	TOTAL ASSETS ($MIL)
USAA LIFE INS CO	TX	26,197.9
USABLE LIFE	AR	505.6
VOYA RETIREMENT INS & ANNUITY CO	CT	129,000.0

Rating: A+

INSURANCE COMPANY NAME	DOM. STATE	TOTAL ASSETS ($MIL)
AMERICAN FAMILY LIFE INS CO	WI	5,473.4
CHESAPEAKE LIFE INS CO	OK	251.1
COUNTRY LIFE INS CO	IL	9,442.8
PHYSICIANS MUTUAL INS CO	NE	2,785.1
TEACHERS INS & ANNUITY ASN OF AM	NY	343,000.0

Rating: A

INSURANCE COMPANY NAME	DOM. STATE	TOTAL ASSETS ($MIL)
AMERICAN FAMILY LIFE ASR CO OF NY	NY	1,108.3
BERKLEY LIFE & HEALTH INS CO	IA	478.2
DIRECT GENERAL LIFE INS CO	SC	33.5
FEDERATED LIFE INS CO	MN	2,427.1
FIDELITY INVESTMENTS LIFE INS CO	UT	44,295.4
GARDEN STATE LIFE INS CO	TX	143.5
GUARDIAN LIFE INS CO OF AMERICA	NY	72,127.3
SENTRY LIFE INS CO	WI	9,857.5
SHELTERPOINT LIFE INS CO	NY	392.4

Rating: A-

INSURANCE COMPANY NAME	DOM. STATE	TOTAL ASSETS ($MIL)
AMICA LIFE INS CO	RI	1,465.4
ANNUITY INVESTORS LIFE INS CO	OH	3,225.7
CENTRAL STATES H & L CO OF OMAHA	NE	386.9
COUNTRY INVESTORS LIFE ASR CO	IL	323.0
DELAWARE AMERICAN LIFE INS CO	DE	106.3
FIDELITY SECURITY LIFE INS CO	MO	982.0
NATIONAL BENEFIT LIFE INS CO	NY	075.0
NEW YORK LIFE INS CO	NY	214,000.0
PACIFIC LIFE INS CO	NE	178,000.0
PARKER CENTENNIAL ASR CO	WI	99.1
STANDARD SECURITY LIFE INS CO OF NY	NY	152.8
TRUSTMARK LIFE INS CO	IL	249.3

Rating: B+

INSURANCE COMPANY NAME	DOM. STATE	TOTAL ASSETS ($MIL)
AMERICAN FIDELITY ASR CO	OK	7,628.5
AMERICAN HEALTH & LIFE INS CO	TX	1,264.4
ASSURITY LIFE INS CO	NE	2,660.6
BOSTON MUTUAL LIFE INS CO	MA	1,634.0
CM LIFE INS CO	CT	9,072.1
COMPANION LIFE INS CO	SC	689.7
GERBER LIFE INS CO	NY	5,146.7
HM LIFE INS CO	PA	881.3
ILLINOIS MUTUAL LIFE INS CO	IL	1,595.0
NATIONAL HEALTH INS CO	TX	181.1
NORTHWESTERN LONG TERM CARE INS CO	WI	320.0
NORTHWESTERN MUTUAL LIFE INS CO	WI	335,000.0
NY LIFE INS & ANNUITY CORP	DE	183,000.0
NYLIFE INS CO OF ARIZONA	AZ	159.0
OLD REPUBLIC LIFE INS CO	IL	106.8
OXFORD LIFE INS CO	AZ	2,955.5
PACIFIC LIFE & ANNUITY CO	AZ	8,615.1
PHYSICIANS LIFE INS CO	NE	1,783.0
PRINCIPAL LIFE INS CO	IA	239,000.0
STANDARD INS CO	OR	32,461.1
TRANS WORLD ASR CO	CA	341.0
UNITED FARM FAMILY LIFE INS CO	IN	2,457.7
UNITED WORLD LIFE INS CO	NE	160.3

Michigan

INSURANCE COMPANY NAME	DOM. STATE	TOTAL ASSETS ($MIL)
Rating: A+		
AMERICAN FAMILY LIFE INS CO	WI	5,473.4
CHESAPEAKE LIFE INS CO	OK	251.1
COUNTRY LIFE INS CO	IL	9,442.8
PHYSICIANS MUTUAL INS CO	NE	2,785.1
STATE FARM LIFE INS CO	IL	86,273.0
TEACHERS INS & ANNUITY ASN OF AM	NY	343,000.0
Rating: A		
BERKLEY LIFE & HEALTH INS CO	IA	478.2
FEDERATED LIFE INS CO	MN	2,427.1
FIDELITY INVESTMENTS LIFE INS CO	UT	44,295.4
GARDEN STATE LIFE INS CO	TX	143.5
GUARDIAN LIFE INS CO OF AMERICA	NY	72,127.3
SENTRY LIFE INS CO	WI	9,857.5
SHELTERPOINT LIFE INS CO	NY	392.4
Rating: A-		
AMICA LIFE INS CO	RI	1,465.4
ANNUITY INVESTORS LIFE INS CO	OH	3,225.7
CENTRAL STATES H & L CO OF OMAHA	NE	386.9
COUNTRY INVESTORS LIFE ASR CO	IL	323.0
DELAWARE AMERICAN LIFE INS CO	DE	106.3
FARM BUREAU LIFE INS CO OF MICHIGAN	MI	2,709.6
FIDELITY SECURITY LIFE INS CO	MO	982.0
NATIONAL BENEFIT LIFE INS CO	NY	675.0
NEW YORK LIFE INS CO	NY	214,000.0
PACIFIC LIFE INS CO	NE	178,000.0
PARKER CENTENNIAL ASR CO	WI	99.1
STANDARD SECURITY LIFE INS CO OF NY	NY	152.8
SWBC LIFE INS CO	TX	42.4
TRUSTMARK LIFE INS CO	IL	249.3
Rating: B+		
AMERICAN CONTINENTAL INS CO	TN	439.4
AMERICAN FIDELITY ASR CO	OK	7,628.5
AMERICAN HEALTH & LIFE INS CO	TX	1,264.4
ASSURITY LIFE INS CO	NE	2,660.6
BEST LIFE & HEALTH INS CO	TX	31.3
BOSTON MUTUAL LIFE INS CO	MA	1,634.0
CM LIFE INS CO	CT	9,072.1
COMPANION LIFE INS CO	SC	689.7
FREEDOM LIFE INS CO OF AMERICA	TX	462.4
GERBER LIFE INS CO	NY	5,146.7
HM LIFE INS CO	PA	881.3
ILLINOIS MUTUAL LIFE INS CO	IL	1,595.0
M LIFE INS CO	CO	479.6
NATIONAL FARMERS UNION LIFE INS CO	TX	158.8
NATIONAL HEALTH INS CO	TX	181.1
NORTHWESTERN LONG TERM CARE INS CO	WI	320.0
NORTHWESTERN MUTUAL LIFE INS CO	WI	335,000.0
NY LIFE INS & ANNUITY CORP	DE	183,000.0
NYLIFE INS CO OF ARIZONA	AZ	159.0
OLD REPUBLIC LIFE INS CO	IL	106.8
OXFORD LIFE INS CO	AZ	2,955.5
PACIFIC LIFE & ANNUITY CO	AZ	8,615.1

INSURANCE COMPANY NAME	DOM. STATE	TOTAL ASSETS ($MIL)
PAN AMERICAN ASR CO	LA	26.7
PHYSICIANS LIFE INS CO	NE	1,783.0
PRINCIPAL LIFE INS CO	IA	239,000.0
STANDARD INS CO	OR	32,461.1
SYMETRA NATIONAL LIFE INS CO	IA	24.4
TRANS WORLD ASR CO	CA	341.0
UNITED NATIONAL LIFE INS CO OF AM	IL	52.1
UNITED WORLD LIFE INS CO	NE	160.3
USAA LIFE INS CO	TX	26,197.9
USABLE LIFE	AR	505.6
VOYA RETIREMENT INS & ANNUITY CO	CT	129,000.0

Minnesota

INSURANCE COMPANY NAME	DOM. STATE	TOTAL ASSETS ($MIL)

Rating: A+

INSURANCE COMPANY NAME	DOM. STATE	TOTAL ASSETS ($MIL)
AMERICAN FAMILY LIFE INS CO	WI	5,473.4
CHESAPEAKE LIFE INS CO	OK	251.1
COUNTRY LIFE INS CO	IL	9,442.8
PHYSICIANS MUTUAL INS CO	NE	2,785.1
STATE FARM LIFE INS CO	IL	86,273.0
TEACHERS INS & ANNUITY ASN OF AM	NY	343,000.0

Rating: A

INSURANCE COMPANY NAME	DOM. STATE	TOTAL ASSETS ($MIL)
BERKLEY LIFE & HEALTH INS CO	IA	478.2
DIRECT GENERAL LIFE INS CO	SC	33.5
FEDERATED LIFE INS CO	MN	2,427.1
FIDELITY INVESTMENTS LIFE INS CO	UT	44,295.4
GARDEN STATE LIFE INS CO	TX	143.5
GUARDIAN LIFE INS CO OF AMERICA	NY	72,127.3
SENTRY LIFE INS CO	WI	9,857.5
SHELTERPOINT LIFE INS CO	NY	392.4

Rating: A-

INSURANCE COMPANY NAME	DOM. STATE	TOTAL ASSETS ($MIL)
AMICA LIFE INS CO	RI	1,465.4
ANNUITY INVESTORS LIFE INS CO	OH	3,225.7
CENTRAL STATES H & L CO OF OMAHA	NE	386.9
COUNTRY INVESTORS LIFE ASR CO	IL	323.0
DELAWARE AMERICAN LIFE INS CO	DE	106.3
FIDELITY SECURITY LIFE INS CO	MO	982.0
NATIONAL BENEFIT LIFE INS CO	NY	675.0
NEW YORK LIFE INS CO	NY	214,000.0
PACIFIC LIFE INS CO	NE	178,000.0
PARKER CENTENNIAL ASR CO	WI	99.1
STANDARD SECURITY LIFE INS CO OF NY	NY	152.8
TRUSTMARK LIFE INS CO	IL	249.3

Rating: B+

INSURANCE COMPANY NAME	DOM. STATE	TOTAL ASSETS ($MIL)
AMERICAN CONTINENTAL INS CO	TN	439.4
AMERICAN FIDELITY ASR CO	OK	7,628.5
AMERICAN HEALTH & LIFE INS CO	TX	1,264.4
ASSURITY LIFE INS CO	NE	2,660.6
BOSTON MUTUAL LIFE INS CO	MA	1,634.0
CM LIFE INS CO	CT	9,072.1
COMPANION LIFE INS CO	SC	689.7
FARM BUREAU LIFE INS CO	IA	9,888.5
FREEDOM LIFE INS CO OF AMERICA	TX	462.4
GERBER LIFE INS CO	NY	5,146.7
HM LIFE INS CO	PA	881.3
ILLINOIS MUTUAL LIFE INS CO	IL	1,595.0
NATIONAL FARMERS UNION LIFE INS CO	TX	158.8
NATIONAL HEALTH INS CO	TX	181.1
NORTHWESTERN LONG TERM CARE INS CO	WI	320.0
NORTHWESTERN MUTUAL LIFE INS CO	WI	335,000.0
NY LIFE INS & ANNUITY CORP	DE	183,000.0
NYLIFE INS CO OF ARIZONA	AZ	159.0
OLD REPUBLIC LIFE INS CO	IL	106.8
OXFORD LIFE INS CO	AZ	2,955.5
PACIFIC LIFE & ANNUITY CO	AZ	8,615.1
PAN AMERICAN ASR CO	LA	26.7
PHYSICIANS LIFE INS CO	NE	1,783.0

INSURANCE COMPANY NAME	DOM. STATE	TOTAL ASSETS ($MIL)
PRINCIPAL LIFE INS CO	IA	239,000.0
STANDARD INS CO	OR	32,461.1
SYMETRA NATIONAL LIFE INS CO	IA	24.4
TRANS WORLD ASR CO	CA	341.0
UNITED NATIONAL LIFE INS CO OF AM	IL	52.1
UNITED WORLD LIFE INS CO	NE	160.3
USAA LIFE INS CO	TX	26,197.9
USABLE LIFE	AR	505.6
VOYA RETIREMENT INS & ANNUITY CO	CT	129,000.0

Mississippi

INSURANCE COMPANY NAME	DOM. STATE	TOTAL ASSETS ($MIL)
Rating: A+		
AMERICAN FAMILY LIFE INS CO	WI	5,473.4
CHESAPEAKE LIFE INS CO	OK	251.1
COUNTRY LIFE INS CO	IL	9,442.8
PHYSICIANS MUTUAL INS CO	NE	2,785.1
STATE FARM LIFE INS CO	IL	86,273.0
TEACHERS INS & ANNUITY ASN OF AM	NY	343,000.0
Rating: A		
BERKLEY LIFE & HEALTH INS CO	IA	478.2
DIRECT GENERAL LIFE INS CO	SC	33.5
FEDERATED LIFE INS CO	MN	2,427.1
FIDELITY INVESTMENTS LIFE INS CO	UT	44,295.4
GARDEN STATE LIFE INS CO	TX	143.5
GUARDIAN LIFE INS CO OF AMERICA	NY	72,127.3
NATIONAL FOUNDATION LIFE INS CO	TX	94.2
SENTRY LIFE INS CO	WI	9,857.5
SOUTHERN FARM BUREAU LIFE INS CO	MS	15,730.7
Rating: A-		
AMICA LIFE INS CO	RI	1,465.4
ANNUITY INVESTORS LIFE INS CO	OH	3,225.7
BLUEBONNET LIFE INS CO	MS	71.5
CENTRAL STATES H & L CO OF OMAHA	NE	386.9
COUNTRY INVESTORS LIFE ASR CO	IL	323.0
DELAWARE AMERICAN LIFE INS CO	DE	106.3
FIDELITY SECURITY LIFE INS CO	MO	982.0
FIDELITY SECURITY LIFE INS CO OF NY	NY	39.3
NATIONAL BENEFIT LIFE INS CO	NY	675.0
NEW YORK LIFE INS CO	NY	214,000.0
PACIFIC LIFE INS CO	NE	178,000.0
PARKER CENTENNIAL ASR CO	WI	99.1
STANDARD SECURITY LIFE INS CO OF NY	NY	152.8
TRUSTMARK LIFE INS CO	IL	249.3
Rating: B+		
AMERICAN CONTINENTAL INS CO	TN	439.4
AMERICAN FIDELITY ASR CO	OK	7,628.5
AMERICAN HEALTH & LIFE INS CO	TX	1,264.4
ASSURITY LIFE INS CO	NE	2,660.6
BEST LIFE & HEALTH INS CO	TX	31.3
BOSTON MUTUAL LIFE INS CO	MA	1,634.0
CHRISTIAN FIDELITY LIFE INS CO	TX	44.0
CM LIFE INS CO	CT	9,072.1
COMPANION LIFE INS CO	SC	689.7
ENTERPRISE LIFE INS CO	TX	159.9
FREEDOM LIFE INS CO OF AMERICA	TX	462.4
GERBER LIFE INS CO	NY	5,146.7
HM LIFE INS CO	PA	881.3
ILLINOIS MUTUAL LIFE INS CO	IL	1,595.0
NATIONAL FARMERS UNION LIFE INS CO	TX	158.8
NATIONAL HEALTH INS CO	TX	181.1
NORTHWESTERN LONG TERM CARE INS CO	WI	320.0
NORTHWESTERN MUTUAL LIFE INS CO	WI	335,000.0
NY LIFE INS & ANNUITY CORP	DE	183,000.0
NYLIFE INS CO OF ARIZONA	AZ	159.0

INSURANCE COMPANY NAME	DOM. STATE	TOTAL ASSETS ($MIL)
OLD REPUBLIC LIFE INS CO	IL	106.8
OXFORD LIFE INS CO	AZ	2,955.5
PACIFIC LIFE & ANNUITY CO	AZ	8,615.1
PAN AMERICAN ASR CO	LA	26.7
PHYSICIANS LIFE INS CO	NE	1,783.0
PRINCIPAL LIFE INS CO	IA	239,000.0
STANDARD INS CO	OR	32,461.1
SYMETRA NATIONAL LIFE INS CO	IA	24.4
TRANS WORLD ASR CO	CA	341.0
UNITED NATIONAL LIFE INS CO OF AM	IL	52.1
UNITED WORLD LIFE INS CO	NE	160.3
USAA LIFE INS CO	TX	26,197.9
USABLE LIFE	AR	505.6
VOYA RETIREMENT INS & ANNUITY CO	CT	129,000.0

Missouri

INSURANCE COMPANY NAME	DOM. STATE	TOTAL ASSETS ($MIL)
Rating: A+		
AMERICAN FAMILY LIFE INS CO	WI	5,473.4
CHESAPEAKE LIFE INS CO	OK	251.1
COUNTRY LIFE INS CO	IL	9,442.8
PHYSICIANS MUTUAL INS CO	NE	2,785.1
STATE FARM LIFE INS CO	IL	86,273.0
TEACHERS INS & ANNUITY ASN OF AM	NY	343,000.0
Rating: A		
BERKLEY LIFE & HEALTH INS CO	IA	478.2
DIRECT GENERAL LIFE INS CO	SC	33.5
FEDERATED LIFE INS CO	MN	2,427.1
FIDELITY INVESTMENTS LIFE INS CO	UT	44,295.4
GARDEN STATE LIFE INS CO	TX	143.5
GUARDIAN LIFE INS CO OF AMERICA	NY	72,127.3
NATIONAL FOUNDATION LIFE INS CO	TX	94.2
SENTRY LIFE INS CO	WI	9,857.5
Rating: A-		
AMICA LIFE INS CO	RI	1,465.4
ANNUITY INVESTORS LIFE INS CO	OH	3,225.7
CENTRAL STATES H & L CO OF OMAHA	NE	386.9
COUNTRY INVESTORS LIFE ASR CO	IL	323.0
DELAWARE AMERICAN LIFE INS CO	DE	106.3
FIDELITY SECURITY LIFE INS CO	MO	982.0
NATIONAL BENEFIT LIFE INS CO	NY	675.0
NEW YORK LIFE INS CO	NY	214,000.0
PACIFIC LIFE INS CO	NE	178,000.0
PARKER CENTENNIAL ASR CO	WI	99.1
STANDARD SECURITY LIFE INS CO OF NY	NY	152.8
TRUSTMARK LIFE INS CO	IL	249.3
Rating: B+		
AMERICAN CONTINENTAL INS CO	TN	439.4
AMERICAN FIDELITY ASR CO	OK	7,628.5
AMERICAN HEALTH & LIFE INS CO	TX	1,264.4
ASSURITY LIFE INS CO	NE	2,660.6
BEST LIFE & HEALTH INS CO	TX	31.3
BOSTON MUTUAL LIFE INS CO	MA	1,634.0
CHRISTIAN FIDELITY LIFE INS CO	TX	44.0
CM LIFE INS CO	CT	9,072.1
COMPANION LIFE INS CO	SC	689.7
FREEDOM LIFE INS CO OF AMERICA	TX	462.4
GERBER LIFE INS CO	NY	5,146.7
HM LIFE INS CO	PA	881.3
ILLINOIS MUTUAL LIFE INS CO	IL	1,595.0
NATIONAL FARMERS UNION LIFE INS CO	TX	158.8
NATIONAL HEALTH INS CO	TX	181.1
NORTHWESTERN LONG TERM CARE INS CO	WI	320.0
NORTHWESTERN MUTUAL LIFE INS CO	WI	335,000.0
NY LIFE INS & ANNUITY CORP	DE	183,000.0
NYLIFE INS CO OF ARIZONA	AZ	159.0
OLD REPUBLIC LIFE INS CO	IL	106.8
OXFORD LIFE INS CO	AZ	2,955.5
PACIFIC LIFE & ANNUITY CO	AZ	8,615.1
PAN AMERICAN ASR CO	LA	26.7

INSURANCE COMPANY NAME	DOM. STATE	TOTAL ASSETS ($MIL)
PHYSICIANS LIFE INS CO	NE	1,783.0
PRINCIPAL LIFE INS CO	IA	239,000.0
STANDARD INS CO	OR	32,461.1
SYMETRA NATIONAL LIFE INS CO	IA	24.4
TRANS WORLD ASR CO	CA	341.0
UNITED NATIONAL LIFE INS CO OF AM	IL	52.1
UNITED WORLD LIFE INS CO	NE	160.3
USAA LIFE INS CO	TX	26,197.9
USABLE LIFE	AR	505.6
VOYA RETIREMENT INS & ANNUITY CO	CT	129,000.0

Montana

INSURANCE COMPANY NAME	DOM. STATE	TOTAL ASSETS ($MIL)

Rating: A+

INSURANCE COMPANY NAME	DOM. STATE	TOTAL ASSETS ($MIL)
AMERICAN FAMILY LIFE INS CO	WI	5,473.4
CHESAPEAKE LIFE INS CO	OK	251.1
COUNTRY LIFE INS CO	IL	9,442.8
PHYSICIANS MUTUAL INS CO	NE	2,785.1
STATE FARM LIFE INS CO	IL	86,273.0
TEACHERS INS & ANNUITY ASN OF AM	NY	343,000.0

Rating: A

INSURANCE COMPANY NAME	DOM. STATE	TOTAL ASSETS ($MIL)
BERKLEY LIFE & HEALTH INS CO	IA	478.2
DIRECT GENERAL LIFE INS CO	SC	33.5
FEDERATED LIFE INS CO	MN	2,427.1
FIDELITY INVESTMENTS LIFE INS CO	UT	44,295.4
GARDEN STATE LIFE INS CO	TX	143.5
GUARDIAN LIFE INS CO OF AMERICA	NY	72,127.3
NATIONAL FOUNDATION LIFE INS CO	TX	94.2
SENTRY LIFE INS CO	WI	9,857.5

Rating: A-

INSURANCE COMPANY NAME	DOM. STATE	TOTAL ASSETS ($MIL)
AMICA LIFE INS CO	RI	1,465.4
ANNUITY INVESTORS LIFE INS CO	OH	3,225.7
CENTRAL STATES H & L CO OF OMAHA	NE	386.9
COUNTRY INVESTORS LIFE ASR CO	IL	323.0
DELAWARE AMERICAN LIFE INS CO	DE	106.3
FIDELITY SECURITY LIFE INS CO	MO	982.0
NATIONAL BENEFIT LIFE INS CO	NY	675.0
NEW YORK LIFE INS CO	NY	214,000.0
PACIFIC LIFE INS CO	NE	178,000.0
PARKER CENTENNIAL ASR CO	WI	99.1
STANDARD SECURITY LIFE INS CO OF NY	NY	152.8
TRUSTMARK LIFE INS CO	IL	249.3

Rating: B+

INSURANCE COMPANY NAME	DOM. STATE	TOTAL ASSETS ($MIL)
AMERICAN CONTINENTAL INS CO	TN	439.4
AMERICAN FIDELITY ASR CO	OK	7,628.5
AMERICAN HEALTH & LIFE INS CO	TX	1,264.4
ASSURITY LIFE INS CO	NE	2,660.6
BEST LIFE & HEALTH INS CO	TX	31.3
BOSTON MUTUAL LIFE INS CO	MA	1,634.0
CHRISTIAN FIDELITY LIFE INS CO	TX	44.0
CM LIFE INS CO	CT	9,072.1
COMPANION LIFE INS CO	SC	689.7
COMPANION LIFE INS CO OF CA	CA	34.1
FARM BUREAU LIFE INS CO	IA	9,888.5
GERBER LIFE INS CO	NY	5,146.7
HM LIFE INS CO	PA	881.3
ILLINOIS MUTUAL LIFE INS CO	IL	1,595.0
NATIONAL FARMERS UNION LIFE INS CO	TX	158.8
NATIONAL HEALTH INS CO	TX	181.1
NORTHWESTERN LONG TERM CARE INS CO	WI	320.0
NORTHWESTERN MUTUAL LIFE INS CO	WI	335,000.0
NY LIFE INS & ANNUITY CORP	DE	183,000.0
NYLIFE INS CO OF ARIZONA	AZ	159.0
OLD REPUBLIC LIFE INS CO	IL	106.8
OXFORD LIFE INS CO	AZ	2,955.5
PACIFIC LIFE & ANNUITY CO	AZ	8,615.1

INSURANCE COMPANY NAME	DOM. STATE	TOTAL ASSETS ($MIL)
PAN AMERICAN ASR CO	LA	26.7
PHYSICIANS LIFE INS CO	NE	1,783.0
PRINCIPAL LIFE INS CO	IA	239,000.0
STANDARD INS CO	OR	32,461.1
SYMETRA NATIONAL LIFE INS CO	IA	24.4
TRANS WORLD ASR CO	CA	341.0
UNITED WORLD LIFE INS CO	NE	160.3
USAA LIFE INS CO	TX	26,197.9
USABLE LIFE	AR	505.6
VOYA RETIREMENT INS & ANNUITY CO	CT	129,000.0

Nebraska

INSURANCE COMPANY NAME	DOM. STATE	TOTAL ASSETS ($MIL)

Rating: A+

INSURANCE COMPANY NAME	DOM. STATE	TOTAL ASSETS ($MIL)
AMERICAN FAMILY LIFE INS CO	WI	5,473.4
CHESAPEAKE LIFE INS CO	OK	251.1
COUNTRY LIFE INS CO	IL	9,442.8
PHYSICIANS MUTUAL INS CO	NE	2,785.1
STATE FARM LIFE INS CO	IL	86,273.0
TEACHERS INS & ANNUITY ASN OF AM	NY	343,000.0

Rating: A

INSURANCE COMPANY NAME	DOM. STATE	TOTAL ASSETS ($MIL)
BERKLEY LIFE & HEALTH INS CO	IA	478.2
DIRECT GENERAL LIFE INS CO	SC	33.5
FEDERATED LIFE INS CO	MN	2,427.1
FIDELITY INVESTMENTS LIFE INS CO	UT	44,295.4
GARDEN STATE LIFE INS CO	TX	143.5
GUARDIAN LIFE INS CO OF AMERICA	NY	72,127.3
NATIONAL FOUNDATION LIFE INS CO	TX	94.2
SENTRY LIFE INS CO	WI	9,857.5

Rating: A-

INSURANCE COMPANY NAME	DOM. STATE	TOTAL ASSETS ($MIL)
AMICA LIFE INS CO	RI	1,465.4
ANNUITY INVESTORS LIFE INS CO	OH	3,225.7
CENTRAL STATES H & L CO OF OMAHA	NE	386.9
COUNTRY INVESTORS LIFE ASR CO	IL	323.0
DELAWARE AMERICAN LIFE INS CO	DE	106.3
FIDELITY SECURITY LIFE INS CO	MO	982.0
NATIONAL BENEFIT LIFE INS CO	NY	675.0
NEW YORK LIFE INS CO	NY	214,000.0
PACIFIC LIFE INS CO	NE	178,000.0
PARKER CENTENNIAL ASR CO	WI	99.1
STANDARD SECURITY LIFE INS CO OF NY	NY	152.8
TRUSTMARK LIFE INS CO	IL	249.3

Rating: B+

INSURANCE COMPANY NAME	DOM. STATE	TOTAL ASSETS ($MIL)
AMERICAN CONTINENTAL INS CO	TN	439.4
AMERICAN FIDELITY ASR CO	OK	7,628.5
AMERICAN HEALTH & LIFE INS CO	TX	1,264.4
ASSURITY LIFE INS CO	NE	2,660.6
BEST LIFE & HEALTH INS CO	TX	31.3
BOSTON MUTUAL LIFE INS CO	MA	1,634.0
CHRISTIAN FIDELITY LIFE INS CO	TX	44.0
CM LIFE INS CO	CT	9,072.1
COMPANION LIFE INS CO	SC	689.7
ENTERPRISE LIFE INS CO	TX	159.9
FARM BUREAU LIFE INS CO	IA	9,888.5
FREEDOM LIFE INS CO OF AMERICA	TX	462.4
GERBER LIFE INS CO	NY	5,146.7
HM LIFE INS CO	PA	881.3
ILLINOIS MUTUAL LIFE INS CO	IL	1,595.0
M LIFE INS CO	CO	479.6
NATIONAL FARMERS UNION LIFE INS CO	TX	158.8
NATIONAL HEALTH INS CO	TX	181.1
NORTHWESTERN LONG TERM CARE INS CO	WI	320.0
NORTHWESTERN MUTUAL LIFE INS CO	WI	335,000.0
NY LIFE INS & ANNUITY CORP	DE	183,000.0
NYLIFE INS CO OF ARIZONA	AZ	159.0
OLD REPUBLIC LIFE INS CO	IL	106.8

INSURANCE COMPANY NAME	DOM. STATE	TOTAL ASSETS ($MIL)
OXFORD LIFE INS CO	AZ	2,955.5
PACIFIC LIFE & ANNUITY CO	AZ	8,615.1
PAN AMERICAN ASR CO	LA	26.7
PHYSICIANS LIFE INS CO	NE	1,783.0
PRINCIPAL LIFE INS CO	IA	239,000.0
STANDARD INS CO	OR	32,461.1
SYMETRA NATIONAL LIFE INS CO	IA	24.4
TRANS WORLD ASR CO	CA	341.0
UNITED NATIONAL LIFE INS CO OF AM	IL	52.1
UNITED WORLD LIFE INS CO	NE	160.3
USAA LIFE INS CO	TX	26,197.9
USABLE LIFE	AR	505.6
VOYA RETIREMENT INS & ANNUITY CO	CT	129,000.0

Nevada

INSURANCE COMPANY NAME	DOM. STATE	TOTAL ASSETS ($MIL)	INSURANCE COMPANY NAME	DOM. STATE	TOTAL ASSETS ($MIL)
Rating: A+			PACIFIC LIFE & ANNUITY CO	AZ	8,615.1
			PAN AMERICAN ASR CO	LA	26.7
AMERICAN FAMILY LIFE INS CO	WI	5,473.4	PHYSICIANS LIFE INS CO	NE	1,783.0
CHESAPEAKE LIFE INS CO	OK	251.1	PRINCIPAL LIFE INS CO	IA	239,000.0
COUNTRY LIFE INS CO	IL	9,442.8	STANDARD INS CO	OR	32,461.1
PHYSICIANS MUTUAL INS CO	NE	2,785.1	SYMETRA NATIONAL LIFE INS CO	IA	24.4
STATE FARM LIFE INS CO	IL	86,273.0	TRANS WORLD ASR CO	CA	341.0
TEACHERS INS & ANNUITY ASN OF AM	NY	343,000.0	UNITED NATIONAL LIFE INS CO OF AM	IL	52.1
			UNITED WORLD LIFE INS CO	NE	160.3
Rating: A			USAA LIFE INS CO	TX	26,197.9
			USABLE LIFE	AR	505.6
BERKLEY LIFE & HEALTH INS CO	IA	478.2	VOYA RETIREMENT INS & ANNUITY CO	CT	129,000.0
DIRECT GENERAL LIFE INS CO	SC	33.5			
FEDERATED LIFE INS CO	MN	2,427.1			
FIDELITY INVESTMENTS LIFE INS CO	UT	44,295.4			
GARDEN STATE LIFE INS CO	TX	143.5			
GUARDIAN LIFE INS CO OF AMERICA	NY	72,127.3			
NATIONAL FOUNDATION LIFE INS CO	TX	94.2			
SENTRY LIFE INS CO	WI	9,857.5			

Rating: A-

INSURANCE COMPANY NAME	DOM. STATE	TOTAL ASSETS ($MIL)
AMICA LIFE INS CO	RI	1,465.4
ANNUITY INVESTORS LIFE INS CO	OH	3,225.7
CENTRAL STATES H & L CO OF OMAHA	NE	386.9
COUNTRY INVESTORS LIFE ASR CO	IL	323.0
DELAWARE AMERICAN LIFE INS CO	DE	106.3
FIDELITY SECURITY LIFE INS CO	MO	982.0
NATIONAL BENEFIT LIFE INS CO	NY	675.0
NEW YORK LIFE INS CO	NY	214,000.0
PACIFIC LIFE INS CO	NE	178,000.0
PARKER CENTENNIAL ASR CO	WI	99.1
STANDARD SECURITY LIFE INS CO OF NY	NY	152.8
TRUSTMARK LIFE INS CO	IL	249.3

Rating: B+

INSURANCE COMPANY NAME	DOM. STATE	TOTAL ASSETS ($MIL)
AMERICAN CONTINENTAL INS CO	TN	439.4
AMERICAN FIDELITY ASR CO	OK	7,628.5
AMERICAN HEALTH & LIFE INS CO	TX	1,264.4
ASSURITY LIFE INS CO	NE	2,660.6
BEST LIFE & HEALTH INS CO	TX	31.3
BOSTON MUTUAL LIFE INS CO	MA	1,634.0
CHRISTIAN FIDELITY LIFE INS CO	TX	44.0
CM LIFE INS CO	CT	9,072.1
COMPANION LIFE INS CO	SC	689.7
COMPANION LIFE INS CO OF CA	CA	34.1
FARM BUREAU LIFE INS CO	IA	9,888.5
FREEDOM LIFE INS CO OF AMERICA	TX	462.4
GERBER LIFE INS CO	NY	5,146.7
HM LIFE INS CO	PA	881.3
ILLINOIS MUTUAL LIFE INS CO	IL	1,595.0
NATIONAL FARMERS UNION LIFE INS CO	TX	158.8
NATIONAL HEALTH INS CO	TX	181.1
NORTHWESTERN LONG TERM CARE INS CO	WI	320.0
NORTHWESTERN MUTUAL LIFE INS CO	WI	335,000.0
NY LIFE INS & ANNUITY CORP	DE	183,000.0
NYLIFE INS CO OF ARIZONA	AZ	159.0
OLD REPUBLIC LIFE INS CO	IL	106.8
OXFORD LIFE INS CO	AZ	2,955.5

New Hampshire

INSURANCE COMPANY NAME	DOM. STATE	TOTAL ASSETS ($MIL)
Rating: A+		
AMERICAN FAMILY LIFE INS CO	WI	5,473.4
CHESAPEAKE LIFE INS CO	OK	251.1
PHYSICIANS MUTUAL INS CO	NE	2,785.1
STATE FARM LIFE INS CO	IL	86,273.0
TEACHERS INS & ANNUITY ASN OF AM	NY	343,000.0
Rating: A		
BERKLEY LIFE & HEALTH INS CO	IA	478.2
FEDERATED LIFE INS CO	MN	2,427.1
FIDELITY INVESTMENTS LIFE INS CO	UT	44,295.4
GARDEN STATE LIFE INS CO	TX	143.5
GUARDIAN LIFE INS CO OF AMERICA	NY	72,127.3
SENTRY LIFE INS CO	WI	9,857.5
Rating: A-		
AMICA LIFE INS CO	RI	1,465.4
ANNUITY INVESTORS LIFE INS CO	OH	3,225.7
CENTRAL STATES H & L CO OF OMAHA	NE	386.9
DELAWARE AMERICAN LIFE INS CO	DE	106.3
FIDELITY SECURITY LIFE INS CO	MO	982.0
NATIONAL BENEFIT LIFE INS CO	NY	675.0
NEW YORK LIFE INS CO	NY	214,000.0
PACIFIC LIFE INS CO	NE	178,000.0
PARKER CENTENNIAL ASR CO	WI	99.1
STANDARD SECURITY LIFE INS CO OF NY	NY	152.0
TRUSTMARK LIFE INS CO	IL	249.3
Rating: B+		
AMERICAN FIDELITY ASR CO	OK	7,628.5
AMERICAN HEALTH & LIFE INS CO	TX	1,264.4
ASSURITY LIFE INS CO	NE	2,660.6
BOSTON MUTUAL LIFE INS CO	MA	1,634.0
CM LIFE INS CO	CT	9,072.1
COMPANION LIFE INS CO	SC	689.7
GERBER LIFE INS CO	NY	5,146.7
HM LIFE INS CO	PA	881.3
ILLINOIS MUTUAL LIFE INS CO	IL	1,595.0
NATIONAL HEALTH INS CO	TX	181.1
NORTHWESTERN LONG TERM CARE INS CO	WI	320.0
NORTHWESTERN MUTUAL LIFE INS CO	WI	335,000.0
NY LIFE INS & ANNUITY CORP	DE	183,000.0
NYLIFE INS CO OF ARIZONA	AZ	159.0
OLD REPUBLIC LIFE INS CO	IL	106.8
OXFORD LIFE INS CO	AZ	2,955.5
PACIFIC LIFE & ANNUITY CO	AZ	8,615.1
PHYSICIANS LIFE INS CO	NE	1,783.0
PRINCIPAL LIFE INS CO	IA	239,000.0
STANDARD INS CO	OR	32,461.1
UNITED FARM FAMILY LIFE INS CO	IN	2,457.7
UNITED WORLD LIFE INS CO	NE	160.3
USAA LIFE INS CO	TX	26,197.9
USABLE LIFE	AR	505.6
VOYA RETIREMENT INS & ANNUITY CO	CT	129,000.0

New Jersey

INSURANCE COMPANY NAME	DOM. STATE	TOTAL ASSETS ($MIL)

Rating: A+

INSURANCE COMPANY NAME	DOM. STATE	TOTAL ASSETS ($MIL)
AMERICAN FAMILY LIFE INS CO	WI	5,473.4
PHYSICIANS MUTUAL INS CO	NE	2,785.1
STATE FARM LIFE INS CO	IL	86,273.0
TEACHERS INS & ANNUITY ASN OF AM	NY	343,000.0

Rating: A

INSURANCE COMPANY NAME	DOM. STATE	TOTAL ASSETS ($MIL)
AMERICAN FAMILY LIFE ASR CO OF NY	NY	1,108.3
BERKLEY LIFE & HEALTH INS CO	IA	478.2
DIRECT GENERAL LIFE INS CO	SC	33.5
FEDERATED LIFE INS CO	MN	2,427.1
FIDELITY INVESTMENTS LIFE INS CO	UT	44,295.4
GARDEN STATE LIFE INS CO	TX	143.5
GUARDIAN LIFE INS CO OF AMERICA	NY	72,127.3
SENTRY LIFE INS CO	WI	9,857.5
SHELTERPOINT LIFE INS CO	NY	392.4

Rating: A-

INSURANCE COMPANY NAME	DOM. STATE	TOTAL ASSETS ($MIL)
AMICA LIFE INS CO	RI	1,465.4
ANNUITY INVESTORS LIFE INS CO	OH	3,225.7
CENTRAL STATES H & L CO OF OMAHA	NE	386.9
DELAWARE AMERICAN LIFE INS CO	DE	106.3
FIDELITY SECURITY LIFE INS CO	MO	982.0
NATIONAL BENEFIT LIFE INS CO	NY	675.0
NEW YORK LIFE INS CO	NY	214,000.0
PACIFIC LIFE INS CO	NE	178,000.0
PARKER CENTENNIAL ASR CO	WI	99.1
STANDARD SECURITY LIFE INS CO OF NY	NY	152.8
TRUSTMARK LIFE INS CO	IL	249.3

Rating: B+

INSURANCE COMPANY NAME	DOM. STATE	TOTAL ASSETS ($MIL)
AMERICAN FIDELITY ASR CO	OK	7,628.5
AMERICAN HEALTH & LIFE INS CO	TX	1,264.4
ASSURITY LIFE INS CO	NE	2,660.6
BOSTON MUTUAL LIFE INS CO	MA	1,634.0
CM LIFE INS CO	CT	9,072.1
GERBER LIFE INS CO	NY	5,146.7
HM LIFE INS CO	PA	881.3
ILLINOIS MUTUAL LIFE INS CO	IL	1,595.0
M LIFE INS CO	CO	479.6
NATIONAL HEALTH INS CO	TX	181.1
NORTHWESTERN LONG TERM CARE INS CO	WI	320.0
NORTHWESTERN MUTUAL LIFE INS CO	WI	335,000.0
NY LIFE INS & ANNUITY CORP	DE	183,000.0
NYLIFE INS CO OF ARIZONA	AZ	159.0
OLD REPUBLIC LIFE INS CO	IL	106.8
OXFORD LIFE INS CO	AZ	2,955.5
PACIFIC LIFE & ANNUITY CO	AZ	8,615.1
PAN AMERICAN ASR CO	LA	26.7
PHYSICIANS LIFE INS CO	NE	1,783.0
PRINCIPAL LIFE INS CO	IA	239,000.0
STANDARD INS CO	OR	32,461.1
TRANS WORLD ASR CO	CA	341.0
UNITED FARM FAMILY LIFE INS CO	IN	2,457.7
UNITED WORLD LIFE INS CO	NE	160.3
USAA LIFE INS CO	TX	26,197.9

INSURANCE COMPANY NAME	DOM. STATE	TOTAL ASSETS ($MIL)
USABLE LIFE	AR	505.6
VOYA RETIREMENT INS & ANNUITY CO	CT	129,000.0

New Mexico

INSURANCE COMPANY NAME	DOM. STATE	TOTAL ASSETS ($MIL)

Rating: A+

INSURANCE COMPANY NAME	DOM. STATE	TOTAL ASSETS ($MIL)
AMERICAN FAMILY LIFE INS CO	WI	5,473.4
CHESAPEAKE LIFE INS CO	OK	251.1
COUNTRY LIFE INS CO	IL	9,442.8
PHYSICIANS MUTUAL INS CO	NE	2,785.1
STATE FARM LIFE INS CO	IL	86,273.0
TEACHERS INS & ANNUITY ASN OF AM	NY	343,000.0

Rating: A

INSURANCE COMPANY NAME	DOM. STATE	TOTAL ASSETS ($MIL)
BERKLEY LIFE & HEALTH INS CO	IA	478.2
DIRECT GENERAL LIFE INS CO	SC	33.5
FEDERATED LIFE INS CO	MN	2,427.1
FIDELITY INVESTMENTS LIFE INS CO	UT	44,295.4
GARDEN STATE LIFE INS CO	TX	143.5
GUARDIAN LIFE INS CO OF AMERICA	NY	72,127.3
NATIONAL FOUNDATION LIFE INS CO	TX	94.2
SENTRY LIFE INS CO	WI	9,857.5

Rating: A-

INSURANCE COMPANY NAME	DOM. STATE	TOTAL ASSETS ($MIL)
AMICA LIFE INS CO	RI	1,465.4
ANNUITY INVESTORS LIFE INS CO	OH	3,225.7
CENTRAL STATES H & L CO OF OMAHA	NE	386.9
COUNTRY INVESTORS LIFE ASR CO	IL	323.0
DELAWARE AMERICAN LIFE INS CO	DE	106.3
FIDELITY SECURITY LIFE INS CO	MO	982.0
NATIONAL BENEFIT LIFE INS CO	NY	675.0
NEW YORK LIFE INS CO	NY	214,000.0
PACIFIC LIFE INS CO	NE	178,000.0
PARKER CENTENNIAL ASR CO	WI	99.1
STANDARD SECURITY LIFE INS CO OF NY	NY	152.8
TRUSTMARK LIFE INS CO	IL	249.3

Rating: B+

INSURANCE COMPANY NAME	DOM. STATE	TOTAL ASSETS ($MIL)
AMERICAN CONTINENTAL INS CO	TN	439.4
AMERICAN FIDELITY ASR CO	OK	7,628.5
AMERICAN HEALTH & LIFE INS CO	TX	1,264.4
ASSURITY LIFE INS CO	NE	2,660.6
BEST LIFE & HEALTH INS CO	TX	31.3
BOSTON MUTUAL LIFE INS CO	MA	1,634.0
CHRISTIAN FIDELITY LIFE INS CO	TX	44.0
CM LIFE INS CO	CT	9,072.1
COMPANION LIFE INS CO	SC	689.7
ENTERPRISE LIFE INS CO	TX	159.9
FARM BUREAU LIFE INS CO	IA	9,888.5
FREEDOM LIFE INS CO OF AMERICA	TX	462.4
GERBER LIFE INS CO	NY	5,146.7
HM LIFE INS CO	PA	881.3
ILLINOIS MUTUAL LIFE INS CO	IL	1,595.0
NATIONAL FARMERS UNION LIFE INS CO	TX	158.8
NATIONAL HEALTH INS CO	TX	181.1
NORTHWESTERN LONG TERM CARE INS CO	WI	320.0
NORTHWESTERN MUTUAL LIFE INS CO	WI	335,000.0
NY LIFE INS & ANNUITY CORP	DE	183,000.0
NYLIFE INS CO OF ARIZONA	AZ	159.0
OLD REPUBLIC LIFE INS CO	IL	106.8
OXFORD LIFE INS CO	AZ	2,955.5

INSURANCE COMPANY NAME	DOM. STATE	TOTAL ASSETS ($MIL)
PACIFIC LIFE & ANNUITY CO	AZ	8,615.1
PAN AMERICAN ASR CO	LA	26.7
PHYSICIANS LIFE INS CO	NE	1,783.0
PRINCIPAL LIFE INS CO	IA	239,000.0
STANDARD INS CO	OR	32,461.1
SYMETRA NATIONAL LIFE INS CO	IA	24.4
TRANS WORLD ASR CO	CA	341.0
UNITED NATIONAL LIFE INS CO OF AM	IL	52.1
UNITED WORLD LIFE INS CO	NE	160.3
USAA LIFE INS CO	TX	26,197.9
USABLE LIFE	AR	505.6
VOYA RETIREMENT INS & ANNUITY CO	CT	129,000.0

New York

INSURANCE COMPANY NAME	DOM. STATE	TOTAL ASSETS ($MIL)
Rating: A+		
PHYSICIANS MUTUAL INS CO	NE	2,785.1
STATE FARM LIFE & ACCIDENT ASR CO	IL	3,528.9
TEACHERS INS & ANNUITY ASN OF AM	NY	343,000.0
Rating: A		
AMERICAN FAMILY LIFE ASR CO OF NY	NY	1,108.3
BERKLEY LIFE & HEALTH INS CO	IA	478.2
EMPIRE FIDELITY INVESTMENTS L I C	NY	4,201.6
FEDERATED LIFE INS CO	MN	2,427.1
GARDEN STATE LIFE INS CO	TX	143.5
GUARDIAN LIFE INS CO OF AMERICA	NY	72,127.3
SHELTERPOINT LIFE INS CO	NY	392.4
STANDARD LIFE INS CO OF NY	NY	325.0
Rating: A-		
AMICA LIFE INS CO	RI	1,465.4
DELAWARE AMERICAN LIFE INS CO	DE	106.3
FIDELITY SECURITY LIFE INS CO	MO	982.0
FIDELITY SECURITY LIFE INS CO OF NY	NY	39.3
FIRST RELIANCE STANDARD LIFE INS CO	NY	259.1
NATIONAL BENEFIT LIFE INS CO	NY	675.0
NEW YORK LIFE INS CO	NY	214,000.0
STANDARD SECURITY LIFE INS CO OF NY	NY	152.8
TRUSTMARK LIFE INS CO	IL	249.3
Rating: B+		
BOSTON MUTUAL LIFE INS CO	MA	1,634.0
GERBER LIFE INS CO	NY	5,146.7
LIFE INS CO OF BOSTON & NEW YORK	NY	193.4
NIAGARA LIFE & HEALTH INS CO	NY	20.4
NORTHWESTERN LONG TERM CARE INS CO	WI	320.0
NORTHWESTERN MUTUAL LIFE INS CO	WI	335,000.0
NY LIFE INS & ANNUITY CORP	DE	183,000.0
PACIFIC LIFE & ANNUITY CO	AZ	8,615.1
PRINCIPAL LIFE INS CO	IA	239,000.0
VOYA RETIREMENT INS & ANNUITY CO	CT	129,000.0

North Carolina

INSURANCE COMPANY NAME	DOM. STATE	TOTAL ASSETS ($MIL)

Rating: A+

INSURANCE COMPANY NAME	DOM. STATE	TOTAL ASSETS ($MIL)
AMERICAN FAMILY LIFE INS CO	WI	5,473.4
CHESAPEAKE LIFE INS CO	OK	251.1
COUNTRY LIFE INS CO	IL	9,442.8
PHYSICIANS MUTUAL INS CO	NE	2,785.1
STATE FARM LIFE INS CO	IL	86,273.0
TEACHERS INS & ANNUITY ASN OF AM	NY	343,000.0

Rating: A

INSURANCE COMPANY NAME	DOM. STATE	TOTAL ASSETS ($MIL)
BERKLEY LIFE & HEALTH INS CO	IA	478.2
DIRECT GENERAL LIFE INS CO	SC	33.5
FEDERATED LIFE INS CO	MN	2,427.1
FIDELITY INVESTMENTS LIFE INS CO	UT	44,295.4
GARDEN STATE LIFE INS CO	TX	143.5
GUARDIAN LIFE INS CO OF AMERICA	NY	72,127.3
NATIONAL FOUNDATION LIFE INS CO	TX	94.2
SENTRY LIFE INS CO	WI	9,857.5
SHELTERPOINT LIFE INS CO	NY	392.4
SOUTHERN FARM BUREAU LIFE INS CO	MS	15,730.7

Rating: A-

INSURANCE COMPANY NAME	DOM. STATE	TOTAL ASSETS ($MIL)
AMICA LIFE INS CO	RI	1,465.4
ANNUITY INVESTORS LIFE INS CO	OH	3,225.7
CENTRAL STATES H & L CO OF OMAHA	NE	386.9
COUNTRY INVESTORS LIFE ASR CO	IL	323.0
DELAWARE AMERICAN LIFE INS CO	DE	106.3
FIDELITY SECURITY LIFE INS CO	MO	982.0
NATIONAL BENEFIT LIFE INS CO	NY	675.0
NEW YORK LIFE INS CO	NY	214,000.0
PACIFIC LIFE INS CO	NE	178,000.0
PARKER CENTENNIAL ASR CO	WI	99.1
STANDARD SECURITY LIFE INS CO OF NY	NY	152.8
TRUSTMARK LIFE INS CO	IL	249.3

Rating: B+

INSURANCE COMPANY NAME	DOM. STATE	TOTAL ASSETS ($MIL)
AMERICAN CONTINENTAL INS CO	TN	439.4
AMERICAN FIDELITY ASR CO	OK	7,628.5
AMERICAN HEALTH & LIFE INS CO	TX	1,264.4
ASSURITY LIFE INS CO	NE	2,660.6
BEST LIFE & HEALTH INS CO	TX	31.3
BOSTON MUTUAL LIFE INS CO	MA	1,634.0
CM LIFE INS CO	CT	9,072.1
COMPANION LIFE INS CO	SC	689.7
FREEDOM LIFE INS CO OF AMERICA	TX	462.4
GERBER LIFE INS CO	NY	5,146.7
HM LIFE INS CO	PA	881.3
ILLINOIS MUTUAL LIFE INS CO	IL	1,595.0
NATIONAL HEALTH INS CO	TX	181.1
NORTHWESTERN LONG TERM CARE INS CO	WI	320.0
NORTHWESTERN MUTUAL LIFE INS CO	WI	335,000.0
NY LIFE INS & ANNUITY CORP	DE	183,000.0
NYLIFE INS CO OF ARIZONA	AZ	159.0
OLD REPUBLIC LIFE INS CO	IL	106.8
OXFORD LIFE INS CO	AZ	2,955.5
PACIFIC LIFE & ANNUITY CO	AZ	8,615.1
PAN AMERICAN ASR CO	LA	26.7

INSURANCE COMPANY NAME	DOM. STATE	TOTAL ASSETS ($MIL)
PHYSICIANS LIFE INS CO	NE	1,783.0
PRINCIPAL LIFE INS CO	IA	239,000.0
STANDARD INS CO	OR	32,461.1
SYMETRA NATIONAL LIFE INS CO	IA	24.4
TRANS WORLD ASR CO	CA	341.0
UNITED FARM FAMILY LIFE INS CO	IN	2,457.7
UNITED NATIONAL LIFE INS CO OF AM	IL	52.1
UNITED WORLD LIFE INS CO	NE	160.3
USAA LIFE INS CO	TX	26,197.9
USABLE LIFE	AR	505.6
VOYA RETIREMENT INS & ANNUITY CO	CT	129,000.0

North Dakota

INSURANCE COMPANY NAME	DOM. STATE	TOTAL ASSETS ($MIL)

Rating: A+

INSURANCE COMPANY NAME	DOM. STATE	TOTAL ASSETS ($MIL)
AMERICAN FAMILY LIFE INS CO	WI	5,473.4
CHESAPEAKE LIFE INS CO	OK	251.1
COUNTRY LIFE INS CO	IL	9,442.8
PHYSICIANS MUTUAL INS CO	NE	2,785.1
STATE FARM LIFE INS CO	IL	86,273.0
TEACHERS INS & ANNUITY ASN OF AM	NY	343,000.0

Rating: A

INSURANCE COMPANY NAME	DOM. STATE	TOTAL ASSETS ($MIL)
AMERICAN FAMILY LIFE ASR CO OF NY	NY	1,108.3
BERKLEY LIFE & HEALTH INS CO	IA	478.2
DIRECT GENERAL LIFE INS CO	SC	33.5
FEDERATED LIFE INS CO	MN	2,427.1
FIDELITY INVESTMENTS LIFE INS CO	UT	44,295.4
GARDEN STATE LIFE INS CO	TX	143.5
GUARDIAN LIFE INS CO OF AMERICA	NY	72,127.3
NATIONAL FOUNDATION LIFE INS CO	TX	94.2
SENTRY LIFE INS CO	WI	9,857.5

Rating: A-

INSURANCE COMPANY NAME	DOM. STATE	TOTAL ASSETS ($MIL)
AMICA LIFE INS CO	RI	1,465.4
ANNUITY INVESTORS LIFE INS CO	OH	3,225.7
CENTRAL STATES H & L CO OF OMAHA	NE	386.9
COUNTRY INVESTORS LIFE ASR CO	IL	323.0
DELAWARE AMERICAN LIFE INS CO	DE	106.3
FIDELITY SECURITY LIFE INS CO	MO	982.0
NATIONAL BENEFIT LIFE INS CO	NY	675.0
NEW YORK LIFE INS CO	NY	214,000.0
PACIFIC LIFE INS CO	NE	178,000.0
PARKER CENTENNIAL ASR CO	WI	99.1
STANDARD SECURITY LIFE INS CO OF NY	NY	152.8
TRUSTMARK LIFE INS CO	IL	249.3

Rating: B+

INSURANCE COMPANY NAME	DOM. STATE	TOTAL ASSETS ($MIL)
AMERICAN CONTINENTAL INS CO	TN	439.4
AMERICAN FIDELITY ASR CO	OK	7,628.5
AMERICAN HEALTH & LIFE INS CO	TX	1,264.4
ASSURITY LIFE INS CO	NE	2,660.6
BEST LIFE & HEALTH INS CO	TX	31.3
BOSTON MUTUAL LIFE INS CO	MA	1,634.0
CHRISTIAN FIDELITY LIFE INS CO	TX	44.0
CM LIFE INS CO	CT	9,072.1
COMPANION LIFE INS CO	SC	689.7
FARM BUREAU LIFE INS CO	IA	9,888.5
GERBER LIFE INS CO	NY	5,146.7
HM LIFE INS CO	PA	881.3
ILLINOIS MUTUAL LIFE INS CO	IL	1,595.0
NATIONAL FARMERS UNION LIFE INS CO	TX	158.8
NATIONAL HEALTH INS CO	TX	181.1
NORTHWESTERN LONG TERM CARE INS CO	WI	320.0
NORTHWESTERN MUTUAL LIFE INS CO	WI	335,000.0
NY LIFE INS & ANNUITY CORP	DE	183,000.0
NYLIFE INS CO OF ARIZONA	AZ	159.0
OLD REPUBLIC LIFE INS CO	IL	106.8
OXFORD LIFE INS CO	AZ	2,955.5
PACIFIC LIFE & ANNUITY CO	AZ	8,615.1

INSURANCE COMPANY NAME	DOM. STATE	TOTAL ASSETS ($MIL)
PAN AMERICAN ASR CO	LA	26.7
PHYSICIANS LIFE INS CO	NE	1,783.0
PRINCIPAL LIFE INS CO	IA	239,000.0
STANDARD INS CO	OR	32,461.1
SYMETRA NATIONAL LIFE INS CO	IA	24.4
TRANS WORLD ASR CO	CA	341.0
UNITED FARM FAMILY LIFE INS CO	IN	2,457.7
UNITED NATIONAL LIFE INS CO OF AM	IL	52.1
UNITED WORLD LIFE INS CO	NE	160.3
USAA LIFE INS CO	TX	26,197.9
USABLE LIFE	AR	505.6
VOYA RETIREMENT INS & ANNUITY CO	CT	129,000.0

Ohio

INSURANCE COMPANY NAME	DOM. STATE	TOTAL ASSETS ($MIL)

Rating: A+

INSURANCE COMPANY NAME	DOM. STATE	TOTAL ASSETS ($MIL)
AMERICAN FAMILY LIFE INS CO	WI	5,473.4
CHESAPEAKE LIFE INS CO	OK	251.1
COUNTRY LIFE INS CO	IL	9,442.8
PHYSICIANS MUTUAL INS CO	NE	2,785.1
STATE FARM LIFE INS CO	IL	86,273.0
TEACHERS INS & ANNUITY ASN OF AM	NY	343,000.0

Rating: A

INSURANCE COMPANY NAME	DOM. STATE	TOTAL ASSETS ($MIL)
BERKLEY LIFE & HEALTH INS CO	IA	478.2
DIRECT GENERAL LIFE INS CO	SC	33.5
FEDERATED LIFE INS CO	MN	2,427.1
FIDELITY INVESTMENTS LIFE INS CO	UT	44,295.4
GARDEN STATE LIFE INS CO	TX	143.5
GUARDIAN LIFE INS CO OF AMERICA	NY	72,127.3
NATIONAL FOUNDATION LIFE INS CO	TX	94.2
SENTRY LIFE INS CO	WI	9,857.5

Rating: A-

INSURANCE COMPANY NAME	DOM. STATE	TOTAL ASSETS ($MIL)
AMICA LIFE INS CO	RI	1,465.4
ANNUITY INVESTORS LIFE INS CO	OH	3,225.7
CENTRAL STATES H & L CO OF OMAHA	NE	386.9
COUNTRY INVESTORS LIFE ASR CO	IL	323.0
DELAWARE AMERICAN LIFE INS CO	DE	106.3
FARM BUREAU LIFE INS CO OF MICHIGAN	MI	2,709.6
FIDELITY SECURITY LIFE INS CO	MO	982.0
NATIONAL BENEFIT LIFE INS CO	NY	675.0
NEW YORK LIFE INS CO	NY	214,000.0
PACIFIC LIFE INS CO	NE	178,000.0
PARKER CENTENNIAL ASR CO	WI	99.1
STANDARD SECURITY LIFE INS CO OF NY	NY	152.8
TRUSTMARK LIFE INS CO	IL	249.3

Rating: B+

INSURANCE COMPANY NAME	DOM. STATE	TOTAL ASSETS ($MIL)
AMERICAN CONTINENTAL INS CO	TN	439.4
AMERICAN FIDELITY ASR CO	OK	7,628.5
AMERICAN HEALTH & LIFE INS CO	TX	1,264.4
ASSURITY LIFE INS CO	NE	2,660.6
BEST LIFE & HEALTH INS CO	TX	31.3
BOSTON MUTUAL LIFE INS CO	MA	1,634.0
CHRISTIAN FIDELITY LIFE INS CO	TX	44.0
CM LIFE INS CO	CT	9,072.1
COMPANION LIFE INS CO	SC	689.7
FREEDOM LIFE INS CO OF AMERICA	TX	462.4
GERBER LIFE INS CO	NY	5,146.7
HM LIFE INS CO	PA	881.3
ILLINOIS MUTUAL LIFE INS CO	IL	1,595.0
M LIFE INS CO	CO	479.6
NATIONAL FARMERS UNION LIFE INS CO	TX	158.8
NATIONAL HEALTH INS CO	TX	181.1
NORTHWESTERN LONG TERM CARE INS CO	WI	320.0
NORTHWESTERN MUTUAL LIFE INS CO	WI	335,000.0
NY LIFE INS & ANNUITY CORP	DE	183,000.0
NYLIFE INS CO OF ARIZONA	AZ	159.0
OLD REPUBLIC LIFE INS CO	IL	106.8
OXFORD LIFE INS CO	AZ	2,955.5

INSURANCE COMPANY NAME	DOM. STATE	TOTAL ASSETS ($MIL)
PACIFIC LIFE & ANNUITY CO	AZ	8,615.1
PAN AMERICAN ASR CO	LA	26.7
PHYSICIANS LIFE INS CO	NE	1,783.0
PRINCIPAL LIFE INS CO	IA	239,000.0
STANDARD INS CO	OR	32,461.1
SYMETRA NATIONAL LIFE INS CO	IA	24.4
TRANS WORLD ASR CO	CA	341.0
UNITED FARM FAMILY LIFE INS CO	IN	2,457.7
UNITED NATIONAL LIFE INS CO OF AM	IL	52.1
UNITED WORLD LIFE INS CO	NE	160.3
USAA LIFE INS CO	TX	26,197.9
USABLE LIFE	AR	505.6
VOYA RETIREMENT INS & ANNUITY CO	CT	129,000.0

Oklahoma

INSURANCE COMPANY NAME	DOM. STATE	TOTAL ASSETS ($MIL)
Rating: A+		
AMERICAN FAMILY LIFE INS CO	WI	5,473.4
CHESAPEAKE LIFE INS CO	OK	251.1
COUNTRY LIFE INS CO	IL	9,442.8
PHYSICIANS MUTUAL INS CO	NE	2,785.1
STATE FARM LIFE INS CO	IL	86,273.0
TEACHERS INS & ANNUITY ASN OF AM	NY	343,000.0
Rating: A		
BERKLEY LIFE & HEALTH INS CO	IA	478.2
DIRECT GENERAL LIFE INS CO	SC	33.5
FEDERATED LIFE INS CO	MN	2,427.1
FIDELITY INVESTMENTS LIFE INS CO	UT	44,295.4
GARDEN STATE LIFE INS CO	TX	143.5
GUARDIAN LIFE INS CO OF AMERICA	NY	72,127.3
NATIONAL FOUNDATION LIFE INS CO	TX	94.2
SENTRY LIFE INS CO	WI	9,857.5
Rating: A-		
AMICA LIFE INS CO	RI	1,465.4
ANNUITY INVESTORS LIFE INS CO	OH	3,225.7
CENTRAL STATES H & L CO OF OMAHA	NE	386.9
COUNTRY INVESTORS LIFE ASR CO	IL	323.0
DELAWARE AMERICAN LIFE INS CO	DE	106.3
FARM BUREAU LIFE INS CO OF MICHIGAN	MI	2,709.6
FIDELITY SECURITY LIFE INS CO	MO	982.0
NATIONAL BENEFIT LIFE INS CO	NY	675.0
NEW YORK LIFE INS CO	NY	214,000.0
PACIFIC LIFE INS CO	NE	178,000.0
PARKER CENTENNIAL ASR CO	WI	99.1
STANDARD SECURITY LIFE INS CO OF NY	NY	152.8
SWBC LIFE INS CO	TX	42.4
TRUSTMARK LIFE INS CO	IL	249.3
Rating: B+		
AMERICAN CONTINENTAL INS CO	TN	439.4
AMERICAN FIDELITY ASR CO	OK	7,628.5
AMERICAN HEALTH & LIFE INS CO	TX	1,264.4
ASSURITY LIFE INS CO	NE	2,660.6
BEST LIFE & HEALTH INS CO	TX	31.3
BOSTON MUTUAL LIFE INS CO	MA	1,634.0
CHRISTIAN FIDELITY LIFE INS CO	TX	44.0
CM LIFE INS CO	CT	9,072.1
COMPANION LIFE INS CO	SC	689.7
ENTERPRISE LIFE INS CO	TX	159.9
FARM BUREAU LIFE INS CO	IA	9,888.5
FREEDOM LIFE INS CO OF AMERICA	TX	462.4
GERBER LIFE INS CO	NY	5,146.7
HM LIFE INS CO	PA	881.3
ILLINOIS MUTUAL LIFE INS CO	IL	1,595.0
NATIONAL FARMERS UNION LIFE INS CO	TX	158.8
NATIONAL HEALTH INS CO	TX	181.1
NORTHWESTERN LONG TERM CARE INS CO	WI	320.0
NORTHWESTERN MUTUAL LIFE INS CO	WI	335,000.0
NY LIFE INS & ANNUITY CORP	DE	183,000.0
NYLIFE INS CO OF ARIZONA	AZ	159.0

INSURANCE COMPANY NAME	DOM. STATE	TOTAL ASSETS ($MIL)
OLD REPUBLIC LIFE INS CO	IL	106.8
OXFORD LIFE INS CO	AZ	2,955.5
PACIFIC LIFE & ANNUITY CO	AZ	8,615.1
PAN AMERICAN ASR CO	LA	26.7
PHYSICIANS LIFE INS CO	NE	1,783.0
PRINCIPAL LIFE INS CO	IA	239,000.0
STANDARD INS CO	OR	32,461.1
SYMETRA NATIONAL LIFE INS CO	IA	24.4
TRANS WORLD ASR CO	CA	341.0
UNITED NATIONAL LIFE INS CO OF AM	IL	52.1
UNITED WORLD LIFE INS CO	NE	160.3
USAA LIFE INS CO	TX	26,197.9
USABLE LIFE	AR	505.6
VOYA RETIREMENT INS & ANNUITY CO	CT	129,000.0

Oregon

INSURANCE COMPANY NAME	DOM. STATE	TOTAL ASSETS ($MIL)

Rating: A+

INSURANCE COMPANY NAME	DOM. STATE	TOTAL ASSETS ($MIL)
AMERICAN FAMILY LIFE INS CO	WI	5,473.4
CHESAPEAKE LIFE INS CO	OK	251.1
COUNTRY LIFE INS CO	IL	9,442.8
PHYSICIANS MUTUAL INS CO	NE	2,785.1
STATE FARM LIFE INS CO	IL	86,273.0
TEACHERS INS & ANNUITY ASN OF AM	NY	343,000.0

Rating: A

INSURANCE COMPANY NAME	DOM. STATE	TOTAL ASSETS ($MIL)
BERKLEY LIFE & HEALTH INS CO	IA	478.2
DIRECT GENERAL LIFE INS CO	SC	33.5
FEDERATED LIFE INS CO	MN	2,427.1
FIDELITY INVESTMENTS LIFE INS CO	UT	44,295.4
GARDEN STATE LIFE INS CO	TX	143.5
GUARDIAN LIFE INS CO OF AMERICA	NY	72,127.3
NATIONAL FOUNDATION LIFE INS CO	TX	94.2
SENTRY LIFE INS CO	WI	9,857.5

Rating: A-

INSURANCE COMPANY NAME	DOM. STATE	TOTAL ASSETS ($MIL)
AMICA LIFE INS CO	RI	1,465.4
ANNUITY INVESTORS LIFE INS CO	OH	3,225.7
CENTRAL STATES H & L CO OF OMAHA	NE	386.9
COUNTRY INVESTORS LIFE ASR CO	IL	323.0
DELAWARE AMERICAN LIFE INS CO	DE	106.3
FIDELITY SECURITY LIFE INS CO	MO	982.0
NATIONAL BENEFIT LIFE INS CO	NY	675.0
NEW YORK LIFE INS CO	NY	214,000.0
PACIFIC LIFE INS CO	NE	178,000.0
PARKER CENTENNIAL ASR CO	WI	99.1
STANDARD SECURITY LIFE INS CO OF NY	NY	152.8
TRUSTMARK LIFE INS CO	IL	249.3

Rating: B+

INSURANCE COMPANY NAME	DOM. STATE	TOTAL ASSETS ($MIL)
AMERICAN FIDELITY ASR CO	OK	7,628.5
AMERICAN HEALTH & LIFE INS CO	TX	1,264.4
ASSURITY LIFE INS CO	NE	2,660.6
BEST LIFE & HEALTH INS CO	TX	31.3
BOSTON MUTUAL LIFE INS CO	MA	1,634.0
CHRISTIAN FIDELITY LIFE INS CO	TX	44.0
CM LIFE INS CO	CT	9,072.1
COMPANION LIFE INS CO	SC	689.7
ENTERPRISE LIFE INS CO	TX	159.9
FARM BUREAU LIFE INS CO	IA	9,888.5
FREEDOM LIFE INS CO OF AMERICA	TX	462.4
GERBER LIFE INS CO	NY	5,146.7
HM LIFE INS CO	PA	881.3
ILLINOIS MUTUAL LIFE INS CO	IL	1,595.0
NATIONAL FARMERS UNION LIFE INS CO	TX	158.8
NATIONAL HEALTH INS CO	TX	181.1
NORTHWESTERN LONG TERM CARE INS CO	WI	320.0
NORTHWESTERN MUTUAL LIFE INS CO	WI	335,000.0
NY LIFE INS & ANNUITY CORP	DE	183,000.0
NYLIFE INS CO OF ARIZONA	AZ	159.0
OLD REPUBLIC LIFE INS CO	IL	106.8
OXFORD LIFE INS CO	AZ	2,955.5
PACIFIC LIFE & ANNUITY CO	AZ	8,615.1

INSURANCE COMPANY NAME	DOM. STATE	TOTAL ASSETS ($MIL)
PAN AMERICAN ASR CO	LA	26.7
PHYSICIANS LIFE INS CO	NE	1,783.0
PRINCIPAL LIFE INS CO	IA	239,000.0
STANDARD INS CO	OR	32,461.1
SYMETRA NATIONAL LIFE INS CO	IA	24.4
TRANS WORLD ASR CO	CA	341.0
UNITED WORLD LIFE INS CO	NE	160.3
USAA LIFE INS CO	TX	26,197.9
USABLE LIFE	AR	505.6
VOYA RETIREMENT INS & ANNUITY CO	CT	129,000.0

Pennsylvania

INSURANCE COMPANY NAME	DOM. STATE	TOTAL ASSETS ($MIL)
Rating: A+		
AMERICAN FAMILY LIFE INS CO	WI	5,473.4
CHESAPEAKE LIFE INS CO	OK	251.1
COUNTRY LIFE INS CO	IL	9,442.8
PHYSICIANS MUTUAL INS CO	NE	2,785.1
STATE FARM LIFE INS CO	IL	86,273.0
TEACHERS INS & ANNUITY ASN OF AM	NY	343,000.0
Rating: A		
BERKLEY LIFE & HEALTH INS CO	IA	478.2
DIRECT GENERAL LIFE INS CO	SC	33.5
FEDERATED LIFE INS CO	MN	2,427.1
FIDELITY INVESTMENTS LIFE INS CO	UT	44,295.4
GARDEN STATE LIFE INS CO	TX	143.5
GUARDIAN LIFE INS CO OF AMERICA	NY	72,127.3
NATIONAL FOUNDATION LIFE INS CO	TX	94.2
SENTRY LIFE INS CO	WI	9,857.5
SHELTERPOINT LIFE INS CO	NY	392.4
Rating: A-		
AMICA LIFE INS CO	RI	1,465.4
ANNUITY INVESTORS LIFE INS CO	OH	3,225.7
CENTRAL STATES H & L CO OF OMAHA	NE	386.9
COUNTRY INVESTORS LIFE ASR CO	IL	323.0
DELAWARE AMERICAN LIFE INS CO	DE	106.3
FIDELITY SECURITY LIFE INS CO	MO	982.0
NATIONAL BENEFIT LIFE INS CO	NY	675.0
NEW YORK LIFE INS CO	NY	214,000.0
PACIFIC LIFE INS CO	NE	178,000.0
PARKER CENTENNIAL ASR CO	WI	99.1
STANDARD SECURITY LIFE INS CO OF NY	NY	152.8
TRUSTMARK LIFE INS CO	IL	249.3
Rating: B+		
AMERICAN CONTINENTAL INS CO	TN	439.4
AMERICAN FIDELITY ASR CO	OK	7,628.5
AMERICAN HEALTH & LIFE INS CO	TX	1,264.4
ASSURITY LIFE INS CO	NE	2,660.6
BEST LIFE & HEALTH INS CO	TX	31.3
BOSTON MUTUAL LIFE INS CO	MA	1,634.0
CM LIFE INS CO	CT	9,072.1
COMPANION LIFE INS CO	SC	689.7
FREEDOM LIFE INS CO OF AMERICA	TX	462.4
GERBER LIFE INS CO	NY	5,146.7
HM LIFE INS CO	PA	881.3
ILLINOIS MUTUAL LIFE INS CO	IL	1,595.0
NATIONAL FARMERS UNION LIFE INS CO	TX	158.8
NATIONAL HEALTH INS CO	TX	181.1
NORTHWESTERN LONG TERM CARE INS CO	WI	320.0
NORTHWESTERN MUTUAL LIFE INS CO	WI	335,000.0
NY LIFE INS & ANNUITY CORP	DE	183,000.0
NYLIFE INS CO OF ARIZONA	AZ	159.0
OLD REPUBLIC LIFE INS CO	IL	106.8
OXFORD LIFE INS CO	AZ	2,955.5
PACIFIC LIFE & ANNUITY CO	AZ	8,615.1
PAN AMERICAN ASR CO	LA	26.7

INSURANCE COMPANY NAME	DOM. STATE	TOTAL ASSETS ($MIL)
PHYSICIANS LIFE INS CO	NE	1,783.0
PRINCIPAL LIFE INS CO	IA	239,000.0
STANDARD INS CO	OR	32,461.1
SYMETRA NATIONAL LIFE INS CO	IA	24.4
TRANS WORLD ASR CO	CA	341.0
UNITED FARM FAMILY LIFE INS CO	IN	2,457.7
UNITED NATIONAL LIFE INS CO OF AM	IL	52.1
UNITED WORLD LIFE INS CO	NE	160.3
USAA LIFE INS CO	TX	26,197.9
USABLE LIFE	AR	505.6
VOYA RETIREMENT INS & ANNUITY CO	CT	129,000.0

Puerto Rico

INSURANCE COMPANY NAME	DOM. STATE	TOTAL ASSETS ($MIL)
Rating: A+		
TEACHERS INS & ANNUITY ASN OF AM	NY	343,000.0
Rating: A-		
NEW YORK LIFE INS CO	NY	214,000.0
STANDARD SECURITY LIFE INS CO OF NY	NY	152.8
Rating: B+		
AMERICAN FIDELITY ASR CO	OK	7,628.5
BOSTON MUTUAL LIFE INS CO	MA	1,634.0
CM LIFE INS CO	CT	9,072.1
GERBER LIFE INS CO	NY	5,146.7
OLD REPUBLIC LIFE INS CO	IL	106.8
PAN AMERICAN ASR CO	LA	26.7
PRINCIPAL LIFE INS CO	IA	239,000.0
STANDARD INS CO	OR	32,461.1
TRANS OCEANIC LIFE INS CO	PR	407.4
VOYA RETIREMENT INS & ANNUITY CO	CT	129,000.0

Rhode Island

INSURANCE COMPANY NAME	DOM. STATE	TOTAL ASSETS ($MIL)
USABLE LIFE	AR	505.6
VOYA RETIREMENT INS & ANNUITY CO	CT	129,000.0

Rating: A+

INSURANCE COMPANY NAME	DOM. STATE	TOTAL ASSETS ($MIL)
AMERICAN FAMILY LIFE INS CO	WI	5,473.4
CHESAPEAKE LIFE INS CO	OK	251.1
COUNTRY LIFE INS CO	IL	9,442.8
PHYSICIANS MUTUAL INS CO	NE	2,785.1
STATE FARM LIFE INS CO	IL	86,273.0
TEACHERS INS & ANNUITY ASN OF AM	NY	343,000.0

Rating: A

INSURANCE COMPANY NAME	DOM. STATE	TOTAL ASSETS ($MIL)
BERKLEY LIFE & HEALTH INS CO	IA	478.2
DIRECT GENERAL LIFE INS CO	SC	33.5
FEDERATED LIFE INS CO	MN	2,427.1
FIDELITY INVESTMENTS LIFE INS CO	UT	44,295.4
GARDEN STATE LIFE INS CO	TX	143.5
GUARDIAN LIFE INS CO OF AMERICA	NY	72,127.3
SENTRY LIFE INS CO	WI	9,857.5
SHELTERPOINT LIFE INS CO	NY	392.4

Rating: A-

INSURANCE COMPANY NAME	DOM. STATE	TOTAL ASSETS ($MIL)
AMICA LIFE INS CO	RI	1,465.4
ANNUITY INVESTORS LIFE INS CO	OH	3,225.7
CENTRAL STATES H & L CO OF OMAHA	NE	386.9
COUNTRY INVESTORS LIFE ASR CO	IL	323.0
DELAWARE AMERICAN LIFE INS CO	DE	106.3
FIDELITY SECURITY LIFE INS CO	MO	982.0
NATIONAL BENEFIT LIFE INS CO	NY	675.0
NEW YORK LIFE INS CO	NY	214,000.0
PACIFIC LIFE INS CO	NE	178,000.0
PARKER CENTENNIAL ASR CO	WI	99.1
STANDARD SECURITY LIFE INS CO OF NY	NY	152.8
TRUSTMARK LIFE INS CO	IL	249.3

Rating: B+

INSURANCE COMPANY NAME	DOM. STATE	TOTAL ASSETS ($MIL)
AMERICAN FIDELITY ASR CO	OK	7,628.5
AMERICAN HEALTH & LIFE INS CO	TX	1,264.4
ASSURITY LIFE INS CO	NE	2,660.6
BOSTON MUTUAL LIFE INS CO	MA	1,634.0
CM LIFE INS CO	CT	9,072.1
COMPANION LIFE INS CO	SC	689.7
GERBER LIFE INS CO	NY	5,146.7
HM LIFE INS CO	PA	881.3
ILLINOIS MUTUAL LIFE INS CO	IL	1,595.0
NATIONAL HEALTH INS CO	TX	181.1
NORTHWESTERN LONG TERM CARE INS CO	WI	320.0
NORTHWESTERN MUTUAL LIFE INS CO	WI	335,000.0
NY LIFE INS & ANNUITY CORP	DE	183,000.0
NYLIFE INS CO OF ARIZONA	AZ	159.0
OLD REPUBLIC LIFE INS CO	IL	106.8
OXFORD LIFE INS CO	AZ	2,955.5
PACIFIC LIFE & ANNUITY CO	AZ	8,615.1
PHYSICIANS LIFE INS CO	NE	1,783.0
PRINCIPAL LIFE INS CO	IA	239,000.0
STANDARD INS CO	OR	32,461.1
TRANS WORLD ASR CO	CA	341.0
UNITED WORLD LIFE INS CO	NE	160.3
USAA LIFE INS CO	TX	26,197.9

South Carolina

INSURANCE COMPANY NAME	DOM. STATE	TOTAL ASSETS ($MIL)

Rating: A+

INSURANCE COMPANY NAME	DOM. STATE	TOTAL ASSETS ($MIL)
AMERICAN FAMILY LIFE INS CO	WI	5,473.4
CHESAPEAKE LIFE INS CO	OK	251.1
COUNTRY LIFE INS CO	IL	9,442.8
PHYSICIANS MUTUAL INS CO	NE	2,785.1
STATE FARM LIFE INS CO	IL	86,273.0
TEACHERS INS & ANNUITY ASN OF AM	NY	343,000.0

Rating: A

INSURANCE COMPANY NAME	DOM. STATE	TOTAL ASSETS ($MIL)
BERKLEY LIFE & HEALTH INS CO	IA	478.2
DIRECT GENERAL LIFE INS CO	SC	33.5
FEDERATED LIFE INS CO	MN	2,427.1
FIDELITY INVESTMENTS LIFE INS CO	UT	44,295.4
GARDEN STATE LIFE INS CO	TX	143.5
GUARDIAN LIFE INS CO OF AMERICA	NY	72,127.3
NATIONAL FOUNDATION LIFE INS CO	TX	94.2
SENTRY LIFE INS CO	WI	9,857.5
SHELTERPOINT LIFE INS CO	NY	392.4
SOUTHERN FARM BUREAU LIFE INS CO	MS	15,730.7

Rating: A-

INSURANCE COMPANY NAME	DOM. STATE	TOTAL ASSETS ($MIL)
AMICA LIFE INS CO	RI	1,465.4
ANNUITY INVESTORS LIFE INS CO	OH	3,225.7
CENTRAL STATES H & L CO OF OMAHA	NE	386.9
COUNTRY INVESTORS LIFE ASR CO	IL	323.0
DELAWARE AMERICAN LIFE INS CO	DE	106.3
FIDELITY SECURITY LIFE INS CO	MO	982.0
NATIONAL BENEFIT LIFE INS CO	NY	675.0
NEW YORK LIFE INS CO	NY	214,000.0
PACIFIC LIFE INS CO	NE	178,000.0
PARKER CENTENNIAL ASR CO	WI	99.1
STANDARD SECURITY LIFE INS CO OF NY	NY	152.8
TRUSTMARK LIFE INS CO	IL	249.3

Rating: B+

INSURANCE COMPANY NAME	DOM. STATE	TOTAL ASSETS ($MIL)
AMERICAN CONTINENTAL INS CO	TN	439.4
AMERICAN FIDELITY ASR CO	OK	7,628.5
AMERICAN HEALTH & LIFE INS CO	TX	1,264.4
ASSURITY LIFE INS CO	NE	2,660.6
BEST LIFE & HEALTH INS CO	TX	31.3
BOSTON MUTUAL LIFE INS CO	MA	1,634.0
CHRISTIAN FIDELITY LIFE INS CO	TX	44.0
CM LIFE INS CO	CT	9,072.1
COMPANION LIFE INS CO	SC	689.7
FREEDOM LIFE INS CO OF AMERICA	TX	462.4
GERBER LIFE INS CO	NY	5,146.7
HM LIFE INS CO	PA	881.3
ILLINOIS MUTUAL LIFE INS CO	IL	1,595.0
NATIONAL HEALTH INS CO	TX	181.1
NORTHWESTERN LONG TERM CARE INS CO	WI	320.0
NORTHWESTERN MUTUAL LIFE INS CO	WI	335,000.0
NY LIFE INS & ANNUITY CORP	DE	183,000.0
NYLIFE INS CO OF ARIZONA	AZ	159.0
OLD REPUBLIC LIFE INS CO	IL	106.8
OXFORD LIFE INS CO	AZ	2,955.5
PACIFIC LIFE & ANNUITY CO	AZ	8,615.1

INSURANCE COMPANY NAME	DOM. STATE	TOTAL ASSETS ($MIL)
PAN AMERICAN ASR CO	LA	26.7
PHYSICIANS LIFE INS CO	NE	1,783.0
PRINCIPAL LIFE INS CO	IA	239,000.0
STANDARD INS CO	OR	32,461.1
SYMETRA NATIONAL LIFE INS CO	IA	24.4
TRANS WORLD ASR CO	CA	341.0
UNITED NATIONAL LIFE INS CO OF AM	IL	52.1
UNITED WORLD LIFE INS CO	NE	160.3
USAA LIFE INS CO	TX	26,197.9
USABLE LIFE	AR	505.6
VOYA RETIREMENT INS & ANNUITY CO	CT	129,000.0

South Dakota

INSURANCE COMPANY NAME	DOM. STATE	TOTAL ASSETS ($MIL)	INSURANCE COMPANY NAME	DOM. STATE	TOTAL ASSETS ($MIL)
Rating: A+			PHYSICIANS LIFE INS CO	NE	1,783.0
			PRINCIPAL LIFE INS CO	IA	239,000.0
AMERICAN FAMILY LIFE INS CO	WI	5,473.4	STANDARD INS CO	OR	32,461.1
CHESAPEAKE LIFE INS CO	OK	251.1	SYMETRA NATIONAL LIFE INS CO	IA	24.4
COUNTRY LIFE INS CO	IL	9,442.8	TRANS WORLD ASR CO	CA	341.0
PHYSICIANS MUTUAL INS CO	NE	2,785.1	UNITED NATIONAL LIFE INS CO OF AM	IL	52.1
STATE FARM LIFE INS CO	IL	86,273.0	UNITED WORLD LIFE INS CO	NE	160.3
TEACHERS INS & ANNUITY ASN OF AM	NY	343,000.0	USAA LIFE INS CO	TX	26,197.9
			USABLE LIFE	AR	505.6
Rating: A			VOYA RETIREMENT INS & ANNUITY CO	CT	129,000.0
BERKLEY LIFE & HEALTH INS CO	IA	478.2			
DIRECT GENERAL LIFE INS CO	SC	33.5			
FEDERATED LIFE INS CO	MN	2,427.1			
FIDELITY INVESTMENTS LIFE INS CO	UT	44,295.4			
GARDEN STATE LIFE INS CO	TX	143.5			
GUARDIAN LIFE INS CO OF AMERICA	NY	72,127.3			
NATIONAL FOUNDATION LIFE INS CO	TX	94.2			
SENTRY LIFE INS CO	WI	9,857.5			

Rating: A-

INSURANCE COMPANY NAME	DOM. STATE	TOTAL ASSETS ($MIL)
AMICA LIFE INS CO	RI	1,465.4
ANNUITY INVESTORS LIFE INS CO	OH	3,225.7
CENTRAL STATES H & L CO OF OMAHA	NE	386.9
COUNTRY INVESTORS LIFE ASR CO	IL	323.0
DELAWARE AMERICAN LIFE INS CO	DE	106.3
FIDELITY SECURITY LIFE INS CO	MO	982.0
NATIONAL BENEFIT LIFE INS CO	NY	675.0
NEW YORK LIFE INS CO	NY	214,000.0
PACIFIC LIFE INS CO	NE	178,000.0
PARKER CENTENNIAL ASR CO	WI	99.1
STANDARD SECURITY LIFE INS CO OF NY	NY	152.8
TRUSTMARK LIFE INS CO	IL	249.3

Rating: B+

INSURANCE COMPANY NAME	DOM. STATE	TOTAL ASSETS ($MIL)
AMERICAN CONTINENTAL INS CO	TN	439.4
AMERICAN FIDELITY ASR CO	OK	7,628.5
AMERICAN HEALTH & LIFE INS CO	TX	1,264.4
ASSURITY LIFE INS CO	NE	2,660.6
BEST LIFE & HEALTH INS CO	TX	31.3
BOSTON MUTUAL LIFE INS CO	MA	1,634.0
CHRISTIAN FIDELITY LIFE INS CO	TX	44.0
CM LIFE INS CO	CT	9,072.1
COMPANION LIFE INS CO	SC	689.7
FARM BUREAU LIFE INS CO	IA	9,888.5
FREEDOM LIFE INS CO OF AMERICA	TX	462.4
GERBER LIFE INS CO	NY	5,146.7
HM LIFE INS CO	PA	881.3
ILLINOIS MUTUAL LIFE INS CO	IL	1,595.0
NATIONAL FARMERS UNION LIFE INS CO	TX	158.8
NATIONAL HEALTH INS CO	TX	181.1
NORTHWESTERN LONG TERM CARE INS CO	WI	320.0
NORTHWESTERN MUTUAL LIFE INS CO	WI	335,000.0
NY LIFE INS & ANNUITY CORP	DE	183,000.0
NYLIFE INS CO OF ARIZONA	AZ	159.0
OLD REPUBLIC LIFE INS CO	IL	106.8
OXFORD LIFE INS CO	AZ	2,955.5
PACIFIC LIFE & ANNUITY CO	AZ	8,615.1

Tennessee

INSURANCE COMPANY NAME	DOM. STATE	TOTAL ASSETS ($MIL)

Rating: A+

INSURANCE COMPANY NAME	DOM. STATE	TOTAL ASSETS ($MIL)
AMERICAN FAMILY LIFE INS CO	WI	5,473.4
CHESAPEAKE LIFE INS CO	OK	251.1
COUNTRY LIFE INS CO	IL	9,442.8
PHYSICIANS MUTUAL INS CO	NE	2,785.1
STATE FARM LIFE INS CO	IL	86,273.0
TEACHERS INS & ANNUITY ASN OF AM	NY	343,000.0

Rating: A

INSURANCE COMPANY NAME	DOM. STATE	TOTAL ASSETS ($MIL)
BERKLEY LIFE & HEALTH INS CO	IA	478.2
DIRECT GENERAL LIFE INS CO	SC	33.5
FEDERATED LIFE INS CO	MN	2,427.1
FIDELITY INVESTMENTS LIFE INS CO	UT	44,295.4
GARDEN STATE LIFE INS CO	TX	143.5
GUARDIAN LIFE INS CO OF AMERICA	NY	72,127.3
NATIONAL FOUNDATION LIFE INS CO	TX	94.2
SENTRY LIFE INS CO	WI	9,857.5
SHELTERPOINT LIFE INS CO	NY	392.4
SOUTHERN FARM BUREAU LIFE INS CO	MS	15,730.7

Rating: A-

INSURANCE COMPANY NAME	DOM. STATE	TOTAL ASSETS ($MIL)
AMICA LIFE INS CO	RI	1,465.4
ANNUITY INVESTORS LIFE INS CO	OH	3,225.7
BLUEBONNET LIFE INS CO	MS	71.5
CENTRAL STATES H & L CO OF OMAHA	NE	386.9
COUNTRY INVESTORS LIFE ASR CO	IL	323.0
DELAWARE AMERICAN LIFE INS CO	DE	106.3
FIDELITY SECURITY LIFE INS CO	MO	982.0
NATIONAL BENEFIT LIFE INS CO	NY	675.0
NEW YORK LIFE INS CO	NY	214,000.0
PACIFIC LIFE INS CO	NE	178,000.0
PARKER CENTENNIAL ASR CO	WI	99.1
STANDARD SECURITY LIFE INS CO OF NY	NY	152.8
SWBC LIFE INS CO	TX	42.4
TRUSTMARK LIFE INS CO	IL	249.3

Rating: B+

INSURANCE COMPANY NAME	DOM. STATE	TOTAL ASSETS ($MIL)
AMERICAN CONTINENTAL INS CO	TN	439.4
AMERICAN FIDELITY ASR CO	OK	7,628.5
AMERICAN HEALTH & LIFE INS CO	TX	1,264.4
ASSURITY LIFE INS CO	NE	2,660.6
BEST LIFE & HEALTH INS CO	TX	31.3
BOSTON MUTUAL LIFE INS CO	MA	1,634.0
CHRISTIAN FIDELITY LIFE INS CO	TX	44.0
CM LIFE INS CO	CT	9,072.1
COMPANION LIFE INS CO	SC	689.7
FREEDOM LIFE INS CO OF AMERICA	TX	462.4
GERBER LIFE INS CO	NY	5,146.7
HM LIFE INS CO	PA	881.3
ILLINOIS MUTUAL LIFE INS CO	IL	1,595.0
NATIONAL HEALTH INS CO	TX	181.1
NORTHWESTERN LONG TERM CARE INS CO	WI	320.0
NORTHWESTERN MUTUAL LIFE INS CO	WI	335,000.0
NY LIFE INS & ANNUITY CORP	DE	183,000.0
NYLIFE INS CO OF ARIZONA	AZ	159.0
OLD REPUBLIC LIFE INS CO	IL	106.8

INSURANCE COMPANY NAME	DOM. STATE	TOTAL ASSETS ($MIL)
OXFORD LIFE INS CO	AZ	2,955.5
PACIFIC LIFE & ANNUITY CO	AZ	8,615.1
PAN AMERICAN ASR CO	LA	26.7
PHYSICIANS LIFE INS CO	NE	1,783.0
PRINCIPAL LIFE INS CO	IA	239,000.0
STANDARD INS CO	OR	32,461.1
SYMETRA NATIONAL LIFE INS CO	IA	24.4
TENNESSEE FARMERS LIFE INS CO	TN	2,599.1
TRANS WORLD ASR CO	CA	341.0
UNITED NATIONAL LIFE INS CO OF AM	IL	52.1
UNITED WORLD LIFE INS CO	NE	160.3
USAA LIFE INS CO	TX	26,197.9
USABLE LIFE	AR	505.6
VOYA RETIREMENT INS & ANNUITY CO	CT	129,000.0

Texas

INSURANCE COMPANY NAME	DOM. STATE	TOTAL ASSETS ($MIL)

Rating: A+

INSURANCE COMPANY NAME	DOM. STATE	TOTAL ASSETS ($MIL)
AMERICAN FAMILY LIFE INS CO	WI	5,473.4
CHESAPEAKE LIFE INS CO	OK	251.1
COUNTRY LIFE INS CO	IL	9,442.8
PHYSICIANS MUTUAL INS CO	NE	2,785.1
STATE FARM LIFE INS CO	IL	86,273.0
TEACHERS INS & ANNUITY ASN OF AM	NY	343,000.0

Rating: A

INSURANCE COMPANY NAME	DOM. STATE	TOTAL ASSETS ($MIL)
BERKLEY LIFE & HEALTH INS CO	IA	478.2
DIRECT GENERAL LIFE INS CO	SC	33.5
FEDERATED LIFE INS CO	MN	2,427.1
FIDELITY INVESTMENTS LIFE INS CO	UT	44,295.4
GARDEN STATE LIFE INS CO	TX	143.5
GUARDIAN LIFE INS CO OF AMERICA	NY	72,127.3
NATIONAL FOUNDATION LIFE INS CO	TX	94.2
SENTRY LIFE INS CO	WI	9,857.5
SOUTHERN FARM BUREAU LIFE INS CO	MS	15,730.7

Rating: A-

INSURANCE COMPANY NAME	DOM. STATE	TOTAL ASSETS ($MIL)
AMICA LIFE INS CO	RI	1,465.4
ANNUITY INVESTORS LIFE INS CO	OH	3,225.7
CENTRAL STATES H & L CO OF OMAHA	NE	386.9
COUNTRY INVESTORS LIFE ASR CO	IL	323.0
DELAWARE AMERICAN LIFE INS CO	DE	106.3
FIDELITY SECURITY LIFE INS CO	MO	982.0
NATIONAL BENEFIT LIFE INS CO	NY	675.0
NEW YORK LIFE INS CO	NY	214,000.0
PACIFIC LIFE INS CO	NE	178,000.0
PARKER CENTENNIAL ASR CO	WI	99.1
STANDARD SECURITY LIFE INS CO OF NY	NY	152.8
SWBC LIFE INS CO	TX	42.4
TRUSTMARK LIFE INS CO	IL	249.3

Rating: B+

INSURANCE COMPANY NAME	DOM. STATE	TOTAL ASSETS ($MIL)
AMERICAN CONTINENTAL INS CO	TN	439.4
AMERICAN FIDELITY ASR CO	OK	7,628.5
AMERICAN HEALTH & LIFE INS CO	TX	1,264.4
ASSURITY LIFE INS CO	NE	2,660.6
BEST LIFE & HEALTH INS CO	TX	31.3
BOSTON MUTUAL LIFE INS CO	MA	1,634.0
CHRISTIAN FIDELITY LIFE INS CO	TX	44.0
CM LIFE INS CO	CT	9,072.1
COMPANION LIFE INS CO	SC	689.7
COMPANION LIFE INS CO OF CA	CA	34.1
ENTERPRISE LIFE INS CO	TX	159.9
FREEDOM LIFE INS CO OF AMERICA	TX	462.4
GERBER LIFE INS CO	NY	5,146.7
HM LIFE INS CO	PA	881.3
ILLINOIS MUTUAL LIFE INS CO	IL	1,595.0
NATIONAL FARMERS UNION LIFE INS CO	TX	158.8
NATIONAL HEALTH INS CO	TX	181.1
NORTHWESTERN LONG TERM CARE INS CO	WI	320.0
NORTHWESTERN MUTUAL LIFE INS CO	WI	335,000.0
NY LIFE INS & ANNUITY CORP	DE	183,000.0
NYLIFE INS CO OF ARIZONA	AZ	159.0

INSURANCE COMPANY NAME	DOM. STATE	TOTAL ASSETS ($MIL)
OLD REPUBLIC LIFE INS CO	IL	106.8
OXFORD LIFE INS CO	AZ	2,955.5
PACIFIC LIFE & ANNUITY CO	AZ	8,615.1
PAN AMERICAN ASR CO	LA	26.7
PHYSICIANS LIFE INS CO	NE	1,783.0
PRINCIPAL LIFE INS CO	IA	239,000.0
STANDARD INS CO	OR	32,461.1
SYMETRA NATIONAL LIFE INS CO	IA	24.4
TRANS WORLD ASR CO	CA	341.0
UNITED NATIONAL LIFE INS CO OF AM	IL	52.1
UNITED WORLD LIFE INS CO	NE	160.3
USAA LIFE INS CO	TX	26,197.9
USABLE LIFE	AR	505.6
VOYA RETIREMENT INS & ANNUITY CO	CT	129,000.0

Utah

INSURANCE COMPANY NAME	DOM. STATE	TOTAL ASSETS ($MIL)	INSURANCE COMPANY NAME	DOM. STATE	TOTAL ASSETS ($MIL)
			PAN AMERICAN ASR CO	LA	26.7
			PHYSICIANS LIFE INS CO	NE	1,783.0
			PRINCIPAL LIFE INS CO	IA	239,000.0
			STANDARD INS CO	OR	32,461.1
			SYMETRA NATIONAL LIFE INS CO	IA	24.4
			TRANS WORLD ASR CO	CA	341.0
			UNITED NATIONAL LIFE INS CO OF AM	IL	52.1
			UNITED WORLD LIFE INS CO	NE	160.3
			USAA LIFE INS CO	TX	26,197.9
			USABLE LIFE	AR	505.6
			VOYA RETIREMENT INS & ANNUITY CO	CT	129,000.0

Rating: A+

INSURANCE COMPANY NAME	DOM. STATE	TOTAL ASSETS ($MIL)
AMERICAN FAMILY LIFE INS CO	WI	5,473.4
CHESAPEAKE LIFE INS CO	OK	251.1
COUNTRY LIFE INS CO	IL	9,442.8
PHYSICIANS MUTUAL INS CO	NE	2,785.1
STATE FARM LIFE INS CO	IL	86,273.0
TEACHERS INS & ANNUITY ASN OF AM	NY	343,000.0

Rating: A

INSURANCE COMPANY NAME	DOM. STATE	TOTAL ASSETS ($MIL)
BERKLEY LIFE & HEALTH INS CO	IA	478.2
DIRECT GENERAL LIFE INS CO	SC	33.5
FEDERATED LIFE INS CO	MN	2,427.1
FIDELITY INVESTMENTS LIFE INS CO	UT	44,295.4
GARDEN STATE LIFE INS CO	TX	143.5
GUARDIAN LIFE INS CO OF AMERICA	NY	72,127.3
NATIONAL FOUNDATION LIFE INS CO	TX	94.2
SENTRY LIFE INS CO	WI	9,857.5

Rating: A-

INSURANCE COMPANY NAME	DOM. STATE	TOTAL ASSETS ($MIL)
AMICA LIFE INS CO	RI	1,465.4
ANNUITY INVESTORS LIFE INS CO	OH	3,225.7
CENTRAL STATES H & L CO OF OMAHA	NE	386.9
DELAWARE AMERICAN LIFE INS CO	DE	106.3
FIDELITY SECURITY LIFE INS CO	MO	982.0
NATIONAL BENEFIT LIFE INS CO	NY	675.0
NEW YORK LIFE INS CO	NY	214,000.0
PACIFIC LIFE INS CO	NE	178,000.0
PARKER CENTENNIAL ASR CO	WI	99.1
STANDARD SECURITY LIFE INS CO OF NY	NY	152.8
SWBC LIFE INS CO	TX	42.4
TRUSTMARK LIFE INS CO	II	249.3

Rating: B+

INSURANCE COMPANY NAME	DOM. STATE	TOTAL ASSETS ($MIL)
AMERICAN CONTINENTAL INS CO	TN	439.4
AMERICAN FIDELITY ASR CO	OK	7,628.5
AMERICAN HEALTH & LIFE INS CO	TX	1,264.4
ASSURITY LIFE INS CO	NE	2,660.6
BEST LIFE & HEALTH INS CO	TX	31.3
BOSTON MUTUAL LIFE INS CO	MA	1,634.0
CHRISTIAN FIDELITY LIFE INS CO	TX	44.0
CM LIFE INS CO	CT	9,072.1
COMPANION LIFE INS CO	SC	689.7
FARM BUREAU LIFE INS CO	IA	9,888.5
FREEDOM LIFE INS CO OF AMERICA	TX	462.4
GERBER LIFE INS CO	NY	5,146.7
HM LIFE INS CO	PA	881.3
ILLINOIS MUTUAL LIFE INS CO	IL	1,595.0
NATIONAL FARMERS UNION LIFE INS CO	TX	158.8
NATIONAL HEALTH INS CO	TX	181.1
NORTHWESTERN LONG TERM CARE INS CO	WI	320.0
NORTHWESTERN MUTUAL LIFE INS CO	WI	335,000.0
NY LIFE INS & ANNUITY CORP	DE	183,000.0
NYLIFE INS CO OF ARIZONA	AZ	159.0
OLD REPUBLIC LIFE INS CO	IL	106.8
OXFORD LIFE INS CO	AZ	2,955.5
PACIFIC LIFE & ANNUITY CO	AZ	8,615.1

Vermont

INSURANCE COMPANY NAME	DOM. STATE	TOTAL ASSETS ($MIL)
Rating: A+		
AMERICAN FAMILY LIFE INS CO	WI	5,473.4
PHYSICIANS MUTUAL INS CO	NE	2,785.1
STATE FARM LIFE INS CO	IL	86,273.0
TEACHERS INS & ANNUITY ASN OF AM	NY	343,000.0
Rating: A		
AMERICAN FAMILY LIFE ASR CO OF NY	NY	1,108.3
BERKLEY LIFE & HEALTH INS CO	IA	478.2
FEDERATED LIFE INS CO	MN	2,427.1
FIDELITY INVESTMENTS LIFE INS CO	UT	44,295.4
GARDEN STATE LIFE INS CO	TX	143.5
GUARDIAN LIFE INS CO OF AMERICA	NY	72,127.3
SENTRY LIFE INS CO	WI	9,857.5
Rating: A-		
AMICA LIFE INS CO	RI	1,465.4
CENTRAL STATES H & L CO OF OMAHA	NE	386.9
DELAWARE AMERICAN LIFE INS CO	DE	106.3
FIDELITY SECURITY LIFE INS CO	MO	982.0
NATIONAL BENEFIT LIFE INS CO	NY	675.0
NEW YORK LIFE INS CO	NY	214,000.0
PACIFIC LIFE INS CO	NE	178,000.0
PARKER CENTENNIAL ASR CO	WI	99.1
STANDARD SECURITY LIFE INS CO OF NY	NY	152.8
TRUSTMARK LIFE INS CO	IL	249.3
Rating: B+		
AMERICAN FIDELITY ASR CO	OK	7,628.5
AMERICAN HEALTH & LIFE INS CO	TX	1,264.4
ASSURITY LIFE INS CO	NE	2,660.6
BOSTON MUTUAL LIFE INS CO	MA	1,634.0
CM LIFE INS CO	CT	9,072.1
COMPANION LIFE INS CO	SC	689.7
GERBER LIFE INS CO	NY	5,146.7
HM LIFE INS CO	PA	881.3
ILLINOIS MUTUAL LIFE INS CO	IL	1,595.0
NATIONAL HEALTH INS CO	TX	181.1
NORTHWESTERN LONG TERM CARE INS CO	WI	320.0
NORTHWESTERN MUTUAL LIFE INS CO	WI	335,000.0
NY LIFE INS & ANNUITY CORP	DE	183,000.0
NYLIFE INS CO OF ARIZONA	AZ	159.0
OLD REPUBLIC LIFE INS CO	IL	106.8
PACIFIC LIFE & ANNUITY CO	AZ	8,615.1
PHYSICIANS LIFE INS CO	NE	1,783.0
PRINCIPAL LIFE INS CO	IA	239,000.0
STANDARD INS CO	OR	32,461.1
UNITED WORLD LIFE INS CO	NE	160.3
USAA LIFE INS CO	TX	26,197.9
USABLE LIFE	AR	505.6
VOYA RETIREMENT INS & ANNUITY CO	CT	129,000.0

Virginia

INSURANCE COMPANY NAME	DOM. STATE	TOTAL ASSETS ($MIL)

Rating: A+

INSURANCE COMPANY NAME	DOM. STATE	TOTAL ASSETS ($MIL)
AMERICAN FAMILY LIFE INS CO	WI	5,473.4
CHESAPEAKE LIFE INS CO	OK	251.1
COUNTRY LIFE INS CO	IL	9,442.8
PHYSICIANS MUTUAL INS CO	NE	2,785.1
STATE FARM LIFE INS CO	IL	86,273.0
TEACHERS INS & ANNUITY ASN OF AM	NY	343,000.0

Rating: A

INSURANCE COMPANY NAME	DOM. STATE	TOTAL ASSETS ($MIL)
BERKLEY LIFE & HEALTH INS CO	IA	478.2
DIRECT GENERAL LIFE INS CO	SC	33.5
FEDERATED LIFE INS CO	MN	2,427.1
FIDELITY INVESTMENTS LIFE INS CO	UT	44,295.4
GARDEN STATE LIFE INS CO	TX	143.5
GUARDIAN LIFE INS CO OF AMERICA	NY	72,127.3
NATIONAL FOUNDATION LIFE INS CO	TX	94.2
SENTRY LIFE INS CO	WI	9,857.5
SOUTHERN FARM BUREAU LIFE INS CO	MS	15,730.7

Rating: A-

INSURANCE COMPANY NAME	DOM. STATE	TOTAL ASSETS ($MIL)
AMICA LIFE INS CO	RI	1,465.4
ANNUITY INVESTORS LIFE INS CO	OH	3,225.7
CENTRAL STATES H & L CO OF OMAHA	NE	386.9
COUNTRY INVESTORS LIFE ASR CO	IL	323.0
DELAWARE AMERICAN LIFE INS CO	DE	106.3
FIDELITY SECURITY LIFE INS CO	MO	982.0
NATIONAL BENEFIT LIFE INS CO	NY	675.0
NEW YORK LIFE INS CO	NY	214,000.0
PACIFIC LIFE INS CO	NE	178,000.0
PARKER CENTENNIAL ASR CO	WI	99.1
STANDARD SECURITY LIFE INS CO OF NY	NY	152.8
SWBC LIFE INS CO	TX	42.4
TRUSTMARK LIFE INS CO	IL	249.3

Rating: B+

INSURANCE COMPANY NAME	DOM. STATE	TOTAL ASSETS ($MIL)
AMERICAN CONTINENTAL INS CO	TN	439.4
AMERICAN FIDELITY ASR CO	OK	7,628.5
AMERICAN HEALTH & LIFE INS CO	TX	1,264.4
ASSURITY LIFE INS CO	NE	2,660.6
BEST LIFE & HEALTH INS CO	TX	31.3
BOSTON MUTUAL LIFE INS CO	MA	1,634.0
CHRISTIAN FIDELITY LIFE INS CO	TX	44.0
CM LIFE INS CO	CT	9,072.1
COMPANION LIFE INS CO	SC	689.7
FREEDOM LIFE INS CO OF AMERICA	TX	462.4
GERBER LIFE INS CO	NY	5,146.7
HM LIFE INS CO	PA	881.3
ILLINOIS MUTUAL LIFE INS CO	IL	1,595.0
NATIONAL FARMERS UNION LIFE INS CO	TX	158.8
NATIONAL HEALTH INS CO	TX	181.1
NORTHWESTERN LONG TERM CARE INS CO	WI	320.0
NORTHWESTERN MUTUAL LIFE INS CO	WI	335,000.0
NY LIFE INS & ANNUITY CORP	DE	183,000.0
NYLIFE INS CO OF ARIZONA	AZ	159.0
OLD REPUBLIC LIFE INS CO	IL	106.8
OXFORD LIFE INS CO	AZ	2,955.5

INSURANCE COMPANY NAME	DOM. STATE	TOTAL ASSETS ($MIL)
PACIFIC LIFE & ANNUITY CO	AZ	8,615.1
PAN AMERICAN ASR CO	LA	26.7
PHYSICIANS LIFE INS CO	NE	1,783.0
PRINCIPAL LIFE INS CO	IA	239,000.0
STANDARD INS CO	OR	32,461.1
SYMETRA NATIONAL LIFE INS CO	IA	24.4
TRANS WORLD ASR CO	CA	341.0
UNITED NATIONAL LIFE INS CO OF AM	IL	52.1
UNITED WORLD LIFE INS CO	NE	160.3
USAA LIFE INS CO	TX	26,197.9
USABLE LIFE	AR	505.6
VOYA RETIREMENT INS & ANNUITY CO	CT	129,000.0

Washington

INSURANCE COMPANY NAME	DOM. STATE	TOTAL ASSETS ($MIL)
Rating: A+		
AMERICAN FAMILY LIFE INS CO	WI	5,473.4
CHESAPEAKE LIFE INS CO	OK	251.1
COUNTRY LIFE INS CO	IL	9,442.8
PHYSICIANS MUTUAL INS CO	NE	2,785.1
STATE FARM LIFE INS CO	IL	86,273.0
TEACHERS INS & ANNUITY ASN OF AM	NY	343,000.0
Rating: A		
BERKLEY LIFE & HEALTH INS CO	IA	478.2
DIRECT GENERAL LIFE INS CO	SC	33.5
FEDERATED LIFE INS CO	MN	2,427.1
FIDELITY INVESTMENTS LIFE INS CO	UT	44,295.4
GARDEN STATE LIFE INS CO	TX	143.5
GUARDIAN LIFE INS CO OF AMERICA	NY	72,127.3
NATIONAL FOUNDATION LIFE INS CO	TX	94.2
SENTRY LIFE INS CO	WI	9,857.5
Rating: A-		
AMICA LIFE INS CO	RI	1,465.4
ANNUITY INVESTORS LIFE INS CO	OH	3,225.7
CENTRAL STATES H & L CO OF OMAHA	NE	386.9
COUNTRY INVESTORS LIFE ASR CO	IL	323.0
DELAWARE AMERICAN LIFE INS CO	DE	106.3
FIDELITY SECURITY LIFE INS CO	MO	982.0
NATIONAL BENEFIT LIFE INS CO	NY	675.0
NEW YORK LIFE INS CO	NY	214,000.0
PACIFIC LIFE INS CO	NE	178,000.0
PARKER CENTENNIAL ASR CO	WI	99.1
STANDARD SECURITY LIFE INS CO OF NY	NY	152.8
TRUSTMARK LIFE INS CO	IL	249.3
Rating: B+		
AMERICAN FIDELITY ASR CO	OK	7,628.5
AMERICAN HEALTH & LIFE INS CO	TX	1,264.4
ASSURITY LIFE INS CO	NE	2,660.6
BEST LIFE & HEALTH INS CO	TX	31.3
BOSTON MUTUAL LIFE INS CO	MA	1,634.0
CHRISTIAN FIDELITY LIFE INS CO	TX	44.0
CM LIFE INS CO	CT	9,072.1
COMPANION LIFE INS CO	SC	689.7
FARM BUREAU LIFE INS CO	IA	9,888.5
FREEDOM LIFE INS CO OF AMERICA	TX	462.4
GERBER LIFE INS CO	NY	5,146.7
HM LIFE INS CO	PA	881.3
ILLINOIS MUTUAL LIFE INS CO	IL	1,595.0
NATIONAL FARMERS UNION LIFE INS CO	TX	158.8
NATIONAL HEALTH INS CO	TX	181.1
NORTHWESTERN LONG TERM CARE INS CO	WI	320.0
NORTHWESTERN MUTUAL LIFE INS CO	WI	335,000.0
NY LIFE INS & ANNUITY CORP	DE	183,000.0
NYLIFE INS CO OF ARIZONA	AZ	159.0
OLD REPUBLIC LIFE INS CO	IL	106.8
OXFORD LIFE INS CO	AZ	2,955.5
PACIFIC LIFE & ANNUITY CO	AZ	8,615.1
PAN AMERICAN ASR CO	LA	26.7

INSURANCE COMPANY NAME	DOM. STATE	TOTAL ASSETS ($MIL)
PHYSICIANS LIFE INS CO	NE	1,783.0
PRINCIPAL LIFE INS CO	IA	239,000.0
STANDARD INS CO	OR	32,461.1
SYMETRA NATIONAL LIFE INS CO	IA	24.4
TRANS WORLD ASR CO	CA	341.0
UNITED WORLD LIFE INS CO	NE	160.3
USAA LIFE INS CO	TX	26,197.9
USABLE LIFE	AR	505.6
VOYA RETIREMENT INS & ANNUITY CO	CT	129,000.0

West Virginia

INSURANCE COMPANY NAME	DOM. STATE	TOTAL ASSETS ($MIL)
Rating: A+		
AMERICAN FAMILY LIFE INS CO	WI	5,473.4
CHESAPEAKE LIFE INS CO	OK	251.1
COUNTRY LIFE INS CO	IL	9,442.8
PHYSICIANS MUTUAL INS CO	NE	2,785.1
STATE FARM LIFE INS CO	IL	86,273.0
TEACHERS INS & ANNUITY ASN OF AM	NY	343,000.0
Rating: A		
BERKLEY LIFE & HEALTH INS CO	IA	478.2
DIRECT GENERAL LIFE INS CO	SC	33.5
FEDERATED LIFE INS CO	MN	2,427.1
FIDELITY INVESTMENTS LIFE INS CO	UT	44,295.4
GARDEN STATE LIFE INS CO	TX	143.5
GUARDIAN LIFE INS CO OF AMERICA	NY	72,127.3
SENTRY LIFE INS CO	WI	9,857.5
Rating: A-		
AMICA LIFE INS CO	RI	1,465.4
ANNUITY INVESTORS LIFE INS CO	OH	3,225.7
CENTRAL STATES H & L CO OF OMAHA	NE	386.9
COUNTRY INVESTORS LIFE ASR CO	IL	323.0
DELAWARE AMERICAN LIFE INS CO	DE	106.3
FIDELITY SECURITY LIFE INS CO	MO	982.0
NATIONAL BENEFIT LIFE INS CO	NY	675.0
NEW YORK LIFE INS CO	NY	214,000.0
PACIFIC LIFE INS CO	NE	178,000.0
PARKER CENTENNIAL ASR CO	WI	99.1
STANDARD SECURITY LIFE INS CO OF NY	NY	152.8
TRUSTMARK LIFE INS CO	IL	249.3
Rating: B+		
AMERICAN CONTINENTAL INS CO	TN	439.4
AMERICAN FIDELITY ASR CO	OK	7,628.5
AMERICAN HEALTH & LIFE INS CO	TX	1,264.4
ASSURITY LIFE INS CO	NE	2,660.6
BOSTON MUTUAL LIFE INS CO	MA	1,634.0
CHRISTIAN FIDELITY LIFE INS CO	TX	44.0
CM LIFE INS CO	CT	9,072.1
COMPANION LIFE INS CO	SC	689.7
FREEDOM LIFE INS CO OF AMERICA	TX	462.4
GERBER LIFE INS CO	NY	5,146.7
HM LIFE INS CO	PA	881.3
ILLINOIS MUTUAL LIFE INS CO	IL	1,595.0
NATIONAL HEALTH INS CO	TX	181.1
NORTHWESTERN LONG TERM CARE INS CO	WI	320.0
NORTHWESTERN MUTUAL LIFE INS CO	WI	335,000.0
NY LIFE INS & ANNUITY CORP	DE	183,000.0
NYLIFE INS CO OF ARIZONA	AZ	159.0
OLD REPUBLIC LIFE INS CO	IL	106.8
OXFORD LIFE INS CO	AZ	2,955.5
PACIFIC LIFE & ANNUITY CO	AZ	8,615.1
PAN AMERICAN ASR CO	LA	26.7
PHYSICIANS LIFE INS CO	NE	1,783.0
PRINCIPAL LIFE INS CO	IA	239,000.0
STANDARD INS CO	OR	32,461.1

INSURANCE COMPANY NAME	DOM. STATE	TOTAL ASSETS ($MIL)
SYMETRA NATIONAL LIFE INS CO	IA	24.4
TRANS WORLD ASR CO	CA	341.0
UNITED NATIONAL LIFE INS CO OF AM	IL	52.1
UNITED WORLD LIFE INS CO	NE	160.3
USAA LIFE INS CO	TX	26,197.9
USABLE LIFE	AR	505.6
VOYA RETIREMENT INS & ANNUITY CO	CT	129,000.0

Wisconsin

INSURANCE COMPANY NAME	DOM. STATE	TOTAL ASSETS ($MIL)
Rating: A+		
AMERICAN FAMILY LIFE INS CO	WI	5,473.4
CHESAPEAKE LIFE INS CO	OK	251.1
COUNTRY LIFE INS CO	IL	9,442.8
PHYSICIANS MUTUAL INS CO	NE	2,785.1
STATE FARM LIFE & ACCIDENT ASR CO	IL	3,528.9
TEACHERS INS & ANNUITY ASN OF AM	NY	343,000.0
Rating: A		
BERKLEY LIFE & HEALTH INS CO	IA	478.2
DIRECT GENERAL LIFE INS CO	SC	33.5
FEDERATED LIFE INS CO	MN	2,427.1
FIDELITY INVESTMENTS LIFE INS CO	UT	44,295.4
GARDEN STATE LIFE INS CO	TX	143.5
GUARDIAN LIFE INS CO OF AMERICA	NY	72,127.3
SENTRY LIFE INS CO	WI	9,857.5
Rating: A-		
AMICA LIFE INS CO	RI	1,465.4
ANNUITY INVESTORS LIFE INS CO	OH	3,225.7
CENTRAL STATES H & L CO OF OMAHA	NE	386.9
COUNTRY INVESTORS LIFE ASR CO	IL	323.0
DELAWARE AMERICAN LIFE INS CO	DE	106.3
FIDELITY SECURITY LIFE INS CO	MO	982.0
NATIONAL BENEFIT LIFE INS CO	NY	675.0
NEW YORK LIFE INS CO	NY	214,000.0
PACIFIC LIFE INS CO	NE	178,000.0
PARKER CENTENNIAL ASR CO	WI	99.1
STANDARD SECURITY LIFE INS CO OF NY	NY	152.8
TRUSTMARK LIFE INS CO	IL	249.3
Rating: B+		
AMERICAN CONTINENTAL INS CO	TN	439.4
AMERICAN FIDELITY ASR CO	OK	7,628.5
AMERICAN HEALTH & LIFE INS CO	TX	1,264.4
ASSURITY LIFE INS CO	NE	2,660.6
BOSTON MUTUAL LIFE INS CO	MA	1,634.0
CM LIFE INS CO	CT	9,072.1
COMPANION LIFE INS CO	SC	689.7
ENTERPRISE LIFE INS CO	TX	159.9
FARM BUREAU LIFE INS CO	IA	9,888.5
GERBER LIFE INS CO	NY	5,146.7
HM LIFE INS CO	PA	881.3
ILLINOIS MUTUAL LIFE INS CO	IL	1,595.0
NATIONAL FARMERS UNION LIFE INS CO	TX	158.8
NATIONAL HEALTH INS CO	TX	181.1
NORTHWESTERN LONG TERM CARE INS CO	WI	320.0
NORTHWESTERN MUTUAL LIFE INS CO	WI	335,000.0
NY LIFE INS & ANNUITY CORP	DE	183,000.0
NYLIFE INS CO OF ARIZONA	AZ	159.0
OLD REPUBLIC LIFE INS CO	IL	106.8
OXFORD LIFE INS CO	AZ	2,955.5
PACIFIC LIFE & ANNUITY CO	AZ	8,615.1
PAN AMERICAN ASR CO	LA	26.7
PHYSICIANS LIFE INS CO	NE	1,783.0
PRINCIPAL LIFE INS CO	IA	239,000.0

INSURANCE COMPANY NAME	DOM. STATE	TOTAL ASSETS ($MIL)
STANDARD INS CO	OR	32,461.1
SYMETRA NATIONAL LIFE INS CO	IA	24.4
TRANS WORLD ASR CO	CA	341.0
UNITED NATIONAL LIFE INS CO OF AM	IL	52.1
UNITED WORLD LIFE INS CO	NE	160.3
USAA LIFE INS CO	TX	26,197.9
USABLE LIFE	AR	505.6
VOYA RETIREMENT INS & ANNUITY CO	CT	129,000.0

Wyoming

INSURANCE COMPANY NAME	DOM. STATE	TOTAL ASSETS ($MIL)

Rating: A+

INSURANCE COMPANY NAME	DOM. STATE	TOTAL ASSETS ($MIL)
AMERICAN FAMILY LIFE INS CO	WI	5,473.4
CHESAPEAKE LIFE INS CO	OK	251.1
COUNTRY LIFE INS CO	IL	9,442.8
PHYSICIANS MUTUAL INS CO	NE	2,785.1
STATE FARM LIFE INS CO	IL	86,273.0
TEACHERS INS & ANNUITY ASN OF AM	NY	343,000.0

Rating: A

INSURANCE COMPANY NAME	DOM. STATE	TOTAL ASSETS ($MIL)
BERKLEY LIFE & HEALTH INS CO	IA	478.2
FEDERATED LIFE INS CO	MN	2,427.1
FIDELITY INVESTMENTS LIFE INS CO	UT	44,295.4
GARDEN STATE LIFE INS CO	TX	143.5
GUARDIAN LIFE INS CO OF AMERICA	NY	72,127.3
NATIONAL FOUNDATION LIFE INS CO	TX	94.2
SENTRY LIFE INS CO	WI	9,857.5

Rating: A-

INSURANCE COMPANY NAME	DOM. STATE	TOTAL ASSETS ($MIL)
AMICA LIFE INS CO	RI	1,465.4
ANNUITY INVESTORS LIFE INS CO	OH	3,225.7
CENTRAL STATES H & L CO OF OMAHA	NE	386.9
COUNTRY INVESTORS LIFE ASR CO	IL	323.0
DELAWARE AMERICAN LIFE INS CO	DE	106.3
FIDELITY SECURITY LIFE INS CO	MO	982.0
NATIONAL BENEFIT LIFE INS CO	NY	675.0
NEW YORK LIFE INS CO	NY	214,000.0
PACIFIC LIFE INS CO	NE	178,000.0
PARKER CENTENNIAL ASR CO	WI	99.1
STANDARD SECURITY LIFE INS CO OF NY	NY	152.8
TRUSTMARK LIFE INS CO	IL	249.3

Rating: B+

INSURANCE COMPANY NAME	DOM. STATE	TOTAL ASSETS ($MIL)
AMERICAN CONTINENTAL INS CO	TN	439.4
AMERICAN FIDELITY ASR CO	OK	7,628.5
AMERICAN HEALTH & LIFE INS CO	TX	1,264.4
ASSURITY LIFE INS CO	NE	2,660.6
BEST LIFE & HEALTH INS CO	TX	31.3
BOSTON MUTUAL LIFE INS CO	MA	1,634.0
CHRISTIAN FIDELITY LIFE INS CO	TX	44.0
CM LIFE INS CO	CT	9,072.1
COMPANION LIFE INS CO	SC	689.7
COMPANION LIFE INS CO OF CA	CA	34.1
FARM BUREAU LIFE INS CO	IA	9,888.5
FREEDOM LIFE INS CO OF AMERICA	TX	462.4
GERBER LIFE INS CO	NY	5,146.7
HM LIFE INS CO	PA	881.3
ILLINOIS MUTUAL LIFE INS CO	IL	1,595.0
NATIONAL FARMERS UNION LIFE INS CO	TX	158.8
NATIONAL HEALTH INS CO	TX	181.1
NORTHWESTERN LONG TERM CARE INS CO	WI	320.0
NORTHWESTERN MUTUAL LIFE INS CO	WI	335,000.0
NY LIFE INS & ANNUITY CORP	DE	183,000.0
NYLIFE INS CO OF ARIZONA	AZ	159.0
OLD REPUBLIC LIFE INS CO	IL	106.8
OXFORD LIFE INS CO	AZ	2,955.5
PACIFIC LIFE & ANNUITY CO	AZ	8,615.1

INSURANCE COMPANY NAME	DOM. STATE	TOTAL ASSETS ($MIL)
PHYSICIANS LIFE INS CO	NE	1,783.0
PRINCIPAL LIFE INS CO	IA	239,000.0
STANDARD INS CO	OR	32,461.1
TRANS WORLD ASR CO	CA	341.0
UNITED NATIONAL LIFE INS CO OF AM	IL	52.1
UNITED WORLD LIFE INS CO	NE	160.3
USAA LIFE INS CO	TX	26,197.9
USABLE LIFE	AR	505.6
VOYA RETIREMENT INS & ANNUITY CO	CT	129,000.0

Section V

All Companies
Listed by Rating

A list of all rated and unrated

U.S. Life and Annuity Insurers

Companies are ranked by Weiss Safety Rating
and then listed alphabetically within each rating category.

Section V Contents

This section sorts all companies by their Weiss Safety Rating and then lists them alphabetically within each rating category. The purpose of this section is to provide in one place all of those companies receiving a given rating. Companies with the same rating should be viewed as having the same relative risk regardless of their order in this table.

1. **Safety Rating**

   Our rating is measured on a scale from A to F and considers a wide range of factors. Highly rated companies are, in our opinion, less likely to experience financial difficulties than lower rated firms. See *About Weiss Safety Ratings* for more information.

2. **Insurance Company Name**

   The legally registered name, which can sometimes differ from the name that the company uses for advertising. An insurer's name can be very similar to that of another, so verify the company's exact name and state of domicile to make sure you are looking at the correct company.

3. **Domicile State**

   The state which has primary regulatory responsibility for the company. It may differ from the location of the company's corporate headquarters. You do not have to be living in the domicile state to purchase insurance from this firm, provided it is licensed to do business in your state.

4. **Total Assets**

   All assets admitted by state insurance regulators in millions of dollars. This includes investments, current business assets and separate accounts.

INSURANCE COMPANY NAME	DOM. STATE	TOTAL ASSETS ($MIL)
Rating: A+		
AMERICAN FAMILY LIFE INS CO	WI	5,473.4
CHESAPEAKE LIFE INS CO	OK	251.1
COUNTRY LIFE INS CO	IL	9,442.8
PHYSICIANS MUTUAL INS CO	NE	2,785.1
STATE FARM LIFE & ACCIDENT ASR CO	IL	3,528.9
STATE FARM LIFE INS CO	IL	86,273.0
TEACHERS INS & ANNUITY ASN OF AM	NY	343,000.0
Rating: A		
AMERICAN FAMILY LIFE ASR CO OF NY	NY	1,108.3
BERKLEY LIFE & HEALTH INS CO	IA	478.2
DIRECT GENERAL LIFE INS CO	SC	33.5
EMPIRE FIDELITY INVESTMENTS L I C	NY	4,201.6
FEDERATED LIFE INS CO	MN	2,427.1
FIDELITY INVESTMENTS LIFE INS CO	UT	44,295.4
FRANDISCO LIFE INS CO	GA	121.9
GARDEN STATE LIFE INS CO	TX	143.5
GUARDIAN LIFE INS CO OF AMERICA	NY	72,127.3
NATIONAL FOUNDATION LIFE INS CO	TX	94.2
SENTRY LIFE INS CO	WI	9,857.5
SHELTERPOINT LIFE INS CO	NY	392.4
SOUTHERN FARM BUREAU LIFE INS CO	MS	15,730.7
STANDARD LIFE INS CO OF NY	NY	325.0
Rating: A-		
AMICA LIFE INS CO	RI	1,465.4
ANNUITY INVESTORS LIFE INS CO	OH	3,225.7
BLUEBONNET LIFE INS CO	MS	71.5
CENTRAL STATES H & L CO OF OMAHA	NE	386.9
COUNTRY INVESTORS LIFE ASR CO	IL	323.0
DELAWARE AMERICAN LIFE INS CO	DE	106.3
FARM BUREAU LIFE INS CO OF MICHIGAN	MI	2,709.6
FIDELITY SECURITY LIFE INS CO	MO	982.0
FIDELITY SECURITY LIFE INS CO OF NY	NY	39.3
FIRST RELIANCE STANDARD LIFE INS CO	NY	259.1
NATIONAL BENEFIT LIFE INS CO	NY	675.0
NEW YORK LIFE INS CO	NY	214,000.0
PACIFIC LIFE INS CO	NE	178,000.0
PARKER CENTENNIAL ASR CO	WI	99.1
STANDARD SECURITY LIFE INS CO OF NY	NY	152.8
SWBC LIFE INS CO	TX	42.4
TRUSTMARK LIFE INS CO	IL	249.3
Rating: B+		
ADVANCE INS CO OF KANSAS	KS	78.4
AMERICAN CONTINENTAL INS CO	TN	439.4
AMERICAN FIDELITY ASR CO	OK	7,628.5
AMERICAN HEALTH & LIFE INS CO	TX	1,264.4
ASSURITY LIFE INS CO	NE	2,660.6
BEST LIFE & HEALTH INS CO	TX	31.3
BOSTON MUTUAL LIFE INS CO	MA	1,634.0
CHRISTIAN FIDELITY LIFE INS CO	TX	44.0
CM LIFE INS CO	CT	9,072.1

INSURANCE COMPANY NAME	DOM. STATE	TOTAL ASSETS ($MIL)
COMPANION LIFE INS CO	SC	689.7
COMPANION LIFE INS CO OF CA	CA	34.1
ENTERPRISE LIFE INS CO	TX	159.9
FARM BUREAU LIFE INS CO	IA	9,888.5
FREEDOM LIFE INS CO OF AMERICA	TX	462.4
GERBER LIFE INS CO	NY	5,146.7
HM LIFE INS CO	PA	881.3
ILLINOIS MUTUAL LIFE INS CO	IL	1,595.0
LIFE INS CO OF BOSTON & NEW YORK	NY	193.4
M LIFE INS CO	CO	479.6
NATIONAL FARMERS UNION LIFE INS CO	TX	158.8
NATIONAL HEALTH INS CO	TX	181.1
NIAGARA LIFE & HEALTH INS CO	NY	20.4
NORTHWESTERN LONG TERM CARE INS CO	WI	320.0
NORTHWESTERN MUTUAL LIFE INS CO	WI	335,000.0
NY LIFE INS & ANNUITY CORP	DE	183,000.0
NYLIFE INS CO OF ARIZONA	AZ	159.0
OLD REPUBLIC LIFE INS CO	IL	106.8
OXFORD LIFE INS CO	AZ	2,955.5
PACIFIC LIFE & ANNUITY CO	AZ	8,615.1
PAN AMERICAN ASR CO	LA	26.7
PHYSICIANS LIFE INS CO	NE	1,783.0
POPULAR LIFE RE	PR	70.2
PRINCIPAL LIFE INS CO	IA	239,000.0
STANDARD INS CO	OR	32,461.1
SYMETRA NATIONAL LIFE INS CO	IA	24.4
TENNESSEE FARMERS LIFE INS CO	TN	2,599.1
TRANS OCEANIC LIFE INS CO	PR	407.4
TRANS WORLD ASR CO	CA	341.0
UNITED FARM FAMILY LIFE INS CO	IN	2,457.7
UNITED NATIONAL LIFE INS CO OF AM	IL	52.1
UNITED WORLD LIFE INS CO	NE	160.3
USAA LIFE INS CO	TX	26,197.9
USABLE LIFE	AR	505.6
VOYA RETIREMENT INS & ANNUITY CO	CT	129,000.0
Rating: B		
4 EVER LIFE INS CO	IL	193.1
AAA LIFE INS CO	MI	764.0
AAA LIFE INS CO OF NY	NY	13.0
AETNA LIFE INS CO	CT	25,501.2
AMALGAMATED LIFE INS CO	NY	144.3
AMERICAN BANKERS LIFE ASR CO OF FL	FL	267.8
AMERICAN BENEFIT LIFE INS CO	OK	238.9
AMERICAN EQUITY INVESTMENT LIFE NY	NY	170.4
AMERICAN FARM LIFE INS CO	TX	5.1
AMERICAN FIDELITY LIFE INS CO	FL	385.7
AMERICAN GENERAL LIFE INS CO	TX	217,000.0
AMERICAN HERITAGE LIFE INS CO	FL	2,325.5
AMERICAN MATURITY LIFE INS CO	CT	68.1
AMERICAN MEMORIAL LIFE INS CO	SD	4,034.0
AMERICAN NATIONAL INS CO	TX	23,828.7
AMERICAN PUBLIC LIFE INS CO	OK	100.9
AMERITAS LIFE INS CORP	NE	27,493.5

INSURANCE COMPANY NAME	DOM. STATE	TOTAL ASSETS ($MIL)	INSURANCE COMPANY NAME	DOM. STATE	TOTAL ASSETS ($MIL)
Rating: B (Continued)			LEGACY LIFE INS CO OF MO	MO	6.4
			LIFE INS CO OF NORTH AMERICA	PA	9,002.2
ANTHEM LIFE & DISABILITY INS CO	NY	48.6	LIFE INS CO OF THE SOUTHWEST	TX	27,512.1
ANTHEM LIFE INS CO	IN	869.7	LINCOLN LIFE & ANNUITY CO OF NY	NY	17,305.7
ASSURITY LIFE INS CO OF NY	NY	8.2	LOCOMOTIVE ENGRS&COND MUT PROT ASSN	MI	100.1
BALTIMORE LIFE INS CO	MD	1,299.4	LOYAL AMERICAN LIFE INS CO	OH	403.0
BENEFICIAL LIFE INS CO	UT	1,944.1	MADISON NATIONAL LIFE INS CO INC	WI	236.9
BERKSHIRE LIFE INS CO OF AMERICA	MA	4,680.8	MANHATTAN LIFE INS CO	NY	632.6
BLUE CROSS BLUE SHIELD OF KANSAS INC	KS	2,277.0	MANHATTAN NATIONAL LIFE INS CO	OH	141.2
BLUE SHIELD OF CALIFORNIA L&H INS CO	CA	256.1	MAPFRE LIFE INS CO OF PR	PR	59.3
CARIBBEAN AMERICAN LIFE ASR CO	PR	41.5	MASSACHUSETTS MUTUAL LIFE INS CO	MA	315,000.0
CIGNA NATIONAL HEALTH INS CO	OH	15.1	MEMBERS LIFE INS CO	IA	386.6
CIGNA WORLDWIDE INS CO	DE	59.4	METROPOLITAN LIFE INS CO	NY	404,000.0
CINCINNATI EQUITABLE LIFE INS CO	OH	192.3	MIDLAND NATIONAL LIFE INS CO	IA	74,313.6
CMFG LIFE INS CO	IA	26,335.6	MIDWESTERN UNITED LIFE INS CO	IN	248.1
COMM TRAVELERS LIFE INS CO	NY	12.2	MUTUAL OF AMERICA LIFE INS CO	NY	28,283.4
CONTINENTAL AMERICAN INS CO	SC	933.7	MUTUAL OF OMAHA INS CO	NE	10,341.8
COTTON STATES LIFE INS CO	GA	316.4	MUTUAL TRUST LIFE INS CO	IL	2,259.5
DEARBORN LIFE INS CO	IL	1,647.0	NATIONAL FARM LIFE INS CO	TX	443.8
DELAWARE LIFE INS CO OF NEW YORK	NY	2,151.9	NATIONAL INCOME LIFE INS CO	NY	390.6
EAGLE LIFE INS CO	IA	3,050.9	NATIONAL LIFE INS CO	VT	11,011.8
ELCO MUTUAL LIFE & ANNUITY	IL	993.1	NATIONAL WESTERN LIFE INS CO	CO	10,771.7
EMC NATIONAL LIFE CO	IA	844.9	NORTH AMERICAN CO FOR LIFE & H INS	IA	35,313.3
EMPLOYERS PROTECTIVE INS CO	HI	5.2	NORTH AMERICAN INS CO	WI	19.8
ENCOVA LIFE INSURANCE CO	OH	607.8	NTA LIFE INS CO OF NEW YORK	NY	10.1
EQUITABLE FINL LIFE INS CO	NY	248,000.0	NY LIFE GROUP INS CO OF NY	NY	503.4
EVERLAKE LIFE INS CO	IL	28,147.6	OHIO NATIONAL LIFE ASR CORP	OH	3,181.4
FARM BUREAU LIFE INS CO OF MISSOURI	MO	698.8	OLD UNITED LIFE INS CO	AZ	129.8
FIRST ASR LIFE OF AMERICA	LA	42.6	OMAHA SUPPLEMENTAL INS CO	NE	25.1
FIRST SECURITY BENEFIT LIFE & ANN	NY	556.7	PACIFIC GUARDIAN LIFE INS CO LTD	HI	504.9
FORETHOUGHT LIFE INS CO	IN	47,725.7	PAN AMERICAN LIFE INS CO OF PR	PR	8.4
FUNERAL DIRECTORS LIFE INS CO	TX	1,718.8	PAN-AMERICAN LIFE INS CO	LA	1,236.0
GLOBE LIFE INSURANCE CO OF NY	NY	266.6	PARK AVENUE LIFE INS CO	DE	199.4
GOLDEN RULE INS CO	IN	632.3	PEKIN LIFE INS CO	IL	1,626.3
GPM HEALTH & LIFE INS CO	WA	140.7	PENN INS & ANNTY CO OF NY	NY	385.7
GREATER GEORGIA LIFE INS CO	GA	106.1	PENN MUTUAL LIFE INS CO	PA	27,994.9
GREENFIELDS LIFE INS CO	CO	10.0	PHILADELPHIA AMERICAN LIFE INS CO	TX	390.4
GUARANTEE TRUST LIFE INS CO	IL	791.2	PLATEAU INS CO	TN	28.9
GUARANTY INCOME LIFE INS CO	IA	3,458.1	PRIMERICA LIFE INS CO	TN	2,064.3
GUARDIAN INS & ANNUITY CO INC	DE	14,206.8	PRINCIPAL NATIONAL LIFE INS CO	IA	832.4
HANNOVER LIFE REASSURANCE CO OF AMER	FL	17,746.6	PROTECTIVE LIFE INS CO	TN	80,820.8
HARLEYSVILLE LIFE INS CO	OH	409.2	PROVIDENT AMER LIFE & HEALTH INS CO	OH	11.0
HCC LIFE INS CO	IN	1,491.3	PROVIDENT LIFE & CAS INS CO	TN	861.9
HEALTH NET LIFE INS CO	CA	616.8	PRUDENTIAL INS CO OF AMERICA	NJ	324,000.0
HEARTLAND NATIONAL LIFE INS CO	IN	13.9	RENAISSANCE L&H INS CO OF AMERICA	DE	97.9
HM LIFE INS CO OF NEW YORK	NY	81.4	RIVERSOURCE LIFE INS CO	MN	116,000.0
HOMESTEADERS LIFE CO	IA	3,451.6	SB MUTL LIFE INS CO OF MA	MA	3,563.5
HORACE MANN LIFE INS CO	IL	9,032.1	SECURITY BENEFIT LIFE INS CO	KS	46,517.4
INTRAMERICA LIFE INS CO	NY	--	SENTRY LIFE INS CO OF NEW YORK	NY	168.1
JACKSON NATIONAL LIFE INS CO OF NY	NY	19,048.2	SHELTER LIFE INS CO	MO	1,404.6
JOHN HANCOCK LIFE & HEALTH INS CO	MA	19,441.1	SHELTERPOINT INS CO	FL	13.2
KANSAS CITY LIFE INS CO	MO	3,770.7	SOUTHERN NATL LIFE INS CO INC	LA	23.1
LAFAYETTE LIFE INS CO	OH	6,345.5	STANDARD LIFE & ACCIDENT INS CO	TX	488.4
LEADERS LIFE INS CO	OK	8.7	STATE LIFE INS CO	IN	10,441.4

INSURANCE COMPANY NAME	DOM. STATE	TOTAL ASSETS ($MIL)	INSURANCE COMPANY NAME	DOM. STATE	TOTAL ASSETS ($MIL)
Rating: B (Continued)			GENWORTH LIFE INS CO	DE	41,321.0
			GERMANIA LIFE INS CO	TX	107.9
STATE LIFE INS FUND	WI	112.9	GOVERNMENT PERSONNEL MUTUAL L I C	TX	799.8
STERLING LIFE INS CO	IL	33.7	GREAT AMERICAN LIFE INS CO	OH	38,448.9
SURENCY LIFE & HEALTH INS CO	KS	21.2	HARTFORD LIFE & ACCIDENT INS CO	CT	13,021.6
THE UNION LABOR LIFE INS CO	MD	4,752.2	INVESTORS LIFE INS CO NORTH AMERICA	TX	512.5
TIAA-CREF LIFE INS CO	NY	17,626.1	JEFFERSON NATIONAL LIFE INS CO OF NY	NY	282.3
TIER ONE INSURANCE CO	NE	73.6	JOHN HANCOCK LIFE INS CO (USA)	MI	273,000.0
TRANSAMERICA FINANCIAL LIFE INS CO	NY	35,545.8	KENTUCKY FUNERAL DIRECTORS LIFE INS	KY	25.9
TRANSAMERICA LIFE INS CO	IA	203,000.0	LIBERTY BANKERS LIFE INS CO	OK	2,323.6
TRUSTMARK INS CO	IL	1,807.8	LIBERTY NATIONAL LIFE INS CO	NE	8,756.8
TRUSTMARK LIFE INS CO OF NEW YORK	NY	11.7	LIFE OF AMERICA INS CO	TX	8.8
UNICARE LIFE & HEALTH INS CO	IN	957.9	LIFEMAP ASR CO	OR	107.2
UNION SECURITY INS CO	KS	3,149.8	LIFESECURE INS CO	MI	582.7
UNION SECURITY LIFE INS CO OF NY	NY	55.8	LINCOLN HERITAGE LIFE INS CO	IL	1,118.1
UNITED AMERICAN INS CO	NE	714.5	MEDICO CORP LIFE INS CO	NE	72.9
UNITED HERITAGE LIFE INS CO	ID	682.2	MEDICO INS CO	NE	75.0
UNITED HOME LIFE INS CO	IN	193.7	MEDMUTUAL LIFE INS CO	OH	60.0
UNITED OF OMAHA LIFE INS CO	NE	31,183.6	MML BAY STATE LIFE INS CO	CT	5,462.8
UNIVERSAL LIFE INS CO	PR	2,445.4	MONY LIFE INS CO	NY	6,597.6
US FINANCIAL LIFE INS CO	OH	373.7	MUTUAL SAVINGS LIFE INS CO	AL	110.1
USAA LIFE INS CO OF NEW YORK	NY	665.9	NATIONAL GUARDIAN LIFE INS CO	WI	4,698.1
UTIC INS CO	AL	165.0	NATIONAL SECURITY INS CO	AL	55.2
VARIABLE ANNUITY LIFE INS CO	TX	95,249.3	NATIONAL SECURITY LIFE & ANNUITY CO	NY	482.6
WEST COAST LIFE INS CO	NE	4,377.3	NATIONAL TEACHERS ASSOCIATES L I C	TX	657.1
WESTERN & SOUTHERN LIFE INS CO	OH	12,681.6	NATIONWIDE LIFE INS CO	OH	179,000.0
WESTERN-SOUTHERN LIFE ASR CO	OH	19,537.6	NEW ENGLAND LIFE INS CO	MA	9,856.9
WYSH L&H INSURANCE CO	AZ	9.5	NEW ERA LIFE INS CO	TX	641.7
Rating: B-			OLD AMERICAN INS CO	MO	303.1
			OMAHA INS CO	NE	114.7
ALLIANZ LIFE INS CO OF NORTH AMERICA	MN	174,000.0	OPTUM INS OF OH INC	OH	251.7
ALLIANZ LIFE INS CO OF NY	NY	5,071.6	PACIFICARE LIFE & HEALTH INS CO	IN	--
AMER MONUMENTAL LIFE INS CO	LA	37.1	PERFORMANCE LIFE OF AMERICA	LA	26.5
AMERICAN INCOME LIFE INS CO	IN	4,889.9	PRENEED REINS CO OF AMERICA	AZ	22.7
AMERICAN NATIONAL LIFE INS CO OF NY	NY	2,874.9	PRUCO LIFE INS CO OF NEW JERSEY	NJ	20,574.7
AMERICAN REPUBLIC INS CO	IA	1,561.0	PRUDENTIAL RETIREMENT INS & ANNUITY	CT	100,000.0
AMERICAN UNITED LIFE INS CO	IN	39,048.1	RELIABLE LIFE INS CO	MO	38.2
AMERICO FINANCIAL LIFE & ANNUITY INS	TX	6,268.1	RELIASTAR LIFE INS CO	MN	15,173.4
AMERITAS LIFE INS CORP OF NY	NY	1,818.3	RELIASTAR LIFE INS CO OF NEW YORK	NY	2,258.6
ATHENE ANNUITY & LIFE ASR CO OF NY	NY	4,008.7	RENAISSANCE L&H INS CO OF NY	NY	15.6
BRIGHTHOUSE LIFE INSURANCE CO	DE	201,000.0	RGA REINSURANCE CO	MO	49,440.5
CAPITOL LIFE INS CO	TX	540.9	S USA LIFE INS CO INC	AZ	1,514.6
CHURCH LIFE INS CORP	NY	309.4	SBLI USA MUT LIFE INS CO INC	NY	2,554.3
CINCINNATI LIFE INS CO	OH	4,966.1	SECU LIFE INS CO	NC	75.7
CLEAR SPRING LIFE & ANNTY CO	DE	14,709.5	SECURIAN LIFE INS CO	MN	2,066.0
COMPANION LIFE INS CO	NY	1,193.1	SECURITY LIFE OF DENVER INS CO	CO	34,605.0
CONNECTICUT GENERAL LIFE INS CO	CT	21,459.7	SETTLERS LIFE INS CO	WI	413.8
CSI LIFE INS CO	NE	23.6	STANDARD LIFE & CAS INS CO	UT	45.3
EQUITRUST LIFE INS CO	IL	25,685.5	SYMETRA LIFE INS CO	IA	46,627.5
FAMILY HERITAGE LIFE INS CO OF AMER	OH	1,588.1	TALCOTT RESOLUTION LIFE	CT	36,351.0
FARMERS NEW WORLD LIFE INS CO	WA	5,670.8	TALCOTT RESOLUTION LIFE INS CO	CT	101,000.0
FIRST COMMAND LIFE INS CO	TX	48.1	TEXAS DIRECTORS LIFE INS CO	TX	4.8
FIRST PENN-PACIFIC LIFE INS CO	IN	1,157.8	UNIMERICA INS CO	WI	427.6
FORTITUDE LIFE INS & ANNTY CO	AZ	48,354.5	UNIMERICA LIFE INS CO OF NY	NY	35.6

INSURANCE COMPANY NAME	DOM. STATE	TOTAL ASSETS ($MIL)

Rating: B- (Continued)

INSURANCE COMPANY NAME	DOM. STATE	TOTAL ASSETS ($MIL)
UNION NATIONAL LIFE INS CO	LA	21.4
UNITED INS CO OF AMERICA	IL	5,067.0
UNITED LIFE INS CO	IA	2,915.1
UNIVERSAL FIDELITY LIFE INS CO	OK	18.8
VERSANT LIFE INS CO	MS	5.2
WESTERN UNITED LIFE ASR CO	WA	1,473.0
WINDSOR LIFE INS CO	TX	3.3

Rating: C+

INSURANCE COMPANY NAME	DOM. STATE	TOTAL ASSETS ($MIL)
ACCORDIA LIFE & ANNUITY CO	IA	12,709.0
ACE LIFE INS CO	CT	37.0
AMERICAN EQUITY INVEST LIFE INS CO	IA	60,422.4
AMERICAN FEDERATED LIFE INS CO	MS	26.2
AMERICAN NATIONAL LIFE INS CO OF TX	TX	137.2
AMERICAN RETIREMENT LIFE INS CO	OH	147.8
AUTO-OWNERS LIFE INS CO	MI	4,655.6
AUTOMOBILE CLUB OF SOUTHERN CA INS	CA	1,676.3
BERKSHIRE HATHAWAY LIFE INS CO OF NE	NE	23,719.2
CANADA LIFE REINSURANCE COMPANY	PA	54.1
CIGNA HEALTH & LIFE INS CO	CT	13,549.9
CITIZENS FIDELITY INS CO	AR	79.8
COLONIAL LIFE & ACCIDENT INS CO	SC	3,861.4
COLUMBIAN MUTUAL LIFE INS CO	NY	1,478.1
COLUMBUS LIFE INS CO	OH	4,628.7
COMBINED LIFE INS CO OF NEW YORK	NY	586.3
CONTINENTAL LIFE INS CO OF BRENTWOOD	TN	629.5
EQUITABLE FINL LIFE & ANNUITY CO	CO	587.0
EQUITABLE FINL LIFE INS CO OF AMER	AZ	6,242.0
ERIE FAMILY LIFE INS CO	PA	3,055.6
EVERLAKE ASSURANCE COMPANY	IL	172.7
FIDELITY LIFE ASSN A LEGAL RESERVE	IL	418.7
FIRST ALLMERICA FINANCIAL LIFE INS	MA	3,262.6
FIRST BERKSHIRE HATHAWAY LIFE INS CO	NY	250.6
FIRST HEALTH LIFE & HEALTH INS CO	TX	150.0
FIRST SYMETRA NATL LIFE INS CO OF NY	NY	3,477.6
FIRST UNUM LIFE INS CO	NY	4,405.9
FORTITUDE US REINSURANCE COMPA	AZ	9.8
GRANGE LIFE INS CO	OH	470.1
HERITAGE LIFE INS CO	AZ	7,707.6
IDEALIFE INS CO	CT	20.3
INTEGRITY LIFE INS CO	OH	9,956.3
JACKSON NATIONAL LIFE INS CO	MI	303,000.0
JAMESTOWN LIFE INS CO	VA	5.2
JEFFERSON NATIONAL LIFE INS CO	TX	10,807.0
JOHN ALDEN LIFE INS CO	WI	181.7
JOHN HANCOCK LIFE INS CO OF NY	NY	19,494.3
LIFE INS CO OF ALABAMA	AL	130.7
LIFESHIELD NATIONAL INS CO	OK	78.6
LINCOLN BENEFIT LIFE CO	NE	12,067.4
LINCOLN LIFE ASSR CO OF BOSTON	NH	--
LINCOLN NATIONAL LIFE INS CO	IN	317,000.0
MANHATTANLIFE INS & ANNUITY CO	AR	792.0

INSURANCE COMPANY NAME	DOM. STATE	TOTAL ASSETS ($MIL)
METROPOLITAN TOWER LIFE INS CO	NE	43,883.0
MINNESOTA LIFE INS CO	MN	66,996.4
NATIONAL INTEGRITY LIFE INS CO	NY	4,580.3
NEW ERA LIFE INS CO OF THE MIDWEST	TX	188.9
OHIO NATIONAL LIFE INS CO	OH	28,854.3
OPTIMUM RE INS CO	TX	282.9
OZARK NATIONAL LIFE INS CO	MO	849.9
PATRIOT LIFE INS CO	MI	30.7
PAUL REVERE LIFE INS CO	MA	745.4
PENN INS & ANNUITY CO	DE	9,532.6
PROFESSIONAL LIFE & CAS CO	AZ	11.6
PROTECTIVE LIFE & ANNUITY INS CO	AL	6,210.6
PROVIDENT LIFE & ACCIDENT INS CO	TN	6,214.2
RELIANCE STANDARD LIFE INS CO	IL	18,943.6
RESERVE NATIONAL INS CO	OK	50.8
SCOR GLOBAL LIFE USA RE CO	DE	787.5
SELECTED FUNERAL AND LIFE INS CO	AR	194.3
STERLING INVESTORS LIFE INS CO	IN	96.8
SWISS RE LIFE & HEALTH AMER INC	MO	13,957.8
TEXAS LIFE INS CO	TX	1,632.4
TRIPLE S VIDA INC	PR	810.1
UNIFIED LIFE INS CO	TX	206.8
UNITED STATES LIFE INS CO IN NYC	NY	32,282.1
UNIVERSAL GUARANTY LIFE INS CO	OH	360.0
UNUM LIFE INS CO OF AMERICA	ME	22,629.7
VANTIS LIFE INS CO	CT	542.5

Rating: C

INSURANCE COMPANY NAME	DOM. STATE	TOTAL ASSETS ($MIL)
AETNA HEALTH & LIFE INS CO	CT	656.5
ALFA LIFE INS CORP	AL	1,642.9
AMALGAMATED LIFE & HEALTH INS CO	IL	--
AMERICAN FARMERS & RANCHERS LIFE INS	OK	33.3
AMERICAN LIFE & ACC INS CO OF KY	KY	300.0
AMERICAN LIFE INS CO	DE	13,159.6
AMERICAN PROGRESSIVE L&H I C OF NY	NY	350.4
AMERICAN REPUBLIC CORP INS CO	IA	19.4
AMERICAN SAVINGS LIFE INS CO	AZ	73.3
AMERICAN-AMICABLE LIFE INS CO OF TX	TX	465.9
ARKANSAS BANKERS LIFE INS CO	AR	2.5
ATHENE ANNUITY & LIFE ASR CO	DE	37,921.8
ATHENE ANNUITY & LIFE CO	IA	106,000.0
ATHENE LIFE INS CO OF NEW YORK	NY	971.0
AURORA NATIONAL LIFE ASR CO	CA	2,954.8
AUTO CLUB LIFE INS CO	MI	973.1
BANKERS FIDELITY ASR CO	GA	10.1
BANKERS LIFE OF LOUISIANA	LA	20.8
BRIGHTHOUSE LIFE INS CO OF NY	NY	11,631.9
BROOKE LIFE INS CO	MI	6,432.0
CANADA LIFE ASSURANCE CO-US BRANCH	MI	3,928.3
CENTRAL SECURITY LIFE INS CO	TX	81.2
CENTRE LIFE INS CO	MA	1,450.2
CICA LIFE INS CO OF AMERICA	CO	151.5
CITIZENS SECURITY LIFE INS CO	KY	36.3
COMBINED INS CO OF AMERICA	IL	2,672.9

INSURANCE COMPANY NAME	DOM. STATE	TOTAL ASSETS ($MIL)

Rating: C (Continued)

INSURANCE COMPANY NAME	DOM. STATE	TOTAL ASSETS ($MIL)
COMMONWEALTH ANNUITY & LIFE INS CO	MA	60,138.2
CONTINENTAL GENERAL INS CO	OH	4,340.3
CORPORATE SOLUTIONS LIFE REINS CO	DE	20,868.3
DELAWARE LIFE INS CO	DE	44,380.7
ELIPS LIFE INS CO	MO	81.0
EMPOWER ANNTY INS CO AM	CO	75,889.8
EMPOWER LIFE & ANNTY INS CO NY	NY	4,138.8
FAMILY LIFE INS CO	TX	140.0
FIDELITY & GUARANTY LIFE INS CO NY	NY	556.8
FIVE STAR LIFE INS CO	NE	324.2
GENERAL RE LIFE CORP	CT	5,020.2
GENWORTH LIFE & ANNUITY INS CO	VA	19,843.6
GENWORTH LIFE INS CO OF NEW YORK	NY	7,569.5
GLOBE LIFE & ACCIDENT INS CO	NE	5,236.5
GREAT SOUTHERN LIFE INS CO	TX	191.1
HAWKEYE LIFE INS GROUP INC	IA	11.4
HUMANA INS CO OF KENTUCKY	KY	234.1
HUMANA INS CO OF PUERTO RICO INC	PR	79.6
IA AMERICAN LIFE INS CO	TX	267.4
IBEXIS LIFE & ANNUITY INS CO	MO	49.0
INDIVIDUAL ASR CO LIFE HEALTH & ACC	OK	18.7
INDUSTRIAL ALLIANCE INS & FIN SERV	TX	295.2
INVESTORS HERITAGE LIFE INS CO	KY	1,398.4
LANDMARK LIFE INS CO	TX	49.1
LEWER LIFE INS CO	MO	34.9
LIFE ASSURANCE CO INC	OK	3.7
LIFECARE ASSURANCE CO	AZ	2,933.0
LUMICO LIFE INSURANCE CO	MO	201.9
MEDAMERICA INS CO	PA	1,146.3
MEDAMERICA INS CO OF FL	FL	74.9
MEDICO LIFE & HEALTH INS CO	IA	14.0
MERIT LIFE INS CO	TX	56.9
MID-WEST NATIONAL LIFE INS CO OF TN	TX	42.9
MONITOR LIFE INS CO OF NEW YORK	NY	20.4
MUNICH AMERICAN REASSURANCE CO	GA	9,176.0
NATIONWIDE LIFE & ANNUITY INS CO	OH	42,615.4
OCCIDENTAL LIFE INS CO OF NC	TX	295.3
OCEANVIEW LIFE AND ANNUITY CO	TX	3,661.7
OLD SPARTAN LIFE INS CO INC	SC	28.3
OLD SURETY LIFE INS CO	OK	40.7
PARTNERRE LIFE RE CO OF AM	AR	417.3
PAVONIA LIFE INS CO OF MICHIGAN	MI	1,005.1
PAVONIA LIFE INS CO OF NEW YORK	NY	27.2
PELLERIN LIFE INS CO	LA	1.7
PIONEER MUTUAL LIFE INS CO	ND	63.9
PREFERRED SECURITY LIFE INS CO	TX	8.0
PRUCO LIFE INS CO	AZ	167,000.0
PRUDENTIAL LEGACY INS CO OF NJ	NJ	55,451.9
PURITAN LIFE INS CO OF AMERICA	TX	271.6
REINSURANCE CO OF MO INC	MO	2,697.7
RESOLUTION LIFE COLORADO INC	CO	1,510.0
RIVERSOURCE LIFE INS CO OF NY	NY	8,277.9

INSURANCE COMPANY NAME	DOM. STATE	TOTAL ASSETS ($MIL)
SECURITY MUTUAL LIFE INS CO OF NY	NY	2,996.8
SHENANDOAH LIFE INS CO	VA	1,850.5
SOUTHERN FINANCIAL LIFE INS CO	KY	16.0
SOUTHERN LIFE & HEALTH INS CO	WI	34.3
STARMOUNT LIFE INS CO	ME	132.1
TRANSAMERICA PACIFIC RE INC	VT	2,280.3
UNION FIDELITY LIFE INS CO	KS	19,882.4
UNITED FIDELITY LIFE INS CO	TX	1,121.1
UNITED HEALTHCARE INS CO	CT	22,699.4
UNITED SECURITY ASR CO OF PA	PA	55.4
UNUM INS CO	ME	117.9
VENERABLE INS AND ANNTY CO	IA	38,977.6
WEA INS CORP	WI	786.8
WESTERN AMERICAN LIFE INS CO	TX	25.1
WILCAC LIFE INS CO	IL	5,581.8
WILLIAM PENN LIFE INS CO OF NEW YORK	NY	1,356.2
WILTON REASSURANCE CO	MN	22,558.5
ZALICONY HNW PPVA SERIES ACT	NY	149.5

Rating: C-

INSURANCE COMPANY NAME	DOM. STATE	TOTAL ASSETS ($MIL)
AMERICAN HOME LIFE INS CO	KS	283.7
ATLANTIC COAST LIFE INS CO	SC	1,076.9
BANKERS FIDELITY LIFE INS CO	GA	162.5
BANNER LIFE INS CO	MD	7,266.8
BEST MERIDIAN INS CO	FL	399.4
CITIZENS NATIONAL LIFE INS CO	TX	11.9
COLUMBIAN LIFE INS CO	IL	387.9
EMPLOYERS REASSURANCE CORP	KS	22,443.7
FAMILY SECURITY LIFE INS CO INC	MS	6.7
FIDELITY & GUARANTY LIFE INS CO	IA	38,358.1
FIDELITY STANDARD LIFE INSURANCE COM	TX	9.9
GREAT WESTERN INS CO	UT	1,191.0
KENTUCKY HOME LIFE INS CO	KY	5.3
KILPATRICK LIFE INS CO	LA	206.7
LIFE OF THE SOUTH INS CO	GA	143.9
MOUNTAIN LIFE INS CO	TN	4.8
MULTINATIONAL LIFE INS CO	PR	132.4
NATIONAL FAMILY CARE LIFE INS CO	TX	15.6
NORTH AMERICAN NATIONAL RE INS CO	AZ	39.7
PIONEER AMERICAN INS CO	TX	122.3
PIONEER SECURITY LIFE INS CO	TX	192.0
PRESIDENTIAL LIFE INS CO	NC	9.8
PROVIDENT AMERICAN INS CO	TX	36.9
PURITAN LIFE INS CO	TX	31.1
RUSH LIFE INS CO	LA	30.1
SCOR GLOBAL LIFE AMERICAS REIN CO	DE	738.5
SCOR GLOBAL LIFE REINS CO OF DE	DE	347.8
SILAC INSURANCE CO	UT	6,778.9
SURETY LIFE & CASUALTY INS CO	ND	14.8
TEXAS SERVICE LIFE INS CO	TX	120.9
THE EPIC LIFE INSURANCE CO	WI	31.6
TOWN & COUNTRY LIFE INS CO	UT	10.6
TRANS CITY LIFE INS CO	AZ	20.5
UNITY FINANCIAL LIFE INS CO	OH	345.1

INSURANCE COMPANY NAME	DOM. STATE	TOTAL ASSETS ($MIL)

Rating: C-   (Continued)

INSURANCE COMPANY NAME	DOM. STATE	TOTAL ASSETS ($MIL)
USA INS CO	MS	5.2
USA LIFE ONE INS CO OF INDIANA	IN	31.0
WILTON REASSURANCE LIFE CO OF NY	NY	7,515.8
ZURICH AMERICAN LIFE INS CO	IL	16,900.4

Rating: D+

INSURANCE COMPANY NAME	DOM. STATE	TOTAL ASSETS ($MIL)
AMERICAN CENTURY LIFE INS CO	OK	92.5
AMERICAN CENTURY LIFE INS CO TX	TX	69.9
AMERICAN LIFE & ANNUITY CO	AR	53.9
AMERICAN LIFE & SECURITY CORP	NE	1,121.1
BANKERS LIFE & CAS CO	IL	18,541.7
CHESTERFIELD REINS CO	MO	342.2
COLONIAL PENN LIFE INS CO	PA	884.8
COLONIAL SECURITY LIFE INS CO	TX	2.8
FEDERAL LIFE INS CO	IL	270.5
FLORIDA COMBINED LIFE INS CO INC	FL	39.0
GULF GUARANTY LIFE INS CO	MS	34.9
INDEPENDENCE LIFE & ANNUITY CO	DE	3,445.7
JACKSON GRIFFIN INS CO	AR	14.3
MAGNOLIA GUARANTY LIFE INS CO	MS	11.2
MARQUETTE INDEMNITY & LIFE INS CO	AZ	4.8
MEDAMERICA INS CO OF NEW YORK	NY	1,128.1
MEDICAL BENEFITS MUTUAL LIFE INS CO	OH	17.3
MULHEARN PROTECTIVE INS CO	LA	12.2
PROFESSIONAL INS CO	TX	84.5
SENIOR LIFE INS CO	GA	89.0
SOUTHERN FINANCIAL LIFE INS CO	LA	169.4
SUN LIFE & HEALTH INS CO	MI	1,078.5
T J M LIFE INS CO	TX	18.2
TRIPLE-S BLUE II	PR	18.2
WASHINGTON NATIONAL INS CO	IN	5,828.8

Rating: D

INSURANCE COMPANY NAME	DOM. STATE	TOTAL ASSETS ($MIL)
ALABAMA LIFE REINS CO INC	AL	19.0
AMERICAN FINANCIAL SECURITY L I C	MO	23.0
AMERICAN LABOR LIFE INS CO	AZ	12.4
BANKERS CONSECO LIFE INS CO	NY	559.3
BANKERS LIFE INS CO OF AMERICA	TX	6.1
BENEVOLENT LIFE INS CO INC	LA	2.0
COOPERATIVA DE SEGUROS DE VIDA DE PR	PR	610.0
FAMILY BENEFIT LIFE INS CO	MO	252.3
FAMILY LIBERTY LIFE INS CO	TX	34.7
FIRST GUARANTY INS CO	LA	52.1
FIRST NATIONAL LIFE INS CO	NE	6.1
FOUNDATION LIFE INS CO OF AR	AR	4.7
FOXO LIFE INS CO	AR	5.0
GRANULAR INSURANCE CO	SC	69.3
HAWTHORN LIFE INS CO	TX	11.2
INDEPENDENT LIFE INSURANCE CO	TX	468.3
LANGHORNE REINSURANCE AZ LTD	AZ	9.7
LIFE INS CO OF LOUISIANA	LA	12.0
LIVE OAK INSURANCE CO	LA	9.9
MAJESTIC LIFE INS CO	LA	16.2

INSURANCE COMPANY NAME	DOM. STATE	TOTAL ASSETS ($MIL)
MEMORIAL LIFE INS CO	LA	3.8
MOLINA HEALTHCARE OF TEXAS INS CO	TX	10.1
NASSAU LIFE & ANNUITY CO	CT	1,935.6
OHIO STATE LIFE INS CO	TX	148.7
ROYALTY CAPITAL LIFE INS CO	MO	3.5
SECURICO LIFE INS CO	TX	29.3
SECURITY NATIONAL LIFE INS CO	UT	702.8
SECURITY PLAN LIFE INS CO	LA	317.9
SENIOR LIFE INS CO OF TEXAS	TX	2.1
SENTINEL SECURITY LIFE INS CO	UT	858.0
SOUTHERN SECURITY LIFE INS CO INC	MS	1.6
STATE MUTUAL INS CO	GA	217.6
SUN LIFE ASR CO OF CANADA	MI	19,675.7
SURETY LIFE INS CO	NE	29.5
TRINITY LIFE INS CO	OK	349.6
UNITED FUNERAL BENEFIT LIFE INS CO	OK	54.4
UNITED FUNERAL DIR BENEFIT LIC	TX	154.8
WICHITA NATIONAL LIFE INS CO	OK	13.4

Rating: D-

INSURANCE COMPANY NAME	DOM. STATE	TOTAL ASSETS ($MIL)
ABILITY INS CO	NE	915.1
CAPITOL SECURITY LIFE INS CO	TX	3.9
DAKOTA CAPITAL LIFE INS CO	ND	24.7
FIRST CONTINENTAL LIFE & ACC INS CO	TX	--
HAYMARKET INS CO	NE	2,707.8
INTERNATIONAL AMERICAN LIFE INS CO	TX	3.3
MCS LIFE INS CO	PR	90.5
NASSAU LIFE INS CO OF KS	KS	77.9
NASSAU LIFE INSURANCE CO	NY	14,014.5
NETCARE LIFE & HEALTH INS CO	GU	34.6
REGAL LIFE OF AMERICA INS CO	TX	6.9
RELIABLE LIFE INS CO	LA	7.0
SAGICOR LIFE INS CO	TX	2,997.6
SOUTHWEST SERVICE LIFE INS CO	TX	9.6
UNITED ASR LIFE INS CO	TX	2.3
US ALLIANCE LIFE & SECURITY CO	KS	85.6

Rating: E+

INSURANCE COMPANY NAME	DOM. STATE	TOTAL ASSETS ($MIL)
DIRECTORS LIFE ASR CO	OK	39.9
PHL VARIABLE INS CO	CT	5,173.0
UPSTREAM LIFE INS CO	TX	218.9

Rating: E

INSURANCE COMPANY NAME	DOM. STATE	TOTAL ASSETS ($MIL)
ATLANTA LIFE INS CO	GA	36.3
CROWN GLOBAL INS CO OF AMERICA	DE	846.8
CYRUS LIFE INSURANCE CO	AR	25.8
INVESTORS PREFERRED LIFE INS CO	SD	1,011.5
LOMBARD INTL LIFE ASR CO	PA	7,923.8
SMITH BURIAL & LIFE INS CO	AR	4.5
TEXAS REPUB LIFE INS CO	TX	31.4
WILLIAMS PROGRESSIVE LIFE & ACC I C	LA	11.9

Rating: E-

INSURANCE COMPANY NAME	DOM. STATE	TOTAL ASSETS ($MIL)
AMERICAN INDEPENDENT NETWORK INS CO	NY	14.8
DELTA LIFE INS CO	GA	70.9

INSURANCE COMPANY NAME	DOM. STATE	TOTAL ASSETS ($MIL)	INSURANCE COMPANY NAME	DOM. STATE	TOTAL ASSETS ($MIL)
			FIRST DIMENSION LIFE INS CO INC	OK	--
Rating: F (Continued)			FIRST LANDMARK LIFE INS CO	NE	--
			GAINBRIDGE LIFE INSURANCE CO	TX	--
AMERICAN COMMUNITY MUT INS CO	MI	--	GENWORTH INSURANCE CO	NC	--
BANKERS LIFE INS CO	FL	--	GMHP HEALTH INS LMTD	GU	--
COLORADO BANKERS LIFE INS CO	NC	--	GRIFFIN LEGGETT BURIAL INS CO	AR	--
CONCERT HEALTH PLAN INS CO	IL	--	GULF STATES LIFE INS CO INC	LA	--
FIDELITY MUTUAL LIFE INS CO	PA	--	IBC LIFE INS CO	TX	--
GERTRUDE GEDDES WILLIS LIFE INS CO	LA	--	INDEPENDENCE INS INC	DE	--
GREAT REPUBLIC LIFE INS CO	WA	--	JRD LIFE INS CO	AZ	--
HIGGINBOTHAM BURIAL INS CO	AR	--	LANDCAR LIFE INS CO	UT	--
INDY HEALTH INSURANCE COMPANY	AR	8.4	LIFE ASR CO OF AMERICA	IL	--
JORDAN FUNERAL & INS CO INC	AL	--	LOMBARD INTL LIFE ASR CO OF NY	NY	--
LADDER LIFE INSURANCE CO	CA	10.3	LUMICO LIFE INSURANCE CO OF NY	NY	--
LONE STAR LIFE INS CO	TX	--	MELLON LIFE INS CO	DE	--
MONARCH LIFE INS CO	MA	627.8	METLIFE INSURANCE LTD	GU	--
NORTH CAROLINA MUTUAL LIFE INS CO	NC	--	MILILANI LIFE INS CO	HI	--
SCOTTISH RE US INC	DE	--	MUNICH RE US LIFE CORP	GA	--
SENIOR HEALTH INS CO OF PENNSYLVANIA	PA	--	OLD SURETY INSURANCE CO	OK	--
SOUTHLAND NATIONAL INS CORP	NC	--	PACIFIC CENTURY LIFE INS CORP	AZ	--
TIME INS CO	PR	--	PAN AMERICAN ASR CO INTL INC	FL	--
Rating: U			PILLAR LIFE INSURANCE CO	PA	--
ACADEME INC	WA	--	PINE BELT LIFE INS CO	MS	--
AGC LIFE INS CO	MO	--	PIONEER MILITARY INS CO	NV	--
ALL SAVERS LIFE INS CO OF CA	CA	--	PRCPL RE CO OF VERMONT II	IA	--
ALLIED FINANCIAL INS CO	TX	--	PROGRESSIVE LIFE INSURANCE CO	OH	--
AMERICAN CREDITORS LIFE INS CO	DE	--	REGAL REINSURANCE COMPANY	MA	--
AMERICAN SERVICE LIFE INS CO	AR	--	RELIABLE SERVICE INS CO	LA	--
ASPIDA LIFE INSURANCE CO	CA	--	RELIANCE STANDARD LIFE INS CO OF TX	TX	--
BESTOW LIFE INS CO	IA	--	RESOURCE LIFE INS CO	IL	--
BESTOW NATL LIFE INS CO	TX	--	ROYAL STATE NATIONAL INS CO LTD	HI	--
BLUE SPIRIT INS CO	VT	--	SENTINEL AMERICAN LIFE INS CO	TX	--
CALPERS LONG-TERM CARE PROGRAM		--	SERVICE LIFE & CAS INS CO	TX	--
CANOPY INSURANCE CORP	AL	--	SHERIDAN LIFE INS CO	OK	--
CANYON STATE LIFE INS CO	AZ	--	SOUTHERN FIDELITY LIFE INS CO	AR	--
CAREAMERICA LIFE INS CO	CA	--	SOUTHWEST CREDIT LIFE INC	NM	--
CATERPILLAR LIFE INS CO	MO	--	SQUIRE REASSURANCE CO LLC	MI	--
CIGNA ARBOR LIFE INS CO	CT	--	STATE FARM HEALTH INS CO	IL	--
CIGNA INSURANCE CO	OH	--	STERLING NATL LIFE INS CO	CT	--
CL LIFE AND ANNUITY INS CO	TX	--	STRUCTURED ANNUITY RE CO	IA	--
COMMONWEALTH DEALERS LIFE INS CO	VA	--	TALCOTT RESOLUTION INTL LIFE	CT	--
CONSECO LIFE INS CO OF TX	TX	--	TRANS-WESTERN LIFE INS CO	TX	--
DAYFORWARD LIFE INSURANCE CO	TX	--	UNIVANTAGE INS CO	UT	--
DEARBORN NATIONAL LIFE INS CO OF NY	NY	--	US ALLIANCE LIFE & SEC CO (MT)	MT	--
DESERET MUTUAL INS CO	UT	--	USIC LIFE INS CO	PR	--
DESTINY HEALTH INS CO	IL	--			
DL REINSURANCE CO	DE	--			
EDUCATORS LIFE INS CO OF AMERICA	IL	--			
EVERENCE INS CO	IN	--			
EVERGREEN LIFE INS CO	TX	--			
FAMILY SERVICE LIFE INS CO	TX	--			
FARMERS LIFE INS CO	TN	--			
FINANCIAL AMERICAN LIFE INS CO	KS	--			

Section VI

Rating Upgrades
and Downgrades

A list of all

U.S. Life and Annuity Insurers

receiving a rating upgrade or downgrade
during the current quarter.

Section VI Contents

This section identifies those companies receiving a rating change since the previous edition of this publication, whether it be a rating upgrade, rating downgrade, newly-rated company or the withdrawal of a rating. A rating may be withdrawn due to a merger, dissolution, liquidation or lack of information. A rating upgrade or downgrade may entail a change from one letter grade to another, or it may mean the addition or deletion of a plus or minus sign within the same letter grade previously assigned to the company. Each rating upgrade and downgrade is accompanied by a brief explanation of why the rating was changed. Ratings are normally updated once each quarter of the year. In some instances, however, a company's rating may be downgraded outside of the normal updates due to overriding circumstances. The tables for new and withdrawn ratings will contain some or all of the following information:

1. **Insurance Company Name**
The legally registered name, which can sometimes differ from the name that the company uses for advertising. An insurer's name can be very similar to that of another, so verify the company's exact name and state of domicile to make sure you are looking at the correct company.

2. **Domicile State**
The state which has primary regulatory responsibility for the company. It may differ from the location of the company's corporate headquarters. You do not have to be living in the domicile state to purchase insurance from this firm, provided it is licensed to do business in your state.

3. **Total Assets**
All assets admitted by state insurance regulators in millions of dollars. This includes investments, current business assets, and separate accounts.

4. **New Safety Rating**
The rating assigned to the company as of the date of this Guide's publication. Our rating is measured on a scale from A to F and considers a wide range of factors. Highly rated companies are, in our opinion, less likely to experience financial difficulties than lower-rated firms. See *About Weiss Safety Ratings* for more information.

5. **Previous Safety Rating**
The rating assigned to the company prior to its most recent change.

6. **Date of Change**
The date that the rating upgrade or downgrade officially occurred. Normally, all rating changes are put into effect on a single day each quarter of the year. In some instances, however, a rating may have been changed outside of this normal update.

New Ratings

INSURANCE COMPANY NAME	DOM. STATE	TOTAL ASSETS ($MIL)	NEW RATING	PREVIOUS RATING	DATE OF CHANGE
TIER ONE INSURANCE CO	NE	73.6	B		10/28/22
WYSH L&H INSURANCE CO	AZ	9.5	B		10/28/22
BROOKE LIFE INS CO	MI	6,432.0	C		10/28/22
SOUTHERN LIFE & HEALTH INS CO	WI	34.3	C		10/28/22
PRESIDENTIAL LIFE INS CO	NC	9.8	C-		10/28/22
PURITAN LIFE INS CO	TX	31.1	C-		10/28/22
LANGHORNE REINSURANCE AZ LTD	AZ	9.7	D		10/28/22

www.weissratings.com

Withdrawn Ratings

INSURANCE COMPANY NAME	DOM. STATE	TOTAL ASSETS ($MIL)	NEW RATING	PREVIOUS RATING	DATE OF CHANGE
AMERICAN SERVICE LIFE INS CO	AR	1.9	U	B	10/28/22
COOPERATIVE LIFE INS CO	AR	2.4	U	D	10/28/22
FUNERAL DIRECTORS LIFE INS CO	LA	6.6	U	B-	10/28/22
PACIFIC CENTURY LIFE INS CORP	AZ	373.4	U	C-	10/28/22
RHODES LIFE INS CO OF LA INC	LA	4.1	U	E-	10/28/22
STERLING NATL LIFE INS CO	CT	9.0	U	D+	10/28/22
USIC LIFE INS CO	PR	5.8	U	C+	10/28/22

Rating Upgrades

ABILITY INS CO was upgraded to D- from E in October 2022 based on a greatly improved capitalization index, a higher five-year profitability index and a greatly improved stability index.

AETNA HEALTH & LIFE INS CO was upgraded to C from C- in October 2022 based on capitalization index, a higher five-year profitability index, an improved liquidity index and a markedly improved stability index.

AMERICAN HEALTH & LIFE INS CO was upgraded to B+ from B in October 2022 based on an improved capitalization index, a higher five-year profitability index and a greatly improved stability index.

AMERICAN MEMORIAL LIFE INS CO was upgraded to B from B- in October 2022 based on a higher capitalization index, a higher liquidity index and a higher stability index., notably the recent upgrade of affiliated company CMFG LIFE INS CO to B from B-.

ATLANTA LIFE INS CO was upgraded to E from E- in October 2022 based on a greatly improved capitalization index, a greatly improved investment safety index and a markedly improved five-year profitability index.

CENTRAL STATES H & L CO OF OMAHA was upgraded to A- from B+ in October 2022 based on a markedly improved stability index.

CMFG LIFE INS CO was upgraded to B from B- in October 2022 based on a greatly improved five-year profitability index.

EMPOWER LIFE & ANNTY INS CO NY was upgraded to C from C- in October 2022 based on a greatly improved liquidity index. enhanced financial strength of affiliates in Great West Life Asr Group.

ENCOVA LIFE INSURANCE CO was upgraded to B from B- in October 2022 based on a markedly improved five-year profitability index, a higher liquidity index and a greatly improved stability index.

JACKSON NATIONAL LIFE INS CO OF NY was upgraded to B from C+ in October 2022 based on a higher five-year profitability index. enhanced financial strength of affiliates in Prudential plc Group.

JAMESTOWN LIFE INS CO was upgraded to C+ from C in October 2022 based on a greatly improved capitalization index, a greatly improved investment safety index and a higher stability index. enhanced financial strength of affiliates in Genworth Financial Group.

KILPATRICK LIFE INS CO was upgraded to C- from D in October 2022 based on a markedly improved capitalization index, a greatly improved investment safety index, a greatly improved five-year profitability index, an improved liquidity index and a greatly improved stability index.

LIFE OF AMERICA INS CO was upgraded to B- from C+ in October 2022 based on an improved capitalization index, a greatly improved investment safety index, a greatly improved five-year profitability index, a greatly improved liquidity index and a markedly improved stability index. composite rating for affiliated New Era Life Group rose to B- from C+.

LIFESECURE INS CO was upgraded to B- from C+ in October 2022 based on a greatly improved five-year profitability index.

NATIONAL HEALTH INS CO was upgraded to B+ from B in October 2022 based on a greatly improved capitalization index and a greatly improved stability index.

PHL VARIABLE INS CO was upgraded to E+ from E in October 2022 based on a markedly improved investment safety index and a markedly improved stability index.

PROVIDENT LIFE & CAS INS CO was upgraded to B from B- in October 2022 based on a higher investment safety index and a higher five-year profitability index.

STERLING INVESTORS LIFE INS CO was upgraded to C+ from C in October 2022 based on an improved capitalization index, a higher investment safety index, a greatly improved five-year profitability index, a greatly improved liquidity index and a greatly improved stability index.

TEXAS REPUB LIFE INS CO was upgraded to E from E- in October 2022 based on a greatly improved capitalization index, a greatly improved investment safety index, a markedly improved five-year profitability index and a greatly improved liquidity index., notably the recent upgrade of affiliated company TRINITY LIFE INS CO to D from D-.

TRINITY LIFE INS CO was upgraded to D from D- in October 2022 based on a markedly improved investment safety index and a markedly improved stability index.

UNION SECURITY LIFE INS CO OF NY was upgraded to B from B- in October 2022 based on a greatly improved stability index.

UNITED NATIONAL LIFE INS CO OF AM was upgraded to B+ from B in October 2022 based on a higher liquidity index.

UPSTREAM LIFE INS CO was upgraded to E+ from E in October 2022 based on a greatly improved capitalization index, a greatly improved investment safety index, a higher five-year profitability index and a markedly improved stability index.

WILCAC LIFE INS CO was upgraded to C from C- in October 2022 based on a higher capitalization index, a greatly improved five-year profitability index, a greatly improved liquidity index and a greatly improved stability index.

Rating Downgrades

ALLIANZ LIFE INS CO OF NY was downgraded to B- from B+ in October 2022 due to a significant decline in its capitalization index and a substantially lower five-year profitability index.

AMALGAMATED LIFE INS CO was downgraded to B from A in October 2022 due to a declining capitalization index, a substantially lower five-year profitability index, a declining liquidity index and a significant decline in its stability index.

AMERICAN EQUITY INVEST LIFE INS CO was downgraded to C+ from B- in October 2022 due to a substantially lower five-year profitability index and a substantially lower liquidity index.

ANTHEM LIFE INS CO was downgraded to B from B+ in October 2022 due to a declining capitalization index, a substantially lower five-year profitability index and a declining stability index.

AUTO-OWNERS LIFE INS CO was downgraded to C+ from B- in October 2022 due to capitalization index, a substantially lower investment safety index and a significant decline in its five-year profitability index.

BANKERS LIFE INS CO OF AMERICA was downgraded to D from D+ in October 2022 due to a declining capitalization index and a significant decline in its five-year profitability index.

CHRISTIAN FIDELITY LIFE INS CO was downgraded to B+ from A- in October 2022 due to a substantially lower capitalization index, a significant decline in its five-year profitability index, a declining liquidity index and a substantially lower stability index.

CIGNA HEALTH & LIFE INS CO was downgraded to C+ from B in October 2022 due to a declining capitalization index, a significant decline in its five-year profitability index, a substantially lower liquidity index and a substantially lower stability index.

CITIZENS NATIONAL LIFE INS CO was downgraded to C- from C in October 2022 due to a lower five-year profitability index. In addition, the composite rating for affiliated Citizens Inc Group fell to D+ from C-.

DEARBORN LIFE INS CO was downgraded to B from B+ in October 2022 due to a declining capitalization index, a substantially lower five-year profitability index and a lower liquidity index.

DELTA LIFE INS CO was downgraded to E- from E in October 2022 due to a significant decline in its investment safety index and a significant decline in its five-year profitability index.

FARM BUREAU LIFE INS CO OF MISSOURI was downgraded to B from A- in October 2022 due to a substantially lower five-year profitability index.

FEDERAL LIFE INS CO was downgraded to D+ from C- in October 2022 due to a declining five-year profitability index.

FORTITUDE LIFE INS & ANNTY CO was downgraded to B- from B in October 2022 due to a declining five-year profitability index and a significant decline in its stability index.

FOUNDATION LIFE INS CO OF AR was downgraded to D from D+ in October 2022 due to a substantially lower capitalization index, a substantially lower five-year profitability index, a significant decline in its liquidity index and a substantially lower stability index.

GRANULAR INSURANCE CO was downgraded to D from C- in October 2022 due to a substantially lower investment safety index, a significant decline in its five-year profitability index, a substantially lower liquidity index and a declining stability index.

GREAT SOUTHERN LIFE INS CO was downgraded to C from C+ in October 2022 due to a declining capitalization index, a lower investment safety index, a declining five-year profitability index and a significant decline in its stability index., per the recent downgrade of affiliated company INVESTORS LIFE INS CO NORTH AMERICA to B- from B.

GULF GUARANTY LIFE INS CO was downgraded to D+ from C in October 2022 due to a substantially lower capitalization index, a lower investment safety index, a substantially lower five-year profitability index, a substantially lower liquidity index and a substantially lower stability index.

HUMANA INS CO OF KENTUCKY was downgraded to C from B- in October 2022 due to a declining capitalization index, a substantially lower five-year profitability index, a substantially lower liquidity index and a substantially lower stability index.

HUMANA INS CO OF PUERTO RICO INC was downgraded to C from C+ in October 2022 due to a declining capitalization index, a substantially lower five-year profitability index and a significant decline in its stability index.

INVESTORS LIFE INS CO NORTH AMERICA was downgraded to B- from B in October 2022 due to capitalization index, a declining liquidity index and a significant decline in its stability index.

LANDMARK LIFE INS CO was downgraded to C from C+ in October 2022 due to a significant decline in its capitalization index, a substantially lower five-year profitability index and a significant decline in its liquidity index.

LIFE INS CO OF BOSTON & NEW YORK was downgraded to B+ from A- in October 2022 due to a lower capitalization index and a declining five-year profitability index.

LIFE INS CO OF NORTH AMERICA was downgraded to B from B+ in October 2022 due to a significant decline in its capitalization index, a substantially lower five-year profitability index and a substantially lower stability index.

LINCOLN NATIONAL LIFE INS CO was downgraded to C+ from B in October 2022 due to a substantially lower five-year profitability index and a substantially lower stability index.

MEDMUTUAL LIFE INS CO was downgraded to B- from B in October 2022 due to a declining capitalization index, a substantially lower five-year profitability index, a significant decline in its liquidity index and a substantially lower stability index.

MIDLAND NATIONAL LIFE INS CO was downgraded to B from B+ in October 2022 due to a substantially lower stability index.

NATIONAL FAMILY CARE LIFE INS CO was downgraded to C- from C in October 2022 due to a lower capitalization index, a lower investment safety index, a significant decline in its five-year profitability index and a declining liquidity index.

NATIONAL GUARDIAN LIFE INS CO was downgraded to B- from B in October 2022 due to a significant decline in its stability index.

NORTH AMERICAN INS CO was downgraded to B from B+ in October 2022 due to a substantially lower capitalization index, a substantially lower five-year profitability index and a declining liquidity index., per the recent downgrade of affiliated company CHRISTIAN FIDELITY LIFE INS CO to B+ from A-.

OCEANVIEW LIFE AND ANNUITY CO was downgraded to C from C+ in October 2022 due to a substantially lower capitalization index, a substantially lower investment safety index, a substantially lower liquidity index and a significant decline in its stability index.

PHYSICIANS LIFE INS CO was downgraded to B+ from A- in October 2022 due to a lower capitalization index, a lower investment safety index and a significant decline in its five-year profitability index.

RESERVE NATIONAL INS CO was downgraded to C+ from B- in October 2022 due to a significant decline in its five-year profitability index.

SCOR GLOBAL LIFE REINS CO OF DE was downgraded to C- from C in October 2022 due to a substantially lower five-year profitability index, a significant decline in its liquidity index and a significant decline in its stability index.

SECU LIFE INS CO was downgraded to B- from B in October 2022 due to a lower five-year profitability index, a substantially lower liquidity index and a substantially lower stability index.

SECURIAN LIFE INS CO was downgraded to B- from B in October 2022 due to a substantially lower five-year profitability index and a declining liquidity index. In addition, the financial strength of affiliates in Securian Financial Group is declining.

SELECTED FUNERAL AND LIFE INS CO was downgraded to C+ from B- in October 2022 due to a substantially lower five-year profitability index.

SILAC INSURANCE CO was downgraded to C- from C in October 2022 due to a substantially lower capitalization index, a substantially lower investment safety index, a declining five-year profitability index and a substantially lower stability index.

STERLING LIFE INS CO was downgraded to B from B+ in October 2022 due to a substantially lower capitalization index and a significant decline in its stability index.

UNIFIED LIFE INS CO was downgraded to C+ from B- in October 2022 due to a significant decline in its five-year profitability index, a substantially lower liquidity index and a substantially lower stability index.

UNITED LIFE INS CO was downgraded to B- from B in October 2022 due to a lower capitalization index, a substantially lower five-year profitability index and a significant decline in its stability index.

UNIVERSAL LIFE INS CO was downgraded to B from B+ in October 2022 due to a declining capitalization index, a substantially lower investment safety index and a significant decline in its five-year profitability index.

USAA LIFE INS CO was downgraded to B+ from A in October 2022 due to a declining capitalization index, a declining five-year profitability index and a significant decline in its stability index.

WICHITA NATIONAL LIFE INS CO was downgraded to D from D+ in October 2022 due to a declining capitalization index, a declining five-year profitability index and a lower liquidity index.

WILTON REASSURANCE LIFE CO OF NY was downgraded to C- from C+ in October 2022 due to a substantially lower five-year profitability index, a declining liquidity index and a substantially lower stability index.

Appendix

State Guaranty Associations

The states have established insurance guaranty associations to help pay claims to policyholders of failed insurance companies. However, there are several cautions which you must be aware of with respect to this coverage:

1. Most of the guaranty associations do not set aside funds in advance. Rather, states assess contributions from other insurance companies after an insolvency occurs.

2. There can be an unacceptably long delay before claims are paid.

3. Each state is governed by its own legislation, providing a wide range of coverage and conditions that may apply. According to the National Organization of Life and Health Guaranty Associations (NOLHGA), the issues are extremely complex with unique variables for each individual state.

4. The table on the following page is designed to help you sort out these issues. However, it is not intended to handle all of them. If your carrier has failed and you need a complete answer, we recommend you contact your State Insurance Official or NOLHGA at 703-481-5206.

State guaranty associations are set up to cover policyholders residing in their own state. This essentially means that each individual state is responsible for policyholders residing in that state, no matter where the insolvent insurer is domiciled.

Non-resident coverage is provided only under certain circumstances listed in the state's statutes. The general conditions are typically as follows:

a) The insurer of the policyholder must be domiciled and licensed in the state in which the non-resident is seeking coverage;

b) When the contracts were sold, the insurers that issued the policies were not licensed in the state in which the policyholder resides;

c) The non-resident policyholder is not eligible for coverage from his or her state of residence;

d) The state where the policyholder resides must have a guaranty association similar to that of the state in which he or she is seeking non-resident coverage.

Warning: Be sure to contact the specific state guaranty association for information in that state's laws. Conditions and limitations are subject to individual state statutes and can change.

Following is a brief explanation of each of the columns in the table.

1. **Maximum Aggregate Benefits for All Lines of Insurance**   The maximum amount payable by the State Guaranty Fund to cover all types of insurance including life insurance, health insurance, disability and annuities.

2. **Maximum Death Benefit with Respect to Any One Life**   The maximum amount payable by the State Guaranty Fund for a death claim on a single life. If the policy benefits are higher than the Guaranty Fund's coverage limits, policyholders may typically be able to file a claim with the court-appointed Liquidator of the insolvent insurance company to try to recover the difference. But success is uncertain.

3. **Liability for Cash or Withdrawal Value of Life Insurance Policy**   The maximum cash value or withdrawal value the Guaranty Fund will assume responsibility for related to an individual life insurance policy.

4. **Maximum Liability for Present Value of an Annuity Contract**   The maximum cash value or withdrawal value the Guaranty Fund will assume responsibility for related to an individual annuity contract. The coverage may be higher if the annuity is in the payout phase.

Coverage of State Guaranty Funds

State	Max. Aggregate Benefits for All Lines of Insurance	Max. Death Benefit with Respect to Any One Life	Max. Liability for Cash or Withdrawal Value of Life Insurance Policy	Max. Liability for Present Value of an Annuity Contract	State Guaranty Association Phone Numbers	State Guaranty Web Address
Alabama	$300,000	$300,000	$100,000	$250,000	(205) 879-2202	www.allifega.org
Alaska	$300,000	$300,000	$100,000	$100,000	(907) 243-2311	www.aklifega.org
Arizona	$300,000	$300,000	$100,000	$250,000	(602) 364-3863	www.id.state.az.us
Arkansas	$300,000	$300,000	$300,000	$300,000	(501) 375-9151	www.arlifega.org
California	80% not to exceed $300,000	80% not to exceed $300,000	80% not to exceed $100,000	80% not to exceed $250,000	(323) 782-0182	www.califega.org
Colorado	$300,000	$300,000	$100,000	$250,000	(303) 292-5022	www.colifega.org
Connecticut	$500,000	$500,000	$500,000	$500,000	(860) 647-1054	www.ctlifega.org
Delaware	$300,000	$300,000	$100,000	$250,000	(302) 456-3656	www.delifega.org
Dist. of Col.	$300,000	$300,000	$100,000	$300,000	(202) 434-8771	www.dclifega.org
Florida	$300,000	$300,000	$100,000	$250,000	(904) 398-3644	www.flahiga.org
Georgia	$300,000	$300,000	$100,000	$250,000	(770) 621-9835	www.gaiga.org
Hawaii	$300,000	$300,000	$100,000	$100,000	(808) 528-5400	www.hilifega.org
Idaho	$300,000	$300,000	$100,000	$250,000	(208) 378-9510	www.idlifega.org
Illinois	$300,000	$300,000	$100,000	$250,000	(773) 714-8050	www.ilhiga.org
Indiana	$300,000	$300,000	$100,000	$100,000	(317) 692-0574	www.inlifega.org
Iowa	$300,000	$300,000	$100,000	$250,000	(515) 248-5712	www.ialifega.org
Kansas	$300,000	$300,000	$100,000	$250,000	(785) 271-1199	www.kslifega.org
Kentucky	$300,000	$300,000	$100,000	$250,000	(502) 895-5915	www.klhiga.org
Louisiana	$500,000	$300,000	$100,000	$250,000	(225) 381-0656	www.lalifega.org
Maine	$300,000	$300,000	$100,000	$250,000	(207) 633-1090	www.melifega.org
Maryland	$300,000	$300,000	$100,000	$250,000	(410) 248-0407	www.mdlifega.org
Massachusetts	$300,000	$300,000	$100,000	$250,000	(413) 744-8483	www.malifega.org
Michigan	$300,000	$300,000	$100,000	$250,000	(517) 339-1755	www.milifega.org
Minnesota	$500,000	$500,000	$130,000	$250,000	(651) 407-3149	www.mnlifega.org
Mississippi	$300,000	$300,000	$100,000	$100,000	(601) 981-0755	www.mslifega.org
Missouri	$300,000	$300,000	$100,000	$100,000	(573) 634-8455	www.mo iga.org
Montana	$300,000	$300,000	$100,000	$250,000	(262) 965-5761	www.mtlifega.org
Nebraska	$300,000	$300,000	$100,000	$250,000	(402) 474-6900	www.nelifega.org
Nevada	$300,000	$300,000	$100,000	$250,000	(775) 329-8387	www.nvlifega.org
New Hampshire	$300,000	$300,000	$100,000	$100,000	(603) 472-3734	www.nhlifega.org
New Jersey	$500,000	$500,000	$100,000	$100,000	(732) 345-5200	www.njlifega.org
New Mexico	$300,000	$300,000	$100,000	$250,000	(505) 820-7355	www.nmlifega.org
New York	$500,000	$500,000	$500,000	$500,000	(212) 202-4243	www.nylifega.org
North Carolina	$300,000	$300,000	$300,000	$300,000	(919) 833-6838	www.nclifega.org
North Dakota	$300,000	$300,000	$100,000	$250,000	(701) 235-4108	www.ndlifega.org
Ohio	$300,000	$300,000	$100,000	$250,000	(614) 442-6601	www.olhiga.org
Oklahoma	$300,000	$300,000	$100,000	$300,000	(405) 272-9221	www.oklifega.org
Oregon	$300,000	$300,000	$100,000	$250,000	(855) 378-9510	www.orlifega.org
Pennsylvania	$300,000	$300,000	$100,000	$100,000	(610) 975-0572	www.palifega.org
Puerto Rico	$300,000	$300,000	$100,000	$100,000	(787) 765-2095	www.ocs.gobierno.pr
Rhode Island	$300,000	$300,000	$100,000	$250,000	(401) 273-2921	www.rilifega.org
South Carolina	$300,000	$300,000	$300,000	$300,000	(803) 783-4947	www.sclifega.org
South Dakota	$300,000	$300,000	$100,000	$250,000	(605) 336-0177	www.sdlifega.org
Tennessee	$300,000	$300,000	$100,000	$250,000	(615) 242-8758	www.tnlifega.org
Texas	$300,000	$300,000	$100,000	$250,000	(512) 476-5101	www.txlifega.org
Utah	$500,000	$500,000	$200,000	$200,000	(801) 302-9955	www.utlifega.org
Vermont	$300,000	$300,000	$100,000	$250,000	(802) 249-0284	www.vtlifega.org
Virginia	$350,000	$300,000	$100,000	$250,000	(804) 282-2240	www.valifega.org
Washington	$500,000	$500,000	$500,000	$500,000	(360) 426-6744	www.walifega.org
West Virginia	$300,000	$300,000	$100,000	$250,000	(304) 733-6904	www.wvlifega.org
Wisconsin	$300,000	$300,000	$300,000	$300,000	(608) 242-9473	www.wilifega.org
Wyoming	$500,000	$300,000	$100,000	$250,000	(303) 292-5022	www.wylifega.org

State Insurance Commissioners'
Website and Departmental Phone Numbers

State	Official's Title	Website Address	Phone Number
Alabama	Commissioner	www.aldoi.org	(334) 269-3550
Alaska	Director	https://www.commerce.alaska.gov/web/ins/	(800) 467-8725
Arizona	Director	https://insurance.az.gov/	(602) 364-2499
Arkansas	Commissioner	www.insurance.arkansas.gov	(800) 282-9134
California	Commissioner	www.insurance.ca.gov	(800) 927-4357
Colorado	Commissioner	https://www.colorado.gov/dora/division-insurance	(800) 886-7675
Connecticut	Commissioner	http://www.ct.gov/cid/site/default.asp	(800) 203-3447
Delaware	Commissioner	http://delawareinsurance.gov/	(800) 282-8611
Dist. of Columbia	Commissioner	http://disb.dc.gov/	(202) 727-8000
Florida	Commissioner	www.floir.com/	(850) 413-3140
Georgia	Commissioner	www.oci.ga.gov/	(800) 656-2298
Hawaii	Commissioner	http://cca.hawaii.gov/ins/	(808) 586-2790
Idaho	Director	www.doi.idaho.gov	(800) 721-3272
Illinois	Director	www.insurance.illinois.gov/	(866) 445-5364
Indiana	Commissioner	www.in.gov/idoi/	(317) 232-2385
Iowa	Commissioner	www.iid.state.ia.us	(877) 955-1212
Kansas	Commissioner	www.ksinsurance.org	(800) 432-2484
Kentucky	Commissioner	http://insurance.ky.gov/	(800) 595-6053
Louisiana	Commissioner	www.ldi.la.gov/	(800) 259-5300
Maine	Superintendent	www.maine.gov/pfr/insurance/	(800) 300-5000
Maryland	Commissioner	http://insurance.maryland.gov/Pages/default.aspx	(800) 492-6116
Massachusetts	Commissioner	www.mass.gov/ocabr/government/oca-agencies/doi-lp/	(877) 563-4467
Michigan	Director	http://www.michigan.gov/difs	(877) 999-6442
Minnesota	Commissioner	http://mn.gov/commerce/	(651) 539-1500
Mississippi	Commissioner	http://www.mid.ms.gov/	(601) 359-3569
Missouri	Director	www.insurance.mo.gov	(800) 726-7390
Montana	Commissioner	http://csimt.gov/	(800) 332-6148
Nebraska	Director	www.doi.nebraska.gov/	(402) 471-2201
Nevada	Commissioner	www.doi.nv.gov/	(888) 872-3234
New Hampshire	Commissioner	www.nh.gov/insurance/	(800) 852-3416
New Jersey	Commissioner	www.state.nj.us/dobi/	(800) 446-7467
New Mexico	Superintendent	www.osi.state.nm.us/	(855) 427-5674
New York	Superintendent	www.dfs.ny.gov/	(800) 342-3736
North Carolina	Commissioner	www.ncdoi.com	(800) 546-5664
North Dakota	Commissioner	www.nd.gov/ndins/	(800) 247-0560
Ohio	Lieutenant Governor	www.insurance.ohio.gov/	(800) 686-1526
Oklahoma	Commissioner	www.ok.gov/oid/	(800) 522-0071
Oregon	Insurance Commissioner	www.oregon.gov/dcbs/insurance/Pages/index.aspx	(888) 877-4894
Pennsylvania	Commissioner	www.insurance.pa.gov/	(877) 881-6388
Puerto Rico	Commissioner	www.ocs.gobierno.pr	(787) 304-8686
Rhode Island	Superintendent	www.dbr.state.ri.us/divisions/insurance/	(401) 462-9500
South Carolina	Director	www.doi.sc.gov	(803) 737-6160
South Dakota	Director	http://dlr.sd.gov/insurance/default.aspx	(605) 773-3563
Tennessee	Commissioner	www.tn.gov/insurance/	(615) 741-2241
Texas	Commissioner	www.tdi.texas.gov/	(800) 252-3439
Utah	Commissioner	www.insurance.utah.gov	(800) 439-3805
Vermont	Commissioner	www.dfr.vermont.gov/	(802) 828-3301
Virgin Islands	Lieutenant Governor	http://ltg.gov.vi/division-of-banking-and-insurance.html	(340) 774-7166
Virginia	Commissioner	www.scc.virginia.gov/boi/	(804) 371-9741
Washington	Commissioner	www.insurance.wa.gov	(800) 562-6900
West Virginia	Commissioner	www.wvinsurance.gov	(888) 879-9842
Wisconsin	Commissioner	oci.wi.gov	(800) 236-8517
Wyoming	Commissioner	http://doi.wyo.gov/	(800) 438-5768

Risk-Adjusted Capital for Life and Annuity Insurers in Weiss Rating Model

Among the most important indicators used in the analysis of an individual company are our two risk-adjusted capital ratios, which are useful tools in determining exposure to investment, liquidity and insurance risk in relation to the capital the company has to cover those risks.

The first risk-adjusted capital ratio evaluates the company's ability to withstand a moderate loss scenario. The second ratio evaluates the company's ability to withstand a severe loss scenario.

In order to calculate these risk-adjusted capital ratios, we follow these steps:

1. Capital Resources

First, we add up all of the company's resources which could be used to cover losses. These include capital, surplus, the Asset Valuation Reserve (AVR), and a portion of the provision for future policyholders' dividends, where appropriate. Additional credit may also be given for the use of conservative reserving assumptions and other "hidden capital" when applicable.

2. Target Capital

Next, we determine the company's target capital. This answers the question: Based upon the company's level of risk in both its insurance business and its investment portfolio, how much capital would it need to cover potential losses during a moderate loss scenario? In other words, we determine how much capital we believe this company *should* have.

3. Risk-Adjusted Capital Ratio #1

We compare the results of step 1 with those of step 2. Specifically, we divide the "capital resources" by the "target capital" and express it in terms of a ratio. This ratio is called RACR #1. (See next page for more detail on methodology.)

If a company has a Risk-Adjusted Capital Ratio of 1.0 or more, it means the company has all of the capital we believe it requires to withstand potential losses which could be inflicted by a moderate loss scenario. If the company has less than 1.0, it does not currently have all of the basic capital resources we think it needs. During times of financial distress, companies often have access to additional capital through contributions from a parent company, current profits or reductions in policyholder dividends. Therefore, an allowance is made in our rating system for firms with somewhat less than 1.0 Risk-Adjusted Capital Ratios.

4. Risk-Adjusted Capital Ratio #2

We repeat steps 2 and 3, but now assuming a severe loss scenario. This ratio is called RACR #2.

5. Capitalization Index

We convert RACR #1 and #2 into an index. It is measured on a scale of zero to ten, with ten being the best and seven or better considered strong. A company whose capital, surplus and AVR equal its target capital will have a Risk-Adjusted Capital Ratio of 1.0 and a Risk-Adjusted Capital Index of 7.0.

How We Determine Target Capital

The basic procedure for determining target capital is to ask these questions:

1.   What is the breakdown of the company's investment portfolio and types of business?

2.   For each category, what are the potential losses which could be incurred in the loss scenario?

3.   In order to cover those potential losses, how much in capital resources does the company need? It stands to reason that more capital is needed as a cushion for losses on high-risk investments, such as junk bonds, than would be necessary for low-risk investments, such as AAA-rated utility bonds.

Unfortunately, the same questions we have raised about Wall Street rating systems with respect to how they rate insurance companies can be asked about the way they rate bonds. However, we do not rate bonds ourselves. Therefore, we must rely upon the bond ratings of other rating agencies. This is another reason why we have stricter capital requirements for the insurance companies. It accounts for the fact that they may need some extra protection in case an AAA-rated bond may not be quite as good as it appears to be.

Finally, target capital is adjusted for the company's spread of risk in the diversification of its investment portfolio, the size and number of the policies it writes and the diversification of its business.

Table 1 on the next page shows target capital percentages used in Weiss Risk-Adjusted Capital Ratios #1 and #2 (RACR #1 and RACR #2).

The percentages shown in the table answer the question: How much should the firm hold in capital resources for every $100 it has committed to each category? Several of the items in Table 1 are expressed as ranges. The actual percentages used in the calculation of target capital for an individual company may vary due to the levels of risks in the operations, investments or policy obligations of that specific company.

Table 1. Target Capital Percentages

Asset Risk	Weiss Ratings	
	RACR#1 (%)	RACR#2 (%)
Bonds		
Government guaranteed bonds	0	0
Class 1	.5-.75	1-1.5
Class 2	2	5
Class 3	5	15
Class 4	10	30
Class 5	20	60
Class 6	20	60
Mortgages		
In good standing	0.5	1
90 days overdue	1.7-20	3.8-25
In process of foreclosure	25-33	33-50
Real Estate		
Class 1	20	50
Class 2	10	33
Preferred Stock		
Class 1	3	5
Class 2	4	6
Class 3	7	9
Class 4	12	15
Class 5	22	29
Class 6	30	39
Class 7	3-30	5 39
Common Stock		
Unaffiliated	25	33
Affiliated	25-100	33-100
Short-term investment	0.5	1
Premium notes	2	5
Collateral loans	2	5
Separate account equity	25	33
Other invested assets	5	10
Insurance Risk		
Individual life reserves*	.06-.15	.08-.21
Group life reserves*	.05-.12	.06-.16
Individual Health Premiums		
Class 1	12-20	15-25
Class 2	9.6	12
Class 3	6.4	8
Class 4	12-28	15-35
Class 5	12-20	15-25
Group Health Premiums		
Class 1	5.6-12	7-15
Class 2	20	25
Class 3	9.6	12
Class 4	6.4	8
Class 5	12-20	15-25
Managed care credit	5-40	6-50
Premiums subject to rate guarantees	100-209	120-250
Individual claim reserves	4	5
Group claim reserves	4	5
Reinsurance	0-2	0-5
Interest Rate Risk		
Policy loans	0-2	0-5
Life reserves	1-2	1-3
Individual annuity reserves	1-3	1-5
Group annuity reserves	1-2	1-3
Guaranteed interest contract reserves	1-2	1-3

All numbers are shown for illustrative purposes. Figures actually used in the formula vary annually based on industry experience.
*Based on net amount at risk.

Investment Class   Descriptions

Investment Class		Descriptions
Government guaranteed bonds		Guaranteed bonds issued by U.S. and other governments which receive the top rating of state insurance commissioners.
Bonds	Class 1	Investment grade bonds rated AAA, AA or A by Moody's or Standard & Poor's or deemed AAA - A equivalent by state insurance commissioners.
	Class 2	Investment grade bonds with some speculative elements, rated BBB or equivalent.
	Class 3	Noninvestment grade bonds, rated BB or equivalent.
	Class 4	Noninvestment grade bonds, rated B or equivalent.
	Class 5	Noninvestment grade bonds, rated CCC, CC or C or equivalent.
	Class 6	Noninvestment grade bonds, in or near default.
Mortgages		Mortgages in good standing
		Mortgages 90 days past due
		Mortgages in process of foreclosure
Real Estate	Class 1	Properties acquired in satisfaction of debt.
	Class 2	Company occupied and other investment properties.
Preferred stock	Class 1	Highest quality unaffiliated preferred stock.
	Class 2	High quality unaffiliated preferred stock.
	Class 3	Medium quality unaffiliated preferred stock.
	Class 4	Low quality unaffiliated preferred stock.
	Class 5	Lowest quality unaffiliated preferred stock.
	Class 6	Unaffiliated preferred stock, in or near default.
	Class 7	Affiliated preferred stock.
Common stock		Unaffiliated common stock.
		Affiliated common stock.
Short-term investments		All investments whose maturities at the time of acquisition were one year or less.
Premium Notes		Loans for payment of premiums.
Collateral loans		Loans made to a company or individual where the underlying security is in the form of bonds, stocks, or other marketable securities.
Separate account assets		Investments held in an account segregated from the general assets of the company, generally used to provide variable annuity benefits.
Other invested assets		Any invested assets that do not fit under the main categories above.
Individual life reserves		Funds set aside for payment of life insurance benefits under an individual contract rather than a company or group, underwriting based on individual profile.
Group life reserves		Funds set aside for payment of life insurance benefits under a contract with at least 10 people whereby all members have a common interest and are joined for a reason other than to obtain insurance.
Individual health premiums	Class 1	Usual and customary hospital and medical premiums which include traditional medical reimbursement plans that are subject to annual rate increases based on the company's claims experience.
	Class 2	Medicare supplement, dental, and other limited benefits anticipating rate increases.
	Class 3	Hospital indemnity plans, accidental death and dismemberment policies, and other limited benefits not anticipating rate increases.
	Class 4	Noncancelable disability income.
	Class 5	Guaranteed renewable disability income.

Group health premiums	Class 1	Usual and customary hospital and medical premiums which include traditional medical reimbursement plans that are subject to annual rate increases based on the company's claims experience.
	Class 2	Stop loss and minimum premium where a known claims liability is minimal or nonexistent.
	Class 3	Medicare supplement, dental, and other limited benefits anticipating rate increases.
	Class 4	Hospital indemnity plans, accidental death and dismemberment policies, and other limited benefits not anticipating rate increases.
	Class 5	Disability Income.
Managed care credit		Premiums for HMO and PPO business which carry less risk than traditional indemnity business. Included in this credit are provider compensation arrangements such as salary, capitation and fixed payment per service.
Premiums subject to rate guarantees		Health insurance premiums from policies where the rate paid by the policyholder is guaranteed for a period of time, such as one year, 15 months, 27 months or 37 months.
Individual claim reserves		Accident and health reserves for claims on individual policies.
Group claim reserves		Accident and health reserves for claims on group policies.
Reinsurance		Amounts recoverable on paid and unpaid losses for all reinsurance ceded; unearned premiums on accident and health reinsurance ceded; and funds held with unauthorized reinsurers.
Policy loans		Loans against the cash value of a life insurance policy.
Life reserves		Reserves for life insurance claims net of reinsurance and policy loans.
Individual annuity reserves		Reserves held in order to pay off maturing individual annuities or those surrendered before maturity.
Group annuity reserves		Reserves held in order to pay off maturing group annuities or those surrendered before maturity.
GIC reserves		Reserves held to pay off maturing guaranteed interest contracts.

Table 2. Bond Default Rates - potential losses as a percent of bond portfolio

	(1)	(2)	(3)	(4)	(5) Weiss	(6)	(7)	(8)
Bond Rating	Moody's 15 Yr Rate (%)	Moody's 12 Yr Rate (%)	Worst Year (%)	3 Cum. Recession Years (%)	15 Year Rate (%)	Assumed Loss Rate (%)	Losses as % of Holdings (%)	RACR #2 Rate (%)
Aaa	0.73	0.55	0.08	0.24	0.79	50	0.95	1.00
Aa	1.39	1.04	0.13	0.39	1.43	50	1.09	1.00
A	4.05	2.96	0.35	1.05	4.02	55	2.02	1.00
Baa	7.27	5.29	0.67	2.02	7.31	60	5.15	5.00
Ba	23.93	19.57	2.04	6.11	25.68	65	23.71	15.00
B	43.37	39.30	4.99	14.96	54.26	70	43.57	30.00

Comments On Target Capital Percentages

The factors that are chiefly responsible for the conservative results of our Risk-Adjusted Capital Ratios are the investment risks of bond Classes 2 - 6, mortgages, real estate and affiliate common stock as well as the interest rate risk for annuities and GICs. Comments on the basis of these figures are found below. Additional comments address factors that vary, based on particular performance or risk characteristics of the individual company.

Bonds

Target capital percentages for bonds are derived from a model that factors in historical cumulative bond default rates from the last 45 years and the additional loss potential during a prolonged economic decline. **Table 2** shows how this was done for each bond rating classification. A 15-year cumulative default rate is used (column 1), due to the 15-year average maturity at issue of bonds held by life insurance companies. These are historical default rates for 1970-2015 for each bond class, taken from *Moody's Annual Default Study*.

To factor in the additional loss potential of a severe three-year-long economic decline, we reduced the base to Moody's 12-year rate (column 2), determined the worst single year experience (column 3), extended that experience over three years (column 4), and added the historical 12-year rate to the 3-year projection to derive Weiss Ratings 15-year default rate (column 5).

The next step was to determine the losses that could be expected from these defaults. This would be equivalent to the capital a company should have to cover those losses. Loss rates were assigned for each bond class (column 6), based on the fact that higher-rated issues generally carry less debt and the fact that the debt is also better secured, leading to higher recovery rates upon default. Column 7 shows losses as a percent of holdings for each bond class. Column 8 shows the target capital percentages that are used in RACR #2 (Table 1, RACR #2 column, Bonds - classes 1 to 6).

Regulations limiting junk bond holdings of insurers to a set percent of assets are a tacit acknowledgement that the reserve requirements used by State Insurance Commissioners are inadequate. If the figure adequately represented full loss potential, there would be no need to limit holdings through legislation since an adequate loss reserve would provide sufficient capital to absorb potential losses.

Mortgages

Mortgage default rates for the Risk-Adjusted Capital Ratios are derived from historical studies of mortgage and real estate losses in selected depressed markets. The rate for RACR #2 (Table 1, RACR #2 column, Mortgages – 90 days overdue) will vary between 3.8 and 25%, based on the performance of the company's mortgage portfolio in terms of mortgage loans 90 days or more past due, in process of foreclosure and foreclosed during the previous year.

Real Estate

The 33% rate (Table 1, RACR #2 column, Real Estate – Class 2) used for potential real estate losses in Weiss ratios is based on historical losses in depressed markets.

Affiliate Common Stock

The target capital rate on affiliate common stock for RACR #2 can vary between 33% and 100% (Table 1, RACR #2 column, Common stock - Affiliate) depending on the financial strength of the affiliate and the prospects for obtaining capital from the affiliate should the need arise.

Insurance Risk

Calculations of target capital for insurance risk vary according to categories. For individual and group life insurance, target capital is a percentage of net amount at risk (total amount of insurance in force less reserves). Individual and group health insurance risk is calculated as a percentage of premium. Categories vary from "usual and customary hospital and medical premiums" where risk is relatively low, because losses from one year are recouped by annual rate increases to "noncancellable disability income" where the risk of loss is greater because disability benefits are paid in future years without the possibility of recovery.

Reinsurance

This factor varies with the quality of the reinsuring companies and the type of reinsurance being used (e.g. co-insurance, modified co-insurance, yearly renewable term, etc.).

Interest Rate Risk On Annuities

The 1 - 5% rate on individual annuities as a percentage of reserves (Table 1, RACR #2 column 3, Individual annuity reserves) and the 1 - 3% rate for group annuities as a percentage of reserves (Table 1, RACR #2 column 3, Group annuity reserves and GICs) are derived from studies of potential losses that can occur when assets and liabilities are not properly matched.

Companies are especially prone to losses in this area for one of two reasons: (1) They promise high interest rates on their annuities and have not locked in corresponding yields on their investments. If interest rates fall, the company will have difficulties earning the promised rate. (2) They lock in high returns on their investments but allow policy surrenders without market value adjustments. If market values decline and surrenders increase, liquidity problems can result in substantial losses.

The target capital figure used for each company is based on the surrender characteristics of its policies, the interest rate used in calculating reserves and the actuarial analysis found in New York Regulation 126 filing or similar studies where applicable.

RECENT INDUSTRY FAILURES
2022

Institution	Headquarters	Industry	Date of Failure	Total Assets ($Mil)	Safety Rating
				At Date of Failure	
Freelancers Ins. Co	New York	Health	01/11/2022	0.00	U (Unrated)
Americas Ins. Co	Louisiana	P&C	01/14/2022	19.2	C (Fair)
St. Johns Ins. Co	Florida	P&C	02/25/2022	152.9	D+ (Weak)
Avatar P&C Ins. Co	Florida	P&C	03/14/2022	82.9	D (Weak)
Southern Fidelity Ins. Co	Florida	P&C	06/15/2022	310.2	E- (Very Weak)
Weston P&C Ins. Co	Florida	P&C	08/08/2022	39.5	U (Unrated)
Fednat Ins. Co	Florida	P&C	09/27/2022	623.2	C (Fair)

2021

Institution	Headquarters	Industry	Date of Failure	At Date of Failure	
				Total Assets ($Mil)	Safety Rating
Global Hawk PPTY Cas Ins. Co	Delaware	P&C	01/07/2021	0.00	U (Unrated)
New Mexico Hlth Connections	New Mexico	Health	01/26/2021	41.4	E- (Very Weak)
Emergency Physicians Ins RRG	Wisconsin	P&C	02/24/2021	13.6	E (Very Weak)
Bedivere Ins. Co.	Connecticut	P&C	03/11/2021	309.5	E- (Very Weak)
American Integrity Life Ins. Co	Arkansas	Life	03/18/2021	8.4	D (Weak)
Hospitality RRG Inc	Vermont	P&C	04/08/2021	4.9	E (Very Weak)
American Capital Assr Corp.	Florida	P&C	04/14/2021	119.0	C+ (Fair)
Western General Ins. Co	California	P&C	05/26/2021	76.1	C- (Fair)
Lighthouse Property Ins. Corp	Florida	P&C	07/21/2021	198.5	D (Weak)
Lighthouse Excalibur Ins. Co	Florida	P&C	07/21/2021	31.9	D (Weak)
Gulfstream P&C Ins. Co	Florida	P&C	07/28/2021	110.0	D+ (Weak)
Global Liberty Ins. Co of NY	New York	P&C	10/12/2021	42.4	E- (Very Weak)
Access Home Ins Co	Louisiana	P&C	11/12/2021	30.0	C (Fair)
State National Fire Ins. Co	Louisiana	P&C	11/12/2021	7.5	C (Fair)
Park Insurance Co	New York	P&C	11/30/2021	69.4	E (Very Weak)

2020

Institution	Headquarters	Industry	Date of Failure	At Date of Failure Total Assets ($Mil)	At Date of Failure Safety Rating
Senior Health Ins. Co of PA	Indiana	L&A	1/29/2020	1,097.00	E- (Very Weak)
Maidstone Ins. Co	New York	P&C	2/13/2020	36.31	E- (Very Weak)
Windhaven National Ins. Co	Florida	P&C	3/05/2020	119.96	C (Fair)
Physicians Indemnity RRG Inc.	Nevada	P&C	03/13/2020	5.1	E- (Very Weak)
Time Ins Co	Puerto Rico	L&A	5/18/2020	18.36	C (Fair)
Nextlevel Health Partners Inc	Illinois	Health	06/09/2020	77.9	E- (Very Weak)
Houston General Ins. Exch	Texas	P&C	8/11/2020	15.12	C- (Fair)
Quality Health Plans of NY Inc.	Florida	Health	9/09/2020	4.82	E- (Very Weak)
ACCC Ins. Co	Texas	P&C	10/21/2020	191.5	E- (Very Weak)

2019

Institution	Headquarters	Industry	Date of Failure	Total Assets ($Mil)	Safety Rating
				At Date of Failure	
Capson Physicians Ins Co	Texas	P&C	02/11/19	25.3	D (Weak)
Atlantis Health Plan	Florida	Health	02/27/19	3.0	U (Unrated)
Sottish Re US Inc	North Carolina	L&A	03/06/19	1,056.0	E+ (Very Weak)
Integrand ASR Co	Puerto Rico	P&C	03/07/19	94.2	D+ (Weak)
Family Health Network Inc	Illinois	Health	03/18/19	69.4	U (Unrated)
Lancet Indemnity RRG Inc	Florida	P&C	04/12/19	7.2	E- (Very Weak)
Physicians Casualty RRG Inc	Alabama	P&C	05/03/19	7.9	E- (Very Weak)
Southland National Ins Corp	North Carolina	L&A	06/27/19	354.0	D+ (Weak)
Bankers Life Ins Co	North Carolina	L&A	06/27/19	397.4	C- (Fair)
Colorado Bankers Life Ins Co	North Carolina	L&A	06/27/19	2,068.0	C (Fair)
American Country Ins Co	Illinois	P&C	07/08/19	92.6	E+ (Very Weak)
American Service Ins Co	Illinois	P&C	07/08/19	157.4	D (Weak)
Pavonia Life Ins. Co of MI	New Jersey	L&A	07/09/19	1080.0	C (Fair)
Physicians Standard Ins Co	Missouri	P&C	08/19/19	7.8	E+ (Very Weak)
Florida Specialty Ins Co	Florida	P&C	10/12/19	55.4	D- (Weak)
Gateway Ins Co	Missouri	P&C	10/16/19	67.3	E+ (Very Weak)
California Ins Co	Nebraska	P&C	11/04/19	1,015.0	B (Good)
Windhaven Ins Co	Florida	P&C	12/12/19	148.8	D- (Weak)

2018

Institution	Headquarters	Industry	Date of Failure	At Date of Failure	
				Total Assets ($Mil)	Safety Rating
Healthcare Providers Ins. Exch	Pennsylvania	P&C	01/12/18	32.6	E- (Very Weak)
Access Ins. Co	Texas	P&C	03/18/18	214.1	C (Fair)
Touchstone Health HMO Inc	New York	Health	04/09/18	12.5	E+ (Very Weak)
Reliamax Surety Co	South Dakota	P&C	06/27/18	63.0	C (Fair)
Paramount Ins. Co	Maryland	P&C	09/13/18	13.2	D- (Weak)
Real Legacy Asr Co Inc	Puerto Rico	P&C	09/28/18	230.4	D+ (Weak)
Merced Property & Casualty Co	California	P&C	12/03/18	23.6	C (Fair)
North Carolina Mut Life Ins. Co	North Carolina	L&A	12/03/18	26.7	E- (Very Weak)
Geneva Ins Co	Indiana	P&C	12/12/18	3.7	U (Unrated)

2017

Institution	Headquarters	Industry	Date of Failure	At Date of Failure	
				Total Assets ($Mil)	Safety Rating
IFA Ins Co	New Jersey	P&C	03/07/17	8.4	E (Very Weak)
Public Service Ins. Co	New York	P&C	03/16/17	278.5	E (Very Weak)
Zoom Health Plan Inc	Oregon	Health	04/26/17	6.0	U (Unrated)
Galen Ins Co	Missouri	P&C	05/31/17	10.0	E- (Very Weak)
Fiduciary Ins. Co of America	New York	P&C	07/25/17	13.9	E- (Very Weak)
Evergreen Health Inc	Maryland	Health	07/27/17	37.2	E- (Very Weak)
Minuteman Health Inc	Massachusetts	Health	08/02/17	111.7	E- (Very Weak)
Sawgrass Mutual Ins. Co	Florida	P&C	08/22/17	32.3	D+ (Weak)
Guarantee Ins. Co	Florida	P&C	08/28/17	400.4	E+ (Very Weak)
Oceanus Ins. Co A RRG	South Carolina	P&C	09/04/17	52.9	D- (Weak)

Glossary

This glossary contains the most important terms used in this publication.

Admitted Assets	The total of all investments and business interests that are acceptable under statutory accounting rules.
Asset/Liability Matching	The designation of particular investments (assets) to particular policy obligations (liabilities) so that investments mature at the appropriate times and with appropriate yields to meet policy obligations as they come due.
Asset Valuation Reserve (AVR)	A liability established under statutory accounting rules whose purpose is to protect the company's surplus from the effects of defaults and market value fluctuation on stocks, bonds, mortgages and real estate. This replaces the Mandatory Securities Valuation Reserve (MSVR) and is more comprehensive in that it includes a mortgage loss reserve, whereas the MSVR did not.
Average Recession	A recession involving a decline in real GDP which is approximately equivalent to the average of the postwar recessions of 1957-58, 1960, 1970, 1974-75, 1980, 1981-82,1990-1991, 2001, and 2007-2009. It is assumed, however, that in today's market, the financial losses suffered from a recession of that magnitude would be greater than those experienced in previous decades. (See also "Severe Recession.")
Capital	Strictly speaking, capital refers to funds raised through the sale of common and preferred stock. Mutual companies have capital in the form of retained earnings. In a more general sense, the term capital is commonly used to refer to a company's equity or net worth, that is, the difference between assets and liabilities (i.e., capital and surplus as shown on the balance sheet).
Capital Resources	The sum of various resources which serve as a capital cushion to losses, including capital, surplus and Asset Valuation Reserve (AVR).
Capitalization Index	An index, expressed on a scale of zero to ten, with seven or higher considered excellent, that measures the adequacy of the company's capital resources to deal with a variety of business and economic scenarios. It combines Risk-Adjusted Capital Ratios #1 and #2 as well as a leverage test that examines pricing risk.
Cash and Demand Deposits	Includes cash on hand and on deposit. A negative figure indicates that the company has more checks outstanding than current funds to cover those checks. This is not an unusual situation for an insurance company.

Collateralized Mortgage Obligation (CMO)	Mortgage-backed bond that splits the payments from mortgage pools into different classes, called tranches. The investor may purchase a bond or tranche that passes through to him or her the principal and interest payments made by the mortgage holders in that specific maturity class (usually two, five, 10 or 20 years). The risk associated with a CMO is in the variation of the payment speed on the mortgage pool which, if different than originally assumed, can cause the total return to vary greatly.
Common and Preferred Stocks	See "Stocks".
Deposit Funds	Accumulated contributions of a group out of which immediate annuities are purchased as the individual members of the group retire.
Direct Premiums Written	Total gross premiums derived from policies issued directly by the company. This figure excludes the impact of reinsurance.
Safety Rating	Weiss Safety Ratings grade insurers on a scale from A (Excellent) to F (Failed). Ratings are based on five major factors: investment safety, policy leverage, capitalization, profitability and stability of operations.
Five-Year Profitability Index	See "Profitability Index."
Government Securities	Securities issued and/or guaranteed by U.S. and foreign governments which are rated as highest quality (Class 1) by state insurance commissioners. Included in this category are bonds issued by governmental agencies and guaranteed with the full faith and credit of the government. Regardless of the issuing entity, they are viewed as being relatively safer than the other investment categories. See "Investment Grade Bonds" to determine which items are excluded from this category.
Health Claims Reserve	Funds set aside from premiums for the eventual payment of health benefits after the end of the statement year.
Insurance Risk	The risk that the level of claims and related expenses will exceed current premiums plus reserves allocated for their payment.
Interest Rate Risk	The risk that, due to changes in interest rates, investment income will not meet the needs of policy commitments. This risk can be reduced by effective asset/liability matching.
Invested Assets	The total size of the firm's investment portfolio.
Investment Grade Bonds	This covers all investment grade bonds other than those listed in "Government Securities" (above). Specifically, this includes: (1) nonguaranteed obligations of governments; (2) obligations of governments rated as Class 2 by state insurance commissioners; (3) state and municipal bonds; plus (4) investment grade corporate bonds.

Investment Safety Index	Measured on a scale of zero to ten, with ten being the best and seven or better considered strong. Each investment area is rated as to quality and vulnerability during an unfavorable economic environment (updated using quarterly data when available).
Investments in Affiliates	Includes bonds, preferred stocks and common stocks, as well as other vehicles which many insurance companies use to invest in, and establish a corporate link with, affiliated companies
Life and Annuity Claims Reserve	Funds set aside from premiums for the eventual payment of life and annuity claims.
Liquidity Index	An index, expressed on a scale from zero to ten, with seven or higher considered excellent, which measures the company's ability to raise the necessary cash to meet policyholder obligations. This index includes a stress test which considers the consequences of a spike in claims or a run on policy surrenders. Sometimes a company may appear to have the necessary resources, but may be unable to sell its investments at the prices at which they are valued in the company's financial statements.
Mandatory Security Valuation Reserve (MSVR)	Reserve for investment losses and asset value fluctuation mandated by the state insurance commissioners for companies registered as life and health insurers. As of December 31, 1992, this was replaced by the Asset Valuation Reserve.
Moderate Loss Scenario	An economic decline from current levels approximately equivalent to that of the average postwar recession.
Mortgages in Good Standing	Mortgages which are current in their payments (excludes mortgage-backed securities).
Net Premiums Written	The total dollar volume of premiums retained by the company. This figure is equal to direct premiums written, plus reinsurance assumed less reinsurance ceded.
Noninvestment Grade Bonds	Low-rated issues, commonly known as "junk bonds," which carry a high risk as defined by the state insurance commissioners. These include bond Classes 3 - 6.
Nonperforming Mortgages	Mortgages which are (a) 90 days or more past due or (b) in process of foreclosure.
Other Investments	Items not included in any of the other categories such as premium notes, collateral loans, short-term investments and other miscellaneous items.
Other Structured Securities	Nonresidential mortgage related and other securitized loan-backed or asset-backed securities. This category also includes CMOs with noninvestment grade ratings.

Policy Leverage

A measure of insurance risk based on the relationship of net premiums to capital resources.

Policy Loans

Loans to policyholders under insurance contracts.

Profitability Index

Measured on a scale of zero to ten, with ten being the best and seven or better considered strong. A composite of five factors: (1) gain or loss on operations; (2) consistency of operating results; (3) impact of operating results on surplus; (4) adequacy of investment income as compared to the needs of policy reserves; and (5) expenses in relation to industry averages. Thus, the overall index is an indicator of the health of a company's current and past operations.

Purchase Money Mortgages

Mortgages written by an insurance company to facilitate the sale of property owned by the company.

Real Estate

Direct real estate investments including property (a) occupied by the company; (b) acquired through foreclosure and (c) purchased as an investment.

Reinsurance Assumed

Insurance risk acquired by taking on partial or full responsibility for claims on policies written by other companies. (See "Reinsurance Ceded.")

Reinsurance Ceded

Insurance risk sold to another company.

Risk-Adjusted Capital

The capital resources that would be needed in a worsening economic environment (same as "Target Capital").

Risk-Adjusted Capital Ratio #1

The capital resources which a company currently has, in relation to the resources that would be needed to deal with a moderate loss scenario. This scenario is based on historical experience during an average recession and adjusted to reflect current conditions and vulnerabilities (updated using quarterly data when available).

Risk-Adjusted Capital Ratio #2

The capital resources which a company currently has, in relation to the resources that would be needed to deal with a severe loss scenario. This scenario is based on historical experience of the postwar period and adjusted to reflect current conditions and the potential impact of a severe recession (updated using quarterly data when available).

Separate Accounts

Funds segregated from the general account and valued at market. Used to fund indexed products, such as variable life and variable annuity products.

Severe Loss Scenario

An economic decline from current levels in which the loss experience of the single worst year of the postwar period is extended for a period of three years. (See also "Moderate Loss Scenario".)

Severe Recession

A prolonged economic slowdown in which the single worst year of the postwar period is extended for a period of three years. (See also "Average Recession".)

Stability Index Measured on a scale of zero to ten. This integrates a wide variety of factors that reflects the company's financial stability and diversification of risk.

State of Domicile Although most insurance companies are licensed to do business in many states, they have only one state of domicile. This is the state which has primary regulatory responsibility for the company. Use the state of domicile to make absolutely sure that you have the correct company. Bear in mind, however, that this need not be the state where the company's main offices are located.

State Guaranty Funds Funds that are designed to raise cash from existing insurance carriers to cover policy claims of bankrupt insurance companies.

Stocks Common and preferred equities, including ownership in affiliates.

Surplus The difference between assets and liabilities, including paid-in contributed surplus, plus the statutory equivalent of "retained earnings" in non-insurance business corporations.

Target Capital See "Risk-Adjusted Capital."

Total Assets Total admitted assets, including investments and other business assets. See "Admitted Assets."